NGLADESH
BAHRAIN
BAHAMAS
AUSTRIA
AUSTRALIA
ARGENTINA
AFGHANISTAN
ALBANIA
ALGERIA
COLOMBIA
CONGO
COSTA RICA
CUBA
CYPRUS
CZECHOSLOVAKIA
DAHOMEY

WHITNEY SMITH

EXECUTIVE DIRECTOR, FLAG RESEARCH CENTER, WINCHESTER, MASSACHUSETTS

DESIGNED BY EMIL BÜHRER

McGRAW-HILL BOOK COMPANY

NEW YORK ST. LOUIS SAN FRANCISCO AUCKLAND JOHANNESBURG KUALA LUMPUR LONDON MONTREAI

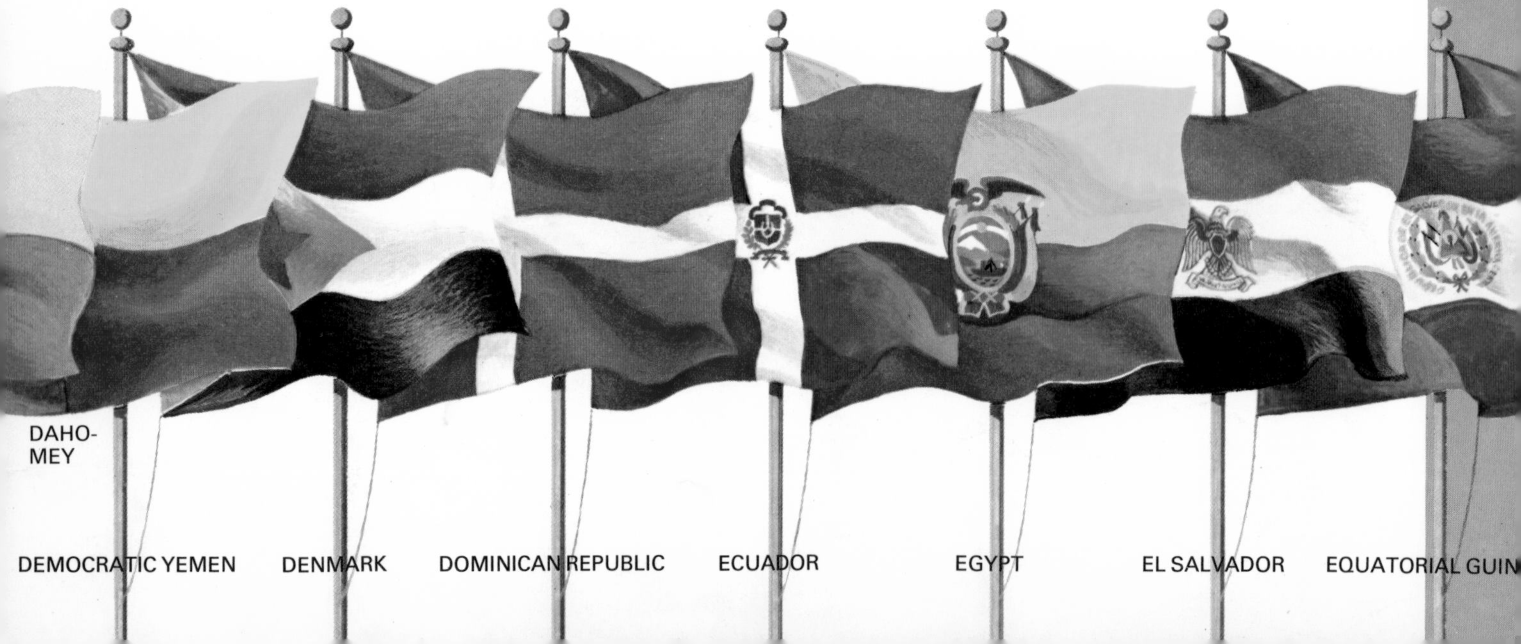

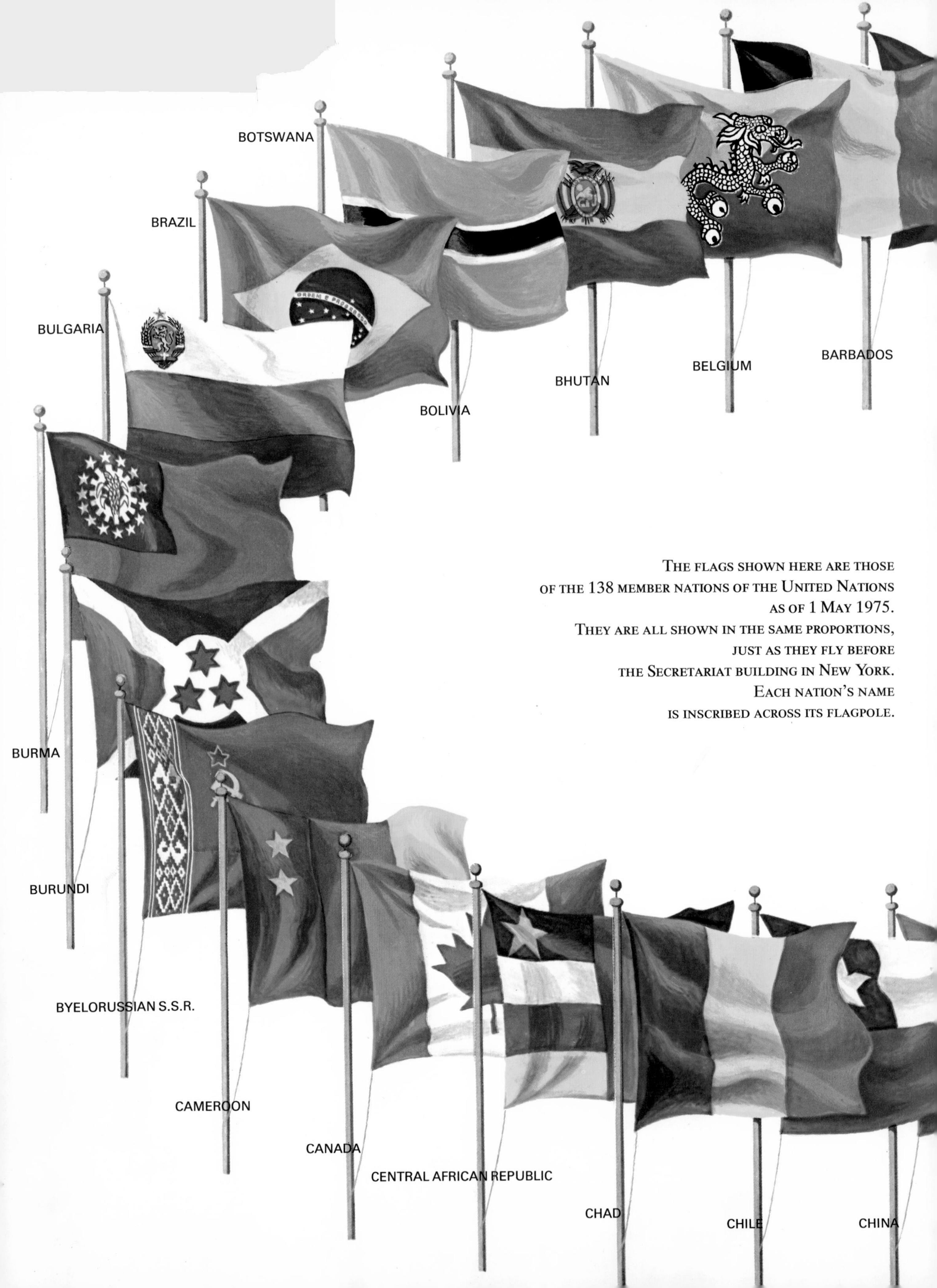

The flags shown here are those of the 138 member nations of the United Nations as of 1 May 1975. They are all shown in the same proportions, just as they fly before the Secretariat building in New York. Each nation's name is inscribed across its flagpole.

FLAGS

THROUGH THE AGES AND ACROSS THE WORLD

NEW DELHI SÃO PAULO SINGAPORE SYDNEY TORONTO

Library of Congress Cataloging in
Publication Data

Smith, Whitney.
Flags.

1. Flags – History. I. Title.
JC345.S57 929.9 75-12602
ISBN 0-07-059093-1

The original concept for this book
was formulated
by Hans-Heinrich Isenbart
and Emil Bührer.
The editor of the book was
Floyd Yearout;
the layouts were done
by Robert Tobler;
the managing editor and
picture researcher was
Francine Peeters;
the copy-editor,
Janine Parson;
the production supervisor,
Franz Gisler.

A McGraw-Hill Co-Publication

Composition
by Hertig & Co. AG,
Biel, Switzerland;
photolithography
by Arnoldo Mondadori,
Verona, Italy,
and Kreienbühl AG,
Lucerne, Switzerland;
printed and bound
by Arnoldo Mondadori in
Verona, Italy.

1234567890AMAM74321098765

Included here are 2257 pieces
of artwork created especially for this book.

Franz Coray
painted the historic flags
found throughout the book,
the United Nations flags below,
and the "flying" flags in
Flags Across the World.

Alfred Znamierowski
drew the flags and coats of arms
of all the nations in
Flags Across the World.

Werner Luzi,
in addition to painting flags
in various sections of the book,
provided the mosaic of symbols
in the last chapter.

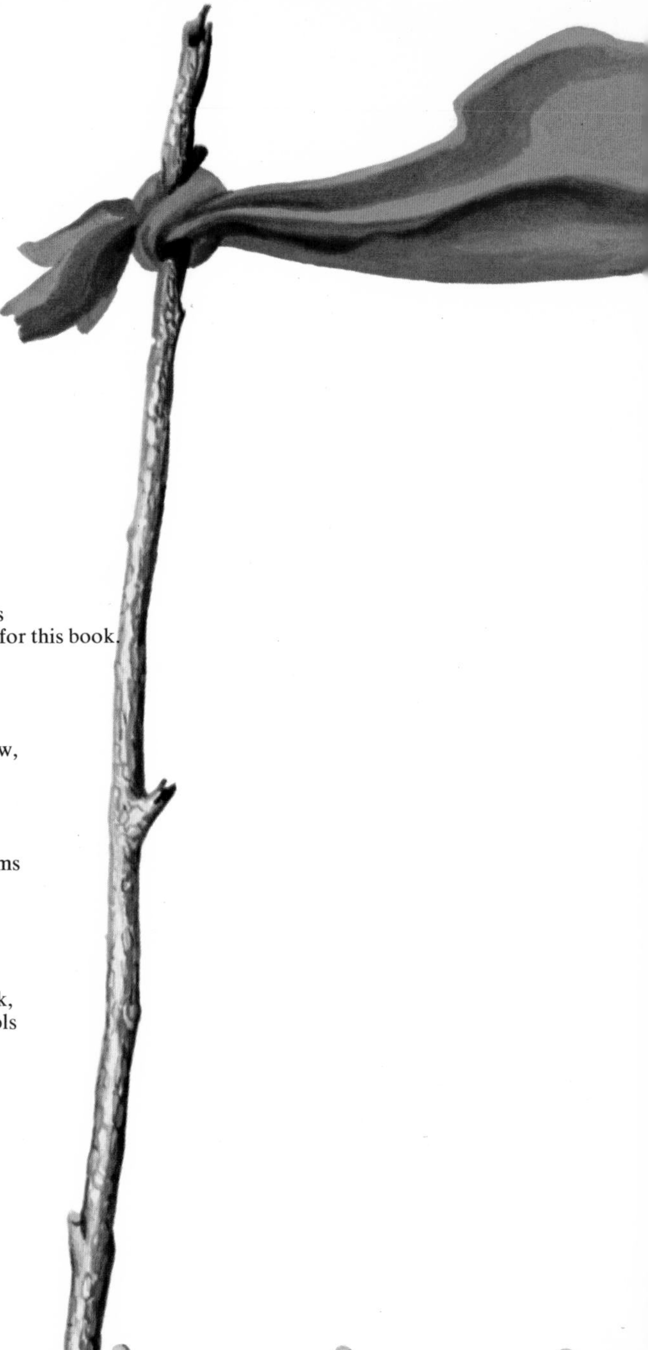

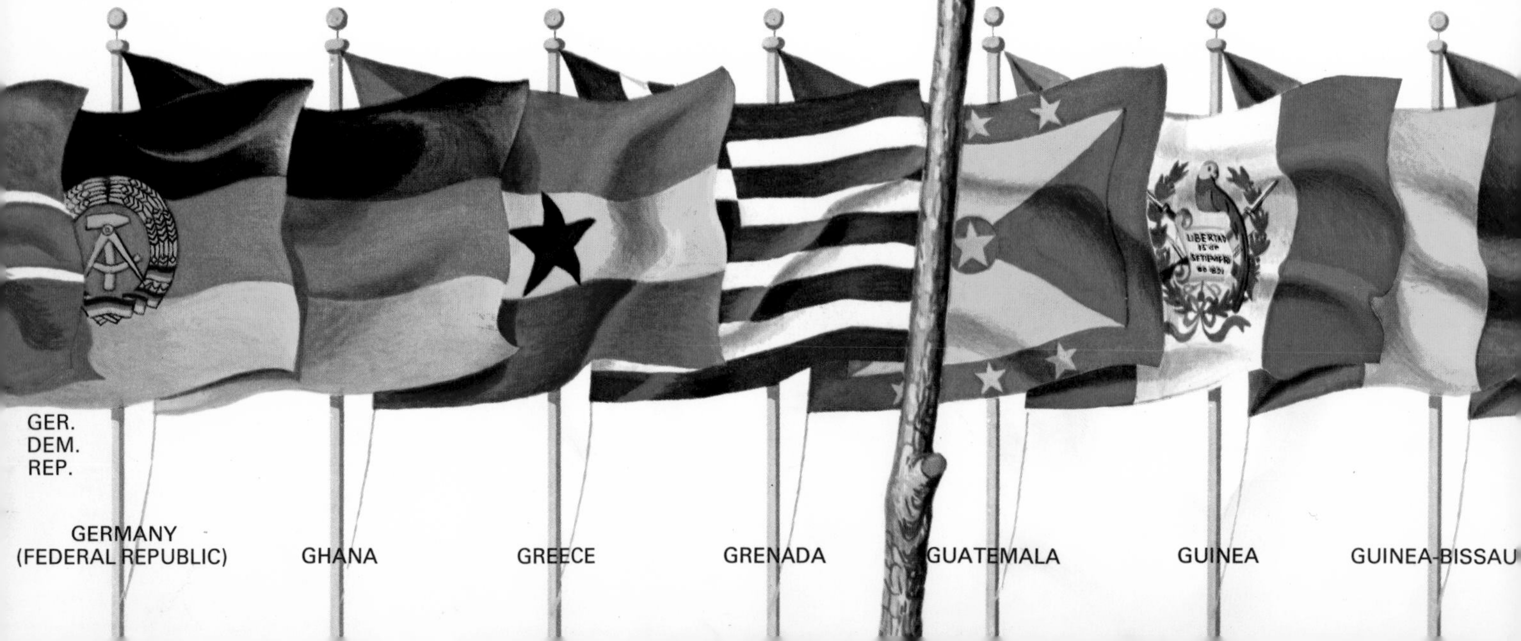

TABLE OF CONTENTS

INDO-
NESIA
IRAN
IRAQ
IRELAND
ISRAEL
ITALY
IVORY COAST
JAMAICA

INTRODUCTION

"IT IS WITH SUCH BAUBLES THAT MEN ARE LED." NAPOLEON I

"In battle all appears to be turmoil and confusion," wrote Sun Tzu twenty-six hundred years ago in his *Art of War,* "but the flags and banners have prescribed arrangements; the sounds of the cymbals, fixed rules." So it is today: all the flags and banners of the world have prescribed arrangements. That great mass of fluttering colors in all shapes and sizes and designs is far more meaningful than decorative, for every flag is a communication from one human being or group of people which may be received and responded to by others.

The primordial rag dipped in the blood of a conquered enemy and lifted high on a stick – that wordless shout of victory and dominion – is a motif repeated millions of times in human existence. Flags incarnate the overcoming of nature, of fellow humans, of self – but an overcoming through comprehension and assimilation as often as by conquest and obliteration. Moreover the themes inherent in the national banners massed before the United Nations headquarters are equally to be found in the paper flag the child sticks on a sand castle. Even the sense of necessity to plant such flags on buildings great and small seems to well from a profound human impulse. It is scarcely possible to conceive of the world, of human society, without flags.

For all this, the fact remains that flags are little understood in their forms, their functions, their origins, and their messages. Some flags, of course, have practical purposes only; they provoke no emotional involvement on the part of those who use them or who see them in use. The decorative pennant in a meeting hall or a warning flag in the street has an obvious practical use, but would scarcely be worth comment. Yet it is possible to take that very same piece of cloth and to endow it, through the circumstances of its display, with a condensed power capable of touching the hearts of millions and of reaching across time. The vast majority of flags are nonreferential, nondecorative: rather they are hortative, their appearance stimulating the viewer to feel and act in a calculated way. Such flags represent or identify the existence, presence, origin, authority, possession, loyalty, glory, beliefs, aspirations, or status of a person, an organization, or a political entity. They are employed to honor and dishonor, warn and encourage, threaten and promise, exalt and condemn, commemorate and deny; they remind and incite and defy the child in school, the soldier, the voter, the enemy, the ally, and the stranger. Other flags of this kind authenticate claims, dramatize politi-

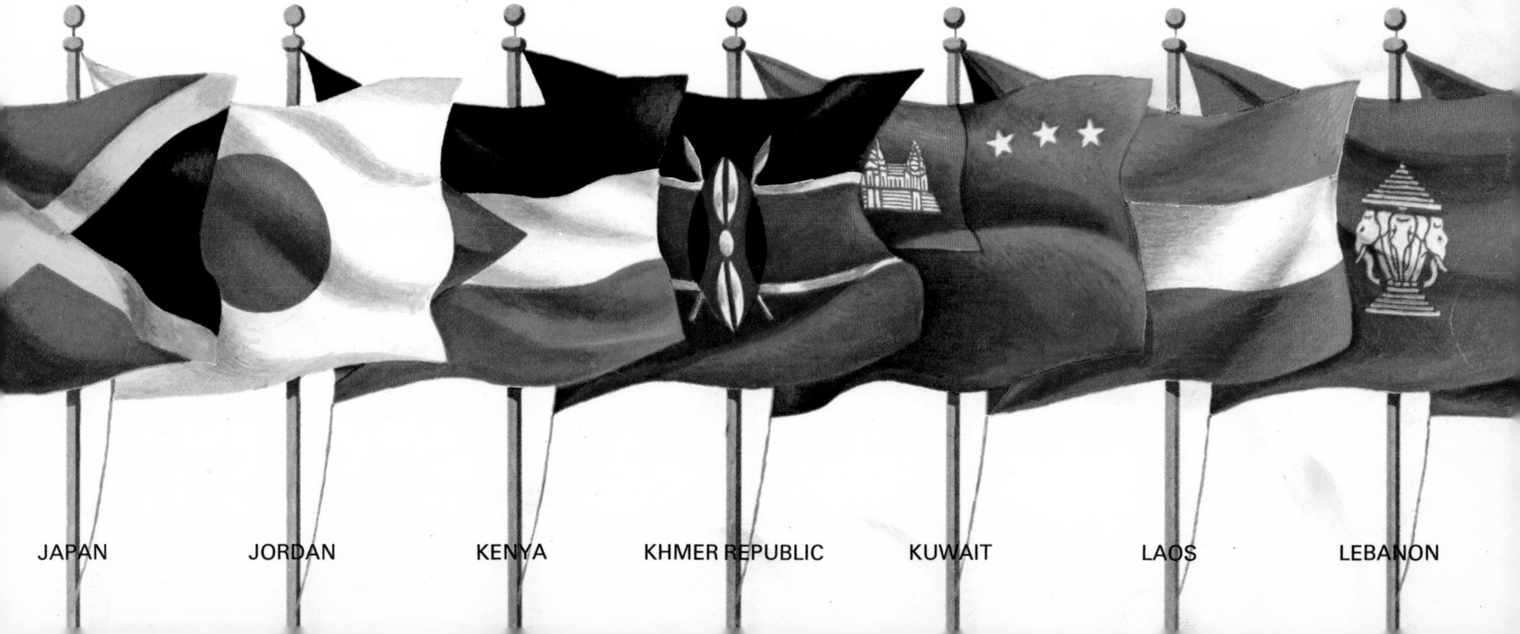

"...TERRIBLE AS AN ARMY WITH BANNERS." SONG OF SOLOMON

cal demands, establish a common framework within which interest groups are willing to confront one another and work out mutually agreeable solutions – or postulate and maintain irreconcilable differences that prevent such agreements from occurring.

There are, in addition, symbols which are related to flags and sometimes used in their stead. Cockades, coats of arms, armbands, uniforms, lapel pins, salutes – these are instruments which help to provide the emotional core needed by groups ranging in size from a troop of scouts to the largest of international associations. Yet flags have certain inherent advantages which have made them among the oldest of human symbols and at the same time the most modern.

The plasticity of a flag allows it to attract, hold, and focus attention on a particular message in a meeting hall, in the street, at a sports event, in a classroom, on a battlefield, at sea, and even in outer space. Individuals and groups at every level of literacy and political sophistication are affected by the compactness of flags, their brilliant colors and designs, simplicity of form, and arresting mobility. Flags are a basic component in innumerable social settings. Sometimes noticed only when missing, they may also be deployed – as in a parade or rally – as a major factor in the molding of attitudes.

Flags have a direct and influential role in many political events. Within the past half century numerous examples come to mind where flags have been pivotal – the definition of South African nationality in the 1920s, the rise to power of Hitler and other fascists, the victory of nationalist movements throughout the Third World, successes and failures of national integration in Cyprus and in the Arab world, the overthrow of Ngo Dinh Diem in Viet-Nam, Panamanian relations with the United States.

These points are stressed because so little attention has been paid to the serious nature of flag usage. Nothing need be said about the visual and artistic appeal of flags; words could scarcely improve on the impact made by a handsome flag floating in the breeze, even as represented by an artist on the printed page. The fascination which young children instinctively have for the infinite variety of flag patterns and colors and shapes is argument enough for publication of a flag book. Nor is it surprising that pieces of cloth embodying the essence of so much human effort tell fascinating stories.

The browser needs no excuse for opening this book to any page and

"FLAGS ARE A BRAVE SIGHT BUT NO TRUE EYE EVER WENT BY ONE STEADILY." EMILY DICKINSON

following as far as his mood carries him. The more interested reader, however, may require some explanations not only about the nature of flags but also about the nature of the book itself. Remarkably, in light of the graphic strength of flags, relatively few books have made use of the illustrative possibilities in dealing with the subject. Every illustration in the present volume has a specific intention, both independently of and jointly with its caption and with the main text of the chapter. While intended to be pleasing to the eye, these same illustrations have been required to serve a didactic function as well. Thus the size, placement, progression, and mode of presentation of the illustrations should be kept in mind by readers seeking the fullest understanding of the subject. Photographs have been used to communicate the texture and "presence" of actual flags and flag usages, particularly where these are unique. Conversely, artwork has been employed throughout the book for reconstructed flags and type flags, i.e., ones reproduced in the real world in great quantity and with more or less standardized format.

No book this size could possibly convey every detail about every flag; moreover, what may be of interest and value for one reader may bore another if overemphasized. To overcome this dilemma in the reference chapters the author and designers have made use of a series of unobtrusive symbols which convey in the most succinct manner possible basic information about a particular flag. Has a design been reconstructed, possibly from brief written descriptions? Is the reverse side of the flag the same as its obverse? Are two flags which appear to have the same proportions in fact alike? These are among the many questions answered by these symbols.

The symbols are not the only language which needs some explanation. The specialized terminology associated with flag study is not great – nor, unfortunately, has it in the past been very precise. Nevertheless there are aspects of the subject which demand a prior understanding of terms and concepts, such as those associated with heraldry, that cannot be conveniently mentioned at each point of usage throughout the book. The reader, therefore, may want to read *Terms Defined* before venturing elsewhere in the volume. Likewise the special sections identified with a key have been prepared as special guides within the reference sections. The intention has been to make it possible for the book simultaneously to serve as a useful reference tool for someone who needs an imme-

THE MOON
20 JULY 1969

diate answer to a specific question as well as a book of enlightenment and entertainment for every reader.

It is a characteristic of national flags (which comprise a large section of this book) that they change – radically or subtly, but without warning and at a steady rate that confounds the most diligent vexillologist. Because the minimum amount of time between writing and publishing a book involves some months, it should be observed that the information presented here constitutes the best available knowledge as of 1 May 1975. Anyone seeking more up to date material – or fuller details on some particular point – is encouraged to write to the author at the Flag Research Center (Winchester, Mass. 01890 U.S.A.). Criticisms and corrections are also solicited.

In the matter of selecting and ordering materials, attention has been paid to those aspects of the flag useful and interesting to the average reader as well as the specialist. Of course, no one book can answer all the possible questions on such a vast subject. Nevertheless somewhere in the book most questions about flags have been considered: for example, under what conditions may a historical flag be flown with a current national flag? How does a standard differ from a banner? Why is the Union Jack asymmetrical? Does a particular head of state have a personal flag?

It is in these and the many other diverse aspects of flags dealt with in different chapters that the importance of this phenomenon becomes clear. Flags may themselves rarely be the center of human political and social activity, yet throughout history flags of one kind or another have always expressed the deepest feelings of those at the center – and of those who want to be. Understanding then why and how certain shapes, designs, colors, and usages have prevailed in flags can give us remarkable insights into wider aspects of human endeavor.

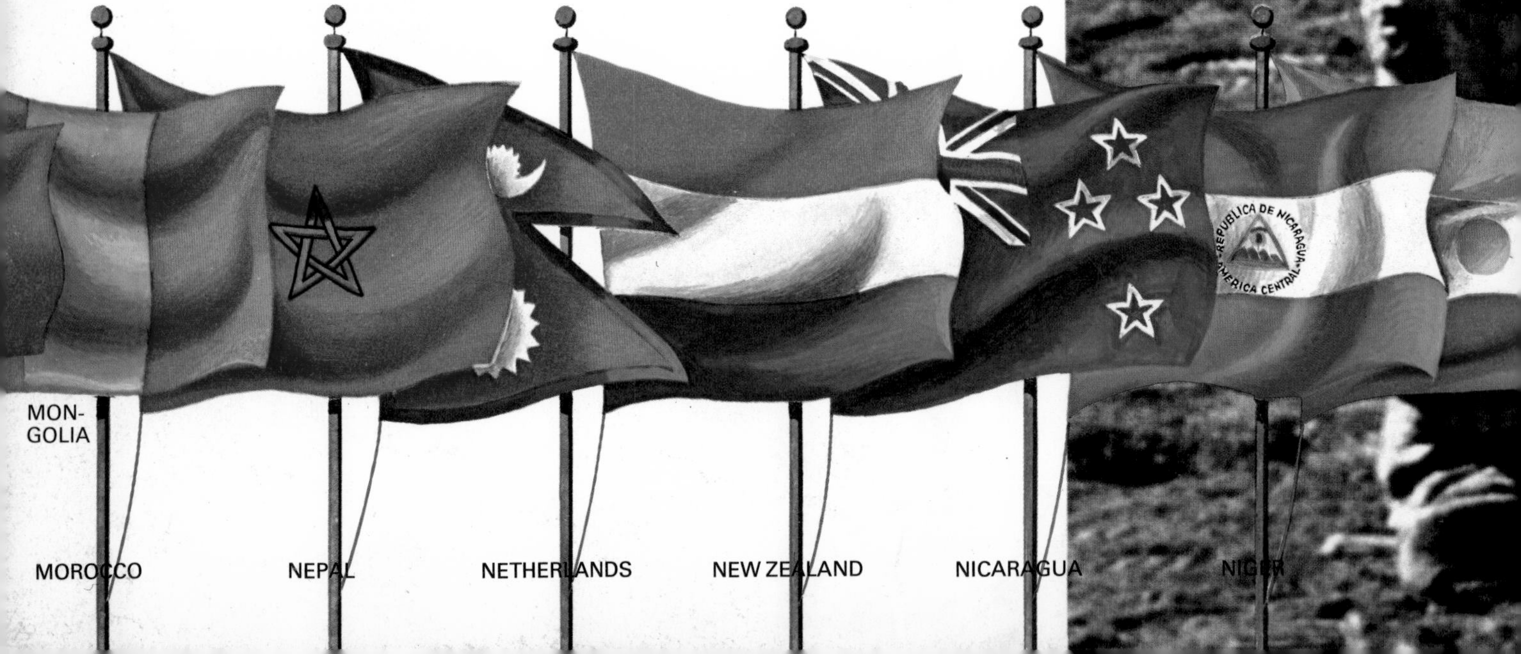

MON-
GOLIA

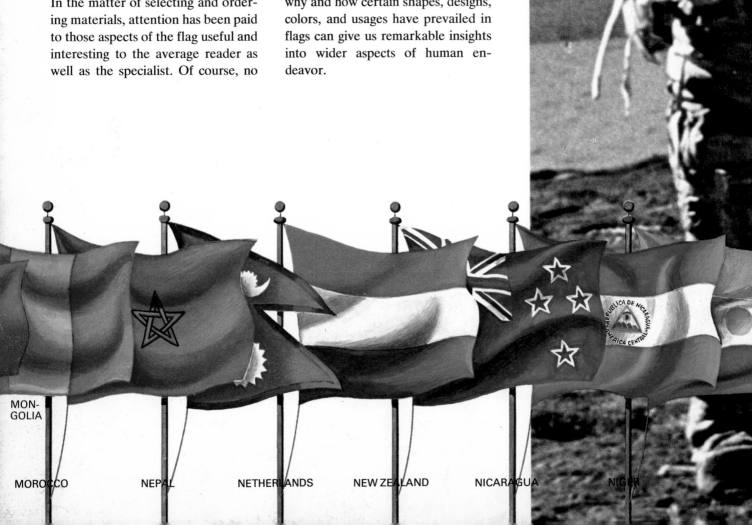

MOROCCO NEPAL NETHERLANDS NEW ZEALAND NICARAGUA NIGER

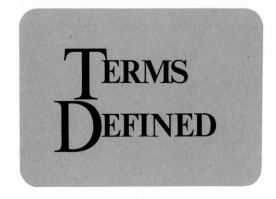

TERMS DEFINED

A KEY TO THE BETTER UNDERSTANDING OF FLAGS...

THE KEY SYMBOL USED THROUGHOUT THIS BOOK signals special reference sections designed to help reveal the world of vexillology to the nonspecialist. This particular key section is the glossary, in which you will find concise explanations of important flag-related words. In other chapters the sections cover flag customs, heraldry, national flags, and flag symbols. A complete list of all the key sections in the book is found on page 348.

Words in SMALL CAPITALS in the glossary and words in *italics* in the captions of this chapter refer to terms that are defined. The numbers in parentheses (e.g. 25-1) refer to page and illustration sequence within the chapter where terms have been illustrated.

About 1634 Sir Nathaniel Boteler put the following words into the mouth of a sailor in his *Six Dialogues about Sea Services:* "Colours and Ensignes I take to be all one, but where are they to be placed and wherefore serve they?" Here in a nutshell are the two key questions covered in the following pages – what are the different kinds of flags, and "wherefore serve they"?

Although it encompasses accessories, flag customs, and heraldic terms, the following vocabulary is not large and technical for the novice. Nevertheless the author has faced difficulties that the reader should be aware of, affecting as they do almost every page of the book.

While the *use* of flags goes back to the earliest days of human civilization, the *study* of that usage in a serious fashion is so recent that the term for it (*vexillology,* coined by the author of this book) did not appear in print until 1959. This has resulted in a lack of uniformity in flag terms and, worse still, a lack of source material concerning actual usage on which standardization might be based.

While the International Federation of Vexillological Associations has begun the task of precisely defining words and phrases for the future, it cannot of course ever hope to standardize historical definitions. Three and a half centuries ago Boteler confidently asserted, "Colours and Ensignes I take to be all one"; yet in truth the number of variations in these two words alone, over time, presents us with considerable confusion – and they are by no means the most difficult flag terms to be defined. "Banner" and "standard" have had so many meanings since their introduction into English that one is tempted to recommend they not be used at all in the future, except in a poetic sense. Changes within one language – and fortunately there are relatively few differences between British and American English that need to be dealt with – shrink into relative insignificance before the problems to be faced in comparing English vexillological terminology with its counterparts in foreign languages. History has dictated that each word have special connotations based on long usage, rendering impossible all kinds of apparent parallels. Often such similarities turn out to be very misleading. The English *banner* cannot be equated with the Italian *bandiera,* the French *bannière,* the Spanish *bandera,* the Malaysian *bendera,* or the German *Banner*; and the Russian *flag* and Pidgin *plak* are closer to the English *flag* than to the German *Flagge.*

Not every term relating to flags will be found here, nor will terms included be given every conceivable definition. Nevertheless, this chapter stands as the most comprehensive flag dictionary ever compiled. Moreover, an attempt has been made to render it as useful a vexillological glossary as possible by clearly indicating problem areas, obsolete uses, variances of spelling, and the likelihood of meeting a term in nautical or land usage. Where appropriate, geographical peculiarities are noted. Perhaps most importantly, the author has sought to be consistent throughout the volume in his own use of words.

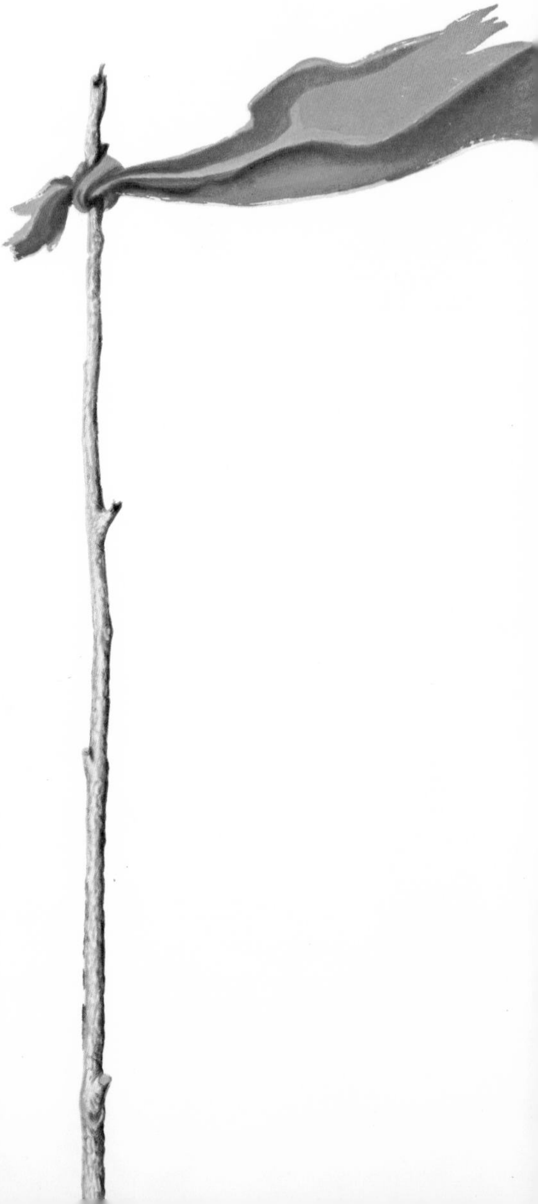

ACHIEVEMENT
A complete coat of arms (27-1).

ANCIENT
Obsolete term for COLOR or STANDARD-BEARER.

APPLIQUÉ
A mode of flag manufacture in which one or more pieces of cloth are stitched on the FIELD to form the design.

ARMORIAL BANNER
A flag whose field corresponds exactly to the shield of a coat of arms (21-1).

ARMORIAL SAIL
The sail of a ship bearing some or all of a coat of arms (16-3).

AUGMENTATION OF HONOR
A CHARGE added to a coat of arms or flag to indicate special recognition for some service (20-1).

BADGE
A distinctive emblem added to an existing flag. Although not necessarily a coat of arms, the badge normally may be used apart from the flag as well as on it (unlike the CHARGE).

BANDEROLE / BANDEROL / BANDROL / BANDROLE
Originally a small banner, now more commonly a streamer or ribbon – often with an inscription – normally used alone (as on a crosier) rather than an as accessory to a flag. In heraldry a banderole is a streamer attached to a helmet or crest. Because of confusion with BANNEROL, "banderole" is rare today.

BANNER
A flag of any kind, but especially a flag (1) in a figurative expression; (2) bearing as its sole CHARGE a coat of arms (see ARMORIAL BANNER); (3) hanging from a CROSSBAR or suspended between two poles; (4) made with great care and displaying a costly and/or complicated design. Because the meaning of the word has changed over the years, it is usually preferable to use a more specific term: ROYAL BANNER, TRUMPET-BANNER, etc.

BANNERET (*ban*-ner-et)
A civil officer of northern Italy and Switzerland, from the title originally given knights entitled to lead men onto the battlefield under their own banners.

BANNERET / BANNERETTE (ban-ner-*et*)
A small flag such as a PIPE-BANNER or TRUMPET-BANNER.

BANNEROL
A small flag, usually square, displaying a single quartering from the coat of arms of a deceased person and employed as a funeral flag; now obsolete.

BATTLE HONOR
A mark added to a COLOR to show its military service. It may take the form of an inscription (often on a ribbon) on the flag itself, a metal band on the STAFF, a metal clip added to a STREAMER, or the streamer itself (30-2).

BEND ON A FLAG
To fasten a flag to HALYARDS in order to hoist it.

BICOLOR
A flag whose field is divided horizontally, vertically, or diagonally into two different colors.

BORDER
A wide band surrounding a field of a different color (24-5); not to be confused with FIMBRIATION.

BREADTH (British)
WIDTH.

BREAK OUT A FLAG / BREAK A FLAG
To unfurl a flag which has been rolled and tied in such a way that a sharp tug on the HALYARD will cause it to open out.

BROAD PENNANT
A short SWALLOWTAILED flag used by navies and yacht clubs as a RANK FLAG.

BUNTING
Strong, loosely woven material used for making flags, originally of wool but sometimes of other fibers; by extension, bunting material used as decoration or, figuratively, flags collectively.

BURGEE
The small DISTINGUISHING FLAG of a yacht club, usually triangular or SWALLOWTAILED.

CANTON
The area in the upper HOIST corner of a flag or a rectangular FIELD filling that area (24-2). Although in heraldry "canton" refers to a specific size, in a flag it may be one-quarter the total area, larger, or smaller.

CASE
A narrow sack with ties at its open end for slipping over a PARADE FLAG to protect it in inclement weather or when not in use.

CHARGE
Any object placed on the FIELD of a flag or shield (31-1). Unlike the BADGE, the charge usually is not employed separately. CHARGED, TO CHARGE.

CHECKY / CHEQUY
Bearing squares of alternating colors (27-1).

CHIEF
The top horizontal third of a shield.

CIVIL ENSIGN
The NATIONAL FLAG flown on commercial and privately owned vessels; also called MERCHANT FLAG.

CIVIL FLAG
The NATIONAL FLAG flown on land by private citizens.

Victory over nature and victory over fellow human beings are common themes in flags throughout history. These prehistoric *vexilloids* are only earlier, less sophisticated versions of the modern flagpole topped with a golden eagle (or lion or similar beast) and of the flag bearing emblems of warfare and power.

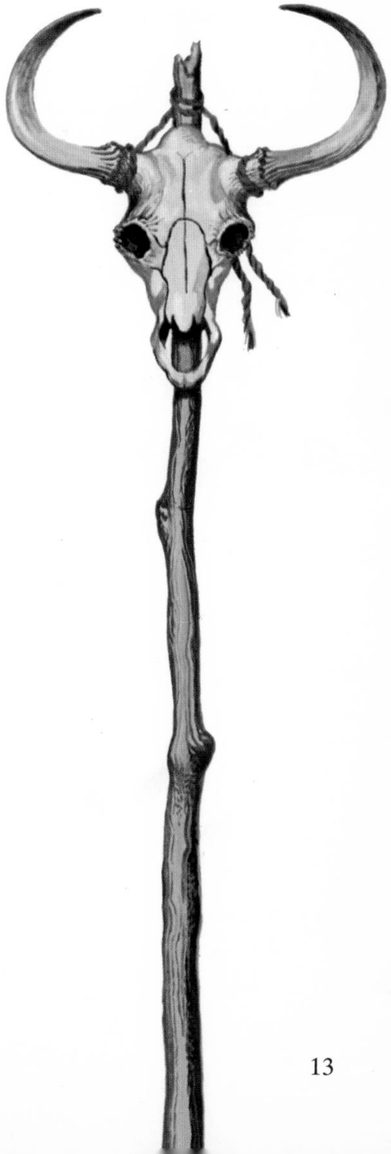

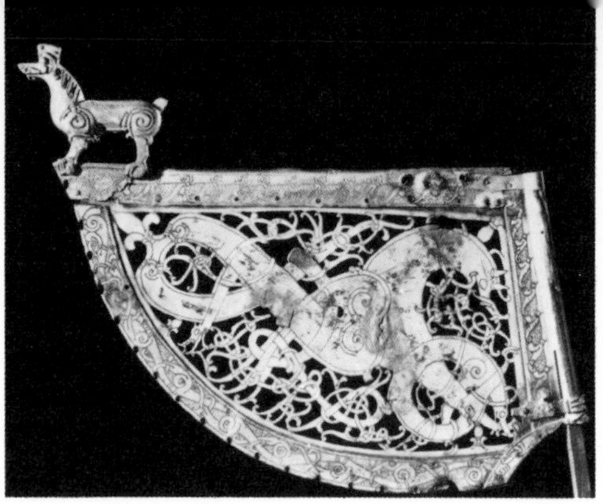

1

Norsemen made extensive use of metal *vanes* as flags. Ribbons were probably attached to the holes along the edge.

2

The *standard* is always a proclamation, whether by an individual or a group: "Here I stand, and this is what I stand for." This Roman *signum* was the standard of a military unit.

CLEAT
A metal device with two arms, attached near the bottom of a STAFF, to which HALYARDS are attached.

COACHWHIP
See PENNANT.

COCKADE
A rosette or bow, usually in national or LIVERY colors, sometimes used to decorate a STAFF below the FINIAL. Cockades were popular during the eighteenth and nineteenth centuries as patriotic symbols on hats and coats.

COLOR / COLOUR
The flag of a military unit (originally infantry only). The plural "colors" is often used, even for a single flag, because the name derives from the colors composing the FIELD of the flag, as well as the British and American practice of issuing two flags simultaneously to the same unit. The regimental (company, battalion, etc.) color represents the unit itself, while a higher allegiance is symbolized by the king's color, or, in countries with a republican form of government, the national or presidential color (20-2).

COLOR-BEARER
The same as STANDARD-BEARER.

COLOR GUARD
The group in a military or paramilitary ceremony responsible for displaying the flag(s).

COLORS
Figuratively, any flag; especially one or a pair of military flags or, at sea, an ENSIGN or SUITE OF FLAGS. The term may refer to the ceremony of hoisting or lowering flags on a vessel, also known as "making colors."

COMMISSION PENNANT
A long narrow flag flown on a warship to indicate its commissioned status. See MASTHEAD PENDANT, HOMEWARD-BOUND PENNANT.

COMPARTMENT
An object such as a panel, mound, or scrollwork on which the shield and the supporters of a coat of arms rest (27-1).

CONSECRATION
The dedication ceremony of a COLOR.

CORD
A piece of twisted material used to finish the edge of a flag or (with tassels and tied at the middle) to decorate a STAFF just below the FINIAL (19-1).

CORNET
A cavalry STANDARD; a cavalry STANDARD-BEARER; in naval usage a BROAD PENNANT. In all three senses the word is obsolete.

COUNTERCHANGED
Having two colors alternating on either side of a line drawn through a flag or coat of arms.

COURTESY FLAG
The flag of a country being visited by a ship from a different nation, as flown by that vessel.

CRAVAT
A scarf, usually in the national LIVERY colors and richly decorated, tied to a STAFF below the FINIAL; normally used with military flags (30-2).

CREST
An object or objects in a coat of arms appearing above the TORSE, sometimes used alone as a BADGE. Popularly, especially in the United States and Malaysia, crest is synonymous with ACHIEVEMENT.

CROSS
Unless otherwise specified, a cross concentric with a flag, its arms extending to the edges of the flag (24-7).

CROSSBAR
A rod bearing a flag (especially a GONFALON or PENNANT) attached directly or by rope to a STAFF (23-12).

DEFACE
To add a BADGE to an existing flag (18-1).

DESECRATION
Disrespectful treatment of a flag.

DEXTER
The right-hand part of a flag or shield from the viewpoint of the bearer; the antonym of SINISTER (27-1).

DIFFERENCED
Having a slight difference from the design of another, related flag or shield.

DIMENSIONS
The actual size (width to length measurements, unless otherwise specified) of a flag, as opposed to its PROPORTIONS.

DIPPING
The custom of lowering a flag briefly to honor an important person, another vessel, etc.

DISC
A circular area of a single color used as a CHARGE.

DISTINGUISHING FLAG
The flag identifying an institution, military or naval service, or official and generally used in addition to a NATIONAL FLAG.

DRAPING
The decoration of a STAFF with a black CRAVAT as a sign of mourning.

1 The flag motif is popular in all kinds of art and decoration: this philatelic curiosity is known as a *flag cancel,* used chiefly in the United States.

DRESS SHIP
To decorate a vessel with flags for a special occasion (18-1).

DRUM-BANNER
A small flag decorating a military parade drum.

EAGLE
A VEXILLOID characterized by a representation of an eagle on a STAFF, used especially by armies of imperial Rome and France.

ENSIGN (*en*-sign)
A generic term for flag, especially associated with naval flags of nationality (CIVIL ENSIGN, NAVAL RESERVE ENSIGN, etc.) and by extension in British usage with distinguishing flags of government services on land. In the seventeenth and eighteenth centuries ensign was the normal term for COLOR and for COLOR-BEARER (18-1).

EX-VOTO FLAG
A flag, usually small and plain, displayed (especially by Hindus) to fulfill a religious vow.

FALSE FLAG / FALSE COLORS
An ENSIGN displayed by a vessel not entitled to it, figuratively applied to persons misrepresenting their true affiliations.

FAN
A semicircular patriotic decoration in bunting of flag design and/or colors.

FANION
A small surveyors' SIGNAL FLAG, originally of military usage.

FIELD
The background of a flag or shield.

FIMBRIATION
A narrow line of a contrasting color separating two areas of similar colors, such as a CHARGE and its FIELD (24-10); not to be confused with BORDER.

FINIAL
The ornament at the top of a STAFF above the TRUCK (19-1).

FLAG
A graphic and plastic medium of social communication, usually but not necessarily political in nature. Although a generic term, flag frequently refers specifically to the typical rectangular flag hoisted on buildings and ships as a symbol of national identification.

FLAG BELT
A leather device worn around the waist and neck which holds the bottom end of a STAFF to assist a marching STANDARD-BEARER.

FLAG CANCEL
A printed invalidation for postage stamps, resembling a flag (15-1).

FLAG CARRIER
Within a given country, an airline or shipping line registered to display its national flag.

FLAG DAY / FLAG WEEK
A holiday for the affirmation of patriotic values expressed in and through the national flag.

FLAG DISCRIMINATION
Choice of a FLAG CARRIER over a foreign line, especially when required by law.

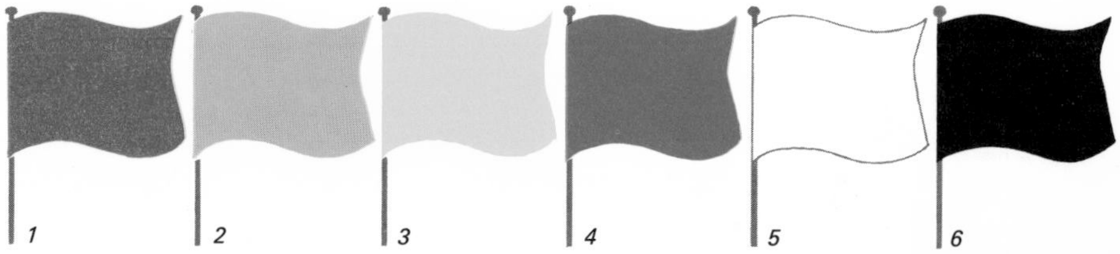

FLAG OF CONVENIENCE
Registration of a ship in a country without stringent maritime regulations.

FLAG OFFICER
A naval officer entitled to display a RANK FLAG.

FLAG SALUTE / FLAG PLEDGE
An oath of allegiance to a nation required of its military and sometimes its civilians, rendered through a ritual involving the national flag. Flag salute can also refer to a salute made with a flag, usually at sea; see DIPPING.

FLAG-TOSSING
A sport and folk custom of Central Europe involving flags twirled and tossed through the air.

FLAG-WAVER
A person literally or figuratively using the national flag as a justification for actions or principles. FLAG-WAVING.

FLAMMULE
A flame-shaped flag edge (26-1) characteristic of the Far East.

FLY
That part of the flag opposite the STAFF (24-1); also a synonym for LENGTH.

FOLK FLAG
A homemade NATIONAL FLAG of simplified design.

FRAME
A metal or wood device, normally along the top edge of a flag (but sometimes along the outer and/or bottom edges as well; 22-11), similar in function to a TANGLE ROD.

FRINGE
A decoration of twisted thread or metal attached to the edges of a flag, usually a COLOR or PARADE FLAG (19-1). Normally used only on the three outer edges,

2

In addition to political meanings (not indicated here), modern monochromatic flags may convey diverse messages. Some are based on traditions that go back thousands of years, while others are of comparatively recent conventional symbolism.

1 Danger, warning, stop; war, martial law, no quarter; revolution, protest.

2 Buddhism; Hinduism; distress.

3 Quarantine, sickness; caution.

4 Islam; safety; proceed.

5 Peace, truce, parley; surrender.

6 Death, mourning, protest; anarchy.

3

Officers of the Royal Belgian Air Force display *rank flags* which (like similar flags around the world) indicate seniority by variations of a common pattern.

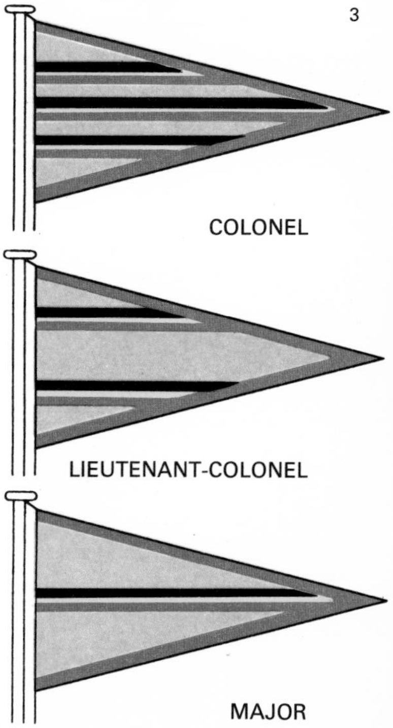

The 28-yard (26-meter) *streamer* of this sixteenth-century English ship presaged the even longer *homeward-bound pennant* of today.

1

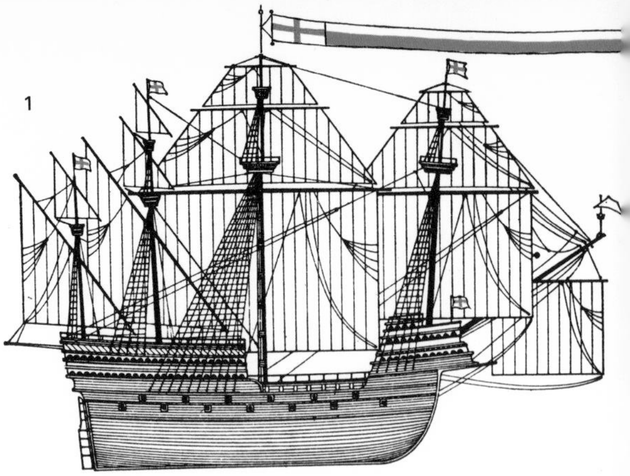

it may appear on from one to four of the sides of a flag and at the ends of a CRAVAT.

GAFF
A spar from which a flag is hoisted, jutting from the mizzenmast of a ship or from a STAFF on land (18-1).

GARRISON FLAG
The largest-size United States flag flown at army posts (20 by 38 feet; 6.1 by 10.9 meters).

GONFALON
A flag characteristic of Italy and of associations

2 The medieval Italian shield known as a "pavis," often arranged in great numbers to form a protective wall, was the inspiration for the decorative *pavisade* of ships.

(particularly religious ones) in Western Europe, hung from a CROSSBAR and generally terminating in TAILS (23-12); often confused with GONFANON.

GONFALONIERATE
The office held by a STANDARD-BEARER (gonfalonier).

GONFANON
A war flag of preheraldic Western Europe, generally attached to a lance and ending in squared tails (22-7); often confused with the later GONFALON.

GOVERNMENT FLAG
STATE FLAG.

GREEK CROSS
An equal-armed cross (24-6).

GROMMET
A hole reinforced by stitching or a metal ring, usually found at both ends of the HEADING, through which clips attached to the HALYARDS pass.

GROUND
FIELD.

GUIDON
A small military flag, usually SWALLOWTAILED, serving as a guide to troops; a DISTINGUISHING FLAG, and/or decoration.

GUMPHION / GUMPHEON
A small funeral flag bearing a death's head.

GYRONNY
Divided into triangles whose apices meet at the center of the flag or shield; formerly characteristic of Swiss military flags.

HALF-STAFF A FLAG
To fly a flag at any point below its normal position at the top of a STAFF, usually to signify mourning or protest.

HALYARD
The rope by which a flag is hoisted.

HANGING FLAG
A flag, normally rectangular, attached to a CROSSBAR which is hoisted on a vertical STAFF, a practice characteristic of German-speaking countries.

HEADING
A piece of heavy material, usually canvas, into which a rope is sewn or into which GROMMETS are put to facilitate hoisting the flag.

3

Never a practical substitute for a flag, the *armorial sail (right)* was nevertheless one of the most handsome displays of heraldry the oceans of the world have ever seen.

1

Contrary to popular imagination, the real *Jolly Roger* of the pirate was unlikely to have a skull und crossbones for a symbol. The hourglass was a reminder to the pirate's victim that his time had run out.

HOIST
That part of a flag nearest the STAFF; also a group of SIGNAL FLAGS to be flown together; also a synonym for WIDTH (24-1).

HOMEWARD-BOUND PENNANT
A COMMISSION PENNANT of a vessel returning home after an extended period of service, with up to 80 yards (73.9 meters) of extra material added to the length, an unofficial custom *(above)* also known among merchant vessels. See PAYING-OFF PENDANT.

HORSETAIL
A decoration for military flags, especially in China where it is usually red, made of real or simulated horsetail (21-2).

HOUSE FLAG
The DISTINGUISHING FLAG of a commercial firm, flown especially at sea; sometimes used in reference to the personal flag of the owner of a yacht or home.

INESCUTCHEON
A shield appearing within another, usually at its center (27-1).

INGLEFIELD CLIPS
A metal device attached at either end of a HALYARD, quickly unfastened to BEND ON A FLAG but also easy to fasten securely.

JACK
A small flag flown under certain circumstances at the prow of a vessel, usually a warship (18-1).

JOLLY ROGER
Any black flag bearing white symbols and associated with piracy (17-1); by extension a flag of similar design used for some other purpose, such as the unofficial flags of British submarines in World War II.

KING'S / QUEEN'S COLOR
See COLOR.

LANCE FLAG
A small flag, usually triangular or SWALLOWTAILED, formerly displayed at the end of a lance by soldiers.

LAPEL FLAG
A metal or plastic flag, often bejeweled, worn on dress or coat lapel as a patriotic or political symbol, characteristic of the United States and Communist countries; also a small paper or cloth flag worn in the lapel as a token of a contribution to a charitable organization.

LAY UP COLORS
To deposit ceremoniously (in a church or other building) old military flags, a European and Commonwealth tradition.

LENGTH
The dimension of a flag measured from its HOIST to the opposite extreme (24-1); see also WIDTH, FLY.

LIVERY
Characterized by the principal colors of a coat of arms.

LOZENGY
Covered with diamonds of alternating colors.

MALTESE CROSS
A cross resembling four arrowheads meeting at the points.

MANTLING
A decoration resembling drapery in a coat of arms, attached to the helmet by a TORSE.

MASTHEAD PENDANT (British)
COMMISSION PENNANT.

MERCHANT FLAG
CIVIL ENSIGN.

METAL
The heraldic term for gold (yellow) or silver (white), an antonym to color (see pages 28 and 29).

3

On ships there normally are a number of flags flown together *(above)* to indicate nationality and rank. The *suite of flags* for a warship includes *jack* (at the prow), *commission pennant* or *rank flag* (at the mainmast), and the *ensign* at the stern. A commercial vessel flies the *house flag* of the shipping company which owns it on the foremast.

The French Tricolor has been *defaced* here by the imperial arms and golden bees to form the personal flag of Emperor Napoleon III. The mainmast on which it flies normally carries the *commission pennant* or the *rank flag* of the vessel's commanding officer.

In anticipation of a visit by royalty, the order has gone out to *"dress ship."* In addition to French *national flags, signal flags* are in evidence.

The largest flag of all, the ship's *ensign,* is hoisted at the *gaff* where its halyards will not interfere with the rigging of the ship.

The custom of manning the yardarms was common in the days of square-rigged ships.

In France as in many other countries, the *jack* is a miniature version of the ensign.

The *Bretagne,* docked in Cherbourg, awaits a visit from Queen Victoria of Great Britain in 1856 with a gala display of naval flags.

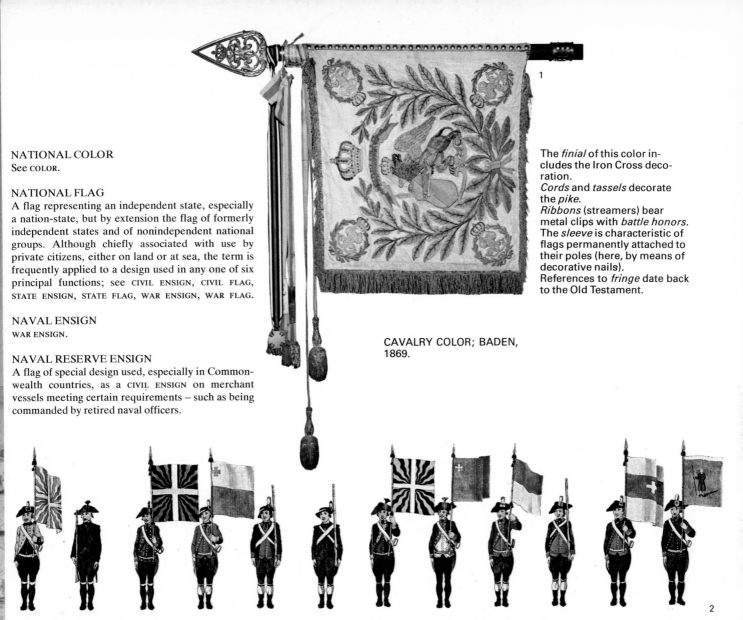

NATIONAL COLOR
See COLOR.

NATIONAL FLAG
A flag representing an independent state, especially a nation-state, but by extension the flag of formerly independent states and of nonindependent national groups. Although chiefly associated with use by private citizens, either on land or at sea, the term is frequently applied to a design used in any one of six principal functions; see CIVIL ENSIGN, CIVIL FLAG, STATE ENSIGN, STATE FLAG, WAR ENSIGN, WAR FLAG.

NAVAL ENSIGN
WAR ENSIGN.

NAVAL RESERVE ENSIGN
A flag of special design used, especially in Commonwealth countries, as a CIVIL ENSIGN on merchant vessels meeting certain requirements – such as being commanded by retired naval officers.

1

The *finial* of this color includes the Iron Cross decoration.
Cords and *tassels* decorate the *pike.*
Ribbons (streamers) bear metal clips with *battle honors.*
The *sleeve* is characteristic of flags permanently attached to their poles (here, by means of decorative nails).
References to *fringe* date back to the Old Testament.

CAVALRY COLOR; BADEN, 1869.

2

OBVERSE
The more important side of a flag, normally seen when the STAFF is to the DEXTER; the antonym of REVERSE.

ORNAMENT
FINIAL.

PARADE FLAG
A flag intended to be carried outdoors by a marcher and made with appropriate material and accessories.

PARLEY FLAG
A plain white flag displayed during war to request negotiations.

PAVILION
A stylized drapery, usually red lined with ermine, against which a coat of arms is displayed (27-1).

PAVISADE
The display of shields, or by extension of flags, along the side of a ship for decoration purposes (16-2).

PAYING-OFF PENDANT (British)
HOMEWARD-BOUND PENNANT.

PEACE FLAG
Any of a number of flags designed to symbolize peace, including a plain white flag, a national flag surrounded by a white border, and a flag incorporating the Peace Symbol (a ring bearing a combined I and inverted V).

PENCEL / PENCIL / PENNONCEL / PENNONCELLE
A small flag such as a LANCE FLAG, made in various shapes and designs (but often bearing a BADGE against LIVERY colors); now obsolete in function and as a term, except as a poetical term for a small triangular flag.

PENNANT / PENDANT
(both, *pen*-ant; the second spelling is obsolete). A term referring to flags that are so diverse that a more technical term (see BANDEROLE, BROAD PENNANT, BURGEE, COMMISSION PENNANT, GUIDON, LANCE FLAG, PENCEL, PENNON, STREAMER) is almost always preferable. From its etymology ("hanging"), it appears that pennants originally always hung from a crossbar, and many continue to do so; others are attached in the usual fashions to a vertical STAFF or are mounted against a flat surface such as a wall. Pennants are extensively used at sea, where they apparently originated, for signaling, for decoration, and as RANK FLAGS. Today they are also used on land, especially as souvenir flags, award flags, and flags of business, fraternal, sports, and other associations.

These *vexillaries* or *standard-bearers* display *armorial banners* of the cantonal arms of Switzerland. Their simplicity makes it possible for a precise heraldic description to be given from which any artist familiar with heraldry can reconstruct the design.

The normal order for describing a flag divided quarterly is upper hoist, upper fly, lower hoist, and lower fly. However, when the field is gyronny (with or without the cross which typifies many Swiss military colors) it is customary to begin in the upper hoist, continuing clockwise and end with the lower hoist.

1

His title has varied over the centuries and in different lands – *ensign, cornet, vexillary, color-bearer, standard-bearer,* – but his position has always been an honorable one. This sixteenth-century Swiss standard-bearer holds a color that has been granted an *augmentation of honor* by the pope.

Originally long and tapering – whence the name still sometimes used, WHIP or COACHWHIP – pennants are now often short, sometimes even the same length as width. In the latter case, however, they are normally distinguished from other flags by being triangular or SWALLOWTAILED or of small size (such as an automobile flag). The common denominator distinguishing a pennant from a flag seems to be that the former is always secondary to the latter in importance and differs in shape, proportions, size, and/or manner of display (15-3).

PENNON
An armigerous LANCE FLAG (obsolete).

PENNONCEL / PENNONCELLE
See PENCEL.

PIKE
A STAFF ending in a spearhead FINIAL, intended to be carried by a soldier and displaying a COLOR.

PILOT FLAG
A DISTINGUISHING FLAG flown by a vessel requiring or carrying a pilot.

PIPE-BANNER
A BANNERET worn on bagpipes.

POLE
STAFF.

PRAYER FLAG
A small flag, often used in groups and decorated with inscriptions, intended to express a prayer as it flies; characteristic of Buddhists in the Himalayan region.

2

In addition to the traditional king's *color (left)* and regimental color *(right)*, the 74th Regiment had a third color displaying its *badge*, an elephant. Raised in Scotland, the 74th saw extensive service in India in the nineteenth century.

1 A massing of colors takes place as men from different parts of Switzerland gather under their cantonal banners in this sixteenth-century print.

The oldest heraldic (or armorial) banners were simple, colorful, and easy to identify. The entire field of each such flag corresponded exactly to the shield from a coat of arms, all accessories to the shield being omitted. Later such accessories were often included in armorial flags (see below), and the shields themselves grew more complicated.

This *Schellenbaum* (Baden Light Grenadiers, 1874) appeals to the ear as well as the eye.

2

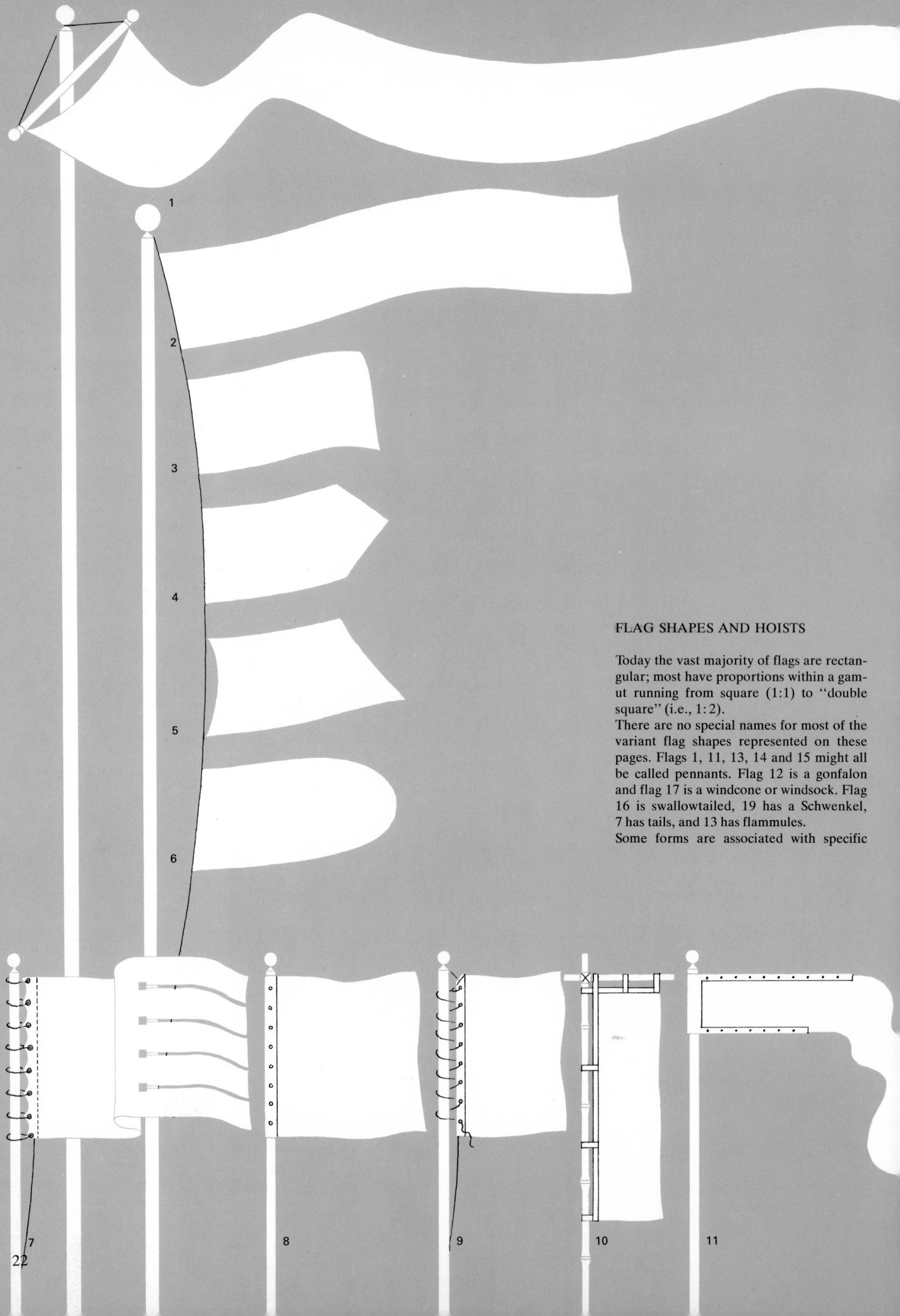

FLAG SHAPES AND HOISTS

Today the vast majority of flags are rectangular; most have proportions within a gamut running from square (1:1) to "double square" (i.e., 1:2).

There are no special names for most of the variant flag shapes represented on these pages. Flags 1, 11, 13, 14 and 15 might all be called pennants. Flag 12 is a gonfalon and flag 17 is a windcone or windsock. Flag 16 is swallowtailed, 19 has a Schwenkel, 7 has tails, and 13 has flammules.

Some forms are associated with specific

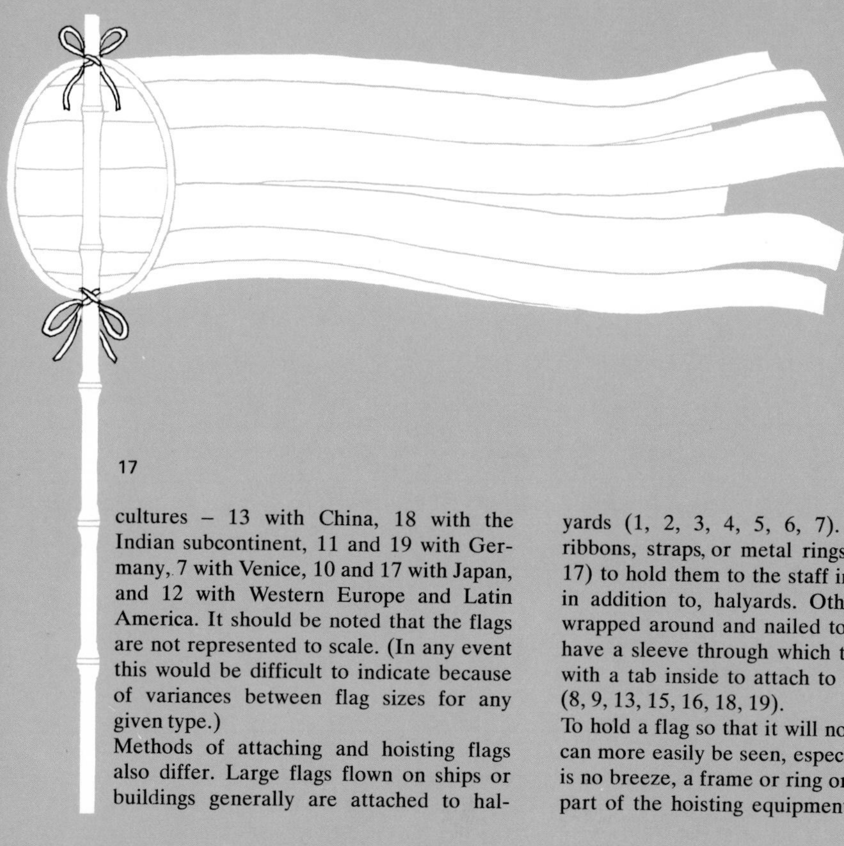

17

18

19

cultures – 13 with China, 18 with the Indian subcontinent, 11 and 19 with Germany, 7 with Venice, 10 and 17 with Japan, and 12 with Western Europe and Latin America. It should be noted that the flags are not represented to scale. (In any event this would be difficult to indicate because of variances between flag sizes for any given type.)

Methods of attaching and hoisting flags also differ. Large flags flown on ships or buildings generally are attached to halyards (1, 2, 3, 4, 5, 6, 7). Some have ribbons, straps, or metal rings (7, 10, 14, 17) to hold them to the staff instead of, or in addition to, halyards. Other flags are wrapped around and nailed to the pole or have a sleeve through which the pole fits, with a tab inside to attach to a screwhead (8, 9, 13, 15, 16, 18, 19).

To hold a flag so that it will not tangle and can more easily be seen, especially if there is no breeze, a frame or ring or bar may be part of the hoisting equipment (1, 10–12, 17). In order to facilitate hoisting with halyards, the flag heading may have grommets to which spring clips are attached. Alternately, a rope may be sewn through the heading, ending in spring clips or Inglefield clips or in a running eye and toggle – whatever corresponds to the halyards by which it is to be hoisted.

Large flagpoles, sometimes 60 meters (160 feet) or taller, often require steel cables as halyards, or some other special hoisting device may be needed.

12

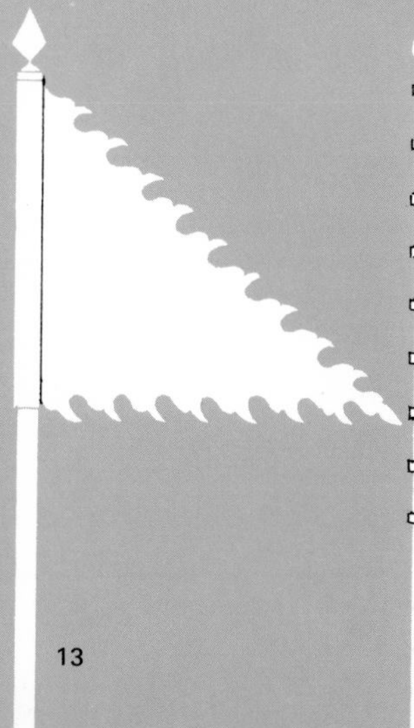

13

14

15

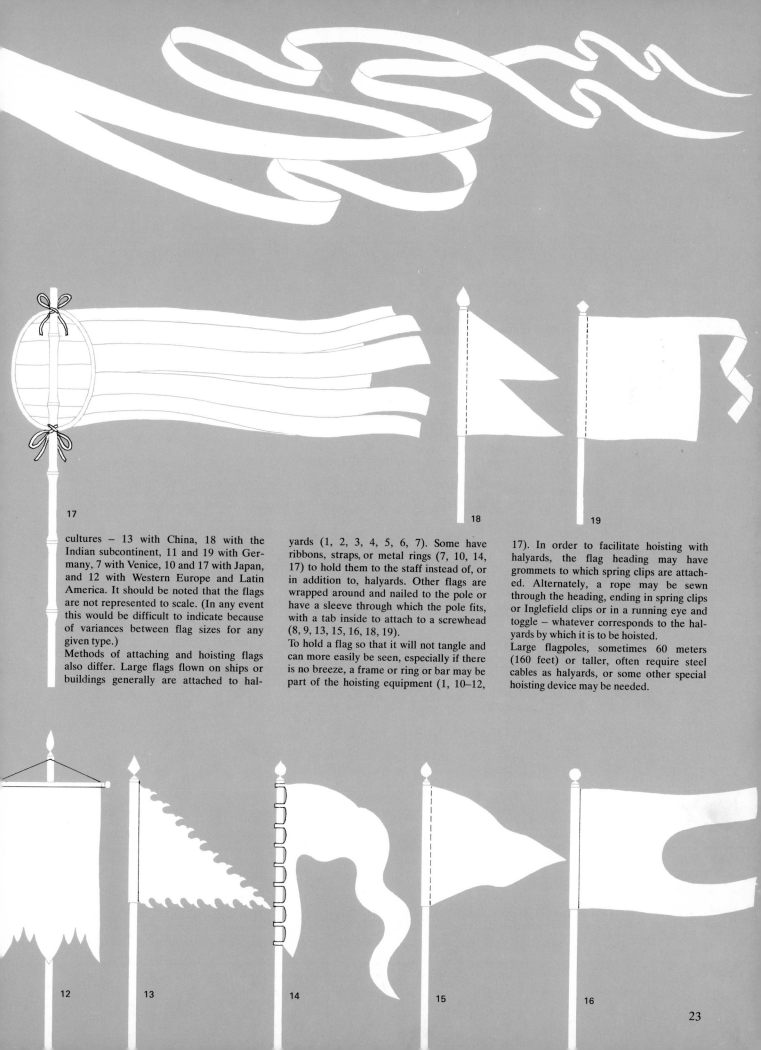

16

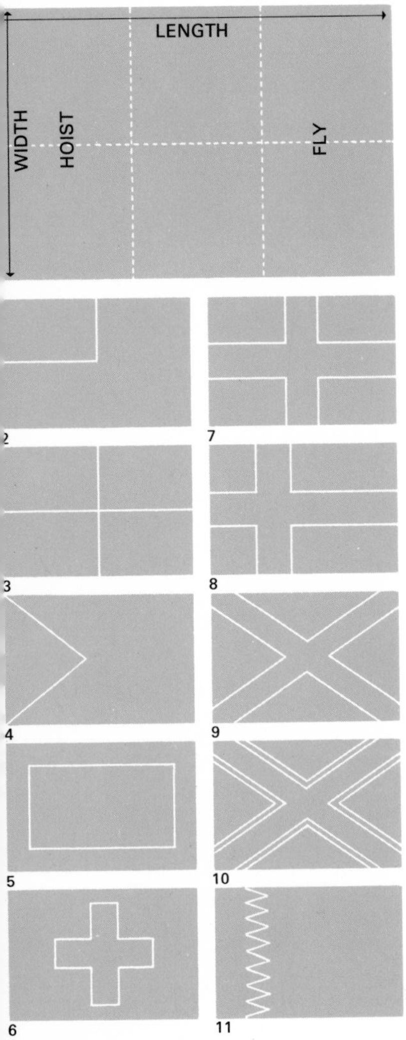

BASIC DESIGN COMPONENTS

1 PROPORTIONS 2 : 3
DIMENSIONS 3.6 × 5.4 cm
2 CANTON
3 QUARTERLY
4 TRIANGLE
5 BORDER
6 GREEK CROSS
7 CROSS THROUGHOUT
8 SCANDINAVIAN CROSS
9 SALTIRE
(or St. Andrew's cross)
10 FIMBRIATIONS
(fimbriated saltire)
11 SERRATION
(serrated border at hoist)

PRECEDENCE
The system of placing flags for a ceremony or display in order of importance; see page 95–97.

PRESIDENTIAL COLOR
See COLOR.

PRIZE FLAG
A special flag flown by a yacht which has won a race.

PROPORTIONS
The relative size of a flag, expressed in terms of its width to length ratio, e.g., 1:2 *(left)*; not to be confused with DIMENSIONS.

PULLDOWN
A flag (or BUNTING in flag colors) attached flat against a building or wall as decoration, the bottom sometimes flying free.

QUARTERLY
Divided into four equal segments crosswise (27-1). Unless the background is GYRONNY, the design or colors are described as follows: (1) upper hoist, (2) upper fly, (3) lower hoist, (4) lower fly.

RACING FLAG
A special flag flown by a yacht when racing.

RANK FLAG
The DISTINGUISHING FLAG of an individual's official position, civil or (usually) military (15-3).

REGIMENTAL COLOR
See COLOR.

REVERSE
The less important side of a flag, normally seen when the STAFF is to the SINISTER; the antonym of OBVERSE. A distinctive REVERSE design is usually found only in a COLOR.

RIBBON
A narrow piece of material serving as a decoration – especially of a military flag (19-1) – or as a means of attaching the flag to its STAFF. See STREAMER.

RING
A circular piece of wood or metal for attaching a WINDSOCK to a STAFF and for keeping it open (23-17); also a CHARGE of similar shape, not to be confused with the DISC.

ROUNDEL
A circular emblem of nationality employed on military aircraft and air force flags, generally consisting of concentric rings of different colors.

ROYAL STANDARD / ROYAL BANNER
The RANK FLAG, frequently an ARMORIAL BANNER, symbolizing the presence or authority of a monarch (25-2).

RUNNING EYE AND TOGGLE
A method of hoisting a flag by means of a rope sewn into its HEADING, which has a wooden toggle at the top and a loop of rope at the bottom that fasten to their opposites at the ends of the HALYARD.

SAFE CONDUCT FLAG
A special flag of recognized design, such as that of the Red Cross, which protects the bearer in wartime or while traveling.

ST. ANDREW'S CROSS
The SALTIRE, generally white on a blue flag or shield, symbolic of St. Andrew and used in Scotland, imperial Russia, and elsewhere (24-9); by extension, a cross of similar design regardless of colors.

ST. GEORGE'S CROSS
A red CROSS on a white flag or shield, symbolic of St. George and used in England, Genoa, and elsewhere; by extension, a flag cross of the same design regardless of color (25-2).

SALTIRE
A diagonal cross whose arms extend to the edges of a flag or shield (24-9).

SASH
A band of material, usually in the national colors and often bearing the national arms, worn across the chest by a head of state, especially in Latin America; a similar symbol used by political organizations.

SCALLOPS
Semicircles used to edge a flag (26-1).

SCANDINAVIAN CROSS
A flag design, often fimbriated (26-8), resembling a normal CROSS except that the vertical arms are set nearer the hoist than the fly.

SCHELLENBAUM
A VEXILLOID carried by soldiers, especially in Germany (21-2).

SCHWENKEL
A single long tail extending from the upper fly corner of a flag (23-19); a Central European custom, now obsolete.

SEMAPHORE
A system of signaling by means of two flags held in various positions.

SEMÉ
Strewn with an indeterminate number of certain objects such as stars or fleurs de lis.

SERRATED
Characterized by a jagged edge or division line (24-11).

SIGNAL FLAG
Any of a number of flags of recognized (and usually simple) design, such as the International Code of Signals, used to transmit messages, especially at sea.

SINISTER
The left-hand side of a flag or shield from the point

1

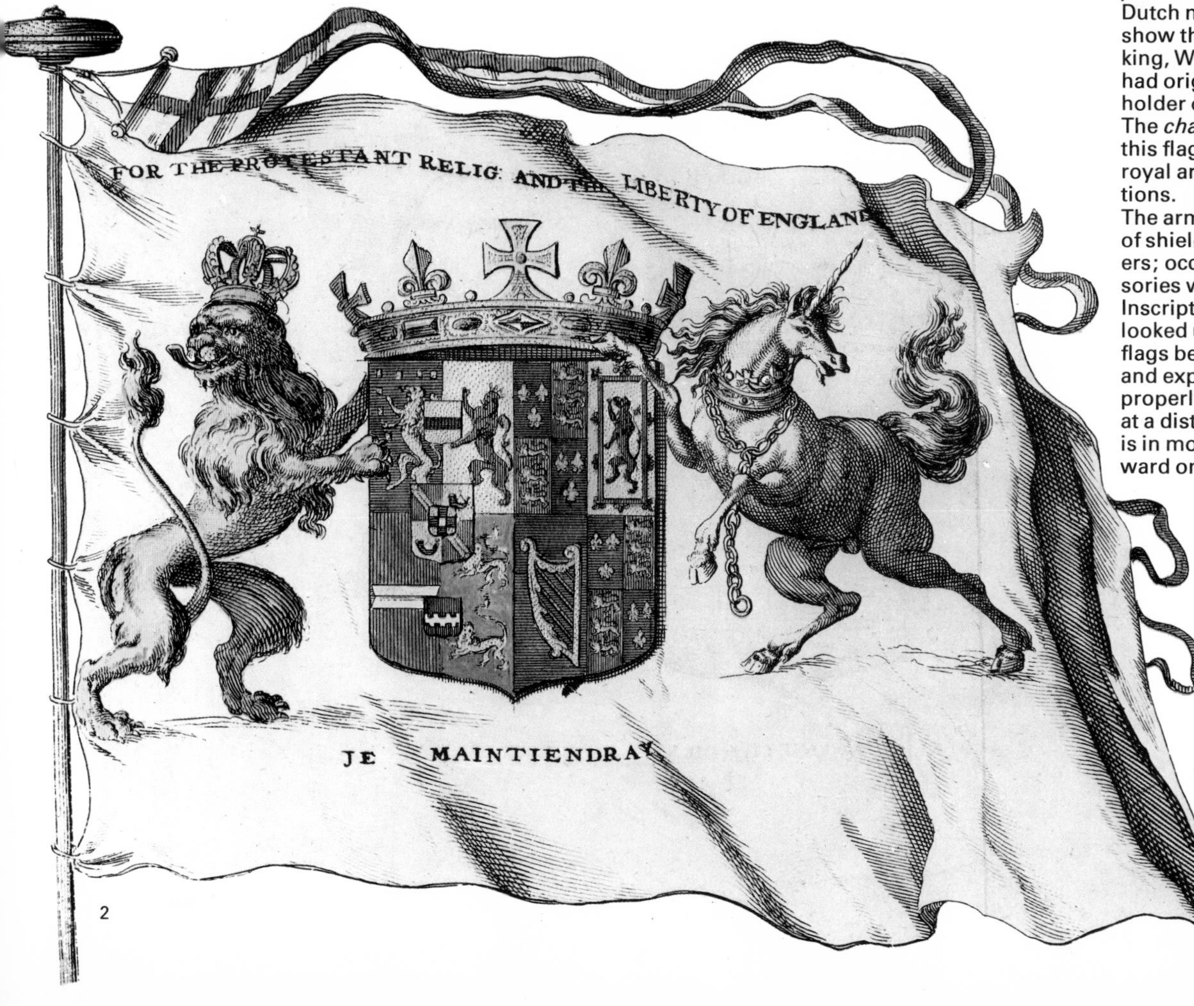
FOR THE PROTESTANT RELIG: AND THE LIBERTY OF ENGLAND
JE MAINTIENDRAY

2

ANALYSIS OF FLAGS.

The national flag of Tibet 1912–1959 *(left)* combines two modes of manufacture: the background and border are pieced together while the lion, yin-yang, and flaming jewels are painted on. In analyzing this flag the vexillologist would also be interested in its exact dimensions, proportions (2:3 in this case), the exact color shades, the design of the reverse (in this case a mirror image of the obverse), and, of course, the exact dates of usage, the manner of hoisting, the design symbolism and its historical development, as well as the rules for its proper usage.

The distinctive *finial* at left is of a pattern no longer in use. The *crossbar* bears a union *pennant* of the English and Dutch national symbols to show that England's new king, William III (1689–1702), had originally been stadholder of the Netherlands. The *charges* on the field of this flag consist of William's royal arms and two inscriptions.
The arms of William consist of shield, crest, and supporters; occasionally other accessories were added.
Inscriptions are generally looked upon with disfavor in flags because they are difficult and expensive to render properly, are difficult to read at a distance or when the flag is in motion, and read backward on the reverse of the flag.

1

In addition to tails of various shapes, the edges of the flag may be decorated with flammules, scallops, or incisions, although all are rare in modern flags.

of view of the bearer; the antonym of DEXTER (27-1).

SLEEVE
A tube of material along the HOIST of a flag through which the STAFF is inserted, used especially for a PARADE FLAG or COLOR.

SOUTHERN CROSS
A stylized representation of the constellation Crux Australis, used as a symbol in flags in the Southern Hemisphere.

STAFF
A cylindrical piece of wood or metal to which a flag is attached or from which it is hoisted (22); also called POLE or MAST. See also GAFF, TRUCK, CROSSBAR, PIKE, and FINIAL.

STANDARD
One of a number of different kinds of flags: (1) a pole with an emblem at the top (see VEXILLOID) around which soldiers could rally in battle, especially one fixed in place (rather than carried by a soldier) or transported in a large vehicle of its own (14-2); (2) a flag of heraldic design, generally long and tapering, used by noblemen in medieval battles and pageantry; (3) a rectangular flag, usually of heraldic design, still in use by cavalry and certain other military units such as the Royal Air Force in Britain; (4) the official RANK FLAG of a sovereign or other high official (see ROYAL STANDARD). The first two types are rarely if ever used today and the most common meaning of standard is the figurative or poetical – any flag around which people rally.

STANDARD-BEARER
One who carries a standard, especially as defined in STANDARD (2) and (3); a synonym for VEXILLARY, ENSIGN, CORNET, and COLOR-BEARER (20-1).

STATE ENSIGN
The NATIONAL FLAG flown on nonmilitary government vessels; often a basic design with special BADGES added for individual services (post office, customs, fishery inspection).

STATE FLAG
The NATIONAL FLAG flown on land over nonmilitary property; also called GOVERNMENT FLAG.

STREAMER
A long, narrow flag formerly used as decoration on vessels; by extension, any long, narrow ribbon attached to a STAFF, such as those on which BATTLE HONORS are inscribed.

SUITE OF FLAGS
A group of flags to be used together under certain circumstances; specifically, the JACK, PENNANT, and ENSIGN of a commissioned warship (18-1).

SWALLOWTAILED
Having a large triangular section cut from the fly end, a characteristic of PENNANTS and of WAR ENSIGNS of Northern Europe. War ensigns sometimes have a third tail between the other two; such a flag may be referred to as swallowtailed with a tongue.

TAB
A small piece of leather sewn within the SLEEVE of a flag and fastened to a screwhead protruding from the STAFF, designed to keep the flag from slipping from the staff.

TABLE FLAG
A small flag, frequently mounted on a CROSSBAR, whose STAFF and stand make it suitable for display on a desk or podium.

2

The armorial is a book showing the arms of individuals or territories entitled to bear them. Such armorials *(above)* were kept by heralds to prevent duplications of design and to eliminate fradulent claims. Heraldry had close relationships with flags during the centuries it flourished in medieval Europe. Many vexillological terms derive from heraldic experience.

Literally hundreds of specialized terms have evolved for use in describing special heraldic forms; even specialized heraldic dictionaries exist. Nevertheless very few of these have relevance to the subject of flags, except in limited instances. The following three pages present those terms which are most useful for an under standing of flags.
The illustration here presents the *achievement* (complete heraldic emblem) of the nineteenth-century Principality of Schwarzburg-Sondershausen. The *greater arms* is known as such not because it is larger but because it is more comp cated than the *lesser arms* (not shown here), a distinction still made by some nations today. Among its elements are the: *pavilion,* a decorative background; *tilting-lance with pennant,* such as was carried in tournaments by knights; *mantling,* a decorative cloth found on the helmet; *crests,* emblems over the helmet; *supporters,* a man on the *dexter* and a woman on the *sinister;* a shield divided *quarterly,* and bearing three *inescutcheons* and two *quarterings* which are *checky,* the whole resting on a *compartment.*

An important distinction should be made between the arms of political units (state heraldry) as treated in this book and personal or family heraldry.

BASIC ELEMENTS OF THE SHIELD.

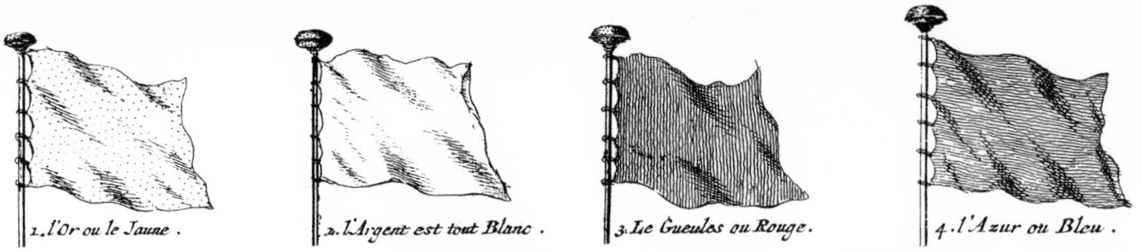

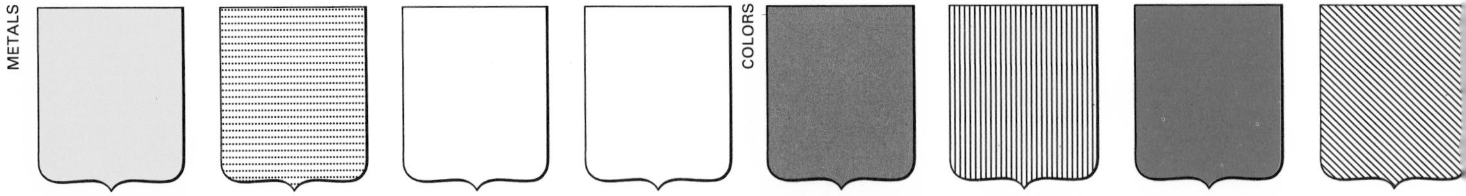

OR (GOLD OR YELLOW) ARGENT (SILVER OR WHITE) GULES (RED) VERT (GREEN)

FURS. The stylized heraldic designs shown here are extremely rare in flags; the best known example is the traditional flag of Brittany, which was plain ermine.

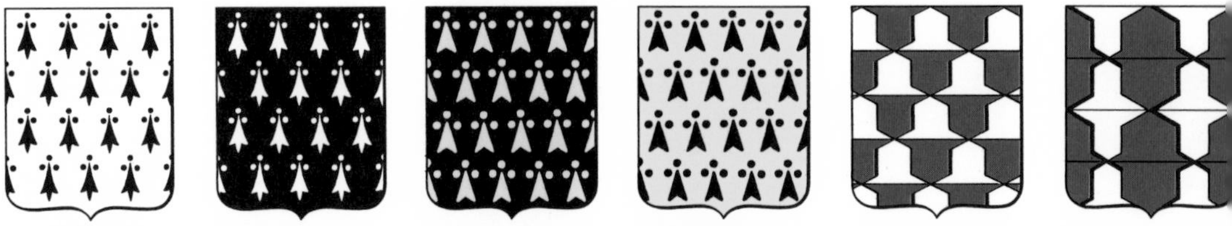

ERMINE ERMINES PEAN ERMINOIS VAIR COUNTER-VAIR

PARTITIONS OF THE SHIELD. A few of the names used in heraldry are also found in flags, as indicated by an asterisk.

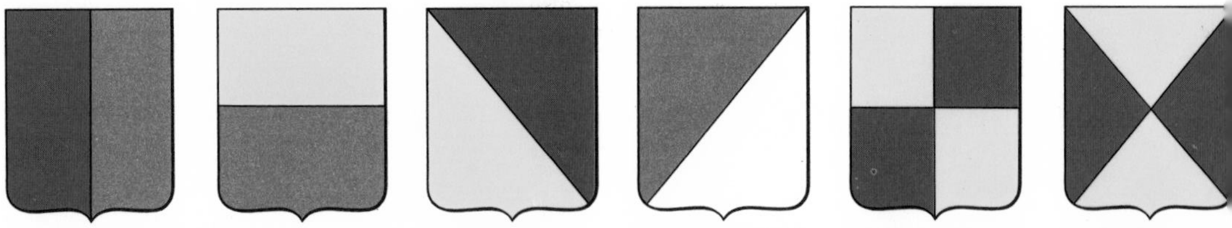

PER PALE PER FESS PER BEND PER BEND SINISTER QUARTERLY* PER SALTIRE

ORDINARIES. This name is given to geometric divisions of a shield, while other emblems (e.g., a lion) are known as charges.

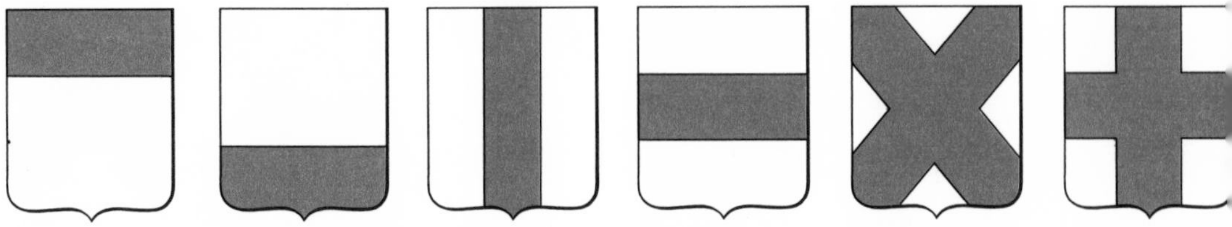

CHIEF BASE PALE FESS SALTIRE CROSS

AMERICAN STATE ARMS. These eighteenth-century arms, many still in use, derive from sigillographic as well as heraldic sources.

NEW HAMPSHIRE MASSACHUSETTS RHODE ISLAND CONNECTICUT NEW YORK NEW JERSEY

RUSSIAN CITY ARMS. These and the arms above and below show the great design similarities which tend to exist within a single country, despite the basic heraldic rule that arms should be clearly distinguishable from one another.

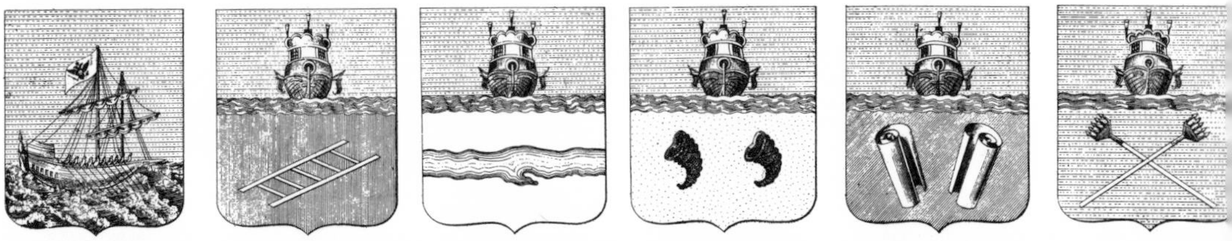

THE KASTROM DISTRICT'S OWN ARMS *(ABOVE, EXTREME LEFT)* WERE COPIED IN THE ARMS OF THE DISTRICT TOWNS AND VILLAGES.

JAPANESE *MON*. The most striking of modern designs are found in the civic heraldry of Japan and Scandinavia and in the commercial graphics of the United States.

THE FORMS SHOWN IN THESE *MON* (JAPANESE FAMILY ARMS, *ABOVE*) ARE ONLY A FEW OF THE THOUSANDS IN EXISTENCE.

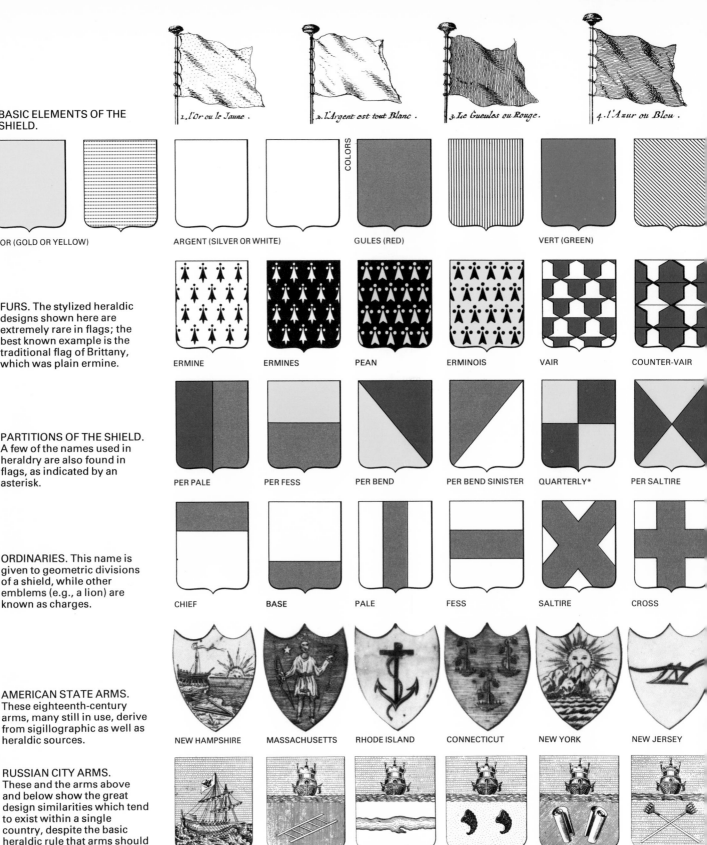

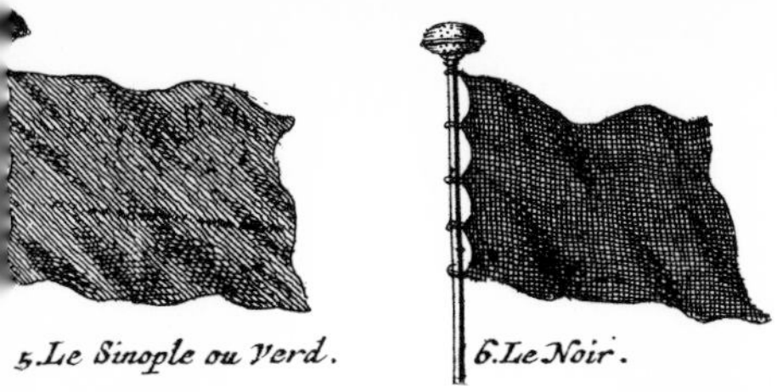

For further information on the relationship between heraldry and flags, see pages 41–55.

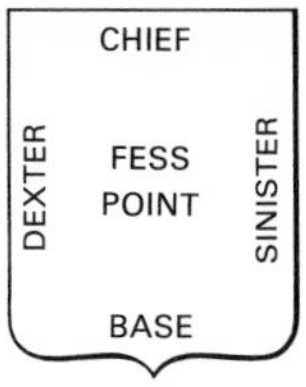

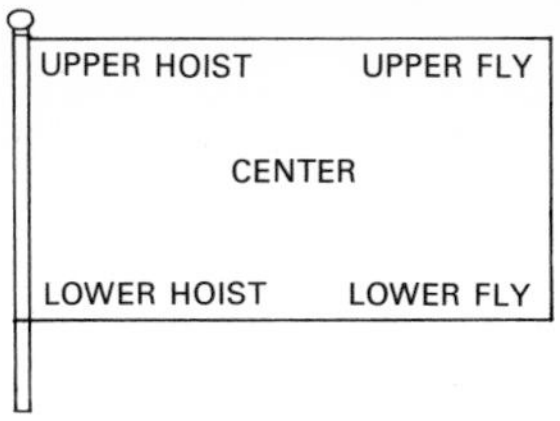

AZURE (BLUE) SABLE (BLACK) PURPURE (PURPLE) TENNÉ (ORANGE)

POTENT

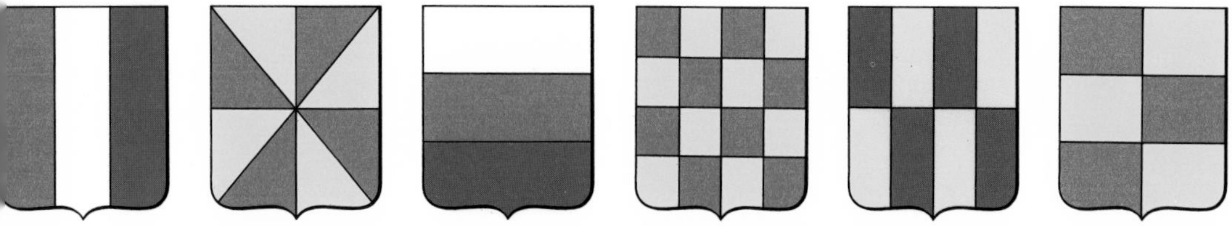

TIERCED IN PALE GYRONNY* OF EIGHT TIERCED IN FESS CHECKY*/CHEQUY

The last two shields are among the many possible elaborations of the basic heraldic shield partitions.

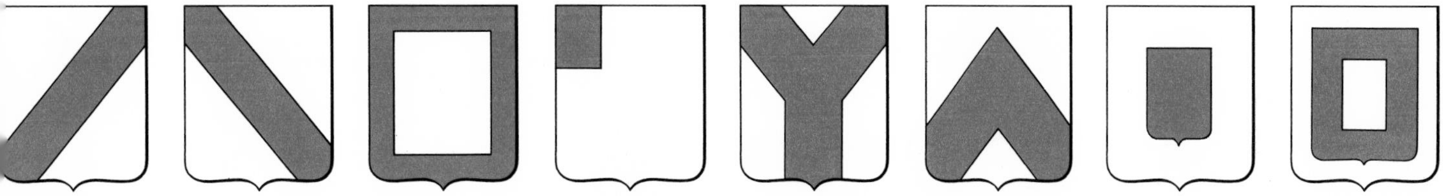

BEND SINISTER BEND BORDER CANTON PALL CHEVRON INESCUTCHEON ORLE

PENNSYLVANIA DELAWARE MARYLAND VIRGINIA NORTH CAROLINA SOUTH CAROLINA GEORGIA

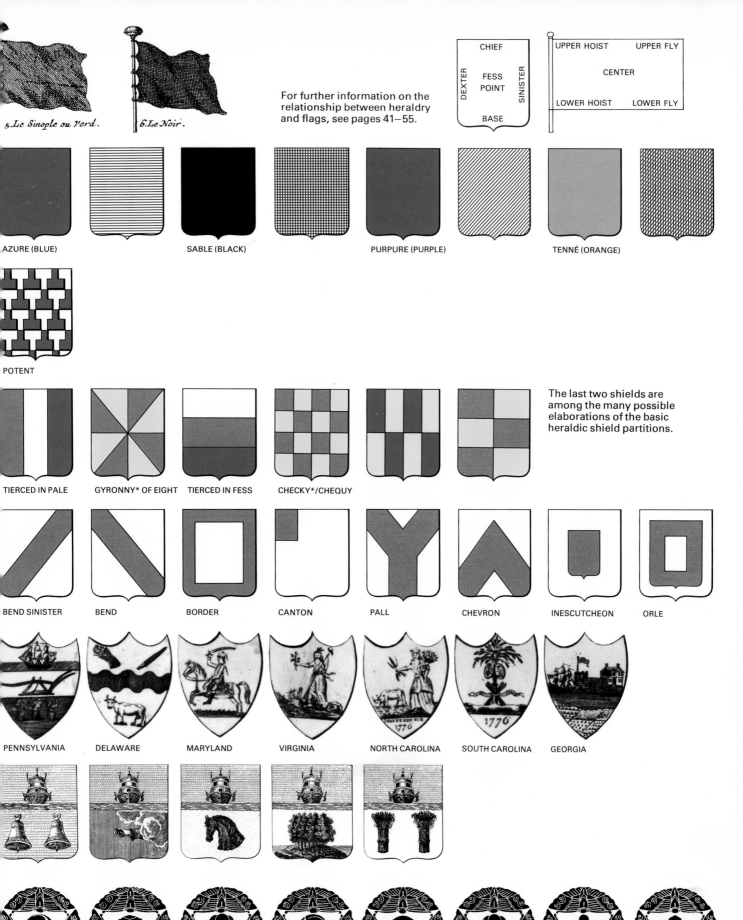

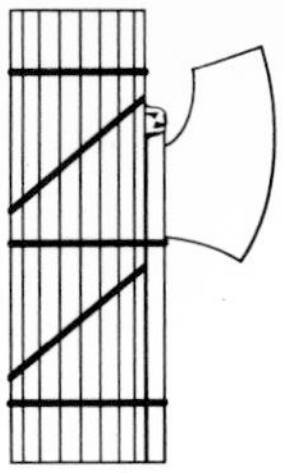
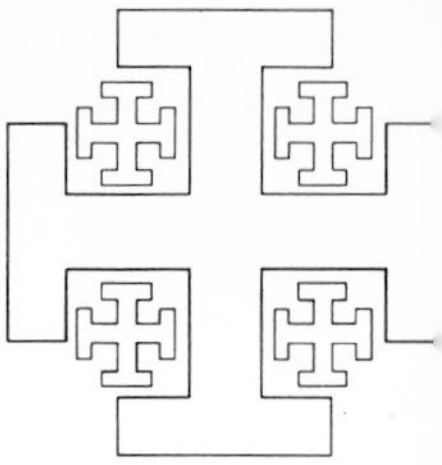

TAIL
A squared or pointed piece of material, long or short, decorating the edge of a flag (22 and 23). See SCHWENKEL.

TANGLE ROD
A metal device attached to a STAFF, particularly one set at an angle from a building, which clasps a flag and prevents it from wrapping around the staff.

TASSELS
A decoration of twisted thread or metal, often surrounding a wooden core and hanging from a cord, attached to a STAFF or directly to a flag – especially a COLOR or PARADE FLAG.

TOGGLE
See RUNNING EYE AND TOGGLE.

TORSE
A representation of a bar of twisted silk, normally in the LIVERY colors of a shield, set below the CREST and above the helmet in a coat of arms.

TRICOLOR
A flag whose FIELD is divided horizontally, vertically, or diagonally into three different colors.

TROOPING THE COLOR
A British ceremony in which the colors are marched past assembled troops.

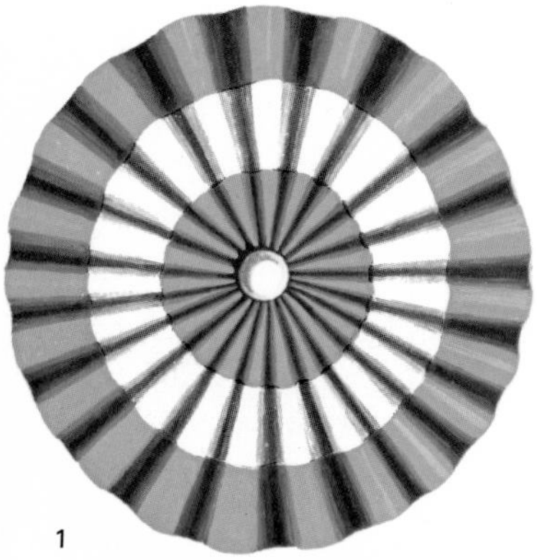

1

Cockades (like those of Argentina, *above*) were very common in the late eighteenth and early nineteenth centuries as political symbols – so much so that some countries adopted official colors for their cockades and made no mention of a national flag. Generally, however, the two or three colors of such a cockade translated directly into a bicolor or tricolor flag.

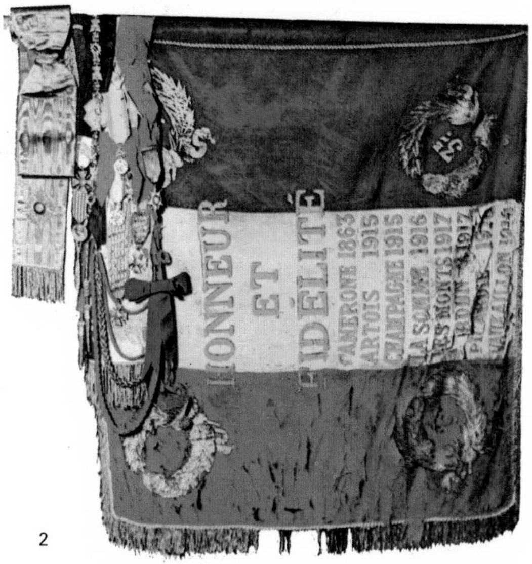

2

The color of the Third Regiment of Infantry of the Foreign Legion *(right)* is the most decorated military flag of France and provides an unusual example of flag accessories. *Battle honors* are inscribed on the white stripe; *fringe* surrounds the flag itself; the *pike* or *staff* is decorated below the *finial* with a *cravat* to which orders and decorations are pinned, while above are the ribbons or collars of other military orders and fourragères. Although they are supposed to remain at headquarters, military *colors* occasionally appear on battle fields even today.

TRUCK
A device at the top of a STAFF below the FINIAL which provides, usually through a pulley, for the raising and lowering of the HALYARDS.

TRUMPET-BANNER
A BANNERET used to decorate a ceremonial trumpet.

TUGH
The VEXILLOID of Mongolian and Turkic usage symbolizing civil or military authority and generally consisting of one or more HORSETAILS at the top of a STAFF.

TYPE FLAG
A model of pattern and color, often sanctioned by law, after which actual flags are manufactured; the antonym is UNIQUE FLAG.

UNION MARK
A symbol expressing political unification of two or more territories, such as the British Union Jack, generally employed both alone and as a CHARGE in other flags.

UNIQUE FLAG
A flag intended in design and usage to be the only one of its kind. If such a flag becomes famous in battle or as a symbol, it may eventually become a TYPE FLAG.

UNIT DESIGNATION
An inscription on a COLOR indicating the military group to which it belongs.

VAILING
The DIPPING of a COLOR as a salute.

VANE
A small metal flag, generally set to swivel on a rod on the top of a building or, formerly, a vessel (14-1).

VENETIAN ENTASIS TAPER
A distinctive design invented in Venice which provides for an esthetically pleasing tapering of a tall STAFF.

VEXILLARY
(Noun) A STANDARD-BEARER; originally a member of a special Roman military unit under a separate VEXILLUM. (Adj.) Of or pertaining to flags.

VEXILLATRY / VEXILLOLATRY
Treatment of the flag as a fetish or sacred object.

VEXILLOID
An object which functions as a flag but differs from it in some respect, usually appearance. Vexilloids are characteristic of traditional societies and often consist of a STAFF with an emblem, such as a carved animal, at the top (13-1).

VEXILLOLOGY (vex-il-*lol*-o-gy)
The scientific study of the history, symbolism, and usage of flags or, by extension, any interest in flags in general. VEXILLOGICAL/VEXILLOLOGICAL, VEXILLOLOGIST, VEXILLOGRAPHER, VEXILLOPHILIST.

VEXILLUM (vek-*sil*-lum; pl. VEXILLA)
A Roman cavalry flag suspended from a CROSSBAR, or the cavalry unit carrying such a flag.

WAFT / WHEFT
A flag tied in a knot and displayed (at sea) as a signal of some emergency; now obsolete.

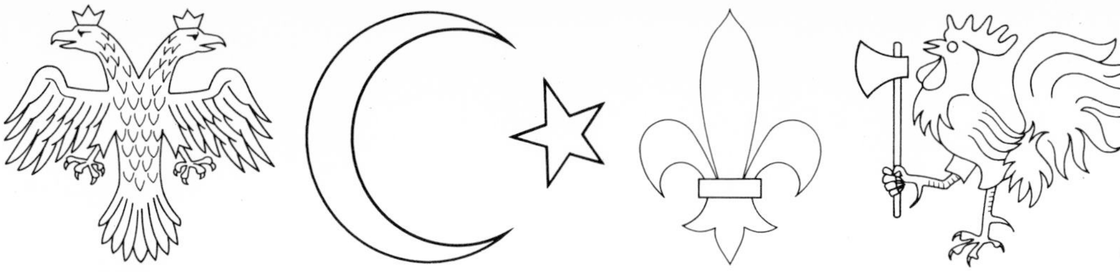

1

Not included in this chapter on terminology are specific symbols found in certain flags and coats of arms, such as those shown *(left)* – the Tudor rose, Sun of May, fasces, Cross of Jerusalem, double-headed eagle, star and crescent, fleur-de-lis, and golden cockerel. Such emblems are analyzed in the chapter entitled "Symbols."

WAR ENSIGN
The NATIONAL FLAG flown on armed vessels; also called NAVAL ENSIGN.

WAR FLAG
The NATIONAL FLAG flown over camps and other military establishments on land, often in conjunction with the STATE FLAG; not to be confused with a COLOR.

WIGWAG
To signal by waving a single flag according to an established code; also signaling in this manner.

WINDSOCK / WINDCONE
A flag shaped like a sleeve, attached at one end to a RING and STAFF and open at the other end (23-17). The windsock is characteristic of traditional societies and of modern Japan.

2

Flags are often employed in conjunction with other symbols, as in this painting by Douanier Rousseau, *The Centenary of Independence.* The liberty cap and the liberty tree are ancient symbols revived by the French and American Revolutions of the late eighteenth century.

WEAR A FLAG
To display a flag; said of a vessel.

WHIP
See PENNANT.

WIDTH
The measurement of a flag along its HOIST (British BREADTH); the antonym of LENGTH.

YACHT FLAG
Any of a number of special flags (see PENNANT, PRIZE FLAG, RACING FLAG), but especially the BURGEE.

YARDARM
A bar attached horizontally to a STAFF on the mizzenmast of a ship or on shore in imitation of naval usage. Flags are flown from it attached to HALYARDS.

FLAGS THROUGH THE AGES

Flags are a universal characteristic of human civilization. With the exception of the most primitive societies and of nomadic peoples, it appears that every culture has invented for itself flags of one kind or another – with a remarkable similarity of form observable throughout the world. The functions of flags are nearly identical in all societies, and parallels in flag usages may be observed in diverse regions and eras.

So strong is the tradition of flags, we may not be far from the truth in surmising that there is a law – not of nature, but of human society – which impels man to make and use flags. There is perhaps no more striking demonstration of this than the fact that, despite the absence of any international regulation or treaty requiring the adoption of a national flag, without exception every country has adopted at least one. Nations have made it clear through elaborate ceremonies that their flags are objects of special reverence and high regard.

The similarities between flags at different times and at different places cannot obscure the profound differences that exist. The knight's attendant with his banners *(right)* is worlds away from the Aztec standard-bearer, both of whom lived in the fifteenth century, and neither would fit into our own world without considerable adaptation. Thus one purpose of the following pages is to introduce the development of flags in a way that will make more comprehensible the modern usages dealt with further on.

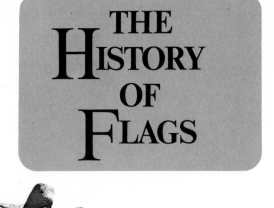

THE HISTORY OF FLAGS

"HAVE NOT I MYSELF KNOWN FIVE HUNDRED LIVING SOLDIERS SABRED INTO CROWS' MEAT FOR A PIECE OF GLAZED COTTON, WHICH THEY CALL THEIR FLAG; WHICH HAD YOU SOLD IT AT ANY MARKET-CROSS, WOULD NOT HAVE BROUGHT ABOVE THREE GROSCHEN?"

Thomas Carlyle, *Sartor Resartus*

Man's earliest flags were generally vexilloids. This form of standard still is used in some parts of the world. The vexilloids shown here *(left to right)* are, respectively, from fourth-century Iran, seventh-century England, thirteenth-century Mongolia, fourteenth-century Ethiopia, and sixteenth-century Mexico.

Probably the oldest flag still in existence, the metal standard from Iran *(right)* dates back five thousand years. The eagle finial is similar to those used in modern German and American flags; and Iran's own modern national symbol, the lion and sun, figures in the design.

Ships with vexilloids *(below)* were represented on predynastic Egyptian pottery dating back fifty-five centuries.

We do not know when or where mankind's first flag was raised, but the antiquity of flags is hinted at by the fact that every example so far uncovered by archeologists, even ones dating back five thousand years, gives evidence of a sophistication built on elaboration over time. In a more important sense the whole question of the "first flag" is irrelevant because flags are a manifestation of a wider and still older form of human activity, the making of symbols. Moreover, societies little developed in the material sphere may nevertheless have sophisticated symbol systems belied by their external forms. Just as the graphic simplicity of the Tricolor of France in no way makes it less interesting than the complicated royal standards of the Old Regime, so the "simple" vexilloids of primitive peoples can rival more complex flags in social significance.

Because they are not an isolated phenomenon, in either function or form, flags are best understood if one has some appreciation for the alternate forms of symbolism that have been devised. However diverse, these may be categorized in one of four groups – active, verbal, concrete, or graphic symbols. Active symbolism involves motion: the upraised clenched fist, the triumphal parade, the coronation ceremony, and a salute to the flag are all examples. Verbal symbols convey their meaning through written or spoken words – the propaganda pamphlet, national anthem, and oaths of allegiance coming to mind under this category. A concrete symbol is any object which, in addition to its practical purposes, has been imbued with a special symbolic meaning. When protesters gather under a tree which recalls an event that is sacred for them, when a building or mountain is the object of reverent pilgrims, or when some other ordinary object acquires a mystic force in the minds of people it constitutes a concrete symbol.

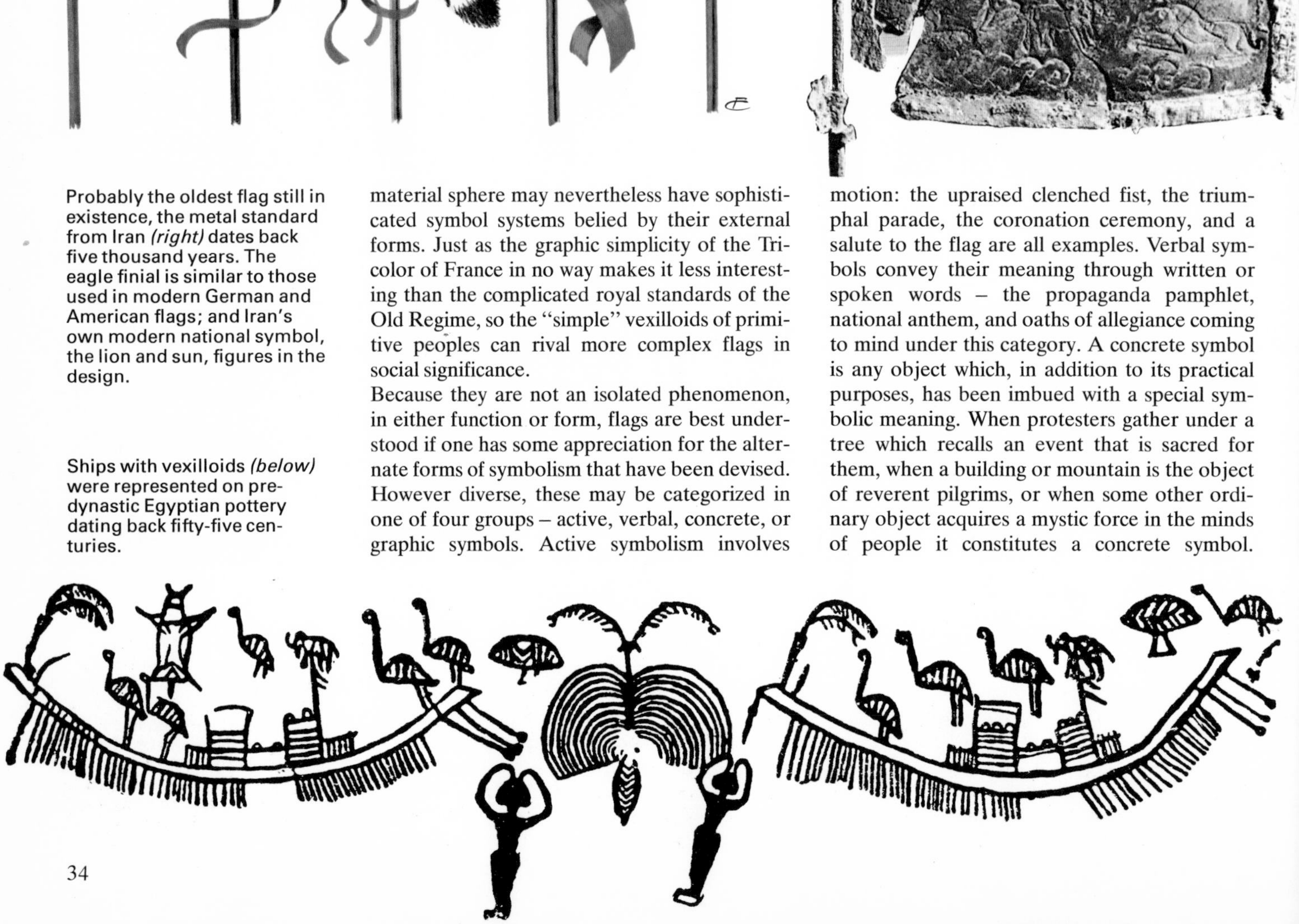

Somewhat crude by modern standards, these vexilloids quite adequately symbolized the different provinces of Egypt millenia ago. The designs resemble those of medieval Japanese warriors (pages 164-165 and 168-169).

Graphic symbols involve the use of illustrative material, colors and patterns, whereas the medium which bears them is of secondary importance.

King Narmer, uniter of Egypt in ca. 3200 B.C., advances on his decapitated enemies in the representation *(above)* carved in stone. He is preceded by the vexilloid standards of three *nomes* or provinces: the Two Falcon Province had the privilege of being represented by two similar vexilloids.

The most potent symbols are those which combine all four aspects simultaneously. This has long been understood in religion, where worshippers may gather in a temple (concrete symbol) decorated with holy icons (graphic symbols), while they perform rituals (active symbolism) by reading from holy scriptures (verbal symbolism). Many political activities are based on the model of religious worship; hence the same elements of symbolism are repeated in China when the Red Guard marches (active symbolism) past the Gate of Heavenly Peace (concrete symbol) displaying revolutionary slogans (verbal symbolism) on huge banners (graphic symbols). Of course there are many situations in which it is difficult (and pointless) to distinguish between forms of symbolism.

There are two basic kinds of graphic symbols. In one type the design itself holds the meaning, regardless of how or where it is represented – in print, clothing, on walls or streets, on coins or posters or banners, or even as formed by air-

Early Chinese vexilloids featured the phoenix, a symbol in the Orient of peace, prosperity, and beauty.

planes or massed athletes. Among the best-known symbols of this type have been the cross, the swastica, and the star. Color combinations have been increasingly important since the rise of nationalism: the red shirts of Garibaldi's men and red-black-green of American blacks are examples. The second type of graphic symbol combines design and/or colors with specific material to produce one of a number of related symbolic forms, including seals, coats of arms, medals, decorations, uniforms, posters, armbands, cockades, and flags.

It is probable that the plasticity of flags has made their use so extensive for so long. An embossed seal on a document may be impressive but can only be seen by a very limited number of persons at any one time. A uniform identifies the wearer to outsiders and gives him a feeling of belonging to a strong and purposeful group; but it is not easy to express nuances of meaning nor to change one's symbolic communication through the medium of the uniform. On the contrary flags are capable of being used and seen by great numbers of people simultaneously. Flags can be easily and quickly made, altered, transmitted – and disposed of. To display a flag is to participate in a group or a philosophy that spans time and distances; it is to express one's own views to others in a concise but dramatic form. In a word the flag is a powerful instrument for social participation and communication.

All this has been stressed in part because of the misconceptions many hold concerning flags. Even in books on the subject there is frequently an implicit assumption that flags are mere decoration, a colorful but insignificant expression of patriotism. Explicitly, many of these books view flags as merely a derivative from and adaptation of heraldry. On the contrary flags, far from being merely a colorful exterior to the world of real events, constitute factors affecting that world directly as they manipulate and are manipulated by groups of people. Examples of

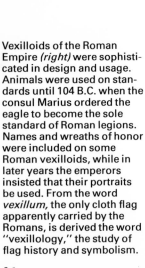

Vexilloids of the Roman Empire *(right)* were sophisticated in design and usage. Animals were used on standards until 104 B.C. when the consul Marius ordered the eagle to become the sole standard of Roman legions. Names and wreaths of honor were included on some Roman vexilloids, while in later years the emperors insisted that their portraits be used. From the word *vexillum,* the only cloth flag apparently carried by the Romans, is derived the word "vexillology," the study of flag history and symbolism.

Naval flags of ancient Rome *(below)* closely paralleled types used on land *(left)*.

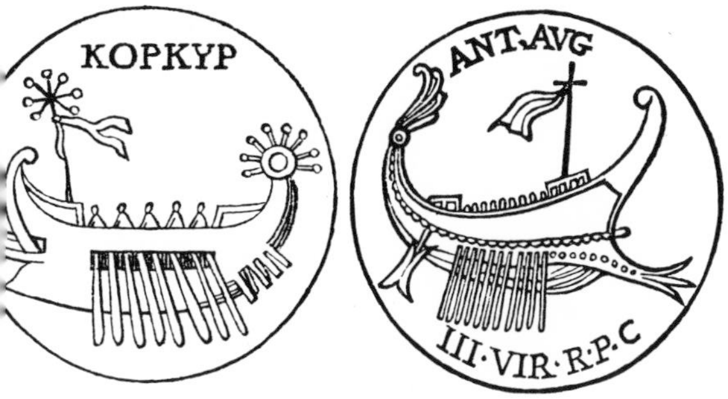

this can be found in even the most ancient societies. Like other symbols, flags express the unity and identity of one group as against all others; it is a way of asserting the bonds which link people despite differences in their wealth, social standing, power, or age. Just as important is the function of the flag and its symbolism in interpreting the unknown forces of the universe, assuring people that their frailty is somehow compensated for by an eternal invisible realm from which they may draw strength. The flag is then an externalization of the fears and hopes, the myths, and the magic of those who carry it.

It should not be surprising that the earliest flags of which we have record place great emphasis on the staff and its finial, sometimes even to the exclusion of the cloth it bears. The staff is a symbol of power; it corresponds to clubs, swords, and other weapons as well as to the erect male organ – which simultaneously embodies regeneration of the race and male dominance over the female, the prototype of other master-slave relationships. From the practical standpoint, the flag staff is an object which can readily be carried aloft in battle, planted beside the throne of a chief, or made the central element in an altar. It is a portable version of the trees under which many societies have traditionally gathered in council or in worship. Its height makes the pole easy to see at a distance, to follow, and to rally around especially in military engagements. In form it expresses the aspiration of earth-bound mankind toward the heavens, which undoubtedly accounts for the prevalence of the eagle as a finial motif.

While the earliest flags were vexilloids, the emblem at the top of the staff varied. It might have been the tail of a tiger, a metal vane, a ribbon, a carved animal, a windsock of woven grasses or crude cloth, or a construction combining more than one material. Since kinship, real or imagined, constitutes the principal organizing technique of primitive societies, very frequently we find the animal from which the clan claims descent and for which it is named – i.e., its totem – as the chief symbol of the vexilloid. The people who carried the totem believed they derived their powers from it; hence vexilloids very early acquired a religious significance they have never lost.

In many instances the protection of the vexilloid spread gradually from the kinship group to all those living within its geographical area. Fictional kinship ties were invented and sanctified by modifications and adaptations of the totemic emblem. Thus flags helped to create a new entity corresponding to (and often named for) the flag it recognized as supreme. From earliest times to the present we find political entities named for their symbols – from the Black Bull and Two Shields Provinces of predynastic Egypt to the banners (political-military districts) of medieval France and Mongolia and the Bear Flag Republic of 1846 in California.

The line is difficult to draw between a flag as a sacred object to be worshipped and one rather to be employed simply as an instrument for communication with the gods. In the Roman Empire, for example, the Eagles and other vexilloids were worshipped; for soldiers thousands of miles from Rome, these portable deities formed a link to the divinity of the emperor and the sacred devotions performed in his name. Like Roman religion, these vexilloids were not jealous or exclusivistic: official recognition was given in the Roman pantheon to the totemic

The Greek vase above is typical of the sources from which our knowledge of ancient flags is reconstructed.

The Chinese were probably the first to use silk flags. They have been used both at sea and on land *(right)* for thousands of years, much longer than in the West.

The vexilloid may take different forms in different cultures. In Southeast Asia *(above)* and West Africa, the parasol is an alternate political symbol of great importance. In China fans *(right)* also played a role as vexilloids.

vexilloids of barbarian troops serving in the Roman army. It was a matter of great surprise to the Romans when the monotheistic Jews rioted in ca. 26 A.D. upon the introduction of the sacred Roman vexilloids into the Temple on order of Pilate.

The Romans also appreciated other attributes of their symbols. Like their language, legal system, coinage, weights and measures, and roads and water systems, the vexilloids of Rome were means of substituting a political and cultural unity for the military strength which had originally created the empire. Wherever they appeared, the ensigns of the legions were a visible sign of the power and majesty of the Roman state; they indicated that the protection of its laws and courts was available, that peace and order would reign so long as they remained. The Roman technique of overawing citizenry by the parade of soldiers in full battle dress with standards displayed, as a compensation for a rather thin distribution of actual military resources, has been followed by many societies since. Quite intentionally, few public spectacles were so lavishly conceived and executed as the Roman triumph, and the sight of the legionary Eagles irrevocably implanted a belief in conqueror and vanquished alike that Rome had a divine mission, that it was invincible, and that it would remain forever. These impressions were reinforced by the sight of flags and regalia captured from other peoples which were always paraded in Rome.

On the battlefield Roman standards were expected to play specific functions. As an incitement to his troops a commander would sometimes order his legion's Eagles thrown into the ranks of the enemy, forcing his men to recapture them. The very massing of the troops with their glittering standards helped create a sense of awe and trepidation in the enemy. Some flags – such as the Dragon, which made a shrill whistling

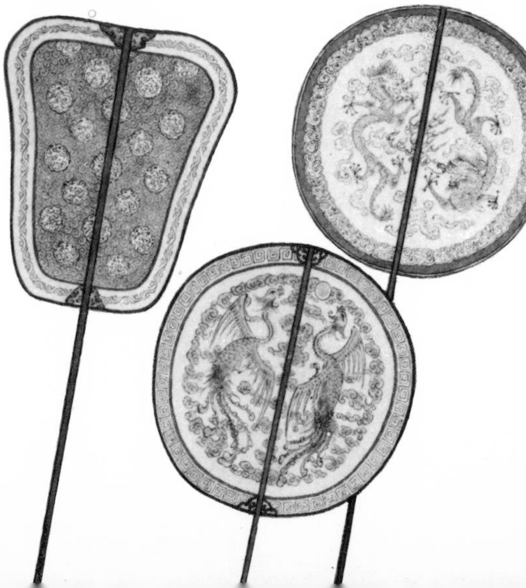

noise when the wind blew through it – were particularly effective in this regard. Signal flags were also employed to indicate tactical maneuvers, the position of troops, and the general progress of an engagement.

Both the vexilloid form and the political, military, and religious functions characteristic of Roman flags are repeated in many other contemporary or earlier civilizations of Asia from the eastern end of the Mediterranean to the Pacific Ocean. Standards with astral symbols of religious significance appeared in Indian and Mesopotamian cultures some four thousand years ago. A sun and moon standard was recorded in Phoenicia in the fifth century B.C.; in the same era Greek navies were known to have used a signal flag to mark the ship of an admiral or the command to attack. Vexilloids from Iran dating to the fourth and third centuries B.C. include both a totemic animal at the top of the pole and a cloth flag (hanging from a crossbar) that bears a distinctive emblem – eagles, falcons, suns, stars, and geometric designs apparently being the most common.

From extant records it is obvious that cloth did not at first have the primacy as a flag medium that it has held over the last thousand years. Leather, wood, metal, and other materials were used quite frequently, leading to a diversity of flag shapes which has also since been lost. On the other hand it must be kept in mind that our documentation on any of these ancient civilizations is fragmentary. Not only are distortions in our understanding possible because we have so little to rely on, but it is frequently difficult even to determine how to translate a word correctly. While the Bible says (Numbers II:2) "Every man of the children of Israel shall pitch by his own standard with the ensign of their father's house," we do not know for certain what these emblems looked like – although that question is not very relevant to an appreciation of their social function.

It would appear that we owe to the Chinese two characteristics of flags which are now universal –

19
٢١

ويحك الفص والجبالة · والفس والذبالة انها لضغث على ابالة فانضاعت نفس مدرجها

وتنشد مدرجها فلما دانتني قرنت بالرقعة درهما وقطعة وقلت لها ان رغبت في المشوف المعلم

واشيري الى الدرهم فبوحي بالسر المدهم وان ابيت ان تشري فخذي القطعة وابري

مالت الى استخلاص البدر التم والابلج الهم وقالت دع جدالك وسل عما بدا لك فاستطلعت

طلع الشيخ وبلدته والشعر وناسج بردته فقالت ان الشيخ من اهل سروج وهو الذي وشى

their lateral attachment to the staff and a focus on the cloth of a flag rather than on its staff and finial. While vexilloids of diverse and imaginative shapes are seen in early Chinese manuscripts, the importance of sericulture very early (perhaps 3000 B.C.) introduced the possibility of a flag that could be light in weight yet large, strong enough to last for a reasonable amount of time in outdoor usage, and capable of being dyed or painted to achieve symbolic variations. While best known for their military uses – signaling, indicating rank, and terrorizing the enemy – Chinese flags also appear in temples and religious processions.

Whether, as seems likely, silk flags spread from China to the Near East – or whether it was simply the silk which made the journey, to be fashioned by peoples who had independently arrived at the idea of a rectangle of cloth attached to a pole – it does seem clear that multicolored flags in the Western world are basically an innovation introduced at the time of the Crusades and inspired by Arab use. Arabs had had vexilloids, including an eagle standard apparently based on the Roman model; yet even before the rise of Islam in the early seventh century they were displaying flags of white and black. Islamic

Turkish and other Muslim flags of the Middle Ages were often as large as 2.5 × 3.75 meters (8 × 13 feet).

Opposite
Since Islam has strong injunctions against the representation of living things, paintings like the one on page 40 are rare and are more common to Persian than Arab traditions. As might be expected, Muslim flags rely on graphic design and calligraphy rather than on the beasts and flowers which tend to predominate in Western European and Japanese heraldry, respectively.

strictures against representational art encouraged the development on flags of abstract patterns and calligraphic designs in embroidery, appliqué, or painting. Moreover, whereas the Chinese tended to associate every color with philosophical and religious concepts, the Arabs seemed to have invented the concept of associating specific colors with dynasties and individual leaders. This latter concept very gradually became the basis for all modern flag designs. Muhammad used at least two flags, one of white and another of black, while flags of white and

The above manuscript of Alfonso X the Wise, King of Leon and Castile (1252–1284) illustrates the lance pennants carried by Spanish knights of that era.

Pope Urban II at the Synod of Clermont in 1095 called for the liberation of Christian shrines in the Near East *(above),* suggesting that spiritual and material rewards would accrue to those who joined the enterprise.

red are associated respectively with Abu Bakr and Umar, the first two caliphs (successors). In commemoration both of Muhammad and Abu Bakr, the flags of the first Muslim dynasty, the Ummayads, were of white. The Abbassids, who transferred the Arab capital from Damascus to Baghdad, chose the color black for their flag; they saw it as the true color of Muhammad's flag – and it made sharp contrast with Ummayad banners. Subsequently the Fatimids, tracing their lineage to Muhammad's daughter Fatima, selected green because of a tradition that the Prophet wore a cloak of this color. Red was the color of the Kharijites ("Secessionists") and later of the Ottoman Turks. How substantial any of these traditional sources may be is open to question; but the symbolic importance of the colors, legendary or not, is clear.

It is indeed a principle of vexillology that symbolic truth generally takes precedence over historical reality. The scholar may be interested to find out what exact designs and usages existed at various periods, in specific battles, or as emblems of certain leaders. To the general public the significance of a design is rather in the affirmation it makes about the propriety of the dominant ethos. Cooperative action in any society requires communication; this in turn is dependent upon a common medium of discourse. Symbols of all kinds, including flags, posit relationships among individuals within a society, between them and other societies, and between all humans and the realms of nature and spirit. It is a primary function of symbolism to reduce to manageable proportions, by distinguishing between the significant and insignificant, the great number of sense impressions we receive. (The very word "insignificant" means non-symbol-making). In this sense one might almost view the Arab flags, which differ from one another in colors and inscriptions more effectively than the rather inflexible vexilloids, as a necessary stage in social development.

How can such flags help to order society? Popular traditions of flag symbolism are not arbitrary; they are promoted and reinforced (if not actually invented) by governments, their rulers finding advantage in one interpretation over another. Regardless of actual origin, the dynastic colors of the Arab flags were claims to legitimacy through association with the Prophet. Today a new interpretation has arisen among Arabs, based on the words of the poet Safi al-Din al-H'ily: "White are our deeds, black our fields of battle; our pastures are green, but our swords are red with the blood of the enemy." Thus in the present century the four traditional colors have been given equal recognition as "authentic"; religious sanction is now seen as less important than Arab honor and the promotion of common political goals.

The development of heraldry in the Western world demonstrates in a slightly different way the rich potentialities for the exploitation of symbolism in the manipulation of political power. Fundamental to the control of economic resources and political processes in any society is an ability to command the allegiance of large numbers of people. That requires rulers to create and maintain an aura of legality for themselves and a hierarchy based on traditional privileges. Few people have ever expressed it so well as Rousseau: "The strongest is never strong enough to be always the master, unless he transforms strength into right, and obedience into duty." There are three major sources of authority – tradition (it has always been thus), religious sanction (the gods will it thus), and ideology (science proves it best thus), the latter in effect being a modern version of religious sanction.

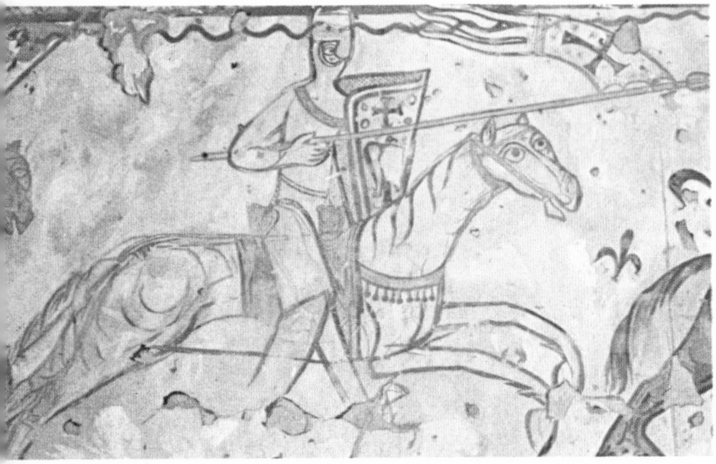

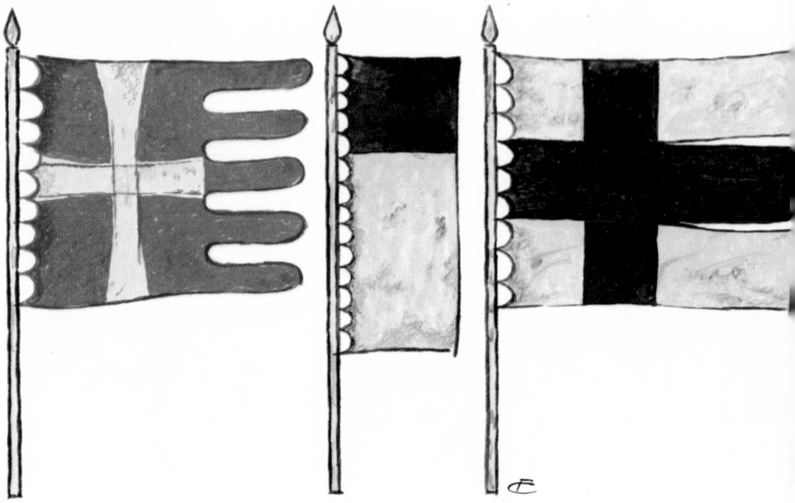

The Templar *(above)* was a member of one of the three great orders founded in Palestine which had substantial influence in European countries throughout the following centuries. The flags illustrated *(left to right)* are, respectively, those of the Knights of St. John, Knights Templar, and Teutonic Knights.

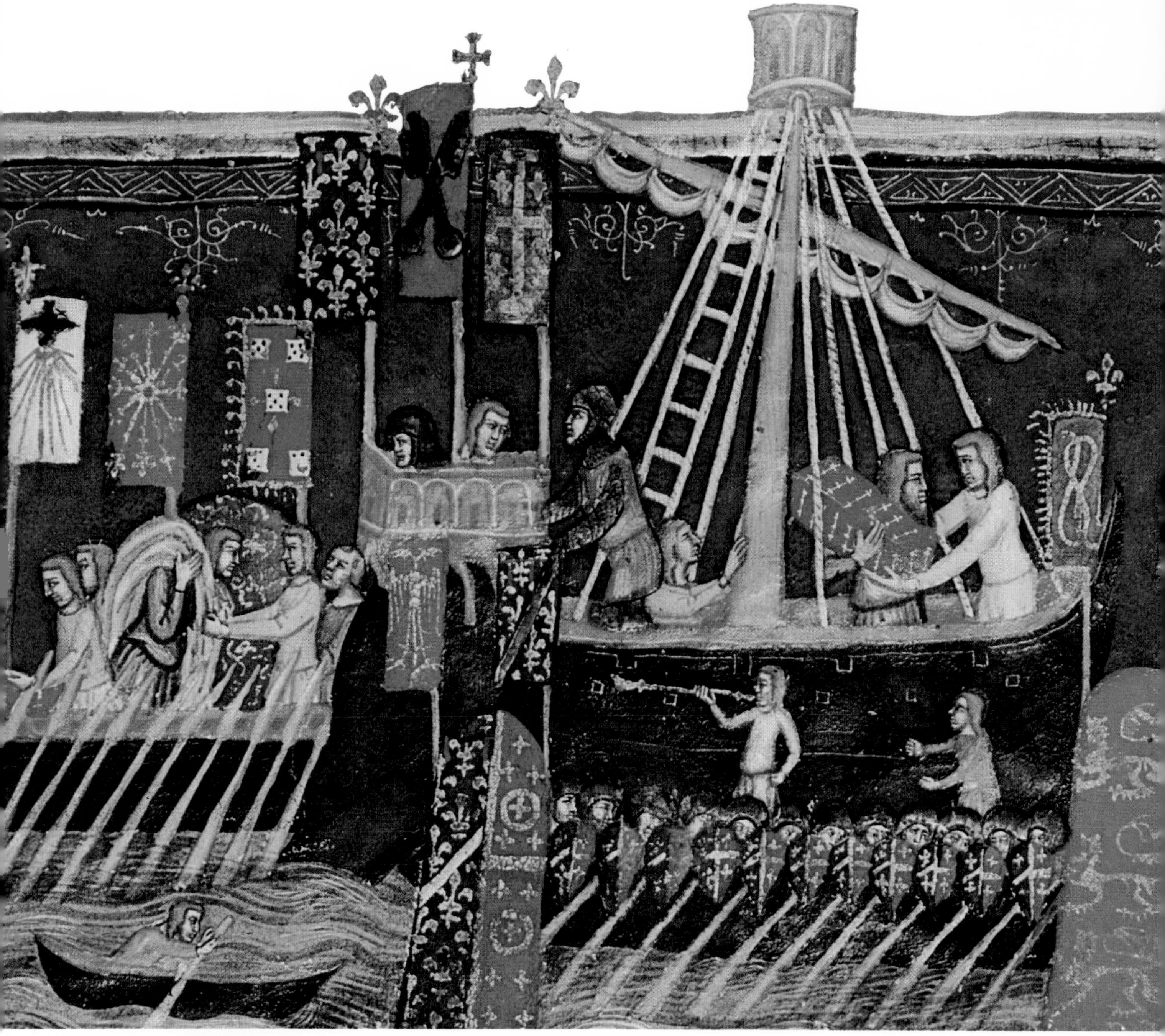

The flags and shields in this fourteenth-century manuscript of the debarcation of the Knights of the Holy Spirit *(above)* probably reflect usages familiar to the artist, rather than those actually characterizing crusaders in the previous century.

The first crusade realized victories at Nicaea and Ascalon *(left)* which eventually resulted in profound changes to medieval society.

All three manipulate symbols in order to justify the division of society into groups whose power decreases proportionately to the number of individuals in the group. Hierarchy, which allows the smallest group in the country (its ruling elite) to maintain a monopoly of power, relies on a myth of superiority. Symbols of all kinds suggest that the rulers are not ordinary mortals. Since earliest times therefore rulers have created distinctions – titles, medals and decorations, extraordinary privileges, uniforms, etc.; these are conferred upon their own families and on supporters in the (usually successful) attempt to endow them with an aura of majesty and dignity. It was precisely this role that heraldry played in the twelfth through the fifteenth cen-

According to tradition, in 1098 at the battle of Antioch the Christians were aided by angelic hosts dressed in white and riding white horses: their banners, copied by the Crusaders, were white with red crosses. The flag above is also a typical crusader's flag.

Battle flags and shields of various designs existed at the time of the battle of Dorylaeum in 1097 (the first major Christian victory in the first crusade).

King Richard I effortlessly subdues an evil-looking Saladin *(right)*, to whom the artist has given an imaginary shield. Another manuscript artist presents a more sympathetic view of Saladin *(above, right)*.

turies in Europe; similar systems, like heraldry in more ways than not, existed in Japan and elsewhere.

Heraldry had its origin in the practical need for recognition of soldiers on the battlefield, following development of helmets which covered the face. In the historic Bayeux Tapestry, which records the Norman invasion of England, Duke William is shown lifting his helmet to assure his men during battle that he is still alive and fighting. Among the flags represented on the tapestry none seems to identify a particular leader by its design or usage. The Dragon is the old war flag of the English forces, and the Normans carry flags with crosses indicating the sanction of the pope in their enterprise, yet the flags and shields of both appear to be largely decorative. They seem to have been arbitrarily chosen without regard for symbolism, distinctiveness, or continuity.

The Crusades and their aftermath in Western Europe altered all of this permanently. Cognizances were added first to flags and then to other attributes of the warrior – his shield, helmet, surcoat, and later his personal possessions – even the clothing of his servants. Because the flag was already recognized as the formal means of transferring title to land or to some privilege, it was logical that it should be first to bear the distinctive colors and charges which came to characterize heraldry. The short pennants and long narrow gonfanons seen in the Bayeux Tapestry, seals, and other preheraldic documents were replaced by the more suitably shaped banner – usually square or wider than it was long. On the other hand as a symbol of the hereditary warrior class, the shield became the preferred medium for representing arms. It predominates even today in the arms of nations where the shield is without logical function and reflects artistic convention.

Heraldic charges had to be simple in form, unvarying over time, and distinctive from all other emblems with which they might be confused: these concepts still form the core of heraldic style. Following the Crusades the nobility, recognizing that it would never enjoy the legitimacy conferred by divine sanction on the clergy, not only insisted on maintaining their coats of arms but also transformed them into the formal system we know as heraldry. This involved establishing the personal and hereditary nature of arms, severely restricting the percentage of the population permitted to assume them, and placing the systematization of arms in the hands of professional heralds. Elaboration grew, such as certain sizes of flags to correspond to different ranks, regularized alterations to arms to indicate different members of the family, augmentations of honor to the otherwise inviolate shield, the

FRANCE (1188).

ENGLAND (1188).

attribution of external decorations (crests, supporters, compartment, motto, etc.). In many respects European flags tended to become subordinated to coats of arms during the era when heraldry flourished; certainly their designs were regulated by the conventions which even today are referred to as heraldic laws.

After heraldry's loss of practical relevance on the battlefield and the growth of new social classes whose power depended on wealth and royal favor as much as on military prowess, coats of arms began to suffer from an artistic degeneration evident in some of the exaggerated designs of the sixteenth century and lat-

er. Even before this, heraldry had become a plaything for the ruling classes. While one can appreciate the color and the drama of the tournament, its ostentatious theatrics had little relevance to practical affairs of state or warfare. Yet even today the concepts and artistic style and at-

FLANDERS (1188).

ENGLAND (1277).

FRANCE (1375).

On 13 January 1188 it was decided that King Philip Augustus of France, King Henry II of England, and Count Philip of Flanders should have certain colors for the crosses displayed on their flags. Later, however, the red and white crosses were reversed and a tradition grew in England of a red cross on white and in France of a white cross – first on a red flag, later on blue.

titudes of heraldry are influential in the designing and usage of flags, and while that influence is not so widespread or beneficial as many heraldists believe, it should not be ignored. Most important is the core of commonsense principles exemplified in the very earliest arms: flags are generally more effective when they are simple, employ distinctive designs and colors, remain relatively fixed over time, and are unlike other flags in design.

Developments of symbols on land in Europe were paralleled by fundamental changes at sea. Until roughly 1500 most vessels did not travel great distances. Naval flags consequently did not come into their own until the age of wind-powered craft, or roughly from the sixteenth century through the nineteenth. (Flag usage has decreased in the era of powered vessels, partly because of the speed at which they travel and partly because radio and other systems have altered radically the traditional visual identification of ships.) Moreover, early warships did not act in a coordinated fashion as a fleet but attacked the enemy ship by ship. Consequently the only flags displayed were those of the noblemen in command; in the assault on Constantinople in 1203, for example, the ship of the Doge of Venice flaunted the Venetian standard but none of the other ships in the fleet had flags.

From the ninth through the thirteenth centuries it was the custom for ships on the North Sea to carry a cross at the top of the mast as a symbol of the king's peace and protection, paralleling the cross of peace on land which protected the market and its goods. The earliest flags were accessories (pennants or streamers of a single color) to the cross; like the banners which replaced vexilloids in military engagements on land, they only gradually supplanted the original emblem. It is not entirely clear why the cross gave way to the flag; perhaps the increase in the absolute number of ships or the length of their trips and likelihood of meeting foreign ships or

SEAL OF BALDWIN III, KING OF JERUSALEM.

SEAL OF BOHEMUND III, PRINCE OF ANTIOCH.

SEAL OF PONCIUS, COUNT OF TRIPOLI.

SEAL OF WILLIAM PRINCE OF GALILEE.

perhaps the spread of heraldry on land were influential. Nevertheless during the late twelfth century in the Mediterranean and the mid-thirteenth century in northern Europe, flags began to appear on ships, substituting for emblems on sails and shields attached along the gunwales which previously had been used for marking nationality. The flag was easier to make and to identify; it was inexpensive and its design was easily changed; finally it was a very striking and handsome object.

The symbol of the Byzantine Empire in the 1300s was a cross between four symbols which probably originally were crescents, but which were variously interpreted as broken chain links or the

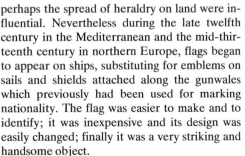

Greek letters standing for the phrase "King of Kings, Ruling over Kings." The Christian cross has been omitted, but the modern socialist republic of Serbia uses these same symbols *(above)*, interpreting them as Cyrillic letters meaning "Only Unity Will Save the Serbs."

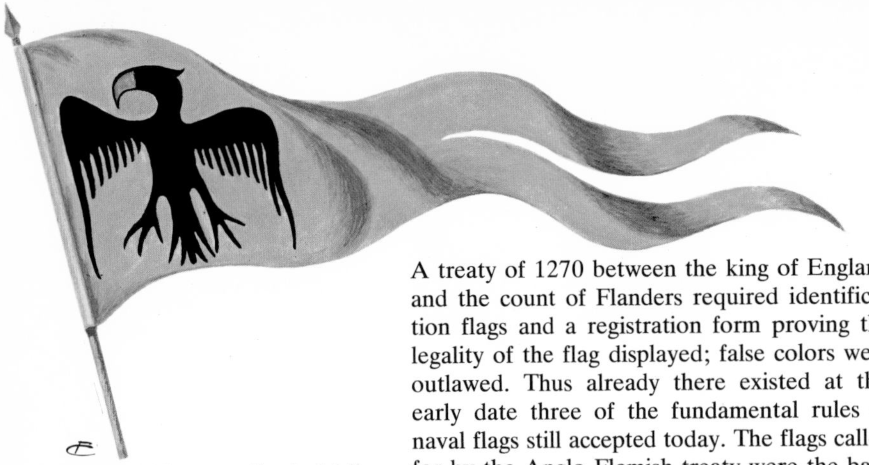

Troops of Emperor Frederick II in 1228 carried the imperial eagle flag *(above).*

Though the cross was the most common religious symbol found on the armor of knights, some even used the Virgin and Child *(below).*

A treaty of 1270 between the king of England and the count of Flanders required identification flags and a registration form proving the legality of the flag displayed; false colors were outlawed. Thus already there existed at this early date three of the fundamental rules of naval flags still accepted today. The flags called for by the Anglo-Flemish treaty were the banners of arms of the two sovereigns, but other flag types existed. From at least the late thirteenth century we have evidence in the Mediterranean of the use of flags with crosses, the red cross on white of Genoa being the most famous. Earlier, representations of saints were prominent – as in 1238 when Genoa and Venice agreed to a joint display of their flags on ships to indicate that the two states were allies. Venice in this case used not its later famous lion of St. Mark, but rather a flag showing the saint himself, Genoa having a banner of red with St. George slaying the dragon.

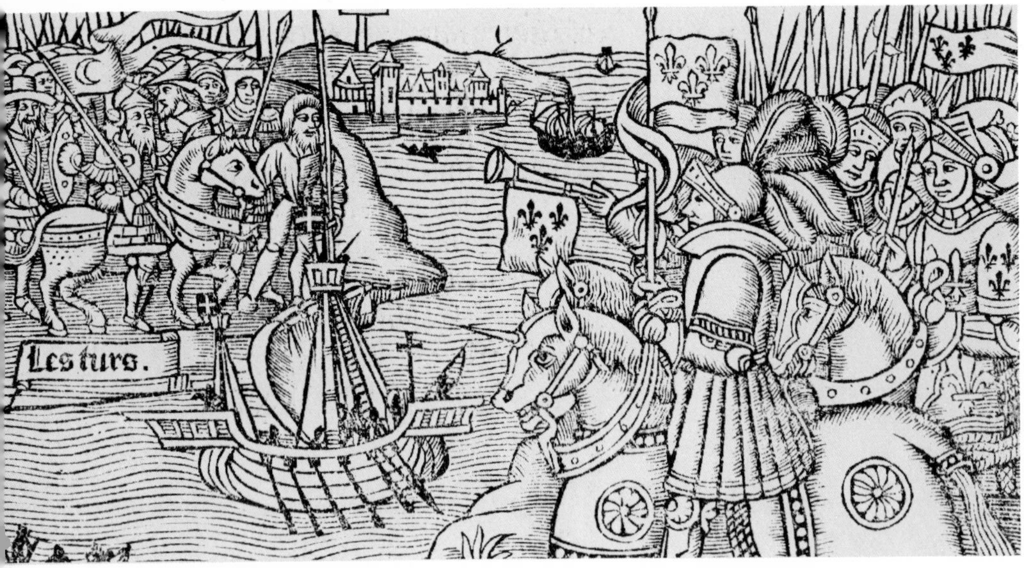

King Louis IX of France (St. Louis) died in 1270 during the eighth crusade in Tunis *(above).* The crusaders' cross has been added to his royal tunic in the illustration below.

These early designs were not national flags in the modern sense: they were not used to any degree on land and, more importantly, they symbolized the state rather than the citizenry. Since medieval society was organized around corporations, the common people rather looked to church banners and guild flags as symbols of their own. These flags tended to be unique examples, and it was possible to have very elaborate and costly designs made. Among the materials used for such flags were linen, leather, and sendal, a fabric of linen warp and silk weft. It was common to appliqué or paint emblems on the field; embroidery developed later. Other techniques were employed in that era in other parts of the world; in the Mayan Empire, for example, vexilloids, shields, and actual flags were often constructed from the brilliant feathers of rare birds.

In discussing the development of flags mention must certainly be made of the portolanos of the fourteenth and fifteenth centuries. These navi-

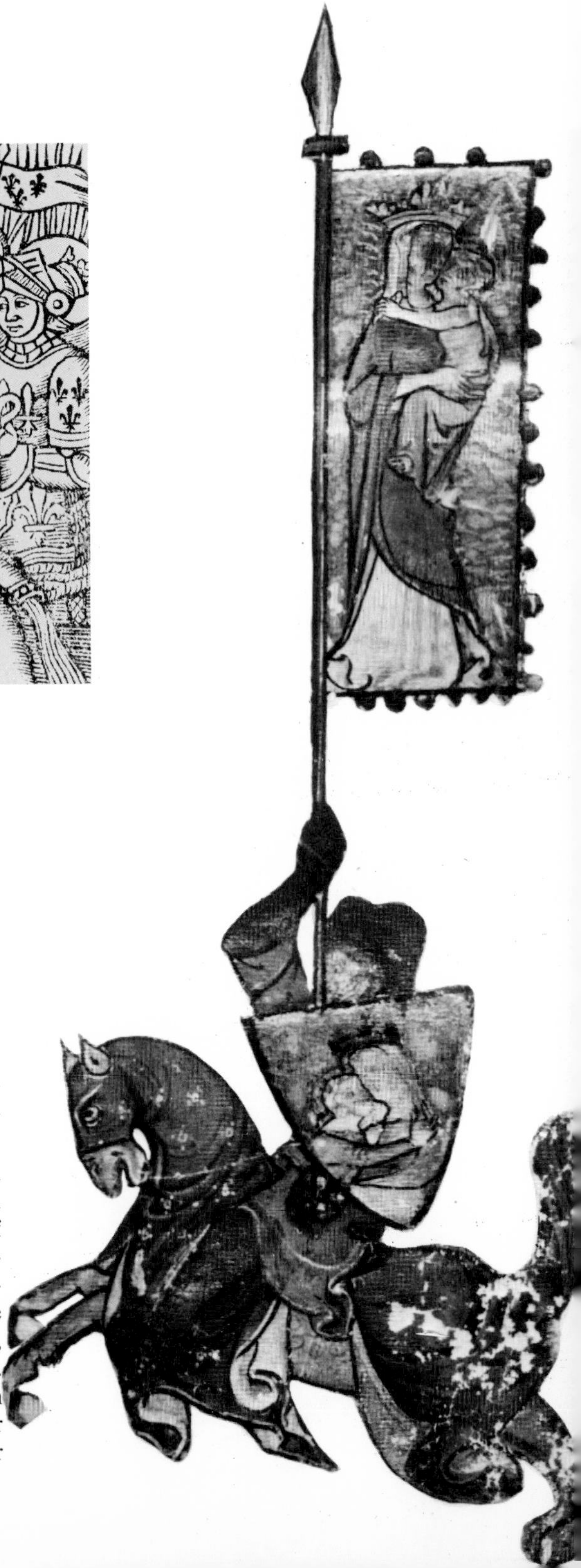

"THE HEARTS OF THE SOLDIERS WOULD BE FILLED WITH THE FEAR THAT THEIR LEADER HAD BEEN OVERCOME IF THEY DID NOT SEE HIS BANNER BORNE ALOFT. . . . WHILE THAT STANDARD REMAINED ERECT THE PEOPLE HAD A SURE PLACE OF REFUGE."

Itinerary of King Richard (1191)

gational charts are more to be recommended for artistic style than geographical accuracy, but they are of enormous interest to the vexillologist because they correspond to the armorials of the heraldist on land. To the extent that the portolano painter had any knowledge, each principal city or sovereign realm along the coast is represented by an ensign. ("Ensign" is used advisedly, since it is not entirely certain that all the designs shown were displayed in flag form.) Some of the designs are pure speculation, while others are obviously based on first-hand accounts collected by the compilers of the portolanos directly or through travelers.

The simple heraldic flags shown in these portolanos gave way by the fifteenth and sixteenth centuries to other modes of artistic style. Particularly in military colors, two trends which are to be important in modern flags begin to develop at the time of the Reformation and Counter Reformation. Sharp ideological divisions and the military encounters based on them quite

It is not always easy to prove direct links, but it is clear that many symbols still in use today derive from the time of the struggles between Christians and Muslims, as suggested below.

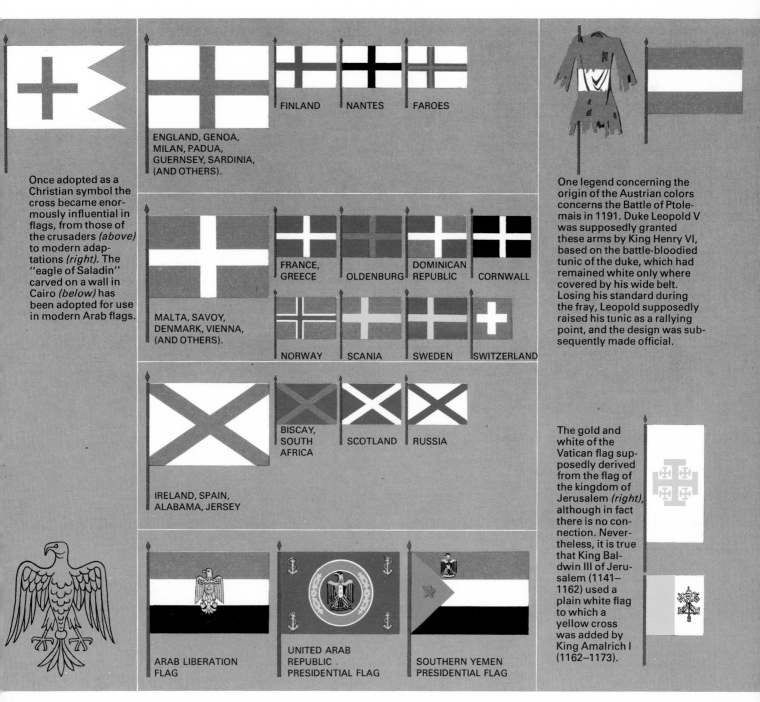

Once adopted as a Christian symbol the cross became enormously influential in flags, from those of the crusaders *(above)* to modern adaptations *(right)*. The "eagle of Saladin" carved on a wall in Cairo *(below)* has been adopted for use in modern Arab flags.

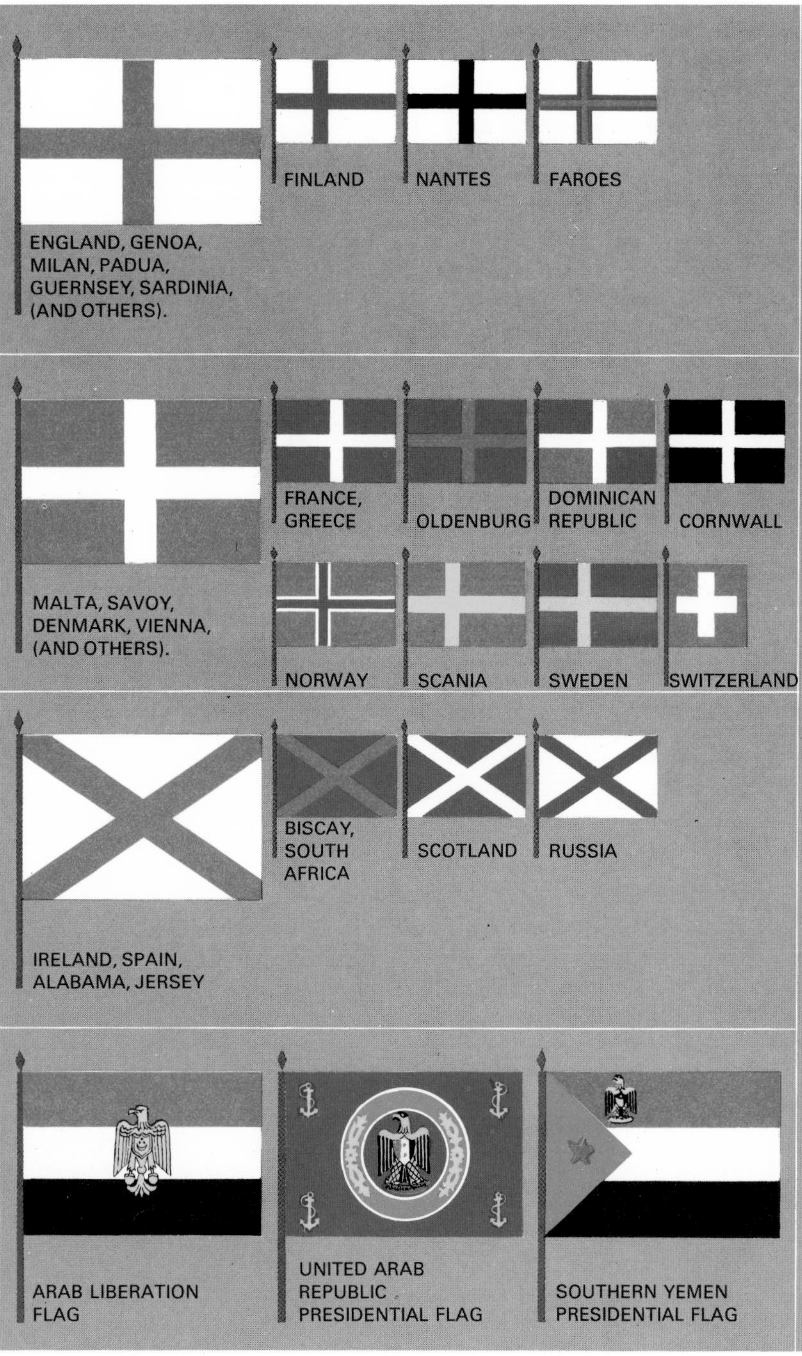

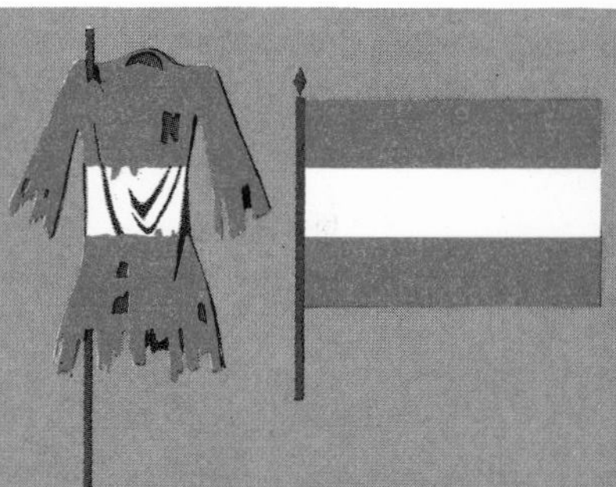

One legend concerning the origin of the Austrian colors concerns the Battle of Ptolemais in 1191. Duke Leopold V was supposedly granted these arms by King Henry VI, based on the battle-bloodied tunic of the duke, which had remained white only where covered by his wide belt. Losing his standard during the fray, Leopold supposedly raised his tunic as a rallying point, and the design was subsequently made official.

The gold and white of the Vatican flag supposedly derived from the flag of the kingdom of Jerusalem *(right)*, although in fact there is no connection. Nevertheless, it is true that King Baldwin III of Jerusalem (1141–1162) used a plain white flag to which a yellow cross was added by King Amalrich I (1162–1173).

Carved and sculpted crests of elaborate design and shape were frequently incorporated in the medieval helmets placed over sepulchers *(right)*.

The arms of Styria *(below)*, today part of Austria, have remained basically unchanged for almost 800 years. The heraldic panther whose breath is fire has been variously interpreted over the centuries, while retaining the same basic characteristics.

naturally are reflected in the banners carried by troops. Emblems such as the peasant's shoe, the cross of Burgundy, the saltire of St. Andrew, and the arm of God are matched by complicated allegorical scenes promising victory and salvation for those who have chosen the one true path. The elaborate parade banners of modern labor organizations and the simple protest flags of political parties and movements in the twentieth

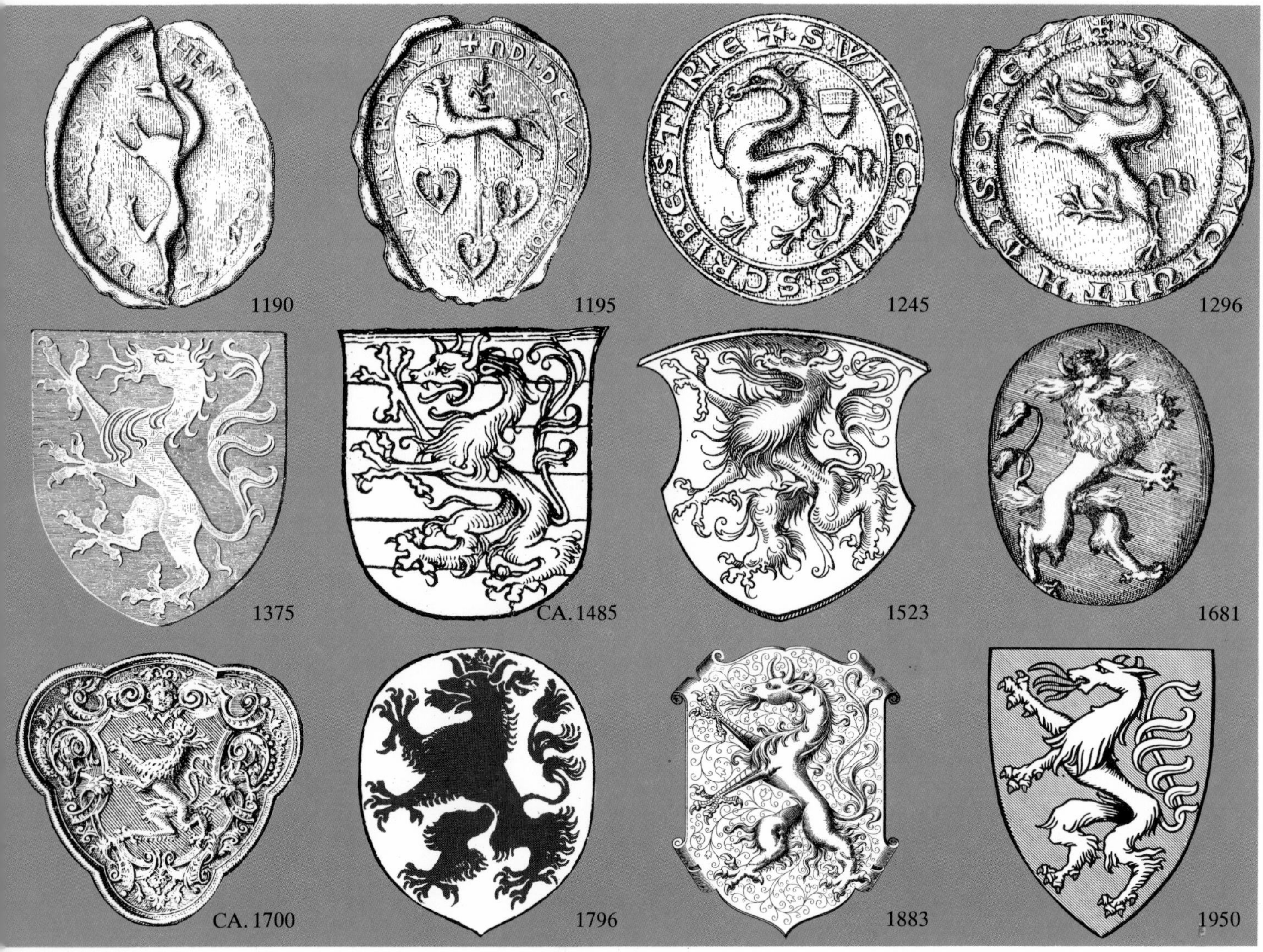

century find their roots in these flags. Certain colors came to be associated with specific religious sects, dynastic causes, and even nationalities, providing the basis for the choices that would be made a few centuries hence when tricolors and bicolors were adopted by revolutionaries. At first these were essentially heraldic livery colors associated with individual monarchs and noblemen; later they took on a more fixed character and had symbolic meanings attributed to them that were truly national in character.

At sea the increased range of ships, both in distance and in time between calls in port, greatly increased the significance of naval flags, their size, and the variety of their design. Elaborating on the armorial banners of an earlier age, Euro-

Although encased in armor, the king of Castile and Leon is immediately recognizable because his arms are repeated on his surcoat, trappings, and crest. The illustration *(left)* is from a fifteenth-century manuscript.

Medieval city dwellers formed guilds to regulate not only economic activities but political and military affairs as well. Frequently there were distinctive banners for these guilds – such as those of the blacksmiths *(top)* and of the wine industry *(bottom)* both

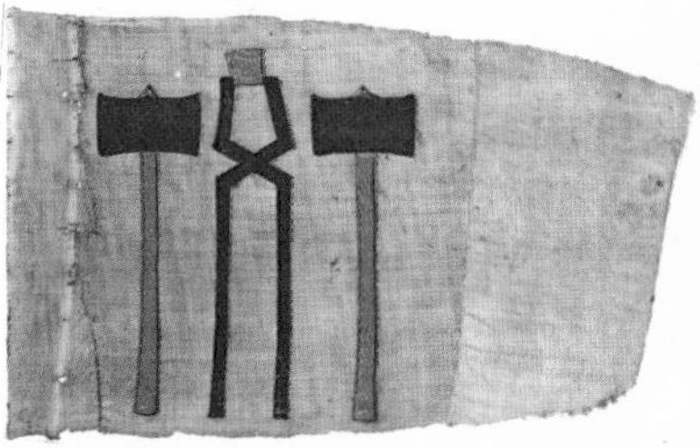

of Basel. The latter represented the vintners, wine merchants, and tavern owners. Their flag honored Pope Urban I, their patron. Since the people represented were not armigerous, such banners were generally nonheraldic in form.

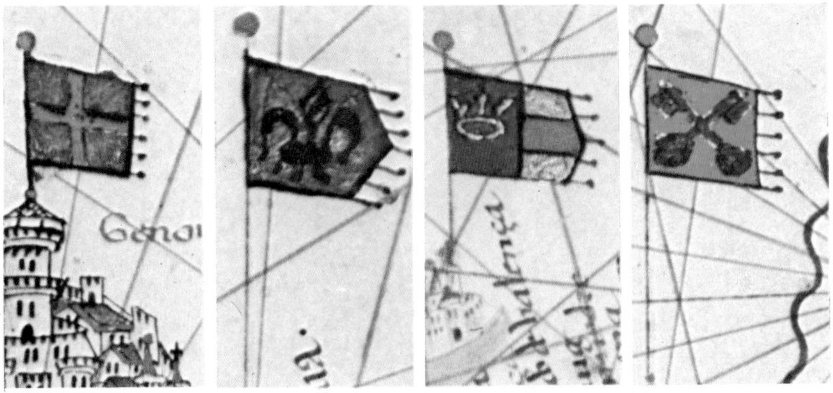

Many of the simple heraldic emblems used by cities in the Middle Ages continue to serve them today. The above flags from a portolano of 1480 are those of Genoa, Livorno, Valencia, and Avignon (residence of the popes in the previous century). The first two are discolored, their fields should be white (the silver paint has turned blue) and the lily on the second should be red.

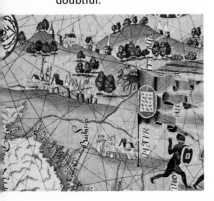

peans of the sixteenth through the eighteenth centuries created a profusion of long streamers in the livery colors of the king, huge flags with royal arms emblazoned with all their conceivable accessories, and special flags of command and rank. The first flag books and charts began to appear in the late 1600s, a further homage to the absolute monarchs of that era. These also performed a practical function, aiding navigators in the recognition of strange vessels in port or on the high seas. There developed a sharp dichotomy between two types of flags: the minute details of armorial bearings and the popularity in many countries of a white flag to display these arms rendered the complicated ensigns rather ineffective for identification purposes. Consequently a parallel system of very simple flags arose and eventually became dominant. On land the two types of symbols – the

The flags and arms in this Spanish manuscript *(right)* of 1503 are no more accurately drawn than the elephant and camel.

The artist of this 1559 map *(below)* has not hesitated to attribute a flag to Mauritania, but whether he had first-hand knowledge of such a flag is doubtful.

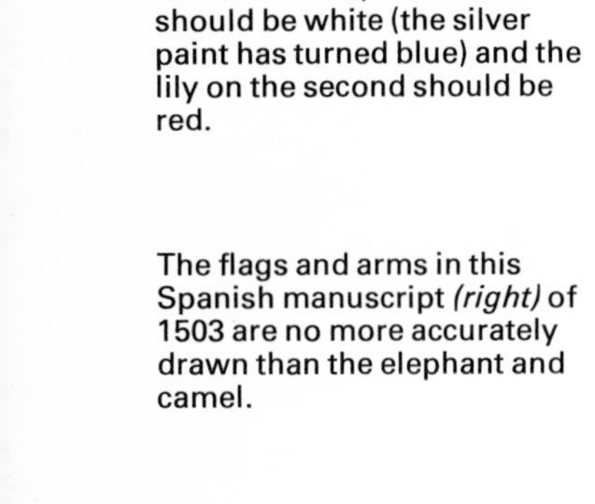

complex honorific and the simple mark of identification – tended to figure within the same design. Mounted troops were still the preserve of the wealthy; their flags were rich and complicated designs, often flattering the patron of the regiment or other unit. Nevertheless the growth of standing armies and the need for ordering infantry by company and battalion led to a certain standardization: in France a white cross figured through the center of most infantry colors, while in England it was a canton of St. George's cross which identified the nationality.

The eighteenth century saw a number of important developments in flag usage and design. The

Of little practical use for navigation, the magnificent portolanos of the fourteenth and fifteenth centuries provide us with knowledge of contemporary flags and an appreciation for the world view of the Europeans who first began to explore Africa and Asia.

"FIRSTLY, THE BANNERS OF ALL PRINCES MUST BE BORNE BY ONE OF THEIR KNIGHTLY CHAMBERLAINS AND THE PENNANTS OF THE SAID LEADERS BY THEIR CHIEF VALETS OR BY BRAZEN EQUERRIES AND THE BANNERS OF THE OTHER BANNERETS BY THEIR GENTLEMEN – AS IT PLEASES THEM."

Treatise of the Form and Specification of a Tournament ("Book of Tournaments of King René," ca. 1460).

While changing tactics of warfare were making the use of heraldry of lesser importance on the battlefield, the tournament of the fifteenth century became the justification for the display of arms and banners. Here was an appreciation for the beauty and majesty of standards, pennants, trumpet banners, crests, tabards, horse trappings, and similar armorial displays for their own sake.

first signal codes were devised at sea, allowing fleets to act as a coordinated unit in battle; commanders and their ranks were indicated by special flags. There was some reduction in the size and number of flags on ships, and alterations in ship architecture led to the standardization of the jack and ensign as the chief flags of nationality. As the modern system of halyards for hoisting was introduced, fewer flags were nailed or tied to poles or attached by means of rings. As might be expected, flag regulations were increasingly required, although monarchs found themselves generally unsuccessful in their efforts to restrict usage of the war ensign, which private merchants insisted on displaying because of the greater prestige and protection it afforded.

Far and away the most significant innovation of the eighteenth century was the national flag. This concept is a difficult one to define precisely, and in most countries the acquisition of a national flag was a gradual process, official government recognition generally coming long after the flag had been accepted in the hearts of the people. Moreover, many countries had developed more than one national flag, although the same basic design usually figured in the special forms used on warships, unarmed government vessels, and privately owned crafts; over forts and military encampments; on state buildings; and by private businesses and individuals.

The propagation of egalitarian and democratic philosophies and the mobilization of the masses into politics beginning in the late eighteenth century were preconditions for the development of national flags. There is no doubt that the struggle for Dutch independence of 1568–1648 (see pages 156–163) and the civil wars in England in the mid-seventeenth century were influential in the process, and while John Locke, Jean-Jacques Rousseau, and Thomas Paine do not mention flags specifically, they may be looked at in some sense as fathers of the national flag.

The actual stages in growth and spread of the national flag have been documented in a number of places in the book, but it will be useful to outline its distinguishing characteristics here. It may seem axiomatic to say that a national flag cannot exist where there is no nation, but in our world of nation-states it is easy to forget that not every state is a nation. Some nationalities, like the Somalis, live in several states. Some supranational states, such as India and the Soviet Union, encompass numerous nationalities which

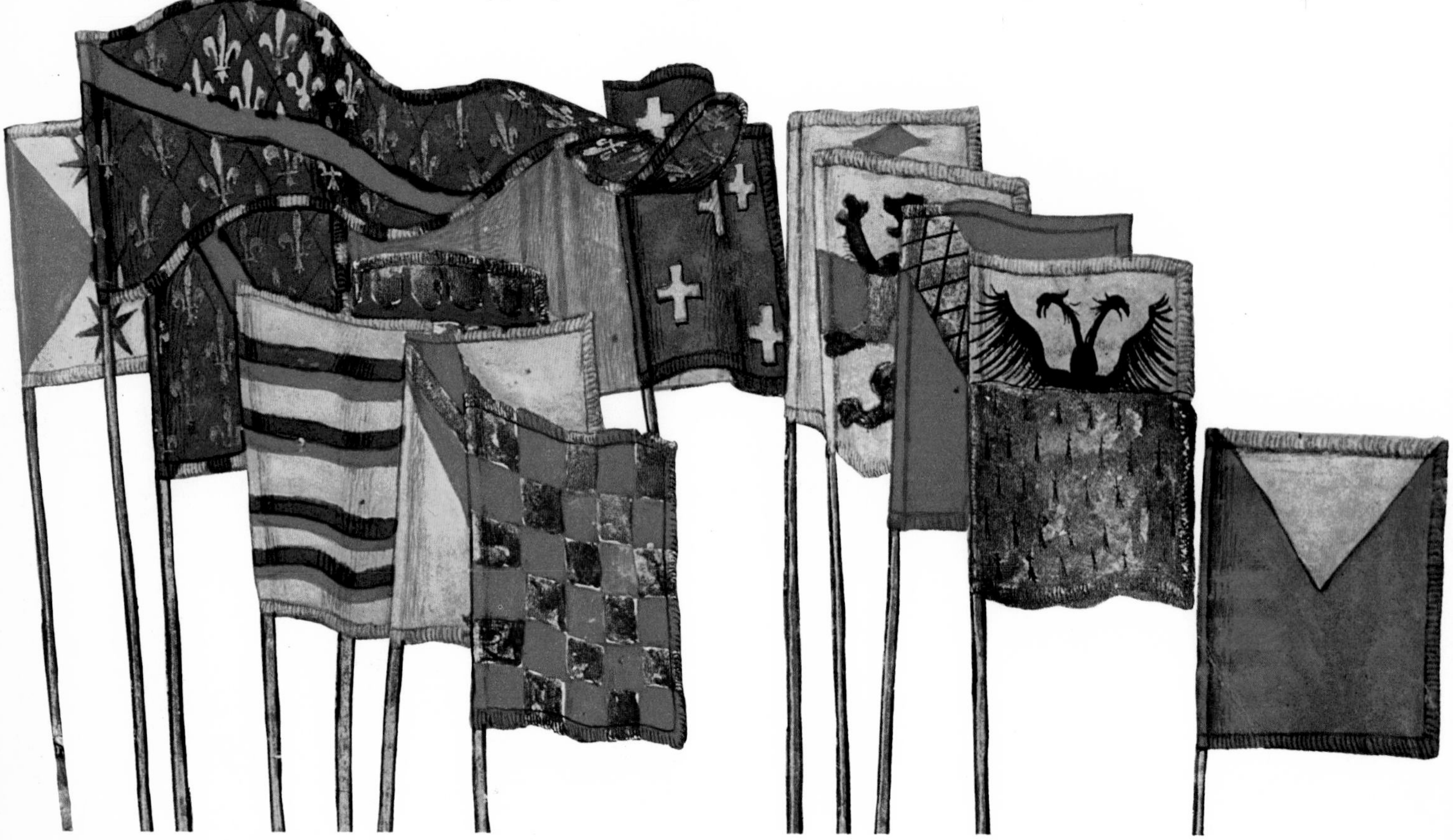

While only two of the flags in the illustrations *(above* and *right)* which appear in the manuscript quoted above were designs belonging to real persons, the artist successfully captured the spirit of the era. The death of King Henry II of France in 1559 from wounds received in a tournament largely ended the popularity of this sport.

This detail from a sixteenth-century Swiss flag (see page 71) is typical of the fine craftsmanship that characterized both painted and embroidered flags in the pre-industrial era.

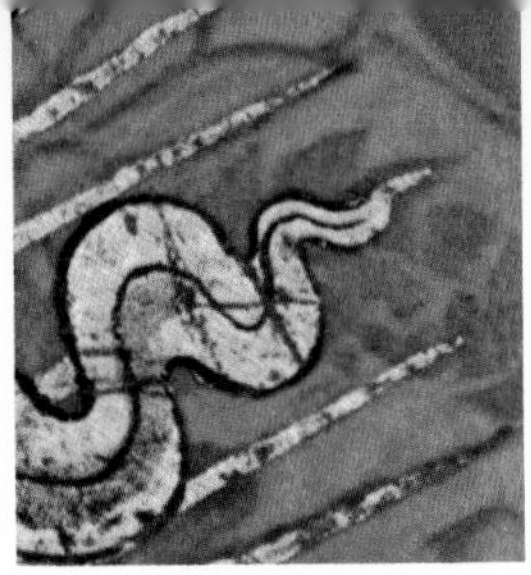

The standard of King Louis XII of France as Count of Pavia *(below)* includes a view of the city of Pavia, its arms and those of Brittany and France.

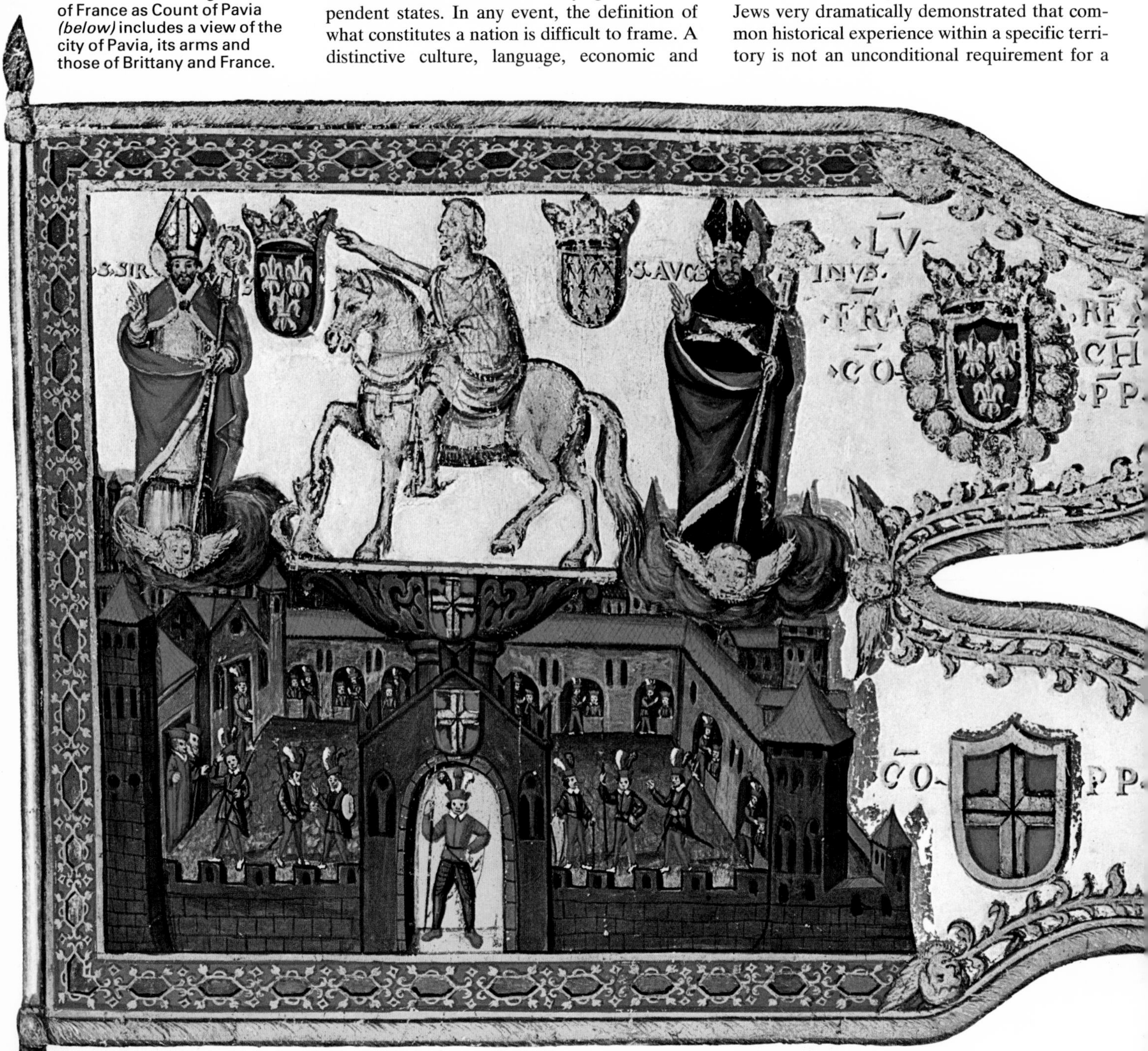

The reverse side of the flag was an entirely different design. The banner was captured by Swiss troops in 1512 and recorded in a book of trophies from which the above illustration was taken.

have been and could conceivably again be independent states. In any event, the definition of what constitutes a nation is difficult to frame. A distinctive culture, language, economic and political system, or common historical tradition may distinguish a nation from its neighbors, but it appears the only characteristic which can be taken in every case as the certain definition of a nation is adherence of its people to common symbols – and first and foremost a national flag. The Swiss and South Africans have shown that a single language is not an absolute necessity; the Americans and Australians have made it clear that a common religion need not exist; and the Jews very dramatically demonstrated that common historical experience within a specific territory is not an unconditional requirement for a sense of nationality. Important as all these factors may be, nationalism in fact relies most heavily on the willingness of people to define themselves as a distinct group, actively to seek the creation of a state in which to manifest that will, and to realize both a common program for the future and interpretation of the past. French unity on the eve of the Revolution was based on common experiences under common rulers;

Europeans were not the only ones with magnificent banners; this standard of the Bey of Tunis, which includes the sword of Ali as well as stars and crescents, dates from the nineteenth century. Similar designs were used earlier and continued to be official until the mid-twentieth century.

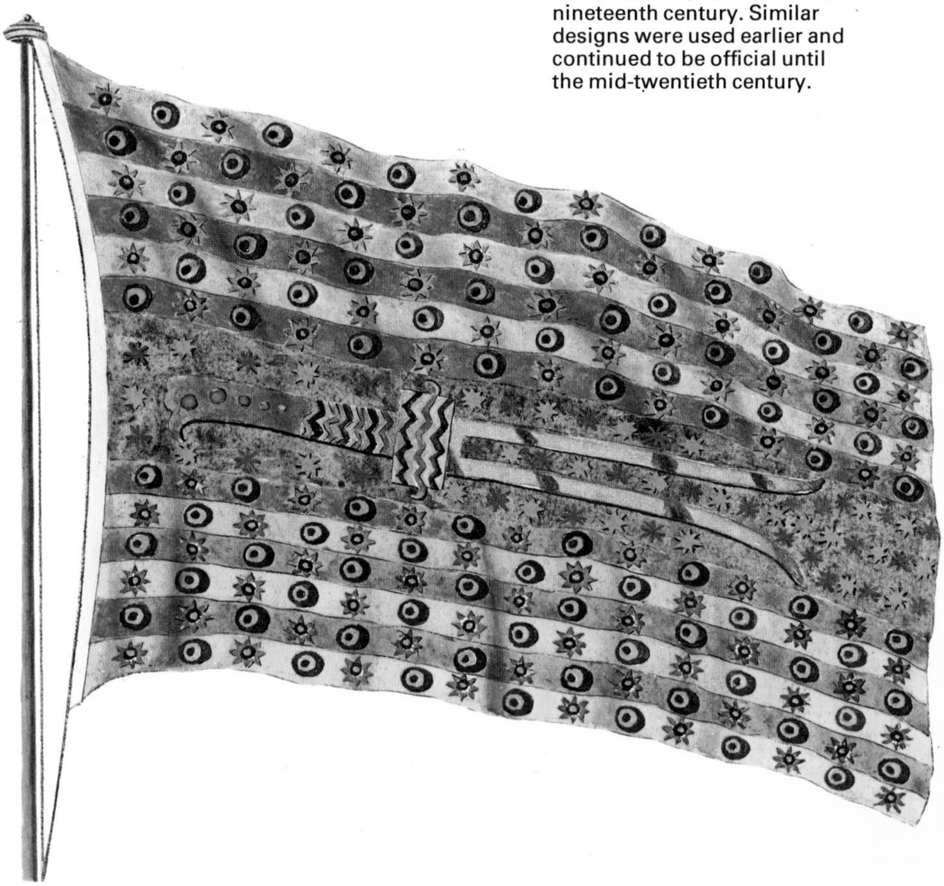

South American nations created borders according to economic factors and population densities. Religion was a unifying factor for the nationalisms of Greece and Pakistan, language for Mongolia and Italy, colonial political institutions for Nigeria and Malaysia. Ireland and Bangladesh have shown that nationalism is still a potent force in the world today.

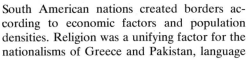

The national flag always reflects the supremacy of the national ideal; neither religion, dynasty, political ideology, history, nor logic is given greater consideration by the nationalist. Since their first use in the American and French Revolutions of 1775 and 1789, national flags have tended to be graphic manifestations of political programs. Their designs explain succinctly which people are to be unified, why, and what their avowed goals are. The Kurdish minority finds no symbol in the professedly Arab flag of Iraq; the Israeli flag espouses a permanent commitment to Judaism. The flag of Ceylon (now Sri Lanka) originally represented only the majority Singhalese; stripes were later added for Muslim and Hindu minorities. The simplicity of many modern designs, particularly in tricolor

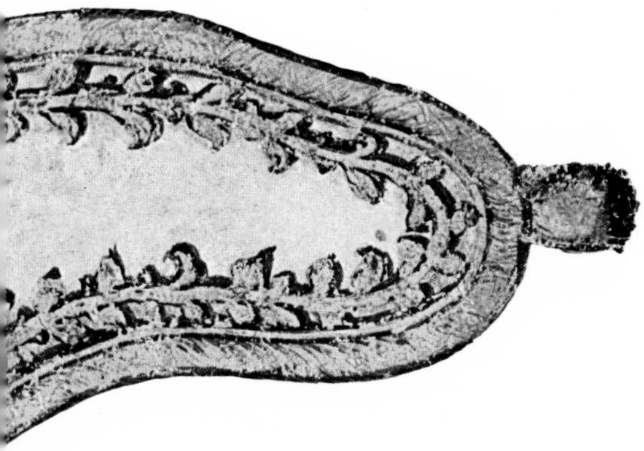

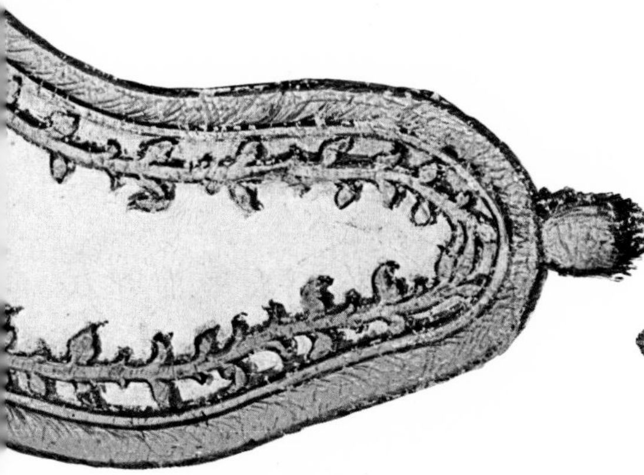

The examples above and at left illustrate how elaborate some ceremonial flags were, whereas those flown at sea *(below)* became simple in design and striking in color to be more easily identified. The eagle flag of Brandenburg *(below, left)* is another example of this development, which led to the national flags of today.

The American and French Revolutions of 1775 and 1789 introduced radical changes in flags as well as in established patterns of thought and action. Flags were no longer exclusively a privilege of the ruling classes on the one hand or functional signals for naval usage on the other: private individuals and their political organizations now freely designed and flew flags expressing their aspirations. The modern concept of the national flag's design, usage, and meaning took root and spread with nationalism itself to Latin America, Asia, Africa, and the Pacific. Today, two centuries later, the national flag is familiar to every people and has taken precedence over all other forms of political symbolism. In a great number of cases, however, acceptance of the concept or of a specific design has been achieved only after long and bitter civil war and/or struggle against foreign powers.

flags, is often a conscious reduction of the national program to a slogan. By definition, the national flag is available to all citizens rather than restricted to special occasions, situations, or individuals. It is subject to modification at the hands of the people as their definition of national goals or the means of achieving them alters. Finally, as the highest expression of nationality, the flag is likely to be the center of a cult, replacing the king or high priest who received adulation in prenationalist days.

Beginning with the revolutionary, democratic, and egalitarian philosophies of the Americans and French, nationalism and its flags have spread relentlessly – first to the rest of Europe, then to South America, and finally to Asia, Africa, and the Pacific. In the chapter *Flags Across the World* only a few reminders will be seen of the era of imperialism, the age of absolute monarchy, and earlier political forms. There are, however, expressions of other modern flag developments in that chapter: within the past century there has been a standardization of all aspects of flag design and use; flags have been subject to conscious exploitation as a

Often the very earliest form of the national flag of a particular country differs from that eventually established by law. For example, the Italian flag flown in the streets of Milan in 1848 in the illustration above has horizontal stripes, whereas the Tricolor of Italy officially established for the first time later that year – and still in use today – has vertical stripes.

tool of coercion and propaganda; their manufacture has been commercialized; and flags have been widely interpreted and used as a motif in art, advertising, literature, architecture, entertainment, and other realms of life.

Through the process of their deification and politicization, flags have come to be predominant over other forms of political symbolism. It is possible that in the future flags will be museum relics (which, for the most part, personal coats of arms are today) but the prolifera-

NINETEEN MONTHS OF FLAG CHANGES
Revolution and reaction in nineteenth-century Italy

EVENTS	SARDINIA
29 JANUARY 1848 On the eve of the revolution	
22 MARCH 1848 The outbreak of the independence war of Italy	
30 JUNE 1848 First victories for Italy	
27 AUGUST 1848 The Austrian counter-attack	
15 MARCH 1849 The revolution spreads to Rome and Parma	
12 APRIL 1849 The defeat at Novara and its aftermath	
27 AUGUST 1849 Restoration of the *status quo ante*	

The "March Days" of 1848 in Berlin saw fighting in the streets between Prussian troops and liberal revolutionaries *(left)*. Within a week the revolutionary black-red-gold was being paraded through the same streets by King Frederick William, although it would be seventy-one years before that tricolor would become established throughout Germany as the national flag.

tion of flags of all kinds – for private organizations, sports events, cities and other small political units, businesses, labor unions and other organizations – makes it seem unlikely. The flexibility of flags rather suggests adaptations to meet new circumstances; space exploration has already led to the creation of several forms of neovexilloids.

Another aspect of flags existing only in rudimentary form in the past has been a recognition that they are a subject worthy of serious study. To date most vexillological work has been in collecting and organizing information, but analysis of the data by sociologists, political scientists, and social psychologists has also begun. Since the early 1960s in particular, vexillology as a social science has established some significant landmarks referred to elsewhere in this book.

This summary history of flags should suggest that the intimacy between them and political life

The frequency and extent of change made in Italy's national flag in the nineteen months from January of 1848 to August of 1849 has never been equaled *(below)*. However, a similar pattern of alternation between flags of revolution and reaction may be traced in many nations in Europe and elsewhere in the world.

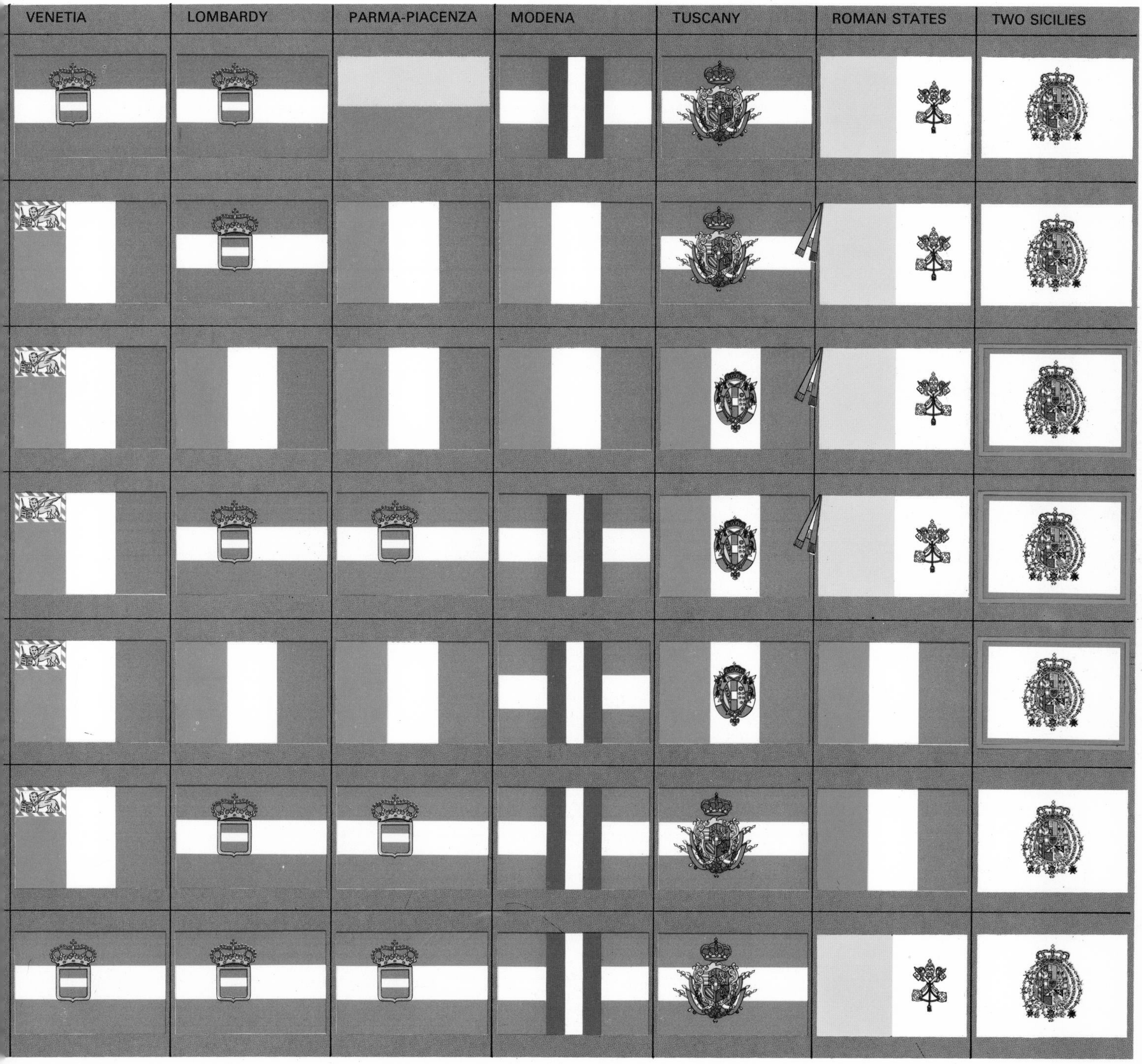

makes it altogether unlikely that flags will disappear as long as human society exists. Writing in 1875, Frederic Marshall in his *International Vanities* recognized the predominance of flags over all other political symbols, but suggested this trend might have reached a peak in his own time: "It is not unlikely," he wrote, "that our successors will look back with a sort of envy to what, in their time, will be geologically known as the 'flag period' of the earth's existence." If flags are to diminish in importance or disappear completely in the future, it must be our own twentieth century rather than any period in the past which will deserve to be known as the Age of Flags.

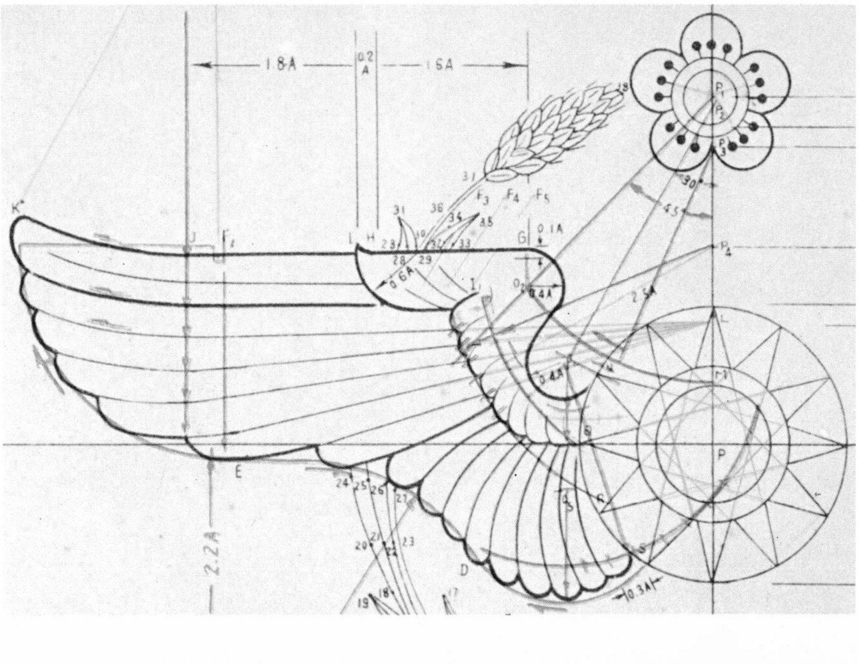

The twentieth century has seen a greater number and variety of flag types and uses than any other period in world history. From the Japanese-made Canadian souvenir flag to the flag in clothing and home decoration average men and women have asserted rights in the design and display of flags, a privilege usually denied them in earlier times. Yet the masses have been manipulated by flags in the twentieth century as well; countless propaganda items (such as the World War I flag scarves, *below)* have demanded the sacrifice of freedom, property, and even life on behalf of the principles supposedly embodied in a national flag. Perhaps no more sophisticated exploitation of flags for propaganda – nor more cruel disillusionment – can be found than in the annals of fascism from the 1930s and 1940s, as typified by the Nueremberg rallies *(far right).* The twentieth century has also seen the commercialization of flags and a growing sophistication of design specifications – as in the official pattern *(right)* for the emblem on the flag of the Republic of China's air force. Indeed, the flag has insinuated itself into every facet of life on land, at sea, and even in the air – as at the funeral of France's Marshal Juin *(opposite page)* where vapor trails from jet planes form the French Tricolor.

IN HOC SIGNO VINCES ("In This Sign You Shall Conquer")

FLAGS THAT MADE HISTORY

THE FOLLOWING PAGES REPRESENT A SELECTION OF A FEW OF THE MANY HUNDREDS THAT MIGHT PROPERLY BE CALLED "FLAGS THAT MADE HISTORY."

The Labarum of Constantine

The Labarum, like many famous flags throughout history, began as a single unique standard, a sacred and precious object. The original eventually was captured in battle, destroyed by fire or decay, or perhaps simply lost among other ancient relics. Because its memory remained strong, replicas were later made, and thus it became a flag that continued to influence men's lives.

Basically the Labarum was only an adaptation of the vexillum that had long served as a Roman battle standard. It first appeared in 312 A.D.

In this sixteenth-century painting of the Battle at the Milvian Bridge, Constantine is shown with standards already displaying the cross – although history records that it was his success at the battle that prompted him to employ the symbol thereafter.

when the Emperor Constantine defeated his rival, Maxentius, at Saxa Rubra near Rome. The historian Eusebius records that Constantine had seen a flaming cross in the heavens and the motto "In This Sign You Shall Conquer" as he had entered Italy. The night before Constantine's battle the Christian deity appeared to him, promising him victory and domination over the Roman Empire.

Sensing the growing power of Christians in his empire and army, the following year in Milan Constantine ordered an end to the persecution of Christians, at least those sects which supported his interpretation of the new state religion. This union of church and state, not to be seriously challenged in the Western world for more than a millennium, was well symbolized by the "monogram of Christ" (composed of the Greek letters *X* and *P* for chi and rho) and the representations of Constantine and his children which appeared jointly on the Labarum.

The Labarum illustrated here *(right)*, like certain other flags in this section, is a modern reconstruction based on best available historical documents – coins, monuments, manuscripts, verbal descriptions, etc.

"Y DDRAIG GOCH DDYRY CYCHWYN"

("The Red Dragon Gives Impetus," the motto of Wales)

The Dragon Flag

Perhaps no single flag of the ancient world was more widely used than the Dragon flag. Varying only slightly in form and use as it appeared in countries from Persia to Britain, the Dragon flag was carried in battles over the course of a thousand years.

Of windsock construction, the light fabric of the Dragon flowing from its gaping jaws snapped and twisted in the lightest breeze. Often containing a device which produced a shrill whistling sound, the Dragon was waved high above the heads of on-charging cavalry with the intention of spreading terror in the ranks of the foe and inspiring the men who followed it.

The Dragon flags shown here reflect a few of the countless instances of its use. The legendary King Arthur *(above)* used it to honor his father, Uther Pendragon. The ninth-century *Codex Aureus* records an example from Central Europe *(right)*. A modern heraldic dragon appears in a Welsh military color *(below)*.

"AS THERE IS ONLY ONE SUN IN HEAVEN, THERE SHOULD BE ONLY ONE GREAT KHAN ON EARTH."

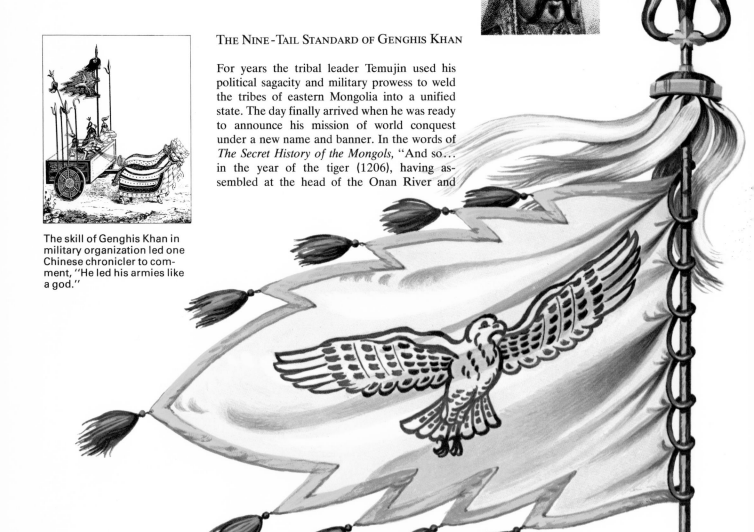

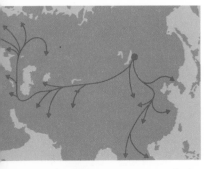

The skill of Genghis Khan in military organization led one Chinese chronicler to comment, "He led his armies like a god."

The Nine-Tail Standard of Genghis Khan

For years the tribal leader Temujin used his political sagacity and military prowess to weld the tribes of eastern Mongolia into a unified state. The day finally arrived when he was ready to announce his mission of world conquest under a new name and banner. In the words of *The Secret History of the Mongols,* "And so... in the year of the tiger (1206), having assembled at the head of the Onan River and having had planted a great white standard having nine feet, they then gave unto Jinghis Qahan the title Khan."

The "feet" were in fact flammules along the sides of the triangular banner, copied from a century-old Chinese tradition. There could be no mistaking this flag as the banner of the great Mongol chief, however. His guardian spirit, the gyrfalcon, was represented in the center. Each of the flammules was decorated with the tail of a yak, recalling at once the importance of this domestic beast to the peoples of central Asia and the nine tribes whose leaders served in the councils of the Great Khan.

At the top of the flagpole bearing this standard was a special gold finial in the shape of a flaming trident. Below it were attached four white horsetails, the whole symbolizing the power of the Khan over the four corners of the earth. It is said that horsetails were chosen because the Mongols believed that the world could only be conquered on horseback.

This special standard was symbolic of Genghis Khan personally and as such probably remained before his tent or mounted on his personal chariot. Numerous other flags of rank existed in the Mongol empire, however, and flags were extensively used for signaling in battle maneuvers. Indeed the administration of territory was directly related to the grant of flags to district chiefs known as bannermen. Such a leader continued in power only so long as he successfully defended the banner (as his territory came to be called) and provided men for the armies led by the Great Khan in his pursuit of further conquests.

Even after the death of Genghis, the tradition of his flag was preserved through oral tradition. The Kalmuck people have maintained its usage even into the twentieth century.

As they spread through Asia and Europe, ending their threat to Vienna only when word was received that the Great Khan had died, the Mongols recalled a special prayer, repeated even today in Mongolia: "You shall accomplish a long and successful

journey; a prosperous wind shall blow in your flag."

The Oriflamme of Charlemagne

The flag of Charlemagne was known as the Oriflamme, presumably because of its golden red color. Its form appears to have been of the gonfanon type common in early medieval Europe – a long flag with swallowtails.

The original mosaic from the Triclinium of St. John of the Lateran in Rome, showing Charlemagne receiving his banner, has been lost. Some authors claim that there were two mosaics – one in which a green standard, symbol of power over Rome, is given to Charlemagne and another in which the red flag of empire is presented to him. The truth can probably never be determined with certainty since the mosaics have been "restored."

The important thing is the historical tradition of an oriflamme used by Charlemagne as the symbol of the empire. It may or may not have been the flag deposited in the Abbey of St. Denis and associated with the war cry "Montjoie," but later French dynasties revered the tradition that the popes had given to their predecessor, Charlemagne, a red standard symbolizing temporal authority, which they themselves still carried in battle (at least in replica).

Of the design on the flag nothing can be said with certainty, particularly concerning its possible significance. It appears that there were six gold discs (perhaps roses), each bordered in dark blue and red. The red, white, and blue colors of a tassel below the spearhead suggested to later generations a continuity with the Tricolor that arose a thousand years later; but the simple fact is that any symbolism the elements in the flag of Charlemagne may originally have had is now forever lost to us.

The revived Roman Empire established by Charlemagne on Christmas Day in the year 800 was finally ended by Napoleon 1,006 years later.

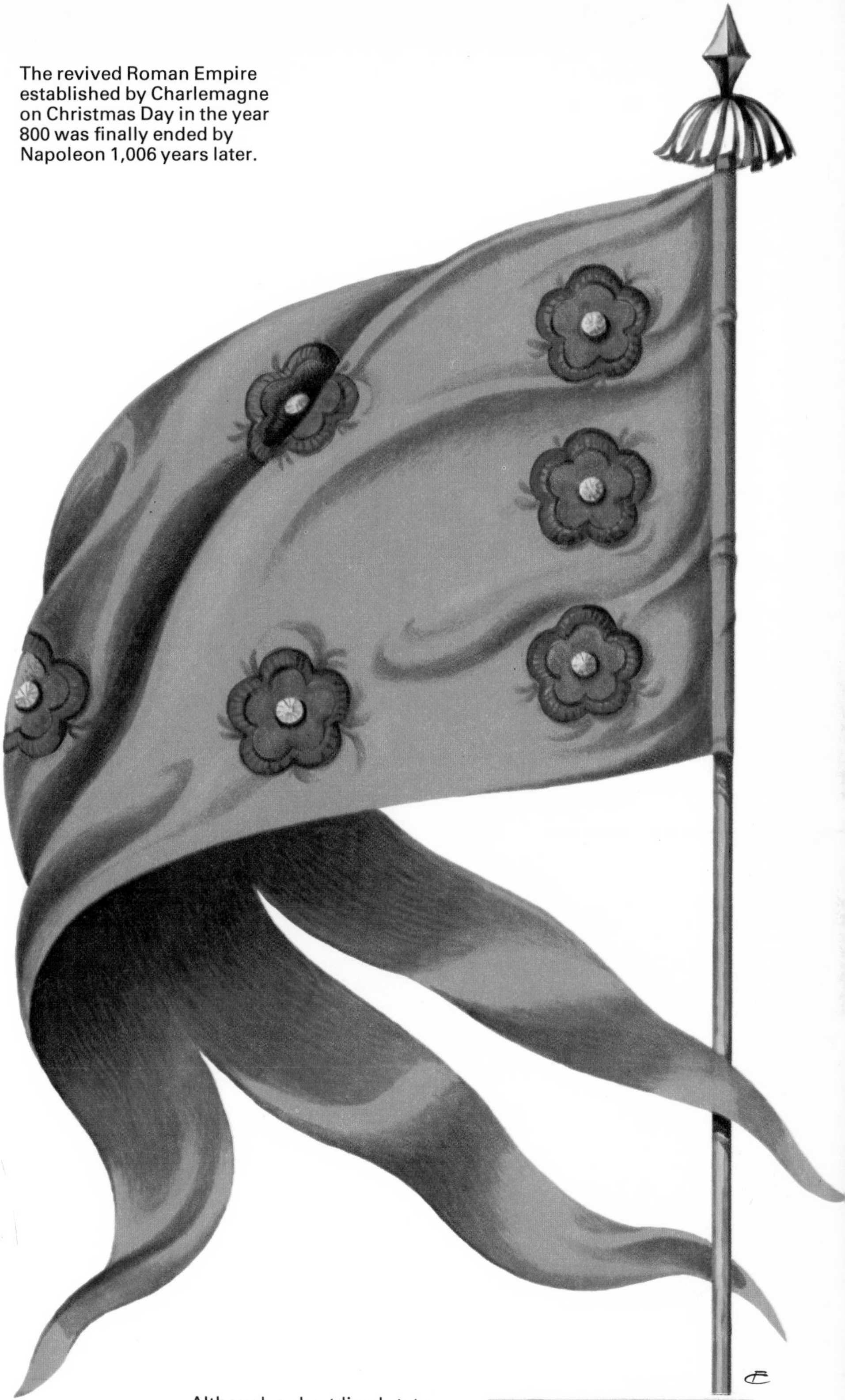

Although a short-lived state, the union of much of what constitutes modern France, Germany, and Italy by Charlemagne still provides inspiration for European unity.

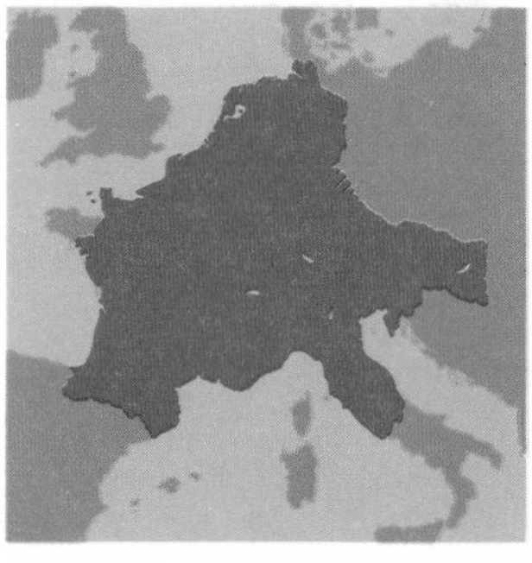

A modern reconstruction of a ninth-century mosaic *(left)* shows St. Peter granting symbols of religious and civil authority to Pope Leo III (on the left) and Charlemagne.

"OF DANNEBROG IT'S KNOWN, IT FELL FROM HEAVEN DOWN"

(popular Danish song)

A seal *(right)* from the Schleswig county of Everschip, dating from at least 1414, is one of the oldest indicating use of the Dannebrog at sea. In a royal seal of Erik of Denmark *(far right)* from 1398 the Danish cross separates the arms of his kingdoms in exactly the same fashion found in today's royal arms of Denmark. Arms *(below)* from the *Gelre Armorial* of the late fourteenth century show the oldest known representation of the Dannebrog.

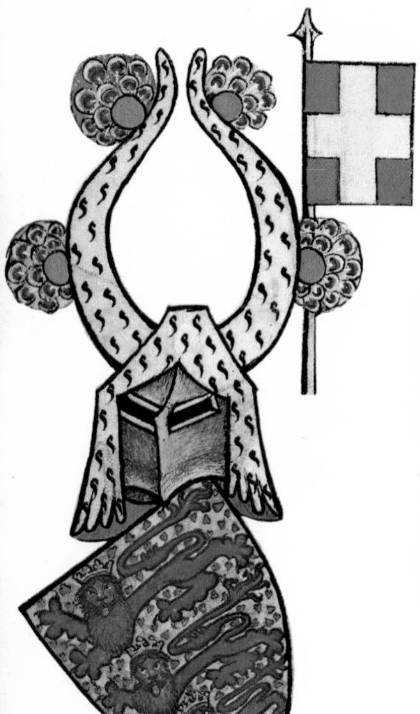

The Dannebrog

The Dannebrog is (at least in its modern form) an extremely simple flag, consisting of an off-center white cross in a red field – yet its history makes it one of the most remarkable of national flags in existence today.
It has frequently been claimed that the Dannebrog is the oldest national flag in the world, continuously in use; but that is an extremely difficult distinction to determine. We can trace the basic design back for 600 years, perhaps even 750 years or more. On the other hand, national flags in the modern sense did not come into existence until the American and French Revolutions of the late eighteenth century, and although the Dannebrog design was chosen for this purpose in Denmark, official usage as a national flag on land did not begin until 1854. Moreover, there have been variations over the centuries in the exact form of the flag as used for naval and military purposes – a rich variety only hinted at in the examples given on these pages.
Nevertheless it must be recognized that the white cross on red has been employed consistently as the chief Danish symbol for at least 600 years. A coin suggests it may date from the second half of the twelfth century, while another source gives it origin in a battle in 1208. It may be related to red flags used in the Baltic Sea as early as the ninth century.

The most famous story – one known to every schoolchild in Denmark – relates that the Dannebrog fell from heaven on 15 June 1219 during a battle in which King Waldemar II was victorious against the pagan Estonians. The situation that day at Lyndanisse seemed hopeless until the Danish bishops who accompanied the army prayed to God for victory. As a sign that he would favor their cause, God sent the Dannebrog to the Danes, who have cherished it ever since.
More recent scholarship indicates that the likely origin of the design may be linked with the war flag of the Holy Roman Emperors, who considered Denmark a vassal state. A red war flag charged with the white cross of Christianity can be documented not only in the "Danish Marches" (i.e., in Denmark), but also in the "Eastern Marches" (i.e., in Austria, where it still serves in the shield of Vienna) and in Savoy, Utrecht, Danzig, Pisa, Barcelona, and numerous other areas of Europe. It is even retained in two other contemporary national flags – those of Malta and Switzerland.
Another possibility is that the first Dannebrog was a gift from one of the popes, who were in the habit of giving special banners to kings undertaking military campaigns (to extend their own royal dominions) in the name of Christianity.

In the eighteenth century a lonely Danish ship sailing along the Gold Coast of West Africa could take heart at the sight of its national flag over the fort at Christiansborg.

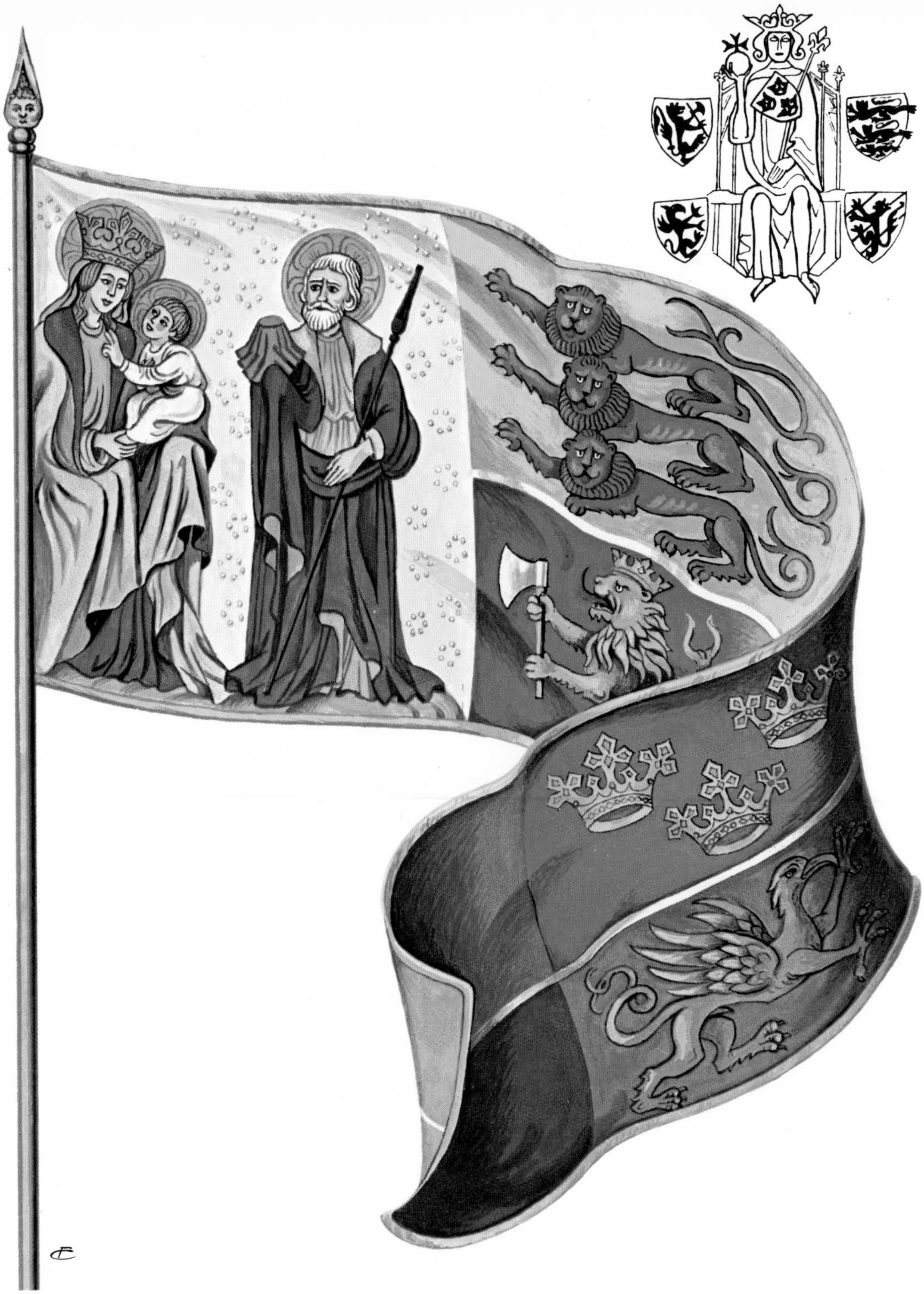

Erik of Pomerania, shown here on his Great Seal (1398), was king of Norway, Denmark, and Sweden. His flag (left), the oldest known Dannebrog, was an elaborate version. Until its destruction during World War II, it hung in St. Mary's church in Lübeck, Germany.

To show his territorial claims, between the arms of the cross on his flag Erik inserted the arms *(top to bottom)* of Denmark, Norway, Sweden, and Pomerania.

In short we are faced, as is often the case in vexillology, with contradictory and confusing sources of documentation concerning a matter of great importance. New evidence may some day be unearthed which will allow us to know once and for all when the Dannebrog arose and for what reasons. More likely, as the attention of scholars is focused again on known details, new theories will be put forward which will help us to understand better what may have happened. In the case of the Danish flag, historical questions have a special interest because it is not simply a vexillological curiosity from ages past, but is still in daily use. The Dannebrog exists in two forms – the *splitflag* officially reserved for the navy and royal institutions since 1625 and the rectangular version, for private display on land and at sea. Since 1690 special badges have been added to indicate a particular government office or private institution – such as the great trading companies which briefly established a Danish colonial empire. The Dannebrog has also been the basis for regimental colors, since 1842 to the exclusion of alternate designs.

The influence of the Dannebrog, like certain other "flags that made history," continues unabated today: it is mentioned in poems and songs and flown on Christmas trees and from flagpoles in private gardens. In fact it expresses in graphic form a highly condensed version of the events and principles of an entire nation.

"BETTER, FORTY TIMES BETTER, MY BANNER THAN MY SWORD"

(Joan of Arc at her trial)

Burned as a heretic by the English, to whom she had been betrayed by her own king, Joan of Arc later became a national hero. In 1920 she was sainted by the Catholic Church, more than 400 years after having been put under its anathema. The arms of France and "Long Live King Louis" appear over the door of her family home *(above).*

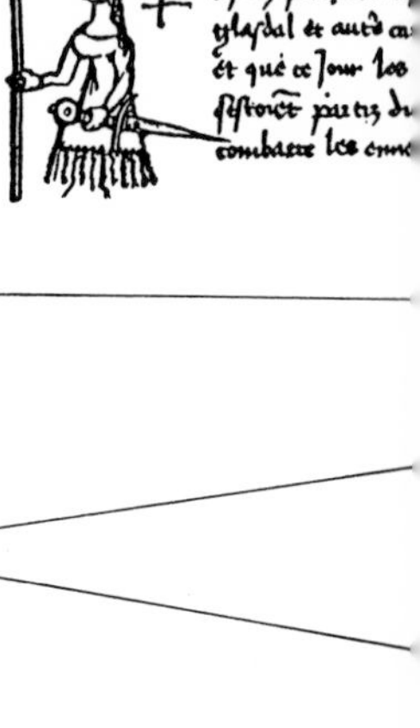

La Pucelle, "the maiden," was a familiar name for Joan of Arc *(right* and *far right)* in the fifteenth century when two manuscripts recorded her appearance and her flag.

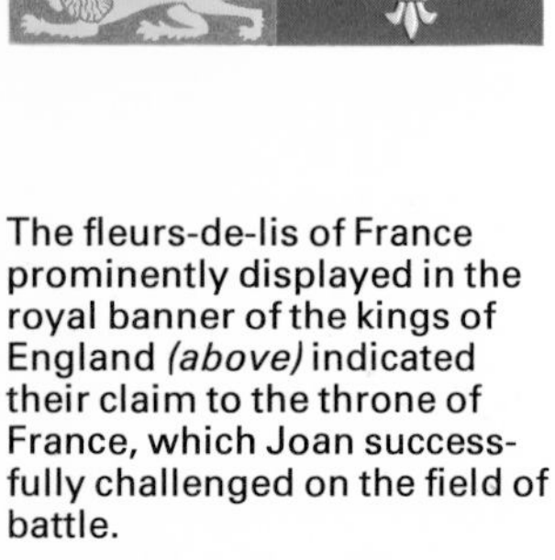

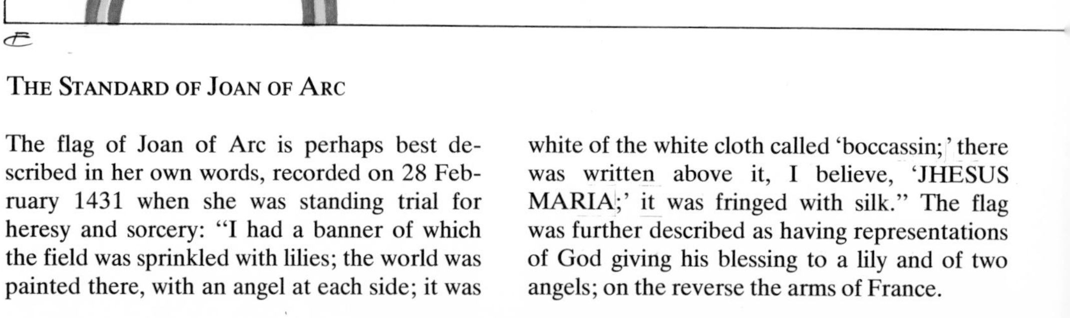

The Standard of Joan of Arc

The fleurs-de-lis of France prominently displayed in the royal banner of the kings of England *(above)* indicated their claim to the throne of France, which Joan successfully challenged on the field of battle.

The flag of Joan of Arc is perhaps best described in her own words, recorded on 28 February 1431 when she was standing trial for heresy and sorcery: "I had a banner of which the field was sprinkled with lilies; the world was painted there, with an angel at each side; it was white of the white cloth called 'boccassin;' there was written above it, I believe, 'JHESUS MARIA;' it was fringed with silk." The flag was further described as having representations of God giving his blessing to a lily and of two angels; on the reverse the arms of France.

King Charles VII of France *(left)* was crowned in Rheims in July 1429 after the city was liberated by forces commanded by Joan. His personal flag *(below)* was red, but later French royal flags favored the color white.

Joan's judges were interested in all the details of the flag design, hoping that they could thereby prove their case that she had imputed magical powers to it. They also asked who was responsible for having the flag made; Joan replied simply that SS. Catherine and Margaret had appeared to her in a vision, commanding that she "take the standard in the name of the King of Heaven."

The role of her flag on the battlefield – where she won eternal honor for the French army by breaking the English siege at Orleans, thereby preventing their capture of the remaining unoccupied parts of French territory – was also sharply questioned. Joan had, she admitted, boasted of the good fortune that followed those marching behind her standard, insisting that she loved her flag "forty times better" than her sword.

At the coronation of Charles VII her standard was carried into the cathedral at Rheims because "it had been present in the perils; that was reason enough for it to be honored." Yet through all her interrogations Joan steadfastly maintained innocence of those charges brought against her implying disloyalty to her land, her king, or her religion.

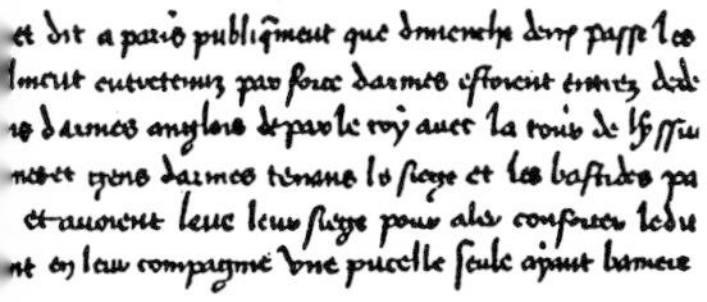
et dit a paris publiquement que dimenche derr passe les
lmeut entretenuz par force darmes estoient entrez ded
us darmes anglois de par le roy avec la tour de ...
...ers gens darmes tenans le siege et les bastides pa
et avoient leve leur siege pour aler combatre le...
nt en leur compagnie une pucelle seule ayant banniere

The arms of Burgundy *(below)* were borne by John the Fearless and Phillip the Good, Burgundian leaders who allied with the English to oppose the accession to the French throne of Charles, head of the House of Orleans.

Although she did not live to see the day, Joan of Arc achieved honor among succeeding generations of French soldiers and statesmen. No vexillological history of France is complete without her: it was her influence which determined that white should serve as the principal French national color from shortly after her death in 1431 until the French Revolution almost 350 years later.

Christopher Columbus, Hernan Cortés, Francisco Pizarro – the three most important early Spanish empire builders in the New World.

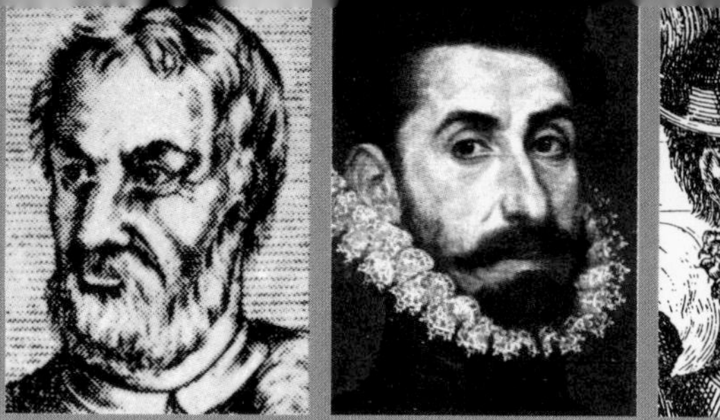

"THERE WILL COME A TIME AFTER MANY YEARS WHEN THE OCEAN WILL LOOSE THE CHAINS THAT FETTER THINGS AND THE GREAT WORLD WILL LIE REVEALED AND A NEW MARINER ...WILL REVEAL A NEW WORLD." (Seneca, *Medea*)

The expeditionary flag of Columbus *(right)*, like many other historical banners, is known to us only by verbal descriptions. The reconstruction is our best knowledge of what the flag actually looked like.

On his way to conquering Mexico City, Cortés's chronicler noted on 5 September 1519: "We left the camp with our banner unfurled *[above]* and four of our company guarding its bearer...."

THE EXPEDITIONARY FLAG OF COLUMBUS

Columbus's expeditionary flag, perhaps the first true flag to be seen in the New World, was described by a contemporary record as an "ensign with an F and a Y; above each letter its crown and one [letter] is on one side of the + and the other on the other." The original flag was not considered of importance at the time and has long since been lost.

Little remains of Pizarro's banner *(right)*, which featured the Spanish royal arms in the center.

Although his ideas had in part inspired German peasants to revolt, Martin Luther *(left)* sided with the princes against them: "My dear friends," he wrote, "Christians are not so numerous that they can get together in a mob."

The title page *(below)* is from a booklet on the history of the Bundschuh movement.

Der Bundtschu
Disz biechlein sagt von dem bő
sen fürnemen der Bundtschuher/wye es sich
angefengt geendet vnd aus kumen ist.

Pamphilus Gengenbach R · G S

The Bundschuh Flag

The plain Bundschuh flag contrasts sharply with the rich heraldic banners against which it contended in early sixteenth-century Germany. Nevertheless, it rallied thousands to its cause and affected the subsequent course of European history.

The Bundschuh movement flourished from 1502 to 1517. Small groups of rural Germans began to demand an end to serfdom and a lessening of the repressive taxes and restrictions imposed by the clergy and nobility. Suppressed, the movement arose again even stronger in 1524, encouraged by the winds of change that the growth of Lutheranism had initiated.

The leaderless Peasant's Revolt and its Bundschuh flag were finally crushed in the battle of Frankenhausen on 15 May 1525. Luther's broadside "Against the Murdering, Thieving Hoards of Peasants," which supported the prerogatives of the established order, was largely responsible. In the twentieth century milder peasant protests have hoisted a black flag displaying a plow and sword.

It has been estimated that 100,000 of the 300,000 peasants who rose in the early sixteenth century to demand improved conditions were

killed in battle or in revenge for attacking Imperial knights *(above).*

"DEFENDERS OF THE LIBERTY OF THE CHURCH"

(Title conferred on the Swiss Confederation by Pope Julius II)

The banner of Uri *(right)* shows elements often found in the Julius Banners – the cantonal emblem, a special canton as an augmentation of honor, and the crossed keys of the papacy.

This scene of the Annunciation, forming the canton of the Julius banner from Basel, epitomizes the unsurpassed craftsmanship that went into the making of flags in the late fifteenth and early sixteenth centuries.

The Julius Banners

It was a proud moment for Matthew Cardinal Schiner when he presented more than thirty Julius banners to the Swiss troops assembled at Alessandria on 24 July 1512. An honor for them, a victory for Pope Julius, and a tribute to Schiner himself were all involved in the ceremony.

Already at that time for more than 200 years, Swiss soldiers had carried their proud (if simple) banners triumphantly into battle, sometimes to defend themselves and sometimes in the service of others. In the Burgundian wars of the late fifteenth century the Swiss had proved so strong that every European power wanted them on its side. Louis XII of France with their aid conquered the Duchy of Milan and was threatening to extend his power further when Pope Julius made Schiner, then Bishop of Sitten, a Cardinal in 1511. The latter's skillful negotiations brought the Swiss over to the side of the Papacy; in 1512 not only Milan, but also the whole of Lombardy was wrested from French control.

To honor this remarkable victory and insure the future loyalty of his new allies, Pope Julius conferred upon the confederation the title "Defenders of the Liberty of the Church" and through Cardinal Schiner presented two special banners. The Swiss, however, jealously preserved the rights of their individual cantons, and it became necessary to have a separate augmentation of honor for each of the cantonal banners. A special badge added to the upper corner of a flag was not the only means of enhancing it. St. Gall, for example, was allowed to change the claws of its heraldic bear from red to gold and to add a gold collar to his neck.

In later years, particularly during the Reformation, many of these flags were mutilated, destroyed, or lost. Nevertheless, those which remain attest not only to the political intrigues of the era but also to the loving care that painters, embroiderers, and other artisans bestowed on the construction of flags in this era. Some of the original Julius banners may be appreciated today in the archives and town halls across Switzerland. Others are preserved only in documents or stained glass windows.

To the damask crimson of the banner of Schwyz has been added a representation of the Madonna, a motto, and a canton incorporating the "coat of arms" attributed to Christ.

Ivan IV (1530–1584) is usually known as "the Terrible." A better translation of the Russian term would be "the Dread" or "the Awe-Inspiring."

The Flag of Ivan the Terrible

This flag of Ivan the Terrible is typical of the fantastical religious motifs found in several banners flown during the course of Ivan's career. Each was an inspiration to the men who fought under it through the affirmation it made of the prevailing political, spiritual, and social ideologies.

This flag, a huge 2.2 by 6.3 meters (7 by 20 feet), is still preserved in the Kremlin. Christ the Savior is emblazoned above the heavenly army of mounted angels, ready to come to the aid of Ivan in battle. His Asian conquests were indeed impressive. While not successful in creating a Russian outlet on the Baltic as he wanted, Ivan set a precedent for future expansion. Moreover, his external victories were matched by fundamental internal changes following his proclamation as tsar in 1547.

Against the glory brought to many handsome banners bearing his name must be set Ivan's record for cruelty and autocracy. Whether due to insanity (as some have claimed) or not, the murder of thousands of his fellow Russians – including his own son – is an ineradicable stain on Ivan's standard.

The Archangel Michael, considered the standard-bearer of heaven, is represented in the triangular portion of Ivan the Terrible's flag of 1560 *(above)*. Instead of a banner Michael bears a Russian Orthodox cross, symbolizing victory for the church of which Ivan was the protector. The same cross figures on a flag in a fifteenth-century battle *(right)*.

BY THE RUDE BRIDGE THAT ARCHED THE FLOOD,
THEIR FLAG TO APRIL'S BREEZE UNFURLED,
HERE ONCE THE ENBATTLED FARMERS STOOD,
AND FIRED THE SHOT HEARD ROUND THE WORLD.

Ralph Waldo Emerson's *Hymn sung at the completion of the Battle Monument, Concord, Massachusetts (19 April 1836)*

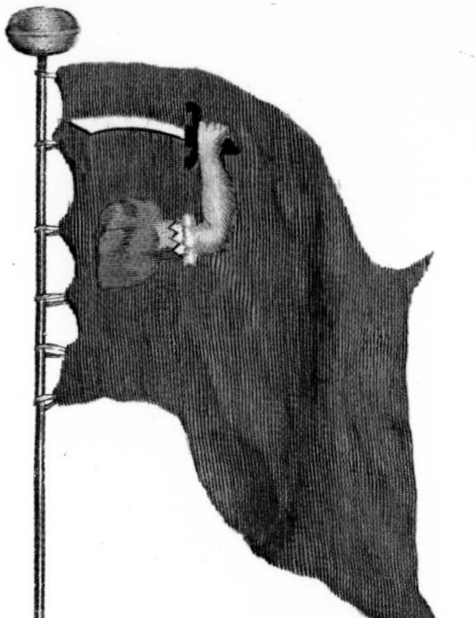

The Bedford flag *(above)* resembles a seventeenth-century Polish naval flag *(left).* Similar flags incorporating the "arm of God" had been used in England, Hungary, Algeria, Bosnia, Sweden, and the Netherlands.

The Bedford Flag

According to tradition, the Bedford flag was the only American banner displayed on the first day of the American Revolution. Cornet (standard-bearer) Nathaniel Page of the Bedford minutemen (a militia company) took it from a closet in his home when he left for neighboring Concord early on the morning of 19 April 1775. Later in the day, after helping tend the dead and wounded, he found a group of children playing with the flag. The historic flag was returned to Page's home closet and was not to be seen again publicly until the centennial celebration of the battle of Concord.
Donated in 1885 to the town of Bedford, it may be seen today in the public library of that small New England town, its Latin motto ("Conquer or Die") scarcely dimmed by age. This flag – probably the oldest one existing in the United States – was already almost a century old at its moment of glory in the battle of Concord. Originally painted in England in the mid-seventeenth century, it had been a cavalry standard of the Three County Troop organized in eastern Massachusetts in 1659 to defend the colonists against Indians.

The British regulars counted 273 casualties in the battles of Lexington and Concord, while their American opponents (mostly farmers and tradesmen) counted 95.

Spanish conquerors substituted worship of the Virgin of Guadalupe *(right)* for the Aztec goddess Tonantzin in the early sixteenth century. She was subsequently represented in various Mexican revolutionary flags *(below)*.

"LONG LIVE THE VIRGIN OF GUADALUPE!
LONG LIVE AMERICA!
DEATH TO BAD GOVERNMENT!"

She has continued to be depicted in flag form *(right)* in political and religious processions of the nineteenth and twentieth centuries.

The Standard of the Virgin of Guadalupe

The flag of the Virgin of Guadalupe, hoisted on 16 September 1810 by Father Miguel Hidalgo (with its Battle Cry of Dolores, *above*), marked the beginning of the revolutionary movement in Mexico against Spanish colonial rule.

Although final success was not achieved for eleven years, Father Hidalgo and his flag have never been forgotten in Mexico. Both have become permanent parts of the political iconography of the Mexican nation (see also pp. 148-151).

As Pope Benedict XIV said about the apparition of the Virgin of Guadalupe itself, "(God) has not acted in such fashion for any nation." The Virgin (speaking Nahuatl) is said to have appeared to the Indian peasant Juan Diego in 1531, on Tepeyacac Hill north of Mexico City. Subsequently her picture was miraculously imprinted on his cloak, which is still preserved in the Basilica at Dolores Hidalgo. The wings of the angel at the Virgin's feet are in the colors (green, white, and red) that later became the Mexican national flag.

"HENRY V CANNOT ABANDON THE WHITE FLAG OF HENRY IV"

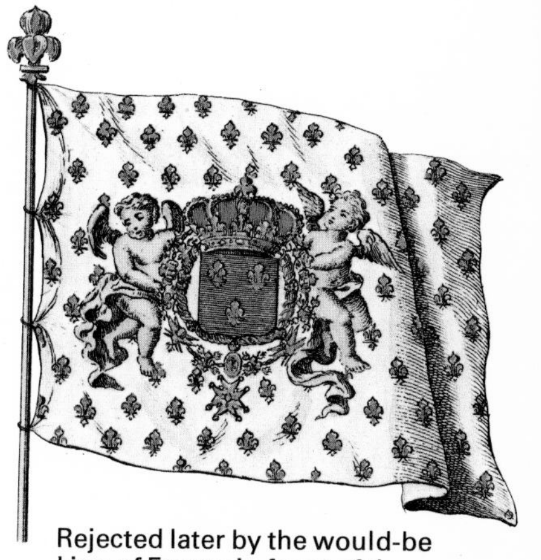

Rejected later by the would-be king of France in favor of the white flag *(above)*, the Tricolor *(left)* had apparently been accepted by the Count of Chambord when he was younger, modified only slightly – perhaps by his own hand. This picture is enlarged ten times from a book that belonged to the count.

The Tricolor of the Count of Chambord

The flag of the Count of Chambord held the fate of France in the balance for two years. The Franco-Prussian War had brought the Second Empire of Napoleon III down in shambles. The French Assembly elected in February 1871 was overwhelmingly in favor of restoring the monarchy, although delegates were about evenly split between support for the Orleanists and the legitimist pretender, the Count of Chambord. The count, who would have become King Henry V, had been living in exile since 1830 when he was ten.

The Paris Commune defeated, the count returned to Paris in the summer of 1871 and seemed likely to be proclaimed king despite the Orleanists. As the grandson of Charles X, however, he might be expected to insist on the restoration of the Bourbon flag of white – with or without the fleurs-de-lis and the arms of France. Knowing that the public was now firmly attached to the Tricolor (even if the restoration of the monarchy were accepted as a means of uniting and rebuilding the nation), members of the nobility approached the Count of Chambord with trepidation.

Their worst fears were realized in his statements to them, made known publicly on 7 July in his newspaper *L'Union:* "France will call me and I shall come to her complete with my devotion, my principle, and my flag.... I shall not allow to be torn from my hands the standard of Henry IV, of Francis I, and of Joan of Arc. I have received it as a sacred trust from the old king, my grandfather (Charles X), who died in exile; it has always been inseparable for me from the memory of my absent fatherland; it floated over my birthplace and I wish it may shadow my tomb. Henry V cannot abandon the white flag of Henry IV."

Although everyone had hoped that some compromise might be found, in the end such hopes were defeated: the count said "Never" to the Tricolor and the formal birth of the Third Republic was thereby guaranteed.

The irony is that some fifteen years before the count apparently had been willing to accept the Tricolor. This flag appears twice in a book that belonged to him, which is now in the library of the Flag Research Center, Winchester, Massachusetts. Although they could as easily have been replaced by the white flag, these Tricolors are modified – perhaps by the count's own hand – only to the extent of having the royal arms of France added on the white central stripe. When the count died in exile, the flag that might have gained him a kingdom remained hidden in his bookshelves.

Memories of past revolutions – such as the one dramatized by Delacroix in his *Liberty Leading the People (28 July 1830)* – made the Tricolor a very distasteful symbol among some French monarchists.

"I DESTROY THIS WORLD
AND I CONSTRUCT
THE WORLD TO COME."

(The Mahdi, on beginning his *jihad)*

No authentic portrait exists of the Mahdi, who, as a strict Muslim, never allowed his picture to be made.

The Mahdi had five flags made for his chief lieutenants – one each of black, white, red, green, and yellow. Except for the last sentence, the inscriptions on these flags were all the same: " O God, O Merciful One, O Compassionate One, O Living One, O Subsisting One, O Lord of Majesty and Honor. There is no god but God. Muhammad is the Apostle of God. Muhammad al-Mahdi is the Successor of the Apostle of God. Ahmad al-Rifa'i is the Saint of God."

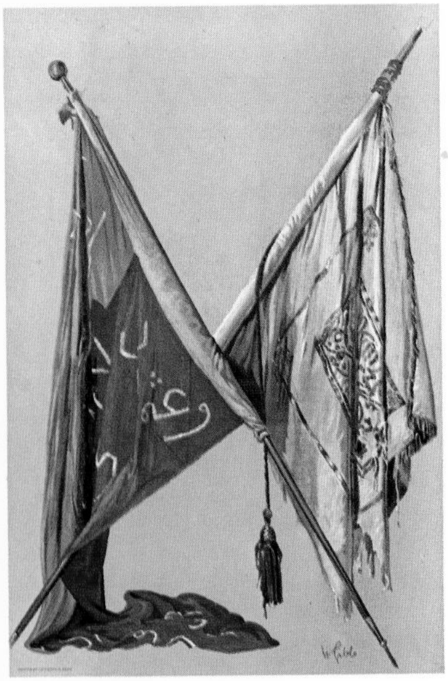

The flag on the left was captured by the British from Mahdist forces in 1884, the other from the Egyptians in 1882.

The Flag of the Mahdi

The flag of the Mahdi called forth the highest adoration and loyalty on the part of millions, while stirring the profoundest disgust and enmity in millions of others. For European society of the late Victorian era in general and England in particular, the imposition of colonial rule in Africa, Asia, and the Pacific was a sacred mission of Christianity and Civilization. The death of the lonely, heroic General Charles Gordon in Khartoum, capital of the Sudan, was an unparalled tragedy for them. In contrast the leader of the "barbarian hordes," Muhammad

"SO LITTLE DONE – SO MUCH TO DO." (Cecil Rhodes's last words)

In 1919 Britain made the final linkup of territories under its control from Cairo to the Cape. But Cecil Rhodes's flag was never officially used and the railroad of his dreams was never built.

Ahmad who called himself the Mahdi ("the Guide"), saw his conquest of Khartoum in January 1885 as a vindication of the *jihad* or holy war that he had begun four years earlier when (he claimed) Allah called on him to expel the infidels and purify Islam.

THE CAPE-TO-CAIRO FLAG OF CECIL RHODES

The Mahdi died later in 1885 and his state survived only thirteen years. By that time a new empire was being built in Africa from the south northward: the Cape-to-Cairo flag appeared as a graphic manifestation of the dreams of empire builder Cecil Rhodes.

Uniting the heraldic emblem of Cape Province (South Africa) and the Egyptian flag – to symbolize the termini of the railroad Rhodes intended to have constructed – was the British Union Jack. Those who did not respect that flag were brushed aside or crushed – a fate that successively befell the Boer farmers of South Africa, the Bantu peoples of Central Africa, and the Arab and European imperialists who competed with Britain. Within seventy years, however, the entire eastern coast of Africa was once again in the hands of native populations. Rhodes's flag is preserved today at Groote Schuur in South Africa.

Elements from Rhodes's personal coat of arms appear in the shield of his namesake, Rhodesia *(right)*.

"OH! BLUE'S THE SKY THAT IS FAIR FOR ALL, WHOEVER, WHEREVER HE BE,
AND SILVER'S THE LIGHT THAT SHINES ON ALL
FOR HOPE AND LIBERTY."

The Eureka Stockade flag of 1854 *(right)* has inspired many Australian flags since that time, including the one *(above)* carried at the Lambing Flat riots of 1860.

The Eureka Stockade Flag

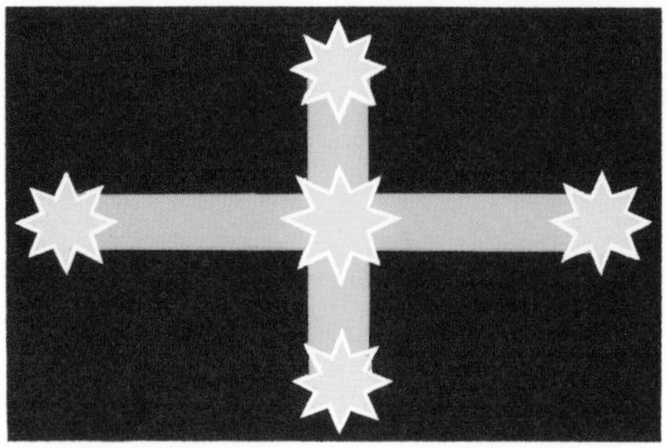

The Eureka Stockade flag, perhaps because of its association with labor riots and a time of political crisis in Australian history, was long forgotten. A century after it was first hoisted, however, Australian authors began to recognize that it had been the inspiration, both in spirit and design, for many banners up to and including the current official civil and state flags of the nation.

Now preserved in the Ballarat Art Gallery in Ballarat, Victoria, the blue and white Eureka Stockade flag originally flew over the camp of goldminers when they took their stand against a corrupt police force in late 1854.

Demanding the release of imprisoned compatriots, abolition of a restrictive licensing system, institution of universal suffrage and vote by ballot, as well as many other reforms, the miners gathered under the leadership of Peter Lalor. Their flag flew only briefly – from 29 November until 3 December, when the stockade was overwhelmed by policemen.

In the 1890s a flag with white stars on a blue cross became associated with the federation movement, which won the battle for a united Australia at the turn of the century. Their slogan was "One People, One Destiny, One Flag."

Without rejecting their loyalty to the British Crown, Australians then sought to emphasize their own nationality by creating a distinctive flag. A competition in 1901 produced a dark blue flag with the Union Jack, a large white "Commonwealth star," and a representation of the Southern Cross composed of five stars not unlike those of the original Eureka Stockade flag. The current Australian flag design was confirmed in 1909.

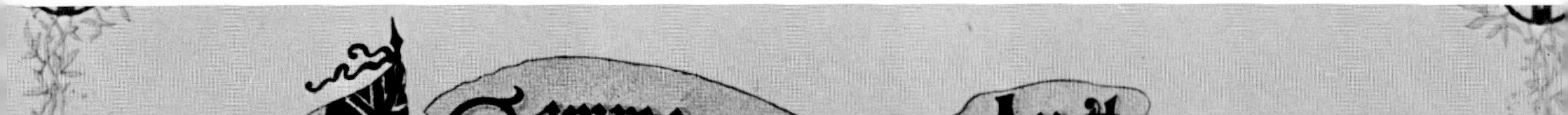

The Commonwealth of Australia had no official flag when it came into being on 1 January 1901, although unofficially the British Union Jack and Eureka Stockade flag were combined *(above)*. A different design was chosen for the national flag in a contest nine months later. The current flag *(right)* shows little change from that version.

The Charkha Flag of Gandhi

The Charkha flag of Gandhi is one of the earliest of numerous banners used by political movements that have evolved into national flags dúring the course of the twentieth century. Dear to the people from the years of struggle they symbolized, these flags were made official at the time of independence (sometimes with minor modifications) as an expression of aspirations for the future.

The flag of the All India Congress Committee, adopted in 1931 at the behest of M. K. Gandhi, contained a representation of a spinning wheel or *charkha.* The national flag of 1947 substituted a slightly different wheel. While the latter may be more dignified for an independent nation, the spinning wheel was a reminder to the followers of Gandhi that they must become self-reliant – making their own cloth and similar goods, raising their own food, and otherwise freeing themselves of industrial products imported by the British. Even today cotton, wool, and silk flags in India are made of *khadi* or homespun cloth.

In contrast to the heraldic symbols which characterized colonial flags, the *charkha* of India's liberation movement flag was recognized instantly by the humblest citizens.

The *chakra* or wheel emblem *(below left)* is a motif in Indian art and architecture going back at least 2,000 years and found in the modern national flag.

The circular form of both the *charkha* and *chakra* is a characteristic of many other national symbols and probably has a psychological appeal based on prehistoric experiences of mankind. They both are related more or less directly to symbols of the sun, moon, the yin-yang symbol, the chrysanthemum emblem of the Japanese emperors, and the peacock of the Burmese.

Although the orange (or saffron) officially stands for courage and sacrifice and the green for faith and chivalry, India's flag colors originated with the two main religious groups of India – the Hindus and the Muslims. White, said to stand for truth and peace, indicates a desire for harmony between them.

IN ALL WISE GOVERNMENTS, THERE HAVE BEEN THESE DISTINCTIONS, WITHOUT WHICH... NO BODY POLITIC OR COMMONWEALTH CAN EXIST.

John Prestwich, *Respublica* (1787)

CUSTOMS AND ETIQUETTE

As inseparable from the soldier as his weapons, the flag has been intimately linked with warfare since the earliest battles on record. Shown at right is a soldier of the Helvetian Republic, ca. 1798.

The flag has gone to sea ever since vessels large enough for more than a few persons have been built. If royal galleys (like that of France, *below*) no longer exist, other ships carry on the traditions of the flag at sea.

In November 1776 during the American war against Britain for independence, vessels belonging to the new United States navy sailed into the harbor of Oranjestad on St. Eustatius in the Netherlands Antilles. The *Andrea Doria* was flying the United States flag (the Continental Colors), at that time unrecognized by any country. When the *Andrea Doria*'s salute to the fort was returned, that action was reported to British authorities in the West Indies and a formal protest lodged with the Dutch government by London. The refusal of the Dutch to retract their salute (which gave de facto recognition to American independence) prompted a British attack on Oranjestad which ended its career as a

leading commercial port in the New World and netted the British over $200 million in booty. A great number of vessels were captured because the British continued to fly Dutch flags in the harbor even after their seizure, thus luring further unsuspecting vessels to easy capture.

Here are elements which to this day continue to be the basis of much ceremony: an institution (or person) of importance and power expresses this status by displaying symbols, in accord with certain established formulas and in situations where they will create or enhance an aura of majesty. A fundamental concept which pervades much of ceremonial is the desire to pay respect to an idea or individual or institution

The most important questions of proper flag display in modern times arise in private usage on businesses, homes, and vessels. This etiquette is as extensive and complex as anything met on a medieval battlefield – a fact suggested by the boats *(opposite page)* in the Dutch harbor of Den Oever.

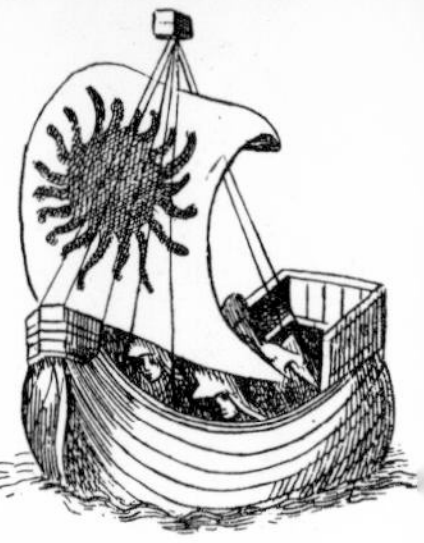

Before the flag was popularized as the principal symbol of a ship, carvings at the prow, crosses and other figures at the top of the mast, and emblems painted on the sails were common means of signaling and identification. Much of our early documentation on their usage and designs stems from the seals used by maritime cities such as those seen above, right.

through the medium of that supreme political symbols, the flag.

Each nation has its own flag customs and etiquette, some of which are based on long-standing traditions such as the American code established by Congress in 1942 and others which are very new (the 1974 flag code of Afghanistan, for example, makes provision for the use of national symbols on any space vehicles Afghanistan may launch). Some rules are merely pleasant procedures which have never been codified, some are backed by law or by international treaty, and some are derived from common sense. This chapter analyzes flag traditions according to the categories already de facto established in the real world.

After reading the chapter, the reader will appreciate why it is impossible to anticipate every circumstance in which flag protocol may be required. Nevertheless the growing standardization of customs throughout the world and the increasing need for codification of basic rules applicable everywhere has resulted in the formulation of the following guidelines for those who must draft or rewrite flag etiquette codes:

The armigerous have always been proud of their right to heraldic emblems: on ships, such as the vessels *(above)*, the logical place for their display was along the gunwales. This system of decorating a warship continued long after its practical usefulness ended. Such a display is known as a *pavisade* from the special shield called a *pavis.*

1. The purpose of any rule of flag usage should be to render, through its display, respect to the country, person, political ideology, religion, event, or institution it represents. (Such a purpose should not include making a fetish of the flag.)

2. In a free country restrictions on display of a national flag (distinguishing flags of specific government officers or departments excepted) should be limited to preventing clear and direct fraud, incitement to violence, or other acts which would be criminal in nature even if the flag were not involved. Bad taste in flag display should be corrected not by law but by public opinion and good example.

3. Flag etiquette regulations should be flexible; economic, technological, and political changes might require modification of flag usage rules over time.

4. The purpose of the rules of flag etiquette should be to facilitate proper display, not to eliminate the use of flags. Simplicity and common sense should be fundamental to every workable flag etiquette code.

5. While courtesy calls for correct flag display, tolerance should exist for honest error and for differences in opinion as to good taste and propriety.

6. The flag of the nation-state generally takes precedence over all others. The chief exceptions are certain royal and imperial standards or, under limited conditions, the flag of an international organization.

7. Flags of equal rank deserve equal honors; generally this means they should be displayed in equal size, at equal height, and in proper design and proportions.

8. Flags or their symbols will fail to command respect if introduced at the wrong time or place; the misjudged expectations of the one who raises the flag may be as much at fault in any resulting disrespect as the behavior of the actual denier of honor due.
9. As symbols of ideas or institutions, flags can command respect only to the same extent as their referents themselves do.

NAVAL FLAG TRADITIONS

Once outside local waters, every vessel is a representative of the country in which it is registered, and for this reason from very earliest days ship flags and signals have been of importance. Behind the rules for naval flag etiquette have always been certain fundamental considerations: the ship must be clearly identifiable, it must be able to communicate effectively with other vessels, and it must uphold the dignity and rights of the country it represents.
The range of circumstances in which naval flags may be displayed is exceeded only by the possible positions on a vessel for such display. Naval etiquette concerns itself with situations in port and out, on holidays and regular occasions, in races and regattas, and when encountering other vessels or signalling, among other circumstances. Private boating may involve a mastless motorboat, a cruiser with temporary staff on the forward deck, a cruiser with bow and stern staffs plus signal mast and yardarm, a cruiser with signal mast plus gaff and yardarm, single and double-masted sailing vessels, double-masted motor boats, and yawls and ketches – to mention only a few varieties.
Types of flags at sea also exceed what normally would be found in a single situation on land. On the private yacht the national ensign, a special distinguishing flag, a yacht club burgee, personal pennants, officers' flags, signal flags, racing pennants, and special flags and pennants may be flown. Naturally, there are variations from one country to the next and over time, particularly as required by changes in naval architecture, which must be kept in mind whether one is actually sailing or simply making a model or a painting of a ship. Not surprisingly, even those books which devote a hundred pages or more to the subject of naval flag etiquette do not exhaust it. The material presented here is thus intended to provide an overview rather than a comprehensive guide to practical usage.

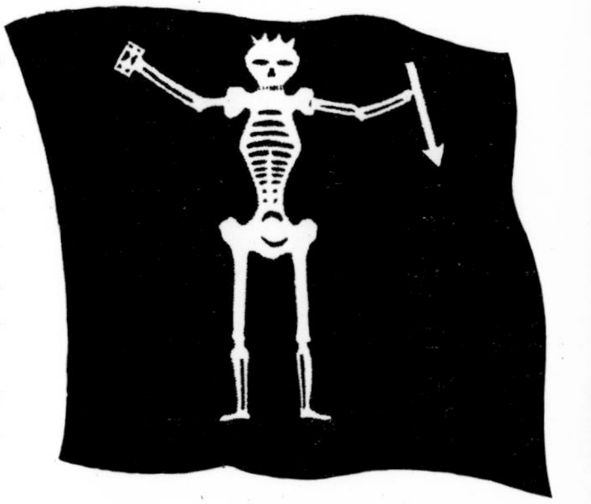

The deathly black flags of piracy seen in the seventeenth and eighteenth centuries were not alone in striking fear into the hearts of sailors. A green flag indicated shipwreck; a yellow flag warned of some highly infectious disease aboard; a plain red flag was the sign that no quarter would be given in battle. The yellow quarantine flag is the only one with the same meaning today.

LEAVING PORT.

A blue flag with a square of white in the center, formerly known as the Blue Peter and now corresponding to signal P in the International Code of Signals, is flown to indicate that a ship is about to leave port.

SHIP COMMISSIONING.

A long, narrow flag flown at the mainmast indicates that a warship is in active service but does not have a commanding officer higher than a certain rank (in which case his command flag would be flown instead).

RENDERING COURTESY ABROAD WITH A FLAG.

The national flag of a foreign country, flown in honor of that country, is known as the *courtesy flag, complimentary ensign,* or *trading flag.* Generally speaking, the civil ensign (which may or may not differ from the civil flag) is the appropriate one to use; it should be flown from the foremast or some other position easily visible and inferior in rank and size only to the ensign of the ship itself and the rank flag of its commander. Courtesy flags are used on entering a

The size and placement of flags on ships has altered over the years, but invariably they are displayed where they can best be seen.

Signal flags, as in the vessel at right, do not always communicate a specific message. In the past when the order "dress ship" was given, it was expected that every piece of bunting in the ship's store would be raised on every available mast and halyard as a salute to royalty, a holiday, or a victory.

National flags of the late eighteenth century are employed to dress this American ship *(right).* Nevertheless its own ensign and commission pennant and the contemporary American rank flags are clearly visible at the ensign staff and on the three principal masts.

The elimination of traditional rigging on the modern ship has not completely done away with flags. Dressing ship is, nevertheless, a more formal matter; the exact order of the signal flags *(above)* is now subject to strict regulations laid down by naval authorities. Owners of private vessels, of course, are still free to choose the flags they prefer for such occasions.

foreign port, and occasionally a home port, as an indication of destination.

DRESSING SHIP.

The custom of decorating a vessel on a special occasion has ancient origins. Current practice is to employ only flags from the International Code of Signals, although ensigns or distinguishing flags of owners and yacht clubs should be flown from the stern and mast. The practice of dressing ship is restricted to ships in harbor and to prearranged occasions.

INDICATING NATIONALITY.

The most important flag flown by a ship indicative of its nationality is the *ensign.* A special design may exist, especially in British Commonwealth countries. The ensign should be larger than any other flag on a vessel and more prominently displayed, usually at the stern. It is regularly flown during daylight hours when a ship is in port or underway or when it encounters another vessel on the high seas. "Ensign" also is frequently but incorrectly used to refer to certain distinguishing flags, which in fact never properly replace the civil ensign and which

"LET THERE BE SOME STANDARD IN YOUR SHIP... SUCH THAT YOU MAY USE IT TO MAKE KNOWN WHAT NEEDS TO BE DONE."

Byzantine Emperor Leo VI (886–912 A. D.), *Basilika.*

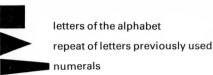

SEMAPHORE

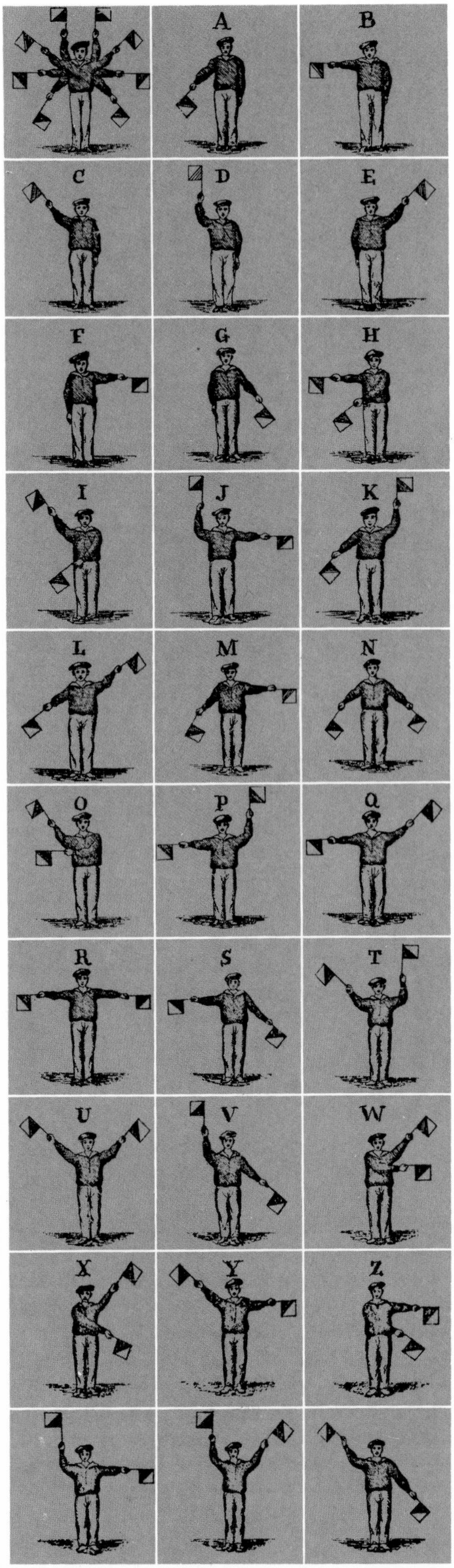

INTERNATL. SIGNAL FLAGS AND PENNANTS

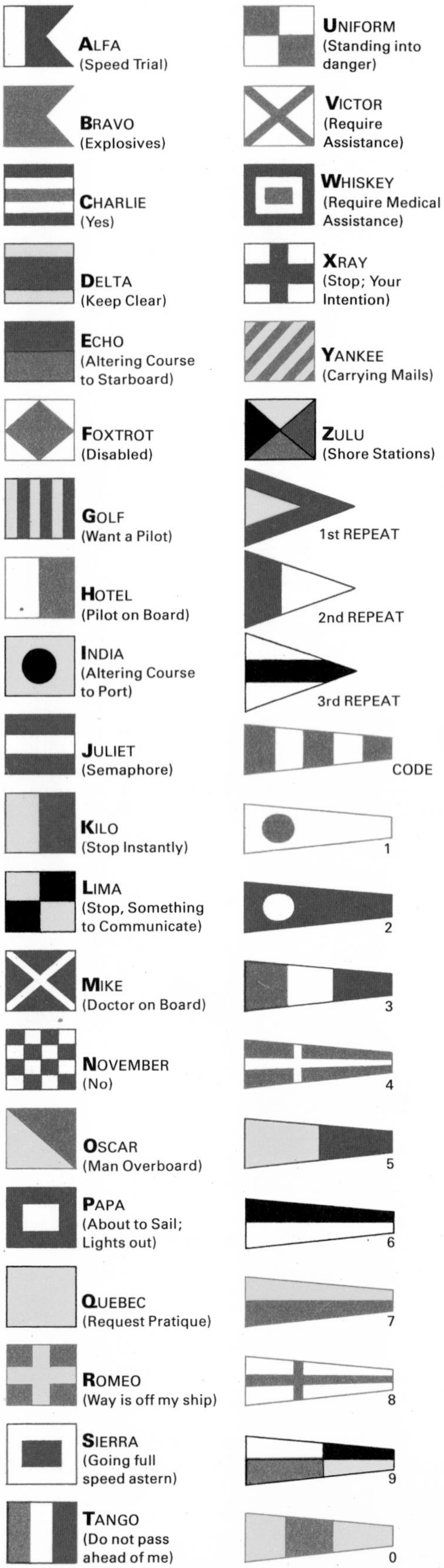

While the private signals of a merchantman – like the *Themistocles (opposite page)* – required special signal books for sender and receiver, the need for universal comprehension early spurred the development of standardized signal flag designs and uses *(right).*

"England Expects That Every Man Will Do His Duty." The inspiration provided by this message, hoisted by Admiral Lord Nelson at the commencement of the Battle of Trafalgar on 21 October 1805, has tended to obscure the brilliance Nelson demonstrated in maneuvering his fleet into a winning position through the use of other

signal flags. His flagship, *H.M.S. Victory,* is today in drydock, but its signal flags repeat the famous battle message. (In a different battle, when ordered by a superior to cease fire, Nelson is said once to have put his telescope to his blind eye exclaiming, "I really do not see the signal.")

Α αριστείδης.
Β ἐπαμινώνδα
Γ θεμιστοκλής
Δ ἀλέξανδρος

Ε σωκράτης
Ζ ξενοφῶν
Η λεωνίδας
Θ αθηνα.

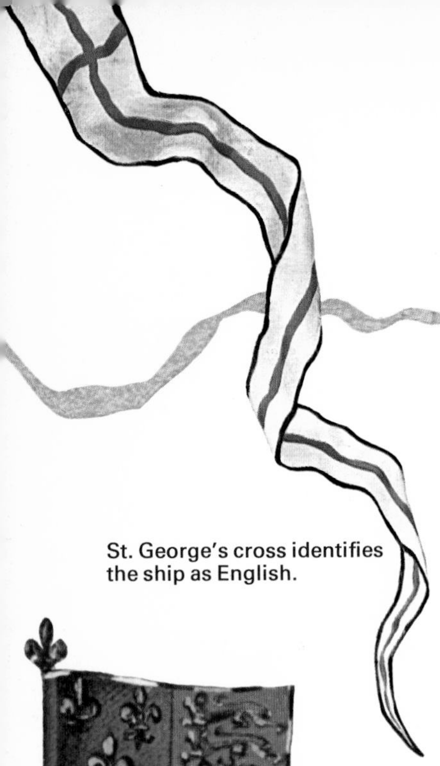

Since time immemorial a festive event has called for the display of special flags.

King Henry VIII departs from Dover for his meeting with King Francis I of France on the *Field of the Cloth of Gold.* The gold sails and pennants are in keeping with the conspicuous opulence of the occasion; most ships would display half as many symbols.

St. George's cross identifies the ship as English.

The positioning of flags is determined by the naval architecture of the era; there is neither ensign nor jack here.
In design each pennant, shield, and flag makes a calculated assertion about the lineage, power, or majesty of the king – the human equivalent of a preening peacock.

The royal banner proclaims sovereignty over France and England.

Decorative shields bear the badges of Edward III, York, and Lancaster and the portcullis badge of Beaufort.

Henry *(above)* showed his Welsh ancestry in the use of white and green as livery colors: a green border frames the cross of St. George, and pennants of white and green serve as back-grounds for other symbols. His ship is probably the 1,500-ton *Henri Grace à Dieu.*

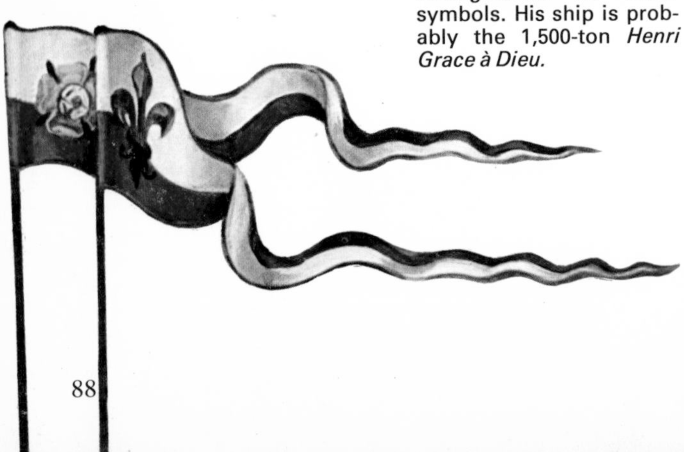

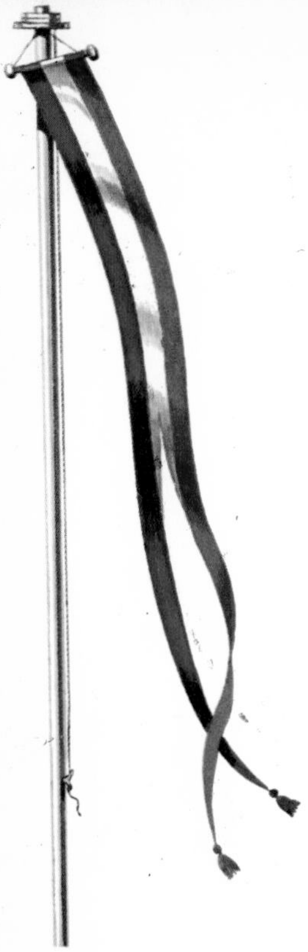

In order that the flagpole will not be completely bare when no flag is displayed on it, the custom prevails in many countries to hoist a pennant of the national colors. Here is the Dutch red-white-blue.

should be flown in smaller size and subordinate position, usually on the foremast. In the United States such flags include the United States Power Squadron ensign, yacht ensign, and United States Coast Guard Auxiliary ensign.

SALUTING.

Rendering honors between two vessels or between a vessel and a naval establishment on shore as a mark of respect often involves a flag salute. No other naval custom associated with flags has brought so much political turmoil. The concept of a courtesy salute is a recent one; the salute originally always had the implication of deference to a superior power. Gun salutes supposedly originated because they temporarily rendered the weapons ineffective for combat and thus showed one's peaceful intentions.

HOISTING A FLAG AT THE GAFF.

A staff with a short spar jutting from it at an angle near the top is said to be gaff-rigged; usually there is a yardarm attached to the same staff. Originally this hoisting arrangement was characteristic of ships; the national flag was flown at the gaff, that being the most easily visible point as well as the one to which a flag could most easily be raised without interfering with other rigging or sails. The gaff-rigged pole has come into increasing usage on land where conditions and etiquette are entirely different. Although the national flag should always take precedence over other flags, which on land means flying at the highest position, it is frequently flown at the gaff (or with another national flag on the yard-arm) rather than at the truck (top) of such a pole.

Many flag etiquette traditions (such as the use of signal flags, *above*) which originated at sea have been brought ashore – first by those living along the coast and later by those far inland. Even the construction of flagpoles in two parts began as an adaptation of nautical usage.

FLAG USAGE

⚑ indicates usage is permitted without official approval; absence of ⚑ may indicate flag is inappropriate rather than forbidden.

TYPE	USAGE: ON PRIVATE HOMES	USAGE: ON COMMERCIAL BUILDINGS
CIVIL FLAG*	⚑	⚑
STATE FLAG*		
PRIVATE RANK FLAG	⚑	
MUNICIPAL FLAG	⚑	⚑
BUSINESS HOUSE FLAG		⚑
HISTORICAL FLAGS	⚑	⚑
FOREIGN FLAGS	⚑	⚑
FLAGS OF ORGANIZATIONS (INCLUDING POLITICAL PARTIES)	⚑	
BUNTING	⚑	⚑

*distinction exists between civil and state flag.

Gradually gun salutes were replaced by a dipping of the ensign and lowering of the sails. In wide areas off its coast, however, Great Britain for centuries demanded that foreign vessels completely take in their ensigns and lower the topsails and do so before any salute was rendered by the British vessel, as a sign that British sovereignty over the seas was recognized. An ancient writer states: "The salute of the cannon is majestic, that of the flag lowered is humble, and if the flag is completely taken in it is of the greatest humility, even debasing." Current practice is for warships to dip on an equal basis to one another but to salute a private or commercial vessel by dipping the ensign only if the latter does so first.

USING SPECIAL FLAGS.

The distinguishing flag of a commercial firm, normally flown on the foremast, is known as a *house flag*. In Britain the term also refers to the private distinguishing flag of a yacht owner. The Jack is a small flag of nationality worn at the prow of a warship when in port. Rank flags indicate the presence on board a vessel of an individual (not necessarily the commander) entitled to fly a personal distinguishing flag. Government and military officers are entitled to specific flags; some private commercial firms and yacht clubs have instituted similar flags of their own.

USING FALSE COLORS.

The use of another's national ensign in wartime

The yardarm and gaff-rigged pole allow for the simultaneous display of a large number of flags.

to deceive an enemy is a *ruse de guerre;* proper flags are supposed to be raised when action is engaged.

FLAG USAGE AND ETIQUETTE ON LAND

While the invention of flag etiquette must be as old as the earliest flags, the subject is as vital today as any aspect of vexillology. Quite simply, the political importance of that cloth we call the flag which expresses the ranking of individuals, the honors of the regiment, the privileges of the state, and similar distinctions is always a function of its setting as well as of its design.
Examination of ancient carvings and paintings

AT RALLIES, PARADES	ON PUBLIC BUILDINGS	ON MISSIONS ABROAD	AT HALFSTAFF	OTHER THAN ON HOLIDAYS	RESTRICTION ON USAGE MAY EXIST
⚑			⚑	⚑	
⚑	⚑	⚑	⚑	⚑	⚑
⚑	⚑		⚑	⚑	⚑
⚑	⚑		⚑	⚑	⚑
⚑			⚑	⚑	
⚑	⚑			⚑	⚑
⚑				⚑	⚑
⚑			⚑	⚑	⚑
⚑	⚑	⚑			

of flags in use will readily confirm the fact: rarely is any flag purely a decorative element, as easily omitted as included. Nor has their use on ships overshadowed that of armies and royal courts and other official events and situations on land. If anything – although the priority is a difficult one to resolve – customs pertaining to flags seem to have originated on land and to have spread from there to the oceans of the world (and more recently to outer space).
In the past the very life of an individual might depend on correct display or recognition of a flag; deep at the core was always that life-or-death struggle for supremacy which is inherent in the very purpose of most flags.
Today observance of etiquette is usually a

The first flag to be used on land may well have been a scrap of material dyed with the blood of an enemy or slain animal.

matter of prestige. Sports persons contend for the honor of the victory pennant, worshippers parade with sacred ensigns, improperly rendered military salutes become the basis for diplomatic incidents, political banners are flaunted or outlawed in accord with national principles of "proper display."

Such incidents are in fact more widespread, more diverse in nature, more frequent, and certainly better publicized than anything known in centuries past. In modern times the hoisting

Trenches on the battlefield, fortresses, pavilions and tents, towers and buildings – wherever the flag most obviously asserts the presence of those who defend it, we may expect to find that flag flying, today as in the past.

of a flag has for the most part become a joyous occasion, a celebration in which all ways of doing things (whether or not they have been codified into formal flag etiquette rules) are no more than a form of courtesy to others, or of common sense and good taste as perceived over time.

Military regulations and those applying to government buildings (including diplomatic missions) tend to be lengthy and detailed; they would fill this entire book if reprinted in full. Fortunately, there are great similarities in flag codes around the world which allow for their essence to be presented here in a form appropriate for the nonspecialist – particularly for the private citizen whose concern is with flag display on a home or business. Moreover, it is precisely here that the greatest guidance is required, for civil flag codes are usually quite inadequate.

A case in point is the code adopted by the United States Congress in 1942. Originally drafted in 1923, it contains anachronisms such as the instruction that an automobile flag must be firmly clamped to the radiator cap! – and inconsistencies, especially concerning the honoring of the United States flag jointly with those of other nations. Major considerations such as the display of historical flags or of the national flag at night, periodic updating of the code itself, and use of the flag in political demonstrations are completely absent. Nevertheless, for lack of an alternative this code has been modified for use in many other countries and in many American states.

The selection of customs here does not exhaust the subject, but does present an analysis of all the major questions likely to occur in normal flag display situations. Wherever applicable, an indication has been given of national peculiarities and of obsolete forms. For the sake of convenience there have been special sections devoted to those specific areas of etiquette (e.g., flags of distress and mourning) where land and sea traditions overlap.

DISPLAYING AUTOMOBILE FLAGS.

Flags flown on vehicles are restricted by law to government officials in some lands, elsewhere limited only by good taste. In addition to flags flown from antennas and front fenders, the flag design may appear on any part of the vehicle.

DECORATING WITH BUNTING.

Material known as bunting and made especially for draping is used as patriotic decoration. In some countries specific colors in a specific order are required. The flag itself may be displayed on a wall or podium either horizontally or vertically with its hoist uppermost. Some countries expressly forbid the flag to be draped or used as covering (e.g. for a plaque or monument).

BURNING A FLAG.

The most dignified way to dispose of a flag when

it is no longer serviceable is to burn it – unless its historic value suggests preservation regardless of condition. Flag burning is also a means of political protest and of preventing the capture of military colors by enemy forces. No special ceremony is associated with burning the flag.

HONORING A FLAG.

A distinctive addition is often made to a military flag or its staff, indicating a special achievement. A head of state or his deputy often presents such

Good taste is the only rule concerning the number of flags that may be flown simultaneously in the same place. However, international custom now restricts the use of national flags for pure decoration – especially where (as in the nineteenth-century museum shown here) some of the flags are smaller or are flying at a lower position than others.

battle honors on the parade ground, the standard-bearer kneeling while the award is attached to the flag in the presence of the unit being honored.

A ritual flag pledge is repeated as an affirmation of loyalty to that which a flag symbolizes, not only in the military but in republican countries where the supreme national symbol is a flag rather than the sovereign. In the United States the pledge of allegiance is often repeated by schoolchildren and by audiences at political and social gatherings. The pledge is rendered in the presence of the flag by standing, facing it with head uncovered (excepting women and those in military service), and rendering a salute.

PARADING COLORS.

Three or more individuals in a military or paramilitary formation detailed to carry its flag(s), generally at the head of a parade are called the *color guard.* From one to five flags may be paraded in a single line, with at least one individual not carrying a color at each end of the line. In the United States civilian color guard units perform precision drill exercises. In the past, defense of the colors was the highest duty of a soldier; if a member of the color guard was

The automobile flag used today for identification corresponds to the coat of arms on the carriage door in centuries past.

killed, another soldier immediately took his place.

Almost any flag may be carried in a procession; generally it is with the pole held aloft, but sometimes at a 45° angle in front of marchers or over their shoulders. Cased colors are carried in a practice march or during inclement weather; very large flags are sometimes carried flat by a number of persons holding the edges. The massing of flags reduces the respect it is possible to render to an individual flag and is generally reserved for special ceremonies.

FLAG PRESERVATION.

A flag should be handled, whether or not it has historic value, in a way which will maintain its appearance and usefulness for as long as possible. Modern synthetic fabrics can be cleaned without damaging, but professional advice is recommended before cleaning if any doubt exists. Except in the worst weather, modern flags can be flown outdoors with impunity. Direct sunlight, excessive heat, dirt, insects, excessive handling, storage with acidic paper or when moist, and prolonged display with stress on the fabric (as when the flag is nailed to a wall) are all harmful. Mending or repairing flags without historic value is recommended, but the preservation of historic flags should be entrusted to a special laboratory associated with a national, historic, or art museum.

FOLDING A FLAG.

An American custom obtains whereby the national flag is folded twice lengthwise, then folded in triangular sections until reduced to a small bundle, convenient for storage. The useful life of a flag, as well as its dignity, are protected by folding it when not in use.

DISPLAYING HOLIDAY FLAGS.

Restriction of use of the national flag to official holidays is made in some countries; others encourage display on holidays without a ban on display on other occasions. In some countries historic flags are flown on specific days as reminders of past events.

The right to be in the van of the army, and to strike the first blow in battle, was a high privilege during the Middle Ages. Across the world, the office of standard-bearer has been an honorable one, and no greater shame is known in battle than the loss of regimental colors.

DISPLAYING HISTORICAL FLAGS.

The display of obsolete flags is always a political act, but not always of protest and not necessarily forbidden by law. Where unrestricted, private citizens may fly historic flags as they see fit on land, even in place of the current national flag, to commemorate a special building, event, or situation. Such flag usage is especially common (and legal) in the United States.

Few sights are more dramatic than the mounted standard-bearer, even if his flag is at times a small pennant or guidon.

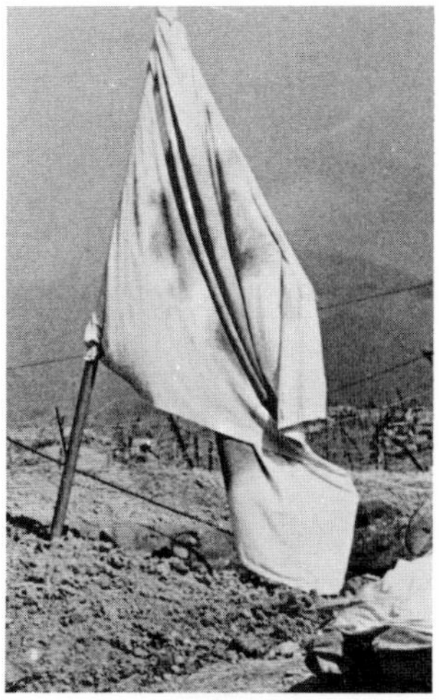

Never issued to troops in advance, the white flag of surrender or truce is universally recognized. The peaceful symbolism of white is also internationally recognized in the Red Cross flag *(bottom)*.

DISPLAYING FOREIGN FLAGS.
Use of another national flag, with or without one's own national flag, is allowed in some countries, forbidden in others, or restricted to use by diplomatic representatives under specified conditions. Such use may be a provocative political act or simply a way of honoring an ally or the fatherland of one's ancestors.

HOISTING THE FLAG.
When a flag is raised on its staff a person indicates respect by standing at attention, facing the flag, saluting if in uniform, and remaining silent until the flag has been fully hoisted.

NIGHTTIME FLAG FLYING.
Use of flags at night is feasible since flags so flown can now be illuminated (although this is not required). Flags are regularly used at night during sports events, political rallies, and parades.

The dramatic forward plunge of the flag toward the enemy is an injunction against ever letting the flag be dishonored.

PRECEDENCE.
The display of flags in order of importance, perhaps the most important aspect of flag etiquette still observed today, is known as precedence or ranking. The general rule is: flags of equal rank should be given equal honors, and flags of un-

Swiss Guards at the Vatican *(right)* are among many to swear allegiance to a regimental color upon induction. Flags are a common sight even in the most modern and mechanized army. Other ceremonies involve the presentation of colors to a unit, the rendering of honors to a sovereign with the flag, the awarding of decorations to the flag of a unit which has performed extraordinary services, and the laying up of colors which are no longer serviceable. The designs of

equal rank should be ordered according to their standing. Today alphabetical order is generally followed for flags of equals, although some older protocol rankings exist. As long as the flags are of equal size and are flown at the same height, it is considered permissible to place the national flag of a host country at an international event first and/or last in a display of flags. Equal size refers to flags of a common surface area or of a common width dimension; common proportions, which grossly distort the correct design of longer and shorter flags, is an unfortunate but frequent expedient. National flags generally take precedence over all others, except occasionally a royal flag or that of an international organization. A current national flag takes precedence over historical flags, which may be flown in chronological or alphabetical order. Generally, flags of political entities are ranked according to their political importance (e.g., national flag, state flag, county flag, city flag), followed by flags of the political or military leaders in similar order (president, governor, county commissioner, mayor); flags of political, religious, commercial, and other institutions follow. Simultaneous display of too many flags, particularly of dissimilar institutions, is a mistake.

the flags and the uniforms of the men who carried them *(right)* may be diverse, but the inspiration behind military customs and etiquette relating to the flag is universal.

Many flag ceremonies involve actually touching the flag, a relic of the belief from antiquity that magic powers can come from direct contact with sacred objects. Even the contemporary Soviet soldier *(above, right)* kneels to kiss the flag when he leaves his regiment.

Flags of lower rank may be flown on the same pole below those of higher rank and/or may be smaller in size, but no more than two flags should be flown on a single pole unless it is gaff-rigged. The ranking of flags for display assumes that they are all visually on the same level; ranking flags on top of a building is separate from ranking those in front of it.

The rules set forth here also apply to flags displayed on the march (where those which come first have a higher rank) or displayed against a wall. No flag should be to the dexter (i.e., the observer's left) of the highest ranking flag. In a meeting hall flags go to the right of the group with which they are associated, as determined by that imaginary line between audience and program leaders. When a flag presentation is made at such a meeting, the ranking flag should be brought in or raised first and taken out or lowered last.

SALUTING THE FLAG.

To honor the country, principles, or person for which a flag stands, one may salute that flag. Usually flags are saluted when being formally hoisted, lowered, posted in a meeting hall, passed in parade review, and when the national anthem is played or a flag pledge is rendered.

Military personnel generally place the right hand to the head without removing headgear, civilians generally stand at attention and/or place the right hand over the heart or lift the entire right arm at a 45° angle. Courtesy suggests respectful attention during a salute rendered to a foreign flag, but every salute is a political act and refusal to salute is a means of expressing a political or religious belief.

SALUTING WITH THE FLAG.

A flag may be used to render homage to an individual or institution. On land a salute (known sometimes as dipping or vailing) is rendered only with a parade flag. Standard-bearers lower their flags (sometimes to the ground) before the reviewing stand on which military and/or civil authorities stand at attention, until ordered to raise them by the reviewing authority. The United States national flag is never dipped on land, even to the president.

PROVIDING SANCTUARY UNDER A FLAG.

Certain flags are recognized as affording protection under specific circumstances to travelers, medical personnel, cultural institutions, etc., according to a special privilege granted by a head of state or international treaty. Such a flag must be prominently displayed to afford protection to the individuals or institutions concerned; violation of a sanctuary flag is considered a criminal act. Among the recognized sanctuary flags are those of the Geneva Convention, the United Nations flag, and a plain white flag. During war or riot conditions foreign nationals in a country usually receive some protection from flying their own national flag or painting it on a building or vehicle.

TOPPING OUT.

Hoisting a tree and flag on the last and highest beam of a building signals completion of the basic structure.

TRAILING.

Marching with a flag dragging on the ground, or standing in that position, is employed as a mark of respect at funerals or as a token of victory in a parade of captured enemy colors.

TROOPING THE COLOUR.

A British custom, formerly known as lodging the colour, involves regimental flags formally paraded before troops who salute it as it passes. It is part of the mounting of the guard ceremony and regularly takes place on the sovereign's birthday in Britain.

Among the more detailed laws on flag etiquette were those issued by the Russian empire in the nineteenth century. Above, the instructions indicate the proper way simultaneously to ride a horse, carry a flag, and fire a pistol. Below, they illustrate flag salutes.

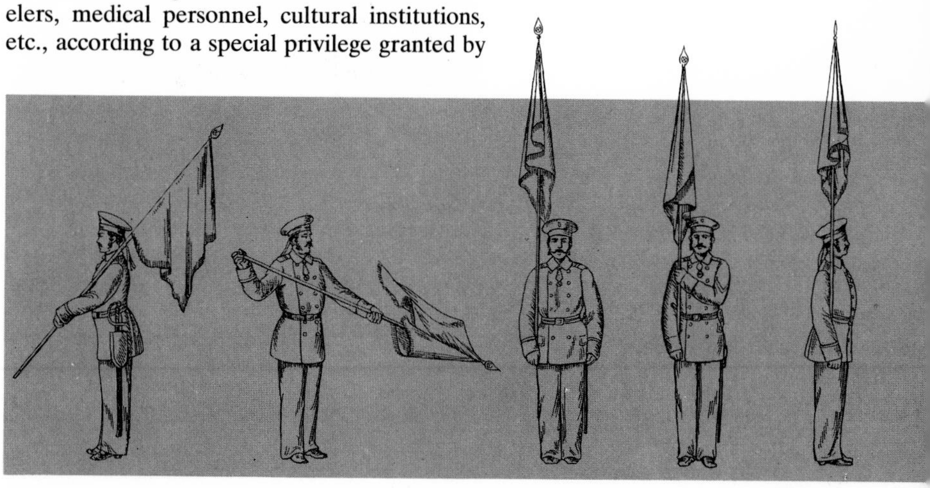

The bemedaled uniform of the veteran and his banner are reminders of a war long after it is over.

Flag tossing is a common folk activity in Central Europe. The ends of the flag poles are weighted, but the flag tosser must still be highly skilled to execute the elaborate ceremonies involved.

Wherever masses of people gather – at sports events, political rallies, or religious processions – flags are likely to be involved. The audience *(below)* forms the imperial crown of Iran as sports organizations with their colors gather on the field before an event.

THE FLAG IN SPORT

In the past, flags were limited mostly to naval usage, to military display, or at least to formal ceremonies and parades: today they can be seen everywhere. Not surprisingly, they are frequently employed in sports events. Flags directly involved in sports include signal flags in races, flag-tossing banners in Europe, and precision drill color guard flags in North America.

The flag of the Olympic Games *(right)* originally was designed as a substitute for competitive national emblems. Although the Olympic flag has not been forgotten, from the very beginning the flags of participating countries have played a dominant role in those quadrennial sports events.

Both outdoors and indoors it is customary to decorate with national flags and/or club flags when teams gather for competition; such flags are often also paraded before and after the event takes place. In the United States it is customary to begin sports events by playing the national anthem; the audience and the players stand at attention and face the national flag during its rendition.

In the quadrennial Olympic Games the original concept of honoring individual men and women for athletic achievement has been submerged in the extensive recognition given to nations and their flags. The Olympic flag itself is flown, and athletes take a vow before it; but a national flag is always hoisted to signal a victory. National flags are frequently sewn on uniforms for easier identification.

The fourteenth-century French knight *(right)* and the twentieth-century president of Somalia *(above)* are both encased in steel; consequently both require flags to be recognized.

Clusa iubet qȝ sic in equo rex stem mō sessor
Militis armati signi sum nacȝ professor
Pratensis reseracȝ suam sic stando figuram
Indulge fidei subiecte respice puram
Mentem deflexam tibi semper ubiqȝ paratam
Nam dn̄o micchi te dn̄m qȝ rē fore gratam
Esse meum noscas m̄ preacinctis quia cerno
Rex quia uirtutes sequeris nunqȝ tua sperno
Iussa · pretor dignare preces audire precantis
Sponte tibi uero fidei celo famulantis
Pracȝ mea tibi matre preces cū supplici mēte
Porrigo pro Roma genitrīce mea mō flente
Nunc eget ipā parens tutelā nuncqȝ senatus
Sensato senio rex ciuis tu trabeatus
Quondam consul amor quia saris urbē Senator
Te rogat ut culpe ne crescat sis medicator
Indiget ipā tui presenti conditione +

Supplico pnate qui regia carmina audit ·
Hec tua que trudit in uincla pro breuitate
Exaudire uelis que poscat nomine prati
Ut tibi sint grati uiuentes rex pie celis
Gloria lausqȝ deo tibi rex decus inde paratur
Detantoqȝ datur exnunc spes magna tropheo
Res facienda leui uerbor̄ sato labore
Iusta salus fore qua poscitur ut mala leui
Nunc patrare putent sȝ formido uideatur
Ipsa necis dantur sic prelia dum fore mitet
Vel quasi re nimi contingere qȝ meditant
Unde retardantur. ne figant uulnera circa
Res ea completa sedabit bella uetusta
Cuncqȝ uia iusta reddet comota quieta
Non fiunt faale que nō in pace petuntur
Donacȝ planguntur senio q̄ iam iuuenile
Tempus uidebat rex dapsilis · pius esto
Ut facias presto tuus ut pater ipē solebat ·

+ Cum manet ancapi^ti mentis luctantis agone
Si uirtute tua quam sperat pace fruetur
Confidas felix qȝ te fortuna sequetur
Scilicet ipā dei que grā ꝓspera reges
Sublimat ꝓuat letatur condere leges ·
Sic ego spero quidem timor hinc orietur in orbe
Oqȝ discedes longe tu pessime morbe
Plene doli q̄tum te falso putasse pudebit
Et q̄ qui sequitur tua pessima nota dolebit :

Renaissance artists represented Christ as a king carrying a flag to show his dominion, such as in this painting by Piero della Francesca. Perhaps not surprisingly, in English paintings this was a white flag with a red cross, in German paintings a red flag with a white cross – corresponding to actual flags used in those countries.

RELIGIOUS FLAG CUSTOMS

In different countries and different ages one might expect to find flags carried on pilgrimages, displayed on church steeples, hanging in the nave of a cathedral, hanging from sticks or strings as a decoration at outdoor shrines, or serving as reminders of religious duty in homes. Almost every flag, except one which serves purely as a referential signal, contains a religious element. Nevertheless a large class of flags is specifically designed to enhance religious ceremonies, express religious principles, or conversely to derive from contact with religion a value they did not previously possess. This is true especially (but not exclusively) where religion is a formal part of the national government.

BETHEL FLAG.

Merchant ships in the nineteenth century flew one of a number of designs all usually called the Bethel flag to indicate religious services were being held on board.

CHRISTIAN FLAG.

A number of designs were used to symbolize (Protestant) Christianity. Generally, a Christian flag is white, bearing a red cross on a dark blue canton designed for that purpose by Charles Overton in 1897 and used extensively today in the United States.

CHURCH PENNANT.

In the United States, contrary to the constitutional separation of church and state and to other flag traditions, the church pennant, a distinctive flag flown at sea during church services, flies above the national flag. The American church pennant is white with a blue cross; the British version has horizontal stripes of red, white, blue with the Union Jack at the hoist. This supposedly dates from the Anglo-Dutch wars of the seventeenth century; the combination of the British and Dutch flags indicated the two powers were at peace during religious services.

CONSECRATION.

Military colors are often consecrated by religious authorities. The consecration ceremonies were originally based on the desire of church leaders to maintain their influence over secular rulers through the threat of withholding their blessing from battle flags. Although the custom of consecration dates back to at least the eleventh century, the actual nature of the ceremony in the Christian tradition has varied over the years – sometimes taking place within a church, sometimes in the field, sometimes on the presentation of the colors, sometimes only immediately before a battle. In some countries consecration of a flag is undertaken in nonmilitary situations: the first official raising of the Baha-

Flags are intimately associated with religion. The vexilloids used by the pope and made from ostrich feathers *(above)* are known as flabella. A flag appears at the coronation of the shah of Iran, Spanish trophy flags are hung by the Dutch in praise of divine assistance, and French pilgrims parade beneath a banner bearing a cross.

mian national flag, for example, was preceded by its consecration.

LAYING UP.

There is a tradition strong in British Commonwealth countries of retiring military colors from usage by formally placing them in a church (or other public building). The epistle side of a cathedral is considered more honorable than the gospel side up to the altar rail, beyond which the situation is reversed. In some countries, including the United States, it is customary to display two flags within a church – the national flag and that of a sect, but these are less likely to be hung from the upper walls than trophy flags or flags which have been laid up.

TROPHY FLAG.

Displaying flags captured in battle as a reminder of victory is another old tradition. The custom arose in Europe during the Middle Ages of depositing such trophies in cathedrals, in appreciation for the divine favor which had allowed them to be captured. Although such flags tended to deteriorate, record books and paintings made in some cases have provided valuable historical information. Today trophy flags are generally placed in museums.

The gonfalon is a popular form for a banner with religious motifs *(above* and *left)*. Often such a gonfalon may have a holy relic sewn directly onto its field. In certain countries political protest marchers display such flags when explicit symbols of opposition to government policy might lead to their arrest.

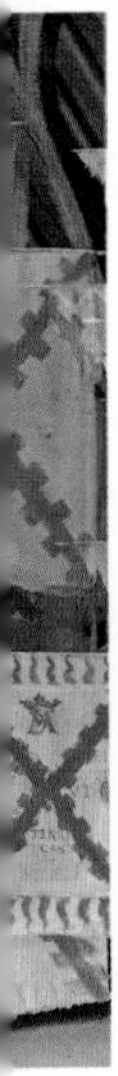

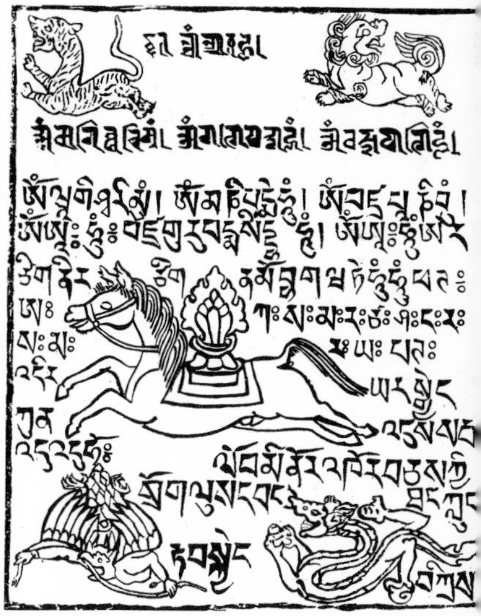

The Tibetan prayer flag above combines traditional animals – tiger, lion, tortoise, and dragon – with religous inscriptions. The horse in the center bears the Wishing Gem, a characteristic Buddhist symbol that also figures in the former national flag of Tibet (see page 25). The use of prayer and good luck flags is common in the Himalayan region; many are of plain color and long and narrow in shape. Generally, they are left flying until completely destroyed by the elements.

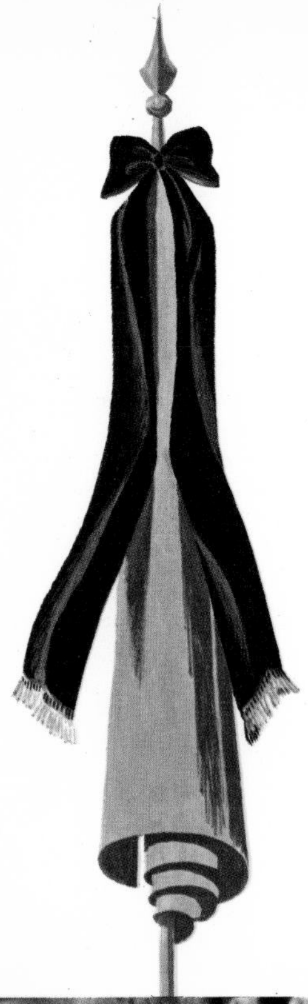

MOURNING, DISTRESS, DANGER

The association of flags with funerals probably began in very ancient times when the caskets of royalty were decorated with the symbols of the authority they held in life. Today in the age of nationalism such customs are even more extensive and are considered particularly appropriate for a person who spent considerable time in government or military service.

The use of red as a symbol of danger is also very ancient and is undoubtedly based on the association of that color with blood and fire. Nevertheless such a custom is not universal: the Chinese regard white as the color of mourning and red as a color of joy.

Charles De Gaulle's casket was covered with the Tricolor. From prehistoric times funerals of important leaders have featured the chief symbols of their power and dignity.

The space above a flag flying at half-staff (as at *right*) is said to be reserved for Death's invisible banner. The first use of the custom dates back to at least the early seventeenth century.

BLACK FLAG.

In certain countries a black flag is carried or flown to indicate mourning or political protest, although more commonly the plain black flag is a symbol of anarchy. Related symbols of mourning include a black border added to the national flag or a draped color.

CEMETERY FLAG.

Often, a flag of special design is used at the graves of police officers, club members, etc.; or a small version of the national flag may be permanently planted over a grave, especially that of a veteran.

DANGER FLAG.

Normally, a plain red flag is flown to indicate the presence of explosives, a slow-moving vehicle, a pedestrian crossing, or a similar condition of danger on land or sea. Such a red flag, but with a white saltire, or diagonal stripe, is flown over diving operations. Other special designs exist also, such as weather signals.

In accord with American custom, the casket flag of a state or military person is sent to the next of kin. The widow *(far left)* of President John F. Kennedy receives the casket flag of her late husband.

The soldier *(left)*, returning home in defeat from Russia, still proudly bears the flag.

DISTRESS FLAG.
When one needs assistance at sea, it is international convention to fly a distress flag, which is orange with or without a black square or disc or both in the center. A red flag, inverted flag, or wheft were formerly used for this purpose.

DRAPED COLOR.
A cravat of black material (usually crepe) is frequently attached to the staff as a symbol of mourning. This custom is usually limited to parade colors of military units following the death of a head of state.

FUNERAL FLAGS.
Any of a number of flags of special design are used at funerals, including an armorial bannerette; a gumphion; a draped color (as *above*); or a small pennant, often of dark blue bearing a white cross or Shield of David, displayed on a hearse.

HALF-STAFFED FLAG.
To symbolize mourning, usually for the death of a prominent individual, but occasionally to make a political protest, a flag is flown below its normal height. Many governments specify the length of time the flag should be half-staffed following the death of persons of specific ranks; they also give special orders for half-staffing on the death of an esteemed foreign leader. In some countries specific days are designated for regular half-staffing, e.g., in memoriam for war veterans. It is appropriate that all flags flown together be half-staffed if one of them is, especially those of lesser importance. The rank of an individual should determine which flag is half-staffed; that is, a city flag should be half-staffed on the death of a mayor, a provincial or state flag on the death of a governor, and the national flag only on the death of a national figure. In such a situation flags of greater precedence should not be flown until the lower ranking flag is full-staffed again. The tradition exists in some monarchies never to half-staff the royal flag, since succession to the crown is immediate through the heir apparent. Only flags hoisted by means of halyards are ever half-staffed. Half-staffing does not necessarily mean flying a flag at the exact center of the pole, but at any distance below the normal full-staff position.

INVERTED FLAG.
As a symbol of mourning or of protest against some political event or situation, such as a military defeat or a state visit by an unpopular foreign leader, a flag is sometimes flown upside down. Very rarely, an inverted flag is a symbol of distress (such as a shipwreck or fire): the custom has never been widespread because many inverted national flags appear the same as when flown normally.

Different lands mourn their dead with different types of flag ceremonies. The Swiss soldier *(left)* in procession to the burial carries a furled and draped flag. The flag is unfurled and waved over the grave before being displayed again in the normal fashion as a sign that the service lives on. Wreathes and small flags are set on graves by American sailors at Pearl Harbor in a yearly memorial ritual.

PALL FLAG.
The national flag is almost always used as a pall flag to drape the casket in military and government funerals. It is usually removed before the casket is lowered into the grave (or dropped into the sea). It is also used when a casket lies in

Not all flag customs are universal: in salute, the Egyptian flag is touched to the ground *(right)*, whereas this would be considered disrespectful treatment in some other lands.

state or is carried in a funeral procession. In some societies it is the custom to wrap the body itself in the flag or to paint a representation of the flag on the casket.

THE FLAG IN POLITICS

By definition, those flags which seek to change the political status quo, through agitation or propaganda, do not usually conform to the rules of etiquette. The key question in any country is whether such political flags are allowed at all. The authoritarian state fears the freedom of individual citizens to display in their own fashion flags of their own design. It rigidly prescribes permissible types of flags and manners of display in order to preserve its own dignity through protection of its symbols.

Since World War I, fascism, communism, anti-imperialism, and other mass ideologies have demonstrated the effectiveness of flags and other symbols in creating the aura of invincibility, in intimidating opponents of certain political philosophies, and in glorifying the will of the ruling elite.

Major incidents have often involved political flags. Consider the refusal in 1963 of President Ngo Dinh Diem of the Republic of Viet-Nam to allow Buddhists of that country to fly their own flag: his death occurred in the rioting that ensued. Bitter public and parliamentary debate raged in 1964 over the question of adopting a national flag in Canada. In 1958 after a student in Japan tore down the flag of the People's Republic of China, diplomatic relations between those countries were severed for several years. Forbidden flags have been displayed as provocations in Spain, the Soviet Union, and elsewhere; international incidents have arisen over the display of particular flags (e.g., that of Palestine or of South Viet-Nam) at a conference or exhibition.

The vexilloid is far from obsolete; indeed it seems to be enjoying a revival in the twentieth century. Dictators in all parts of the world have learned the effectiveness of the flag as a propaganda tool and as a means of intimidating opponents. The Nazi standards paraded here demonstrate key aspects of the symbol as a political weapon – the massing of men and flags, use of a striking design, repetition of a simple yet forceful theme, emphasis on uniformity of construction and presentation, and involvement of the audience in the presentation.

The chief flag dispute since the ones which embroiled Germany (see page 120) and South Africa in the 1920s occurred in the United States between 1967 and 1973. Through legislation and otherwise, President Richard Nixon and a large following sought to monopolize the United States flag as an emblem exclusively of one point of view; the Stars and Stripes began to appear extensively in lapel pins, on bumper stickers, and elsewhere. Many others, especially students and those opposed to American involvement in Indo-China, protested American policies by adding the peace symbol or inscriptions to the flag, flying it upside down, or sometimes by burning or otherwise "desecrating" the flag. Industries have exploited heightened interest in the flag by using its motif in clothing, home decoration, advertising, packaging, and publishing – even in films and the theater.

The end of American involvement in the Viet-Nam war and revelations of the moral and political bankruptcy of those officials who had used the flag for their own purposes eventually terminated public debate on the question. Nevertheless an important precedent for the future was set when a number of courts, including the Supreme Court of the United States, determined that in a free country the flag symbolizing liberty belonged to the people; that respect for that flag and the principles it symbolizes could not be created by legislation or enforced by criminal prosecution; that misuse of the flag brought dishonor on the desecrator, not on the flag or country; and that restrictions on flag display were legitimate chiefly where fraud or destruction of property was involved. Most flag desecration laws attempted to make the government an arbiter of good taste or to make the flag sacred, thus reestablishing in modern guise the concepts of *lèse-majesté* and blasphemy.

The "Viet Cong" flag became an international protest symbol in the 1960s.

Burning flags as a form of political protest has increased substantially since World War II.

The symbolic statement of one group – such as the Palestinians *(above)* – is often attacked by another group – Israelis in this instance – through the use of contrary symbols.

NATIONAL FLAG HISTORIES

A national flag announces authority, victory, threat, solidarity, remembrance. But where does this inspiration come from? Why should certain colors or designs or traditional modes of display be associated with certain nations and not others? Such aspects of flags are rarely arbitrary and while we may not understand the motivations of the past, an appreciation for national flag histories can be a key to better understanding of the nations themselves.

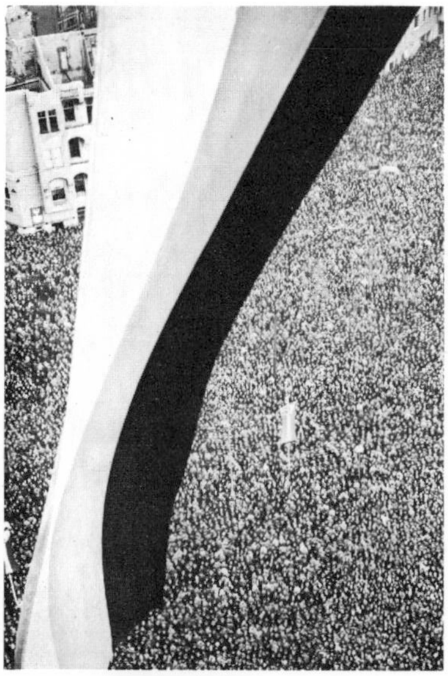

EGYPT: BANNERS OF INSPIRATION FOR THE ARAB WORLD

NETHERLANDS: "ORANJE BOVEN!" ("ORANGE ON TOP")

JAPAN: LAND OF THE RISING SUN

SOVIET UNION: "WORKERS OF THE WORLD UNITE!"

UNITED KINGDOM: THE NOBLE LINEAGE OF THE UNION JACK

UNITED STATES: A BANNER BORN OF REVOLUTION

ZAIRE: THE SEARCH FOR NATIONAL IDENTITY

Just as there is no typical nation, so there is no typical national flag history. The very meaning of "national flag" varies from country to country and within one country over a period of time. Nevertheless there is one characteristic which may be seen as universal: the national flag always embodies an essential part of the spirit of a given land and its people. Indeed for those who know how to read the symbolisms, flags are a condensed expression of all the victories and tragedies of national life – especially the struggle for unity, independence, and supremacy for that philosophy of state which in every country determines not only the constitution and law but the everyday lives of citizens as well. For this reason it would be highly desirable to present a complete history of the national flags of every country. To be done properly this would require literally thousands of pages; yet the selectivity evidenced here has not been arbitrary. The countries chosen and the flags dealt with are intended to provide the reader with a substantial comprehension of the unity or diversity of traditions within a single nation, the variety of vexillological development across the world, the changes in attitude toward flags and consequently of flag usages over time, and above all the fundamental significance of flags in the lives of those men and women who live under them. Readers seeking further information are referred to the bibliographic section on pages 350–351. What has happened in the past cannot help but give an understanding to possible new phases in the life of any country, for the future can never be entirely divorced from the past and no national flag is ever created entirely without historical links and associations.

CHINA: FINDING NEW MEANINGS IN ANCIENT SYMBOLS

GERMANY: FROM THE IMPERIAL EAGLE TO THE BLACK-RED-GOLD

SPAIN: MEDIEVAL HERALDRY IN MODERN FORM

FRANCE: FROM THE ORIFLAMME TO THE TRICOLOR

ITALY: THE TRICOLOR: UNITY OUT OF DIVERSITY

MEXICO: "THERE, WHERE YOU SEE A CACTUS GROWING FROM A ROCK..."

CHINA

FINDING NEW MEANINGS IN ANCIENT SYMBOLS

A bridge across thousands of years of history, the symbolism of five is reflected in the five-starred banner of the People's Republic of China and in the five military colors of Chinese antiquity.

When one is isolated from other lands – or, as the Chinese saw it, when one lives in the Middle Country – it is logical to assume that only the miscellaneous peoples of the far corners and edges of the globe must identify themselves. Thus the dragon flag of imperial China, although it incorporated an ancient symbol, was never intended to rally the Chinese people or even to represent them. As a national flag it was adopted reluctantly as an appeasement for outsiders – those "barbarians" who, having had flags of their own, insisted that the Chinese have one as well.

Prior to European involvement in the affairs of China in the mid-nineteenth century, the most widely used Chinese flags were those of fishing boats and of the army, and both were characterized by a great diversity of shape, color, and design. Chinese armies had traditionally been organized into units carrying flags of five colors – red, yellow, blue, white, and black. Each hue had ancient associations of a philosophical nature. Yellow (perhaps because it was the color of the soil constituting much of the rich agricultural land of northern China) was connected with the earth; red stood for the sun, blue for the sky, and white for the moon. The Blue Dragon of the East corresponded to spring and morning; the Red Phoenix of the South stood for summer and noon; the White Tiger of the West represented autumn and evening, while the tortoise, known as the Black Warrior of the North, was for winter and night. Appropriately, since it was the imperial emblem par excellence, the Yellow Dragon was a symbol of the center. These concepts provided the source symbols for various Chinese flags, particularly ones of a religious character.

CHINESE WAR ENSIGN 1863–CA. 1872.

CHINESE STATE AND WAR ENSIGN 1872–CA. 1890.

The real history of national flags in China begins only in 1863, during one of many incursions by European soldiers designed to exact new concessions from China. A "Chinese" navy – commanded by Europeans and instituted to protect European merchants and missionaries – was authorized (under pressure) by the seven-year-old emperor, T'ung Ch'ih. To express

Icons of modern China – a portrait of Mao Tse-tung and a red banner – are reproduced in millions of lapel flags like the one on the left.

Under threat of punishment, lower officials were forbidden use of the emperor's five-clawed dragon.

The last days of the empire saw the first Chinese national flag – and foreign military occupation.

imperial authority, the jack of this fleet was to be yellow with a blue dragon. But the true state of affairs was nevertheless reflected in the new war ensign in which the imperial dragon and its yellow background were reduced to a very small central emblem. The field design of the ensign was St. Andrew's cross of Scotland, represented in the green and yellow colors of the family tartan associated with the commander of the new navy, Englishman Charles Gordon. In short the new flag was not only imposed on the Chinese, but did not really reflect their own rich vexillological traditions.

On 10 November 1872 the aforementioned jack became the official state and war ensign of China; eighteen years later it was brought into

CHINESE STATE AND WAR ENSIGN CA. 1890–1912.

KUOMINTANG PARTY FLAG SINCE 1895.

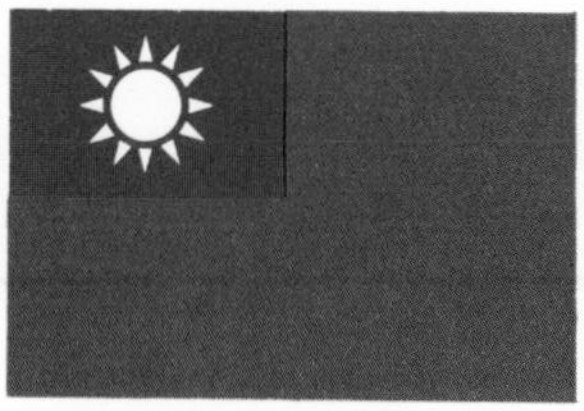

REPUBLIC OF CHINA NATIONAL FLAG SINCE 1928; WAR ENSIGN SINCE 1914.

CHINESE WAR FLAG 1911–1928.

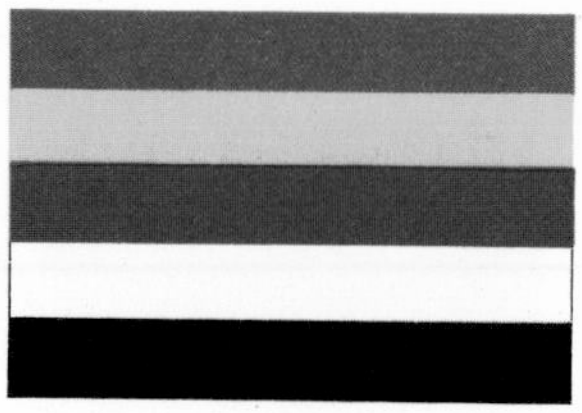

REPUBLIC OF CHINA NATIONAL FLAG 1912–1928.

conformity with European flag patterns by being altered to a rectangular shape. The ensign created in 1863, simplified to its basic yellow saltire on green, became the flag of the Imperial Maritime Customs. This powerful institution raised the money that guaranteed the profitability of China to European imperialists.

The degradation of China in this era led many of the Chinese to seek ways of restoring former national greatness. Foremost among the exponents of a policy of maintaining Chinese independence by westernization of the country from within was Dr. Sun Yat-sen. In 1894 at Honolulu, Hawaii, he founded the Society for Regenerating China; he spent most of the next seventeen years organizing party chapters, writing revolutionary tracts, and preaching the need for a transformation of Chinese culture. On 16 March 1895 Lu Hao-tung's design for a flag was accepted by the society. Known as White Sun in Blue Sky, it reflected the nature of the organization by combining traditional Chinese colors and symbolism with Western concepts of flag design. Its sun was the essence of the *yang* or male principle which Chinese hailed as the positive force of universal existence – associated with life, heaven, vigor, and pure and just administration in government. Several traditional meanings might be associated with the twelve rays of the sun, but they

This fantastical seventeenth-century European conception of a Chinese flag (which fails to show correctly even the simple yin-yang) stands as a warning to the vexillologist who relies on verbal descriptions for his information.

The robe in the imperial portrait at left shows the yellow used to represent the (Manchu) Ching dynasty that ruled China from 1644 to 1912.

This 1933 poster makes clear the fate of those Chinese who refused to accept the flag of the Manchu State and the force that established and maintained it – the Japanese military.

basically bespoke the spirit of unceasing progress throughout the twelve two-hour periods of the day.

Manchuria, Mongolia, Tibet, and the Muslims of China. The latter lived principally in Sinkiang (pronounced as *sin* djahng). Encouraged by Japan, Russia, and Britain, many of these limitrophe areas established autonomous or independent regions with national flags of their own.

Dr. Sun and his followers, who remained in control of the south of the country, organized the Kuomintang (KMT) or Nationalist Party on 25 August 1912 to agitate for the Three Principles of the People that formed the cornerstone of Dr. Sun's political philosophy. The flag symbolizing this ideology incorporated the White Sun in Blue Sky – retained even today as the party flag of the KMT – with a red field for

MANCHU STATE FLAG 1932–1945.

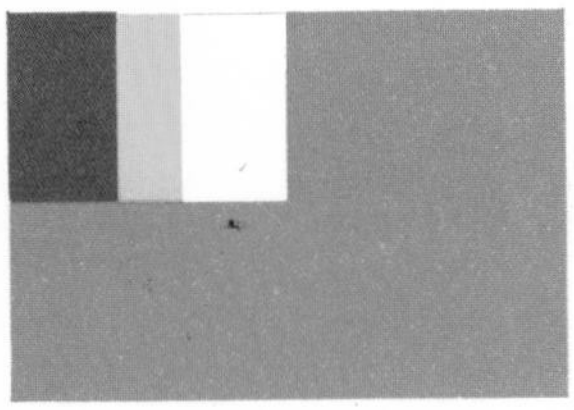

MENG-CHIANG STATE FLAG CA. 1938–1942.

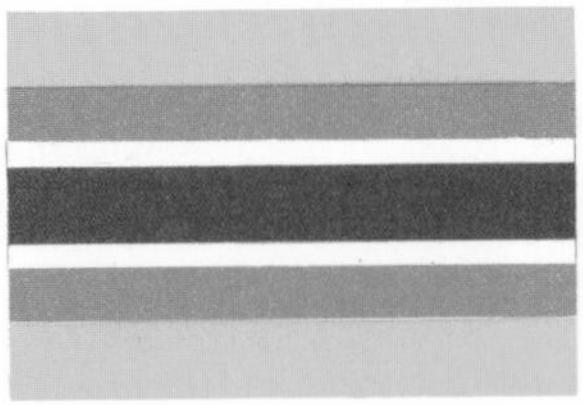

MONGOLIAN FEDERATION STATE FLAG CA. 1942–1945.

KMT REPUBLIC OF CHINA STATE FLAG 1940–1943.

CHINESE SOVIET REPUBLIC STATE FLAG 1932–1935.

Hair styles as well as flags underwent radical transformations after China became a republic in 1912.

Ironically, Dr. Sun and his White Sun in Blue Sky were not involved in the revolution that eventually gave birth to the Republic of China. On 10 October 1911 revolutionaries within the army seized control of Wuhan, raising a new banner to symbolize the dawn of a new day in China. Its red field bore in the center a black star with eighteen gold balls – one for each province of the land. Red corresponded symbolically to the south where the revolution had been raised, but it also was recognized as the national color of the Han or Chinese people, rising against the yellow (Manchu) dynasty to which they had been subjected for two and a half centuries.

Returning to his native land after reading about the Chinese revolution in a Denver, Colorado, newspaper, Dr. Sun was elected provisional president on 29 December 1911. Although the dragon flag disappeared forever when the last emperor abdicated in March 1912, the White Sun in Blue Sky was not chosen as the new Chinese national flag. To avoid conflict with General Yüan Shih-k'ai, who held effective power in the north of the country, Dr. Sun abdicated as president in his favor and accepted the Five-Color Flag to represent the young republic. The Five-Color Flag was composed of stripes in the traditional red, yellow, blue, white, and black that stood for China proper,

Most of the flags of the Republic of China, like this example at right, are derivatives of its state flag.

During World War II aviators sewed flags on their jackets for identification in case they were shot down.

China, thus giving one color each for the Three Principles. Adopted on 1 September 1914, the new White Sun in Blue Sky over Red Land distinguishing flag of the Customs Service, which continued to collect revenues on behalf of foreign imperialists.

Weak and divided, China saw many local warlords hoist varying flags of their own during the following decades. After Dr. Sun's death in 1925, the KMT under the leadership of General Chiang Kai-shek established a national government at Canton and laid plans for the Northern Expedition to unite the country. To signal the success of that campaign in unifying most of China, on 8 October 1928 the KMT abolished the Five-Color Flag in favor of its own White Sun in Blue Sky over Red Land. This has continued to serve as the state and civil flag of the Republic of China.

The 1949 proclamation of the People's Republic of China began a new era in the history of the nation.

CHINESE SOVIET REPUBLIC WAR FLAG 1932–1934.

CHINESE COMMUNIST WAR FLAG CA. 1935–1937.

PEOPLE'S REPUBLIC OF CHINA STATE AND WAR FLAG, NATIONAL ENSIGN SINCE 1949.

became the Chinese war ensign; the red flag with the black star was the war flag. The national Five-Color Flag defaced with a green canton bearing a yellow saltire served as the

In 1931 the Japanese invaded northeastern China and on 18 February 1932 they proclaimed the independent Manchu State (Manchukuo). The old yellow flag with its blue dragon reappeared and the last Manchu emperor of China, Henry P'u-yi, who had abdicated at the age of six in 1912, was installed as a figurehead ruler. The Manchu national flag featured the imperial golden yellow of his dynasty, its canton composed of stripes in the other four colors of the original Chinese republican flag. Officially hoisted on 9 March 1932, this flag continued unchanged when the name of the state was altered in 1934 to Manchu Empire (Manchutikuo). Henry P'u-yi then became Emperor K'ang Te, his dragon flag replaced by a new imperial banner of yellow with a central stylized orchid of gold.

The Japanese invasion of China continued throughout the 1930s; extensive territories along the coast fell under Japanese occupation and Chiang Kai-shek retreated to the interior of the country. The amalgamation of these conquests resulted on 14 December 1937 in the announcement of a Provisional Government of the Republic of China at Peiping, followed by the Reformed Government of the Republic of China created at Nanking on 28 March 1938. Both officially adopted the Five-Color Flag which had disappeared barely a decade before.

Chairman Mao's portrait – often flanked with national flags *(left)* – is a common sight throughout China.

"Arise! Arise! Arise! Millions with but one heart, braving the enemy's fire, march on!" (From *The March of the Volunteers*, national anthem of the People's Republic of China.)

Members of the Youth Corps, an organization within the secondary school system of the Republic of China, parade with their corps flag which incorporates the White Sun in Blue Sky symbol of the Nationalist Party.

The Japanese also sponsored local regimes among Mongols living in occupied Inner Mongolia. On 22 November 1937 the Meng-Chiang [Mongol Borderlands] United Commission was organized; its flag was light blue for the Mongols with stripes of red, yellow, and white to represent other races. The same four colors appeared in the flag of the Mongolian Federation Autonomous Government created on 1 September 1939.

On 1 April 1940 the Japanese-sponsored governments at Peiping and Nanking united their territories and hoisted the flag of their new Nationalist Government of the Republic of China. Its ruling party adopted the name, symbols, and much of the program of the original KMT whose own government still existed at Chungking. Even the state flag differed from that of its rival only in being surmounted by a yellow pennant bearing the inscription "Peace, Anti-Communism, National Construction." After February 1943 the pennant was omitted and for two years the Chinese masses were confronted by the counterclaims of two governments sharing a common name and flag, each insisting it alone was the voice of China. The chief beneficiary of the confusion proved to be the Communist Party of China (CPC).

The capitol building in Taipei on the island of Taiwan features a number of symbols in honor of the founding of the Republic of China. The emblem resembling a double-barred cross is the figure 10 repeated twice, since "Double Ten" (10 October) is the date when the revolution broke out that ended the Chinese Empire. The five-petaled plum blossom appearing in the decorations is China's national flower.

Founded in 1921 and originally an ally of Chiang Kai-shek, the CPC in the 1930s had some success in establishing local governments. On 3 January 1932, for example, a Chinese Soviet Republic was proclaimed in Kiangsi. Chiang did not succeed in overthrowing this state until 10 November 1934 and during the two and a half years of its existence the Chinese Soviet Republic flew a distinctive state flag and a war flag. In late 1937 the CPC agreed to cooperate with the KMT in opposing the Japanese. The Communists abandoned their own symbols in favor of the White Sun in Blue Sky and its variations and recognized Chiang as head of the Republic of China. Nevertheless the CPC took advantage of the war and its aftermath to build a solid base for their own domination over all of mainland China, achieved with the fall of Tibet in 1951.

In 1941 six de facto independent nations (Republic of China, KMT Republic of China, Manchutikuo, Meng-Chiang, Sinkiang, and Tibet) – each with its own flag – existed in China. Barely eight years later the nation knew greater unity and independence from foreign control than it had experienced in more than a century when, on 1 October 1949, the People's Republic of China was proclaimed. Those achievements and the dominant position of the Han people within what they considered their patrimony were reflected in the new state flag designed by Ma Hsu-lun.

Its red field is certainly a symbol of communism, but it also stands for the Han people and is thus in keeping with the other Chinese national flags adopted since 1911. The large star symbolizes the leadership of the Communist party, the four smaller ones standing for the classes of its united front – workers, peasants, petty bourgeoisie, and patriotic capitalists. Nevertheless the five stars can scarcely fail to suggest to the Chinese ancient meanings of the number five. Like the stripes in the Five-Color Flag, the five stars clearly stand for China proper, Manchuria, Mongolia, Sinkiang, and Tibet. Traditionally, the number five in China conveys a sense of strength and completeness – the full gamut of possible or desirable options within a certain sphere of action. Philosophical writings spoke of the Five Rulers, Five Elements, Five Virtues, Five Classics, and so forth.

For a government stressing Chinese nationalism, as well as the political characteristics of communism, there could be few better designs or color choices than those incorporated in the new state flag of the People's Republic of China. Like its rival, the White Sun in Blue Sky over Red Land, the five gold stars on a red field stand for the unity, sovereignty, authority, and dignity of the Chinese state and nation.

更

The Black-Red-Gold and the medieval orb of authority are only two of innumerable German political symbols reflecting the vicissitudes of German history.

GERMANY

FROM THE IMPERIAL EAGLE TO THE BLACK-RED-GOLD

Entire lives have been devoted to the study of German vexillology and state heraldry. Perhaps in no other country in the world has so much scholarly literature been produced on the origins, meaning, and transformation of national symbols as in Germany, and the subject has by no means been exhausted. Even if the individual states, cities, and rulers are ignored insofar as they do not affect the course of German national symbols through the ages, the details available for the historian, the political scientist, the sociologist – even the art historian or anthopologist – are voluminous, significant, and endlessly fascinating. Consequently although German flags are given attention elsewhere in various other parts of this book, only an outline of the subject matter can possibly be presented. Two central themes stand forth in modern German flag history; one involves the cross and the eagle, and the other, the colors black, red, gold, and white. Although these two themes were not historically related, Charlemagne employed both a red flag and a golden eagle, and each has played a lasting role in German symbolism. Both express authority over civil and military affairs, over life and death, and the majesty of a divinely sanctioned ruler. Yet red flags were car-

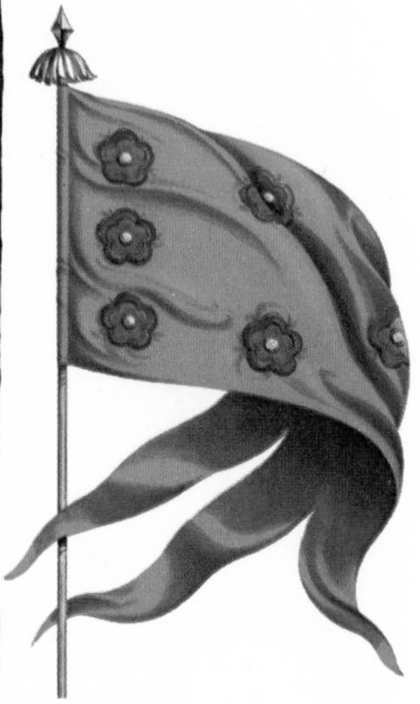

Although his reign preceded the invention of heraldry, Charlemagne's influence on the symbols of imperial Germany was great. The cross, the eagle, and the red gonfanon or war flag *(below)* are among the symbols whose usage was perpetuated in memory of the central European unity and cultural progress associated with Charlemagne's rule.

The imperial eagle flag *(above)* marks King Henry VII as he enters Rome in this fourteenth century illustration. Other German princes are marked by their own banners. The imperial German eagle *(right)* bears a shield quartering the arms of Hungary and Bohemia.

ried by military units or given to subordinates by Charlemagne as testimony of the authority he delegated to them. In contrast, the eagle erected on his palace at Aachen was almost a personal emblem, symbolizing the claim Charlemagne (and later emperors) made to universal dominion as successors to the Roman Empire. The new Holy Roman Empire of the German Nation, as it was called from the fifteenth century on, was not the only state to claim the inheritance of the Caesars or to employ the eagle as a visible outward manifestation of such pretensions; but until 1806, when disbanded by Napoleon, it was the chief contender for that title.

The third important symbol of Charlemagne's empire was the cross: it marked the Christian nature of the state and a view that the ultimate source of the emperor's authority was neither his army nor the pope, but Christ. As the red flag symbolized imperial authority over life and death, so the cross in a marketplace or on a merchant ship indicated the king's peace.

Use of the cross was not limited to those specific usages, however. A state with divine sanction might, by definition, expect intercession in any cause undertaken in the name of the cross. Not only the banners of the Crusaders and of knightly orders, such as the Teutonic Order, come to mind in this regard, but also an imperial flag which was red with a white cross.

IMPERIAL WAR FLAG

TEUTONIC ORDER

GRAND MASTER, TEUTONIC ORDER

STRALSUND

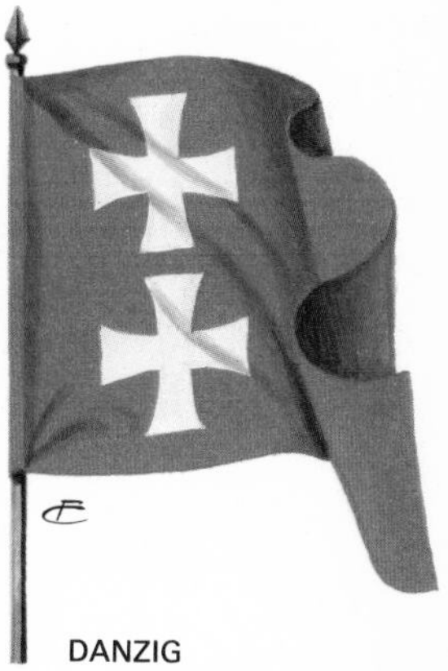

DANZIG

The Teutonic Order had a lasting impact on German flags through its preference for white and black. Red and white were more common in the Hanseatic towns of the North Sea. Riga in the east Baltic records a black pennant with a white cross from 1295 onward, but, already a quarter century before, Hamburg had begun officially to display a plain red pennant. This was followed by the white-over-red of Lübeck and similar flags in Elbing and Stettin, the red flag with white crosses of Danzig, and the white arrowheads on red used by Stralsund. Numerous other examples could be cited. The red and white were not solely a prerogative of the Hansa, but characterized troops in battle from dozens of cities and states as is dramatically evident in the banners captured by the Poles at the Battle of Tannenberg on 15 July 1410. A manuscript record of the booty shows an overwhelming predominance of white and red, followed by black as the third most popular flag color. Important as these traditions might be, it is not yet possible, of course, to speak of German national colors because German nationalism was not fully developed.

During the later Middle Ages heraldry had a profound impact on German flags which has been dealt with elsewhere in this book (see pages 44–59). Whatever their preheraldic sources may have been, the eagle of Prussia, horse of Saxony, lions of Schwabia, and many other charges became standardized in form and usage as emblems of state. Eventually, once the individual states were amalgamated into a unified Germany, only the eagle would prove of national significance; yet so long as the states they represented were independent, all of Europe recognized the sovereign standing of the key of Bremen, the oxhead of Mecklenburg, the eagle of Lübeck, or the lozenges of Bavaria. Indeed the prerogatives of these flags were jealously guarded even after German unification in 1871, especially among the seafaring states. They had the legal right to hoist – within coastal waters – distinctive state and civil ensigns.

Nevertheless the state symbols and colors cited did not serve as national flags in the German states for a number of reasons. Many of the territories were small and without seaports; they were often transferred to other sovereigns; and above all what sense of nationalism did exist was a consciousness of a culture, language, and history that was pan-German rather than local. Just at the time when this situation began to

Three of the greatest dynasties of imperial Germany are recalled by these portraits of Charlemagne (800–814) the Carolingian, Frederick I "Barbarossa" (1152–1190) of the Hohenstaufens, and Rudolph I (1273–1291) of the Hapsburgs.

The flags illustrated below indicate some general characteristics of early German vexillology. Tails or Schwenkels often decorated the fly end, especially of war flags. The cross – in various artistic interpretations each with a special name in heraldry – was not at all limited to religious flags but indicated divine sanction in civil and military banners as well.

Symbols on the earliest heraldic flags often made reference to the name of the locality flying the flag: thus Stralsund bore two arrowheads (*Strahl* being the German word for ray or beam). Red and white, as in the flag of Danzig were the usual royal colors of Hansa merchant ports.

The city flag of Trier *(right)* is recorded in a fifteenth-century manuscript; it shows the municipal patron, St. Peter.

Imperial cities, which enjoyed considerable autonomy, were especially proud of their heraldic banners. The woodcuts below are reproduced from the armorial of Jacob Köbel (1545): the flags shown (*left* to *right*) are those of Brandenburg, Speyer, and Schwäbisch Gmünd.

change, under the impact of the French Revolution and the national uprisings of 1848, alternative foci of allegiance were created. Yet, despite the many political changes that Germany has undergone since 1848, even the abolition of the state flags in the 1930s and the radical redrawing of state borders following World War II, the popularity of regional flags in Germany is stronger today than are similar sentiments in other countries where such local flags exist.

Central to the understanding of German national flags is the imperial banner, the heraldic manifestation of Charlemagne's eagle and of the eagle vexilloids carried by Roman armies. Since the thirteenth century the eagle was "heraldicized" and used in flag form. The imperial banner was a golden yellow cloth, usually square, bearing a black eagle (and sometimes decorated with a Schwenkel). From 1332 the lord of the town and castle Markgroningen claimed the privilege and responsibility of keeping the imperial standard and of presenting it in time of war, a privilege later lost to Württemberg. The right of standard-bearer was at one point the subject of an extensive legal suit, ending with the 1695 decision of the Imperial Council that the title belonged to Württemberg – and to this day the pretender to the throne of that state displays the imperial standard in his arms. The double-headed eagle was finally established by Sigismund as regent of the empire in 1401, but this pattern was always more favored in the similar flags of Austria and Russia. On 1806 the Holy Roman Empire officially disappeared, but the black eagle with its red tongue, all on a golden shield, was not forgotten. It came to be the basis both for the flag of modern Germany and (in various modified forms) for the arms of the land under different constitutions.

Given the variety of arms in Central Europe which might be transformed into tricolors, it is not surprising that black-red-gold flags existed prior to the acceptance of this flag as the German national standard. The Belgians in their revolution of 1830 hoisted such flags, showing the colors from the arms of Brabant. Württemberg had used the same colors from the end of the sixteenth century to the beginning of the nineteenth; the states of Reuss and Waldeck both had cockades of black-red-gold. But the origin of the all-German black-red-yellow stems from the use of those colors in the uniform worn in 1813 by the Lützow Free Corps. Three years later women from Jena presented the Jena Student's Association *(Burschenschaft)* with a flag of crimson-black-crimson horizontal stripes bearing a gold oak branch across the center and gold fringe. At the time of the Wartburg Festival when young men formed a Students' Associa-

This battle in 1532, one of many in Europe that resulted from the Reformation and the division of communities between Catholics and Protestants in the early sixteenth century, pitted Swiss knights against German citizen-soldiers *(Landesknechten)* under flags of similar design.

Behind the apparent fragmentation of the German polity prior to the nineteenth century lay not only cultural and historical links, but the political reality of the Holy Roman Empire whose golden banner bore an eagle *(below)* with a shield combining the arms of Austria and Burgundy.

tion including all parts of Germany, they adopted the black-red-yellow, believing them to be the old colors of Germany. Their society began to popularize the three colors as a German symbol in the second and third decades of the nineteenth century.

Students and others who hoped for German unification, impatient with the conservative policies and dilatory methods of existing rulers, held a great festival in Hambach in May 1832 where the new Black-Red-Gold came into its own as the symbol of their cause. Inspired by the 1830 revolution in Paris, which had reestablished the French Tricolor, thousands demanded the abolition of state borders and the democratization of Germany; they were met by repressive police measures. While no immediate practical results in their campaign were obtained, the spirit of Hambach remained an important force thereafter and the new flag, heralded in popular songs,

For use in rituals such as state funerals, banners of guilds and similar organizations were invariably of complex heraldic designs, richly

painted or embroidered to enhance the prestige and dignity of the individual or institution it represented *(above)*. In contrast, flags of identification at sea tended to be simple in design so they could be easily distinguished even at a great distance. One of the most famous German

flags of this kind was that of Hamburg *(above)* whose white castle normally appeared on a red field. Due apparently to the influence of the British flag system, in the nineteenth century a blue flag with a similar castle was sometimes used.

The oak, symbol of strength, figures both in the branch painted on this early nineteenth century student association flag and in the acorn tassels attached to its decorative cords *(above)*.

At the battle of Zorndorf on 25 August 1758, at the risk of his life, King Frederick the Great of Prussia seized a regimental color and personally led his troops into battle *(above)*.

became firmly entrenched as the rallying symbol of German unity.

The outbreak of the revolution in Paris in 1848 led to a new wave of revolutionary action in Germany. In a very brief time frightened autocrats approved rather liberal constitutions. On 9 March the Federal Assembly meeting in Frankfurt, as a step toward German unification, declared adopted the "old German imperial eagle and the colors of the former German imperial banner black-red-gold." When the king of Prussia, Frederick William, himself paraded through the streets of Berlin on 21 March in the company of such a flag, it seemed to many that the day of German unity was at hand. The historic National Assembly convened on 18 May in Frankfurt in the Church of St. Paul, preparing (in vain, as it turned out) to act as a constituent congress for all of Germany. As such it appointed a German war ensign and civil ensign on 31 July 1848, the latter corresponding to the black-red-gold civil flag, the former bearing the federal arms as a canton added to the same design.

An enormous amount of literature was produced on the question of the new arms and flag. Some felt black, red, and gold were not the true German colors, while others protested that the arrangement was improper according to heraldic rules. More seriously, only the United States, Belgium, the Netherlands, and Naples recognized the ensign – largely because the traditional rulers began to regain their nerve and reassert authority, taking heart from the reversal of revolutionary causes elsewhere. Lacking financial support and an army of its own, the National Assembly found itself unable to command adherence to the constitution it promulgated in March of 1849. Frederick William of Prussia was offered the crown of Germany, but refused it on the principle that the right of kings was by divine rather than popular sanction. The influence of the assembly faded, its flag disappeared, and the leading role in German unification efforts was taken up by Prussia.

Prussian initiatives for German unity did not receive immediate success, but under the firm direction of Chancellor Otto von Bismarck treaties were concluded which resulted in a North German Confederation in 1867. Bismarck took exception to the Black-Red-Gold as a German flag and was personally responsible for the adoption – through the constitution of 25 June 1867 – of a flag which was to become a powerful rival for the allegiance of Germans, the Black-White-Red. The original idea for the three colors appears in the 1848–1851 flag proposals of Prince Adalbert, Prussian Minister of the Marine. The public was told that the red and white were for the Hansa cities and the black and white for Prussia. This coincided conveniently with the colors of the king of Prussia, who was flattered to see black and white for his state and red and white for Brandenburg.

In the new North German war ensign, the Black-White-Red served as a canton while the white field had a black cross, fimbriated in white and black, and a center disc bearing the Prussian eagle on white. This flag combined the ancient German black cross on white of the Teutonic Order and the Iron Cross, which had long served as the chief military decoration for German soldiers and sailors. Not only were the three colors of the new combination long familiar to Germans in various flags, but the flag corresponded graphically to the "blood and iron policy" of Bismarck. Then Germany made a distinction between its civil ensign and war ensign on a pattern roughly corresponding to similar distinctions existing in Britain and among other naval powers. Most importantly, the new flags gave Germans what they had long been seeking

Below are a typical finial and color from Prussia and a flag from Frankfurt, all from the late eighteenth or early nineteenth century.

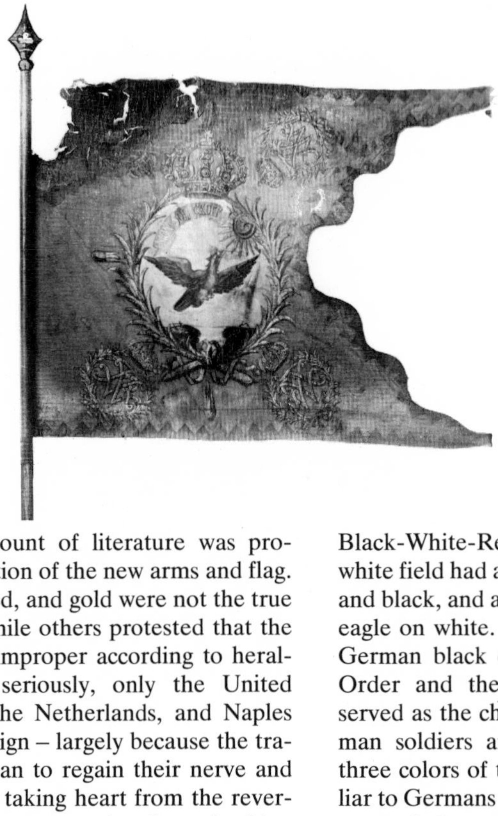

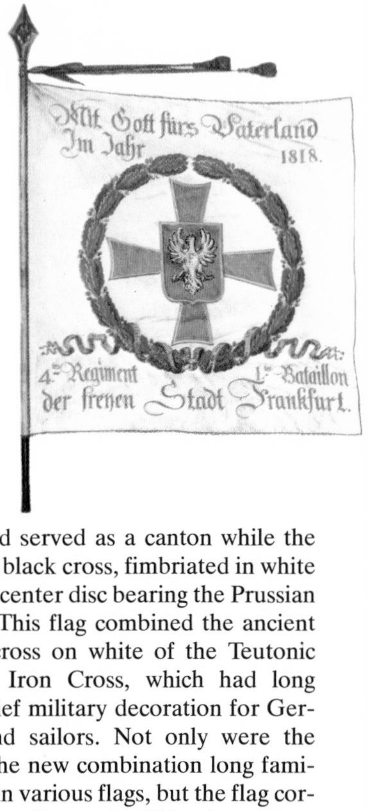

The National Assembly which gathered in St. Paul's church in Frankfurt *(top)* in 1848 raised expectations for German unity. These found graphic expression in a coat of arms *(above)* combining the imperial shield with the German tricolor and a star.

On 11 July 1848 the entrance of Regent of the Empire John into Frankfurt found the streets lined with elaborate flag decoration, typical of that time.

Prussian Chancellor Otto von Bismarck *(right)* saw his dream of German unification realized in 1871 under the black-white-red flag he had designed.

– a flag representing in fact as well as in spirit a united Germany, a nation respected abroad and characterized within by capable leadership.

The creation of a unified Germany (excluding Austria which held extensive non-Germanic territories) was completed in the foundation on 18 January 1871 of the Second Empire. There followed four decades of elaboration of the basic theme of black-white-red. Naval flags, colonial flags, government officials' flags, royal and imperial standards – these and many more were adopted without the least recognition being given to the Black-Red-Gold so dear to the hearts of so many Germans such a short time before. The personal standards of the imperial family with its golden yellow field, black cross, and the imperial shield (based on the medieval one) in the center incorporated the three old colors, but the red elements were so small that the visual impression of the black, red, and gold that had characterized symbols of the First Empire was entirely lost.

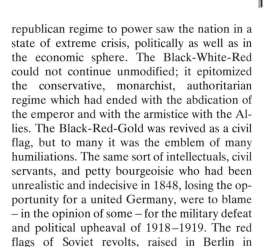

The military defeat of Germany in World War I and the subsequent revolution which brought a republican regime to power saw the nation in a state of extreme crisis, politically as well as in the economic sphere. The Black-White-Red could not continue unmodified; it epitomized the conservative, monarchist, authoritarian regime which had ended with the abdication of the emperor and with the armistice with the Allies. The Black-Red-Gold was revived as a civil flag, but to many it was the emblem of many humiliations. The same sort of intellectuals, civil servants, and petty bourgeoisie who had been unrealistic and indecisive in 1848, losing the opportunity for a united Germany, were to blame – in the opinion of some – for the military defeat and political upheaval of 1918–1919. The red flags of Soviet revolts, raised in Berlin in January 1919 and for almost a month in Bavaria

This regimental standard of 1890 belonging to the Life Guards features the royal cipher in each corner and the Prussian arms and motto ("For Glory and Fatherland"). Similar standards were later used by the Nazi party and German armed forces under the Third Empire.

"Germany's Rebirth" is the promise of the banner carried in the Hambach festival in 1832 *(above, left)*. With a canton of the imperial arms *(above)*, the same tricolor was adopted as the official war ensign of the German Confederation of 1848–1852.

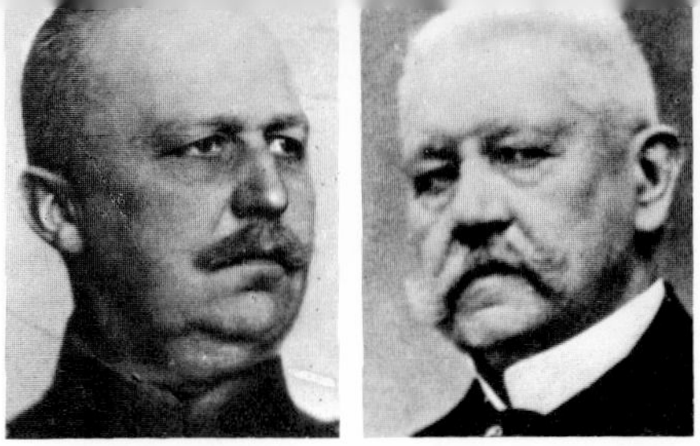

Two German heroes of World War I became involved in politics afterwards. Erich von Ludendorff *(near right)* participated in Hitler's attempted coup of 1923, Paul von Hindenburg appointed Hitler chancellor ten years later.

Seeking to promote the Baghdad to Berlin railway, Emperor William II of Germany *(above)* visited the Ottoman empire in 1898. He is shown here entering Damascus, followed by his personal standards.

later that year, were an ominous sign of things to come.

In the search for a solution to deeply divergent public feelings on the flag question, a compromise was evolved which attempted to express irreconcilable political differences through common symbols. The civil flag was the Black-Red-Gold; the state flag, the same with the new arms

The Iron Cross, traditional German military decoration, inspired the basic design of a number of nineteenth century military colors, including those above of Prussia *(left* and *middle)* and Baden; above right are those of Saxony and Bavaria.

in the center. These arms consisted of the traditional black eagle with red attributes on a gold shield, represented in a modern graphic style. The state ensign placed this shield on the Black-White-Red – adding the civil flag in miniature as a canton in 1926. The combination of the Black-White-Red with a canton of the Black-Red-Gold was adopted in 1919 as the civil ensign, and later the government established the same with the Iron Cross in the center as the war flag and ensign. The complicated choices pleased no one. Each faction saw a betrayal of true Germanism in the retention, even for limited purposes, of the other flag and each group was constantly reminded by the sight of these flags that its aims had not been satisfied.

The Black-Red-Gold and Black-White-Red did not express the full range of German political attitudes, and they were soon joined on the political left and right by red flags. The plain red of the socialists and communists came to be opposed in the late twenties by a new banner – the hooked cross or Swastika Flag of the National Socialist German Workers' Party, the Nazis. This was designed by Hitler himself – although he admits in *Mein Kampf* that a dentist from Starnberg had created a very similar pattern – as were many other Nazi symbols. The red stood for Hitler's brand of socialism, the white for nationalism, and the black swastika indicated "the mission for the fight for the victory of Aryan man." The swastika had indeed been used by ancient "Aryans," but also by nearly every other major ethnic group around the world. It is in fact a sun symbol representing the apparent motion of the solar disc across the skies and as such was a common motif among many traditional societies. It was not even unique as a flag symbol; in the 1930s it could be seen in flags from Estonia, Finland, Latvia, India, and the secessionist Republic of Tule created by Indians in Panama. Nevertheless the lack of originality of the swastika design had no impact on its effectiveness and the Nazis proved extremely skillful in exploiting flags as well as other symbols to intimidate, inspire, and coerce mass action.

During the late 1920s and early 1930s the flag question in Germany went beyond parliamentary debate and commentary in newspapers. Actual battles were fought in the streets between the partisans of different flags, each hoping to impose its conception of Germany, as expressed in its symbols, on the entire nation. When Hitler was named chancellor in 1933 one of his first acts was to reestablish the Black-White-Red and to make the Swastika Flag, which combined

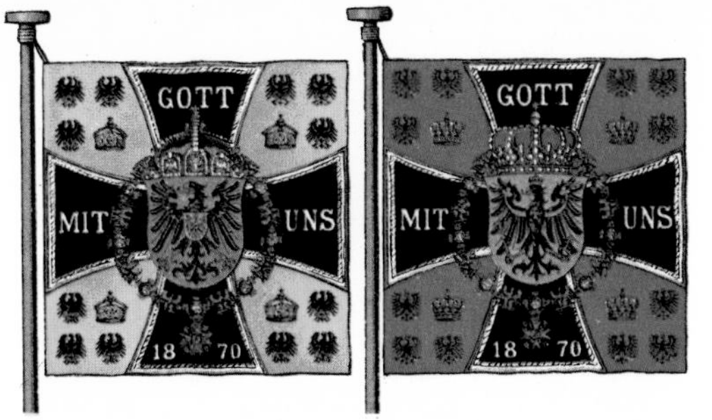

Basically similar in design, the royal banner of the Second Empire and that of the Kingdom of Prussia encompassed (among other symbols) the national German motto "God Is with Us."

The picture below, left shows the dramatic use of powerful symbols made by Hitler's Nazi party.

the same three colors, a coequal. Thus Germany had two national flags simultaneously. The Black-Red-Gold was abolished, the only reminder being the presidential standard which bore, within a border of black-white-red, the traditional black eagle on gold. Even this was abolished in 1934 when President Hindenburg died and Hitler became both head of state and head of government.
An incident in New York the following year involved the Nazi flag. A German ship flying it was attacked by a group vehemently opposed to the anti-Jewish policies of the Nazis; American authorities, insisting that this was only a "party flag," avoided prosecuting the individuals involved. Perhaps partly because of this, on 15 September 1935 a special meeting was held of

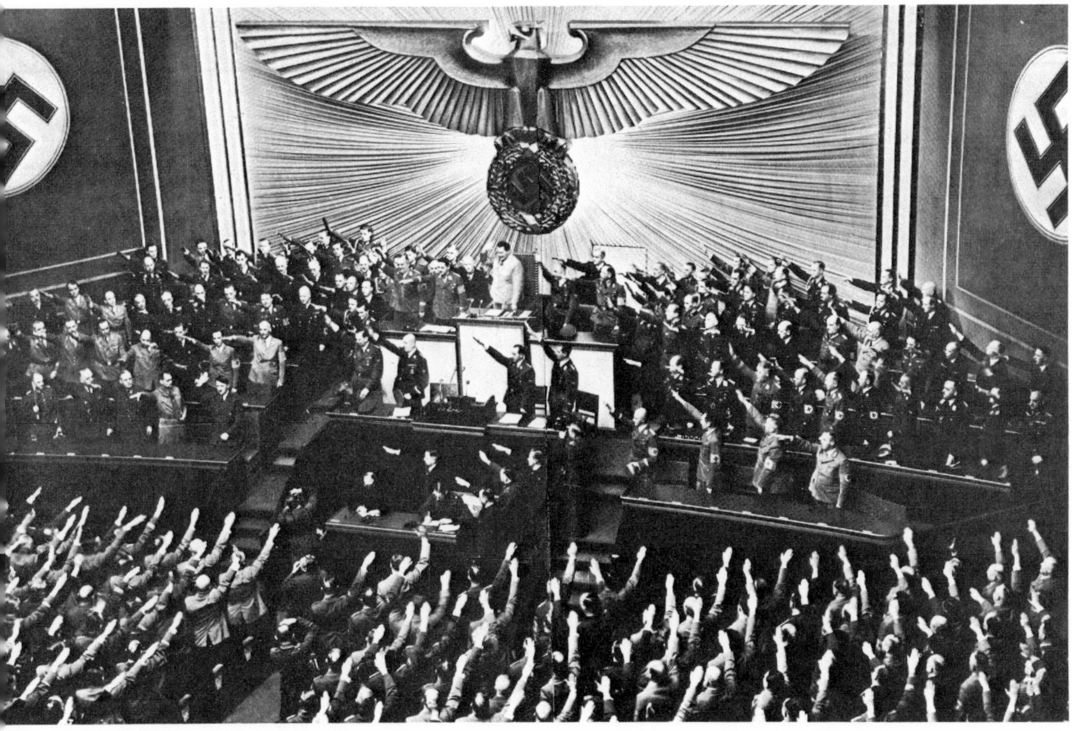

the Reichstag in Nuremberg. It suspended its parliamentary rules and effectively eliminated its own role in German government in favor of the Führer. Hitler Law No. 1 proclaimed that the Swastika Flag was henceforth to be the sole state and civil flag of Germany. Jews were deprived of German citizenship and forbidden to fly the Nazi flag, and Hermann Goering declared that the first step had been taken toward making this, the Third Empire, a thousand-year state.

The consolidation of Nazi power did not in any way lessen their use of flags and related symbolism in the political life of the state. On the contrary, types of flags and flag ceremonies and uses of flags in all aspects of life – art, sports, architecture, student organizations, etc. – intensified enormously. No more pervasive or successful utilization of flags for the ordering of state affairs has been seen through history.
The total defeat of Nazi Germany in World War II brought a strong reaction against flags, regardless of design or symbolism, among the German people. At first, of course, distinctive German flags were outlawed by the Allied occupation authorities. The flag required as a civil ensign on German vessels was simply the C flag of the International Code of Signals with a triangular area cut from its fly. The first postwar German symbols were not national but provincial, when, both in the Soviet and Western Zones of occupation, flags were adopted by the reconstituted German states. While these reflected historical precedence in design, many new elements were introduced. This was especially true in the Soviet Zone where such flags disappeared in the early 1950s with the political reorganization of the country and the suppression of local centers of loyalty.
As new state institutions were created by both the Federal Republic of Germany and the German Democratic Republic, the necessity arose

NATL. FLAG, ENS. 1867–1919, 1933–1935.

WAR ENS. 1903–1921.

STATE ENS. 1892–1918.

NATL. FLAG 1919–1933.

STATE ENS. 1921–1926.

STATE ENS. 1926–1933.

CIVIL ENS. 1919, 1921–1933.

WAR ENS. 1921–1933.

In the 1953 insurrection against the German Democratic Republic marchers before the Brandenburg Gate *(right)* carrying the German tricolor destroyed the red flag and other Communist symbols.

CIVIL ENS. 1935–1945.

WAR FLAG, ENS. 1935–1945.

STATE FLAG, ENS. 1935–1945.

CIVIL ENS. 1945–1952.

NATL. FLAG, ENS. SINCE 1949.

for official national flags, and each chose the Black-Red-Gold. The Black-White-Red had been thoroughly discredited along with the Swastika Flag, and few were interested in the creation of an alternate design. The "flag intoxication" of the previous twelve years – a successor to the "flag strife" of the 1920s – was replaced by a "flag neurosis." This has only very gradually given way to the situation today where flag usage on public and commercial buildings parallels the extent of display in other European countries.

The postwar division of Germany into two states was long looked at as a temporary aberration which, if it could not be reversed, must at least be officially ignored. Nevertheless the German Democratic Republic campaigned vigorously for national recognition, even in the matter of its official state name. Thus the similarity of the two German state flags came to be an embarrassment to the Communist regime, and in 1959 a new design was adopted. Retaining the traditional black-red-gold, this flag added the state arms in the center. Strong but unsuccessful representations were made against this flag by Chancellor Konrad Adenauer of the Federal Republic. Indeed a compromise proved necessary for the participation of a unified German team in the Olympic Games of 1960. The Olympic Committee in the German Democratic Republic refused to accept the plain Black-Red-Gold and, until the last moment, the Federal Republic of Germany Olympic Committee insisted that the traditional flag not be modified in any way. It was finally decided that, for this special purpose alone, the five-ring symbol of the Olympic Games should be added in white to the center stripe of the Black-Red-Gold.

The amount of space it has been possible to devote here to the history of German flags would barely suffice to give a list of the books and articles published on the question of the German flag in the years 1848–1850. Nevertheless the broad lines of development are clear, especially the importance of the Black-Red-Gold in the struggle for German unity and freedom. While often suffering setbacks and defeats at the hands of partisans of alternate symbols, those colors stand as the underlying current of German flag history for more than a century and a half. In the intimate relationship between the designs and usages of its national symbols and the political developments of national life, Germany is ordinary. Nevertheless, the nation is an example of the degree to which flags and similar emblems can serve as substantive forces in human life, rather than as mere decoration.

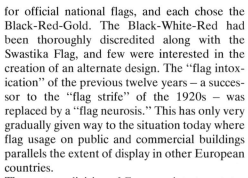

Flags symbolizing peace and communism figure in this East Berlin rally in 1953. The placard at left shows a portrait of Ernst Thälmann, a leader of the Communist Party of Germany; he also appears on the red "honor flag" of the Socialist Unity Party of Germany, presented by its Central Committee in 1973 to the Free German Youth.

On 31 October 1949 two hundred thousand people gathered in Berlin *(far right)* as the president of the Federal Republic of Germany, Theodor Heuss, visited Berlin.

SPAIN

MEDIEVAL HERALDRY IN MODERN FORM

The war ensign and most military colors of Spain include the national coat of arms, as well as inscriptions or other symbols. The national flag, however, remains the starkly simple red-yellow-red, heraldic colors whose traditions in Spain date back to the twelfth century.

Every national flag is an expression of the country over which it flies – its aspirations for the future, its economic conditions, its independence struggle, its political philosophy, or some other significant aspect of national life. Some flags have taken on the telegraphic conciseness affected by other modern communications media. Spain is one of those nations which has chosen the opposite course: its current state and war flag incorporates, in the arms emblazoned across the center, a detailed statement about Spanish history. At the same time certain contemporary Spanish political values have also been enunciated.

The basic red-yellow-red Spanish flag dates back to a royal decree of 28 May 1785. King Charles III had examined a number of designs proposed to him as replacements for the white flags previously displayed on Spanish vessels. His choice was seen as a restoration of the true national colors of Spain, although white had predominated in naval and military flags since the death of Queen Isabella the Catholic in 1504. While the tradition of red and gold in Spain can be traced further back than that of white alone or of white and red – such that the latter were looked upon by many as foreign symbols – no Spanish flag history can be complete without an analysis of the white and red.

New symbols were introduced under the influence of the House of Austria. This began when Philip, son of Maximilian I, a Hapsburg and Holy Roman Emperor, married Joan the Crazy, daughter of Isabella and King Ferdinand. Philip was Duke of Burgundy; his son was King Charles I of Spain but also was elected as Holy Roman Emperor Charles V. He favored the Burgundian symbols of his father, Philip, over purely Spanish symbols – even within his Spanish dominions. The primary Burgundian emblem was the red saltire known as the Cross of St. Andrew; it was traditionally represented in a distinctive fashion known to heraldry as raguly, that is, shown as if two tree trunks with branches cut off had been crossed to form the saltire. Long after the Burgundian cause was lost, a white flag with a red saltire, often bearing the imperial arms in the center, flew over Spain and its dominions, especially in what is today Belgium and in Latin America. The arms were also sometimes featured without the cross on a plain white flag, since white was the color of the Houses of Austria and of Bourbon (the latter providing Spain with monarchs between 1700 and 1931).

In 1843 white was eliminated from Spanish military colors, giving further reinforcement to the red-yellow-red as the Spanish national symbol. The most recent affirmation of this flag is found in the Organic Law of the State dated 10 January 1967. Earlier decrees on the subject

The arms *(above)* of their Catholic Majesties, Ferdinand and Isabella, which decorate this manuscript are set in a border combining their personal emblems, a yoke and bundle of arrows. The phrase "Tanto Monta" is part of a longer formula indicating the equality of Isabella with Ferdinand. The two words appear so frequently on tapestries that people sometimes refer to the hangings themselves as Tanto Montas.

The patriotic loyalty of the Jew who added the castle and lion symbols in this bible in 1491 did not prevent his expulsion from Spain with other Jews the following year.

issued by the government of General Francisco Franco date from 12 October 1945 and from 29 August 1936. Indeed since the decree of 1785, only the Spanish Republic of 1931–1939 has provided a flag tradition contrary to the red and gold. It did so by adding purple to the colors previously in use.

That flag was a typical republican tricolor: the stripes were equal in width, the new color (purple) replacing the bottom red stripe of the previous flag. While there is considerable confusion about the exact shade of color found in old flags, both *morado* (purple) or *carmesí* (crimson) have authentic Spanish roots. One or the other was always found in royal banners, even under the Bourbons. Purple was the color of the lion in the arms of Leon and quite possibly served in the medieval Standard of Castille and in the flags used by the *Comuneros* (the "commoners" who had led an uprising against the Hapsburg King of Spain, Charles I, in 1520–1521). Moreover, during the civil disorders in the nineteenth century liberals used flags incorporating purple. Thus as a symbol of struggle against foreign monarchs, feudal social institutions, and church privileges, purple was a logical choice for the republican movement. It appeared in unofficial flags from the revolution of 1868 through the end of the first Spanish Republic (1873–1874), although officially the latter never went further than to introduce changes into the national coat of arms. Purple may have been the flag color of the king, but on the establishment of the second Spanish Republic in 1931 a red-yellow-purple tricolor became Spain's national flag, disappearing only in March 1939 with the victory of the fascists led by Francisco Franco.

The Reconquest looms as the most significant early chapter in Spanish national history. In the manuscript picture below the Moors are shown attacking a Spanish city under one of their banners with a

religious inscription, but ultimately they were forced out of the peninsula. The last Muslim state fell in 1492, seven centuries after the first invasions from Africa.

From the early thirteenth century to the early sixteenth, the most important Spanish flag was a banner *(left)* combining the arms of Castile and Leon. These are known as canting arms because the charges (the castle and lion) echoed the names of the states they represented.

On 11 February 1938 Franco had decreed, "The arms of Spain are based on the heraldry of the Catholic Monarchs...." This symbolism was intended to recall the days of Isabella and Ferdinand. Under their rule Spain had been united, the Muslims and Jews expelled, an empire in the New World established through the efforts of Spanish explorers and colonizers, and the state firmly dedicated to monarchical and ecclesiastical authority. After the loss of empire, wars both civil and foreign, and a succession of unpopular rulers, the 1938 arms were intended as a call to restoring Spanish greatness. Each element has an important historical and ideological message.

The Hapsburgs introduced new symbols into Spain in the sixteenth century, the most important of which were the raguly saltire of St. Andrew and the flintstone and flames of the Order of the Golden Fleece, such as were used *(below)* by Philip of Burgundy.

Sailors of the Holy League were inspired by the special pennant *(above)*, representing the Crucifixion, which accompanied them into battle against the Turks; yet over the centuries thousands of captured Spaniards and other Christians ended their days enslaved by the Muslims.

On 7 October 1571 the Holy League organized by Pope Pius V won a resounding victory over the Turkish fleet in the Battle of Lepanto. Almost 500 galleys took part – the largest naval battle Europe had seen in fifteen hundred years. It is not known how accurately the Turkish flags were represented by the Christian artist whose work

The dynastic color of the Bourbon monarchs was white and the Burgundy cross a frequent charge against a background of that color in flags. Familiar to three centuries of Latin Americans under Spanish rule, this flag is flown today in Spain by the Requetes movement.

The central shield indicates immediately the source of the red and gold Spanish national colors. Omitting the arms of Sicily and other non-Spanish dominions which had been part of the royal shield from 1516 on, this emblem is now a combination of five shields – those of the kingdoms of Castile, Leon, Aragon, Navarre, and Granada. It should be noted that it is a peculiarity of heraldry that the location of an emblem rather than its size indicates its impor-

appears below, but the diversity of Spanish and Venetian flags is immediately visible. The cross and other religious symbols and dynastic colors are evident, but otherwise there is little uniformity. The confusion among flags closely paralleled the naval tactics of the era: individual vessels fought one another with little coordination between ships in the same fleet. While 80 Turkish galleys were sunk the Spanish were not able to follow up on their victory because of disagreements with their Venetian allies.

tance. The shield is more important than the accessories; within the shield the dexter and chief are more important respectively than the sinister and the base. Consequently, Castile and Leon, the oldest parts of Spain, are given primacy over Aragon, Navarre, and Granada. Arms such as those of Leon and Castile are known to heraldry as canting arms because their charges correspond to the names of the persons (or in this case, states) which bear them. The

The majesty of Spanish imperial power was immediately evident in its eighteenth-century war ensign *(below)*. While the quarterings in the arms represented only its European possessions, it was actually the gold and other resources of huge New World territories which made Spain wealthy and powerful. This flag was replaced in 1785.

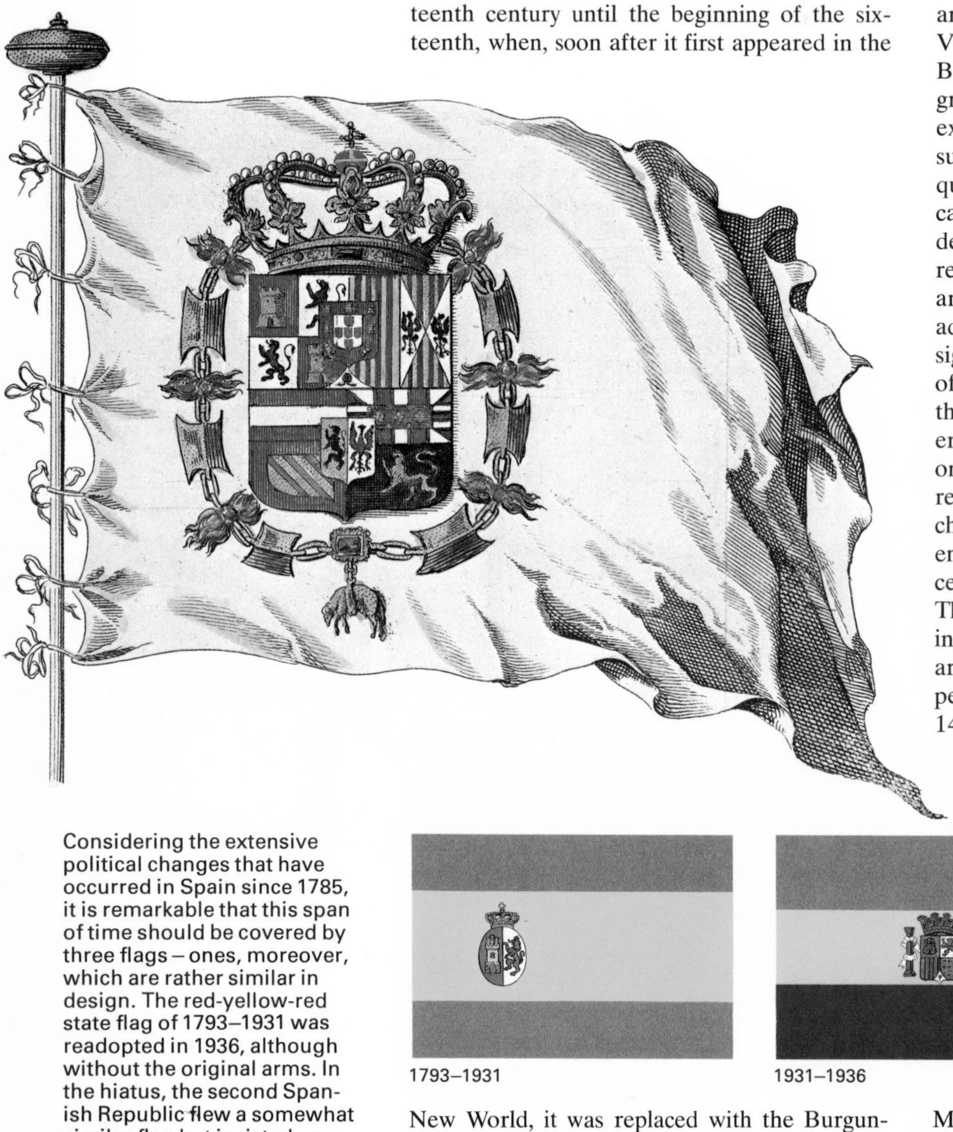

Considering the extensive political changes that have occurred in Spain since 1785, it is remarkable that this span of time should be covered by three flags – ones, moreover, which are rather similar in design. The red-yellow-red state flag of 1793–1931 was readopted in 1936, although without the original arms. In the hiatus, the second Spanish Republic flew a somewhat similar flag but insisted on a tricolor of equal stripes to reflect the republican tradition of other European and American nations.

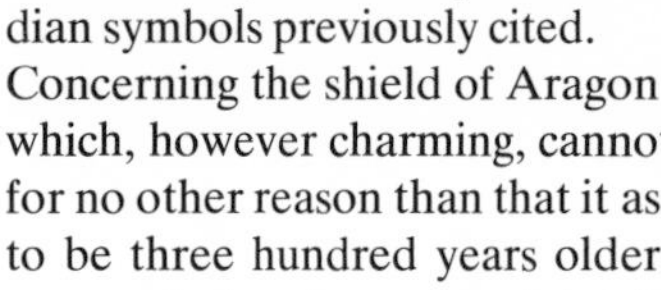

1793–1931

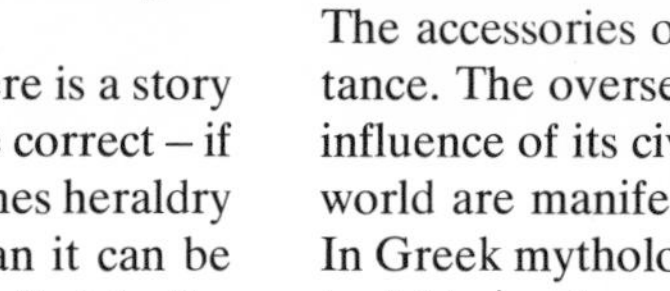

1931–1936

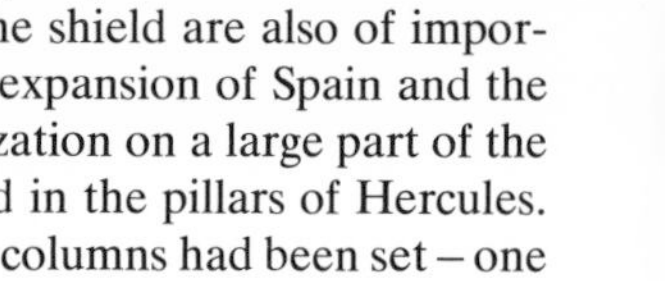

SINCE 1936

first record of the lion as a symbol of Leon seems to be found in coins issued under Alphonso VII (1126–1157). Shortly thereafter Alphonso VIII (1158–1214) introduced the castle of Castile on his own coins. The two arms were united under St. Ferdinand (Ferdinand III, 1230–1252) in the quartered fashion repeated twice in the modern heraldic achievement of Spain. An armorial banner, also quarterly of Castile and Leon, served Spain from the thirteenth century until the beginning of the sixteenth, when, soon after it first appeared in the New World, it was replaced with the Burgundian symbols previously cited.

Concerning the shield of Aragon there is a story which, however charming, cannot be correct – if for no other reason than that it assumes heraldry to be three hundred years older than it can be proven to be. A manuscript relates that in the ninth century the first independent Count of Aragon, Wilfred I (the Hairy) went to aid Charles the Bald, King of France and grandson of Charlemagne. Visiting his wounded ally, Charles is said to have dipped four fingers in Wilfred's blood and then to have drawn them down his plain gold shield. The fact is, however, that the four red bars on the gold of Aragon are not known to predate King Ramon Berenguer IV (1131–1162). It was also under Berenguer in 1137 that the County of Barcelona (i.e., Catalonia) became part of Aragon, making use of the same coat of arms.

The golden chains on the red shield of Navarre are also the subject of a famous legend. Sancho VII (the Strong, 1194–1234) participated in the Battle of Navas de Tolosa on 16 July 1212, a great victory for the Christian princes seeking to expel the Muslims from Spain. King Sancho is supposed to have captured the general headquarters of Muhammad bin Yusuf and to have carried off the chains which protected this camp, depositing them in various churches and adding representations of chains to his own coat of arms. (The emerald in the center is said to have adorned the turban of bin Yusuf.) Nevertheless, sigillographical evidence indicates that the kings of Navarre, including Sancho, used an eagle as their heraldic emblem and that the shields of the era which appear to show chains in fact have only a representation of those metal strips which reinforced actual battle shields. The stylized chains do not seem to have become the heraldic emblem of Navarre until late in the fourteenth century.

The arms of Granada – a pomegranate (*granada* in Spanish) on a silver shield – are also canting arms. This fruit was in use, apparently as the personal emblem of King Henry IV (1454–1474), before the Reconquest by which the Muslims were finally expelled from Granada. The accessories of the shield are also of importance. The overseas expansion of Spain and the influence of its civilization on a large part of the world are manifested in the pillars of Hercules. In Greek mythology columns had been set – one in Africa and one in Europe, both at the mouth of the Mediterranean – at the ends of the known world; they were inscribed with the warning "[There Is] No More Beyond." Emperor Charles V (King Charles I of Spain) adopted

His power firmly established after the Spanish civil war, Generalissimo Francisco Franco in 1940 resurrected an ancient Spanish cavalry standard *(right)* to serve as his personal standard. The dragon-wolves are Spanish symbols of authority, while the Pillars of Hercules recall the spread of Spanish culture throughout the world after Columbus and others realized that the geographical "pillars" of the same name were not in fact the end of the world.

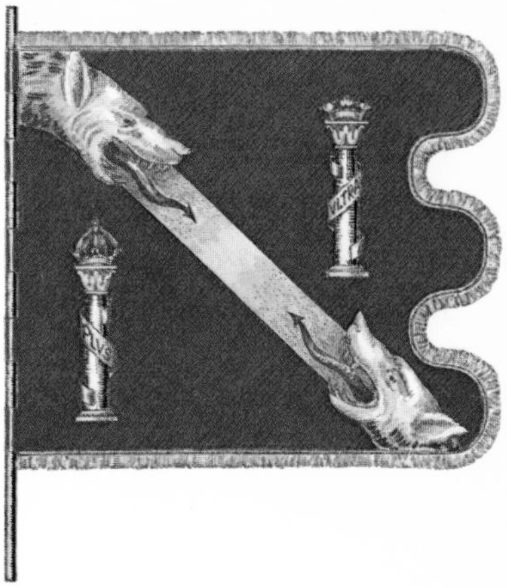

stylized pillars to indicate the universal extent of his imperial domains and, as a tribute to Spanish explorers, the motto inscribed on the ribbons around the pillars was revised to read "[There Is] More Beyond."

Within the pillars is the eagle of St. John who holds the Spanish shield. This supporter first appeared in representations of the royal arms in the church of St. John of the Kings in Toledo, dedicated by Queen Isabella in 1476. The eagle of St. John disappeared after 1516 in the arms of Spain until its modern revival more than four centuries later. In 1938 a ribbon was added behind the eagle head in the black and red colors of the fascist Spanish Phalanx; its motto reads "One, Great, Free." The two elements which combined to form the party symbol of the Phalanx, the yoke and arrows, are prominent but separate in the state arms. Originally the yoke and arrows had been personal badges of the Catholic Monarchs. The first letters of their names correspond to those of the symbols: the yoke or *yugo* is for Isabella (Ysabel) and the arrows or *flechas* for Ferdinand. They are seen today as emblems of unity and strength, respectively. The crown recalls that Spain is officially a kingdom, although without a king since 1931.

No symbol has a constant or implicit meaning; it conveys only such information as the beholder draws from personal experience. Nevertheless over the course of centuries certain symbols have acquired meanings which folklore and more formal institutions (the church, schools, the military, etc.) have perpetuated from generation to generation. Rarely is the choice of a symbol arbitrary or neutral; the inclusion or exclusion of a particular color or charge in a flag or coat of arms indicates a commitment to a particular view and often to a specific plan of action. The arms and flags of Spain are a case in point; in the centuries since the first steps toward the unification of the peninsula and its culture each sovereign or ruling class or political movement has expressed its interpretation of Spanish history and its program for the nation through political symbols.

Characteristic of Spain, the national flags in the photograph above are draped along balconies, as they often are as well on private homes. The length of the flag here is of no concern – only its colors and the widths of the stripes are considered important.

In the days when it was part of the Roman Empire, France was known as *Gallia,* and the vexilloid carried by Gallic troops was in the form of a cock – *gallus* in Latin. For the past two hundred years the Tricolor of France has been one of the best-known national symbols in the world.
Between the cock and the Tricolor, French history

is crowded with diverse and colorful symbols (such as the fleurs-de-lis on the gates of Versailles, *above*) which recall battles, monarchs, and other significant points in French history.

Since 1870 France has had no official coat of arms, but this unofficial version *(right)* was employed during the Fourth Republic (1946–1958). Surrounded by the Order of the Legion of Honor, it bears the republican fasces and the national motto "Liberty, Equality, Fraternity."

FRANCE

FROM THE ORIFLAMME TO THE TRICOLOR

A person not knowing the history of French national flags might imagine, on seeing the chief banners carried by the French through their history, that the famous Tricolor was simply a combination of previous designs. The blue of St. Martin's cloak and the Banner of France, the white of Joan of Arc and the Bourbons, and finally the red of Charlemagne and St. Denis all seem to be reflected directly in the stripes of the Tricolor. There is no doubt that historical precedents to the three chief colors of the modern French national flag have contributed to its popularity, and they may in part account for the strength with which the Tricolor has returned after being officially abolished three times and challenged many other times. Yet important as the flags mentioned above have been to the French, the Tricolor essentially is a derivation from other sources. To understand French flag history, therefore, it is necessary to examine each of the flags separately and to appreciate

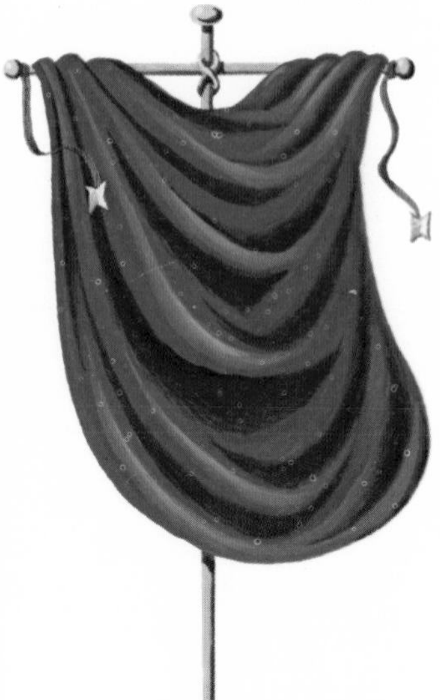

ST. MARTIN'S CLOAK.

THE MONTJOIE OF CHARLEMAGNE.

why one gave way to the next. This review will make it clear why the Tricolor stems from sources other than French flags of the past and yet is seen to be in symbolic continuity with them.
Apart from the vexilloids bearing wild boars and cocks which Gallic soldiers carried in the armies of Rome, the earliest standard of the French seems to have been the cloak of a fourth-century bishop, St. Martin. When King Clovis disinterred St. Martin's grave in the fifth century, one of the relics found was a cloak, which, according to legend, had once been divided with a beggar. This cloak was kept in a portable oratory, carried into battle for the use of French kings from Clovis onward. Its fame as

Early French symbols included the cloak of St. Martin *(far left)*, which he divided with a beggar, and the fleur-de-lis *(left)*, here held by King Henry I.

an aid to military success was won the first time it was displayed, in 507 at the battle of Vouillé. So important did the cloak of St. Martin become, the oratory in which it was carried came to be known as a chapel, from the Latin word for cloak (*cappa* or *capella*), and the priest in charge of it was known as a chaplain.

The same emblem was used by Charles Martel against the Muslims and in battles in the years 838, 1043, 1066, and 1195. It has been suggested that the French word for flag, *pavillon,* came from the fact that the cloak was protected by a pavilion when carried in war. Although this is unsubstantiated, it does seem likely that the cloak itself was not used directly as a vexilloid, certainly not without being replaced by replicas from time to time. There is also some confusion between the cloak and a flag from St. Martin of Tours which the counts of Anjou had the right to carry in battle. Whatever its form or origins, the tradition of St. Martin's cloak as a symbol of victory ended with the defeat suffered by the French at the Battle of Poitiers in 1356.

Concurrently with the cloak of St. Martin as a war flag, the Franks recognized a red imperial flag from the time of Charlemagne on. While this has been dealt with elsewhere in the book (see page 63), a few words about its use in France are appropriate. This flag was known as the oriflamme it seems because of its golden red color and perhaps because of the flamelike tails at its end. It was also known as the Roman standard because it symbolized temporal authority and Charlemagne's title as Holy Roman Emperor which he had obtained from the pope in Rome. Finally, it was known as Montjoie (Mount Joy) from the Mons Gaudii in Rome, the site of its transmission from the pope to Charlemagne. This name became the original battle cry of the French, later modified to "Montjoie St. Denis!"

St. Denis had been the first bishop of Paris, and the oriflamme associated with him – which available records seem to indicate was physically similar to Charlemagne's oriflamme – was first chosen as a war flag by King Louis VI (the Fat) in 1124. It had been a special privilege of the Counts of Vexin to carry the oriflamme of St. Denis; King Philip I (1060–1108) fell heir to their title, which probably accounts for its adoption soon thereafter as the French war flag. Carried during four Crusades and seventeen other wars, the color of the oriflamme of St. Denis may possibly account for the red cross used by early French crusaders. Nevertheless, like the cloak of St. Martin, its career was ended in a dramatic French defeat – in this case the Battle of Agincourt in 1415, in which the English were again successful against the French.

The blue war flag of St. Martin had coexisted with the red imperial standard of Charlemagne; the red war flag of St. Denis was matched by a blue royal flag – the Banner of France. This displayed golden fleurs-de-lis on its square blue field and seems first to have been used under King Louis VI (1108–1137). At first the fleurs-de-lis were semé, but under Charles VI (1380–1422) the number was reduced to three – presumably in honor of the Holy Trinity. The Banner of France ranks with the black eagle on gold of the Holy Roman Empire and the gold

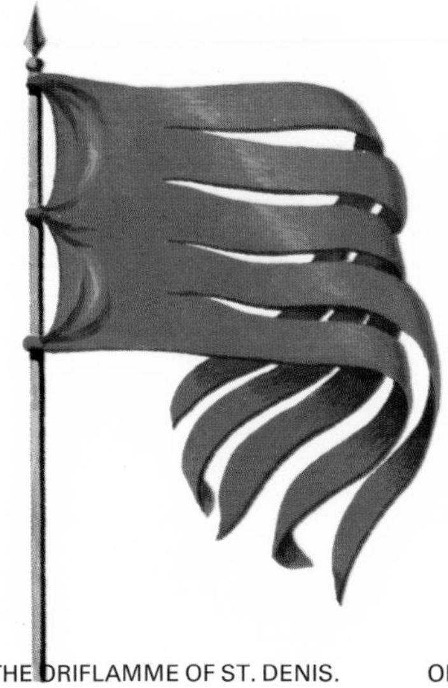

THE ORIFLAMME OF ST. DENIS.

ORIFLAMME (VARIANT).

THE BANNER OF FRANCE.

JOAN OF ARC'S STANDARD.

The origin of the fleur-de-lis symbol is not known for sure. Some have seen it as originally a flower, others a weapon, still others a frog – such as those appearing in the flag *(top)*, from a tapestry in the Cathedral of Reims. The original Banner of France was strewn with fleurs-de-lis *(above)* rather than having only three.

The miniature below represents the defeat by Charles Martel of the Muslim invasion from Spain. The heraldic shield and costumes indicate clearly, however, that the miniature itself was done many centuries after the battle of Poitiers since heraldry was not practiced by either Muslims or Christians until long after 732.

As King Charles VI is laid to rest in 1422 the arms of France are in evidence on his helmet, on the sword of state, on the trappings of the horse, in shields, and on the robe of the wax effigy of the king which rests on his coffin.

lions on red of England as one of the most famous heraldic banners of the Middle Ages, and, although considered the personal emblem of the king, it figured in battles from the Crusades onward.

White is first introduced as a French national color during the fifteenth century, chiefly under the influence of Joan of Arc (see page 66) and the House of Orleans. At the Battle of Ivry in 1590 it gained added fame when Henry IV employed his white scarf as a flag and a symbol of the French national struggle against the Holy League. White crosses were worn on the uniforms of soldiers and white invariably appeared in the personal livery of the kings of France (which took various forms over the years, in contrast to the unchanging Banner of France). King Francis I (1515–1547) made the command flag of the Colonel General of Infantry a white cornet. All regiments recognized it as the national color, and a cross of white was intro-

This piece of embroidery from the Burgundian booty captured by the Swiss shows a stylized version of the emblem of the Order of the Golden Fleece – a flintstone striking fire.

KING FRANCIS I'S FLAG.

LOUIS XIV'S LIFE GUARD CORNET.

FRENCH STATE FLAG CA. 1643–1790.

duced into flags which otherwise had the most diverse colors and designs. By the time of the French Revolution in 1789, all regiments had two colors. The colonel's color was white with a white cross sewn on it; the other was white with regimental colors in the four quarters of the flag.

White was also introduced into French naval flags. We have examples of many different forms without very clear indications as to dates of usage. A plain white flag, a white flag semé of golden fleurs-de-lis, a similar flag with the arms of France in the center, a white (or blue) flag with three golden fleurs-de-lis, a blue flag with a white cross, the same with the arms of the king in the center, simple blue and white horizontal stripes – all these designs were in use at one

The use of white as a French national color began in the sixteenth century and spread from a few royal flags until, in the form of a cross or the background of a flag, it was the predominant flag color both on land and at sea among French forces. Its predominance lasted until 1794 and was briefly revived between 1815 and 1830.

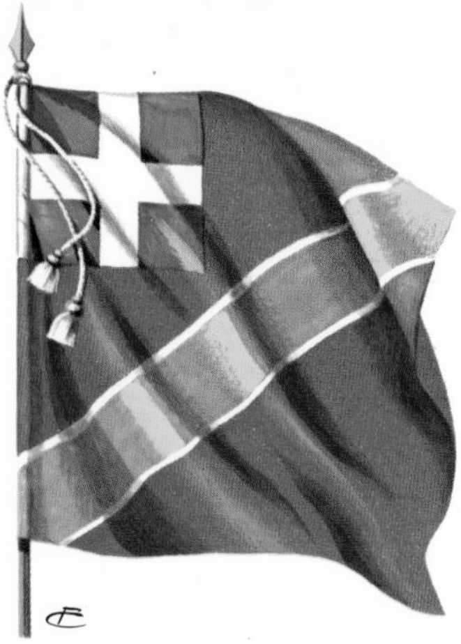

The national holiday of France, 14 July, commemorates the storming of the Bastille prison on that date in 1789. Luckless defenders of that bastion of the Old Regime carried a distinctive flag *(above).*

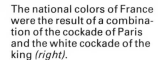

The national colors of France were the result of a combination of the cockade of Paris and the white cockade of the king *(right).*

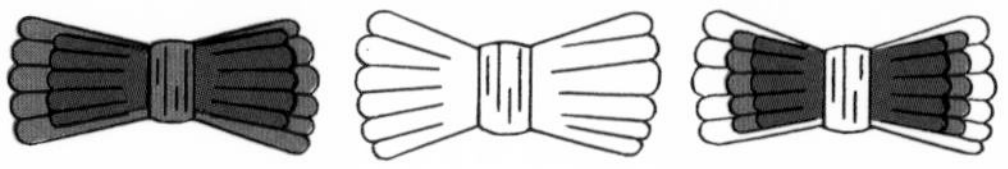

point or another. There was a tendency for merchant vessels to display the white flag of warships, although they were supposed to be restricted to the blue flag with the white cross. The blue flag with three fleurs-de-lis – a rectangular version of the Banner of France – was also displayed on ships and forts, since these were under the authority of the king. The influence of this flag and the blue flag with the white cross is seen in a number of modern flags in the United States and Canada, parts of their territories once being under French domination.

The difficulty facing the vexillologist in defining precisely what was the national flag for France (or any other European country) during the years before standardized designs is suggested by a print from 1636 of the warship *La Couronne.* On the jack staff this vessel flies a square blue flag semé of gold fleurs-de-lis. On the ensign staff is a flag of the same design, but red instead of blue. On the foremast there is a horizontally striped flag of red and white above a long pennant striped blue and white. The mainmast has a white flag elaborately embroidered

The rule of Louis XVI came to an end with the storming of the Tuileries *(right)* on 10 August 1792. While the monarchy was not formally abolished until the next month, the Paris Commune and Jacobin clubs were in effective control of France.

Each of the national guard battalions from different districts of Paris had its own distinctive banner – such as that of St. Victor *(above).* In addition to allegorical scenes of republican sentiment, many of these flags were quartered with the Paris city colors (red and blue) and bore the French national cross of white.

with fleurs-de-lis, royal ciphers, and the arms of France. On the mizzenmast we find a green flag bearing gold fleurs-de-lis and the crowned L symbolic of King Louis XIII. Obviously, if one vessel had so many flags, all indicating French nationality, our list of prerevolutionary French flags is far from complete.

At the time of the revolution not only had individual flags of red, white, and blue been long established in France, but a combination of the three colors had been used as royal livery several times in the past. Nevertheless it is to the coat of arms of the city of Paris that we must look for the inspiration of the first Tricolor. On 13 July 1789 when the Paris Militia (later the National Guard) was organized, the troops were required to wear cockades of the municipal blue and red. Four days later the same revolutionary symbol was presented by the Marquis de Lafayette to the king, who wore it when he greeted the crowd outside the City Hall. It is not clear whether it was Louis or Lafayette who added the white (royal) cockade to the red and blue, but in recommending a combination of these three colors to the revolutionary government Lafayette is said to have asserted, "I bring you a cockade which will make a tour of the world, an institution both civic and military which must triumph over the old tactics of Europe and which will reduce arbitrary governments to the alternative of being beaten if they do not imitate it and overthrown if they dare to imitate it."

Red, blue, and white were officially adopted on 4 October 1789 as a cockade, at that time an important form of political symbol. The National Guard flags were quartered blue and red with a white cross throughout. The colors were an appropriate choice, red and blue having been used at least as early as 1358 by Parisian commoners revolting against royal authority. Nevertheless flags of plain white were displayed at the Festival of the Federation the following year, on the first anniversary of the overthrow of the Bastille. The initiative for completely replacing white, theretofore recognized as the royal and national color of France, with red-white-blue came from rebellious sailors. They

Reorganization of the army as well as ideological changes in post-revolutionary France demanded new military colors. The Napoleonic designs *(above)* are only a few of the hundreds developed between 1799 and 1815. The Tricolor itself *(left)* went through many adaptations before the pattern now familiar was permanently established.

When Napoleon returned from Elba in 1815, one of his most powerful weapons for regaining authority was the appeal which could be made to French soldiers in the tricolored military banners he reestablished. His challenge to them to take up the Tricolor against the white banners of reaction is dramatized in the painting *(below)* "Return from the Island of Elba February 1815" by Karl Steuben.

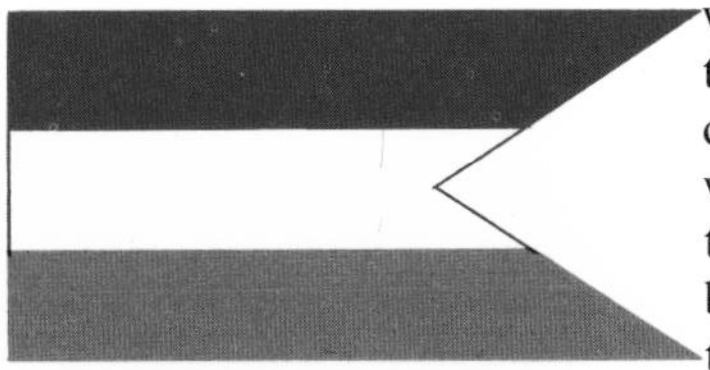

NATL. FLAG CA. 1792 TO CA. 1794.

NATL. FLAG CA. 1792 TO CA. 1794.

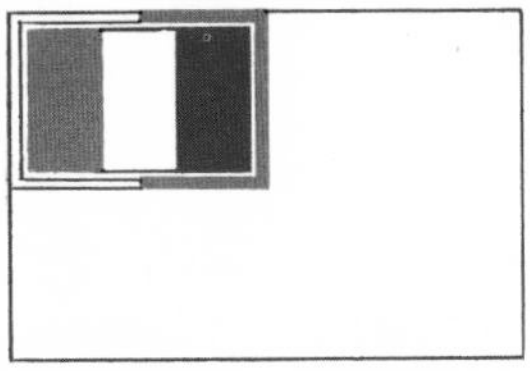

WAR ENSIGN 1790–1794.

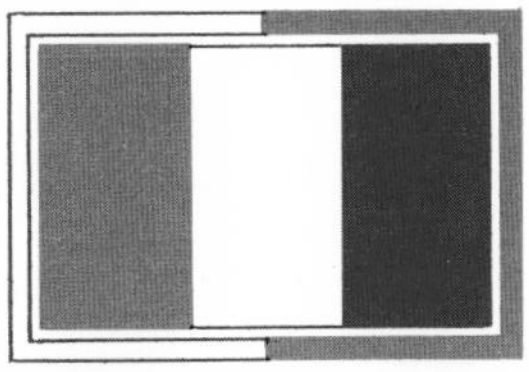

JACK 1790–1794.

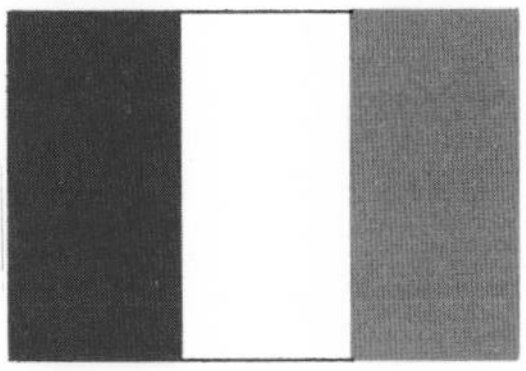

NATL. FLAG 1794–1814, 1815.

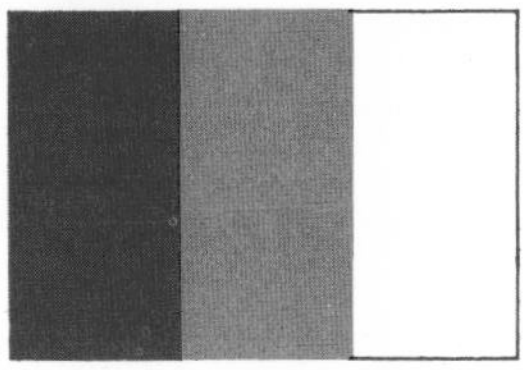

NATIONAL FLAG 1848.

NATIONAL FLAG 1830–1848, SINCE 1848.

Although it is not always possible to prove direct influence, it is clear that the Tricolor has inspired a great number of foreign flags – including the ones shown in this column.

HAITI MAY 1803–1805.

HAITI 1805–1820 SINCE 1964.

HAITI 1806–1964.

LUCCA 1803–8 AUGUST 1805.

LUCCA 8 AUGUST 1805–1814.

MEXICO CA. 1821.

MEXICO 1815–?

NORWAY 1821–1844 SINCE 10 DECEMBER 1898.

URUGUAY 25 AUGUST 1825–16 DECEMBER 1828.

DOMINICAN REPUBLIC SINCE 27 FEBRUARY 1844.

COSTA RICA SINCE 29 SEPTEMBER 1848.

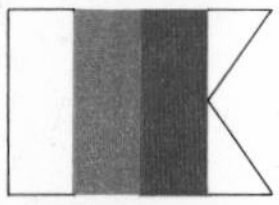
BUGANDA 1880–?

MADAGASCAR 1885–1896.

SAAR 1948–1956.

LOUISIANA 1861.

FRENCH ASSOC. OF INTL. VEXILLOLOGICAL STUDIES SINCE 1969.

Flags of the victorious regiments in the defense of Verdun are reviewed in April 1916 by General Henri Pétain, French President Poincaré, and King Victor Emmanuel III of Italy *(below)*.

protested against having to sail and do battle under the old white flag and demanded that the National Assembly establish as official some kind of naval flag incorporating what had come to be known as the national colors.

Their wish was realized in a law adopted on 24 October 1790. Although three-quarters of the new ensign was still white, its canton (which also served separately as the French jack) repeated the national colors twice: vertical stripes of red-white-blue, the reverse of the modern order, were bordered by the same colors. Two years later a decree was promulgated which required everyone living in or passing through France to wear the tricolor cockade. On 17 September 1792 the death penalty was provided as punishment for selling cockades other than those of red-white-blue; four days later the First Republic was proclaimed. It was hailed with flags of these colors exhibiting a diversity of shapes and designs.

It was again the sailors of the French navy whose protests led to the alteration of the flag in 1794. At their behest a committee recommended to the National Assembly "an ensign formed completely of the three national colors, [a] simple [design] as is appropriate for republican morals, ideas, and principles." The white field and borders of the vertical stripes were eliminated, the order of the latter being altered so that the blue-white-red took the form of the Tricolor as it is known today. According to the revolutionary calendar in use at the time, it was adopted on 29 Pluviose of the year II, which corresponds to 15 February 1794.

The predominance the Tricolor had found at sea was not immediately matched on land, at least in the army. Various tricolored flags of the most diverse geometric patterns imaginable were employed by various units until 1812, in which year the three vertical stripes became official. One early republican military flag pattern, a white lozenge framed by blue and red triangles in the corners, influenced national flags in other countries. Not only several Italian states under French influence (see pages 143–144) but Brazil also appears to have taken it as a model. The

The overwhelming popularity of the Tricolor has not been diminished by adaptations created over the years by strong leaders. The personal standards of Emperor Napoleon III (1852–1871), Head of State Henri Pétain (1940–1944), and President Charles de Gaulle (1959–1968) display, respectively, the imperial eagle and bees first used under Napoleon I, the stars and baton of a marshal (the latter rendered in the form of a medieval weapon, the francisc), and the double-barred Cross of Lorraine. Under the Third and Fourth Republics it was customary to place the initials of the current president in gold on the center of the white stripe of the Tricolor. Each president under the Fifth Republic has had a distinctive flag of his own.

Tricolor itself was even more influential among the flags of revolutionary groups around the world, directly in the colors of many national flags and indirectly in the equal vertical (or horizontal) stripes of still more. Not only former French colonies in Africa, but countries as diverse as Mexico, Romania, and Ethiopia have been affected by the trend first established by the French.

The battle for the Tricolor was not won with its

acceptance in 1812 as the standard pattern for military colors. The restoration of the French monarchy resulted in the decree of 13 April 1814, stating that "the white cockade is the French cockade: it shall be taken up by the whole army." Even the tsar of Russia had suggested it might be acceptable to keep the Tricolor, but Louis XVIII insisted on the supremacy of the white flag. During the Hundred Days, of course, Napoleon reestablished the blue-white-red. His proclamation of 1 March 1815 (followed by a formal decree eight days later) exhorted: "Wear the tricolored cockade; you bore it in our previous days!... Soldiers, fall into place under the flags of your chief.... The eagle with the national colors will fly from steeple to steeple even unto the towers of Notre Dame." Men rallied and Napoleon indeed reached Notre Dame, but following his defeat at Waterloo the white cockade and flag were established once again. The king disdained, however, to recognize the legitimacy of the Hundred Days by issuing a new decree to supplement that of April 1814.

The July Revolution of 1830, which brought constitutionalism to the French monarchy, saw the publication on 2 August of a decree signed by King Louis Philippe: "The French nation takes up again its colors. There shall not be worn any cockade other than the tricolored cockade." The apparent success of the Tricolor ultimately proved to be a danger to its continued acceptance when the revolution of 1848 broke out. Having overthrown the monarchy, the French revolutionaries of that year felt it inconsistent that they should maintain its flag: the Tricolor was to be replaced by the plain red flag of revolution. It was the poet Alphonse de Lamartine who saved the Tricolor. When a crowd entered the hall of the Assembly brandishing red flags and found him one of only two delegates present, he warned them:

"If you take away from me [as Minister of Foreign Affairs] the tricolor flag... you take away from me half of the force of France abroad!... I will resist to the death this flag of blood and you should repudiate it more than I! For the red flag that you bring to us has only been around the Champ-de-Mars [a military training field], dragged through the blood of the people in '91 and '93, while the Tricolor has made a tour of the world with the name, the glory, and the liberty of the fatherland!"

As a compromise, on 26 February 1848 a red rosette was ordered to be added to the top of poles bearing the national flag. Ironically, while

In 1956 General de Gaulle presented a flag to students at the military academy of Saint-Cyr. Speaking of the military career they had chosen, he said on that occasion: "It requires that you renounce liberty and money, but it will give you in exchange the dream which is after all the most beautiful – the dream of glory at the foot of a standard."

Heeding the call of General de Gaulle in 1940 – in what seemed at the time a hopeless effort to rally the French against the Nazi invaders – this lonely Breton fisherman sailed for England. He proudly flew his nation's banner on his small boat, as did thousands of other men and women who crossed the English Channel at the same time.

"preserving" the original colors of the flag, the government decreed they should be ordered blue, red, and white. The preface of the decree indicated that it was justified because "the form of the national flag should be fixed in an invariable manner," but barely two weeks later the original blue, white, and red form was restored and the red rosette omitted. An official decree of 5 March ordered:

"The Gallic cock and the three colors were our venerated symbols when we founded the republic and France; they were adopted by the glorious days of July. Do not think, citizens, to suppress or change them: you will repudiate the most beautiful pages of your history, your immortal glory, your courage which has become known in all points of the globe. Keep thus the Gallic cock, the three colors: the Government demands it of your patriotism."

Since that time there have been no official modifications in the national flag of France. During the Commune in 1871, the plain red flag again laid claim to French loyalty, but its influence was not felt beyond Paris and it disappeared with the defeat of the Commune. For a while it seemed as if the plain white flag might be reestablished (see page 75), but in fact the Tricolor has continued under the Third, Fourth, and Fifth Republics as well as the French State established by Marshal Henri Pétain during World War II. In opposition to his double-bladed ax (the francisc, a medieval weapon), General Charles de Gaulle offered the double-barred cross of Lorraine. This found its way into several flags, including one with a lozenge resembling the military colors of the early nineteenth century. The national flag itself was not officially changed.

While variations of the colors red, white, and blue over the centuries have been substantial, a strong symbolic continuity exists in France. No government or ruler has introduced a design or color combination so out of keeping with French history as to be rejected. The less radical modifications have had to be justified in terms of prior traditions, and old flags have given way to new generally only when the previous regime proved to be inadequate in the political or military sphere. In short, it would be quite wrong to assume a simple process whereby the red flags of Charlemagne and St. Denis and the blue cloak of St. Martin and blue Banner of France were transformed together with the white flag of the Bourbons into the Tricolor. There has rather been a gradual growth and expansion of a consistent symbolic tradition making the Tricolor the unchallenged national symbol of France today.

The French have and have had other symbols – including the Cross of Lorraine and Arch of Triumph apparent in the demonstration of 1968 *(right)*. All, however, are eclipsed in importance by the Tricolor.

TRAVAIL

ITALY

THE TRICOLOR: UNITY OUT OF DIVERSITY

The present Italian Tricolor dates from 1946, but has roots that may be traced to 1796.

The fourteenth-century manuscript illustration *(below, right)* shows Crusaders embarking from Naples. Among the many nationalities represented are Italians, knights of the Holy Spirit. Their flag includes the traditional symbol of the Holy Spirit, a dove with the tongues of fire referred to in Acts II:2-4.

The smaller the organization or political entity, the more complex its flag tends to be. This general rule does not apply everywhere, of course; but it is remarkable that the great powers of the world by and large have simpler flags than the smaller nations which, in turn, have less detailed flags than those of their provinces and cities. The flags of Italy are a case in point: the national Tricolor is a strikingly clean design consisting of green-white-red equal vertical stripes. The naval flags of Italy have added emblems; the flags flown by the independent states which united to form Italy, still more involved patterns; and, finally, the military colors of Italy's past display a complexity matched by its political history.

The politics of the Italian peninsula is a key to its flags. Under the royal houses and communal republics existing in Tuscany, Sicily, the Roman States, Venice (not to mention Parma, Piombino, Massa-Carrara, Menton and Rocquebrun, and many others), flags were an assertion of sovereignty, a defense of traditional rights, a proclamation of the very justification for a separate existence. This was of course especially true of royal and naval flags, but even a civil flag usually incorporated symbols and colors strikingly more complex than the modern Tricolor.

Coats of arms were changed to reflect the acquisition of new territories by marriage or conquest or otherwise; to enhance the majesty of the state, the crest or supporters might be altered, often in correspondence with a change in the title of the local ruler. Before the late eighteenth century no attempt was made to appeal to the patriotism or loyalty of the citizenry, although such themes were sometimes reflected in military colors. In short the flags were an asseveration of state privilege, frequently coupled with a hint of divine favor. It is not surprising therefore that the simple message of Italian unity expressed by the Tricolor was not immediately accepted. It took fully three-quarters of a century from the time of its conception until the green-white-red flew over all parts of the Italian homeland.

Some attention must be given to earlier Italian flags, not simply for the background they provide to our understanding of how the Tricolor arose and achieved preeminence, but also because those old symbols have not entirely today lost their influence. The heraldic components of the shield featured in the civil ensign and war ensign of Italy (page 244) provide excellent examples, although many other famous emblems might merit equal attention – for example, the halberd of Trieste; the lily of Florence; the trinacria of Sicily; or even the snake which grasps its tail, emblem of Fiume under d'Annunzio earlier in this century.

It is scarcely surprising that all four of the emblems on the naval shield – the golden winged lion on red of Venice, the red cross on white of Genoa, the white Maltese cross on blue

Although flags used by the Roman Empire had no lasting impact on later Italian flags, the Latin *vexillum (above)* did provide the basis for the Italian word *vessillo* or banner.

of Amalfi, and the white cross on red of Pisa – are all religious emblems. Not only has Italy been the very heart of Catholic Europe for centuries, but many of its flags and other symbols date back to the early medieval era when almost every flag was an open prayer for the well-being or success of the enterprises of those who bore it.

Each of the apostles and a vast number of saints had specific emblems which were readily identified by the illiterate masses when featured on standards. Many such symbols recalled instruments of torture, others simply referred to an incident in the life of the saint. It is said that the thundering voice of St. Mark was responsible for the choice of a lion as his emblem. It should be noted (see page 244) that a sword accompanies the lion in the Italian war ensign, while the civil ensign has the lion holding a book with the same paw. On the statues, tapestries, paintings, and numerous other artistic representations found throughout the city of Venice and in territories formerly under its control, this book is inscribed with a Latin phrase. The words translate as "Hail to Thee, Mark, My Evangelist," and the story of that quotation relates directly to the political history of Venice and its choice of Mark as a patron saint.

In the late thirteenth century Jacob Varazze wrote a book which was very influential in displacing St. Theodore, the original patron of Venice, and in having the new patron saint figure extensively in municipal iconography. We are told that an angel used the Latin salutation, now inscribed on the lion's book, in hailing St. Mark who had stopped in Venice on a trip from

The figure of St. George slaying the dragon on this gonfanon *(left)* marks it as the standard of Genoa, although that city was not the only one to recognize St. George as its patron. The illustration is taken from a thirteenth-century manuscript history, but the shape of the flag is not very different from the later Venetian banner shown below.

Alexandria to Aquileia, where he was to become bishop. The angel promised veneration for Mark's bones at Venice, and indeed in 828 two Venetian merchants in Alexandria made off with the saint's mortal remains, bringing them back to their home city. Thus, according to Varazze, not only did the island of Rialto provide shelter to the Evangelist during his travels in lifetime, but protected him even after death.

While the basic design has remained the same since about the 1300s, the flag of Venice has been represented in an endless variety of interpretations. In the late seventeenth-century version shown above, the lion stands partly on land and partly on water, indicating Venetian domination of the city's hinterland and of the Adriatic.

In the 1100s and 1200s sphragistic documentation suggests that the flag bore an actual representation of the saint, the lion symbol being adopted about 1300. Gold and red were perhaps chosen as the flag colors because of prior use by the Byzantine Empire, whose territories Venice was in the process of acquiring. The traditional form of the flag, still proudly displayed today in the Place of St. Mark, has four squared tails. The very pole it flies from is of historic importance, being the original model for the Venetian entasis taper which modern flagpoles copy to achieve beauty combined with great height.

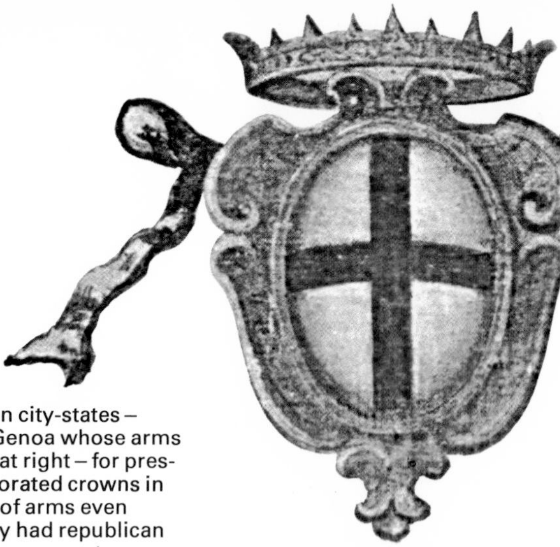

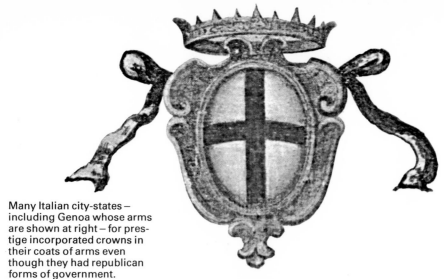

Many Italian city-states – including Genoa whose arms are shown at right – for prestige incorporated crowns in their coats of arms even though they had republican forms of government.

While less dramatic in form than the Venetian ensign, the cross of Genoa is at least as ancient. Earlier references are unsure but by December 1138, when the town achieved the privilege of minting its own coins, we have certain evidence that the cross was used as a symbol. St. George replaced St. Lawrence about that time, probably under the influence of the Crusades. In 1198 a red flag bearing a representation of St. George slaying a dragon distinguished the admiral of the chief galley of the Genoan fleet; a similar banner used on land appears in an illustration of 1227. References in the thirteenth century indicate joint use of the cross of St. George (red on a white shield, i.e., the same emblem adopted in this era by the English) with the lion of St. Mark, to indicate that the two naval powers were at peace. For the next six hundred years through varying fortunes the Genoese continued to honor St. George and his cross, although the motto of the state proclaimed in Latin "Golden Liberty Is the Genoese Flag."

As was common in other European states, elaborations from time to time appeared of the basic design. We have examples of the flag of Genoa in which either the word *justicia* or *Ianua* is written across the top. The former is Latin for "justice," the latter the name of Genoa (from the god Janus) in the same language. In the eighteenth century the elaborate heraldic style of the time produced a white flag with the full armorial bearings of Genoa in the center. Yet even when Napoleon transformed Genoa into the Ligurian Republic in 1798 and later when in 1814 the provisional government of the Most Serene Republic of Genoa was proclaimed under British protection, the red cross on white was universally recognized as the special emblem of the city.

As an independent entity Genoa disappeared

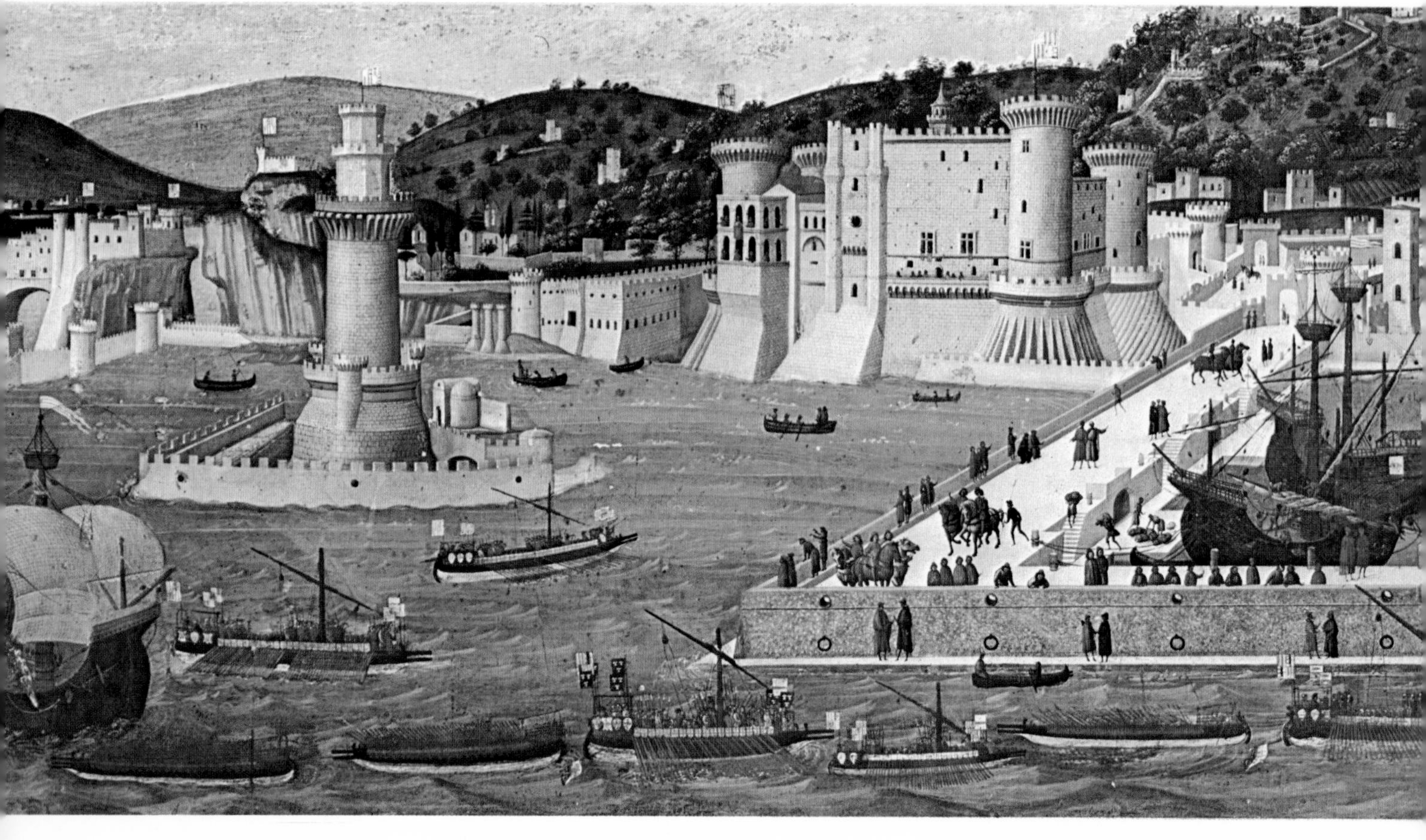

This fifteenth-century view of Naples shows that flags on ships in that era were often attached to poles which were removable, rather than being hoisted on halyards to permanently affixed poles, as in modern vessels.

Napoleon I, King of Italy as well as Emperor of France, personally chose the color green for Italian military flags, such as this faded example *(far left).* He also favored the imperial eagle holding a thunderbolt, a symbol which had been used in the Roman Empire. Another favored emblem was the golden bee, which many Frenchmen in the eighteenth century believed had been the royal symbol of King Clovis of France. Such bees appear in the flag of the island of Elba, which Napoleon ruled after his first fall from the French throne in 1814. That flag, designed by Napoleon himself, continued to be used by Elba *(left)* – as a canton in the state flag of Tuscany – when the island became a part of that nation.

forever in 1814, absorbed by the Kingdom of Sardinia. The Sardinian flag of that era also incorporated an ancient emblem – a white cross on red, the opposite of Genoa's symbol. The Savoy cross used by Sardinia is reputed to go back to 1147, although certain references date only to 1263. It is similar in design to a number of other European flags, notably those of Denmark, Malta, and Switzerland, all of which may have been influenced by the war flag of the Holy Roman Empire (see page 115). At first the flag represented the Counts of Savoy and their domains in the Piedmont; Sardinia was acquired in 1718.

In order to distinguish the Savoyard flag from other similar ones, particularly the Maltese flag frequently seen in the Mediterranean, the letters FERT were added in white to the four quarters of the red field. Some have seen these as an abbreviation for the Latin Motto "His Strength Held Rhodes" (referring to the military bravery of Amadeus V in 1310) or "We Are Bound by Covenant and Religion" (a device appearing on old coins). The red emblem with its white cross was also made more distinctive by adding blue to the flag, possibly in honor of the Virgin Mary. In the mid-eighteenth century, for example, we find the cross emblem in the center of a blue flag narrowly bordered in red; in a red flag with a white cross throughout, the whole narrowly bordered in blue; or in a blue flag with a red canton bearing the white cross. The second pattern, in shield shape, would a century later be added to the Italian national flag where it remained as a reminder of the ruling House of Savoy until King Victor Emmanuel III was deposed in 1946. The third Savoyard banner is also of interest in the story of how the Italian national flag developed.

On 30 December 1814 King Victor Emmanuel I proclaimed as the war ensign and diplomatic flag of the Kingdom of Sardinia a design incorporating the crosses of his various realms. This became the war and state flag in 1848, just a few months before it disappeared forever, giving way to the Tricolor. The field of the flag was blue; the red canton displayed the white cross of Savoy. On top of that cross was placed the red cross of the traditional Sardinian flag, first introduced in 1297 by King James II of Aragon who had received the island from Pope Boniface VIII. (That white Sardinian flag with its red cross would have been exactly similar to those of Genoa and England except for the "Moor's head" added in each of the four quarters to symbolize the struggle against Islamic forces to the south.) A shield of the Sardinian flag design was one of many incorporated into the arms of the Savoyard kings in the eighteenth century. In the flag of 1814, however, there was no place for the Moors' heads: on top of the red cross of Sardinia was placed the red cross of Genoa, fimbriated in white so that it would be visible.

Although this flag reflected the unification of some Italian territories, the spirit in which it did so was clearly one of a past era. Monarchs for hundreds of years had been combining the arms (real or imagined) of territories under their control, formerly under their control, or which they felt they had some proper basis for seeking to control. Family lineage might also be reflected in these arms which, while emphasizing the legitimacy and majesty of the ruler, had little or nothing to say about the achievements and

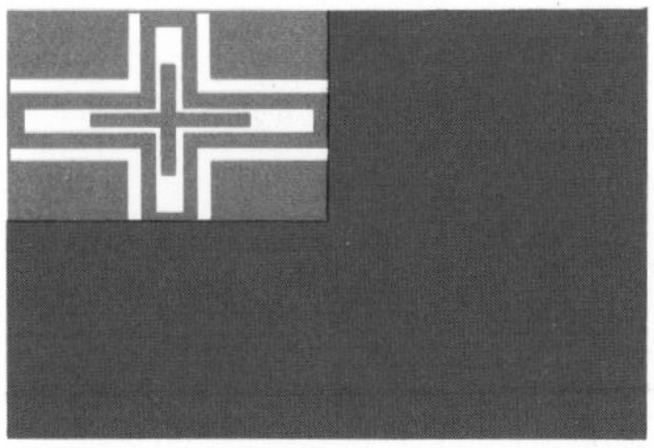

SARDINIA 1814–1848.

White predominated in the flags of the Pontifical State, the temporal territories in Italy ruled by the popes until 1870. Different designs *(below)* were used for warships, merchant vessels, and, in the presence of the pope, on warships and forts, respectively.

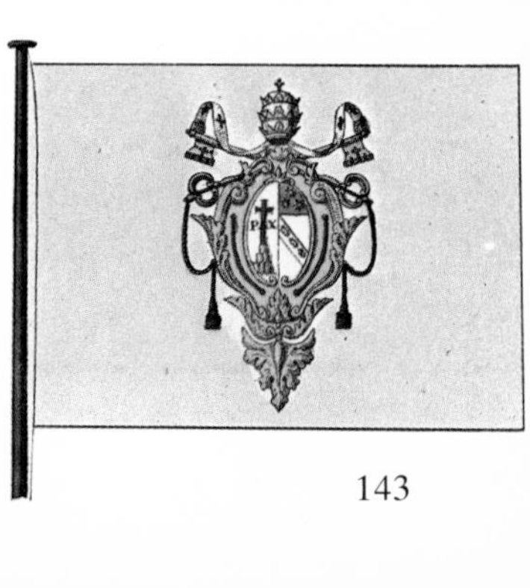

In the early nineteenth century the personal standard of the King of Sardinia *(right)* featured the Savoy coat of arms with the symbols of all those areas which he actually ruled or which he claimed by right of inheritance. In addition to the initials FERT (discussed in the text), the border features the Savoy dynastic badge, the so-called knots of love.

aspirations of those living in the lands represented. Of course what was true of "national" flags in the early nineteenth century was *a fortiori* characteristic of royal banners. The King of Sardinia displayed on a bordered field his royal achievement combining the arms of Sardinia, Jerusalem, Lusignan, Montferrat, Cyprus, Genoa, Piedmont, and two shields for Savoy (Savoy Ancient featured a black eagle on gold in contrast to the cross figuring in Savoy Modern) – but nothing clearly representing Italy.

KINGDOM OF ITALY 1848–1946.

ITALIAN SOCIAL REP. 1944–1945.

SINCE 1946.

The painting above by Quinto Cenni does not represent a specific moment in history, but rather illustrates the changes in uniforms and flags of the Royal Piedmont Regiment from 1692 to 1892.

The spirit of the future was perhaps better expressed by the flag of Carbonari used during numerous liberal revolts in the early nineteenth century. Inspired by the principles of the French Revolution, these "charcoal burners" had formed a secret society dedicated to the overthrow of existing monarchies, expulsion of foreign powers from Italy, and introduction of liberal democratic principles into the constitution of a unified Italy. Their flag, first hoisted in Naples at the proclamation of the Parthenopean Republic in 1789, was composed of black, red, and blue stripes. These symbolized charcoal, its glow when burning, and the smoke it gives off, as well as faith, love, and hope.

Flags of three symbolic colors had become popular in Italy under the influence of the French Revolution. Some were simple tricolors, such as the horizontal red-blue-orange employed by the Republic of Piedmont between 1796 and 1801; some followed the diamond pattern of French military colors, such as the flag of the Republic of Lucca between 1803 and 1805 (see page 136). Perhaps the most striking was the flag of the Parman State of 1851–1859; within a red border was featured a gyronny of eight blue and yellow pieces. None of these tricolors, however, has the historical interest of the green-white-red, whose origin is probably to be found in the uniforms of the Urban Militia of Milan. Since these were white and green, the troops were popularly referred to as "little turnips." Following Napoleon's invasion of Lombardy in 1796 and the erection of a Transpadane Republic, this militia became the new republican National Guard. Crimson accessories were added to the uniform, and on 9 October 1796 each cohort received a standard whose field consisted of vertical green, white, and red stripes. Although itself only a military color, this flag may be looked at as the progenitor of the national Tricolor.

Credit for introducing the same colors into a civil flag belongs to a neighboring state. On 16–18 October 1796 an assembly held in the city of Modena gave birth to the Cispadane Federation. Although French troops established the conditions under which the new state (renamed the Cispadane Republic in December) might develop, a local militia was created under the name of the Italian Legion. Its uniform consisted of a green cloak with red piping and white waistcoat and trousers; plumes of white, green, and red were worn on the hat. On 7 January 1797 the same three colors were adopted for the Cispadane cockade and for the horizontal trico-

lor of the republic. The latter must be considered the first authentic Italian national flag, although it lasted only from 25 February to 19 May of 1797. This flag bore at its center a coat of arms proposed by Napoleon himself: the principal charge was a quiver with arrows representing the towns of Bologna, Ferrara, Modena, and Reggio. Soon afterwards Napoleon ordered the Cispadane Republic united with the Transpadane Republic, forming a new state – the Cisalpine Republic.

On 11 May 1798 the Cisalpine Republic made official the flag it had been using without legal sanction, a plain vertical tricolor of green-white-red, today the Italian national flag. That the Cisalpine flag varied from the French flag of that period only in the color of the stripe nearest the hoist may have been one of the factors leading to a revised design. Differing only in their proportions, the war flag and war ensign were ordered as of 20 August 1802 to be red with a

As Italian head of government, Benito Mussolini displayed a distinctive personal flag *(right)*. The fasces which gave his party its name figures prominently in the center.

The painting below shows Florence in 1865 with a profusion of flags. The event is the dedication of a statue to Dante on his 600th birthday.

This propaganda postcard of 1944 issued by the Italian Social Republic exhorts soldiers to fight in the spirit of the poet Goffredo Mameli who died on 3 June 1849 in the defense of the Roman Republic against the Austrians.

FRATELLI D'ITALIA
L'ITALIA S'È DESTA!
1849-1944
LO SPIRITO DI GOFFREDO MAMELI
DIFENDERA' LA REPUBBLICA SOCIALE

Few flag pageants anywhere in the world match the color and spirit of the Palio of Siena. Every year the seventeen districts of the city, each of which has a distinctive flag of its own, contend for the honor of having the Palio or palladium – an old flag with an image of the Virgin Mary – displayed in its church for the following year. In addition to their use during the brief horse race which decides the question, the flags of the seventeen *contrade* are extensively displayed by the citizens who support them, including flag tossers *(above)* who perform skillfully executed maneuvers with flags on weighted poles.

white diamond throughout bearing a green rectangle. When Napoleon transformed France into an empire he also ordered changes in his Italian dominions. The Cisalpine Republic, in 1802 renamed the Italian Republic, now became the Italian Kingdom and a royal coat of arms was incorporated into its flag between 1805 and 1814.

Following the final overthrow of Napoleon there was a hiatus in the development of Italian unity; the Tricolor, while continually growing in popularity among the masses of people, officially disappeared. The tempestuous events of 1848 not only revived its use but established it permanently as the one flag to which all Italians seeking the liberation and unification of their country could turn. On 23 March 1848 King Charles Albert of Sardinia ordered his troops, about to go to war with the Austrian forces who occupied northern Italy, to carry the Italian Tricolor. In actual practice many variations appeared, but officially the center of the white stripe was to bear the red shield and white cross of the House of Savoy, surrounded by a blue border. The same model on 15 April 1848 replaced the former Sardinian civil ensign and, with the crown above the shield, also became the war ensign. Subsequently, civil and military regulations were issued dealing with certain details of the usage and design of this flag.

The importance of the Tricolor at this time must be measured in the inspiration it provided to the Italian unification movement. The hopes raised early in 1848 were to be cruelly disappointed by the events of the succeeding year – as is graphically documented in the transformation of flags given on pages 56-57. Yet if this green-white-red tide was forced to retreat in the face of superior Austrian military strength, the next one was decisive. In 1858 the Tricolor of the Kingdom of Sardinia swept over much of northern Italy; two years later Giuseppe Garibaldi brought the rest of the country (except for Rome and Venetia) under this banner and the rule of King Victor Emmanuel II. On 18 March 1861 the monarch proclaimed the modern Kingdom of Italy and less than a decade later the Roman States were added to his realm, the pope losing his position as a temporal ruler. In 1929 a very tiny part of the papal territories were restored, but except for the flags of the Vatican and San Marino, the entire Italian peninsula since 1870 has lived under the Tricolor.

In the twentieth century Mussolini's Fascist regime introduced many new symbols in all areas of Italian life, especially the political and military systems. Fasces were added to the coat of arms of the kingdom, but the state and war flag and the civil ensign were untouched. In the last days of World War II, Mussolini fled from advancing Allied troops and found protection in the German-occupied part of northern Italy. There he proclaimed the Italian Social Republic which was endowed with a coat of arms and several flags. The former was simply a shield vertically striped in the national colors and bearing a gold fasces on the white: an eagle was featured as the crest. A similar eagle, grasping a fasces, spread across the three stripes of the Tricolor in the war flag and ensign of the new republic. Its flag staff was to be topped by a special finial in the form of a fasces. The inspiration for the use of the eagle and the fasces may be found in a coin issued by the Roman Republic in 1799; it in turn was derived from a classical motif of imperial Rome found in the Forum of Trajan. The civil flag of green-white-red was without either a Fascist or royal emblem.

With the fall of the Italian Social Republic in May of 1945 the plain Tricolor disappeared officially, to be resurrected the next year and made the state and civil flag, following the proclamation of the Italian Republic. Thus finally the name and flag of the 1798–1802 Italian Republic, which had helped to put Italy on the path toward unity, democracy, and freedom from foreign occupation, were again official symbols. On the other hand the civil ensign and war ensign show that Italians have not forgotten their ancient heritage. Old heraldic charges – many more than can even be mentioned in so brief a résumé of Italian vexillological history – are cherished elsewhere. Cities and regions have adopted them, cultural and sports organizations keep them present in the attention of the public. They have been accorded legitimate recognition as ancient and honorable local symbols. What the past century has established is that no Italian symbol can detract from the primacy of the Tricolor.

Like many other central squares in cities around the world, Piazza San Marco of Venice gives prominence to the national flag as a reminder to all that the nation represented by these flags guarantees the very existence of both city and citizen. Except that the Venetian flag has replaced the central Tricolor, the scene in this painting from ca. 1850 appears almost exactly the same today.

MEXICO

"THERE, WHERE YOU SEE A CACTUS GROWING FROM A ROCK..."

Repeated endlessly in diverse art forms, the eagle and snake and cactus motif of Mexico is a six-hundred-year-old symbol that continually provides fresh inspiration to new generations.

After long wandering, the original Aztecs found the home promised by their gods under the eagle and cactus omen in the middle of a great lake. The traditional theme is interpreted in a sixteenth-century painting *(above)*. The eagle *(left)* recalls Aztec sacrificial practices as it tears apart a human heart.

While the flag histories of many countries are interesting for their diversity of distinctive banners and emblems, Mexico presents an example of the rich possibilities inherent in the reinterpretation of a single theme. Like the peacock in Burma, the lion and sun in Iran, the trinacria in Sicily, the lion in Ethiopia, and similar symbols elsewhere in the world, the eagle and cactus of Mexico may be found in every century and in almost every artistic medium.

Properly speaking, the eagle is always associated with certain other elements – a snake in its beak, a cactus on which it stands, and a rock (from which the cactus grows) rising from water. The whole constitutes a graphic representation of the foundation of Mexico City and, by extension, of the nation itself. According to legend, the Mexica tribesmen were ordered by their sun god Huitzilopochtli to settle where they should see a cactus growing from a rock – which they found about 1325 on an island in a lake. They called their settlement Tenochtitlan (the Place with the Cactus in the Rock). Representations of the founding of Tenochtitlan (Mexico City) invariably show an eagle on a cactus, although instead of a snake he sometimes is tearing apart a small bird or human heart.

It is impossible to calculate how many representations of this iconography are unknown to us today because they were destroyed by the Spanish. Their conquest of Mexico in 1521 was followed by an attempt to eradicate all traces of the Aztec culture. In 1642, for example, we find the viceroy, Dr. Juan de Palafox y Mendoza, writing indignantly to the municipal administration of Mexico City about the prominence of the eagle and snake in art and architecture. He wished to have them all replaced by Christian emblems; the council concurred and many ancient monuments were defaced by the removal of the offensive icon. Nevertheless the traditional arms continued to be popular – the eagle and snake more so than the cactus and rock. Mexican troops who invaded Florida in 1550 carried the earliest known representation of a flag bearing this device. The coat of arms granted Mexico City in 1523 by Emperor Charles V was frequently represented with the eagle as an unofficial crest. Even churches came to be decorated with the emblem.

It is scarcely surprising that the eagle and cactus was recognized as the premier symbol of Mexico when its revolutionary war for independence against Spain began. With a flag showing the Virgin of Guadalupe (see page 74), Father Miguel Hildalgo's Battle Cry of Dolores launched the revolution on 16 September 1810. Following his execution in 1811, another priest,

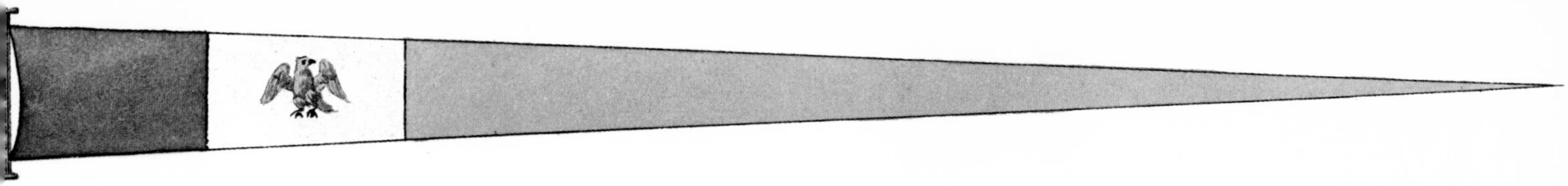

Since 1821 the Mexican flag has remained basically the same. The pennant version *(above)* is from an early nineteenth-century French source.

José María Morelos y Pavón, took up the cause. The colors he chose, light blue and white, were traditionally associated with the royal house of the last Aztec dynasty, Montezuma. A Morelos battle flag still preserved today shows a border of blue and white squares surrounding the eagle and cactus on a white field.

What appears to have been the first official Mexican national flag is reported to have been adopted on 14 July 1815. There were two versions: the war flag and ensign included an eagle and cactus coat of arms as well as the colors white, blue, and red. Documentary evidence is scarce and inconclusive, but it may be that the use of these three colors in revolutionary Mexican flags was due to the influence of the United States, Haiti, and France – three countries to which Latin Americans in that era looked for inspiration when seeking their own liberty. The vertical tricolor adopted by Mexico in 1821 must have been directly inspired by the French model it closely resembles.

The immediate precursor of that flag was a military color established, apparently between 30 April and 3 May 1821, by order of Agustín de Iturbide. He was a soldier sent by the viceroy to put down the decade-old revolt against Spanish authority, Mexican conservatives fearing the 1820 liberal revolution in Spain would spread to their own country. Instead of suppressing the revolutionaries, Iturbide joined them and together they were able to win complete independence for Mexico. Success was due in large part to their program (known as the Plan of Iguala from the town in which it was announced) which made Three Guarantees – religion, independence, union. This slogan meant that, while the conservatives were willing to accept independence, it must not be at the expense of the established religion which guaranteed their social, political, and economic dominance. Moreover, there was to be a union of all Mexicans – Spanish, Indian, and those of mixed blood – rather than a policy of majority rule which would have reversed the previous three hundred years of Spanish cultural domination.

The Flag of the Three Guarantees designed for Iturbide's troops showed white, green, and red diagonal stripes bearing stars (respectively of green, red, and white) and a central emblem. It is not clear if Iturbide had in mind a specific association between the three guarantees and three colors, but traditionally green is said to stand for independence, white for the purity of religion, and red (the Spanish national color) for union. In any event these three colors have been the basis for Mexican flags ever since.

The Mexican arms above are respectively from the sixteenth, eighteenth, nineteenth, and twentieth centuries.

On 21 September 1821 Mexican independence was proclaimed, almost three hundred years to

the day after the Aztec empire had fallen to Cortés and his conquistadores. On 2 November of that year the Provisional Governing Supreme Junta ordered that the flag "should be tricolored, adopting perpetually the colors green, white, and red in vertical stripes and representing on the white a crowned eagle." The national arms were to consist of a cactus with an eagle,

Among the more famous flags of Mexican history are those of Iturbide and Maximilian *(above)*.

Famous for his reform law of 1857 which curtailed military and clerical control of Mexican life, Benito Juárez became the leader of the liberals during the 1858–1860 war of reform. He was elected president of Mexico in 1861, 1867, and 1871, and is honored in Mexico for leadership in the struggle to repel the French. Their army invaded Mexico and attempted to transform it into an empire under a European monarch who would be subservient to French interests.

its head bearing a prophetic crown: on 21 May 1822 Iturbide proclaimed himself emperor.

The empire ended on 1 February 1823 and on 9 April the Mexican arms (and hence flag) were modified. Not only was the crown removed, but the snake which had been omitted from the imperial emblem was restored and branches of laurel and oak were added around the base of the arms. Thus all the elements now included in the Mexican flag were established under the new republic.

In 1863, taking advantage of the American Civil War and the failure of Mexico to pay certain debts, Napoleon III of France sent troops who seized control of Mexico City. The new regime, welcomed by conservatives, was headed by an Austrian Hapsburg who became Emperor Maximilian. In 1863 imperial arms for Mexico were established, the eagle on its blue shield looking – not surprisingly – like the imperial arms of France. This coat of arms was revised in 1864 and on 1 November 1865 three new flags became official – the imperial standard, the war ensign, and the civil ensign. The civil ensign contained only the familiar vertical stripes of green, white, and red. The war ensign and imperial standard displayed the crowned eagle and cactus of the new arms on the central stripe, the latter flag repeating the eagle and cactus motif in each corner of the flag.

While the empire with its resplendent symbols was in control of much of the country, a legitimate republican government still existed under the flag of 1823. Its civil war over, the United States pressured France to withdraw troops from Mexico with the result that the empire of Maximilian collapsed and he himself – to the horror of European ruling classes – was executed at the order of President Benito Juárez, a Zapotec Indian.

The republic was safe, but republicanism was still weak. In 1880 a neoimperial style of eagle was established by President Porfirio Díaz, who controlled the nation until 1911. The revolution of 1910 which forced Díaz from office eventually led as well to a revision in the Mexican arms and flag. Venustiano Carranza, wishing to eliminate vestiges of the previous regimes, on 16 September 1916 officially called for a return to "the Aztec eagle," i.e., to one shown in profile with its head lowered and its body actively engaged in attacking the snake. This contrasted with the rather stiff heraldic eagle, seen front view with head raised, that had characterized the imperial and Díaz models.

The 1916 decree was followed by new laws in 1934 and 1968, the latter inspired by the Olympic Games hosted by Mexico City. Apart from distinctive artistic models for the arms, these laws had little impact in the basic appearance of the flag. Nevertheless the latest law sets forth in detail the etiquette associated with display of the flag and officially abolishes the plain green-white-red civil ensign which corresponded exactly to the Italian national flag in use since 1946.

The history of Mexican symbolism clearly reflects the pervasiveness a particular national emblem may achieve in a country. Modifications can and will appear, frequently corresponding to the artistic style of the day, but the basic image is perpetuated because the vast majority of people feel that it represents their nationality. In such circumstances ideological changes in the government are likely to be reflected only through renditions that emphasize a recognizable republican (or monarchical or communist or other) style, often achieved through the use of accessories. As in Mexico, so in Bulgaria, Cambodia, Malawi, Haiti, and other nations across the globe the flag with such a symbol simultaneously expresses pride in the national past and commitment to a particular national philosophy in the future.

The current official coat of arms *(right)* is the eighth since 1821.

Although angels award President Madero a wreath for his action in the constitutional crisis of 1913, the artist of the flag *(far right)* was determined that future generations not forget the nature of Madero's heroism. Emblazoned across the white stripe is the legend "On 9 February 1913 with this flag Señor President Francisco Madero marched forth from Chapultepec in the company of its cadets to defend our legality."

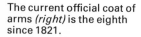

To the sound of drums the salute is given *(opposite page)* to the Mexican national flag, here the version official between 1934 and 1968. "Citizens: I come in the name of the nation to entrust to your civic sense, patriotism, and strict responsibility this flag which symbolizes your independence, your honor, your institutions, and the integrity of your territory. Do you promise to follow it with fidelity and constancy and to defend it until victory is achieved or life lost?" "Yes, we promise."

20 BI
19 BI

EGYPT

BANNERS OF INSPIRATION FOR THE ARAB WORLD

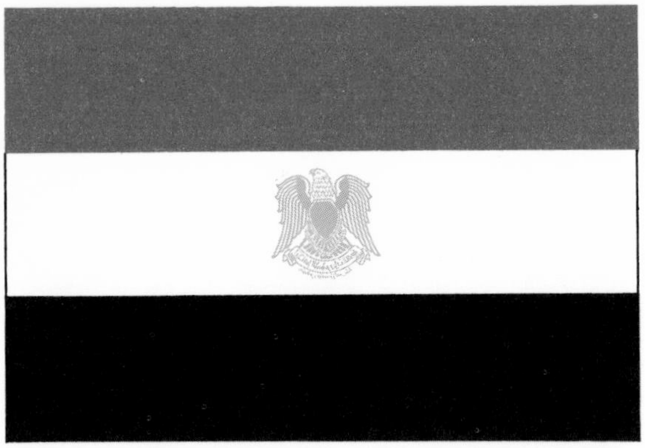

Although they are not united politically, Egypt, Syria, and Libya have flown the same flag *(above)* since 1972.

The nineteenth-century Egyptian flag *(right)* captured in battle by the British has a religious inscription characteristic of flags of that era.

Today the flag of Egypt is a model, both literally and figuratively, for other nations from the Indian to the Atlantic Ocean. This fact is clear from the chart on page 155 and in the flags of Libya, the Sudan, Syria, Iraq, Kuwait, the United Arab Emirates, and both Yemens. The leading role of Egypt is scarcely surprising to those familiar with international events since World

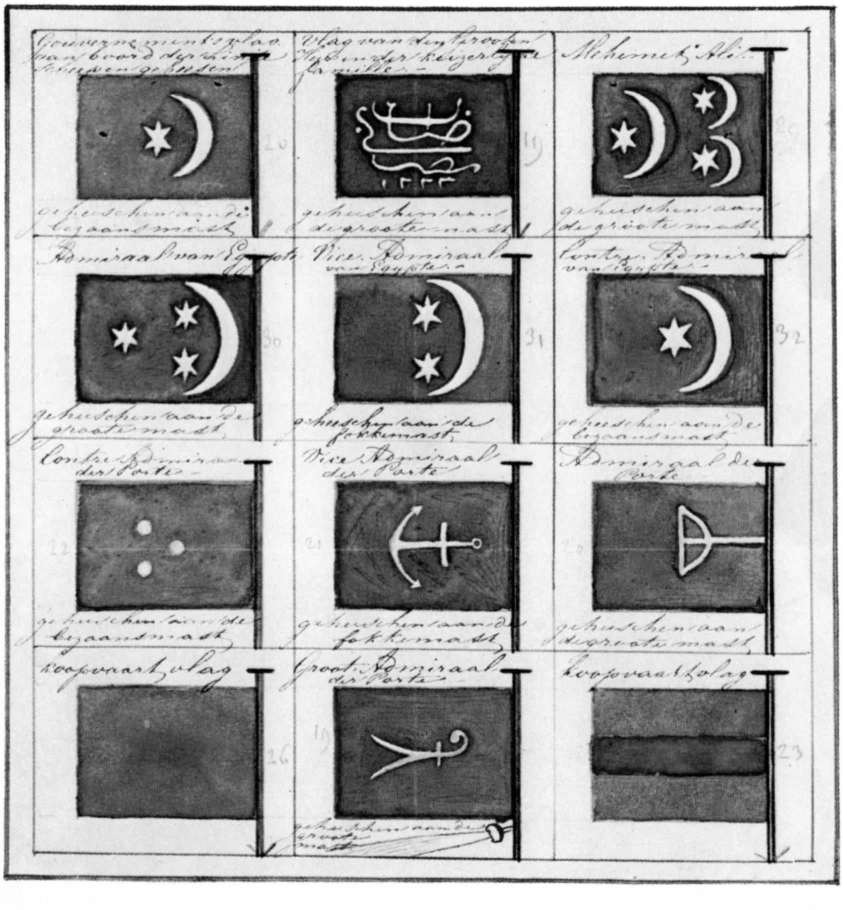

In the nineteenth century, Egyptian flags *(above)* were basically the same as those of the Ottoman empire. While Muslims used a green stripe through their red civil ensign *(bottom right-hand corner)*, the Christians of Greece substituted a blue stripe, and those of Albania, a black one.

War II, yet until the beginning of the twentieth century it seemed to many that Egypt was destined to be a follower of other countries in all things. Its prestige suffered especially because of inevitable contrasts with the achievements of ancient Egyptian civilization.

The troubled history of the past millenium and the transformation that has led to modern Egypt are reflected in the flags of that land. The military colors employed throughout the centuries, with few important exceptions, characterized dynasties imposed on Egypt from abroad. Their flags – including those of the Ummayads (white), Abbasids (black), Fatimids (green), Ayyubids (yellow), and Ottomans (red) – have already been described in *The History of Flags.* Even when the power of the Ottoman sultans was broken by the French invasion of 1798 and a free Egypt seemed possible, power was again seized by a foreigner. Muhammad Ali, an Albanian solider in the Ottoman army that had fought the French, introduced many reforms in the social, political, and economic organization of Egypt. Yet everything was done in the name of the Ottoman empire to which he professed allegiance.

The Ottoman flag in the nineteenth century normally bore a white star and crescent on its red field, although both Turkish and Egyptian ships very frequently displayed the old, plain red ensign. Muhammad Ali did introduce one distinctive new flag which eventually became the first real Egyptian national flag. Perhaps to symbolize the victory of his armies in three continents (Europe, Asia, and Africa) or his own sovereignty over Egypt, Nubia, and the Sudan, Ali set three white crescents and three stars on a red field. Technically only the personal standard of Muhammad Ali – and of those who followed him as hereditary rulers of Egypt under the title of khedive – the flag was at least a mark of distinction between Egypt and Turkey.

While industry, agriculture, education, commerce, and the political and military administration of the nation improved during Muhammad Ali's reign, the strategic and commercial significance of Egypt – and of the Suez Canal in particular – laid the stage for a transfer of effective power from Turkey to Britain. In 1882, Egyptian nationalists, seeking to take leadership in their own land by deposing the khedive, provided the pretext Britain sought for occupying the country. A promise was made that

Emperor Franz Joseph of Austria-Hungary sailed through the Suez Canal on the steamer *Greif* when that Egyptian commercial and military lifeline was first opened in 1869 *(below)*.

Her Majesty's troops would leave "as soon as the state of the country and the organization of proper means for the maintenance of the Khedivial authority will admit of it." But in fact the last British soldier did not abandon Egyptian soil until December 1956.

Technical Ottoman sovereignty over Egypt proved only a minor embarrassment when Britain and Turkey became enemies in World War I; on 18 December 1914 a formal British protectorate over Egypt was declared, followed by the deposition of the ruling khedive and the transformation of his flag into an Egyptian national flag. Agitation for independence began immediately, reaching a peak in the Revolution of 1919. While the red flag with its white crescents and stars was carried by Egyptians protesting British rule, a special banner was also seen in the streets. Its field was green and bore a crescent and cross to show that both Muslims and Coptic Christians supported the independence movement.

Although the revolution was suppressed, continued agitation led to the termination of the British protectorate in 1922. Fuad I became king and the Wafd (Nationalist Party), victorious in the elections of September 1923, adopted a distinctive national flag reminiscent of the one used in the revolt four years previously. Instead of a cross, the flag that became official on 10 December 1923 had three white stars arranged within a single crescent standing for Muslims, Christians, and Jews living in Egypt. Green, color of the nationalist movement and of the Hadji (Muslims who have made a pilgrimage to Mecca), suggested the fertility of the Nile Valley. It also provided a sharp contrast with the red Ottoman flag that Egypt had known for more than four hundred years.

This 1923 design was not replaced by a modern tricolor until some years after the 1952 revolution that overthrew the monarchy. Nevertheless the red-white-black Liberation Flag of the revolution was extensively flown alongside the national flag, often with the state arms added. These consisted of a representation in gold of the eagle of Saladin. This twelfth-century military and political leader represented Arab unity in the face of foreign threats of independence: in 1956 Egyptian soldiers fought under his eagle to repel British, French, and Israeli invasions of their country. The spirit of the Liberation Flag was that the years of past oppression (black) were to be replaced by a shining future (white) through the blood (red) which Egyptians were willing to sacrifice in reaching their goals.

A fourth pan-Arab color – green – was added to the Liberation Flag on 8 April 1958. On that

The flag of the Revolution of 1919 *(above)* influenced the Egyptian national flag of 1923–1958.

The crescent and three stars of the then current national flag were featured on the shield of the Saladin eagle in the Arab Liberation Flag *(above)* hoisted after King Faruq was deposed in 1952. The design of this Arab Liberation Flag soon completely replaced older symbols, however.

From 1899 until 1956 the Sudan was jointly ruled by Great Britain and Egypt. Therefore the flags of these two countries were flown jointly *(left)*, with the Union Jack always taking precedence – except in the city of Suakin, where the Egyptian flag flew alone.

President Gamal Nasser raised the Egyptian war ensign in 1956 when the British finally evacuated the Suez Canal area. This ensign resembled the state flag except that it had crossed white anchors in the upper hoist, as in the decorative pennant above Nasser's head.

Thousands of Egyptians mourned Nasser in 1970 as his flag-draped coffin was moved through the streets in the burial cortege.

Green is still the chief Muslim color in Egypt, and flags with religious inscriptions are used in parades and public ceremonies like the one above.

day it became the official flag of a new nation, the United Arab Republic, its two new stars representing Egypt and Syria, the nucleus for the unity which President Gamal Nasser hoped would eventually encompass all Arab lands. The new state arms repeated the Saladin eagle in a slightly different artistic form. The practical problems of integrating two noncontiguous territories characterized by cultural and historical dissimilarities caused the breakup of the United Arab Republic in 1961. President Nasser and his successor, President Anwar Sadat, nevertheless continued to strive for the unity they believed was necessary to solve Arab problems. The United Arab Republic's name and flag were employed by Egypt alone until replaced by similar emblems on 1 January 1972. On that date the official flag of the Federation of Arab Republics – consisting of Egypt, Syria, and Libya – was formally displayed for the first time at the seat of the confederation, Cairo. Many other attempts had been made at finding a common ground for extending Arab unity beyond symbolic attributes of statehood into substantive matters of economic planning, military coordination, and governmental structure. Some of the bonds, such as those which linked the United Arab Republic with Yemen in the United Arab States, were so tenuous that no common flag was even created. Others – such as the proposed 1963 union between Egypt, Syria, and Iraq – led to a permanent transformation in the state symbolism of two of the countries involved.

Outside observers have often commented on the seemingly insurmountable obstacles to pan-Arab unity. It is true nationalists have overemphasized the importance of the Muslim

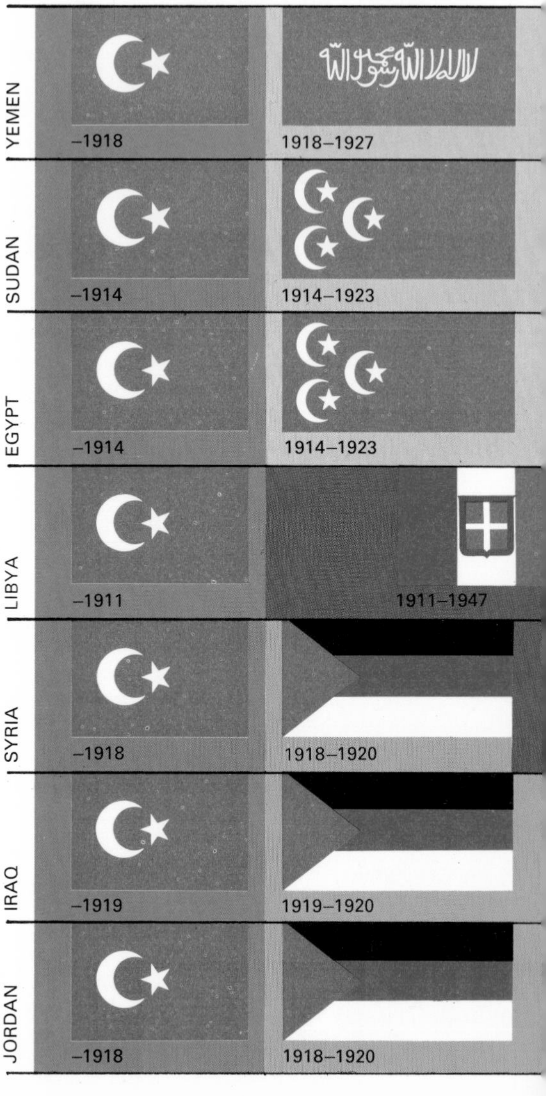

Egyptians welcomed the American president to their capital in 1974 with a display of their own national flag and that of the United States *(left).*

religion and Arabic language they share and have achieved more in the signing of declarations and introduction of unity flags than they have in effecting permanent structural integration of their lands. Nevertheless it is remarkable that, aside from Western Europe, the Arab world is the only area on earth where, since the end of World War II, serious efforts have been made to submerge national sovereignties in favor of a higher union. The future will perhaps allow some analysis to be made of whether the technocratic or symbolic program of integration is the more effective. In any event it is clear from the impact it has had in neighboring lands that the Liberation Flag of Egypt now stands as the premier symbol of political and economic independence, Arab socialism and democracy, the search for a Muslim rebirth through unity, and the other principles stated in Nasser's *Philosophy of the Revolution.*

THE DEVELOPMENT OF ARAB NATIONAL FLAGS, 1900–1975.

At the turn of the century most Arab countries were nominally under the star and crescent flag of the Ottoman empire. Upon gaining independence, some adopted flags which paralleled the Ottoman flag with its plain color background and stars and crescents; others used the Arab Revolt Flag or a variation including its four colors. Since 1958, however, the Arab Liberation Flag has been the basis for an increasing number of red-white-black flags varied with stars, triangles at the hoist, or a hawk. These four major design groupings, as well as non-Arab colonial flags, are indicated in the chart below.

- OTTOMAN EMPIRE
- "NEO-OTTOMAN" FLAGS
- ARAB REVOLT MODEL FLAGS
- NON-ARAB COLONIAL FLAGS
- ARAB LIBERATION MODEL FLAGS

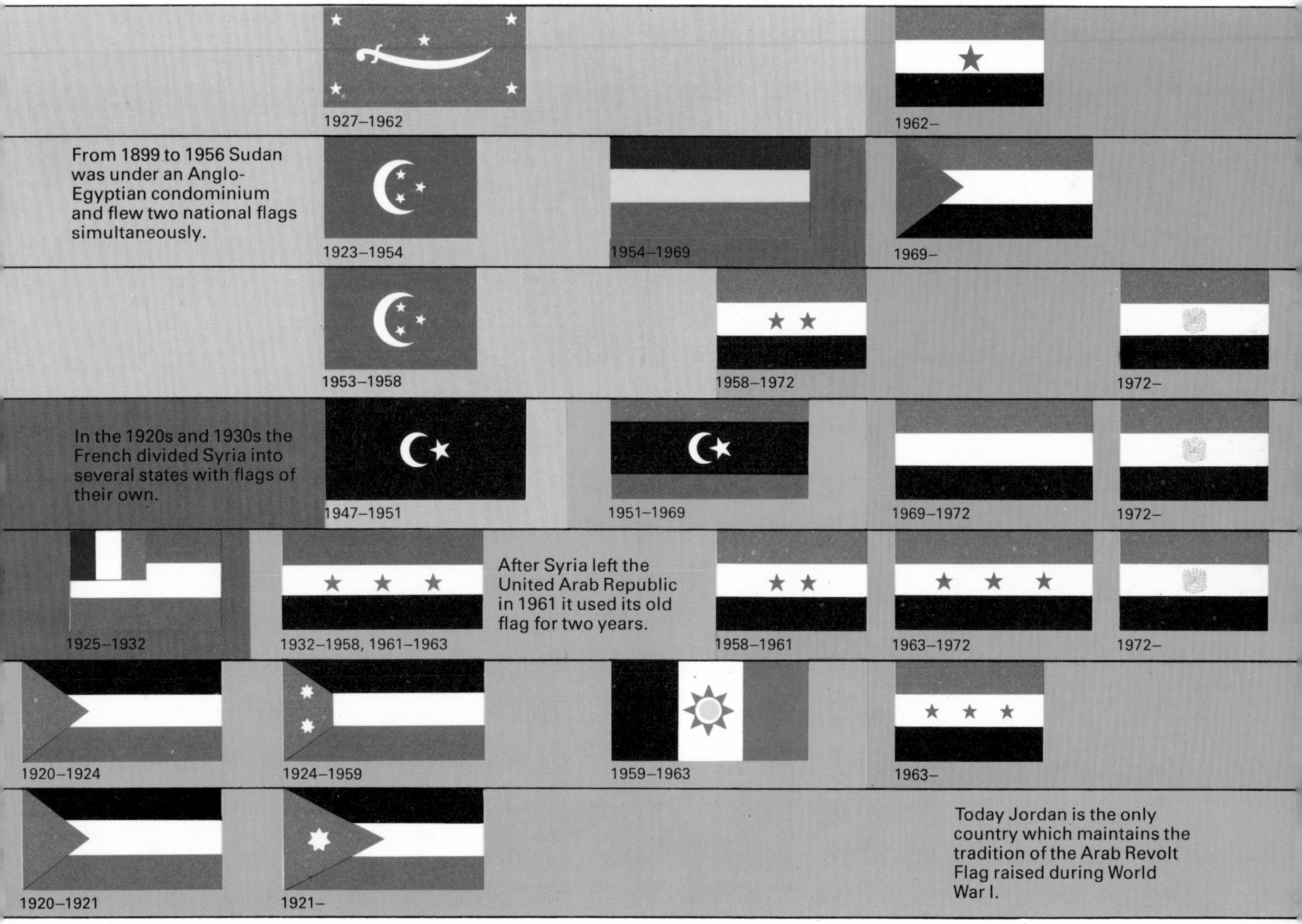

NETHERLANDS

"ORANJE BOVEN!" ("ORANGE ON TOP")

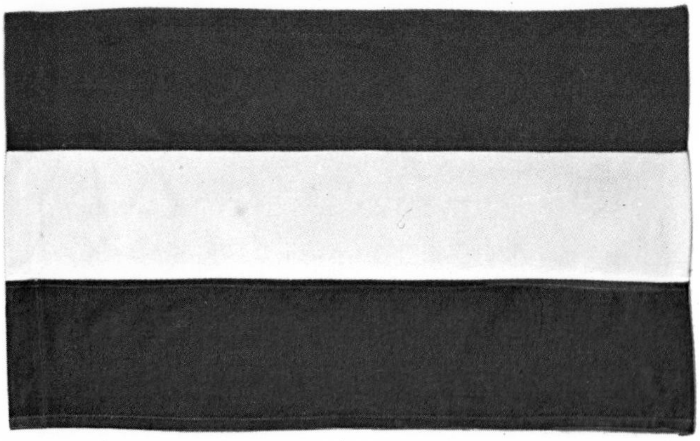

Red, white, and blue have come to be known as the "colors of liberty" because of their use in the national flags of the Netherlands, France, the United States, Britain, and certain other countries. Although the Dutch tricolor may not have directly influenced the choice of those colors by other nations, it is the oldest of them still continuing unmodified in use today.

Equal horizontal stripes of red, white, and blue: what could be more simple? Yet the history of the Dutch national flag is not simple, and the importance of this tricolor extends far beyond the small land area over which it flies. Reflecting the origins and development of Dutch independence and liberty in 1568–1648, this flag, despite its simplicity of form, stands today as a prime subject of vexillological interest.

From the Middle Ages many small territories along the North Sea had been under the Dukes of Burgundy; the Burgundian red raguly saltire on a white flag, also flown in Spain, was therefore common in the Low Countries. We even have reports of Dutch ships flying this flag when fighting against the Spanish, but the suggestion that it may have been the basis for the Dutch flag finds little substantiation beyond the similarity of the gyronny form of early Dutch jacks to the Burgundian saltire. This kind of jack was revived in the Netherlands in 1931; other flags based on the cross of Burgundy are found in Belgium, South Africa, Burundi, and the Basque Lands.

Despite Burgundian overlordship, local rulers and cities took pride in their ancient traditions of autonomy. Among the seventeen states which at the time constituted the Netherlands, the lion was a popular symbol. Henry the Lion in the mid-twelfth century chose a lion as the emblem of his cause, and Count William II of Holland did the same a century later (although some have suggested the beast originally was a wolf). Its popularity throughout the area is clear from the fact that lions appear today as heraldic charges or supporters in the arms of all Netherlands provinces.

One of these provincial shields, that of Sealand, has been suggested by some as the possible origin of the Dutch national flag and certainly few more appropriate emblems for the Netherlands could be found. The traditional red lion on gold appears at the top of the shield (or its banner counterpart); its lower half is hidden by blue and white wavy horizontal stripes representing the sea. The motto of the arms, *Luctor et Emergo* – "I Struggle and Emerge" – expresses the centuries-long effort of the Dutch to secure and expand their land area against the depredations of the North Sea. However, this scarcely proves that the red lion and yellow field of the Sealand arms were somehow transformed into an orange stripe and that the wavy bars below were reduced to equal stripes of white and blue, as has been claimed.

It seems more likely that the colors of this and other provincial and city flags played a different, albeit equally important, role: when orange, white, and blue were introduced from a different source, their similarity to favorite ancient symbols allowed for the interpretation of the new colors as extensions of existing symbols. In countless other countries around the world, such a process of assimilation has taken place; local vexillologists frequently find the colors of a modern flag prefigured in some ancient banner or manuscript or mural (see page 74, for example). Although coincidental, such color parallels help to establish the legitimacy of new symbols in the popular mind.

In the sixteenth century the Hapsburgs began repressive measures in the Netherlands, especially occupation of the area with a standing army recruited from other parts of the empire and massacres of those who did not subscribe to the Catholicism of Philip II. Philip had left his Dutch territories in the hands of William I, Prince of Orange, but William eventually turned

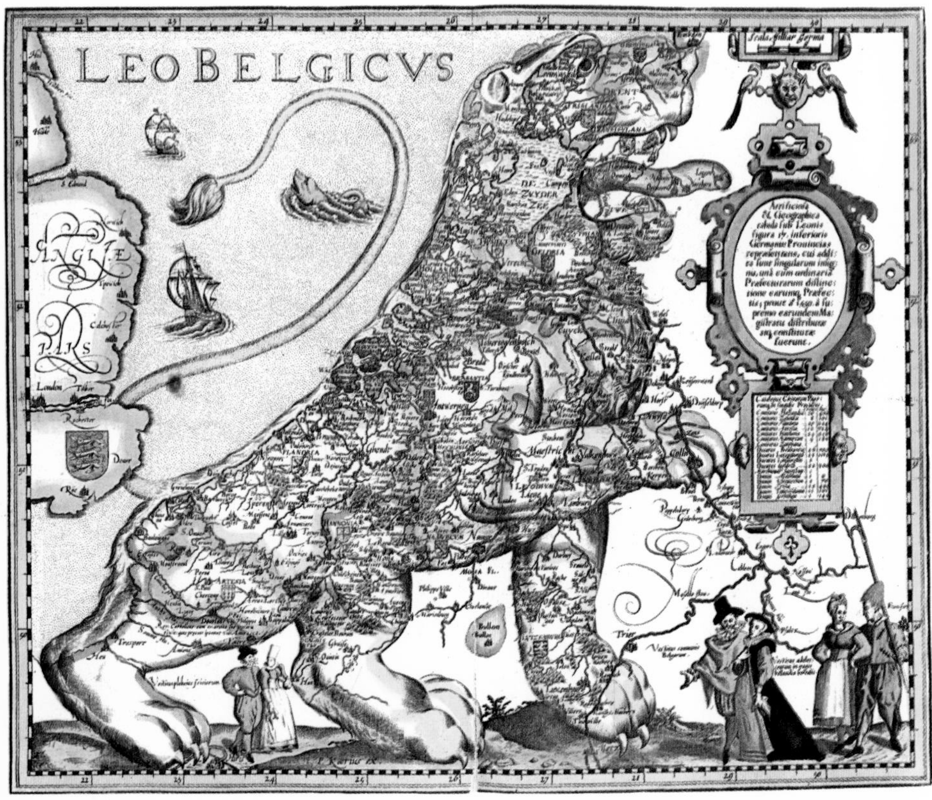

The "Belgian Lion" not only fit the geographic layout of the Low Countries when the seventeenth-century map *(above)* was made, but was appropriate because the lion had long been the political symbol of the Seventeen Provinces.

His refusal to reveal to his nominal Spanish masters his allegiance to the Netherlands, despite his knowledge of Spanish plans to massacre Dutch Protestants, earned Prince William the epithet "the Silent."

The de Gortter manuscript in the Royal Library in Brussels, from which the picture at left is taken, provides our best documentation of the flags used by Dutch and Spanish troops when the Netherlands was fighting for its independence in the late sixteenth and early seventeenth centuries.

King Charles I of Spain – the Holy Roman Emperor Charles V – annexed the Dutch provinces in 1548 to his Burgundian territories. He did not live to see the revolt against Spanish rule, in part inspired by the rise in Protestantism which he had fought against for decades. In his personal standard *(below)* the Netherlands are represented only by a tiny quartering in the shield on the breast of the eagle.

against his lord because of the latter's cruelty. When William was elected stadholder of the Seventeen United Provinces, the Dutch cause seemed hopeless. Behind the Duke of Alva were the armies and wealth of the Holy Roman Empire; Dutch nobles who petitioned the Count of Barlaimont for their historic rights were dismissed as "a bunch of beggars." Dutch patriots fighting on the open seas against Spanish rule took this derogatory comment as a mark of honor and called themselves the Water Beggars. When they seized the port of Briel, it sparked open revolution. The proclamation in 1579 of the Union of Utrecht was followed two years later by assertion of Dutch independence from Spain.

The flag of the Water Beggars was known as the Prince's Flag (in honor of William), and it seems likely that its horizontal stripes of orange-white-blue were taken from his livery. William was received at Ghent in 1577 by figures dressed in these colors and three years previously armbands of orange, white, and blue were worn by soldiers at the siege of Leiden. The Admiralty of Sealand in November of 1587 ordered flags of these colors for the cities of Flushing and Veere; they were recognized for the fleet sailing to Cadiz in 1596; and a manuscript showing soldiers from ca. 1590–1620 confirms the same usage on land. The battle cry of the Dutch, referring both to the stripe in their flag and the princely house to which they had entrusted their fortunes, was "Orange on Top!"

By the time Spain recognized Dutch freedom in 1648, the flag of the United Provinces was beginning to change. The first mention of a red stripe instead of orange dates from 1596; by 1630 the substitution was becoming common and apparently by 1660 the transformation was complete. The impermanence of available orange dyes may have encouraged the substitution of the stabler and more brilliant red, but political considerations are more likely to have been responsible for the alteration. The flag of the Dutch Estates-General was red with a gold lion (the reverse of the traditional Holland flag). In the seventeenth century the Estates-General represented those who opposed the centralization of power in the hands of the stadholder. The death of William II in 1650, following his attack on Amsterdam itself, put the Estates-General and its supporters in effective control of the country for a quarter century. Moreover, in 1654 the Dutch signed a defensive alliance with England and secretly promised Oliver Cromwell, then ruling that country, that members of the House of Orange would be excluded from the stadholdership.

Flags of Spanish design are evident in this detail *(left)* of a painting showing a parade of local troops in 1615 in Brussels, at the time a part of the Spanish Netherlands.

Although not fully documented, it seems likely that these political motivations influenced the substitution of red for orange. Orange was not forgotten, sailors recalling the glorious days of the Water Beggars under the orange-white-blue. That flag had been carried to the ends of the earth by the Dutch who – while still struggling for recognition of their independence – founded a colonial empire. In the East Indies and West Indies, Ceylon and Australia, South Africa and Brazil, New York and Malacca – across the oceans – the orange-white-blue provided a brief but glorious moment for the small republic of northern Europe. The influence is not entirely lost even today: many flags in New York and South Africa show a direct symbolic inheritance from the Netherlands.

The flag *(above)* from the Netherlands East Indies (now Indonesia) shows the arrival of Dutch trading vessels: one such ship (its flag misrepresented) is attacked from shore.

It must not be imagined that the early Dutch flag was standardized, any more than were national flags in other countries. The basic Prince's Flag was often displayed with decorative and symbolic additions – a lion, orange branches, or the abbreviation PPP (*Pugno Pro Patria,* "I Fight For the Fatherland") being especially popular. A plain orange or plain red flag as a symbol of war or of no quarter in battle can be seen in paintings of old Dutch ships. A similar flag with a mailed arm holding a sword emerging from clouds is also common; to the Calvinist Dutch Protestants, this was the vindictive arm of God ready to strike down Dutch enemies (but see page 73). In the late sixteenth and early seventeenth centuries there were, in addition, flags representing towns, provinces, and trading companies such as the United East-India Company and Chartered West-India Company.

In this early seventeenth-century print, troops from Amsterdam march under the slogan which has since become the national motto of Belgium – "Unity Makes Strength."

In the struggle for Dutch independence of 1568–1648, many variations of three basic types of flags were used.

Many of the symbolic themes of the early years were reinforced or readopted later. Thus when the House of Nassau came to the Dutch throne in 1815, its gold lion on a blue shield acquired the arrows and sword characteristic of the lion that had been adopted in 1578 by the Estates-General. Earlier, under the brother of Napoleon I (King Louis) the gold lion on red of Holland had been quartered with the gold imperial eagle on blue of France. The lion was also recognized by the Batavian Republic which replaced the United Provinces.

Following the French Revolution those who favored a republic in the Netherlands on the model of that established in France were known as Patriots. They came to power in 1794–1795 when French troops overran the Netherlands. A Batavian Republic, based on the French model and under French influence, was proclaimed, and on 14 February 1796 it adopted the red-white-blue tricolor in the first official Dutch national flag law. While the civil ensign was a plain tricolor, the war ensign included a white panel near the hoist with the symbolic figure of Liberty, holding a staff with a liberty cap and accompanied by the traditional Dutch lion. From 1802 to 1806 a yellow lion with a sword and arrows on a red shield constituted the official arms. On 5 June 1806, following the establishment of the Kingdom of Holland under Louis, this emblem was amalgamated with the eagle and other imperial symbols.

This new coat of arms caused the king considerable trouble. On 4 July 1806 it was announced that the arms would be introduced into the tricolor. Sailors at Texel refused to pledge loyalty to King Louis and hoisted the old flag; after all, the Patriots had struggled against stadholder William V precisely because their tolerance for monarchy was very limited. Ten days later the king announced in an official decree that the old flag would be preserved – although Vice Ad-

The symbol of the Estates-General was the lion, bearing a sword and a bundle of arrows representing the United Provinces.

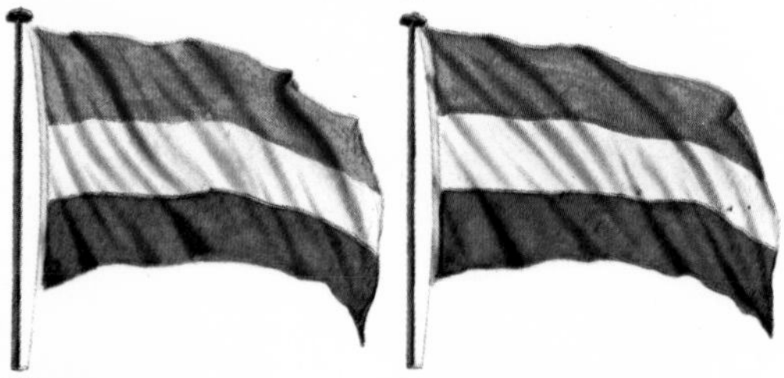

The Prince's flag of horizontal stripes was presumably taken from the orange-white-blue livery of William the Silent.

A variation of the Prince's flag showed the red, white, and blue in one of several gyronny interpretations.

The initials PPP are for the Latin phrase "I Fight for the Fatherland."

The Netherlands had probably a higher percentage of towns and cities with distinctive flags of their own than any other major nation. The municipal flags *(below)* show some of the older designs.

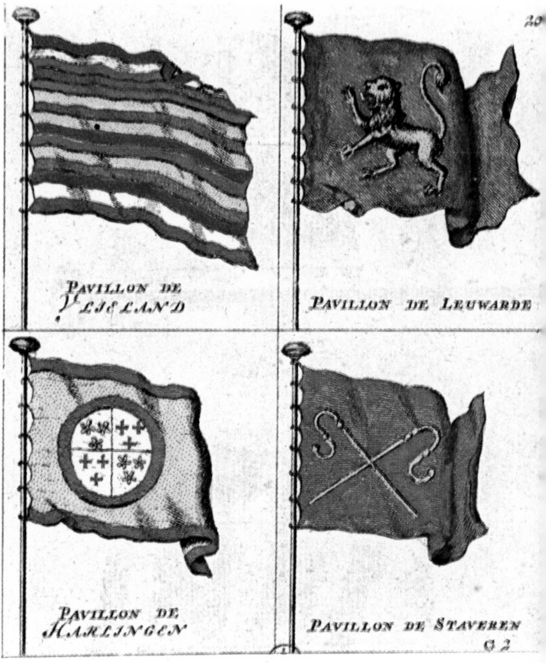

The Dutch stadtholder William III, who had married Mary, daughter of King James II of England, became joint sovereign of Great Britain with his wife in 1689 following the Glorious Revolution. The two principles of that revolution – liberty and Protestantism – are expressed in the flag *(left)* William flew on his ship when he sailed from the Netherlands.

miral Winter was sent to punish the rebellious sailors. The flag originally proposed by Louis, bearing his royal arms, was now limited to use as a jack; the plain red-white-blue reigned supreme as Holland's national flag on land and at sea from 1 December 1807 until 17 July 1810.

It was a twist of ironic fate that brought the Netherlands under the French Tricolor in 1810, when Napoleon annexed the territory. The Dutch flag had been looked at as the "colors of liberty" by French revolutionaries in the 1790s, and indeed one of the earliest of French republican flags was simply a swallowtailed version of the Dutch tricolor. The Patriots for similar reasons had not raised the question of a new flag for the Netherlands when they became the dominant political force. Nevertheless the red-white-blue of the Netherlands was abolished in 1810 in accord with Napoleon's imperial plans. On 24 November 1813, when Dutch independence was again established, the orange-white-blue was raised again, at least in some places. Following the definitive overthrow of Napoleon in 1815 it was the red-white-blue which found

In the late seventeenth century the Netherlands began to produce a great number of books and charts (including the one from which the ship above is taken) illustrating flags from around the world. As in the example shown, these were more decorative than practical in nature, but they did lay the groundwork for modern vexillological studies.

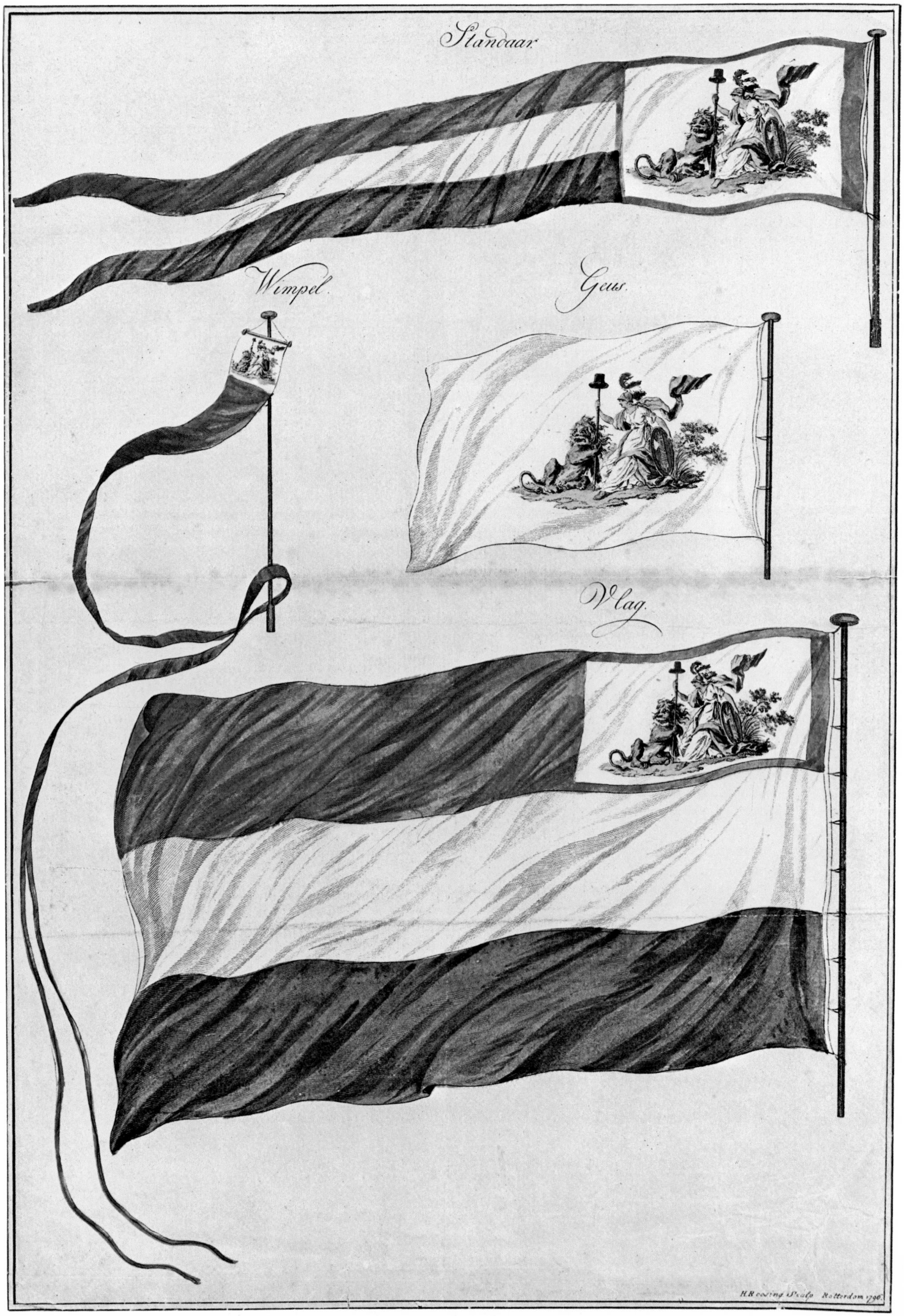

Standaar.
Wimpel.
Geus.
Vlag.
H.Roosing Sculp. Rotterdam 1796.

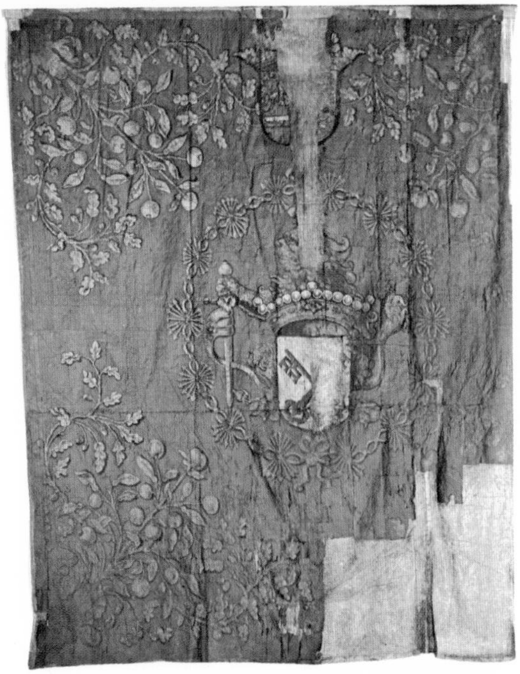

Fruited orange branches were frequent decorations in Dutch flags of the past, honoring the royal House of Orange.

were described as vermilion red, cobalt blue, and (for the pennant) standard orange.

No color has an intrinsic meaning, nor does any simple tricolor flag. For this reason even the simplest of designs, such as the Dutch orange-white-blue and red-white-blue, are susceptible to infinite interpretations. The history of the Netherlands over the past four centuries makes clear that there can be a dedication to the basic design or even meaning of the national flag while disagreement exists between segments of the population over political questions. It also makes clear that the flag itself can become, for one or another group, a means of promoting the policies and views they believe best incarnate the spirit of national life.

The arms of the new Batavian Republic figure in all the flags displayed *(opposite)* in the official government print of 1796. The traditional Dutch lion is combined with the figure of Liberty, whose shield is the Roman symbol of republicanism, the fasces. The pole she holds displays a distinctively Dutch version of the liberty cap.

NATALIA 1839–1843.

NETHERLANDS ANTILLES SINCE 1959.

LYDENBURG REP. 1857–1860.

NEW YORK CITY 1915–1975.

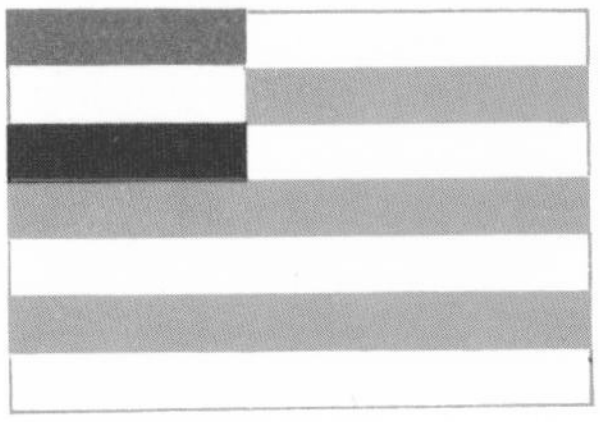

ORANGE FREE STATE SINCE 1857.

SOUTH AFRICA SINCE 1928.

TRANSVAAL 1857–1874, 1875–1877, SINCE 1880.

Flags from Africa, North America, and South America *(above)* show the continuing influence of Dutch flags on symbols of other countries where the Netherlands has had political or cultural involvement.

favor with King William I. The former Prince of Orange had been recognized by the great powers at the Congress of Vienna as the head of a new state, the Kingdom of the Netherlands, combining Holland and the former Austrian Netherlands, i.e., Belgium. A royal decree of 16 March 1816 approved the red-white-blue tricolor, and this has continued to the present day as the official Netherlands flag.

In the 1930s a movement for the reestablishment of the original orange-white-blue of Prince William the Silent gained some favor. Its strongest supporters, however, were the members of the fascistic National Socialist Movement, and the Queen put an end to the question, at least on the official level, by a royal decree of 19 February 1937 stating that the colors of the Kingdom were to be red-white-blue. Orange was to be used separately as a symbol of loyalty to the House of Nassau, being flown in the form of a pennant hoisted above the national flag. During the Second World War when the Netherlands was under Nazi occupation the display of orange to show loyalty to the exiled monarch was forbidden. At first the Dutch placed matches in their coat pockets so that the phosphorous tips would be a reminder of the Queen. Others used orange-tipped tulips or even carrots to show the same devotion to Netherlands independence. After the war precise scientific definitions were given to what

The Queen's Commissioner in Friesland displays six flags from his boat *(left)*. At the stern is the Dutch national flag; at the prow, the provincial flag of Friesland. A pennant of the Dutch national colors is at the head of the sail and the top of the mast bears a decorative streamer. Below it is the pennant of the Oostergo Royal Yacht Club and, below that, the personal rank flag of the Queen's Commissioner.

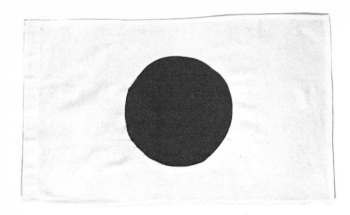

JAPAN

LAND OF THE RISING SUN

RED CIRCLE ON WHITE FIELD
THE RISING SUN FLAG IS
DRAWN; HOW BEAUTIFUL
THE JAPANESE FLAG IS! AS
THE SUN RISES IN THE SKY
IT HAS SUCH INSPIRING
POWER; HOW VIGOROUS
THE JAPANESE FLAG IS!

Japanese children's song

The spirit of the Japanese national flag, known as the Sun Disc, is as clear and simple as its design. Farthest east of any major nation, Japan's very name, which means Source of the Sun, suggested an appropriate symbol centuries before a national flag was developed and made official. So appropriate is the flag chosen in the mid-nineteenth century to represent the Japanese nationality within the country and externally among all the other countries of the world, no modification or alternate design has ever been proposed.

This does not at all mean that the history of the Japanese national flag is uninteresting. Unfortunately, all too little of that history has been revealed and, as in Western countries, many details are uncertain or lacking in substantiation. For example, it would appear that the form and symbolism of early Japanese flags – as well as their very uses – relied on traditions originally developed in China and perhaps transmitted to the Japanese simultaneously with the introduction of Buddhism in the mid-sixth century A.D. or during the reign of Prince Shotoku (593–622) who fostered the influence of Chinese ways in Japan. Two ancient chronicles, the *Jingo Kogo Ki* and the *Kinmei Tenno Ki*, speak of Japanese white flags of surrender used on the battlefield in the fourth century, but this does not rule out Chinese origins since our record of contacts between the two nations goes back to at least the first century.

Certainly from the description of the flags flown on the imperial palace on New Year's Day in

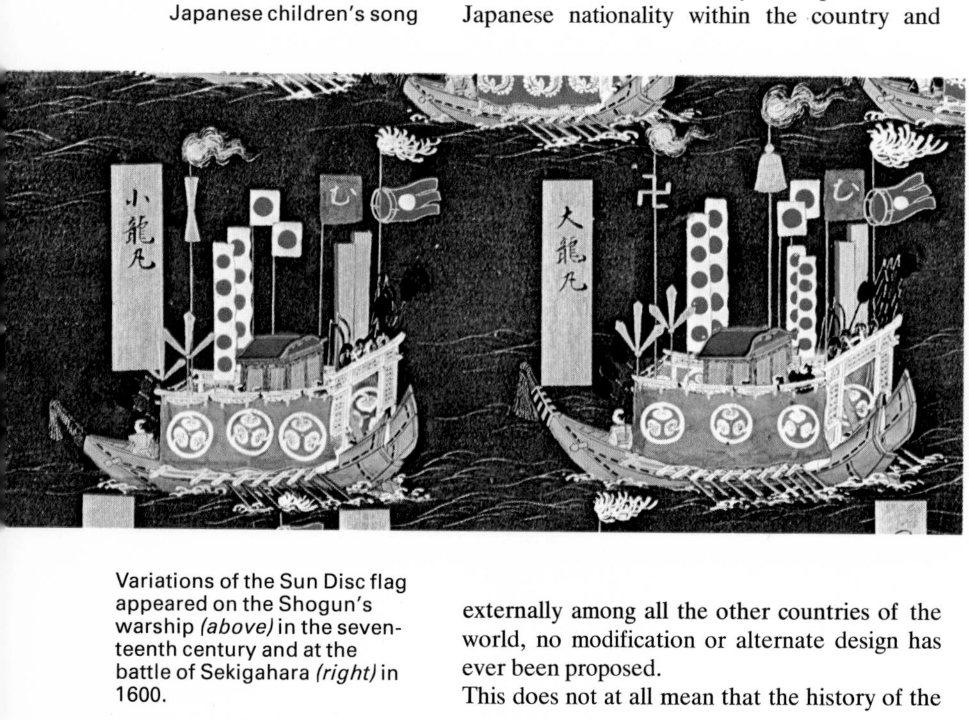

Variations of the Sun Disc flag appeared on the Shogun's warship *(above)* in the seventeenth century and at the battle of Sekigahara *(right)* in 1600.

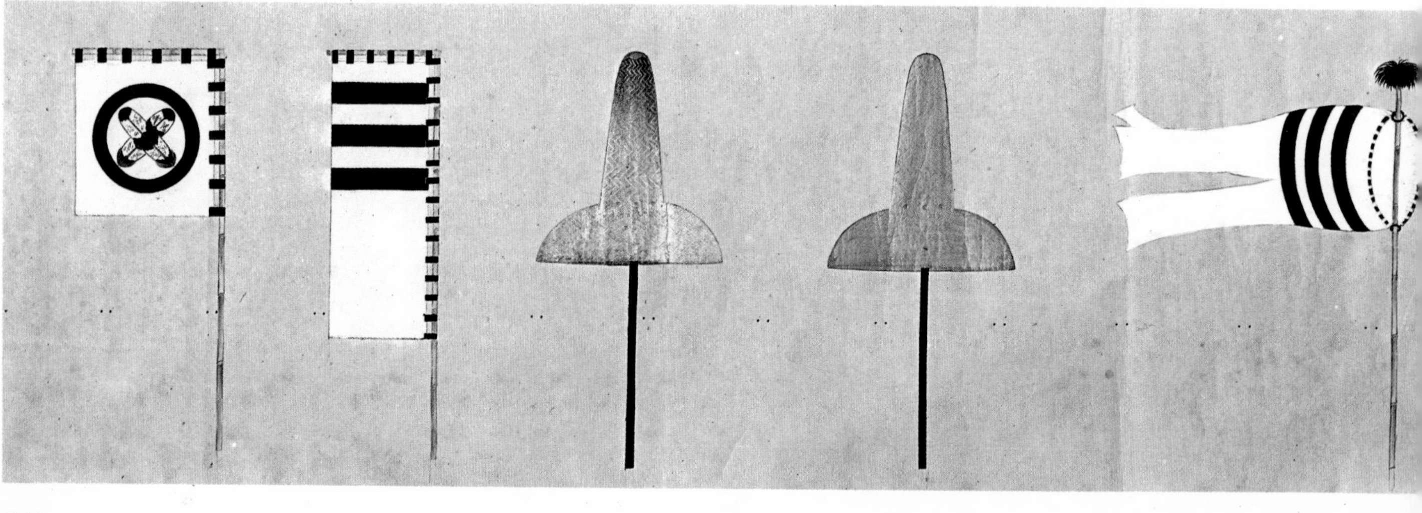

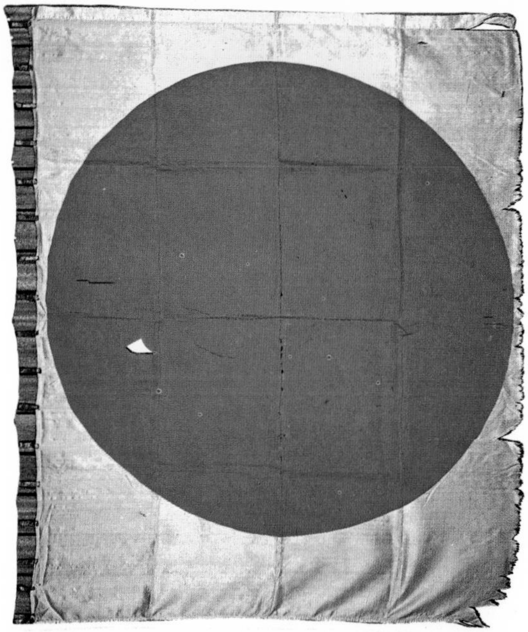

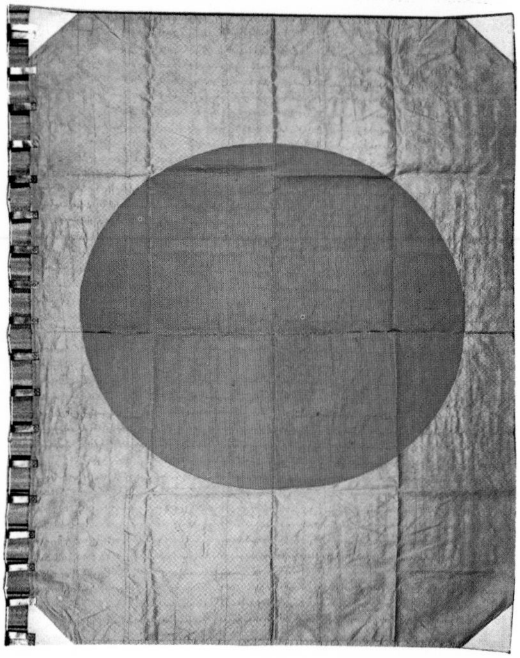

The two flags at left are known as Great Horse Standards. These war flags were always displayed next to the horse of the commander in a battle.

603 by Emperor Suiko, it is clear that the concept of certain colors and beasts being associated with the cardinal points of the compass had been adopted by the Japanese from China. An interesting point in our understanding of the Japanese national flag is that among the banners displayed by Suiko, one represented the sun. Similar flags are described in one of the oldest written historical records of Japan, the *Nihongi,* written about 720. It relates that on the very first day of the first month of the first year of the Taiho era (corresponding to 697 A.D.), Emperor Mommu received his aides and subjects in Taikyoku Hall. Before the court building were displayed various flags bearing representations of a crow, a dragon, a red bird, a tortoise, a tiger, and the sun and the moon.

The symbolism of these two celestial objects is clear: just as they shed their light both day and night over all parts of the world, so the emperor illuminates his nation at all times. Moreover, through the transmission of imperial authority from generation to generation the state is (in theory) assured of the immortality which characterizes the sun and moon. In Eastern philosophy there is further appeal in the use of these symbols together, corresponding as they do to the positive and negative forces of the universe expressed in the familiar yin-yang emblem. The circular form of both has a double meaning: it is all-encompassing and indicative of motion. In this way the state, epitomized by its sovereign, symbolically spreads its influence over every aspect of life, yet it is continually a changing institution.

Japan is far from the only nation in the East to have adopted this form of symbolism for its national flag. Based on long traditions, the Kingdom of Nepal and the People's Republic of Mongolia display both the sun and moon on their current flags. The sun, considered as a positive force, has appeared alone on the flags of the Republic of China (since 1928), Tibet

Overleaf
In the seventeenth century, personal banners with the distinctive *mons* (heraldic badges) of families became widespread in military usage. However, it is believed that the first flags in Japan were derived from a Shinto ritual performed by soldiers before going into battle. A halberd or other poled weapon was driven into the ground forming a "lightning rod" on which the deity invoked by a soldier might descend to his aid. At the top of such a pole was attached a piece of cloth bearing the name of the deity. This eventually developed into the flags we know today.

The sun emblem below, a detail from a flag believed to date from the early fourteenth century, represents the legendary *ho-oh* or phoenix which lives in the sun.

Like the armorial or roll of arms in Western tradition, the scroll of flags (shown at the bottom of this page and on pages 164, 168, and 169) was compiled in order to show which samurai had participated in a particular event.

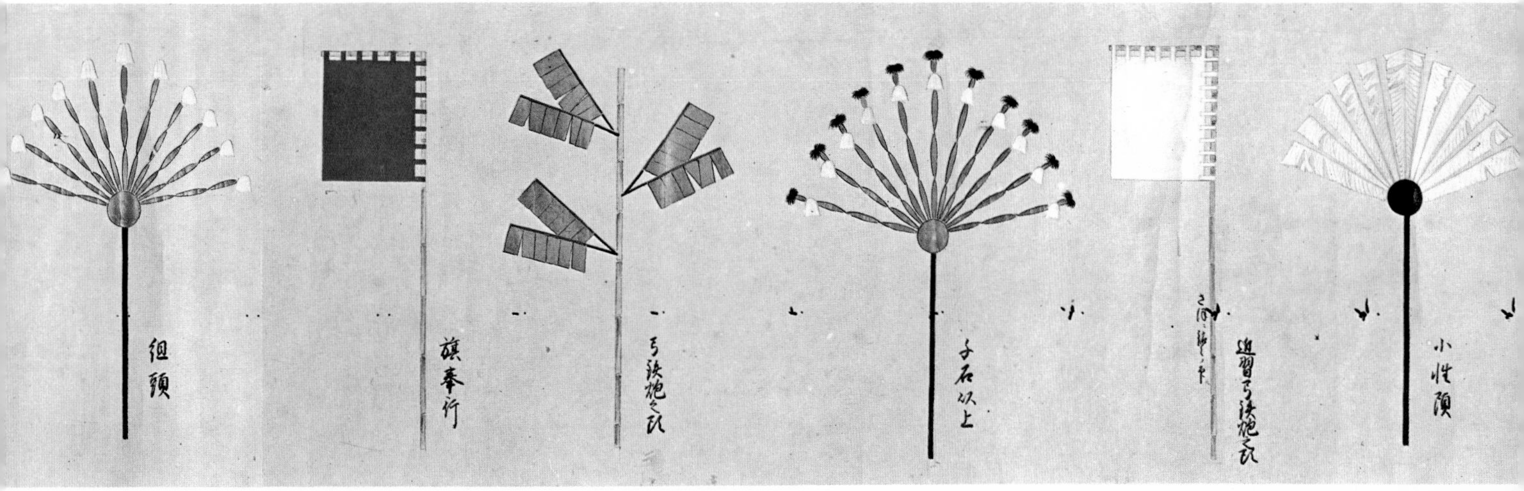

瓢軍談五十四場
三十三
久吉道秀
天王山を
真柴勢
折尾宇助
道秀勢

瓢軍談五十四場
四十五
賤ヶ嶽七本鎗之内和毛坂新内高名
市川藤助
和毛坂新内
和志見堅治

"Wind, woods, fire, mountain" (i.e., speed, silence, fierceness, firmness) is the military maxim of Sun Tzu inscribed on this sixteenth-century Great Horse Standard *(right)* used by Lord Shingin Takeda.

(1912–1959), Burma (until 1886 and between 1939 and 1945), not to mention many former princely flags in the Indian subcontinent. The would-be Republic of Taiwan has a blue flag with a sun and moon in white. The yin-yang symbol or a similar emblem has been featured in the flags of both Korean republics, the former Kingdom of Liuchiu, and the Japanese-sponsored government in Shanghai (1937).
The tradition of a banner with a sun and/or moon was especially strong in Japan because of the legend concerning the descent of the emperor. Traditionally the imperial line was established by the progeny of Amaterasu-Omikami, Heaven Shining Great Deity. From 660 B.C. when she founded Japan to the present day there are supposed to have been 124 emperors following in a direct line from Jimmu. Although the Shinto religion was officially disestablished in 1945, the chief shrine to Amaterasu-Omikami at Ise is still extremely popular. In addition to Son of Heaven, the emperor is called Sun God and Sublime Gate of the Sun; the sun is said to be his brother, the moon his sister.
In light of the constant reinforcement of the divine aura imputed to the monarch, it seems reasonable to surmise that there must have been flags with suns and moons even in times when documentary evidence is lacking. Some records do of course exist: manuscripts relate that under Emperor Godaigo (1319–1339), on the special brocade banner kept in his presence, a golden sun and silver moon were pictured on the obverse and reverse, respectively. There is a tradition that when Takauji of the Ashikaga family raised his revolt against Emperor Godaigo – leading to almost two hundred fifty years of Ashikaga rule in Japan – he began by capturing the sun and moon banner. Because of its close personal association with the divine ruler, Japanese warriors and commoners alike who

Painted on a folding screen *(above)* is one of the twenty-nine festive floats paraded through the streets of Kyoto during the Gion Festival. The flag at the top represents a prayer to a Shinto deity to descend and aid the bearers.

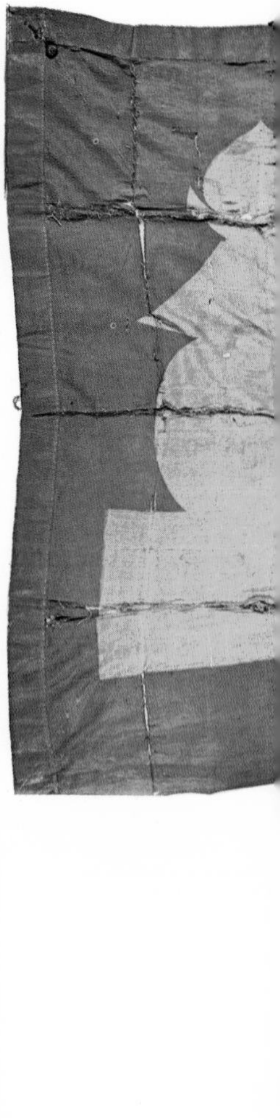

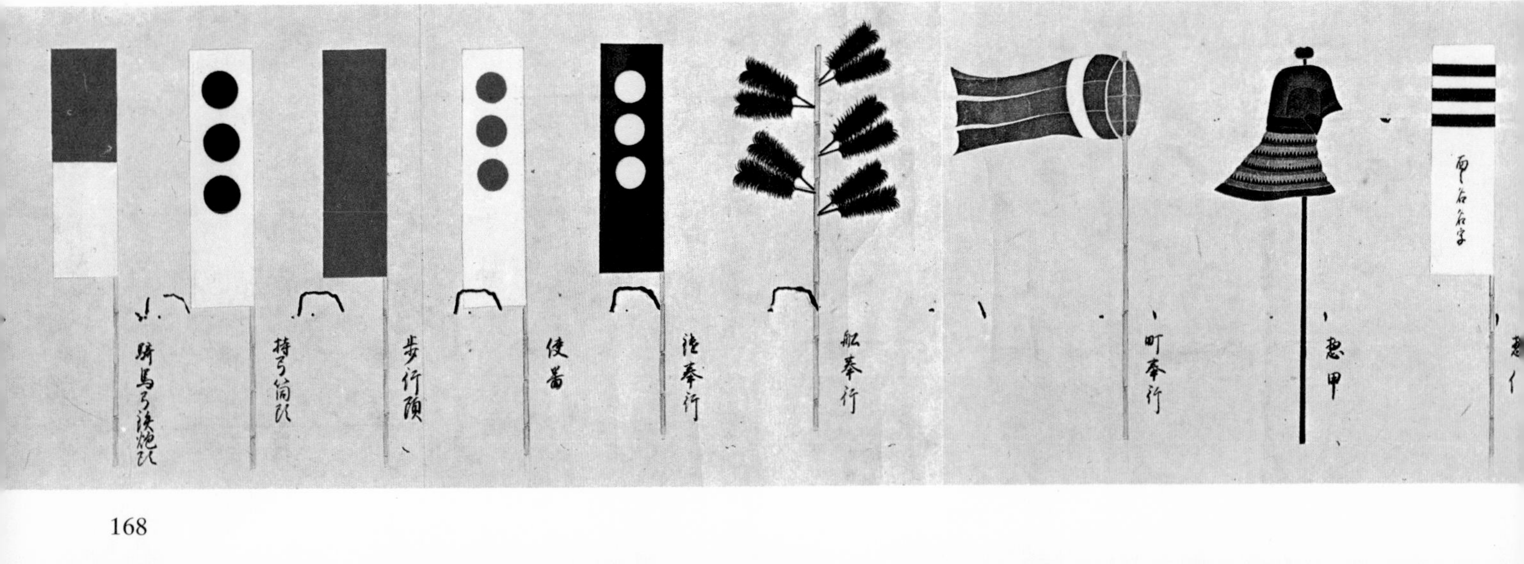

saw the flag believed that Takauji's cause was legitimate and joined him. This recalls similar accounts among the intralacustrine kingdoms of East Africa, except that there the royal symbol whose favor was required for any successful revolt was a drum rather than a flag.

even on swords. The *mon* or Japanese heraldic emblem is associated with a family rather than an individual, but a single family may use more than one *mon*. During the Muromati period the lesser *mon* of the imperial household, the paulownia flower, was assigned to the Ashikaga

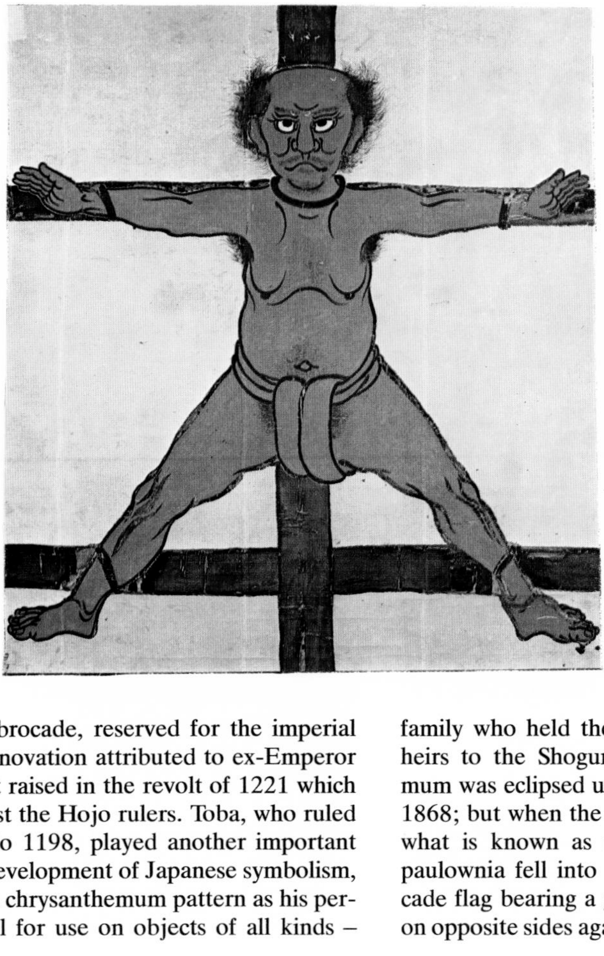

The use of brocade, reserved for the imperial flag, is an innovation attributed to ex-Emperor Toba II, first raised in the revolt of 1221 which he led against the Hojo rulers. Toba, who ruled from 1183 to 1198, played another important role in the development of Japanese symbolism, choosing the chrysanthemum pattern as his personal symbol for use on objects of all kinds – family who held the actual power in Japan as heirs to the Shogunate. Thus the chrysanthemum was eclipsed until the Shogunate ended in 1868; but when the emperor regained power in what is known as the Meiji Restoration, the paulownia fell into disrepute and the red brocade flag bearing a golden sun and silver moon on opposite sides again reigned supreme.

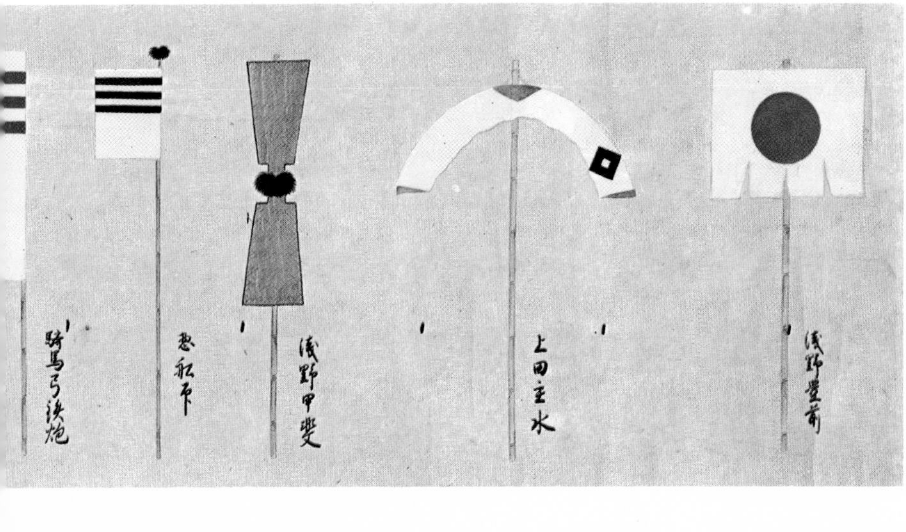

A tomb decoration on the flag preserved at the Zenpukuji temple *(far left)* indicates the willingness of the standard-bearer to die in his cause. In contrast, the flag of Saheiji Ochiai *(left, center)* is a tribute to an enemy who suffered crucifixion rather than betray a friend. The Christians of Kyushu rose in revolt against the Shogunate in 1673 under a flag *(above)* on which were painted angels and symbols of the Eucharist. Portuguese Jesuits in the seventeenth century had boldly attempted to convert the Japanese to their own ways. The ruling Tokugawas sought to preserve traditional Japanese ways by persecuting the Christians. At the "Great Martyrdom" on 10 September 1622, a crowd of 60,000 people at Nagasaki witnessed the beheading of thirty-one Japanese Christians and the burning alive of thirty-four others, following which proponents of the Western religion went underground.

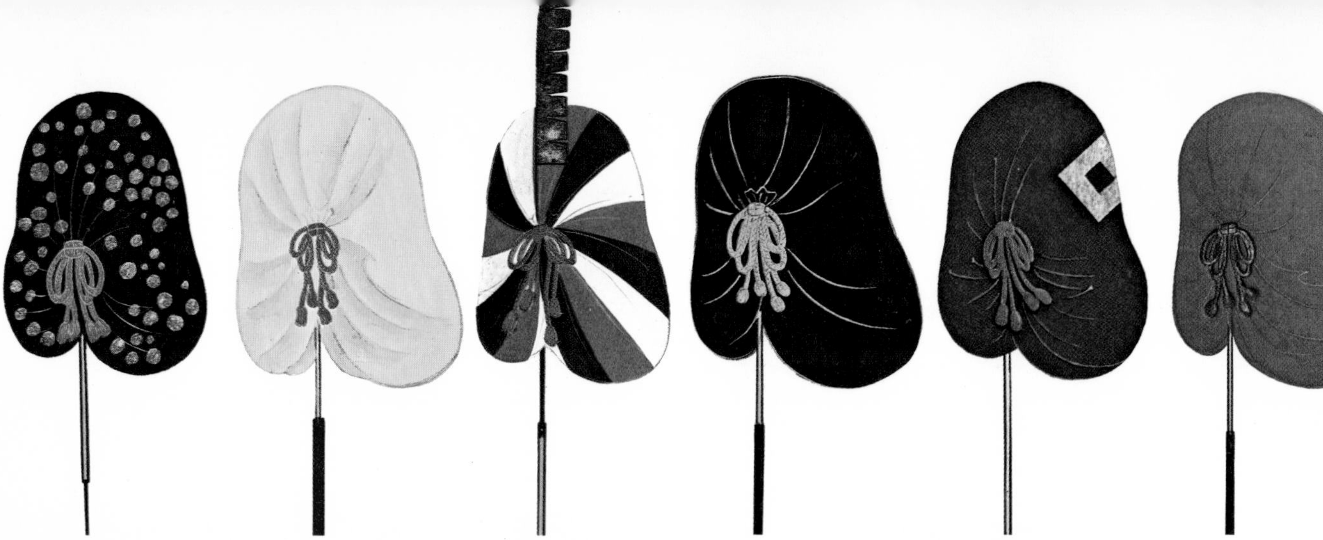

To protect themselves against enemy arrows, Japanese warriors developed hoods to cover the head and back of the neck. These were covered by brilliantly colored cloth, sometimes bearing the *mon* of the family. Such hoods *(above)*, like other attributes of the warrior, came to be stylized into vexilloids having a purely symbolic function after they had ceased to be of practical importance on the battlefield.

Between 1870 and 1873 this pattern served as the emperor's distinguishing flag at sea, but already in 1871 on land it was replaced by a simpler red flag, displaying the golden chrysanthemum in the center of both sides. That flag did not become official at sea until 1889 when the new constitution was written; however, from 1873 to 1889, another naval chrysanthemum flag existed, differing from the land flag in that the charge was white on purple. The old sun and moon banner was given up by the emperor, despite more than a millenium of use, because by

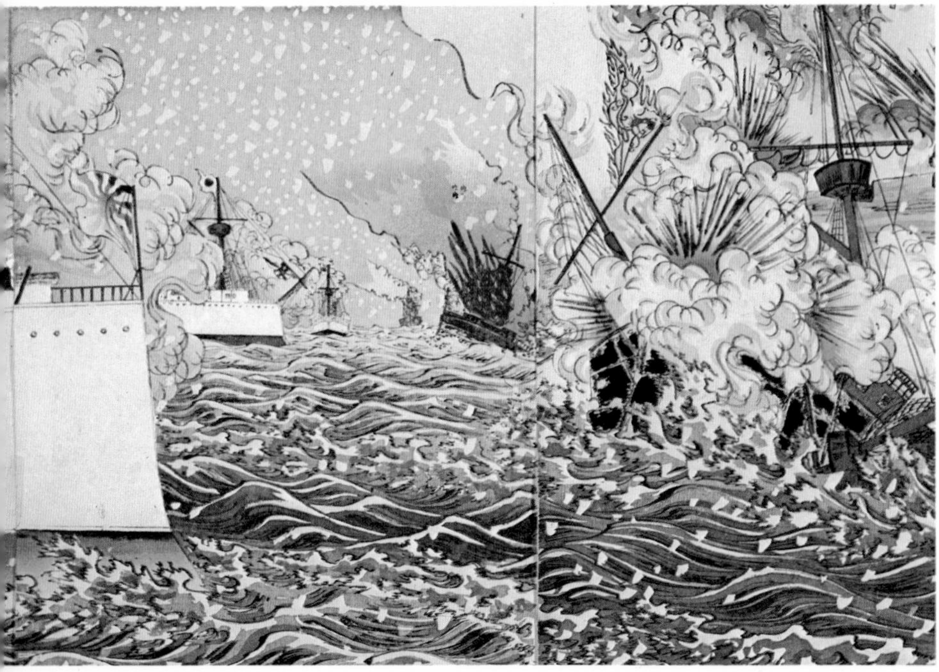

In the late nineteenth and early twentieth centuries Japan became a recognized international power. Its vessels are shown above defeating those of China during a naval engagement in 1894. Following victory in the Sino-Japanese War, Japan went on to conquer Korea and other parts of the mainland under the war version of its Sun Disc flag.

the mid-nineteenth century it was needed for a new function. The emperor continued to personify the Japanese nation, but a modified sun banner was thereafter to symbolize the country in graphic form.

Precedents for the use of a sun flag by other than the emperor are not unknown in Japanese history. The best known and perhaps best substantiated claim is that one or more fans bearing red suns were used by the Taira (or Heike) clan during the civil wars in which it sought, unsuccessfully, to prevent a seizure of power by the Minamoto (or Genji) clan. Two famous engagements in particular – the battles of Yashima (1184) and Dan No Ura (1185) – saw the fate of the Japanese nation sealed in the defeat of the Sun Disc fan. As a challenge to the Genji, during a lull in one of the battles a single Heike ship sailed forth, a vexilloid incorporating the Sun Disc fan at its prow. A young Heike woman taunted the Genji by pointing to the emblem: it fell to Nasu No Yoiti to save Genji honor. When he accomplished the difficult feat of shooting down the tiny target from a great distance with a single arrow, his own family honored him by adopting the Heike *mon* as their own. At the same time we have some indication that white and red were considered as important national colors; the former was associated with the Genji and the latter with the Heike throughout the civil wars of the twelfth century.

The actual combination of colors and designs into a flag resembling the modern Sun Disc may be dated to the early fourteenth century, if a tradition current among members of the Hori family is correct. Until the nineteenth century the Horis preserved a flag of white with a red central disc, strikingly like the modern national flag but supposedly derived from the time of Godaigo. Like the Sun Disc fan vexilloid, this standard had the shape typical of its age rather than of our own, just as European flags which have remained fairly constant in basic design over hundreds of years have nevertheless exhibited variances in proportions, mode of execution and display, size, and accessories.

The "normal" oblong flag – originally flown in Japan from a crossbar but now hoisted with halyards or otherwise affixed to a vertical staff – is known in Japanese as *hata* or *ki.* The former name means "long arm," suggesting the actual appearance of a flag held aloft. The name *ki* is a corruption of the Chinese name for flag (the Chinese character being used in Japanese as well). There are many other nonoblong flag types in Japan, most of them finding substantially greater usage today than their medieval Western counterparts. The Sun Disc flag of the Hori is of the kind known as *nobori,* longer in the hoist than it is horizontally and attached at both top and side by straps going around the pole. The *nobori* is a standard eminently suited to be a *hatajirushi* (armorial banner) and even today

Shinto prayers are inscribed on a flag *(right)* once carried by a Japanese soldier. Never placed directly on the sun symbol itself, these inscriptions spread out like rays in all directions around it. Such flags became popular trophy items with Allied soldiers in the Pacific theater of World War II.

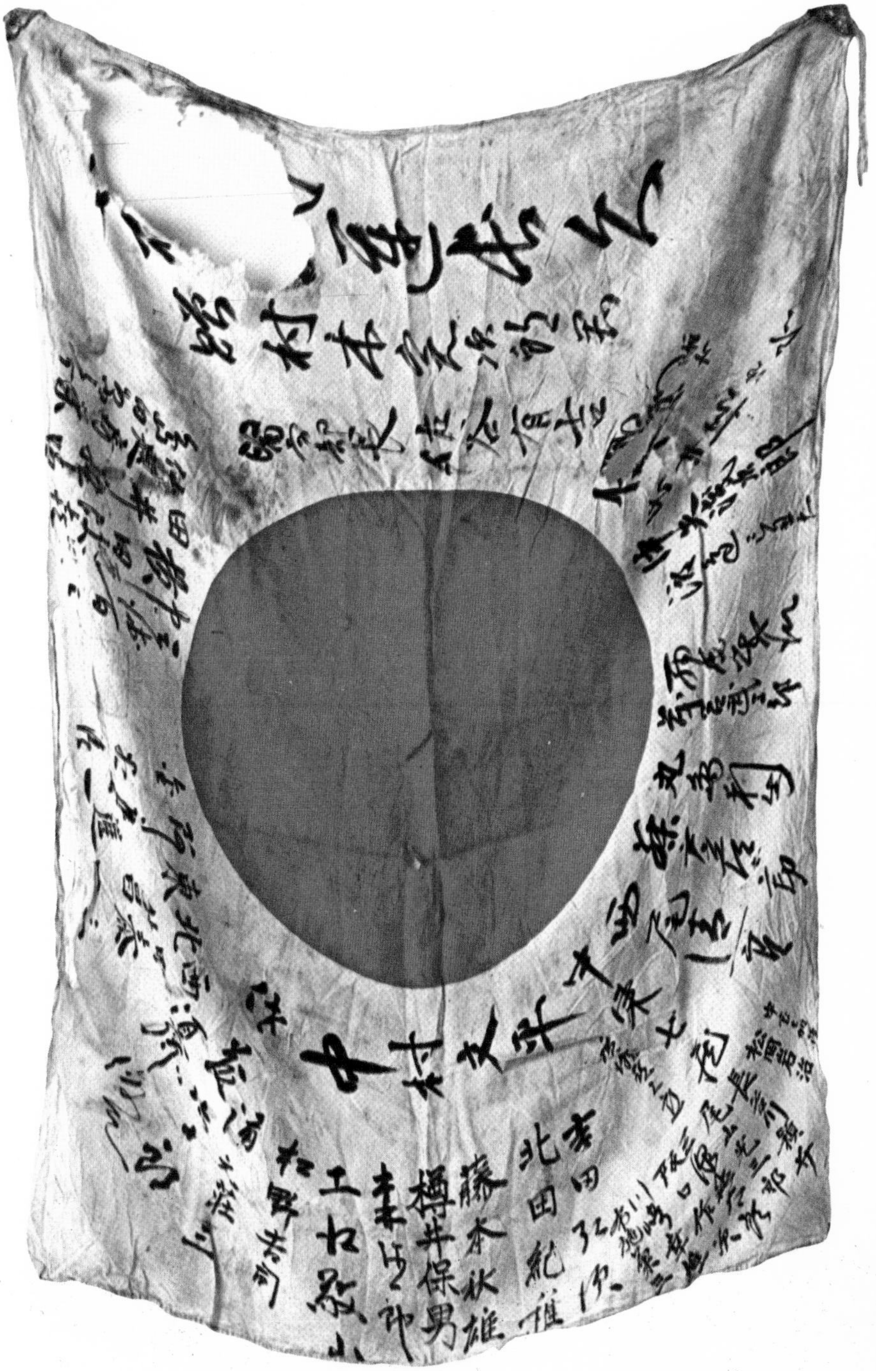

in ceremonies and festivities the family *mon* of ancient Japan are proudly displayed on *nobori.* The armorial sail or *hojirushi* is the naval equivalent.

Vexilloids, known as *matoi* or *umajirushi,* appeared both on land and at sea during military engagements in medieval Japan. Such vexilloids were of the most fantastic shapes and compositions imaginable – helmets, fans, branches, tufts of feathers or tails of animals, almost anything which might be attached to a vertical pole and displayed to cast wonder and fear into the hearts of an enemy. Small flags whose poles were attached to the backs of riders in battle were known as *sashimono* and were supposed to have been introduced by Menjo Tensho (1573–1592). The windsock type of flag, used chiefly in the West today for mundane practical purposes, was elevated by the Japanese to a veritable form of art; such flags are known as *fukinuki.* The Western concept of an ensign to identify the nationality of a ship is a fairly recent innovation in Japan; such a flag is called a *funajirushi* or ship emblem. This does not by any means exhaust the list of flag types, but does serve to explain why one should not be surprised to find the traditions leading to the modern Sun Disc expressed during earlier centuries in unanticipated forms.

The earliest use of the Sun Disc flag in its current form is difficult to determine with precision. It is known that the fleet which sailed against Korea in 1592 carried a sun flag and that in 1673 Empo ordered royal troop carriers to display a sun flag. The Korean diplomatic mission received in Japan in 1810 also saw such a flag displayed. The real question is not whether the sun flag was recognized as a Japanese symbol, but rather when did it achieve preeminence in that function and when was it brought into line with modern notions of the national flag?

The event which was to resolve both those questions was the arrival in Edo Bay of an American, Commodore Matthew C. Perry, and his fleet of four ships on 8 July 1853. On his return the following February a treaty was signed that led to Japan's being opened to Americans; similar treaties followed with European nations. One of numerous results was the lifting of the old ban on intercourse by Japan with foreign countries. Even before Perry made his second trip, the Hyojosho or Great Council discussed at some length the matter of the Japanese flags which

On poles decorated in the Japanese national colors, the flags of Japan and her allies (Italy and Nazi Germany) fly along the Ginza in Tokyo. The three countries first signed a pact against communism in 1937 followed by a full military alliance in 1940, although barely two decades before Japan had been one of the Allies against Germany.

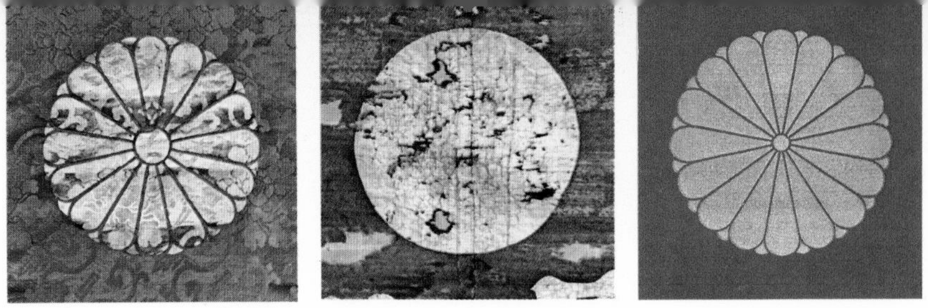

The chrysanthemum emblem of the imperial house was given several interpretations before the present flag design *(far right)* was selected. During the nineteenth century such flags *(above)*, frequently made in gold brocade, sometimes bore the name of the sun goddess, Amaterasu-Omikami, who is credited with having founded the country and imperial dynasty.

Opposite
Together with the Sun Disc flag, Mount Fujiyama (seen in the background) must be considered as one of the fundamental symbols of Japanese nationality. Climbing it is a special pilgrimage performed by thousands annually, and it is among the most photographed and painted objects in the nation. In stylized form it figures in the prefectural flag of Yamanashi (page 268).

The Soma Festival *(below)* is one of many events in which Japanese recall the days of the past by displaying traditional flags, wearing traditional clothing, and performing traditional ceremonies and events. The use of bamboo and silk makes it possible for riders to wear large flags on their backs without discomfort or hindrance to riding maneuvers.

would be required for vessels navigating outside Japanese territorial waters.

Under the Shogunate then in power, a common symbol of authority was one of the Minamoto family's *mons* known as *nakaguro* or Black Middle. Either as a circular emblem or a flag, its horizontal white-black-white was recognized as a badge of high import, and many favored it for a national emblem. On the other hand others felt that the Sun Disc was the only appropriate choice for Japan's national flag; this was especially true of those who supported the emperor, led by Nariakira, Lord of Satsuma. The compromise reached, embodied in the decree of 5 August 1854, provided that large vessels of Japanese nationality should wear the Sun Disc as a *funajirushi* (ensign) with the Black Middle serving as the *hojirushi* (armorial sail); a *fukinuki* (windsock) of blue and white completed the suite of symbols.

The Sun Disc quickly became supreme. In 1855 it was displayed on the Japanese fleet built at Satsuma. In 1860 it was hoisted at the prow of the USS *Powhattan* which carried Japanese diplomats to Washington, exposing the new flag to the rest of the world. The replacement of the *nakaguro* as sail emblem in 1863 presaged the overthrow of the Shogunate and the assumption of direct power by the emperor on 3 January 1868. Following this Restoration, a complete revision was made in all laws concerning the government, civil, and military flags of the empire. The Sun Disc was confirmed on 27 February 1870 and was made the basis for the regimental colors to be carried by the reorganized army. Usage of the flag on land came slowly, in part because many Japanese deeply resented the imperialist activities of foreign powers which were causing so many radical changes in Japanese life. Display of the Sun Disc as a state flag was not formally approved until 5 May 1872 and it is said that the first use of this flag by private citizens came on 17 September of the same year at the inauguration in Yokohama of the first Japanese railroad.

The war flag and ensign, in which the sun was represented off-center and with rays, was adopted on 3 November 1889. This flag became well known during the period of Japanese militarism which led the country to its involvement in World War II. Following surrender to the United States in 1945, Japan found its war ensign outlawed and its national flag greatly restricted in use. In addition to the Sun Disc, Japanese vessels sailing outside home waters were required by the American occupation government to display one of several distinguishing flags to indicate type of registration. The entire prefecture of Okinawa was under a special regime whereby the Americans prevented local ships from using the Japanese national flag at all until 1967.

The Sun Disc expresses the name of the country in graphic terms; the flag, as it were, was bestowed by nature itself on the land of the sunrise. Today this flag is more extensively employed and widely respected than at any time in the past. Its associations with the legendary sun goddess who founded Japan and with its historic use by emperors and warriors is not the basis for its current popularity, however. Its greatest appeal probably lies in its symbolism and artistic beauty, characteristics which the Japanese appreciate in all aspects of life.

White is seen as an expression of purity and integrity, while red suggests fervor, sincerity, and enthusiasm. The concept of *ikioi* – vigor, energy, optimistic vitalism – is important in Japanese culture and the flag seems to embody that spirit. The contrast of circle and oblong is obvious, but the disc is also bright against the neutral background and "hot" to its "cool." The dynamic asymmetry which is embodied in the very character for *ikioi* is also inherent in the flag (at least one made in accord with the decree of 27 January 1870 where the disc is set slightly off-center toward the hoist). This contrasts with the symmetry of the chrysanthemum in the imperial standard, reflecting the dichotomy of progress and stability inherent in the two institutions that display these flags. Even the staff to which the Japanese flag is normally attached has a symbolism of its own. Such poles are made of bamboo painted black every few inches; in contrast to the smooth, shiny, and spherical gold finial, the poles are rough, dull, and cylindrical. In brief the apparent simplicity of form in the Sun Disc flag is not, nor has it ever been, a hindrance to a broad philosophical interpretation.

The red banner of revolution is the basis for the Soviet state flag.

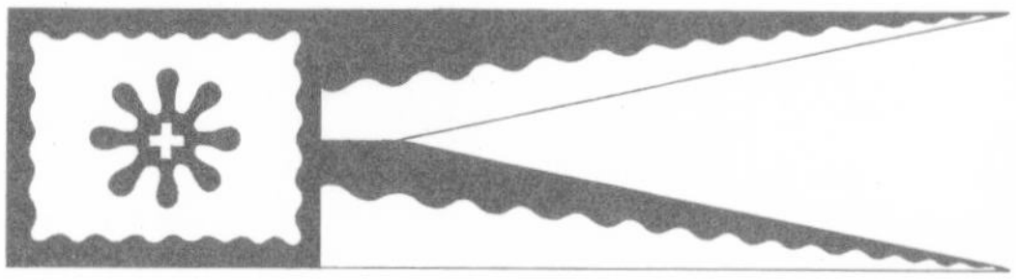

Medieval Russian banners *(right* and *below)* were mostly religious or military in nature and were characterized by unusual shades of color, long inscriptions invoking saints, multipointed stars, or intricate border designs.

SOVIET UNION

"WORKERS OF THE WORLD UNITE!"

At the time of its collapse in 1917, the Russian empire was characterized by one of the most extensive collections of official flags and coats of arms in the world. Small villages in Siberia had blazons of their own and fire-fighting boats in the Black Sea proudly displayed distinctive ensigns. Yet most of these were variants of one or more of four traditional flag themes – the imperial eagle, St. George slaying the dragon, the cross of St. Andrew, and the white-blue-red tricolor. The pervasive use of the last two as Russian national symbols may be attributed to Tsar Peter I (the Great).

The two major symbolic elements of Russian vexillography which predate Peter I were both considered Russian state arms. The older form (a mounted dragon slayer known as George the Victorious) was always associated with the Grand Duchy of Moscovy, later becoming the official arms of the city of Moscow. The earliest graphic representation of a rider with a spear

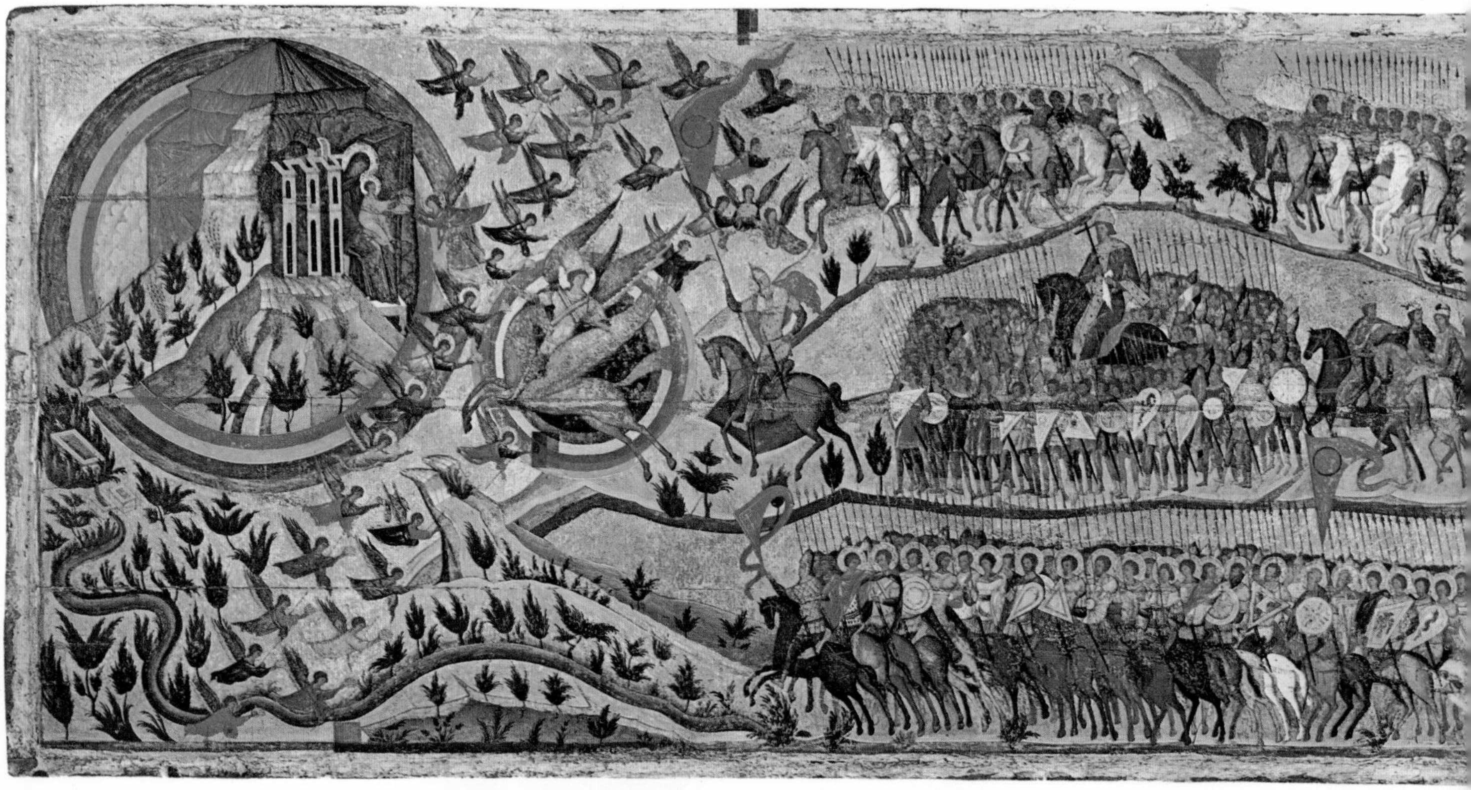

The angelic hosts and triangular flags in the fifteenth-century painting *(above)* recall the standard of Ivan the Terrible (see page 72).

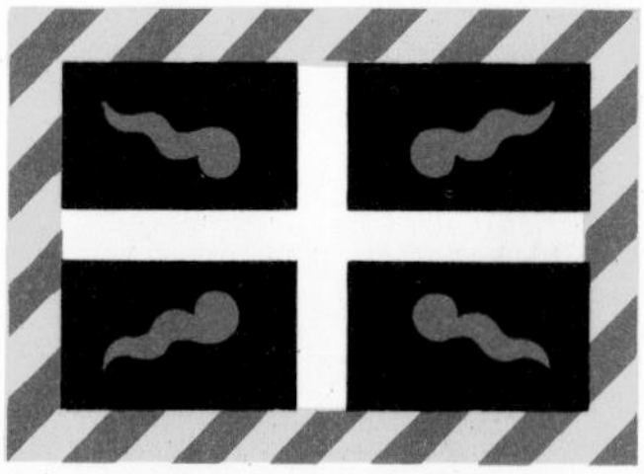

(1390) figures in a seal of the prince of Moscow, Vasilii Dmitriyevich. The serpent or dragon was added under Ivan III (1462–1505), probably to represent the Christians of Russia defeating the pagan hordes of the east – Russia's traditional enemy, the Tatars.

As an augmentation of honor, beginning in 1819, an inescutcheon of George the Victorious was added to Russian flags of military units and other institutions which had performed extraordinary services. This concept was revived in 1942 by the Soviets for their own war ensign. Of course George the Victorious was too reminiscent of the religious and political system the Communists had overthrown to be used directly; nevertheless the Soviet naval augmentation of honor – the "guard ribbon," sometimes employed with the Order of the Red Star – has precisely the same orange and black stripes forming the ribbon of the defunct Order of St. George the Martyr.

The familiar Russian double-headed eagle was in fact a foreign symbol, adopted to demonstrate the imperial pretensions of the Russian tsars beginning with Ivan III (the Great) in 1497. To reinforce his position and that of the state by symbolic means, Ivan replaced the title grand duke with tsar, the Russian equivalent of caesar or emperor; his palace began to take on the form of the modern Kremlin; and Western concepts of autocracy and court ritual were introduced. Most importantly, Ivan married Zoë (Sophia) Paleolog whose uncle Constantine had been the last Byzantine emperor. In the eyes of eastern Christians the worldly empire of the original Caesars was the legitimate inheritance of the Byzantine emperors at Constantinople, following the fall of the Western Empire in 476. Now, a millenium later, Constantinople itself had fallen – conquered by the Turks in 1453.

The responsibility and privilege of defending the holy faith and of ordering civil society could (in his own opinion) rightfully belong only to

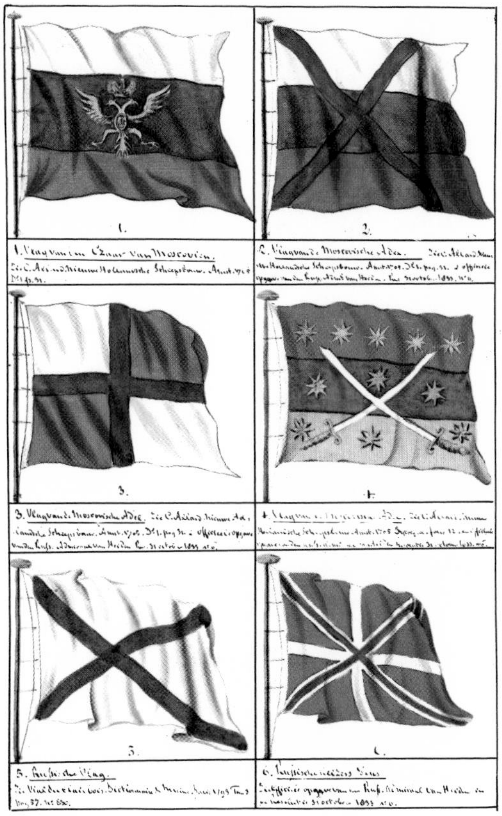

The Order of St. Andrew, instituted by Tsar Peter I in 1699 to honor the patron of Russia, was reflected in numerous flags apparently designed by the tsar himself. The two bottom flags in the manuscript print *(left)* date from that year. The blue saltire on white of both is the reverse of the Scottish version of St. Andrew's cross. The Russian jack shows this saltire against a red field bearing a white cross: the resemblance to the British Union Jack may have been intentional.

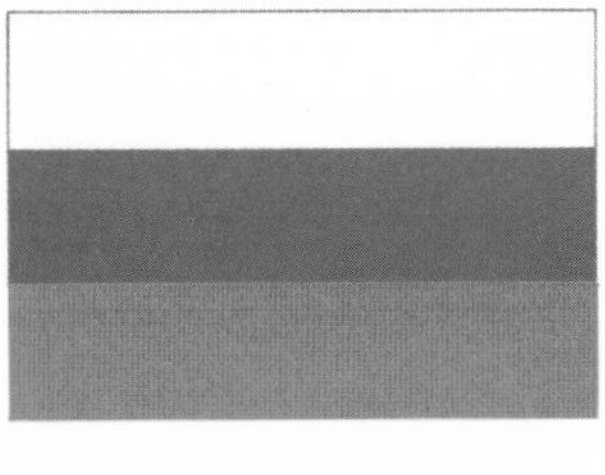

Adopted as a civil ensign in 1799 and as an alternate civil flag in 1883, the white-blue-red was used by imperial Russia until 1917. The Russian Republic of that year used it unofficially as its national flag and ensign.

IMPERIAL FLAG (MODEL OF 1842–1858).

The fact that the Holy Roman Empire of the German Nation had long claimed inheritance to the title of the original Caesars by displaying a gold banner with a black eagle (see pages 114–123) did not deter Ivan the Great from asserting his own rights, following marriage to the niece of the last Byzantine Emperor. "Two Romes have fallen; Moscow is the third Rome and there shall be no fourth" was the philosophy by which he justified placing the traditional arms of Moscow on the Byzantine double-headed eagle to form a new Russian symbol.

Tsarist soldiers went to battle under a flag *(right)* bearing the face of Christ and the motto "God Is with Us." Modern Russians are exhorted *(far right)* to move "Forward to the Victory of Communism!" by a banner bearing the face of Lenin. Similar parallels in tsarist and Soviet iconography appear in their coats of arms *(see below)*.

Typical of the flags of limited usage, which were adopted by imperial decrees illustrated with extravagantly printed color plates, is this flag – used by the Crimean-Caucasus Mountain Climbing Club from 1905 to 1917.

Ivan, both as the defender of Orthodox Christianity and as husband of Zoë. From 1497 on the double-headed eagle proclaimed Russian sovereignty over East and West, which in later years came specifically to mean Europe and Asia. The chief flag in which these arms (embellished over the years) appeared was the imperial standard itself, an armorial banner of golden yellow with the eagle in the center. Nevertheless the eagle was used extensively in other flags – e.g., those of diplomatic representatives, the Russian-American Company, and finally in 1914 even in the national flag of Russia.

Although Peter introduced important new flags, he did not abandon the imperial eagle. In fact he gave it further attributes, adding a naval map in each of the eagle's beaks and talons. This expressed the tsar's determination to make Russia a naval power, freeing it from its traditional landlocked position. In a letter of 2 May 1703 he wrote, concerning addition of the final map (which illustrated the Baltic): "Glory, glory, glory to God for the correction of our standard in the form of the holy Andrew." By this he meant that the diagonal cross of St. Andrew could now be traced between the four maps in the arms – in his eyes no doubt a holy omen of success for his policy of expansion.

For ten years Peter experimented with different naval flags; from the more than thirty varieties developed, the tsar chose the simplest, the blue saltire of St. Andrew on a white field. His source of inspiration is not entirely clear, but a reasonable claim has been put forth by some authors that both this war ensign and its contemporary, a civil ensign of white-blue-red stripes, were derived from a common source. That earlier flag had a quarterly field of white and red, separated by a regular blue cross throughout. Such an ensign may have been used on the first warship of the Russian navy, the *Oryol,* built in 1667.

Regardless of the impact of that flag, the influence of the Dutch on Peter the Great can no more be disregarded in the matter of flags than in naval tactics and policy. The tsar's trip to Western Europe impressed him with the need for modernizing his nation, and it can scarcely have been coincidental that it was precisely upon his return from the Netherlands that he introduced a flag which varied from the Dutch national tricolor only in having the stripes reordered. Moreover, like the Dutch flag, the Russian white-blue-red was at times used in a repeat pattern showing six or nine stripes in all. Of course the Russian version of the tricolor was given new interpretations consistent with Russian history. Some saw a derivation from the red shield displaying George the Victorious with his blue cloak and white horse. The white was said to stand for nobility and frankness; the blue for truthfulness, honor, faultlessness, and chastity; the red for love, courage, boldness, and bigheartedness. It was also pointed out that white had traditionally been associated with the White Russians (Byelorussians), blue with the

RUSSIAN CIVIL FLAG 1858–1914.

RUSSIAN CIVIL FLAG 1914–1917.

The arms of the Russian Empire and of the Soviet Union *(right* and *far right)* are remarkably alike in symbolism. At the top is an emblem of the supreme authority (the tsar's crown, the star of the Communist party) above a symbol of world dominion (the double-headed eagle, a globe) which bears a Russian symbol (St. George, the hammer and sickle), while symbols of non-Russian territories (coats of arms, inscriptions in local languages) are arranged around the outside of the emblem. Both include a sunburst. In the imperial arms the protective wreath is of oak and laurel for strength and honor, however, while the Soviets favor wheat as a symbol of agriculture. The arms also differ in the predominance of the imperial gold in the former, contrasting with the socialist red of the latter.

Soviet Russian civil ensign, 1920–1925.

The Soviet penchant for words and inscriptions in flags is evident in the revolutionary standards below, proclaiming "Land and Liberty," "We Renounce the Old World," and "Down with Monarchy."

Lesser Russians (Ukrainians), and red with the Great Russians. In any event white, blue, and red became so completely integrated into Russian symbolism that in the nineteenth century these three colors in various combinations appeared as a pan-Slavic emblem throughout Eastern Europe.

While no subsequent flag ever challenged either the war ensign or the civil ensign developed by Peter I until a completely new order was established in Russia by the Soviets, some attention must be paid to the "heraldic flag" officially adopted on 11 June 1858 for use as a civil flag. Under the influence of German counselors, the government based it on the livery colors of the imperial arms – black and golden yellow, the latter usually represented as orange. A white stripe was added at the bottom lest the flag be exactly the same as the one then used by Austria, whose arms also featured a black eagle on gold. White, long a symbol of legitimist monarchies in Europe, was specifically attributed here to the cockades of Peter I and Catherine II.

The black-orange-white flag was very unpopular, so much so that the government felt compelled on 7 May 1883 to recognize the white-blue-red as official for use on land during

celebrations. Hence the flag intended for unrestricted use was rarely seen in prerevolutionary Russia, while the flag restricted to special occasions was in fact the most likely to be hoisted whenever private citizens wished to

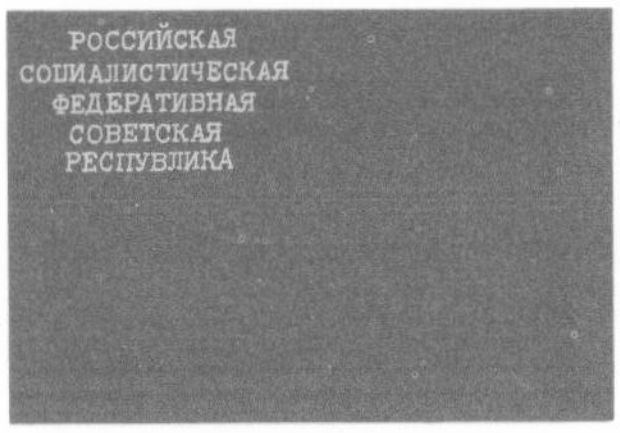

SOVIET RUSSIAN NATIONAL FLAG AND ENSIGN 1918.

SOVIET RUSSIAN NATIONAL FLAG AND ENSIGN 1918–1920.

SOVIET RUSSIAN STATE AND WAR FLAG 1920–1954.

SOVIET UNION STATE FLAG AND ENSIGN, CIVIL ENSIGN (1955 MODEL).

express their nationality by displaying a flag on land. In 1896 and 1910 the Special Commissions established by the government investigated this matter of the dual civil flags.

While no action was taken on the commission reports, World War I witnessed the birth of an entirely new design combining the five colors. To symbolize the close relations the tsar believed existed between the Russian people and himself, on 19 November 1914 Nicolas II, last of his dynasty, authorized that a canton resembling the imperial standard be added to the white-blue-red for use as the nation's new civil flag. War conditions did not allow for the extensive introduction of this design and it disappeared forever with the collapse of the imperial regime in March 1917.

The Provisional Government under Kerensky

Twenty million Soviet citizens died in World War II before this soldier planted his flag on a Berlin rooftop.

Metal flags of various shapes, known in Russian as *vimpely* (pennants), have been sent by the Soviet Union to the Moon, Venus, Mars, and outer space.

scarcely had time to consider flags in the half year it ruled Russia prior to the seizure of power by Lenin and his Bolsheviks. In practice, this period was characterized by three kinds of flags displayed throughout the land with greater or lesser official standing. The Provisional Government itself used the white-blue-red

Communist leaders are a familiar theme in Soviet flag design.

The flag of independent Armenia (1918–1921) resembles the flag adopted by Soviet Armenia in 1952 *(above).*

tricolor while many others (including, of course, the Communists) raised flags of plain red. Elsewhere in the vast empire national groups freed from central authority sought to create autonomous or even independent national states with flags expressing purely local themes. Some scarcely got beyond the stage of being sketched on paper; others flew bravely for a few years before being overwhelmed by the Red Army; the flags of Latvia, Lithuania, and Estonia lasted until 1940, and those of Finland and Poland are still official today.

Although Soviet power introduced a great diversity of flags to Russia following the October Revolution, the variations were largely limited to gold emblems added to a plain red field. As soon as it became apparent to Bolshevik leaders that the entire world was not about to unite in a single communist state, the need arose to distinguish between the different Soviet regimes in Russia, Hungary, Tuva, Armenia, Khorezm, the Far East, and elsewhere. In most cases the distinction was a simple one involving various inscriptions inserted in the upper hoist. Nevertheless some early Soviet flag designs were quite imaginative, involving embroidery patterns from folk costumes, crescents, sheaves of wheat, or entire coats of arms. Moreover, in keeping with the imperial Russian tradition, the central government of the Soviet Union adopted a great number of designs for rank flags of civil and military officers and for distinguishing flags of such institutions as state shipping companies, the Academy of Sciences, and the Hydro-Meteorological Survey.

Just as the white-blue-red tricolor and the Andrew flag stand out among all Russian naval flag varieties in the period 1699–1917, so certain patterns have predominated in Soviet flag history. Military colors have invariably been red with a gold (or gold-bordered) star and inscriptions. Frequently these colors bear as well as the hammer and sickle symbol, developed in 1918 as an emblem of the proletariat and the peasantry. The first Soviet war ensign was red and swallow-tailed, bearing at the hoist a blue anchor charged with a star. When the Russian Soviet Federated Socialist Republic united with three other Soviet states in 1922, the common war ensign developed was a red flag with a red star centered on a white design. The latter resembled a rising sun, but actually had its provenance in the jack invented by Peter the Great mentioned previously. A red star, hammer, and sickle appear on a white field in the war ensign version in use since 1935. This is perhaps most remarkable for the blue stripe along its bottom edge, which strongly recalls the Andrew flag of the old imperial navy.

The state flag of the Soviet Union has remained unchanged from 1923 to the present, except for slight artistic variations in the hammer and sickle pattern. The flag of the largest and most important constituent of the U.S.S.R., the R.S.F.S.R., has been altered more significantly. In anticipation of sending diplomatic missions abroad, the All-Russian Central Executive Committee decreed on 8 April 1918 that the state flag should be red with the name of the country. On 10 July of the same year the initials RSFSR were made an acceptable variation, instead of the full name. The artist S. V. Chekhonin created a stylized rendition, showing the initials framed by gold border, a design that continued to be used for thirty-six years.

In 1954 the R.S.F.S.R. became the last of the Union Republics (then sixteen in number) to eliminate inscriptions from its red banner and substitute a stripe of some symbolic color to distinguish itself from the others. Alone of the Union Republics, the R.S.F.S.R. even today has no horizontal stripe through its red field, limiting its differentiation from the U.S.S.R. flag to a narrow blue vertical stripe at the hoist.

UNITED KINGDOM

THE NOBLE LINEAGE OF THE UNION JACK

Quite properly, many people associate British flags with the sea. The insular position of Britain alone, however, neither provides a good starting point for the understanding of British flags nor accounts for all the major factors that have given the nation a preeminent place in the flag history of the modern world. It seems more to the point to consider the political history of Britain than to treat its naval development, although these two lines are inevitably closely linked.

A system of tolerance and adaptability has enabled the British to preserve their independence for almost a thousand years and to create a stable constitution in which the monarchy does quite well in our era of democracy and dictatorship. It is not surprising, considering the inherent flexibility and pragmatism of that system, that Britain has been able to meld successfully at least four flag traditions.

The oldest flags in Britain are the military standards which can be traced to the Roman invaders of the first century A.D., if not earlier. Then in the twelfth century during the early days of the Norman dynasty, the feudal social structure which resulted from the Crusades developed the rich heraldic tradition which most frequently is recalled today by the royal banner. While naval flags had existed prior to Tudor times, it is precisely the late sixteenth century that saw the flowering of those ensigns and pennants and other special flags that loom so large

King Arthur *(above)* in this early tapestry detail bears the legendary three crowns.
At left are the arms of William III.

Saint Edward the Confessor *(below)*, king of England between 1054 and 1066, holds the typical war flag of his era, a gonfanon.

in British vexillological history. Finally, a growing empire in the nineteenth and twentieth centuries succeeded in introducing seals and other nonheraldic symbols into the realm of British flags.

Of course Britain is not unique in having experienced these four stages of flag growth; in an important sense they are the patrimony of all of the Western European countries. Nevertheless it has been the genius of Britain to absorb large amounts of these really quite diverse trends in such fashion that its flags, like its parliamentary form of government, today represent an accretion and accumulation. In such a situation earlier usages are of interest not simply to the antiquarian. Of course some heraldic principles have little relevance to modern conditions, just as some customs associated with Parliament seem anachronistic, and doubtless the respect which the British manifest for the past has maintained certain conceits and prejudices in the matter of flag design and usage that have a stultifying tendency. Prejudice (among scholars, newspeople, and others) against those graphic artists who create flag designs which lack the blessing of the College of Arms or against headquarters flags which do not fit traditional categories of military flags, are cases in point. Nevertheless the lack of rigidity, the willingness to experiment, and the intellectual tolerance of the British have essentially saved old flag traditions from becoming museum pieces.

It is remarkable how important the vexilloid was in early Britain, considering the almost total desuetude into which it has fallen today. Aside from those standards that were introduced by the Romans, we find at least three important sources of vexilloids in preheraldic Britain. The Angles and the Saxons employed totemic animals; these were not only carried on poles but served as symbols elsewhere. The most dramatic examples are the white horses, carved in limestone, which cover huge areas in the English countryside. A handsome vexilloid (page 34) attributed to King Redwald of East Anglia suggests what the general vexilloid of early times may have looked like.

The Norse invasions from the eighth to the twelfth centuries introduced ship vanes and military standards. Preeminent among these was Raven, Terror of the Land, a vexilloid which consisted of a triangle, curved along one edge and fringed; it bore a representation of the bird that gave it its name. We are assured in Asser's *Life of King Alfred* that when the forces which carried this were to be victorious, the raven would flap its wings; it would hang down motionless if defeat were in store for the Danes. The single most important British vexilloid, the Dragon flag (see page 61), seems to have been a holdover from Roman days. Like its contemporaries, this standard is important today because of the influence it continues to have (through the stylized form heraldry has given to its symbolic animals) on modern civic and military vexillology. The Dragon boasts of a continuity of usage from the investiture of the Prince of Wales in 1969 back through the standards and banners of the Tudor Henrys and of Harold (who was vanquished at the Battle of Hastings) and even further back to the shadowy references of local leaders such as the Wessex lord whose

Although disguised as a woodsman as he returned home from the Near East, Richard I, the Lion-Hearted, was discovered and taken prisoner. Ransomed from captivity, he finally reached England – one of only two visits to his homeland during ten years of his reign.

The oldest known seal of Richard I apparently bore only two lions. But from about 1195 on his device began to consist of three, as in the banner above. The lions continue to this day to be the heraldic emblem of England.

The Battle of Hastings in 1066, as recorded in the Bayeux Tapestry *(left)*, is the earliest point of our certainty about British flags. The figures represented here are a Norman soldier with a gonfanon bearing a cross and a Saxon banner-bearer with the Dragon war standard of King Harold, who died in battle when forces under William the Conqueror carried the day.

Edward III (ruled 1327–1377) was the grandson of King Philip IV of France and laid claim to the throne of that country. To enforce his claims he initiated the Hundred Years War with France and quartered his own arms with those of France *(below).*

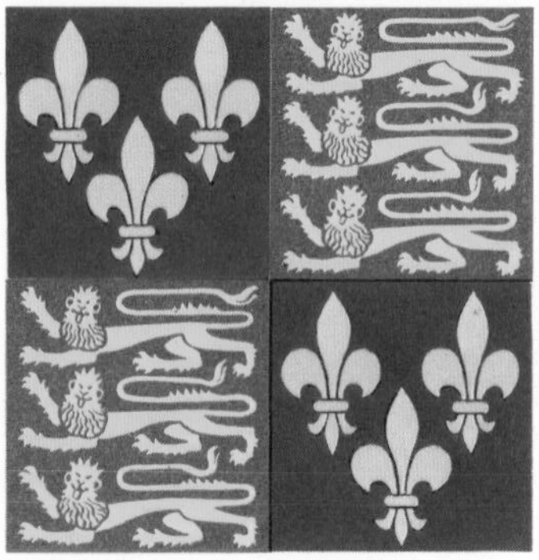

About 1407 King Henry IV (ruled 1399–1413) changed the quartering of his arms from France Ancient to France Modern. Like earlier and later royal arms, these were displayed in banner form, although the proportions were unlike those of the modern royal banner which is twice as long as it is wide.

One of the most important developments in British flags has been the evolution of jacks and ensigns for merchant ships, war ships, unarmed government vessels, and privateers. The general correspondence between jack and ensign in each case is evident in the two series of flags illustrated for merchant ships *(right)* and for war ships (pages 184–185). They reflect all the official variants used from the time of the first Stuart king, James I, who created the Union Jack, to those flags still in use today.

standard at the Battle of Burford in 752 was a dragon.

Many other standards have appeared over the years, although today the number we know about is undoubtedly only a small percentage of those originally existing. The flags associated with the Norman invasion, as represented in the Bayeux Tapestry, have already been discussed at some length (page 44). Their importance is undoubted – although perhaps exaggerated, relative to other flags of the period about which we lack as ready a source of documentation as the Bayeux Tapestry. In particular one wishes more information were available on the banners that eventually evolved into the modern Union Jack. In the early Middle Ages it became the custom for soldiers to carry painted images of saints into battle in the hope of securing divine intercession – a hope that never seems to have been dimmed by knowledge that the opposing army expected the same succor from its own saintly standards. Often these representations were mounted on heavy poles, set in carts, and decorated with streamers; such a vexilloid gave its name to the Battle of the Standard in 1138. The flags originally attached to such standards and later displayed separately cannot at all be considered national flags, yet through them – in their design and in their increasing use both in battle and on ships – we at least can discern the bases from which the modern national flag stems.

Perhaps the most surprising thing is the proliferation of such flags. St. Edmund, St. Edward the Confessor, and later St. George were the most popular in England, but at least a half dozen other saints were likewise common on the battlefield. The eventual primacy of St. George seems to be due in large part to the fact that he had been discovered by Crusaders in the Near East and was popular with the common soldier. He was never really a churchman's saint and in fact was removed from the church calendar in 1970. Soldiers not entitled to wear the livery colors or badge of a noble lord often displayed a red cross on a white armband when in the service of the king. The first certain references to an actual shield and to a flag date respectively from 1249 and 1277, but prominence for the Cross of St. George seems to have come a century later. Edward III made St. George the patron of the Order of the Garter in 1348. The saint's position was enhanced in 1415 when, in his name, troops under Henry V won the day at the Battle of Agincourt. In 1419 the same monarch ordered that "every man of what estate, condition, or nation that he be, of our party, bear a band of St. George, sufficient large, upon the peril if he be wounded or dead in the fault thereof, he that him wounded or slayeth shall bear no pain for him: and that none enemy bear the said sign of St. George... upon pain of death therefor."

The primacy of St. Andrew in Scotland seems to have been achieved earlier, although its white on blue coloring evolved more slowly – perhaps because the saltire shape of St. Andrew was more immediately distinctive than the regular cross used by St. George. The earliest reference (in the twelfth century) to the saltire imputes an origin going back to King Hungus in the eighth century. In 1385 it was ordered that every soldier of a combined French and Scottish army should wear "a white St. Andrew's cross, and if his jack is white or his coat white he shall bear the said white cross in a piece of black cloth round or square." Gradually blue came to be the standard background color for the saltire, yet as late as the seventeenth century a naval flag of green, yellow, and red bearing a white saltire was displayed by the Scots.

The third cross of the modern British Union Jack, which stands for St. Patrick of Ireland, seems to have had no historical association with him. The chief Irish heraldic emblem has long been the harp, and the national color green. One scholar has suggested that the red saltire prominent in the arms of the Geraldines and other important Anglo-Irish families may have been the source of "St. Patrick's Cross." It first appears in the late sixteenth century, being incorporated into the Union Jack on the first day of 1801.

If the flags with crosses representing England and Scotland replaced early battlefield standards and eventually developed into the various British national flags we know today, the process was a gradual one and an important flag development intervened that must be given some attention. While the cross of St. George or saltire of St. Andrew belonged to every Englishman or Scot, actual organization of troops on the battlefield in most cases depended upon noblemen whom the king would call on for support. From the late twelfth century until the institution of the standing army five hundred years

BRITISH CIVIL ENSIGNS AND JACKS

BEFORE 1606

The Union Jack was legal only briefly for merchant vessels, yet long after 1634 it continued to be used unofficially until, with a white border, it was reestablished in 1801. Today use of the merchant jack is infrequent.

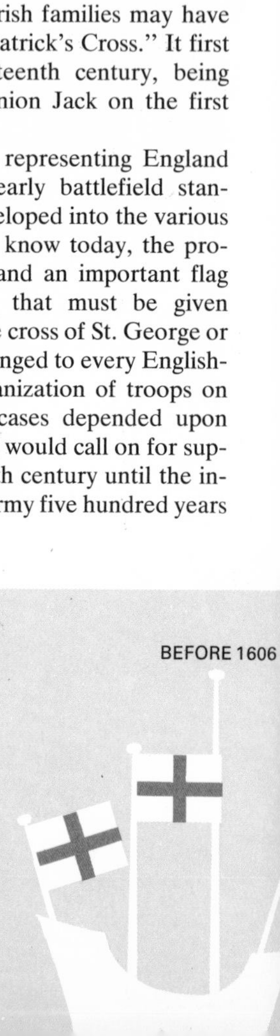

Royal seals – including the one *(below)* of King Edward III – are generally known to us from wax impressions, since the original metal dies were broken on the death of a sovereign to prevent fraudulent use. In Britain it was the practice to have a different design on either side, but invariably the arms of the king were included on one or both of these sides.

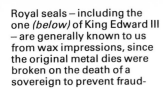

The orb *(left)*, often referred to as the "imperial apple," has prechristian origins and continues today as one of various symbols of royalty in Europe. Others include the crown, the scepter, and the throne.

A great number of distinctive flags were used under the Commonwealth (1649–1660) and its successive Lords Protector, Oliver Cromwell and his son, Richard. The banner of the former combines the colors and shield of his realms, England and Scotland, on a regal pavilion under a regal crown and with a cipher (OP for *Oliverus Protector,* Oliver the Protector). The motto at the bottom translates "Peace Is Sought Through War."

The personal union of Scotland and England under King James I led to the introduction of the Scottish lion into the royal arms and banner.

later, various heraldic flags symbolizing the period's leaders were the principal ones about which soldiers rallied, attacked, or fell back. Heraldry and heraldic flags went through several stages in this period. But as interesting and colorful as these developments are, there are few aspects which affect the national flag of Britain.

On the one hand the rules of heraldry became the basis for much British flag design and usage, continuing to this day to have considerable impact on all kinds of flags, regardless of whether or not they are heraldic in nature or origin. The right to armorial bearings was the

The arms of Nassau *(left)* were added as an inescutcheon *(below, middle)* for King William III.

The harp has been an Irish symbol for centuries. On a green shield it serves as the arms of Leinster County; since 1603 on a blue field it has been the armorial banner for Ireland.

The lion arms of Scotland have been used since King Alexander II (1214–1249). The red "double tressure flory counterflory" was added as a frame by his successor.

1603–1649, 1660–1689, 1702–1707

1689–1694

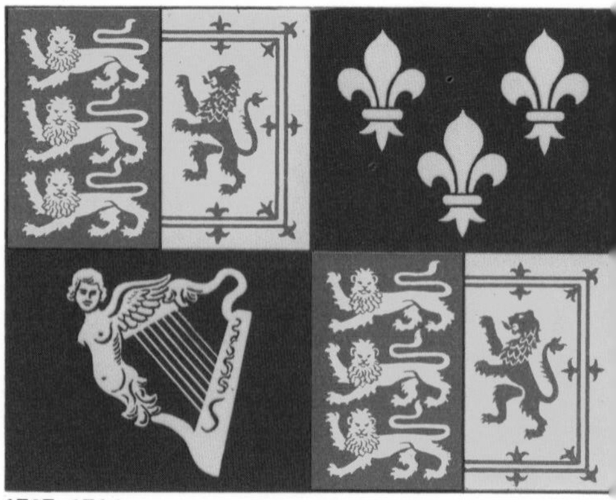

1707–1714

Together with the harp of Ireland, also first introduced under James I, Scottish arms have continued through all subsequent variations of the British royal flag *(above).*

BRITISH ENSIGNS OF WARSHIPS.
British war ensigns *(below)* parallel, but do not match exactly, the civil ensigns of the same period (previous page).

prerogative of the ruling classes in the Middle Ages and it is not surprising that they jealously guarded their privileges.

Heraldry survived in Britain when it died out elsewhere: the prestige attached to a royal warrant granting arms or adding an augmentation of honor or a similar distinction remains today a useful tool in British politics. The mystique surrounding the half-millenium-old College of Arms enhances this considerably.

From the thirteenth century until the beginning of the seventeenth the royal arms constitute per-

The fleur-de-lis symbol of France was abandoned by British kings when they renounced all title to the French throne on 1 January 1801.

The use of three lions as a symbol of England dates from about 1195.

haps the single most important component of the national symbolism of Britain. Technically considered the personal arms of the ruling sovereign, these arms nevertheless stood for the authority of the state in an era when the sovereign personified the land; thus, wherever his or her authority extended, the royal banner might be seen. (This is quite contrary to the modern practice of restricting display of this flag to situations where the sovereign is personally present.) Since they sailed under royal protection, even private merchant vessels hoisted the royal banner as is documented in the seals of certain ports. The practice was confirmed in 1270 by a treaty between King Edward I and the Count of Flanders, Guido. On land in the peasant revolts of the late fourteenth century we find both sides carrying two flags – the cross of St. George and the royal banner. In the sixteenth century there are examples of adaptations: the explorer Martin Frobisher hoisted as a flag the cross of St. George with the royal arms in the center; the Levant Company superimposed the same cross on the royal banner. By the nineteenth century the royal banner was largely restricted to use as a street decoration during holidays and parades and even this practice came to an end under Edward VII.

The death in 1603 of Queen Elizabeth I and succession to the throne of the Stuart dynasty in the person of James VI of Scotland (who became James I of England) initiates a new era of British flags – ones we may consider as national flags. While the new developments probably would have taken place (due to the growth of British naval power and changes in the architecture of the ships themselves) even without this personal union of the crowns of Scotland and England, James certainly played a decisive role in British flag history. In a proclamation which is dated 12 April 1606 and which includes many details concerning flags, he noted:

"Whereas some difference has arisen between our Subjects of South and North Britain, Travelling by Sea, about the bearing of their flags, for the avoiding of all such contentions hereafter, We have with the advice of our Council ordered That from henceforth all our subjects of this Isle and Kingdom of Great Britain and the Members thereof shall bear in their maintop the Red Cross, commonly called St. George's Cross, and the White Cross, commonly called St. Andrew's Cross, joined together, according to a form made by our Heralds."

The Earl of Nottingham approved a design in which the two crosses were set per pale, that is, side by side. "This will be the most fittest for this is like man and wife, without blemish unto other," he commented after reviewing other

The arms of Wales are not included in the royal banner *(middle)*, because Wales is a principality. However, the Prince of Wales displays the Welsh armorial banner with an inescutcheon bearing his crown *(top)*.

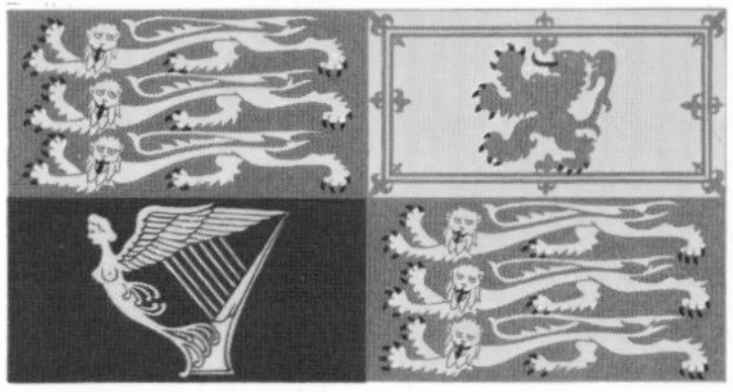

SINCE 1837

1714–1801

1801–1816

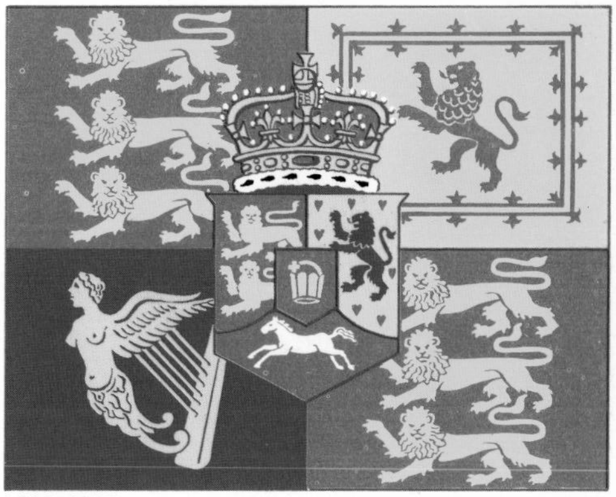

1816–1837

One of the subtle changes introduced into the British royal arms and banners under the Hanoverians concerned the crown of their German territories. Hanover was recognized as a kingdom by the Congress of Vienna in 1814. Prior to that it had been an electorate – entitled only to an electoral cap, not a crown. The inescutcheon of the Hanoverian arms showed the traditional crown of Charlemagne.

Although the dragon is regarded as a benevolent monster in the Orient, it has generally been a symbol of evil in the West. The traditional story of St. George slaying a dragon to save a maiden must therefore be seen as an allegory – the courage and strength of the Christian knight defeating the forces of darkness and evil to save purity and honor. As such, it has been popular as a symbolic motif in many countries from Ethiopia to England and from Russia to Spain. This flag of St. George *(above)* is an example from Stein am Rhein, Switzerland.

proposals in which one or the other cross appeared on top. Nevertheless the design actually chosen set the red cross of the larger kingdom on top of the white saltire of the older realm. Many Scots disliked this and designed new Union Jacks in which the saltire took precedence. In passing, it is interesting to note that special versions of the royal arms and banner, long officially recognized for use in Scotland, give that kingdom symbolic primacy over England.

It is clear that the Union Jack derived the first part of its name from the political event that precipitated its creation, even though it was more than a century later that England and Scotland were submerged into a United Kingdom. Many theories have been put forward concerning the term "jack." Some have seen it as an Anglicized version of Jacques (i.e., James in French, the court language), others as a corruption of the jacket or surcoat displaying the individual national crosses which soldiers formerly wore. Neither seems likely, but we do not know the true source of the word. While jack today continues to refer to a small flag flown on the prow of a ship, only the pedant insists that the familiar Union Jack, if appearing other than on the jack staff of a vessel, be referred to as the Union Flag.

The union of England and Scotland, broken in 1649, was reestablished five years later; but alterations in British flags were also affected by the substitution for the monarchy of the Commonwealth regime under Oliver Cromwell. While the Commonwealth ensigns, jacks, and command flags are of interest for their designs, most important to note is the heavy reliance they made on traditional symbols of authority. Cromwell was quite aware that his position rested largely upon the force of his personality and of his arms, whereas the monarchy that had

ENGLAND
The red cross has been associated with St. George *(left)* since at least the twelfth century. In 1606 it was combined with the saltire of St. Andrew to form the first Union Jack.

SCOTLAND
The diagonal form of the cross of St. Andrew is related to the supposed form of his martyrdom, as represented *(left)* in this fifteenth-century seal. The Scots were long unhappy at having their cross partly obliterated by that of St. George.

IRELAND
The historical traditions of the "saltire of St. Patrick" in Ireland are highly dubious. It was convenient, however, to incorporate such a cross into the Union Jack when in 1800 Ireland was raised to a status equal to the kingdoms of England and Scotland, rather than inserting the Irish shield over the English and Scottish crosses as Cromwell had done in the seventeenth century (see page 184).

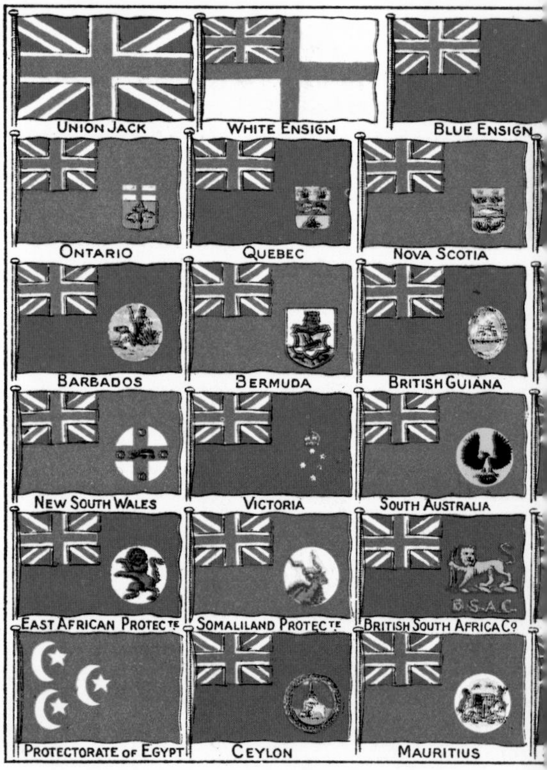

At the end of the nineteenth century, Britain was growing in economic and military strength, confident of its cultural and moral leadership and busy in all parts of the world building an empire. The compiler of the flag chart *(right)* at the turn of the century thus felt no hesitancy in devoting half the space for his "flags of the world" to the red and blue colonial ensigns of Britain's overseas territories.

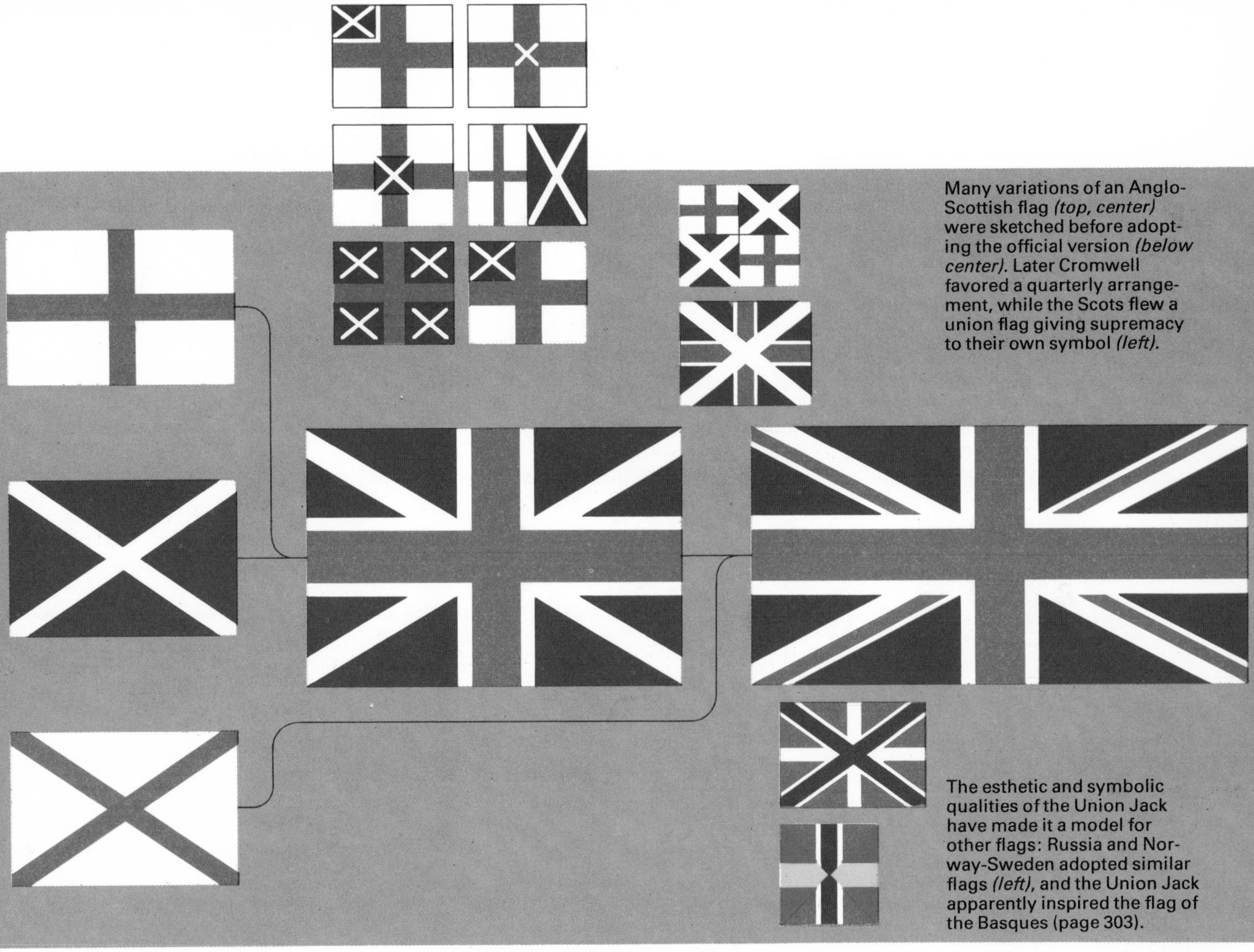

Many variations of an Anglo-Scottish flag *(top, center)* were sketched before adopting the official version *(below center)*. Later Cromwell favored a quarterly arrangement, while the Scots flew a union flag giving supremacy to their own symbol *(left)*.

The esthetic and symbolic qualities of the Union Jack have made it a model for other flags: Russia and Norway-Sweden adopted similar flags *(left)*, and the Union Jack apparently inspired the flag of the Basques (page 303).

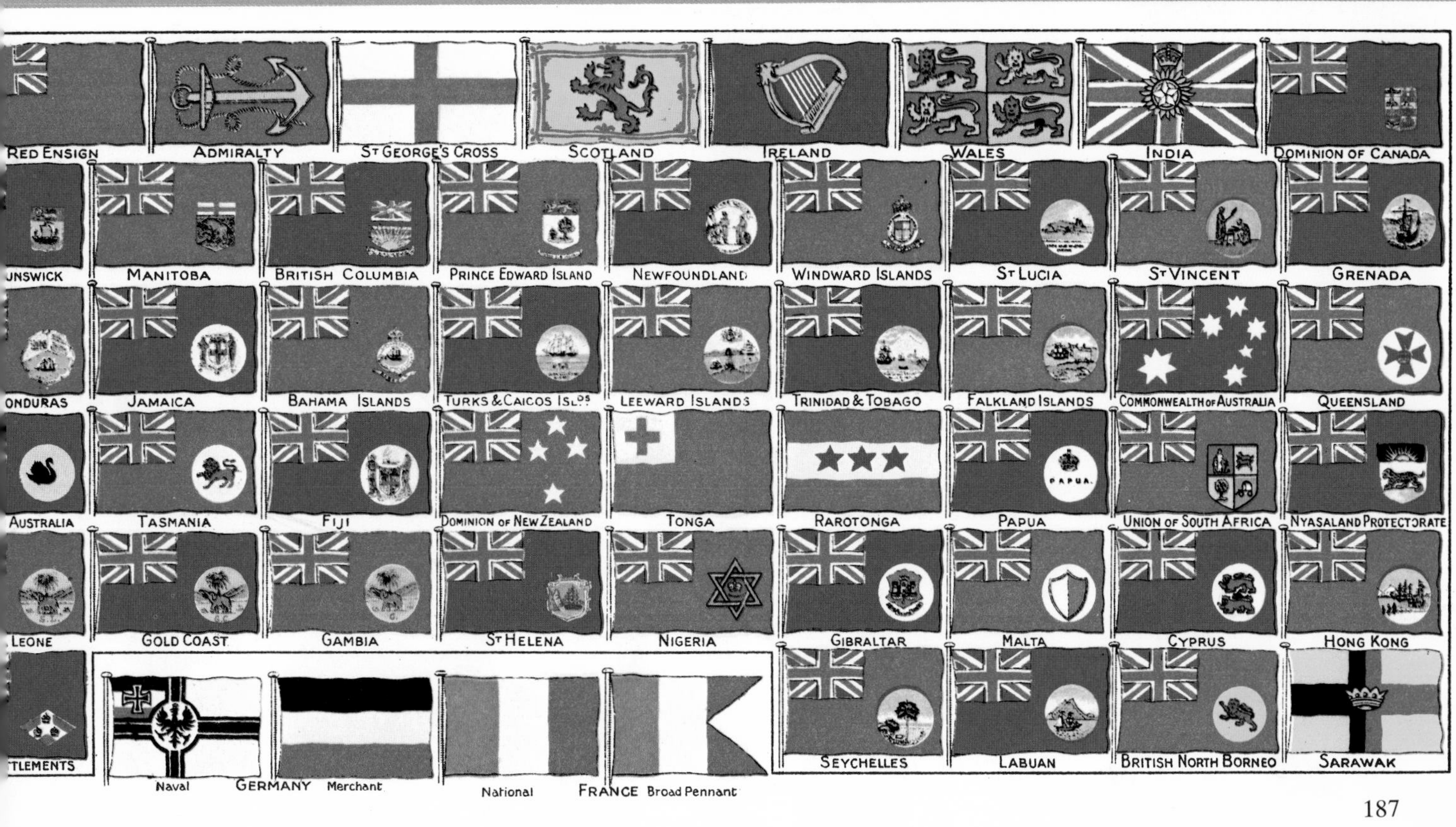

The queen, the royal arms, the Union Jack – these three essential British symbols have been intimately associated with one another and with the British nation through traditions of almost a thousand years.

In this 1957 visit of Queen Elizabeth II and Prince Philip to Paris, the British royal banner flies in the position of honor with the personal standard of French President Coty on the left fender. Prince Philip has his own personal standard, as do other members of the British royal family; in many cases these personal standards change with the age and status of the individuals who fly them. The queen is entitled to display a personal standard distinct from the royal banner when visiting nonmonarchical members of the Commonwealth. In those member nations which continue to recognize her as head of state, there is generally a special banner composed of the local national arms with her cipher superimposed in the center.

As Churchill's casket was carried to its final resting place *(below)*, the Order of the Garter – Britain's highest – rested on a pillow over the Union Jack.

been replaced – whatever might be said about any given sovereign – represented a centuries-old tradition which inspired instant loyalty on the part of great numbers of people. Cromwellian symbols disappeared in 1660 with the Restoration of Charles II and appear today as a brief anomaly in the pattern of British flag development.

While the Glorious Revolution of 1688 and subsequent transformations of Britain's royal and parliamentary structure have had little affect on the basic designs of national symbols, two other important developments have made substantial changes in British flags over the past three hundred years. For various reasons private merchant vessels sought the privilege of displaying the same flags as warships, while the Royal Navy found it desirable to maintain a distinction between the two, although it did provide special symbols for privateers, i.e., merchant vessels with certain rights of warships. Moreover, within the Royal Navy itself, the end of the era of warfare where combat was largely between two ships introduced a need for signals and distinctive ensigns that would allow a great number of ships to operate as a single fleet. Hence for a period of two hundred years, until the question was finally settled in 1864, a great variety of ensigns, jacks, and pennants were devised for both these purposes. Although all were essentially variations of the Union Jack and of the recognized British colors, they worked rather well in identifying instantly the nature of a particular ship and the rank of its commander.

Red had been the senior naval color, but the 1864 regulation reserved the Red Ensign to the merchant fleet and, except in time of war, the Royal Navy since then has flown the White Ensign. The Blue Ensign is for unarmed public vessels, usually more precisely identified by a badge of office inserted in the fly. A Blue Ensign is also the distinctive flag of a merchant ship commanded by a Naval Reserve Officer and the basic pattern for the colonial flag of most British territories. The latter developed in the last decade of the nineteenth century, and even today when the British Empire has largely been replaced by a Commonwealth of independent nations a few territories around the globe still have distinctive Blue Ensigns of their own.

The British tradition of using three distinctive naval flags to indicate nationality and a fourth flag on land was transmitted to countries in all parts of the world, which in turn have developed their own adaptations. Most of the original colonial flag badges were based on seals created by persons with little or no professional heraldic competence. The final stage of their transformation into state heraldry was the responsibility of civil servants in various government departments and of the flag manufacturers. Even the Admiralty itself developed quite a different style from that sanctioned by the College of Arms. These, coupled with the enormous number of other flags involved, result in the Commonwealth's having perhaps one of the most extensive body of vexillological material, ranging from actual flags and their usages and customs to commentary and study about the same.

Despite all other developments, nothing in British flag history in the past three hundred years has rivaled the importance or interest of the Union Jack. Begun as a distinguishing flag – an auxiliary to the principal flag of a ship, it evolved into the state flag of Britain and its empire. As the chief British symbol it was incorporated into dozens of other flags and it became the fond national emblem of millions throughout the world of British ancestry or heritage.

The popularity of the Union Jack is only in part attributable to the vigor with which missionaries, soldiers, and merchants spread its usage (such that a Frenchman was led to comment "An Englishman cannot see an island without planting a Union Jack there"). We must also consider that its striking geometric, almost abstract, form has made the Union Jack as suitable for modern graphic interpretation as for execution in traditional bunting. Moreover, despite heraldic and constitutional strictures, theory has rarely been allowed to interfere with its actual usage. Its adaptations are manifold; it figured as a background in the military colors of the eighteenth century, was inscribed with slogans as a protest flag of the Chartist movement in the nineteenth century (when it became a true national flag), and has been incorporated into clothing and household goods in the current century. It is, then, the prime example of the spirit of adaptation and continuity which to a greater or lesser degree has long characterized British flags.

DIEU ET MON DROIT

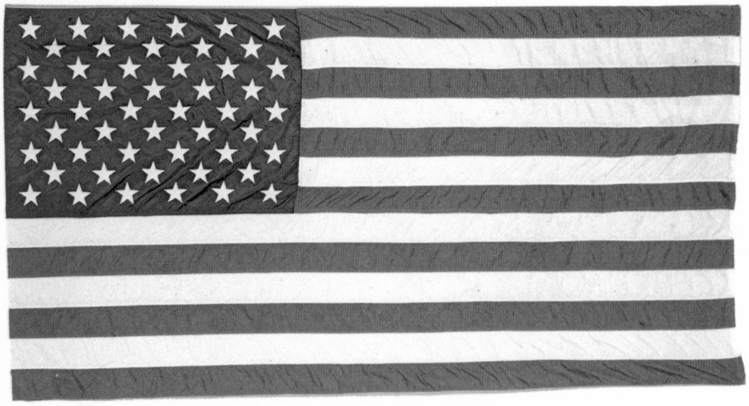

Having origins no longer clear to us, the stars and the stripes of the United States flag developed into one of the world's best-known symbols. Americans also revere their national bird, the bald eagle (*right* with the arrows of war and an Indian peace pipe).

UNITED STATES

A BANNER BORN OF REVOLUTION

The Stars and Stripes – a familiar object, not limited like flags in some countries to official display on select holidays – tends to be taken for granted. Books on the subject often repeat anecdotes rather than analyze history, and patriotic societies are more concerned with promoting the U.S. flag than with understanding it. To the casual observer it might seem that the historical development of the American national flag is a story simply told. In the Revolutionary War (1775–1783) a flag of thirteen red and white horizontal stripes with thirteen white stars in a blue canton was chosen to symbolize the colonies seeking independence from Britain. Later arose the tradition of adding a star to symbolize each newly admitted state, such that the current flag, dating from 1960, simply reflects the small and regular changes of the past two hundred years.

A more critical approach reveals the study of American flags to be an immensely rewarding subject. The sources of the design of the Stars and Stripes; its extensive influence on symbols within and without the United States; the numerous challenges to the design; and above all the manifestations of emotional attachment to this symbol, which has led to unique modes of flag display and usage – all these elements form the fascinating, little understood background to a study of the historical development of the U.S. flag.

Although early explorers and settlers from Spain, France, Sweden, and other European nations brought their flags to America, we must look to the English colonies – and in particular to Massachusetts – as the source of many of the flag trends still current in the United States. The Puritans, who had left England because it would not accept certain religious views, immediately established their own religious intolerance in the Massachusetts Bay Colony of the 1630s. Although relying upon the mother country for almost every aspect of its legal and practical existence, this colony, when barely seven years old, allowed itself the luxury of a debate over flags.

The only known life portrait of Betsy Ross, legendary maker of the first Stars and Stripes.

Flags of exploration and colonization in America from 1492 onward included flags of Spain, France, Great Britain (Union Jack and Red Ensign), the Dutch Chartered West-India Company, and Sweden.

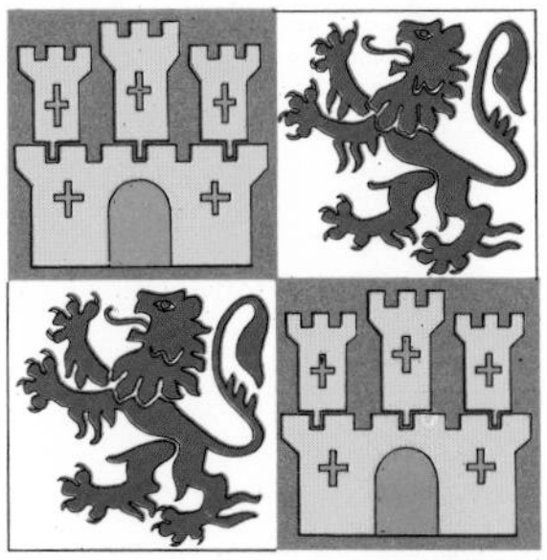

John Endicott, for years the governor or deputy governor of Massachusetts Bay, was sorely troubled by the inclusion of the cross of St. George in the flag raised in forts and carried on ships and by local troops. The Puritans, having stripped their churches and clergy of all symbolism, considered this cross – which in England had long before achieved secular status – a superstitious badge, a papish abomination, a palpable threat to their own salvation. This view, characteristic of American attitudes toward flags (i.e., of showing greater concern for moralism than for political ideology) led to both action and public debate.

When Endicott ordered the cross cut from the local infantry color, he provoked sermons, speeches, and finally a debate in the local legislature. At a time when but a few Europeans existed on the fringe of a huge and hostile continent, Endicott, leader of the colony, was disbarred from public office for a whole year for his "rash, uncharitable, indiscreet act."

Nevertheless, public sentiment rallied behind Endicott, and soon a red flag with a white canton (the red cross of St. George conspicuously absent) was established as the first of a long line of local flags. The early New Englanders were practical, however; realizing that their lifeline to England might be endangered if reports got back that proper flags were not being displayed, they soon gave evidence of another American trait, the love for constant redesigning of flags. Yet, though possible adaptations and modifications of the new flag were hotly debated, the important historical point is that for half a century New Englanders had a flag of their own.

In 1686 Sir Edmund Andros was sent as governor to assert royal authority over the colonies, and the English cross was restored to the flag. By then fresh differences with the mother country led New Englanders to introduce a distinctive local symbol (the pine tree) into English flags. In this fashion began the American tradition of using flags for political expressions of loyalty or dissent, of debating such usage, and of adapting official flags for unofficial purposes; these practices are still vigorous today.

Flags were prominent again in the agitation against arbitrary British rule during the 1760s,

Supposedly captured by Israel Forster on the first day of the American Revolution, the St. George's cross of this flag was replaced with stripes.

French ships captured by the British sail into New York harbor in 1757 under two flags *(above).*

The Bedford flag *(above)* carried on the opening day of the American Revolution is further described on page 73.

The rank flag of George Washington as commander in chief of the American Army during the Revolution was blue with thirteen white stars.

culminating in the Revolution. The British Union Jack and Red Ensign – as well as local banners of various designs – were inscribed with slogans such as "Don't Tread Upon Me" or "Liberty, Property, and No [Tax] Stamps." The hoisting of such a flag on a large "liberty pole" in the center of a town constituted an intentional provocation to established authority. For every liberty pole that was torn down, several new ones arose; correspondingly, it became evident to greater numbers of Americans that the Union Jack and other official symbols no longer stood for the rights the people had exacted from the crown over five hundred years' time.

The actual outbreak of the Revolutionary War in April 1775 did not find Americans united behind a national flag. In fact the only banner apparently carried by Americans that day (see page 73) had been made in England almost a century before. While the Forster flag captured the same day by the Americans from British regulars straggling back to Boston has a canton of thirteen stripes, its alteration from the cross of St. George was probably not effected until later in the Revolution. The truth is that the flags of the Americans were as diverse as their political views – and of course thousands remained loyal to British symbols. Massachusetts radicals may have displayed a plain red flag when George Washington arrived in July 1775 to take command of the newly forming army; but in South Carolina the Fort Moultrie flag simply proclaimed "Liberty," and in Philadelphia the elegant heraldic standard of the Philadelphia City Cavalry loyally featured the Union Jack as its canton. (This is especially important to note, since for the past century the blue and silver stripes later painted over that Union Jack have erroneously been hailed as a possible source of the stripes in the American flag.)

The first national flag of the United States – the British Red Ensign modified by the addition of six white stripes *(above)* – was known as the Continental Colors. It was in unofficial use from 1775 to 1777. Stars replaced the Union Jack in 1777 *(right)*, but it was many years before any uniformity of flag design was achieved.

Constantly misrepresented in flag books, the flag flown at the Battle of Bunker Hill in June 1775 *(right)* was red with the New Englanders' pine tree on its white canton. The English cross of St. George in use on earlier New England flags *(above)* was omitted as Americans took up arms against the British.

When the first truly national American flag was decided upon, apparently in December 1775, its design presented no impediment to possible reconciliation between the combatants. The canton of this flag, properly known as the Continental Colors, bore the Union Jack. The thirteen stripes of its field were symbolic of the colonies united in defense of their liberties. Almost a full year after the Declaration of Independence, Americans finally replaced the Union Jack canton with what the law of 14 June 1777 refers to as a "union [of] 13 stars white in a blue field representing a new constellation."

In view of the extensive public adulation in later years of this flag and of the persons and events surrounding it, it is ironic that we can say little with certainty about its design elements or even the process of their transformation into the now familiar Stars and Stripes. There is no question

The flag of the Philadelphia City Cavalry had a Union Jack canton, still visible today under the stripes painted on at a later date.

Rattlesnake flags *(left)* were popular with Rhode Islanders, including naval commander in chief Esek Hopkins *(above).*

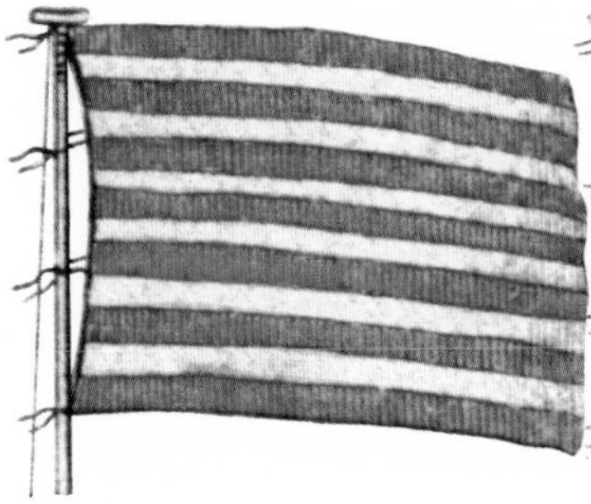
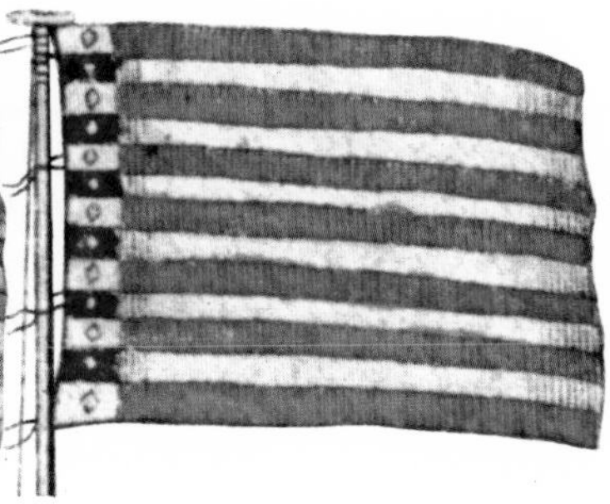

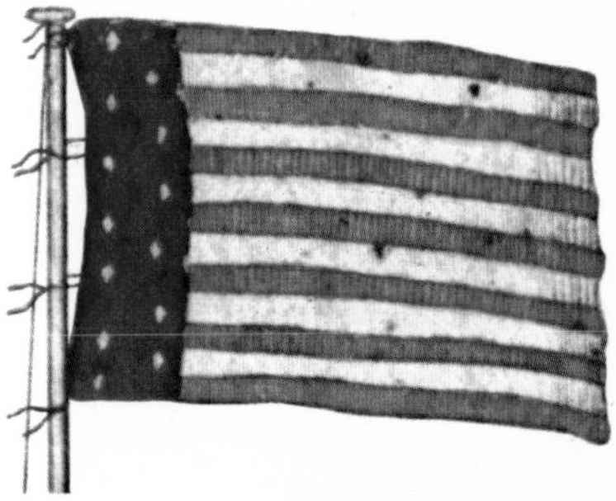

but that red, white, and blue were British colors and that the canton-and-field composition was also based on contemporary models in the mother country. Other than that European and North African flags of the eighteenth century frequently had stripes in the national colors and that striped flags were apparently flown by the radical Sons of Liberty (whose agitation promoted the Revolution), it is difficult to determine why the United States acquired a flag of stripes. If anything, the stars are an even greater enigma. Plausible theories have been advanced concerning possible influences on the national flag of the starry seal of the Portsmouth, Rhode Island, town council or of the personal command flag of General Washington. One might also investigate other hypotheses, such as the speculation that the stars were originally recommended by a Harvard astronomy professor, John Winthrop.

Yet in an important sense it is not the historical truth or falsity of such details about the flag that is so fascinating in American vexillology, but rather the depth of popular emotion on the subject. The prime example is the legend of Betsy Ross, the supposed seamstress of the first flag. Despite the fact that she was unknown outside a small circle in her home city of Philadelphia until almost a century after her alledged sewing of the first Stars and Stripes for George Washington, Betsy Ross probably ranks as the most famous woman in American history. The facts supporting the traditional story are extremely weak; the account relies almost exclusively on family tradition. Nevertheless, doubts by historians have failed to shake the faith of the public in the story.

It should not be imagined from what has been said that nothing is known about early American flags: a considerable amount of evidence exists and indeed the subject has been more thoroughly researched than the flag history of most other countries. Moreover, new evidence which may eventually resolve some of our current questions is continually coming forth. A prime example of this is the portrait of Betsy Ross, heretofore unpublished, appearing on page 190. It is the only one known to have been made during her lifetime, its very existence adding some weight to claims made on her behalf.

Whatever its sources, the United States flag became immensely popular in a very short time. No less popular have been its many variants in

The flag law of 14 June 1777 referred to the stars of the flag as "a new constellation," but failed to indicate how they should be arranged. Manufacturers followed their own fancy.

Benjamin Franklin published a cartoon of a severed snake *(left)* in 1754 when urging the colonists to unite.

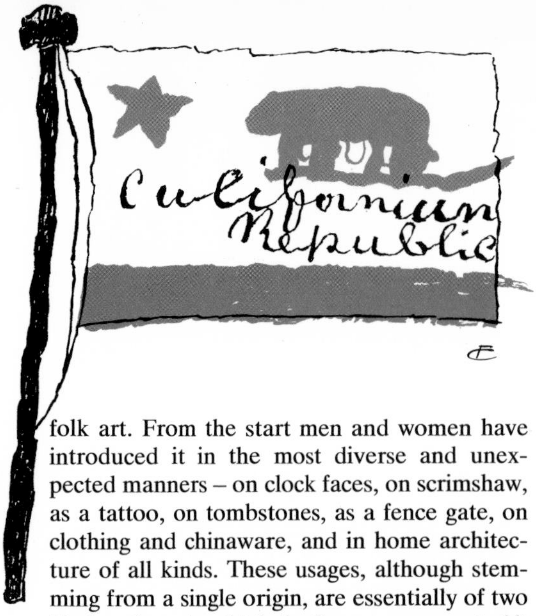

Throughout American history the design motifs of the national flag have been borrowed by local flags. For example, the Bear Flag Republic of 1846 in California combined the animal for which it was named with a single star and single stripe, indicating the American nationality of settlers who wanted California to separate from Mexico and join the United States.

folk art. From the start men and women have introduced it in the most diverse and unexpected manners – on clock faces, on scrimshaw, as a tattoo, on tombstones, as a fence gate, on clothing and chinaware, and in home architecture of all kinds. These usages, although stemming from a single origin, are essentially of two kinds – those in which the flag or some part of it serves as a motif for patriotic decoration and those in which the adaption has taken place within an actual flag still preserving its original functions. Since the late nineteenth century, great concern has arisen about misuse of the United States flag. The distinctions between flag motif and real flag are lost and the old American tradition of protest flags forgotten. For one hundred years, however, there was an unrestricted, brilliant flowering of the stars and stripes pattern.

The American government indirectly encouraged this process. Soon after the Revolution, Vermont and Kentucky became the fourteenth and fifteenth states. Like so much of the American political system, federalism was essentially a new idea in the world, and in the 1790s Congress might have invented any symbolism to represent its principles. Although the star it chose has not become universally associated with federalism, it is today one of the most common of flag symbols and its principle associations – with unity, independence, or the constituent parts of a nation – are all based upon the American model. In 1795, however, the star (particularly the five-pointed variety which Americans soon made their standard form) was extremely rare: the city flag of Norden, Germany, the cantonal banner of Valais, Switzerland, and a few military colors

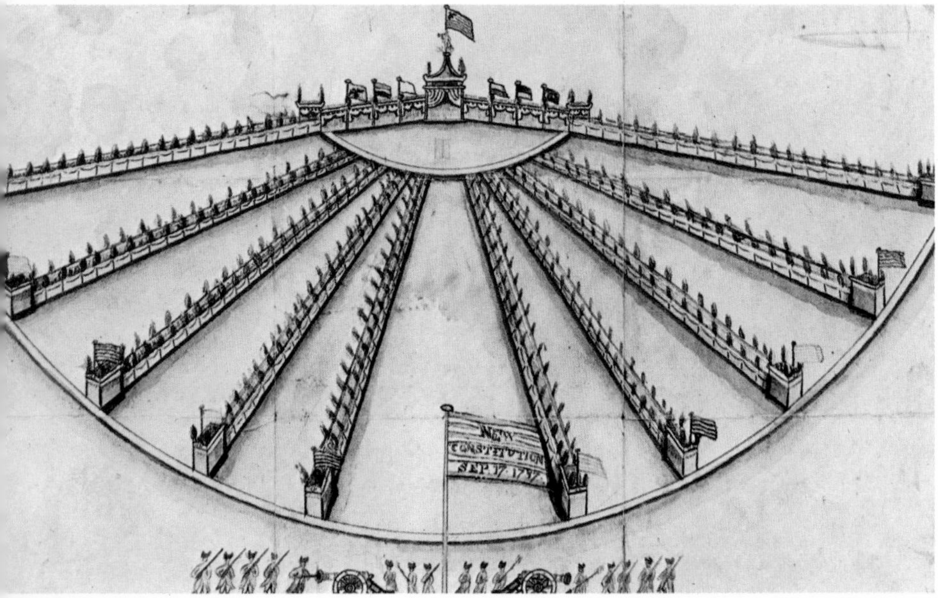

Of all the written constitutions in effect in the world, the American is the second oldest; its promulgation in 1787 is shown *(above)* being celebrated.
The constitution of Massachusetts dates from 1780.

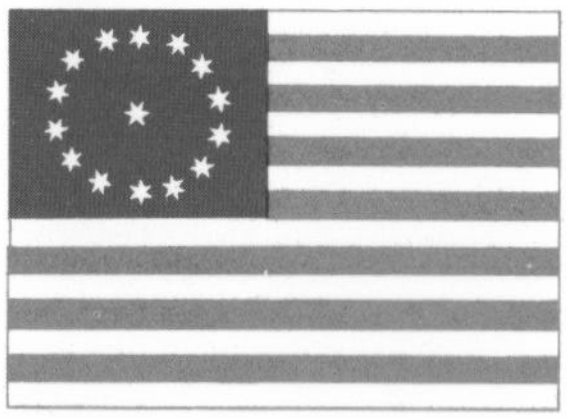

The size and placement of the stars, the shape of the canton, the number of points on the stars, the relative numbers of red and white stripes – these and other details provided the greatest variety in the American national flag throughout the nineteenth century.

Frequent adaptations for political and commercial use were made of the Stars and Stripes, particularly in the period 1870–1890.

were virtually the only examples of its usage in the world.

Nevertheless in 1795 Congress decided to add a new star and stripe for each new state, such that, until 1818, properly made American flags had a total of fifteen stars and fifteen stripes. Costs, lack of news concerning the official change, and disinterest in honoring the new states of the Union – all were reasons why many flags of the period did not conform to the new law. Because the law itself was vague about the exact flag design, each flag maker chose his own pattern until 1912, when official patterns, color shades, and proportions were set forth by the govern-

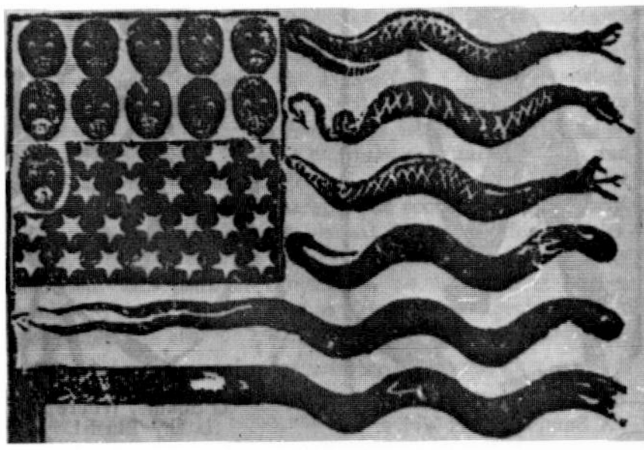

The flag has been a theme in commercial and folk art since its first adoption by the United States.

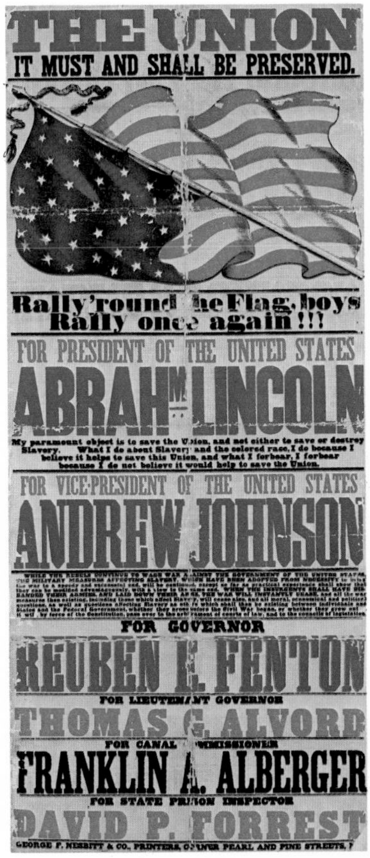

Once common, the liberty cap *(left,* carried by Liberty) is rarely seen in the United States today.

Never officially adopted, the first Confederate national flag had one star for each state recognized by the Confederate government.

The first shot of the American civil war was fired at Fort Sumter. When it fell to the Confederates in April 1861, the new Stars and Bars was hoisted; Confederate flags continued to fly for four years.

ment. The imaginative interpretations Americans had previously given their national flag then disappeared.

The question of an official flag change had arisen in 1816, when it became evident that the nation would continue to grow for some time. Peter Wendover, representative of New York in Congress, deserves credit as the man whose foresight preserved both the original harmony of the flag and the concept of honoring new states. Rather than reverting to thirteen stars and thirteen stripes or, at the other extreme, continuing to add one star and one stripe for each new state, he recommended, and Congress accepted, a concept which is still part of American law. The basic design of the flag would henceforth be thirteen equal horizontal stripes of red and white, honoring the original states; the canton would be blue containing one white star for each state. Each new star was to be added to the flag on the 4th of July (America's independence day) following a state's admission to the Union.

Over the years this has produced a total of twenty-seven different American flags – completely disregarding the endless varieties of unofficial (and sometimes quite incorrect) designs. Whatever might be said about the system of altering the flag from the standpoint of aesthetics or cost, there is no doubt about the method's popularity among the American people. Each state is distinctly honored and the flag constitutes an embodiment in graphic form of the entire history of the country – rather than a single moment of the past, frozen forever in an unchanging form. Of all the proposals suggested for a new design none has found more favor.

The influence of the Stars and the Stripes on other flags – like that of the eagle of the national arms on other emblems – has been enormous. From the very first, Americans developed flags for their states; cities; counties; local military groups; civic, fraternal and educational organizations; and other groups. Such flags frequently embodied some aspect of the Stars and Stripes. A good example is found in the designs that were submitted to the new government organized as the Confederate States of America (C.S.A.) when the southern states seceded (1860–1865). The majority of flag ideas proposed and/or made had red-and-white-stripes and white-stars-on-blue design elements, which found their way into both the original Stars and Bars and the C.S.A. battle flag. The latter served as the basis for the two official national flags of the Confederacy and for the flag of Dixie (the Southern states) still in unofficial use today.

The influence of the United States flag also extends to other countries. It is understandable why the Republic of Texas, the Kingdom of Hawaii, and the American colony in Liberia followed the American flag model, but its influence is also apparent in the flags of Puerto Rico, Cuba, several Brazilian states, Uruguay, Chile, El Salvador (1865–1912), and probably in a number of other flags where the influence is difficult to prove. The appeal of the Stars and Stripes has led innumerable designers of new

During its brief existence, the Confederate States of America had a number of flags – all based on the red, white, and blue colors of the United States flag and all employing its star symbolism.

The Bonnie Blue flag was used unofficially in 1860 throughout the South.

To avoid confusion with Union troops, the Confederates devised the Battle Flag.

The naval jack *(right)* and first official national flag *(below)* date from 1863.

This flag flew for a single month in 1865.

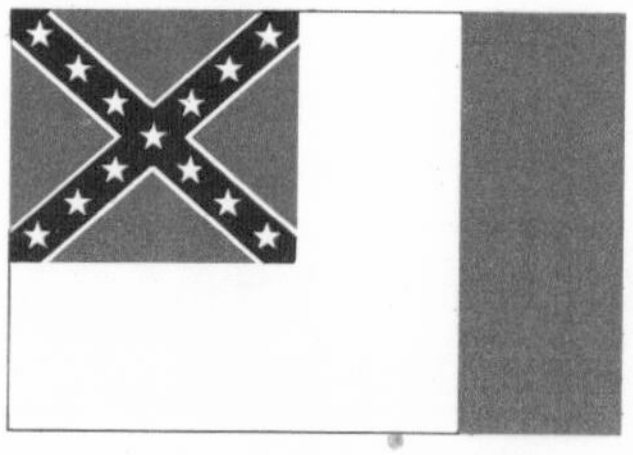

THE STARS
The years the stars were added to the U.S. flag:

13 – 1777	23 – 1820	27 – 1845	31 – 1851	35 – 1863	43 – 1890	48 – 1912
15 – 1795	24 – 1822	28 – 1846	32 – 1858	36 – 1865	44 – 1891	49 – 1959
20 – 1818	25 – 1836	29 – 1847	33 – 1859	37 – 1867	45 – 1896	50 – 1960
21 – 1819	26 – 1837	30 – 1848	34 – 1861	38 – 1877	46 – 1908	

The same Union flag *(below)* lowered at Fort Sumter, South Carolina, in 1861 was hoisted again in victory four years later after the American Civil War.

As they have done in every war since the Revolution, American blacks rallied to the cause of the Union during the Civil War *(left)*. Note the "Confederate flag" with a snake which the soldier tramples underfoot and the flag flown from the school-house, a custom that began during the Civil War.

The canton in the fifty-star flag *(above)* has a specified pattern, but earlier flags varied with the whims of the manufacturer.

For many Americans the flag raising at Iwo Jima epitomized the spirit of their efforts in World War II and their respect for the flag.

national flags in many parts of the world – the Trankei, Belize, Ireland, and Australia, to name but a few – to look to it for inspiration in their own work.

As remarkable for the vexillologist as the flag itself have been the flag traditions developed by the United States. Some of these are mentioned elsewhere in this book, and all deserve greater attention than can be given here. Early in the nineteenth century Americans developed songs about the flag; one, *The Star-Spangled Banner,* was made the national anthem in 1931. Nicknames such as Old Glory evolved from stories and incidents, particularly military engagements involving the flag. By the time of the Civil War (1861–1865) the flag had become the chief national symbol: disrespecting the flag was treason, waving the flag was proof of patriotism, saving the flag in battle or capturing the enemy's flag was heroism.

The custom also arose at the time of displaying flags prominently in schools, building a firm link between the flag and education. A salute to the flag was developed, Flag Day and Flag Week were honored, flag tableaux were enacted, "living flags" composed of hundreds of school children dressed and aranged appropriately were formed. In the twentieth century, as a direct outgrowth of this spirit, laws were adopted and court cases initiated to protect the flag from presumed disrespect. The vigorous efforts of civil libertarians, supported by the good sense of many citizens and of the courts, have prevented the establishment of a state religion with the flag as its chief object of veneration, but such a cult is popular with great numbers of people. Vexillatry – flag worship – is probably to be expected in a country lacking the traditional ruling classes characteristic of most other parts of the world – royalty, nobility, established clergy, a hereditary military class, a land-owning aristocracy. For better or worse, the taste of the American citizen has determined how flags should be used, and the Stars and Stripes is seen as the embodiment of everything Americans believe in. While the United States may lack ideological political parties or long-standing heraldic traditions, the process of democratization has certainly not caused a withering of traditional interest in or use of flags. If anything, Americans seem to be challenged only by the Chinese in the extent of flag usage and by no other country in the originality and spontaneity of flag display.

In the 1960s the flag became the center of bitter political disputes: here the Massachusetts State House flag is half-staffed at the demand of a crowd protesting the killing of students at Kent State University in 1970.

ZAIRE

THE SEARCH FOR NATIONAL IDENTITY

Founded in the fifteenth century in the region bounded by the Kwango, Bengo, and Zaire (now Congo) Rivers, the Kongo Empire had a sophisticated administrative structure when the first Portuguese arrived in 1482. Under the *mani-kongo* or emperor, who also served as a religious leader, were six provincial governors ruling districts divided into villages under hereditary chiefs. As symbols of authority the governors received from the mani-kongo a sword, a bonnet, a carpet, and a flag. The prospects for mutually beneficial commercial relationships

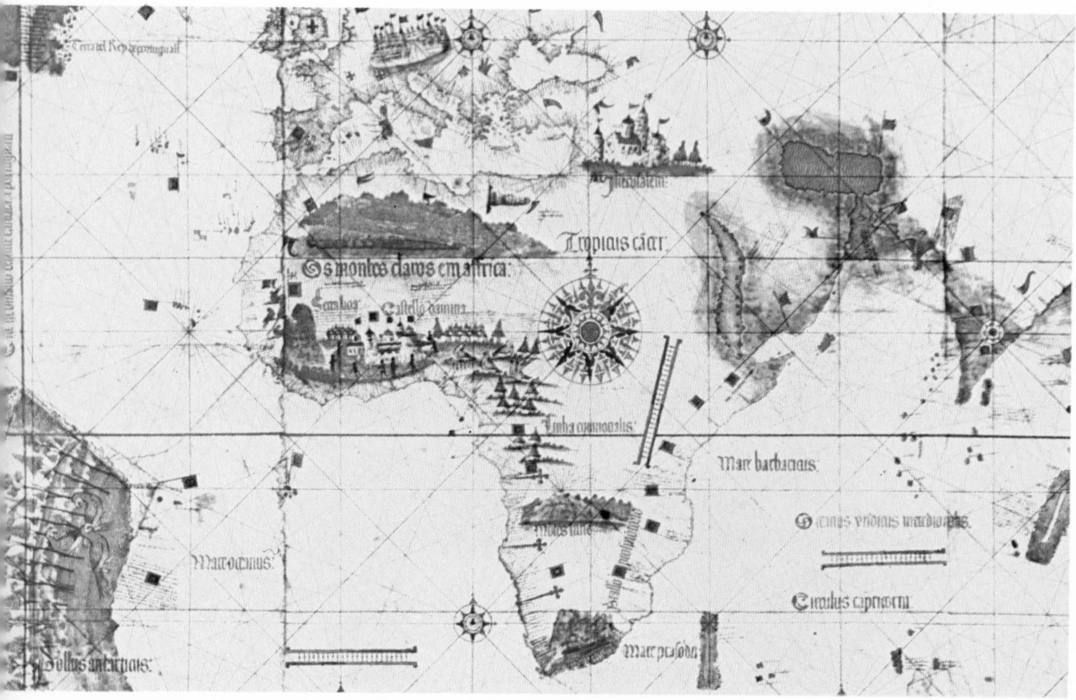

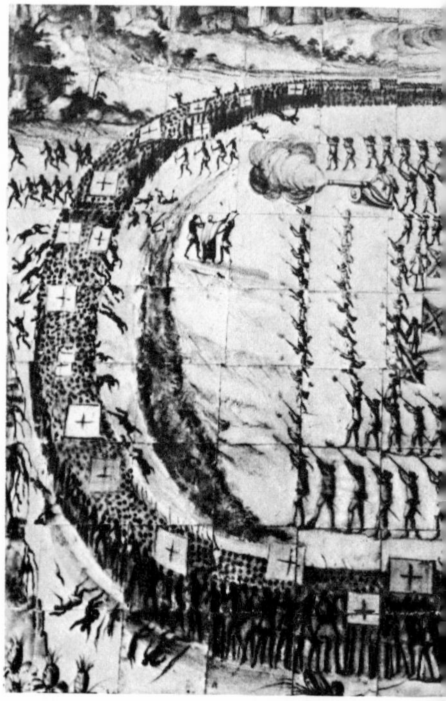

with the Portuguese were enhanced by the willingness of the Kongolese to adopt European customs.

Following his conversion to Christianity, Mani-Kongo Nzinga Mbemba (who reigned 1506–1542) adopted the name Dom Alfonso I. His capital Mbanza became São Salvador, and he accepted from his brother king in Portugal, Manuel I, a coat of arms. Nevertheless the profitability of the slave trade led first to an erosion in relations and, finally, to a successful Portuguese invasion of Kongo in 1665. The demise of the Kongo flag – clearly an adaptation of the contemporary Portuguese banner – marked the end of any hope that the Kongo might develop as an African state freely adapting what it found of use in European civilization.

Few flags were used in the following 300 years, characterized by exploitation of the Congo region by Arabs from the east and Europeans from the west, until the creation in 1876 of the International African Association. Theoretically devoted to the exploration of the Congo River, the International Association of the Congo (as it came to be called) actually laid the basis for a personal empire under Leopold II of Belgium. Its distinctive flag, adopted on 21 June 1877, consisted of a gold star in the center of a blue field. According to Henry M. Stanley, it symbolized the light of hope cast into the darkness of Africa. In fact, the new flag marked an era of cruelty and exploitation rarely matched in any other part of the world, such that eventually Leopold was forced to cede his dominions to the Belgian state in 1908.

The blue and gold flag introduced by Leopold's private army throughout the territory had become the only established symbol of authority in the area; it had been recognized on

10 April 1884 by the United States as the flag of a sovereign power. European states followed this example and on 1 August 1885 Leopold had proclaimed himself Sovereign of the Independent State of the Congo. In effect, the new state had come into existence through the recognition by other states that it was exercising the prerogatives of statehood, including the display of a national flag. After 15 November 1908 in addition to the black-yellow-red Belgian tricolor the new Belgian Congo colony continued to use the flag of the Independent State. In the words of the new Colonial Charter, "The suppression of the flag of the Independent State of the Congo, the only one known by the natives, could not be done without serious drawbacks."
The long tradition of the blue and gold flag and the absence of a unified national liberation movement were to influence the selection of the flag adopted when the Congo first achieved independence. Its provisional government, known as the General Executive College, decided on 21 May 1960 to add six small gold stars – one for each Congolese province – along the hoist of the old flag. The central star was seen as an expression of the hope for unity, the blue background interpreted as a symbol of prosperity. The new banner was raised on 30 June 1960 as the Belgian colonial regime ended. Its brief career was associated with national tragedies due in no small part to the Congo's being unprepared for independence and to the active support of many foreigners for secessionist movements.
The Congo first faced dismemberment less than two weeks after its proclamation of independence, when the State of Katanga was proclaimed on 11 July 1960. The Katanga flag, hoisted on 1 August, flew over this de facto independent nation until 24 May 1963 when United Nations troops intervened. Katanga had a flag which reflected its own mineral wealth, the chief justification for its separate existence. Copper had long been smelted into the form of crosses in Katanga and used for money. Prior to the absorption of Katanga by Leopold's Independent State of the Congo, King Msiri had adopted such a cross as his personal emblem. His grandson, Godefroy Munongo, was to be the powerful Minister of the Interior of the new Katanga state. The Katanga flag featured three crosses in red, a color said to stand for the

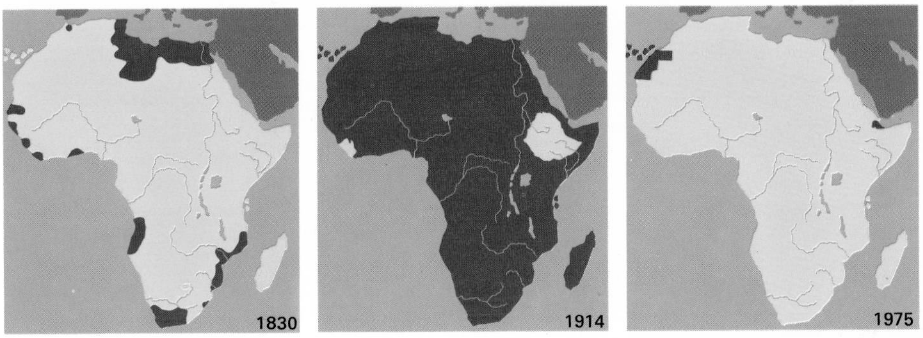

European powers established small outposts along the continent of Africa as early as the fifteenth century, but it was not until after the Berlin Conference of 1884 that the Europeans penetrated inland. At one time or another every part of Africa has been under colonial rule. The borders of modern African states (90 percent of which have gained independence since 1956) were largely established in the twentieth century by the colonizing powers.

Early portolanos *(far left)* show no flags for the Kongo Empire, although it did in fact use flags. These bore crosses and were based on the Portuguese model. They can clearly be seen *(left, center)* in the Battle of Ambuila in 1665, where Portuguese cannon decided the day. Two centuries later King Leopold II of Belgium granted his Congo dominions a coat of arms *(left)* incorporating the gold star on blue also found in its flag.

Inspiration for the Zaire national flag was found in the party emblem of the Popular Movement of the Revolution *(above).*

The yellow V on the green and red flag of South Kasai *(below)* stood for victory, but the flag and the state it represented barely lasted two years. The flag of another successionist state – Katanga – is shown *(bottom)* displayed on the office of one of its missions in Europe.

bravery of its people and the blood they were willing to shed in the defense of their nation. In addition to a triangle of the same color, the flag included white for purity and green for hope. Another province, South Kasai, announced its nationhood to the world on 9 August 1960 and lasted until 2 October 1962. Ruled by President (later King) Albert Kalonji, it was officially known as the Mining State because of its diamonds and other precious minerals.

Secession was not the only political problem facing the Congo. When its first prime minister, Patrice Lumumba, was assassinated some months after being dismissed by President Kasavubu, his supporters organized a rival government in Stanleyville (now Kisangani). Although Lumumba himself had referred to the blue flag with its seven gold stars as an "emblem of colonialism," the rebel government used it because of its associations with Lumumba during his months as prime minister. Even though the rebels were driven from Stanleyville, the central government at Leopoldville (now Kinshasha) felt the national flag should be altered, especially following a decision to increase the number of provinces from six to twenty. The symbolism of the new flag, with its yellow-bordered red stripe added through the center was clear: the red was for the blood of those who had struggled for independence, yellow for prosperity. A single star for unity appeared in the upper hoist.

In January 1964 a new revolt was raised in the east; following their capture of Stanleyville on 7 September 1964, rebels proclaimed the People's Republic of the Congo and threatened to extend their dominion to the remaining two-thirds of the nation. This regime resurrected the blue flag with seven gold stars, again because of the favorable association it had in the minds of many as the flag of Patrice Lumumba. Only in October 1965 did the last urban area controlled by the People's Republic fall to government forces.

A period of national reconstruction and reorganization followed. As part of his program to centralize the political and economic structure, President Joseph Mobutu organized the nationwide Popular Movement of the Revolution in 1967. In seeking an authentic African past, Mobutu has attempted to reverse the psychological dependence his people have had on European ideas for three hundred years. Christian names were converted to autochthonous forms – the president himself becoming Mobutu Sese Seko. Cities were renamed; the country was rebaptized after the original name of its great river, Zaire (pronounced zah *eer*). Like the gold and blue flag, the old name tended to recall the Independent State of the Congo, the Belgian colony, and the years of disunity following independence.

To express the new national identity of Zaire, a new flag design was required and pupils from the Kinshasa Academy were asked to submit ideas. As modified by President Mobutu, the final choice reflects the leading role in Zaire of the Popular Movement of the Revolution: its

INTERNATIONAL ASSOCIATION OF THE CONGO 1877–1885. INDEPENDENT STATE OF THE CONGO 1885–1908. BELGIAN CONGO 1908–1960.

REPUBLIC OF THE CONGO 1960–1963. PEOPLE'S REPUBLIC OF THE CONGO 1964–1965.

DEMOCRATIC REPUBLIC OF THE CONGO 1966–1971.

REPUBLIC OF ZAIRE 1971–PRESENT.

official color (light green) serves as the background. Green is a symbol of hope, faith in the future, and confidence of the people. Unity is symbolized by a disc whose yellow color stands for Zaire's extensive natural resources. The arm bearing a flaming torch graphically expresses the revolutionary spirit the nation aspires to; its red flames honor the nation's martyrs.

Zaire's experience, first of adapting colonial symbols during its early independence and then of recasting completely its symbolic identity –

borrowing both from its own past and from its dominant political organization – is a process found in many nations around the world. Particularly in Africa and Asia, new nations lacking highly integrated economic infrastructures, universally understood national languages, ethnic homogeneity, or even borders established by the will of their own people, have sought to ensure unity and development through the creation of a new national consciousness to supplant previous loyalties. To the degree that their political philosophies, government structures, heroes, symbols, and even names are those whose primary associations lie in the past, the very existence of new nations is endangered. New symbols cannot accomplish the entire task, of course; yet a sophisticated "alternate state" created in the minds and lives of people in part through a distinctive flag can go a long way toward providing the political identification that leads to the stability on which most other progress depends.

In the 1960s the Congolese rallied under a flag associated with their first prime minister, Patrice Lumumba. President Mobutu Sese Seko *(above, center)* was responsible for instituting the current name and flag of Zaire.

FLAGS ACROSS THE WORLD

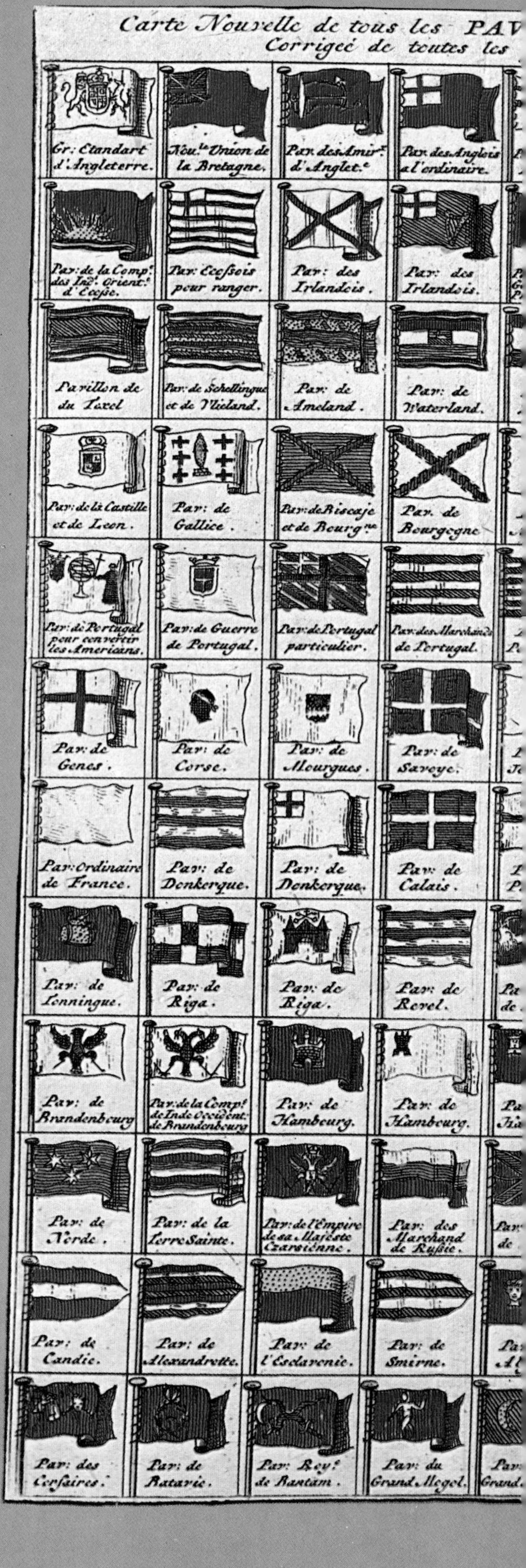

The editor of this mid-eighteenth-century flag chart, included in a Dutch atlas, promises that it is "corrected of all previous errors."

For six hundred years the attempt has been made to produce the perfect flag reference source. Hindered by vast distances and by differences in language and flag traditions as well as lacking a sophisticated audience for their work, early vexillologists, nevertheless, did a remarkable job. We may smile at the rendering of the flag of Genghis Khan (page 62), which the compiler of the chart *(right)* has attempted to show under the name Ensign of Tartary (see the fourth square from the bottom right corner). His overall success, however, is a remarkable one.

The following hundred pages present the flags and state arms of all the countries in the modern world. If there are similarities with this chart, the differences are even more striking. Colors and proportions and designs are now shown with a precision which modern laws require; usage of each design is clearly indicated, eliminating the confusion which existed in past sources where three or more flags might be shown for the same country. The importance of each country's national language, the history of its symbolism, even its geographical location – all are given due recognition. Finally we note, while many European nations retain the same flags they had more than two hundred years ago, no longer do European flags constitute five-sixths of the total as they did when the chart at right was compiled.

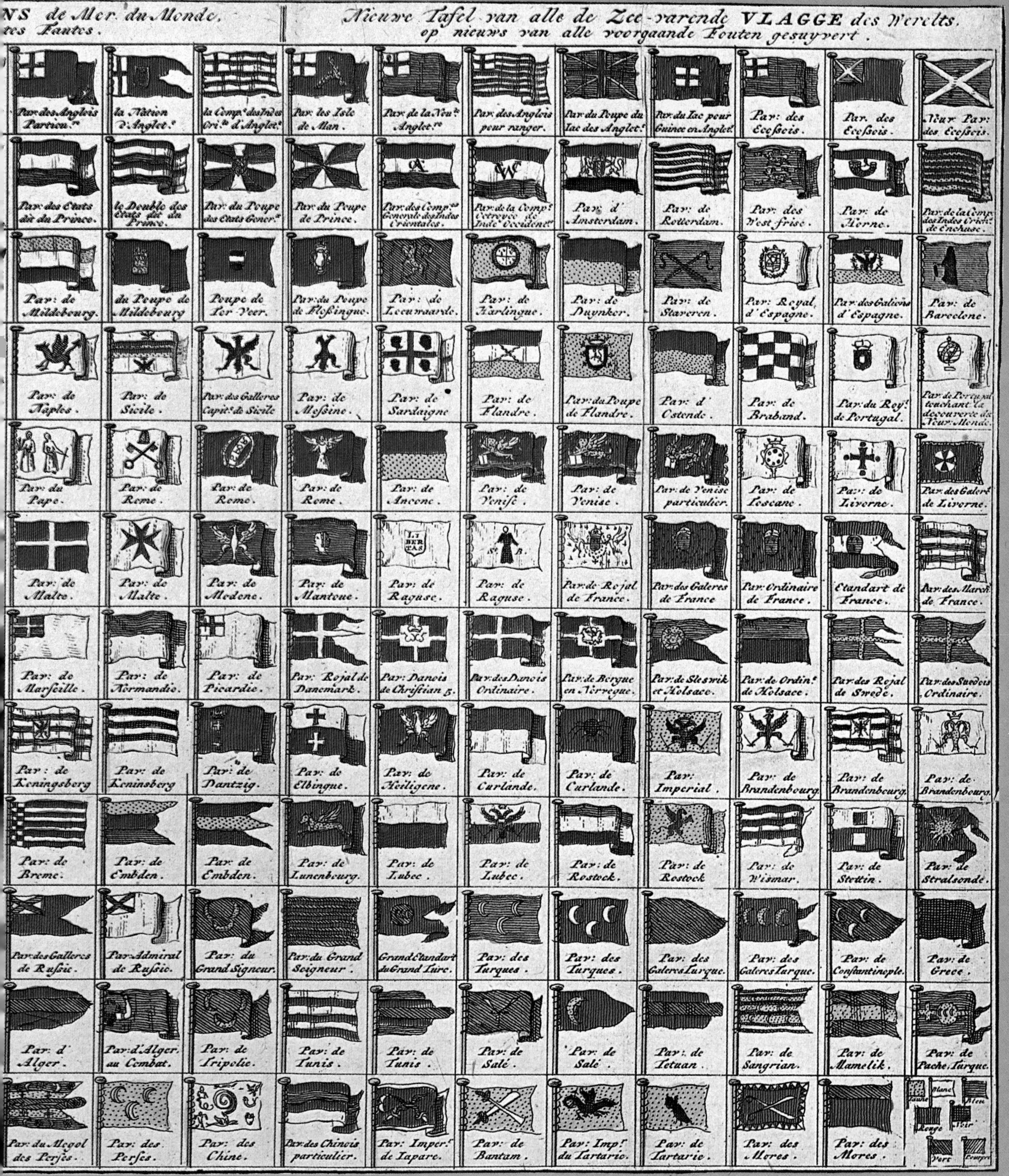
NS de Mer du Monde,
tes Fautes.
Nieuwe Tafel van alle de Zee-varende VLAGGE des Werelts,
op nieuws van alle voorgaande Fouten gesuyvert.
Par: des Anglois Particu.re
la Nation d'Anglet.e
la Comp.e des Indes Ori.le d'Anglet.e
Par: les Isle de Man.
Par: de la Nou.le Anglet.re
Par: des Anglois pour ranger.
Par: du Poupe du Iac des Anglet.s
Par: du Iac pour Guinee en Anglet.e
Par: des Ecossois.
Par: des Ecossois.
Nour Par: des Ecossois.
Par: des Etats dit du Prince.
le Double des Etats dit du Prince.
Par: du Poupe des Etats Gener.x
Par: du Poupe de Prince.
Par: des Comp.es Generale des Indes Orientales.
Par: de la Comp.e Octroyee de Inde Occident.le
Par: d'Amsterdam.
Par: de Rotterdam.
Par: des West frise.
Par: de Horne.
Par: de la Comp. des Indes Orient. de Enchuse.
Par: de Mildebourg.
du Poupe de Mildebourg
Poupe de Ter Veer.
Par: du Poupe de Flessingue.
Par: de Leeuwaarde.
Par: de Harlingue.
Par: de Duynker.
Par: de Stareren.
Par: Royal d'Espagne.
Par: des Galions d'Espagne.
Par: de Barcelone.
Par: de Naples.
Par: de Sicile.
Par: des Galleres Capit.e de Sicile
Par: de Messine.
Par: de Sardaigne
Par: de Flandre.
Par: du Poupe de Flandre.
Par: d'Ostende.
Par: de Braband.
Par: du Roy.l de Portugal.
Par: de Portugal touchant la decouverte de Nouv. Monde.
Par: du Pape.
Par: de Rome.
Par: de Rome.
Par: de Rome.
Par: de Ancone.
Par: de Venise.
Par: de Venise.
Par: de Venise particulier.
Par: de Toscane.
Par: de Livorne.
Par: des Galere de Livorne.
Par: de Malte.
Par: de Malte.
Par: de Medene.
Par: de Mantoue.
Par: de Raguse.
Par: de Raguse.
Par: de Rojal de France.
Par: des Galeres de France
Par: Ordinaire de France.
Etandart de France.
Par: des March. de France.
Par: de Marseille.
Par: de Normandie.
Par: de Picardie.
Par: Rojal de Danemark.
Par: Danois de Christian 5.
Par: des Danois Ordinaire.
Par: de Bergue en Norregue.
Par: de Sleswik et Holsace.
Par: de Ordin.e de Holsace.
Par: des Rojal de Swede.
Par: des Suedois Ordinaire.
Par: de Koningsberg
Par: de Koninsberg
Par: de Dantzig.
Par: de Elbingue.
Par: de Heiligene.
Par: de Curlande.
Par: de Curlande.
Par: Imperial.
Par: de Brandenbourg.
Par: de Brandenbourg.
Par: de Brandenbourg.
Par: de Breme.
Par: de Embden.
Par: de Embden.
Par: de Lunenbourg.
Par: de Lubec.
Par: de Lubec.
Par: de Rostock.
Par: de Rostock
Par: de Wismar.
Par: de Stettin.
Par: de Stralsonde.
Par: des Galleres de Russie.
Par: Admiral de Russie.
Par: du Grand Signeur.
Par: du Grand Seigneur.
Grand Etandart du Grand Turc.
Par: des Turques.
Par: des Turques.
Par: des Galeres Turque.
Par: des Galeres Turque.
Par: de Constantinople.
Par: de Grece.
Par: d'Alger.
Par: d'Alger au Combat.
Par: de Tripolie.
Par: de Tunis.
Par: de Tunis.
Par: de Salé.
Par: de Salé.
Par: de Tetuan.
Par: de Sangrian.
Par: de Mamelik.
Par: de Pache Turque.
Par: du Mogol des Perses.
Par: des Perses.
Par: des Chine.
Par: des Chinois particulier.
Par: Imper.r de Iapare.
Par: de Bantam.
Par: Imp.r du Tartarie.
Par: de Tartarie.
Par: des Mores.
Par: des Mores.
Jaune
Blanc
Bleu
Rouge
Noir
Vert
Pourpre

FLAGS OF ALL NATIONS provides both a quick reference and a leisurely survey of the world's 157 nation-states and their subdivisions and dependencies as of 1 May 1975. Detailed explanations of the illustrations for the essential flags and arms of each country appear at the bottom of this and the next page; their histories and usages are presented in an accompanying text. Each nation appears in alphabetical order according to the official name in its own language. To find any country, simply check the number that determines its position in the following pages by locating the nation's name in the English language index presented here.

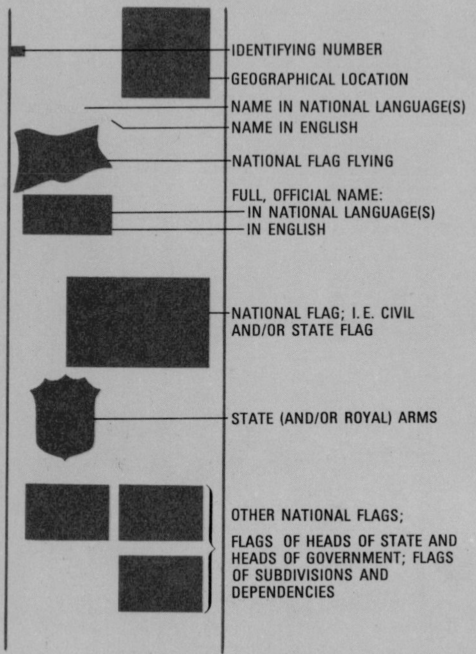

The term "national flag" comprehends six different possible functions. Some countries have one flag, others several, for these functions. The reader may find it useful to refer to *Terms Defined*, page 12.

JAPAN	105	NIHON
JORDAN	148	AL URDUN
KENYA	70	KENYA
KOREA	71,2	KORAI
KUWAIT	74	AL KUWAIT
LAOS	75	LAO
LEBANON	80	LUBNAN
LESOTHO	76	LESOTHO
LIBERIA	77	LIBERIA
LIBYA	78	LIBIYA
LIECHTENSTEIN	79	LIECHTENSTEIN
LUXEMBOURG	81	LUXEMBURG
MALAGASY REPUBLIC	116	RÉPUBLIQUE MALGACHE
MALAWI	84	MALAWI
MALAYSIA	85	MALAYSIA
MALDIVES	36	DIVEHI
MALI	86	MALI
MALTA	87	MALTA
MAURITANIA	94	MURITANIYA
MAURITIUS	88	MAURITIUS
MEXICO	89	MÉXICO
MONACO	92	MONACO
MONGOLIA	93	MONGGOL
MOROCCO	82	AL MAGRIB
MOZAMBIQUE	91	MOÇAMBIQUE
NAMIBIA	97	NAMIBIA
NAURU	98	NAOERO/NAURU
NEPAL	100	NEPAL
NETHERLANDS	99	NEDERLAND
NEW ZEALAND	101	NEW ZEALAND
NICARAGUA	102	NICARAGUA
NIGER	103	NIGER
NIGERIA	104	NIGERIA
NORWAY	106	NORGE
OMAN	145	UMAN
PAKISTAN	108	PAKISTAN
PANAMA	109	PANAMÁ
PARAGUAY	110	PARAGUAY
PERU	111	PERÚ
PHILIPPINES	112	PILIPINAS
POLAND	113	POLSKA
PORTUGAL	114	PORTUGAL
QATAR	115	QATAR
RHODESIA	119	RHODESIA
ROMANIA	120	ROMÂNIA
RWANDA	121	RWANDA
SAN MARINO	123	SAN MARINO
SAUDI ARABIA	6	AL ARABIYA AL SAUDIYAH
SENEGAL	124	SÉNÉGAL
SIERRA LEONE	126	SIERRA LEONE
SINGAPORE	127	SINGAPURA
SOMALIA	128	SUMALIYA
SOUTH AFRICA	129	SUID-AFRIKA
SOVIET UNION	130	SOVYETSKII SOYUZ
SPAIN	42	ESPAÑA
SRI LANKA	131	SRI LANKA
SUDAN	132	AL SUDAN
SWAZILAND	136	SWAZILAND
SWEDEN	135	SVERIGE
SWITZERLAND	58	HELVETIA
SYRIA	134	SURIYAH
TANZANIA	137	TANZANIA
THAILAND	95	MUANG TAI
TOGO	139	TOGO
TONGA	140	TONGA
TRINIDAD/TOBAGO	141	TRINIDAD/TOBAGO
TUNISIA	142	AL TUNISIYA
TURKEY	143	TÜRKİYE
UGANDA	144	UGANDA
UNITED ARAB EMIRATES	2	AMIRAT ARABIYAH MUTAHIDAH
UNITED KINGDOM	146	UNITED KINGDOM
UNITED STATES	147	UNITED STATES
UPPER VOLTA	56	HAUTE-VOLTA
URUGUAY	149	URUGUAY
VATICAN CITY	26	CITTÀ VATICANO
VENEZUELA	150	VENEZUELA
VIET-NAM	151-3	VIỆT-NAM
WESTERN SAMOA	122	SAMOA I SISIFO
YEMEN	154,5	AL YAMAN
YUGOSLAVIA	67	JUGOSLAVIJA
ZAIRE	156	ZAÏRE
ZAMBIA	157	ZAMBIA

NATIONAL FLAGS/IDENTIFICATION SYMBOLS.

The following international standard symbols are used to indicate the functions of a particular flag, its proportions, or some other significant fact about it.

	PRIVATE USE	PUBLIC USE	MILITARY USE
USE ON LAND	CIVIL FLAG	STATE FLAG	WAR FLAG
USE AT SEA	CIVIL ENSIGN	STATE ENSIGN	WAR ENSIGN

- CIVIL FLAG
- STATE FLAG
- WAR FLAG
- CIVIL ENSIGN
- STATE ENSIGN
- WAR ENSIGN
- CIVIL AND STATE FLAG
- STATE AND WAR FLAG
- CIVIL AND STATE ENSIGN
- STATE AND WAR ENSIGN
- CIVIL FLAG AND ENSIGN
- STATE FLAG AND ENSIGN
- WAR FLAG AND ENSIGN
- NATIONAL FLAG
- NATIONAL ENSIGN
- WAR FLAG AND ENSIGN, STATE FLAG
- STATE FLAG, CIVIL AND WAR ENSIGN
- CIVIL AND STATE FLAG AND ENSIGN
- STATE AND WAR FLAG AND ENSIGN
- NATIONAL FLAG, STATE ENSIGN
- NATIONAL FLAG, CIVIL AND STATE ENSIGN
- NATIONAL ENSIGN, STATE AND WAR FLAG
- CIVIL AND STATE FLAG, NATIONAL ENSIGN
- NATIONAL FLAG AND ENSIGN

- PROPOSAL (design never actually used)
- RECONSTRUCTED (design based on written sources only)
- REVERSE (design shown is reverse side of flag)
- VARIANT (one of two or more variants of the same basic design)
- ALTERNATE (one of two flags used simultaneously – or under special conditions – for the same function)
- 1:2 OFFICIAL PROPORTIONS
- 1:2≈ UNOFFICIAL PROPORTIONS (de facto or unknown, but approximate)
- DE FACTO (in actual use but without legal sanction)
- TWO-SIDED (reverse side is unlike design shown)
- SINISTER HOIST (The obverse or more important side of the flag is seen when the hoist is shown to the observer's right.)

1

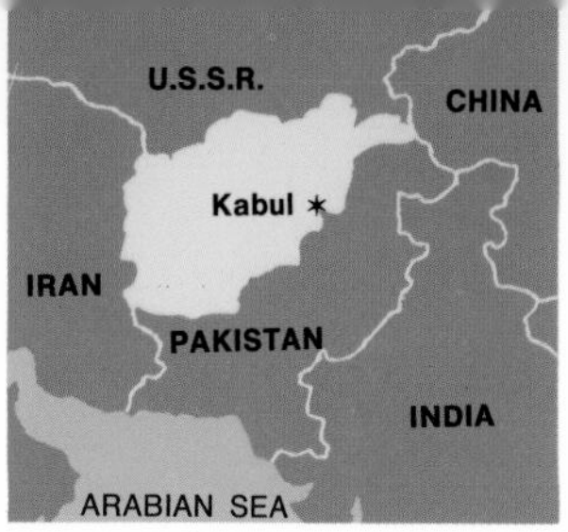

AFGANISTAN

AFGHANISTAN

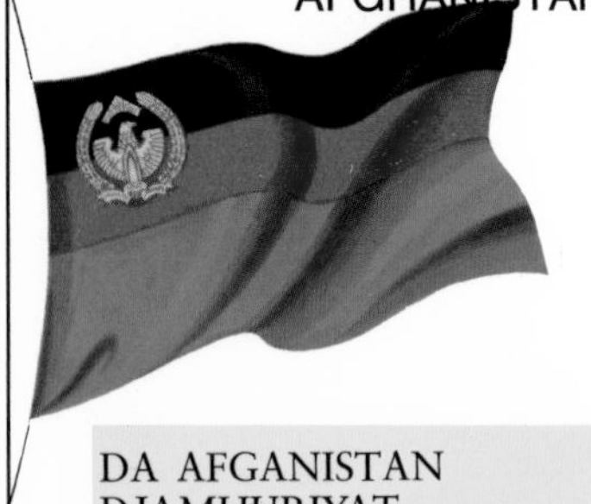

DA AFGANISTAN DJAMHURIYAT

REPUBLIC OF AFGHANISTAN

Until 1929 the field of the Afghan national flag was black – one of very few national flags in world history to employ this color for its background. Until the monarchy was overthrown in 1973, the royal color was red.
After 1928 these two colors were combined with green to form the national flag, although under the monarchy the stripes were vertical.
The state arms include symbols of agriculture and of religion (the stylized mosque in the center). The eagle is the miraculous bird of legend which placed a crown on the head of the first Afghan king, Yama. The ribbon bears the name of the state and the date 26 Changash 1352 (17 July 1973), when the republican revolution took place.

Officially hoisted 9 May 1974.

2:3

STATE ARMS

The rising sun, symbol of a new dawn for the country, was first featured in the Afghan national flag for a few months in 1928. At that time King Amanullah, back from a visit to Europe, introduced sweeping reforms in the social, economic, and political organization of his nation.
The coat of arms and flag Amanullah introduced disappeared very quickly in a counterrevolution led by reactionaries, but they did have influence on later designs. (His was the first Afghan flag of stripes, for example.) The sun may originally have been influenced by the Zoroastrian religion.

2

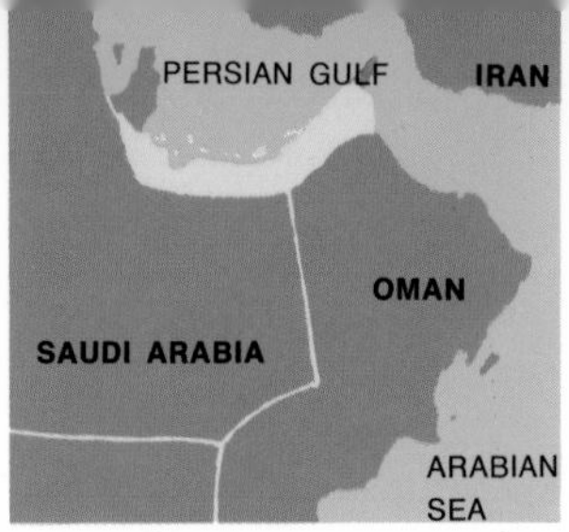

AL AMIRAT AL ARABIYAH AL MUTAHIDAH

UNITED ARAB EMIRATES

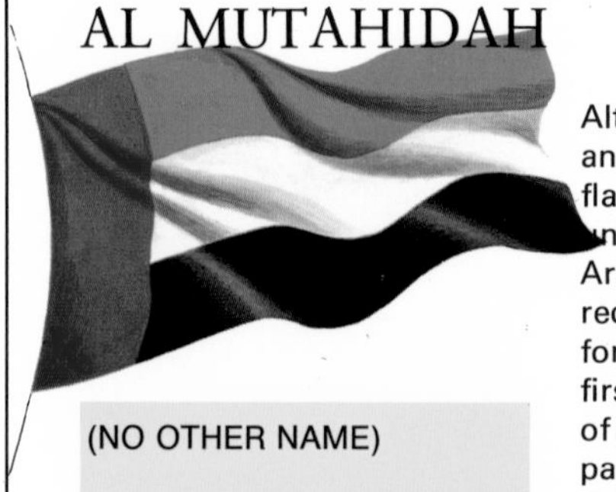

(NO OTHER NAME)

Although only the colors red and white appeared in the flags of the seven states which united to create it, the United Arab Emirates chose the four recognized pan-Arab colors for its national flag. These had first been combined in the flag of the Arab Revolt of 1916 (see page 155).
The red and white flags of the member states are variations of a single flag created in 1820 (see Bahrain). The arms of the United Arab Emirates include the name of the state, the falcon which is popular locally in hunting, and the familiar *dhow* – a ship in which Arabs for centuries have sailed the Indian Ocean.

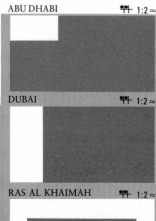

Officially hoisted 2 December 1971.

1:2≈

STATE ARMS

ABU DHABI 1:2≈

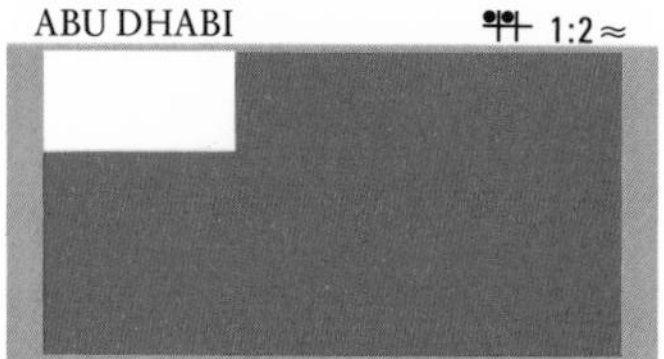

AJMAN 1:2≈

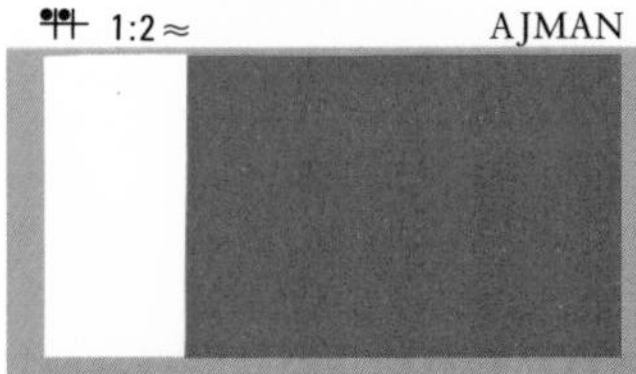

DUBAI 1:2≈

AL FUJAIRAH 1:2≈

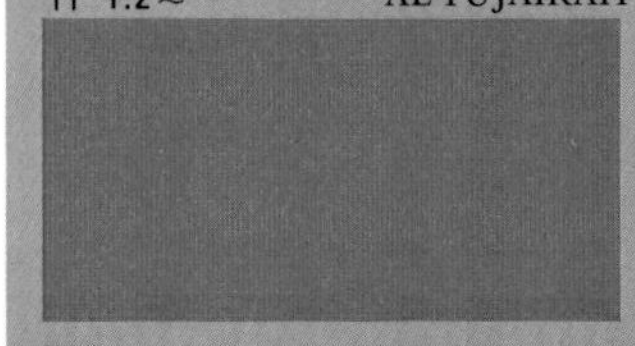

RAS AL KHAIMAH 1:2≈

AL SHARQAH 1:2≈

UMM AL QIWAIN 3:5≈

3

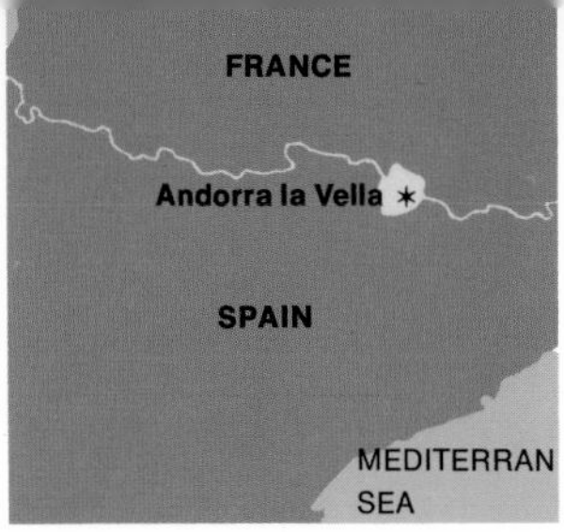

ANDORRA

ANDORRA

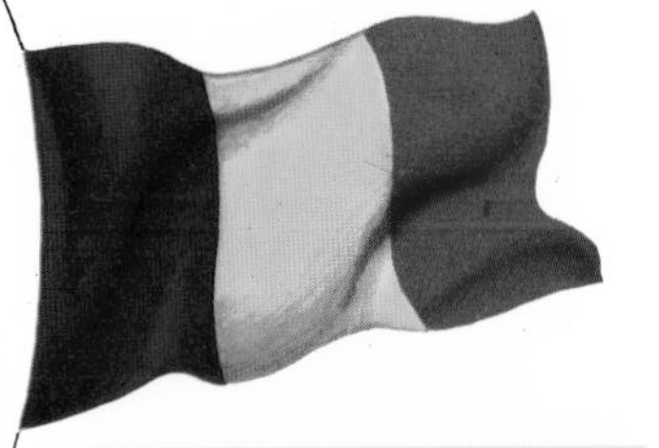

VALLS D'ANDORRA

VALLEYS OF ANDORRA

The colors of the Andorran flag are those of its neighbors, France and Spain.

Napoleon III of France is reputed to have established the flag of Andorra more than a century ago.
The House of the Valleys, meeting place for the General Council of Andorra (its parliament), has a carved representation of the arms inscribed: "Behold: here are the arms of a neutral valley; there are kingdoms more noble by which they rejoice to be guarded. If individually they bless other peoples, Andorra, why should they not, joined, bring to you a golden age?"
The arms of Andorra express its history well. The crozier and mitre are symbols of the Bishops of Urgel; their authority was challenged by the Counts of Foix – whose arms appear in the second quarter of the shield. In 1278 the two signed an agreement and became joint rulers of Andorra.
The arms of Catalonia and of Béarn figure in the third and fourth quarters of Andorra. The motto of Andorra may be translated from the Latin "Strength United Is Stronger."

Usage initiated ca. 1866.

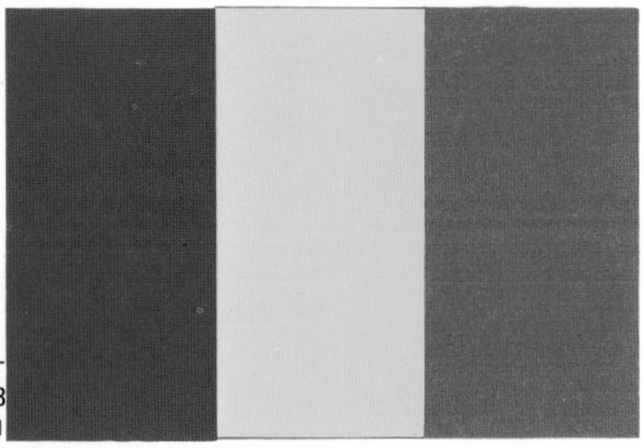

2:3

STATE ARMS

2:3

Andorra is often referred to as a republic or as a principality. In the modern sense of these words, neither one is appropriate. Andorra is rather a condominium ruled jointly by Spain and France. Although not a sovereign nation, it does enjoy considerable local autonomy.

4

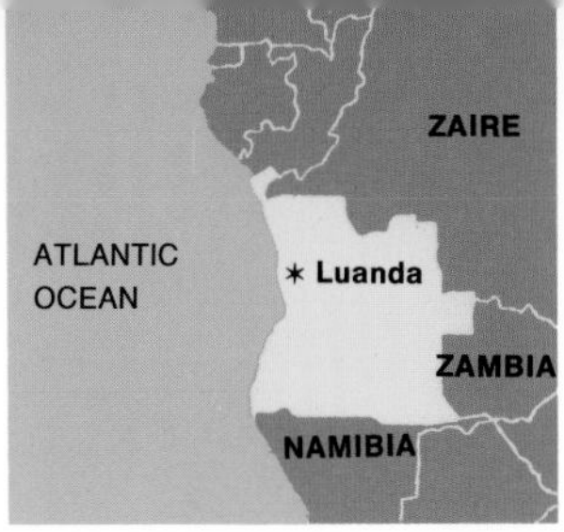

ANGOLA

ANGOLA

(NO OTHER NAME)

In the early 1960s three different national liberation movements began political agitation and military operations designed to establish an independent Angola. Success was achieved, however, only after a revolution in Portugal itself created a new political climate in which the Portuguese were willing to consider that their overseas territories would no longer accept the status of non-self-governing provinces of the homeland.
The arms of Portugal are linked (by the heraldic symbol for water) with native fauna of Angola in the provincial arms used under the colonial regime.

At the time of this writing, the flag of Portugal is still the official state flag of the territory. Angolan independence is scheduled for 11 November 1975.

COLONIAL ARMS

UNION OF ANGOLAN PEOPLES (PARTY FLAG)

2:3≈

POPULAR MOVEMENT FOR THE LIBERATION OF ANGOLA (PARTY FLAG)

2:3

NATIONAL UNION FOR THE TOTAL INDEPENDENCE OF ANGOLA (PARTY FLAG)

1:2

The liberation flags of the three parties now forming the provisional government of Angola proclaim independence through use of a star or rising sun. Red is for the blood shed in the struggle for freedom. Agreement on a national flag is one of many tasks facing the provisional government.

5

ANGUILLA

ANGUILLA

(NO OTHER NAME)

Usage initiated September 1967.

Marvin Oberman, an American graphic designer and a cocreator of the Anguillan flag, explained its symbols as follows: "The flag has a white field for peace, a blue-green band across the bottom symbolizing the sea that surrounds Anguilla, youth, and hope. The three interlocking orange dolphins on the white field (suggested by the red sun on white of the Japanese flag) represent strength and endurance. . . . The total design is meant to represent a bright, new, forward-looking aspect combined with dignity and freedom for a newly emerged independent country." Because of Anguilla's unusual legal status, its flag is not internationally recognized. Originally part of the British colony of St. Christopher-Nevis-Anguilla, Anguilla declared its independence in 1967. Two years later British forces occupied the island and have continued to administer it since.

1:2 ≈

STATE ARMS

COMMISSIONER'S FLAG

1:2

The symbols of the coat of arms reflect the history, Caribbean sun, prosperity, and close ties of Anguilla with the sea. The tree is the native mahogany, known for its strength. The dolphin supporter represents friendship and intelligence.

6

AL ARABIYA AL SAUDIYAH

SAUDI ARABIA

AL MAMLAKAH
AL ARABIYAH
AL SAUDIYAH

SAUDI ARABIAN KINGDOM

This is the only national flag featuring an inscription as its principal charge.

Officially confirmed ca. 30 March 1938.

Green, long symbolic in Islam as the color of the Fatimid dynasty established by the Prophet's daughter, Fatima, was used by early Muslims as a flag. A green turban belonging to the Prophet supposedly was their first such flag.

Abd al-Aziz ibn Saud, leader of the Wahabis (a strict Muslim sect), extended their rule throughout the heartland of Arabia, renaming the country after himself in 1932.

The traditional Wahabi banner is now the official Saudi state flag. It displays the *Shahada* or Word of Unity of Islam: "There is no god but Allah and Muhammad is the Prophet of Allah." The sword, a symbol of Wahabi militancy, is repeated in the coat of arms which also includes the date palm associated with the agricultural livelihood of traditional Saudi society.

2:3

STATE ARMS

1:1

ROYAL FLAG

2:3 ≈

7

ARGENTINA

ARGENTINA

REPÚBLICA ARGENTINA

ARGENTINE REPUBLIC

Officially adopted 25 July 1816.

Cockades of celeste and white were distributed to the crowd which gathered on 25 May 1810 in the Plaza of Buenos Aires, successfully demanding from the Spanish viceroy the creation of a popular local government.
The day had been cloudy, and the people took it as a favorable omen when the clouds parted and the sun shone down on them. That "Sun of May" came to be recognized as a national symbol; added to the celeste-white-celeste civil flag in 1818, it formed the state flag still in use today.
Over the years not only has there been disagreement on whether the Argentine blue should be called celeste, azure, azure-celeste, sky blue, or celeste-blue, but the exact meaning of these terms has never been precisely defined.

2:3≈

STATE ARMS

2:3

PRESIDENTIAL FLAG

3:4

A military color hoisted by General Manuel Belgrano on 12 February 1812 in the city of Rosario is hailed by Argentines as their first national flag.
The United Provinces of the Plate River, as the country was then known, had already begun to employ celeste and white as national colors. The victorious Army of the Andes under José de San Martín used flags of blue and white as it helped liberate South America.

8

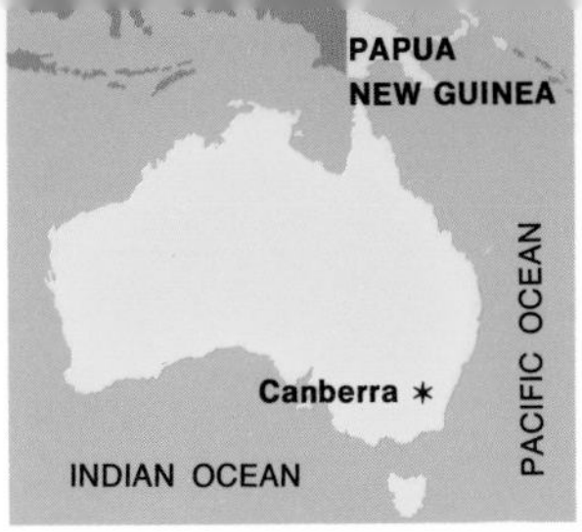

AUSTRALIA

COMMONWEALTH OF AUSTRALIA

Officially adopted 22 May 1909; confirmed in present form 15 April 1954.

The first official flag representing the whole continent was hoisted by the governor-general, the Earl of Hopetoun, on 16 September 1901 in Townsville. Except that the large star has increased from six to seven points – to represent the six states and the territories of Australia – the same banner has flown ever since.
The constellation of the Southern Cross is used not only by Australia but also by two of its states and by New Zealand, Western Samoa, Papua New Guinea, the Falkland Islands, and Brazil and several of its states. In Australia the white stars and blue field may be traced back to the Eureka Stockade flag (see page 78).
Symbols of the Australian states are found both in the national arms and the flag of the queen of Australia. In the former native flora and fauna join the "Commonwealth star" as accessories.

1:2

STATE ARMS

1:2 1:2

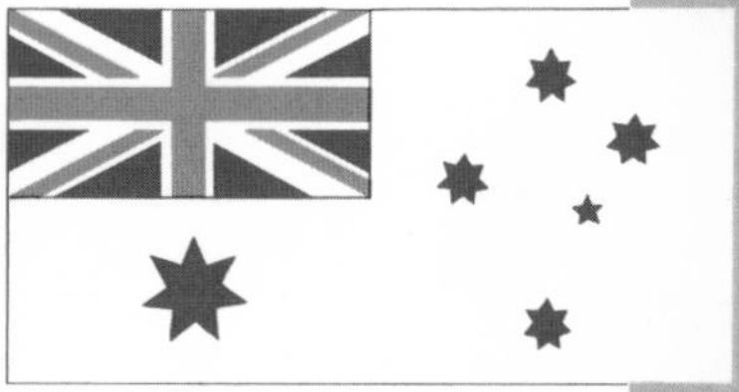

ROYAL FLAG

22:31≈

GOVERNOR-GENERAL'S FLAG

1:2

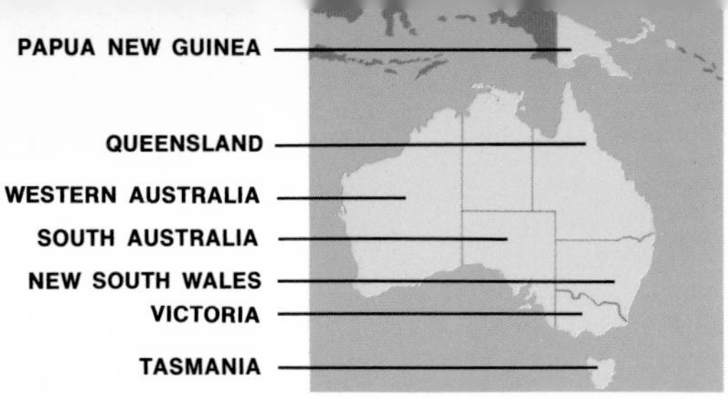

The traditional Blue Ensigns with badges recall the fact that these states were British colonies when the flags were adopted. In contrast Papua New Guinea is an Australian dependency scheduled for independence.

1:2

NEW SOUTH WALES
Officially adopted
15 February 1876.

1:2

QUEENSLAND
Officially adopted
29 November 1876.

1:2

SOUTH AUSTRALIA
Officially adopted
13 January 1904.

1:2

TASMANIA
Officially adopted
25 September 1876.

1:2

VICTORIA
Officially adopted
30 November 1877.

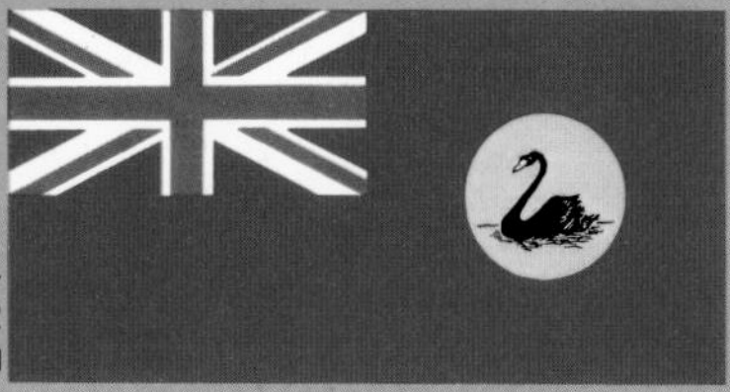
1:2

WESTERN AUSTRALIA
Officially adopted
27 November 1875.

3:4

PAPUA NEW GUINEA
Officially hoisted
1 July 1971; independence is scheduled for the 1970s.

9

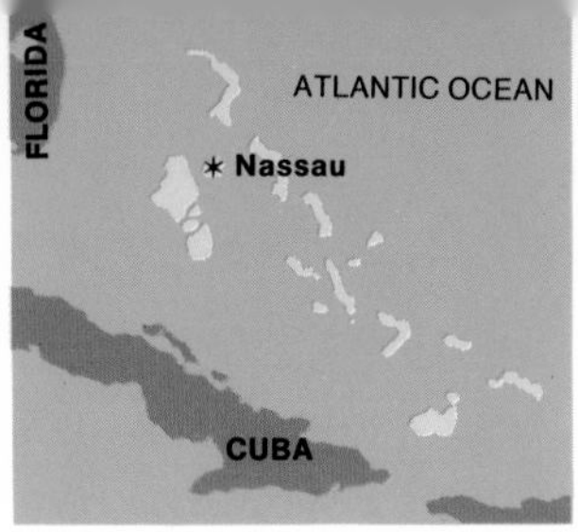

THE BAHAMAS

THE COMMONWEALTH OF THE BAHAMAS

Officially hoisted
10 July 1973.

The golden sands of the 700 Bahamian islands are reflected in the center stripe of the flag, while the aquamarine stripes bring to mind the various shades of ocean waters around those islands. The black triangle indicates the unity of the Bahamian people in their determination to develop the resources of both land and sea.

The other Bahamian flags follow a general British pattern, recalling two and a half centuries under British rule. The mace in the flag of the Prime Minister, symbol of parliamentary authority, indicates the peaceful evolution of the country to independence.

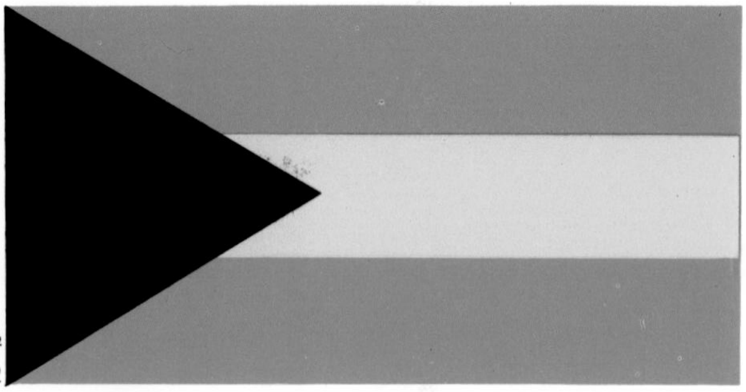
1:2

STATE ARMS

1:2

1:2

1:2

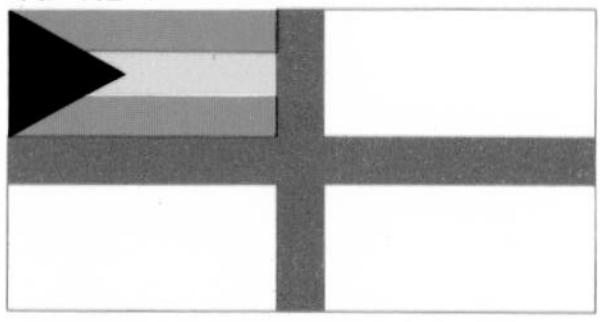

GOVERNOR-GENERAL'S FLAG

1:2

PRIME MINISTER'S FLAG

1:2

10

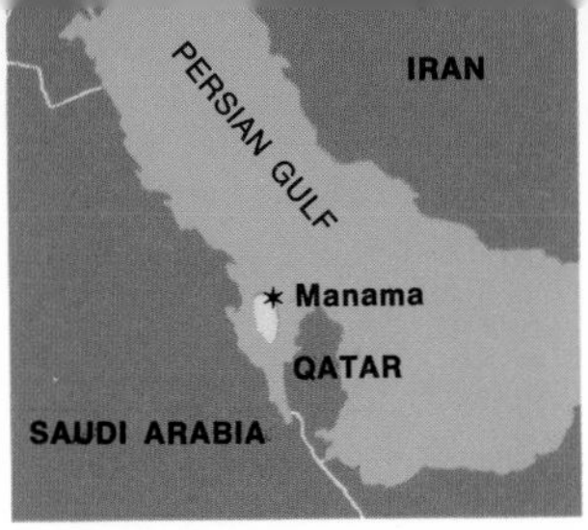

AL BAHRAIN
BAHRAIN

DAULAT AL BAHRAIN

STATE OF BAHRAIN

The name of the country means "Two Seas."

Article 3 of the General Treaty signed by the British and certain states of the Persian Gulf in 1820 required that "the friendly Arabs shall carry by land and sea a red flag, with or without letters in it, at their option, and this shall be in a border of white...."
Bahrain, one of the signatories to the treaty, still flies an adaptation of that flag today. Like the other signatories – the rest now states of the United Arab Emirates – Bahrain has made modifications in the original design. The border, still covering three edges in the standard of the ruler, is found only along the hoist in the national flag. The line between the white and red in that flag may be either straight or serrated, as shown.
No special significance is attached to the variations of the original flag. The red color of the field was originally a symbol of the Kharijite Muslims of the area.

Officially confirmed 1933.

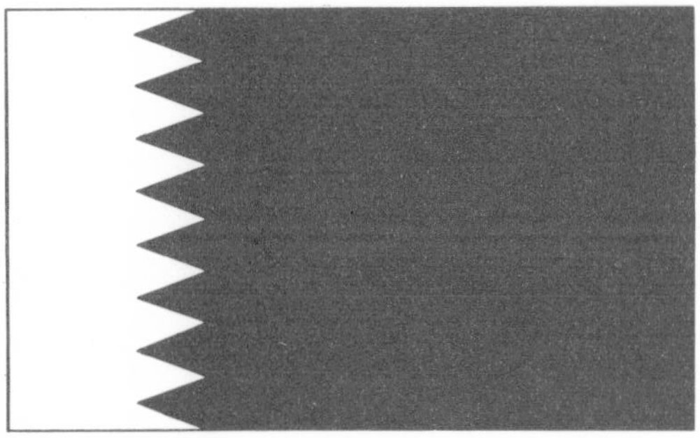

3:5

STATE ARMS

ROYAL FLAG

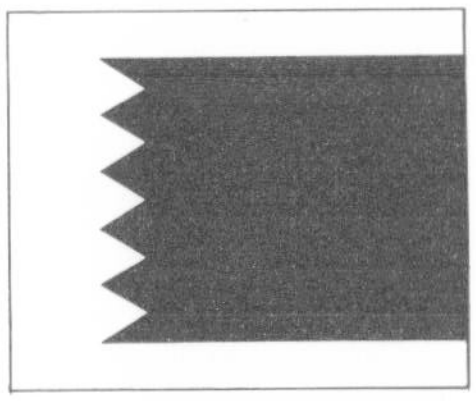

3:4

Although theoretically independent, the Arab states who signed the General Treaty all later agreed to allow the British to conduct their foreign affairs; their independence was regained in the 1970s.
A British advisor to the Shiekh of Bahrain, Sir Charles Belgrave, was responsible in the 1930s for designing the Bahrain coat of arms. The crest consists of an "eastern crown" which symbolizes royalty but which is not in actual use in the country.

11

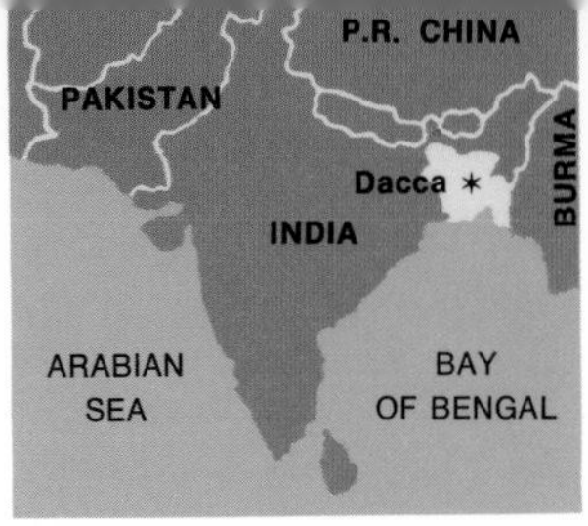

BANGLADESH
BANGLADESH

GANA PRAJATANTRI BANGLADESH

PEOPLE'S REPUBLIC OF BANGLADESH

For almost a quarter of a century Pakistan consisted of two parts separated by Indian territory – as well as by language, economic conditions, and culture. Finally in 1971 East Pakistan proclaimed its independence as Bangladesh.
The green of the new flag may have been inspired by its associations with Islam. During the independence struggle a silhouette map of Bangladesh appeared in gold on the disc; this was later omitted because of difficulties in properly representing it on both sides of the flag.
The verdure of the land is symbolized by the field of the flag; blood shed in the battle for freedom is recalled by the red disc. The flag was designed by Serajul Alam, whose name means "Light of the Flag."
The disc is set slightly toward the hoist so that when the flag is flying it will appear to be in the center.

Officially confirmed 25 January 1972.

3:5

STATE ARMS

The coat of arms of Bangladesh features a water lily (shapla flower) in the center, framed by shoots of padi. Leaves of jute, another important agricultural product, appear at the top. The stars are associated with the social and economic goals of national development. The waters recall Bengali rivers, the national transportation network.

12

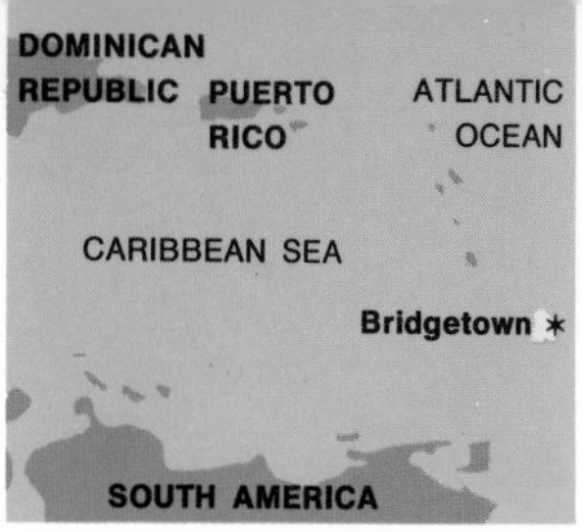

BARBADOS

(NO OTHER NAME)

Under British colonial rule the badge of Barbados included a trident, the traditional symbol of the sea god Neptune. Use of a trident in the national flag thus reflects the nation's past and its association with the sea. The fact that the trident head has been broken from its shaft indicates a break with the colonial past.

The sea and sky surrounding the island are represented by the blue stripes of the flag, its sandy beaches by the gold stripe. Grantley Prescod chose the colors and designed the flag for which he won first prize in a nationwide competition.

A royal warrant dated 21 December 1965 confirmed the arms of Barbados. Its shield includes a bearded fig tree and two flowers known as the red pride of Barbados. The arm in the crest holds sugar cane, an important agricultural resource for Barbados. The dexter supporter is a dolphin rendered in a stylized heraldic form.

Officially hoisted 30 November 1966.

2:3

STATE ARMS

PRIME MINISTER'S FLAG

2:3≈

GOVERNOR-GENERAL'S FLAG

3:4≈

Governors of British colonies generally display a local badge on the Union Jack. After 1931 a new flag was devised for use by the governor-general, the royal agent in independent countries still associated with Britain.

Although some variations exist in certain details, the 1931 flag is flown today by governors-general in Australia, the Bahamas, Canada, Fiji, Jamaica, Mauritius, New Zealand, Trinidad and Tobago, as well as Barbados.

13

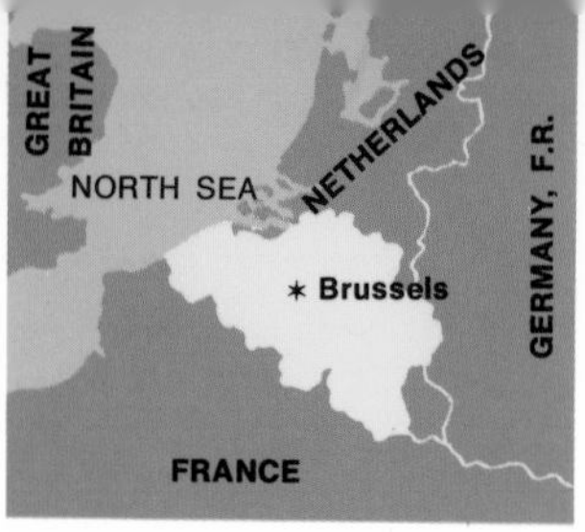

BELGIQUE/BELGIË

BELGIUM

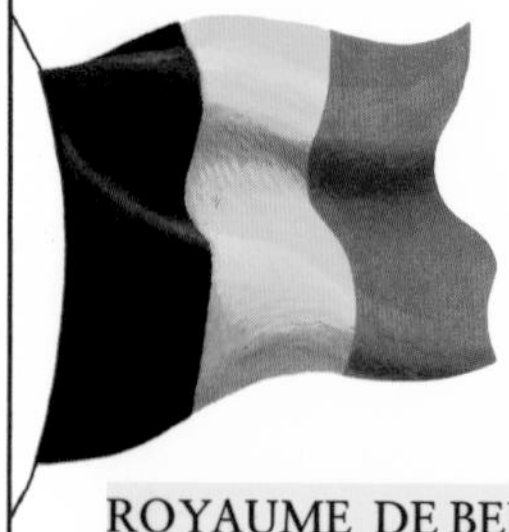

ROYAUME DE BELGIQUE/
KONINKRIJK BELGIË

KINGDOM OF BELGIUM

A black-yellow-red flag was first used by Belgians in 1789 when they revolted, unsuccessfully, against the rule of Austria. The three equal stripes were inspired by the French Tricolor, while the colors were based on the arms of Brabant.

The revolution of 1830 against Dutch rule was successful, and the colors of 1789 were adopted for various Belgian flags. Already in use for centuries in the arms of the provinces, these colors are used by them in flag form today. The Walloon regional flag dates from 1913, while the Flemish lion can be traced to the twelfth century.

Officially adopted 23 January 1831.

13:15≈

STATE AND ROYAL ARMS

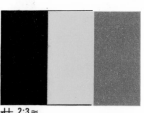

2:3≈
2:3

2:3

ROYAL FLAG 1:1

BELGIAN PROVINCES

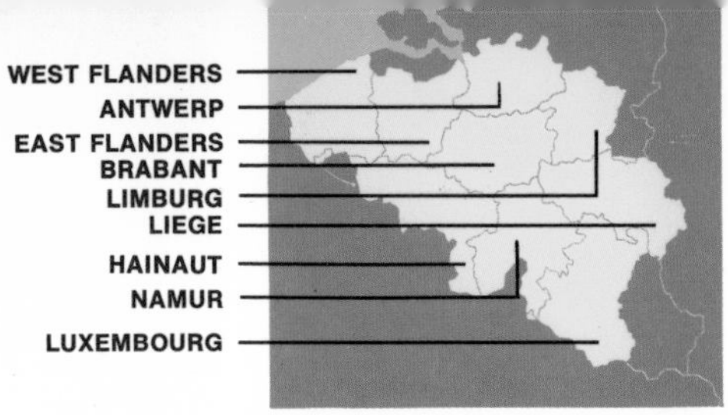

1:1≈

VLAANDEREN
FLANDERS

1:1≈

WALLONIE
WALLONIA

1:1≈

ANTWERPEN
ANTWERP

1:1≈

BRABANT

1:1≈

HAINAUT

1:1≈

LIÈGE

1:1≈

LIMBOURG

1:1≈

LUXEMBOURG

1:1≈

NAMUR

1:1≈

OOST-VLAANDEREN
EAST-FLANDERS

1:1≈

WEST-VLAANDEREN
WEST-FLANDERS

14

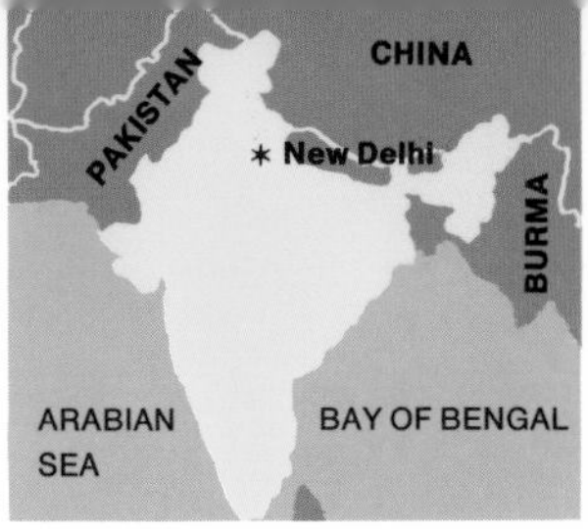

BHARAT

INDIA

BHARAT KA GANATANTRA

REPUBLIC OF INDIA

Further information on Indian flags appears on page 79.

Born in the independence struggle, the flag of India combines the colors of its principal religious groups – the orange of the Hindus and green of the Muslims – with an ancient Buddhist symbol, the wheel. The wheel is repeated in the state arms, modeled after an architectural capital found at Sarnath. It is one of many pillars erected by Emperor Asoka in the third century B.C. Written below in the national Devanagari script is a quotation from the ancient *Mundaka Upanishad,* "Truth Alone Triumphs." The state emblem has no official colors.

Officially adopted 22 July 1947.

2:3

STATE ARMS

2:3

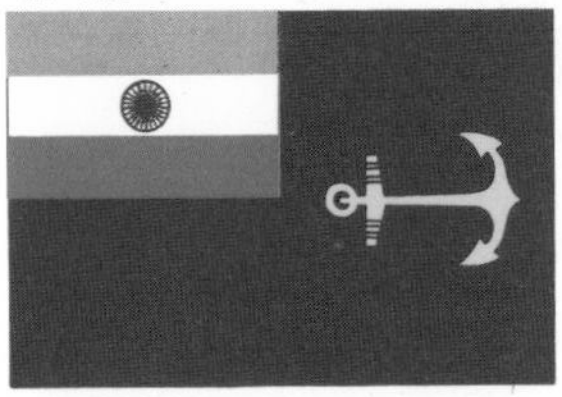

2:3

2:3≈

JAMMU AND KASHMIR

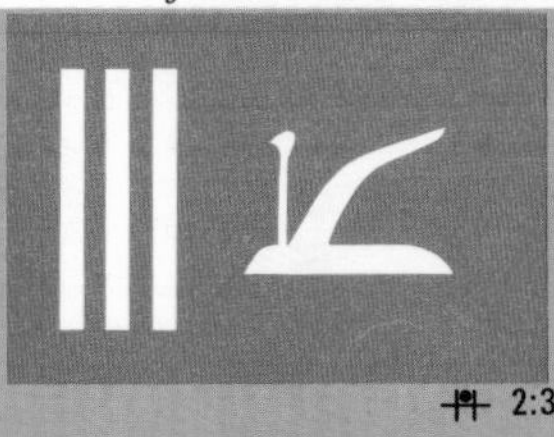

2:3

1:2

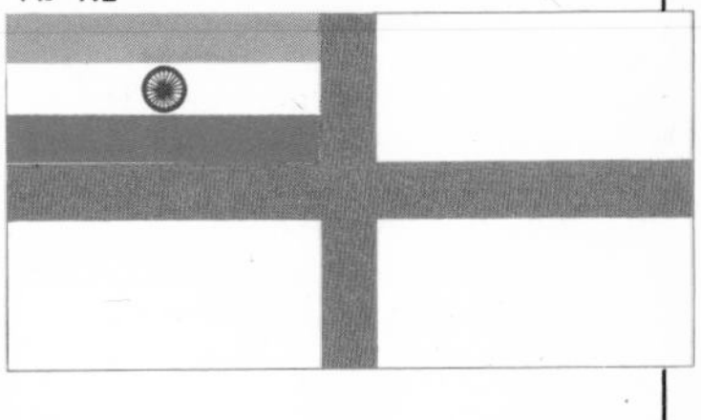

15

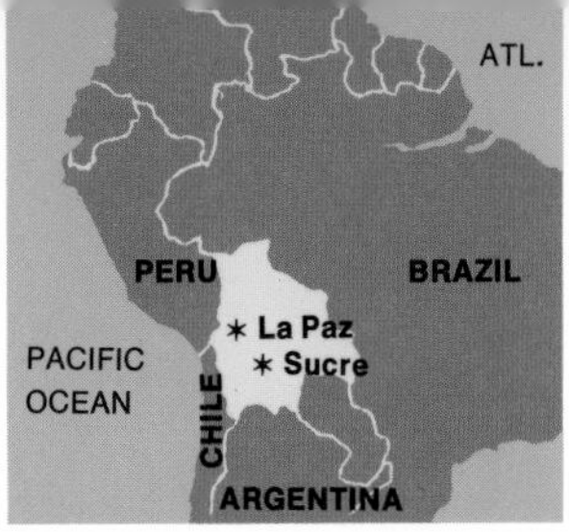

BOLIVIA

BOLIVIA

REPÚBLICA DE BOLIVIA

REPUBLIC OF BOLIVIA

Upper Peru was renamed Bolivia in honor of the Liberator, Simón Bolívar.

The independence of Bolivia was originally achieved in 1825 through the military victories of leaders from the north, Bolívar and Sucre. The horizontal stripes and the colors yellow and red of the flag were undoubtedly influenced by those already existing in Colombia.

Manuel Belzú, the first president of Bolivia to base his power on the Indian majority, established the flag in 1851 in basically the same form as used today. The red has been interpreted as signifying the valor of the Bolivian soldier, green the fertility of the land, and gold the richness of national mineral resources.

Officially adopted 14 July 1888.

2:3

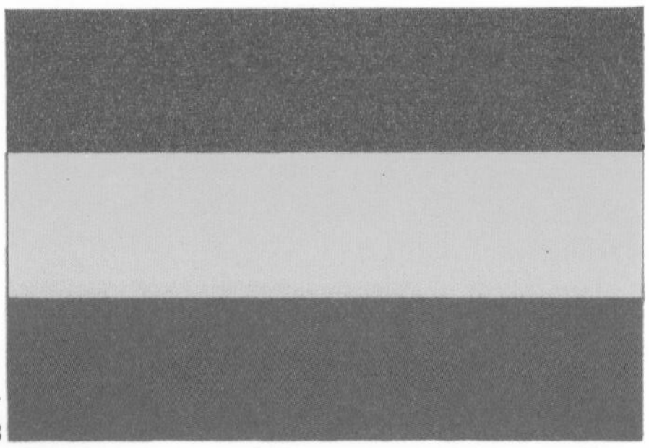

STATE ARMS

Its agricultural and mineral wealth are reflected in the coat of arms by the wheat sheaf, breadfruit tree, and the argentiferous Mount Potosí. Native fauna – the condor and alpaca – are also included. The sun is an ancient Inca symbol.

2:3

3:4 ≈

Since gaining its independence, Bolivia has lost much of its territory to neighboring states. Bolivians are particularly unreconciled to Chilean conquests of the only province which gave Bolivia an outlet to the Pacific Ocean. Although presently restricted to rivers and lakes, the war ensign of Bolivia adopted in 1966 includes a star for the nation's littoral, as well as smaller stars (such as are found in the coat of arms) for its nine departments.

16

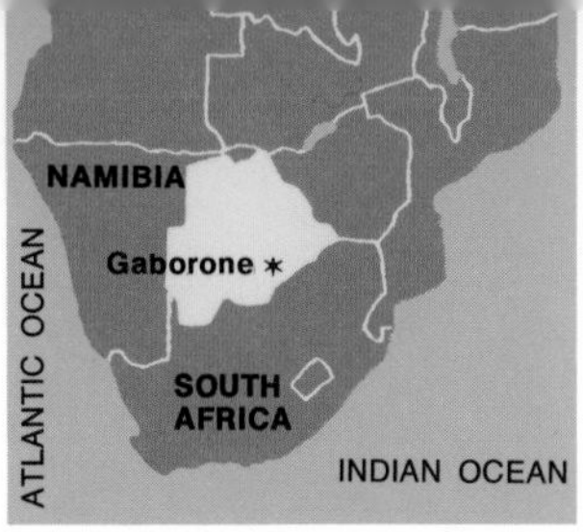

BOTSWANA

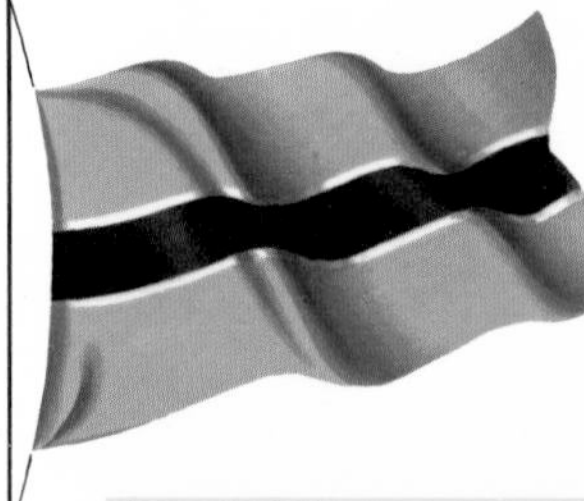

REPUBLIC OF BOTSWANA

The people of the country are called Batswana, their language Tswana.

In submitting the Botswana flag and arms for legislative approval, Prime Minister Dr. Seretse Khama explained: "Rain is our lifeblood, and 'Pula' is a well-known expression which means more than just 'rain.' It expresses a hope and a belief that we will win through in the end and good fortune will be our partner in the years ahead." The blue field of the flag was chosen to represent water as well as the sky. The coat of arms features the traditional heraldic representation of water and includes the Tswana word for "rain."

The black and white stripes of the flag and the zebras reflect a determination to build a society of equal opportunity for persons of all races. The bull's head is an emblem of the livestock industry. Cogwheels suggest the desire for industrialization; the stalk of sorghum recalls that the national economy is still primarily agricultural.

Officially hoisted 30 September 1966.

2:3

STATE ARMS

PRESIDENTIAL FLAG

15:23

President Khama of Botswana has had a special personal interest in racial equality because of his experiences under British colonial rule. As a student in Britain, Khama met and married an Englishwoman. British authorities refused to allow him to return to his native land for five years and then only when he renounced legitimate claims to the chieftainship of the Bamangwato tribe.

BRASIL

BRAZIL

REPÚBLICA FEDERATIVA DO BRASIL

FEDERATIVE REPUBLIC OF BRAZIL

The inscription is supposed to read correctly on both sides of the state flag.

The green of this vast land and its golden mineral wealth are represented in the Brazilian flag, whose diamond shape recalls many French military colors of the early nineteenth century. A similar flag was adopted by Brazil in 1822 upon gaining independence from Portugal.
The historic colors of Portugal, blue and white, appear in the Brazilian flag. The globe shows the constellations as they appear over Rio de Janeiro, but in mirror image. The motto "Order and Progress" is a Positivist slogan.
That the country has looked to the United States as a model may be seen in its flag, whose stars increase as necessary to represent the states of the union (plus one star to indicate its territories).
The arms include the date on which the Brazilian empire was replaced by a republic. Surrounding the central emblem are branches of coffee and tobacco.

Officially adopted 30 May 1968.

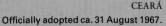

7:10

STATE ARMS

PRESIDENTIAL FLAG

2:3≈

Unlike the geometric arrangements in the United States flag, Brazil's stars correspond to actual constellations. The Southern Cross, Scorpio, the Southern Triangle, and parts of a number of other constellations may be identified. Each star corresponds to a specific political entity, whereas in the American flag the stars represent the states collectively. Each Brazilian star is one of five different sizes, rather than all being the same.

BRAZILIAN STATES

11:20

AMAZONAS
Usage initiated ca. 1897.

7:10≈

CEARÁ
Officially adopted ca. 31 August 1967.

7:10

ESPÍRITO SANTO
Officially adopted 24 April 1947.

7:10

MARANHÃO
Officially confirmed 1 December 1971.

2:3

MINAS GERAIS
Officially adopted 27 November 1962.

7:10≈

ACRE
Officially confirmed 1 March 1963.

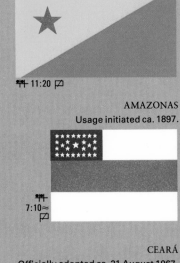

ALAGOAS
Off. adopted 23 September 1963.

4:7≈

BAHIA
Usage initiated 26 May 1889.

7:10≈

DISTRITO FEDERAL
FEDERAL DISTRICT
Off. hoisted 7 September 1969.

13:18≈

GOIÁS
Usage initiated 30 July 1919.

7:10≈

MATO GROSSO
Officially confirmed 11 July 1947.

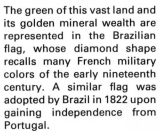

7:10≈

BRAZILIAN STATES

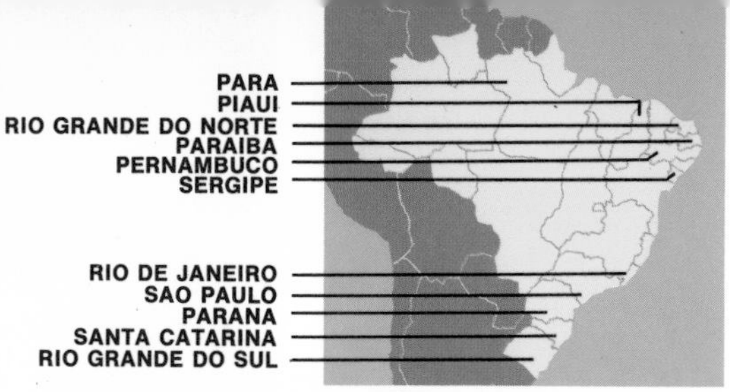

PARÁ
Usage initiated 17 November 1889.

7:10≈

PARAÍBA
Officially hoisted 27 October 1965.

7:10

PARANÁ
Officially adopted 31 March 1947.

2:3

PERNAMBUCO
Usage initiated 23 February 1917.

7:10≈

PIAUÍ
Usage initiated 24 July 1922.

7:10≈

RIO DE JANEIRO
Usage initiated ca. 1947.

7:10≈

RIO GRANDE DO NORTE
Officially adopted 3 December 1957.

2:3

RIO GRANDE DO SUL
Usage confirmed 1947.

7:10≈

SANTA CATARINA
Officially adopted 23 October 1953.

3:4

SÃO PAULO
Officially adopted
3 September 1948.

7:10≈

SERGIPE
Usage initiated ca. 1947.

2:3

18

BULGARIYA
BULGARIA

NARODNA REPUBLIKA BULGARIYA

PEOPLE'S REPUBLIC OF BULGARIA

In 681 Bulgars settled the area they now inhabit, a date commemorated in the modern coat of arms and flag of Bulgaria.

The national flag, adopted in 1878, was based on the then current Russian flag of white-blue-red (see page 175). The colors in the Bulgarian flag are said to stand for peace, love, and freedom; wealth from the soil; and the courage of the Bulgarian people.

Agriculture and industry are reflected in the wheat and cogwheel of the arms. Communism is symbolized by the red star, while the "1944" marks the liberation of Bulgaria from fascism.

Officially hoisted 21 May 1971.

3:5

STATE ARMS

While the lion has officially served as an emblem of Bulgaria since 1879, it is also seen on coins issued by a Bulgarian tsar, Ivan Shishman, in the late fourteenth century.

3:5≈

FLAG OF THE CHAIRMAN OF THE PRESIDIUM

2:3≈

FLAG OF THE CHAIRMAN OF THE COUNCIL OF MINISTERS

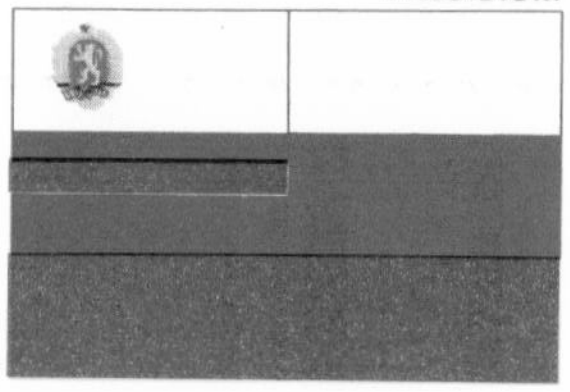

2:3≈

2:3≈

19

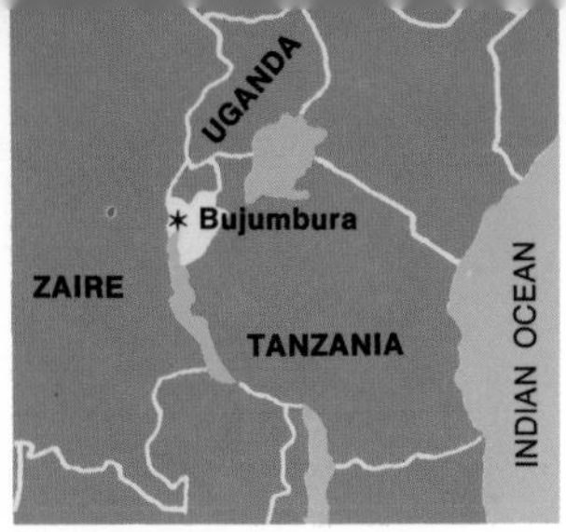

BURUNDI

BURUNDI

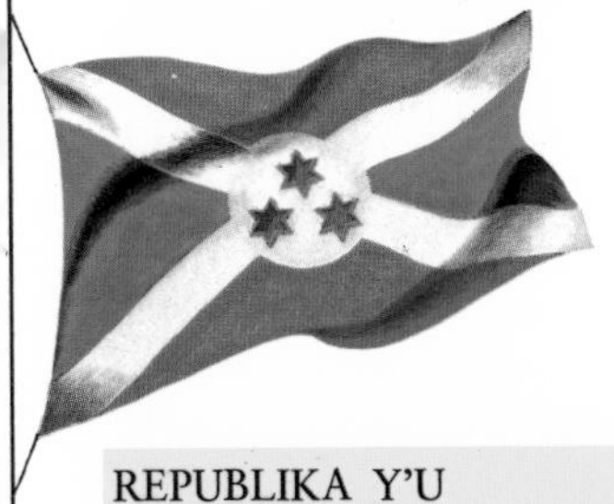

REPUBLIKA Y'U BURUNDI/RÉPUBLIQUE DU BURUNDI

REPUBLIC OF BURUNDI

The three stars in the flag and the three spears in the arms of Burundi are interpreted as symbols of the words in the national motto – "Unity, Work, Progress." However, they may also recall the three races that live in the nation – the Tutsi, Hutu, and Twa.

The colors of the Burundi flag are explained as symbolizing suffering and the struggle for independence (red), peace (white), and hope (green).

Formerly a sorghum plant, emblem of prosperity, and a royal drum were represented in the center of the flag. Because of their close association with the ruling dynasty, these symbols were removed following the republican revolution of 1966. Nevertheless the shield of the national arms was retained, although the lion symbol had been used under the monarchy and, prior to independence, under the Belgian colonial administration.

Officially adopted Spring 1967.

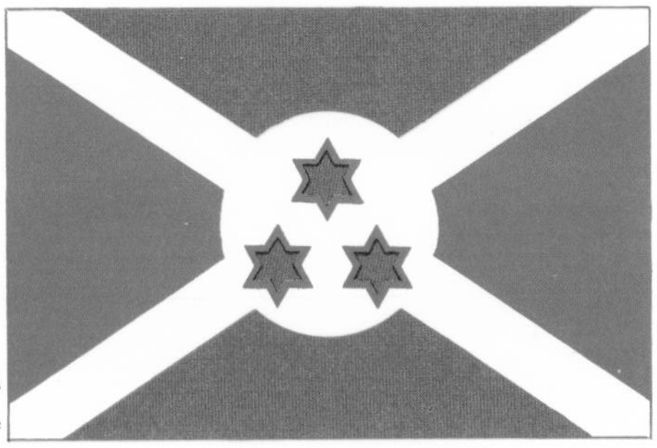

2:3≈

STATE ARMS

The vexillologist frequently finds a plausible or even likely condition which he cannot establish as factually correct because documentation is lacking.

A case in point is the diagonal cross in the flag of Burundi, a pattern unlike any national flag other than Jamaica's. It appears to have been inspired by the old flag of Sabena World Airlines, the Belgian national carrier, but no concrete proof of this exists. Certainly that house flag would have been better known in Burundi than any other flag except the Belgian national tricolor.

The Sabena flag in turn is probably related – like the Belgian war ensign – to the white flag bearing a red saltire which Belgium flew more than two centuries ago when it was the Spanish Netherlands.

20

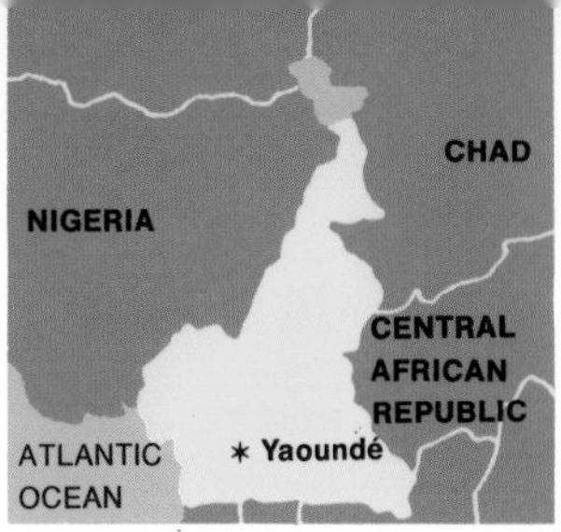

CAMEROUN/CAMEROON

RÉPUBLIQUE UNIE DE CAMEROUN/ UNITED REPUBLIC OF CAMEROON

As part of a program to increase national consciousness, a national flag was adopted in 1957 while Cameroon was still under French rule. Its vertical stripes were like those in the French Tricolor, but the colors were the pan-African green, red, and yellow. Cameroon was the second modern African nation (after Ghana) to adopt these colors, later copied by many other French-speaking African lands.

In 1961 the British territory of Southern Cameroons voted to join Cameroon. This was the basis for adding two gold stars to the Cameroon flag in that year. Although the federal system was replaced by a unitary government in 1972, the flag was only altered in 1975.

The name Cameroon is derived from the Portuguese word *camarões* ("shrimps"). The name was applied by Portuguese explorers to a river in the area, following their discovery of shrimp there. In the 1950s a political organization dedicated to ending French colonial rule proposed a field of red bearing a shrimp for the national flag.

Officially hoisted 1 October 1961.

2:3≈

STATE ARMS

Green and yellow stand for the hope of a prosperous future and the sun. They also symbolize the forests in the south of Cameroon and the savannahs of its north, while red represents unity between them.

In the coat of arms the triangle bearing the map recalls Mount Cameroon, the highest point in West Africa. Also included is the national motto "Peace, Work, Fatherland."

CANADA

DOMINION OF CANADA/ DOMINION DU CANADA

Officially hoisted
15 February 1965.

The importance of flags in expressing national character and aspirations is reflected in the process by which the Canadian flag was selected.
Following debate which had gone on intermittently for almost a century, a definitive flag proposal was submitted to Parliament by Prime Minister Lester Pearson in 1964. Whether any flag should be adopted and what its design might be engrossed Parliament for seven months.
Red and white have been associated with Canada since 1921 as part of its coat of arms. The maple leaf was an unofficial emblem of Canada even before its confederation in 1867.

1:2

STATE ARMS

1:2

ROYAL FLAG 8:13≈

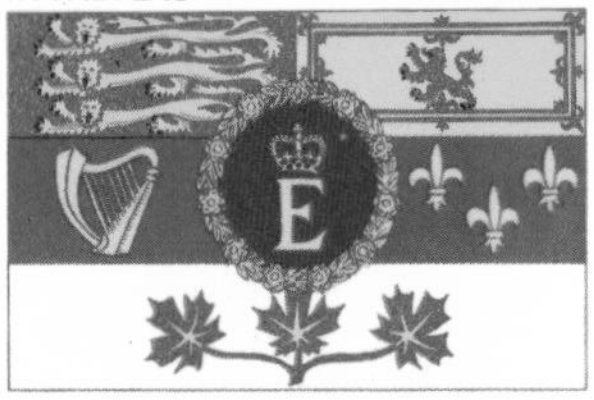

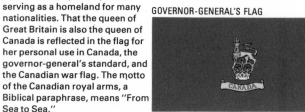

Close symbolic links with Great Britain have not been abandoned by Canada, despite its pride in serving as a homeland for many nationalities. That the queen of Great Britain is also the queen of Canada is reflected in the flag for her personal use in Canada, the governor-general's standard, and the Canadian war flag. The motto of the Canadian royal arms, a Biblical paraphrase, means "From Sea to Sea."

GOVERNOR-GENERAL'S FLAG 1:2

CANADIAN PROVINCES & TERRITORIES

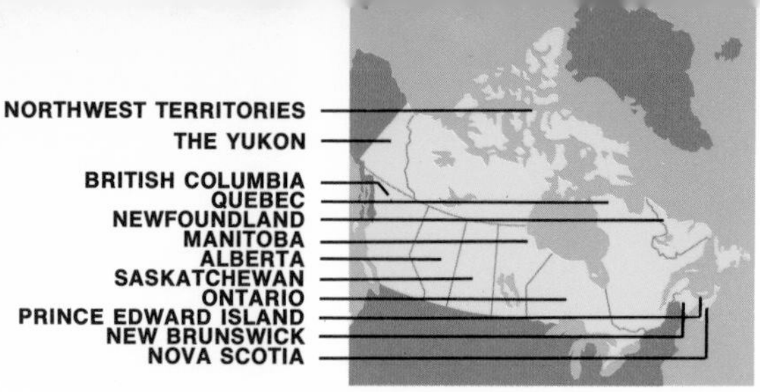

1:2

ALBERTA
Officially hoisted 1 June 1968.

1:2

MANITOBA
Officially hoisted 12 May 1966.

1:2

NEWFOUNDLAND
Officially adopted 15 May 1931.

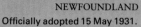

1:2

ONTARIO
Officially hoisted 21 May 1965.

2:3

QUÉBEC/QUEBEC
Officially adopted 21 January 1948.

1:2

NORTHWEST TERRITORIES
Officially hoisted 31 January 1969.

BRITISH COLUMBIA
Officially adopted 20 June 1960.

3:5≈

NEW BRUNSWICK/NOUVEAU-BRUNSWICK
Officially hoisted 25 March 1965.

5:8

NOVA SCOTIA
Officially confirmed 19 January 1929.

3:4≈

PRINCE EDWARD ISLAND
Officially hoisted 24 March 1964.

2:3

SASKATCHEWAN
Officially hoisted 22 September 1969.

1:2

THE YUKON
Officially adopted 1 March 1968.

1:2

22

ČESKOSLOVENSKO

CZECHOSLOVAKIA

ČESKOSLOVENSKÁ SOCIALISTICKÁ REPUBLIKA

CZECHOSLOVAK SOCIALIST REPUBLIC

In 1158 Holy Roman Emperor Frederick Barbarossa granted a coat of arms to Bohemia which is in use to this day – a white rampant lion with a double tail displayed on a field of red. The colors of this emblem became associated with agitation for Czech autonomy in the late nineteenth century when Bohemians and Moravians created a white-over-red bicolor. In 1918 this became the flag of the new Czechoslovak Republic.
Slovaks hoisted a horizontal tricolor in the revolution of 1848 whose white-blue-red colors were recognized as symbolizing pan-Slavic nationalism. In 1920 the color blue was introduced into the Czechoslovak flag to stand for Slovakia – an especially appropriate symbol since the new Slovak arms featured in blue the traditional mountains Tatra, Matra, and Fatra.

Officially adopted 30 March 1920; reestablished 1945.

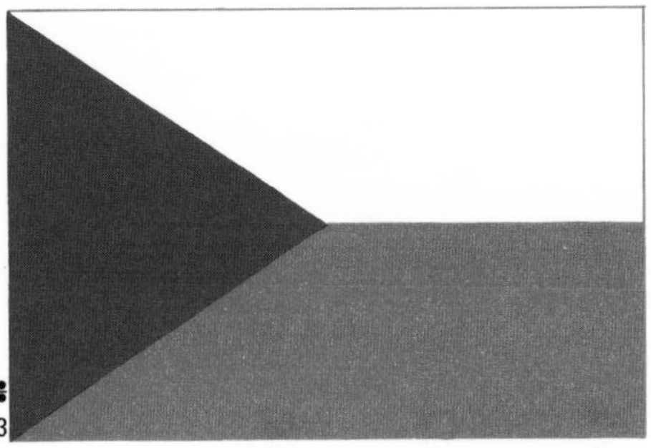

2:3

STATE ARMS

The unusual shape of the Czechoslovak shield approved in 1960 is a traditional design used by Hussite rebels of the early fifteenth century. Here the ancient Bohemian lion is charged on the shoulder with a shield for Slovakia. This bears the "Flame of Freedom" against a stylized representation of the Carpathian Mountains.
"Truth Conquers" is the national motto of Czechoslovakia, figuring among branches of linden leaves in the presidential standard adopted in 1960.

PRESIDENTIAL FLAG

1:1

23

CHILE

CHILE

REPÚBLICA DE CHILE

REPUBLIC OF CHILE

The design of the Chilean flag was inspired by the United States flag.

The national epic of Chile, *La Araucana,* is a sixteenth-century saga of precolonial life by Alonso de Ercilla. This tale of the Araucanian Indians speaks of warriors wearing sashes of white, blue, and red, although they had no flag.
As in many other countries, Chile had many actual flags and proposed designs in the early years of its struggle for independence. Such was the confusion that the Governor of Valparaiso, Col. Francisco Lastra, felt compelled to write the government on 3 October 1817: "In the capital I have seen tricolors of different forms and types which have not provided me with information sufficient to establish them here, for which reason Your Excellency shall inform me on this particular subject all that is convenient for you."
The government's response was a decree (now lost) establishing the current flag of Chile.
Chileans generally see in the white flag stripe the snow of the Andes, which form the eastern border of their land; in the blue they see the sky; and in the red, the blood of those who have died in defense of the country. The white star is a guide on the path of progress and honor.

Officially adopted ca. 18 October 1817.

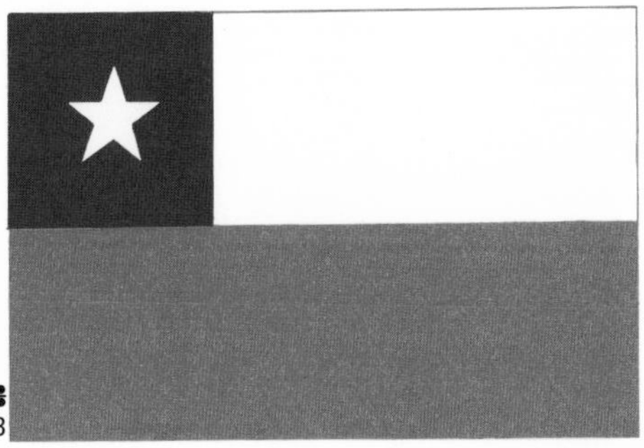

2:3

STATE ARMS

The national coat of arms reflects the flag in its shield and crest. The supporters, each of which wears a naval crown, are indigenous. The condor serves as a symbol in the arms of Bolivia, Ecuador, and Colombia, while the huemal (a deer that lives in the forests and high plateaus of the Andes) is exclusive to the heraldry of Chile. The national motto – "By Right or Might" – is emblazoned across the bottom of the arms.

PRESIDENTIAL FLAG

2:3

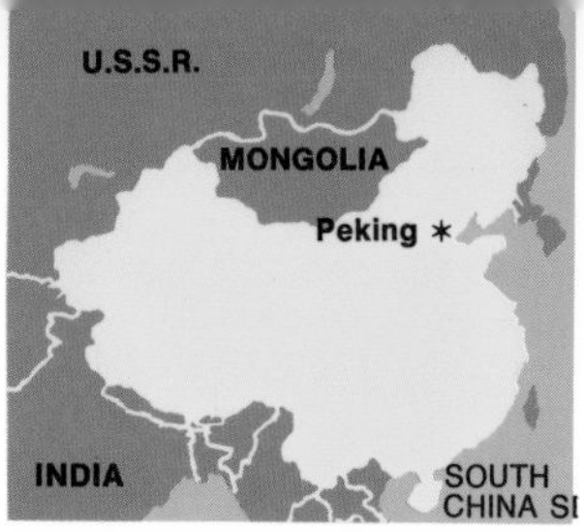

CHUNG KUO
CHINA

CHUNG-HUA JEN-MIN KUNG-HO-KUO

PEOPLE'S REPUBLIC OF CHINA

Further information on Chinese flags will be found on pages 108–113.

Leadership of the Communist Party over the four classes joined in China's united front is the theme embodied in the five stars of the flag. Red is the traditional color of China proper, as well as the symbol of the path toward Communism, which the nation has followed since 1949.

Many official flags in China bear inscriptions in gold or white; all have red fields. Even the name Red Flag is extremely popular: it serves *inter alia* as the name of the chief ideological newspaper and of the largest Chinese automobile.

The star in the People's Liberation Army flag stands for its victories, won during the long struggle to expel foreign powers from China and unite the country. The People's Liberation Army marks the date of its foundation by adding the stylized characters for "8" and "1" (for 1 August 1928) to its red banner.

Officially hoisted 1 October 1949.

2:3

STATE ARMS

The chief agricultural products of China, wheat and rice, frame the state arms, which repeat the colors and symbolism of the flag. Industry is represented by a cogwheel, while the Gate of Heavenly Peace, entrance to the former imperial Forbidden City in Peking, symbolizes restoration of power to the traditional Chinese capital. The four small stars stand for workers, peasants, petty bourgeoisie, and patriotic capitalists.

2:3≈

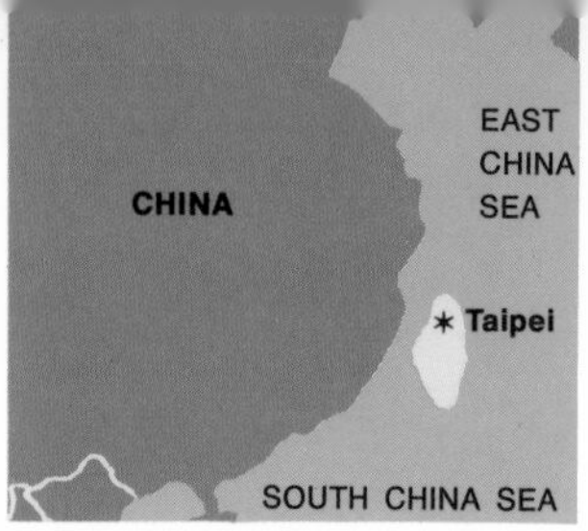

CHUNG KUO
CHINA

CHUNG-HUA MIN-KUO

REPUBLIC OF CHINA

More information on Chinese flags will be found on pages 108–113.

The flag of the Kuomintang (Nationalist Party) served as the inspiration for many flags adopted by the Republic of China in 1928, following Chiang Kai-shek's victorious Northern Expedition. The White Sun in Blue Sky continues today as the party flag and also serves as a jack for naval forces.

Red has long been regarded as the national color of the Han, an ethnic group constituting the overwhelming majority of the Chinese population. The blue of the present flag is said to stand for equality and justice; the white is a symbol of fraternity and frankness. White, blue, and red also correspond to the Three Principles of the People enunciated by the father of the Republic of China, Dr. Sun Yat-sen – popular well-being, popular government, and popular sovereignty (or welfare, democracy, and nationalism).

Officially adopted 28 October 1928.

2:3

STATE ARMS

2:3

8:11≈

Under the imperial regime prior to 1912 the civil ensign of China was red and gold and the standard of the emperor had a gold field. The colors of these flags may have influenced the modern civil ensign and presidential standard.

PRESIDENTIAL FLAG

2:3

CITTÀ DEL VATICANO

VATICAN CITY

STATO DELLA CITTÀ DEL VATICANO

STATE OF THE VATICAN CITY

Saint Peter has frequently been represented bearing the keys referred to in Matthew XVI:19; his successors, the popes at Rome, adopted keys for a symbol as early as the thirteenth century. The two keys on a red shield indicate the papal claim to dominion over both spiritual and temporal matters.
The tiara is another ancient emblem of papal authority, dating back at least to the thirteenth century.

Officially hoisted 8 June 1929.

1:1

STATE ARMS

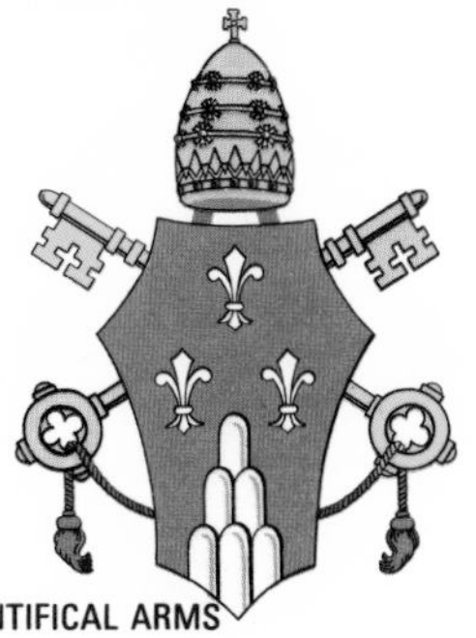

PONTIFICAL ARMS

HOLY SEE FLAG 1:2≈

Throughout the Middle Ages red was the color of the Catholic Church; gold was used for the crossed papal keys. In 1808 Napoleon amalgamated the pontifical army into his own and Pope Pius VII felt that new colors were needed. He chose yellow and white; in 1825 they were approved for various official flags of the Pontifical State. Incorporated into Italy in 1870, this state was revived in 1929 as Vatican City and its flag was resurrected.

COLOMBIA

COLOMBIA

REPÚBLICA DE COLOMBIA

REPUBLIC OF COLOMBIA

For further information see Venezuela and Ecuador.

Reminders of Spanish rule are found in modern symbols of Colombia. Its shield bears at the top a pomegranate (*granada* in Spanish), the heraldic emblem of Granada: until 1861 Colombia was known as New Granada. A stripe of red, the traditional color of Spain, forms the bottom of the Colombian flag. It is separated from the yellow – symbolizing the gold of the New World – by blue, suggestive of the Atlantic Ocean.

Officially adopted 26 November 1861.

2:3≈

STATE ARMS

2:3

PRESIDENTIAL FLAG 3:5≈

2:3

ANTIOQUIA 1:2

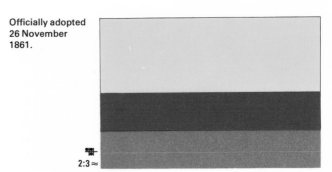

CUNDINAMARCA 2:3≈

HUILA 2:3≈

MAGDALENA 2:3≈

28

CONGO

CONGO

RÉPUBLIQUE POPULAIRE DU CONGO

PEOPLE'S REPUBLIC OF THE CONGO

The former Belgian Congo is now known as Zaire (q. v.).

Following an agreement between the French explorer, Pierre Brazza, and Makoko, king of the Bateke, the area north of the Congo River became a French protectorate in 1880. Under the name of Middle Congo, it knew no official flag until 1958 other than the Tricolor.

In that year it became the Republic of the Congo with a flag of its own, although still linked to France by the Community. The flag adopted in 1958 had diagonal stripes of the pan-African colors – green, yellow, and red. No change was introduced when the Congo became independent on 15 August 1960.

Officially hoisted 30 December 1969.

2:3

In 1963 a socialist government was instituted and on the last day of 1969 a people's republic was proclaimed. To symbolize solidarity with other socialist countries, the flag was altered to the present design in which red predominates. That color is seen as a symbol of the Congolese people's struggle during the colonial era for national independence. The green palm branches stand for peace, and the gold star at the top is for hope. A hammer and hoe indicate the classes united in the building of a new Congo, workers and peasants.

Despite changes, the pan-African colors are still present in the Congo flag; moreover, the hoe is a symbol found in the arms of several African nations, including neighboring Upper Volta.

Commenting on the original Congo flag when it was adopted, the President of the National Assembly stated: "The true personality of the Republic of the Congo will not be its flag, will not be its anthem, but will depend above all on the dignity, civic sense, labor, and patriotism of its citizens. . . . The real personality of the Congo is found rather within us than outside us."

29

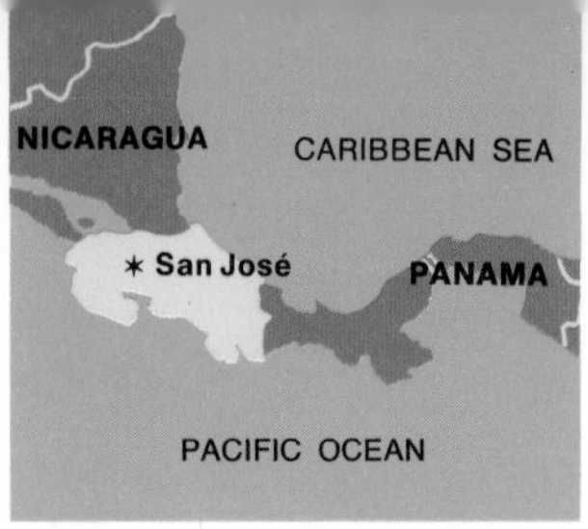

COSTA RICA

COSTA RICA

REPÚBLICA DE COSTA RICA

REPUBLIC OF COSTA RICA

The arms and flags are related to those of other Central American nations.

Alone among the former members of the United Provinces of the Center of America, Costa Rica decided that it was improper to continue to use the flag of that federation following its dissolution. At first a flag of white-blue-white was adopted, but in 1848 the five stripes still found in the national flag were selected.

Blue and white recall the former flag of the Central American federation, as do the volcanoes in the coat of arms. The red was added in tribute to the French revolution of 1848. Since that time the arms of Costa Rica have twice been modified slightly.

At present the arms bear the

Officially adopted 21 October 1964.

3:5

STATE ARMS

name of the country and at the top "Central America," a reminder of past unity and an expression of the hope that Costa Rica may again in the future be part of a larger state. The stars correspond to the number of provinces in Costa Rica.

2:3≈

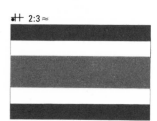

Costa Rica is one of a number of countries which expressly forbids private citizens to display their national flag on land. While a civil ensign exists for merchant vessels, homes and businesses may only be decorated with pennants in the national colors on holidays, according to the Costa Rican law. (In actual practice the civil ensign tends to serve as a civil flag as well.)

30

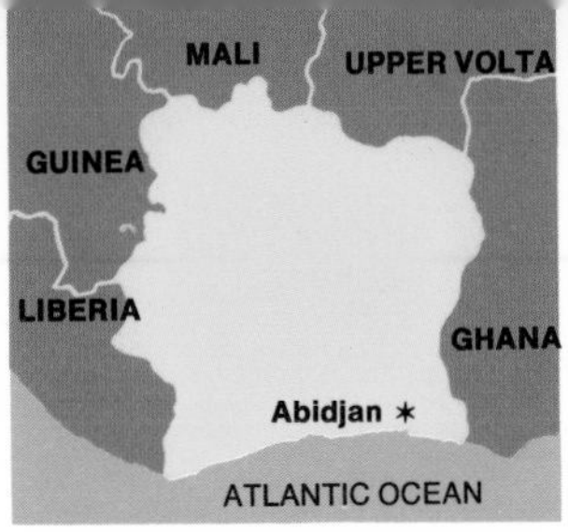

CÔTE D'IVOIRE

IVORY COAST

RÉPUBLIQUE DE CÔTE D'IVOIRE

REPUBLIC OF THE IVORY COAST

The three stripes of the national flag are said to represent the dynamism of the Ivorian youth as they progress in the spirit of the national motto – "Union, Discipline, Work." Certainly the form of the stripes was based on the vertical divisions of the French Tricolor, which for decades flew over the Ivory Coast before it obtained its independence in 1960.
The colors chosen for the national flag are not the pan-African red-yellow-green found in many other African banners. Nevertheless the orange-white-green is found in the flag of Niger, also a former French colony, where the symbolism is the same as in the Ivory Coast flag. The savannas of the north are recalled by the orange stripe, while the green is an expression of the virgin forests of the southern regions.
White symbolically stands for unity between north and south. Orange, white, and green have also been interpreted to mean the spirit of national development, peace and purity, and hope for the future through the utilization of natural resources.

Officially adopted 3 December 1959.

2:3

STATE ARMS

Originally the shield in the national arms was blue, but in 1964 a new decree altered the color to green to conform more closely with the national flag.
The elephant, which figures as the principal charge of the shield, is not only an indigenous beast but also the party emblem of the Ivory Coast Democratic Party that led the country to independence.
The "white gold" of the elephant, which attracted early European traders and conquerors, gave the nation its distinctive name.

31

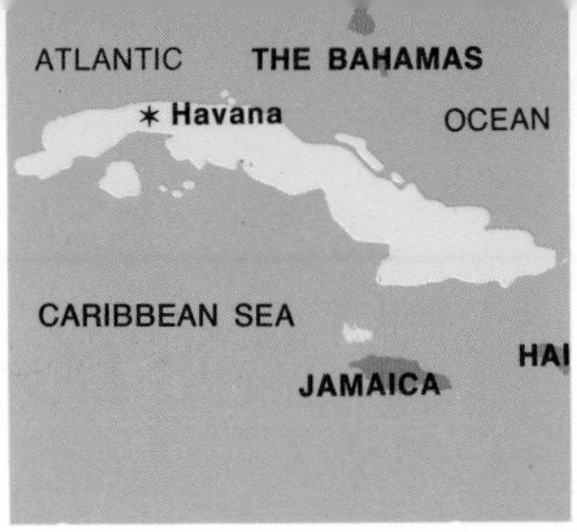

CUBA

CUBA

REPÚBLICA DE CUBA

REPUBLIC OF CUBA

Officially hoisted 20 May 1902.

Exiled from their native island for revolutionary activities, many Cubans in New York in the mid-nineteenth century gathered to talk of their plans for the eventual liberation of their homeland. At such a meeting in early June 1849 the Cuban national flag was born.
Tradition relates that Narciso López was responsible for the design. Emilia Teurbe Tolón, wife of López's host the evening the flag was discussed, executed the first copy. The original banner found its way to Cuba and more than a half century later became the model for the flag of a newly independent republic.

1:2

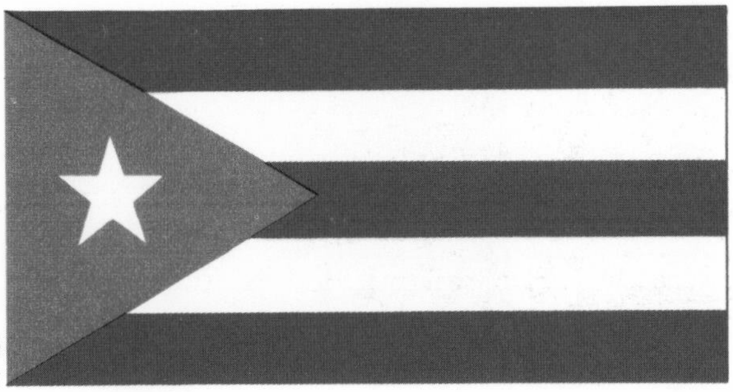

STATE ARMS

The white stripes of the Cuban flag are for the purity of the revolutionary cause, while the three blue stripes correspond to the territorial subdivisions of Cuba at the time the flag was created. A star of independence figures on the Masonic triangle, whose red color suggests the bloody struggles the nation has faced in achieving and preserving independence.

The coat of arms of Cuba, prominently featured in the presidential standard, is said to have been designed by the husband of the woman who sewed the Cuban flag. Miguel Teurbe Tolón in 1849 combined traditional symbols of republicanism – the liberty cap and fasces – with distinctive Cuban emblems. The position of Cuba as the key to the Gulf of Mexico is represented graphically in the chief. As in the flag, stripes correspond to the subdivisions then existing in Cuba. A palm tree on the sinister of the shield bears testimony to the vigor and fertility of the Cuban soil.

PRESIDENTIAL FLAG

1:1

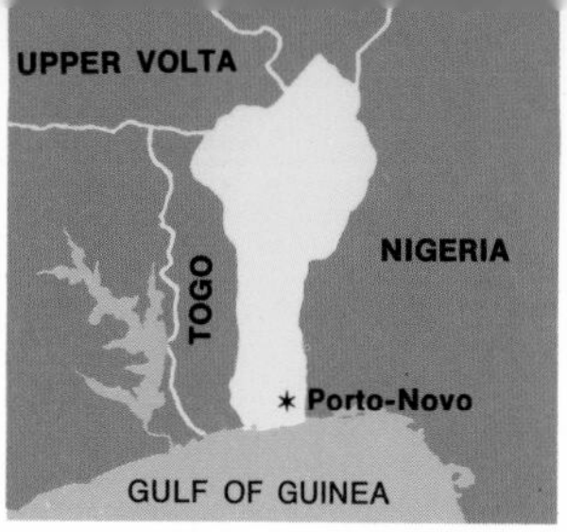

DAHOMEY

DAHOMEY

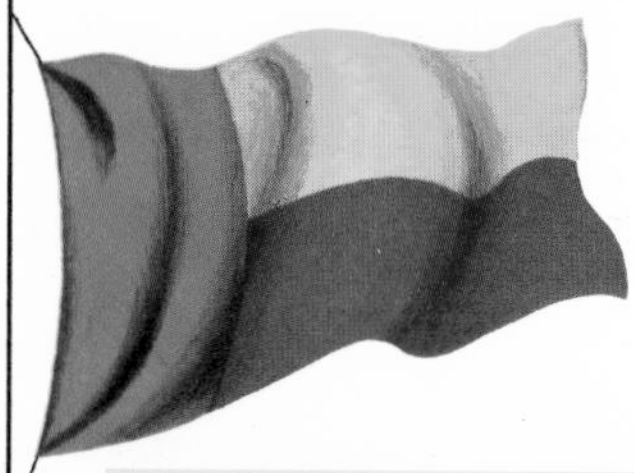

RÉPUBLIQUE
DU DAHOMEY

REPUBLIC OF DAHOMEY

The pan-African colors of the national flag chosen by Dahomey prior to its independence are the same as those found in the flags of many other former members of the French colonial empire. The green and yellow reflect the division of Dahomey between the palm groves of its south and savannahs of the north. The common bond between them, expressed by the red, is the blood of ancestors shed in defense of the homeland.
The flag has not been altered since independence from France was gained on 1 August 1960, although on 3 December 1974 President Mathieu Kerekou announced the transformation of Dahomey into a Marxist-Leninist state.

Officially adopted 16 November 1959.

2:3≈

STATE ARMS

"Fraternity, Justice, Work" is the slogan of Dahomey's coat of arms. Its shield contains a picture of a typical Somba building and the star of the Order of the Black Star, instituted in 1892 by King Toffa of Porto-Novo. The palm oil which provides much of the nation's income is suggested by the palm tree, while the ship in the final quarter recalls the harbors that early attracted European explorers to Dahomey's coasts. Agricultural abundance is the theme of the crest, two cornucopias spilling ears of corn.

Dahomey has a tradition of brightly colored appliqué hangings. In the past these were sometimes used as flags, but today the flag itself is frequently found as a design motif. One such flag was apparently used by the last independent king of Dahomey, Behanzin (1889–1892). French soldiers who seized his royal capital found a blue gonfalon bearing a shield with a shark and egg flanked by a palm tree, tusks, and snakes.

DANMARK

DENMARK

KONGERIGET DANMARK

KINGDOM OF DENMARK

The story of the historic Dannebrog is told in greater detail on pages 64 and 65.

Originally a battle standard and later widely used at sea, the Danish civil flag today is very much the property of the average Danish citizen. It appears on private homes, in parks and gardens, in parades, and on buildings – even as a decoration for Christmas trees.
The swallow-tailed version of the Danish flag, known as the *splittflag,* is used for official purposes. A number of institutions and officials have the right to add a distinctive mark to the basic design.
The huge island of Greenland, which is part of the Danish kingdom, flies the Danish civil flag.

The state arms *(below, right)* date from the twelfth century. The same design is found as a quartering in the royal arms, which assumed their present form in 1972. The national flag dates from the thirteenth or fourteenth century.

28:37

ROYAL ARMS

STATE ARMS

56:107

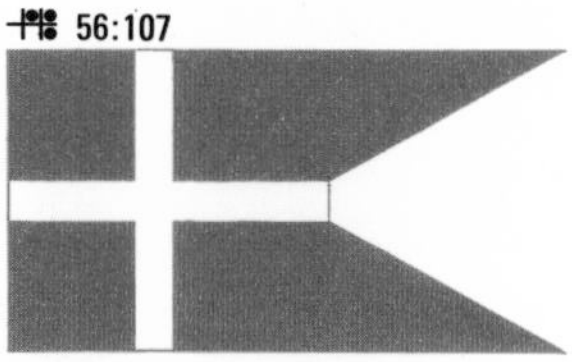

56:107

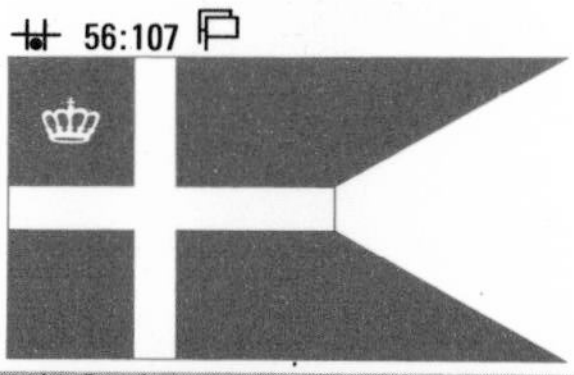

ROYAL FLAG 56:107

FØROYAR/FÆRØERNE
FAROE ISLANDS

8:11

GERMAN STATES

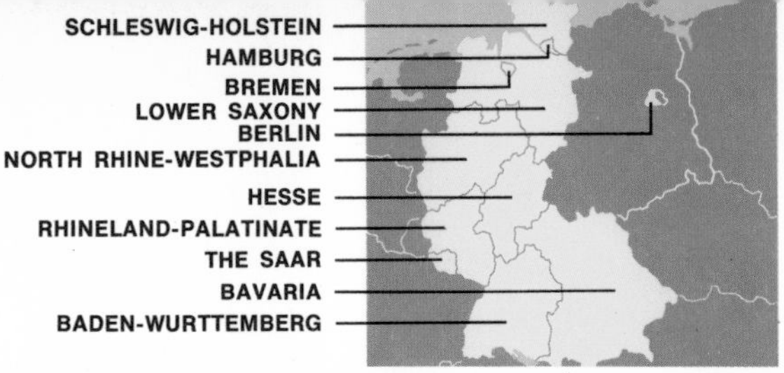

DEUTSCHLAND
GERMANY

BUNDESREPUBLIK DEUTSCHLAND

FEDERAL REPUBLIC OF GERMANY

Further information on German flags will be found on pages 114 to 123.

During the Weimar Republic earlier in the century, use of the black-red-gold national colors was compromised by modifications in various German flags through the incorporation of black-white-red. Today black-red-gold is alone official, even in military colors carried by the federal defense force.

Following the reestablishment of complete sovereignty for Germany on 5 May 1955 the Federal Republic adopted a war ensign; in the tradition of other Baltic lands, this flag is swallowtailed. In this ensign another old custom obtains. Like the state flag, it bears its coat of arms set slightly toward the hoist. When the flag is flying this compensates visually for the twisting of the fly end of the flag in the wind. The emblem appears to be in the center and is more clearly visible than it would otherwise be.

Officially adopted 9 May 1949.

3:5

STATE ARMS

3:5

3:5

CHAIRMAN OF THE STATE COUNCIL

1:1

Because metallic shades are difficult to achieve in textiles, what German law calls "gold" is usually a deep golden yellow. In painted details of coats of arms, however, gold (and silver) may be found in flags.

LAND BADEN-WÜRTTEMBERG

3:5

STATE OF BADEN-WURTTEMBERG

Off. adopted 29 September 1954.

3:5≈

LAND BERLIN

STATE OF BERLIN

Officially adopted 26 May 1954.

2:3≈

FREIE UND HANSESTADT HAMBURG

FREE AND HANSEATIC CITY OF HAMBURG

Usage initiated 8 October 1897.

2:3

LAND NIEDERSACHSEN

STATE OF LOWER SAXONY

Officially adopted 17 October 1952.

2:3

LAND RHEINLAND-PFALZ

STATE OF RHINELAND-PALATINATE

Officially adopted 15 May 1948.

3:5

FREISTAAT BAYERN

FREE STATE OF BAVARIA

Officially adopted 14 December 1953.

FREIE HANSESTADT BREMEN

FREE HANSEATIC CITY OF BREMEN

Off. confirmed 21 November 1947.

15:23≈

LAND HESSEN

STATE OF HESSE

Off. adopted 31 December 1949.

3:5

LAND NORDRHEIN-WESTFALEN

STATE OF NORTH RHINE-WESTPHALIA

Officially adopted 10 March 1953.

3:5

SAARLAND

SAAR STATE

Off. adopted 10 September 1956.

3:5

LAND SCHLESWIG-HOLSTEIN

STATE OF SCHLESWIG HOLSTEIN

Officially adopted 18 January 1957.

35

DEUTSCHLAND
GERMANY

DEUTSCHE DEMOKRATISCHE REPUBLIK

GERMAN DEMOCRATIC REPUBLIC

Further information on German flags will be found on pages 114 to 123.

During the first ten years of its existence the German Democratic Republic flew the traditional black-red-gold German colors. To distinguish its flag from that of the Federal Republic of Germany, the state arms were added in 1959 to various German Democratic Republic (G.D.R.) flags.
The elements in these arms express the ideological orientation of the state. Red shows its commitment to Communism; the tricolored ribbon reflects the national character of the state. Peasants, manual laborers, and intellectuals are represented by the wheat, hammer, and pair of dividers. A wreath of laurel appears in the war flag and war ensign, as well as in several other G.D.R. flags. The national colors also appear in the cord which substitutes for fringe as a decoration in the personal flag of the head of state.

Officially hoisted 1 October 1959.

3:5

STATE ARMS

3:5

3:5

CHAIRMAN OF THE STATE COUNCIL FLAG

1:1

In contrast with the customary British flag proportions of 1:2 and with those of French flags (2:3), German flags since the nineteenth century have frequently had official proportions of 3:5.

36

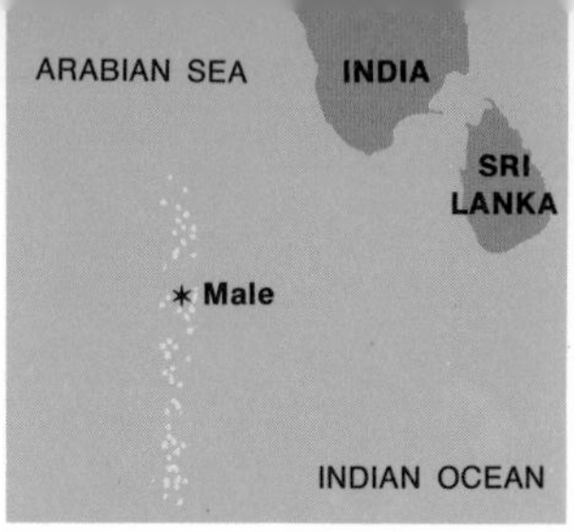

DIVEHI
MALDIVES

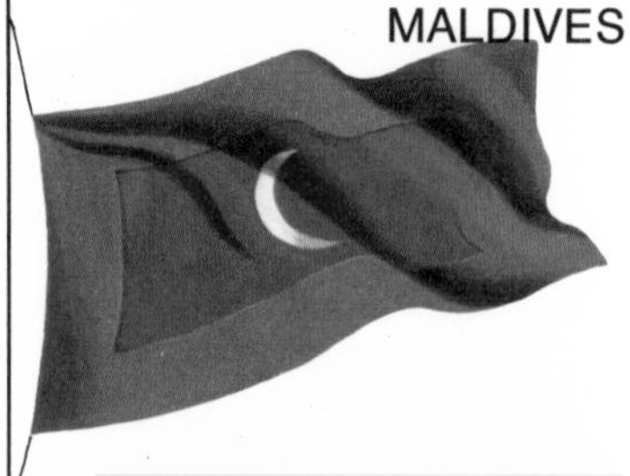

DIVEHI RAAJJE

REPUBLIC OF THE MALDIVES

The name of the country means "A Thousand Islands."

Throughout the Indian Ocean states visited by the Arab ships of the Persian Gulf have used a common national flag of plain red. Gradually these states – Kuwait, Oman, Tadjurah, Zanzibar, the Comoros, and others – changed their flags. The red border of the Maldives flag is thus a reminder of the plain red flag it flew in the past.
The green panel and crescent, both symbols of the Islamic religion of the people, were introduced by Prime Minister Amir Abdul Majid Didi early in the twentieth century.
When the British protectorate established in 1887 was ended in 1965, the flag was modified by the omission of the black and white diagonal striped border along its hoist. No changes occurred when the sultanate was replaced by a republic, then restored, and then again altered to a republic. The arms feature a date palm, national flags, and a star and crescent above the name of the state on a scroll.

Officially hoisted 26 July 1965.

2:3

STATE ARMS

3:5≈

PRIME MINISTER'S FLAG

3:5≈

In addition to those shown, Maldivian flags include those of cabinet ministers and other officials (such as harbormasters) and of the Customs Service. Special flags are used on ceremonial occasions and in the past other flags existed.

37

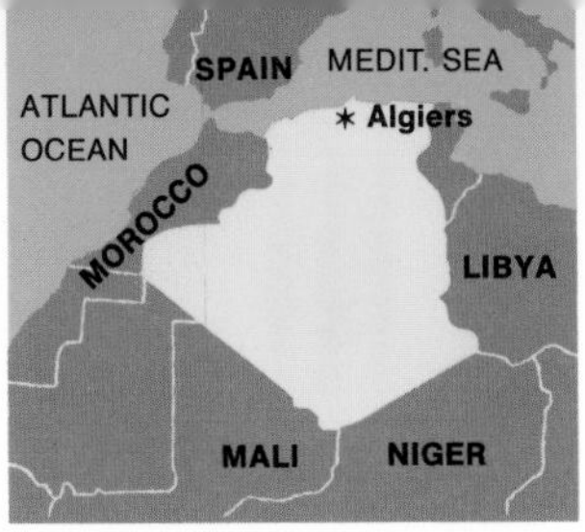

AL DJAZAIR

ALGERIA

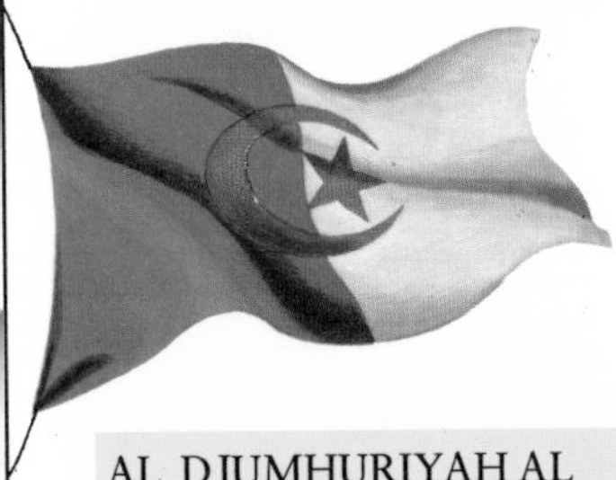

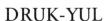

AL DJUMHURIYAH AL DJAZAIRIYAH AL DIMUQRATIYAH AL SHABIYAH

ALGERIAN DEMOCRATIC PEOPLE'S REPUBLIC

From 1832 to 1847 Abd el-Kader led resistance forces struggling to keep Algeria free from French military occupation. Their eventual defeat led to more than a century of French colonial power in Algeria. Today Abd el-Kader is honored by an independent Algeria. He is also popularly credited with having created the design which is now the national flag, although this has not been substantiated. It appears more likely that the flag was designed by Messali Hadj in 1928. His North Africa Star, founded two years before, was the first serious effort to organize Algerian Muslims politically.

Officially hoisted 3 July 1962.

2:3

STATE ARMS

The meaning of the national symbols and agricultural products in the Algerian coat of arms is clear, but the symbol at the top is not familiar to most non-Algerians. It is the Hand of Fatima, a traditional good luck emblem popular throughout North Africa. (Fatima was the daughter of Muhammad and progenitor of the Fatimid dynasty). The Hand of Fatima is found in jewelry, as a flagpole finial, at the tops of minarets, and as a motif in the decorative arts.

Even though the Front of National Liberation (FNL) adopted Messali Hadj's flag in 1954, its own radical program and revolutionary tactics came to dominate the independence struggle. Following the establishment in 1958 by the FLN of the Provisional Government of the Algerian Republic, the flag became known throughout the world. The crescent and star motif has been a common symbol of Islamic culture in North Africa for centuries, particulary under the Ottoman rule which preceded French conquest. Green is also recognized as a traditional Muslim color.

38

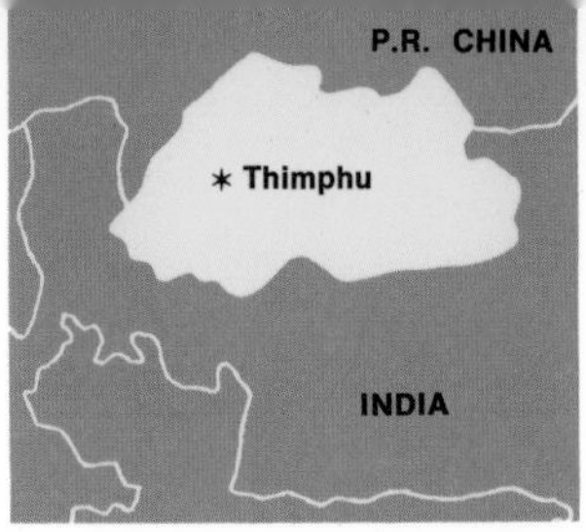

DRUK-YUL

BHUTAN

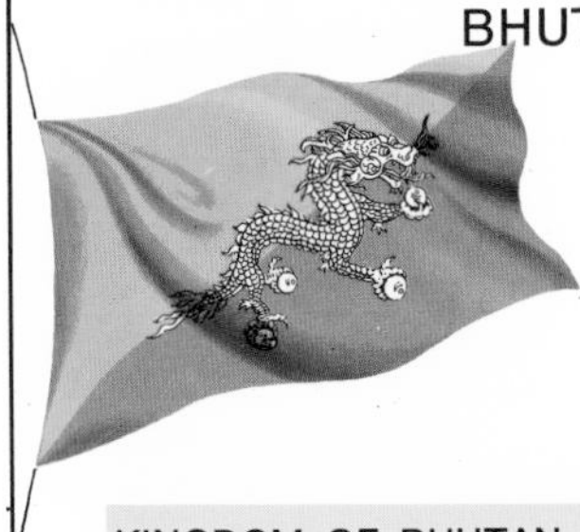

KINGDOM OF BHUTAN

Usage initiated in the nineteenth century.

The yellow or saffron half of the flag is symbolic of the authority of the king and signifies his active role in directing religious and secular affairs. The lower half of the flag symbolizes the spiritual power of Buddhism, represented in Bhutan by the Kagyudpa and Nyingmapa sects. This color formerly was maroon, but was altered in the 1960s to orange-red. White is seen as an emblem of both loyalty and purity.

The dragon in the center has several symbolic functions. It refers to the name of the country, which translates as "Land of the Dragon." It also refers to thunder, often heard in the valleys and mountains of Bhutan and traditionally believed to be the voice of dragons. In the past Bhutan had close relations with the emperors of China whose flag was golden yellow with a dragon.

Bhutan is one of many countries with traditional flags which have only recently been subject to exact specifications. In the past essential design elements were considered of greater concern than details of proportions and color shades.

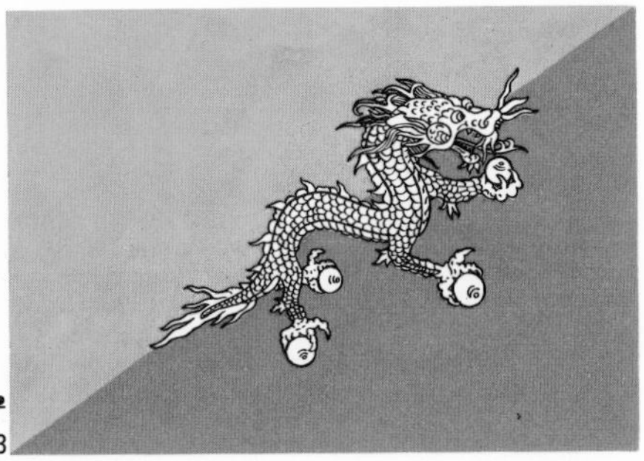

2:3

ROYAL ARMS

In the center of the royal arms is a stylized thunderbolt, associated with the power of the lamas. The head of a monastery, for example, is known as *Dorjéraja* or Wielder of the Thunderbolt. It is seen today as an emblem of power and authority as well as of harmony between spiritual and secular laws. At the top of the royal arms is the triple gem of Buddhist philosophy, which also appeared in the 1912–1959 flag of Tibet (see page 25).

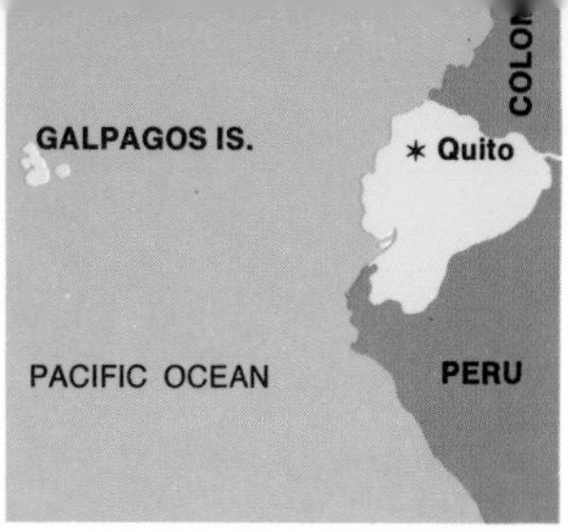

ECUADOR

ECUADOR

REPÚBLICA DEL ECUADOR

REPUBLIC OF ECUADOR

In use since 1860; officially adopted 7 November 1900.

In the first years of its independence, Ecuador was part of a union comprising Colombia and Venezuela. The national flag it hoisted in 1830 when the federation was dissolved retained the same basic design as the federation flag.

As in many other South American countries, private citizens fly a flag of plain stripes while national government buildings and military installations add the national coat of arms. Ecuador is unique, however, in having a special flag for use on municipal buildings with a ring of stars, one for each of the provinces. The arms include "that portion of the Zodiac which contains the signs corresponding to the memorable months of March, April, May and June," recalling the revolution that took place during those months in 1845. It also shows Mount Chimborazo and a ship that stands for navigation and trade.

1:2

1:2

TERRITORIO DE LOS GALAPAGOS

TERRITORY OF THE GALAPAGOS

The flag of Guayas was originally raised in the Guayaquil revolt of 1820, but most of the other provincial flags of Ecuador *(next column)* date from the mid-twentieth century.

PROVINCES OF ECUADOR

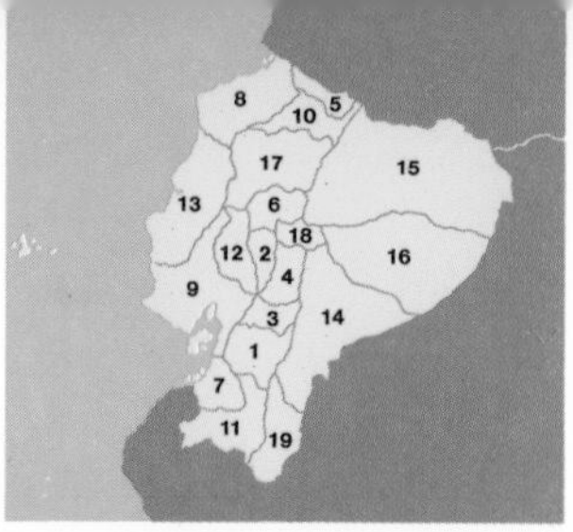

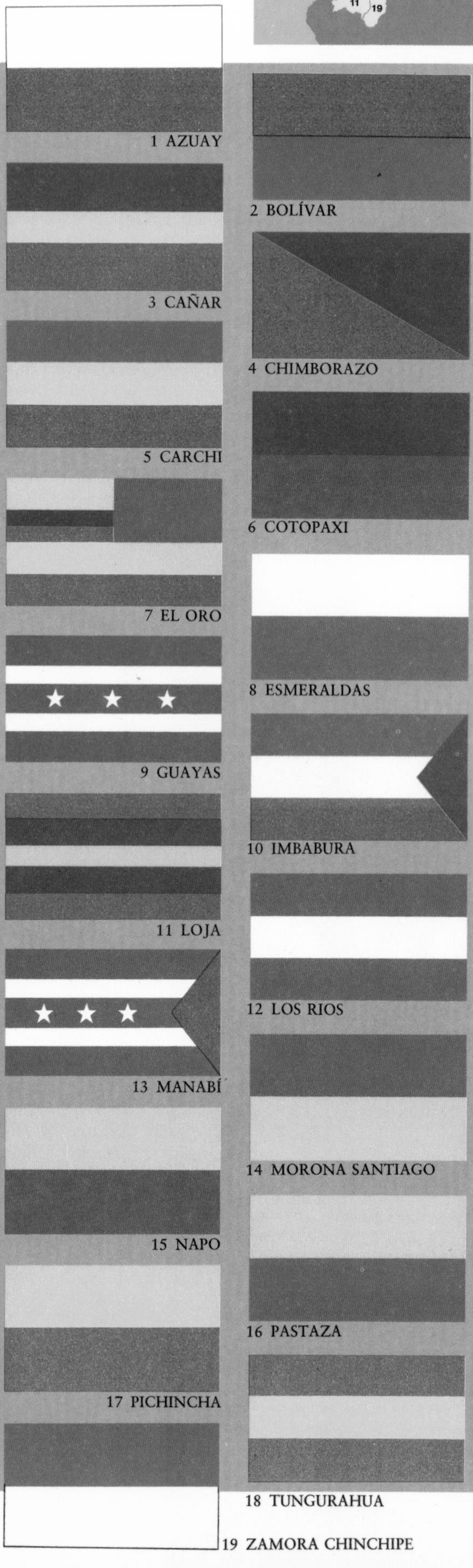

40

EIRE/IRELAND

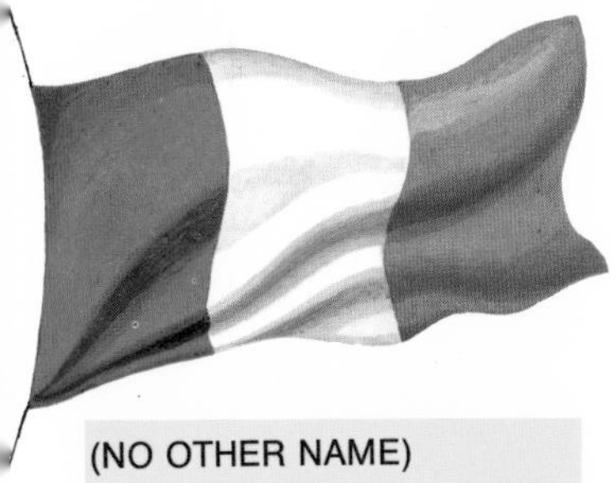

(NO OTHER NAME)

Official confirmed
29 December 1937.

The harp has been an Irish national symbol since at least the fifteenth century. The Brian Boru harp (today at Trinity College in Dublin) is the model for the modern representation of the arms, but variations have existed in the past.
Green figured in almost all flags raised by the Catholic majority as they struggled to end English rule over their land. Irish Protestants, recalling the victory of King William III in the Battle of the Boyne, in 1690, have used his livery color (orange) since that time.
In the nineteenth century under the influence of France the Irish revolutionary movement began to fly a tricolor which included a white stripe for peace. It has been used in Ireland since independence was proclaimed on 21 January 1919.

1:2

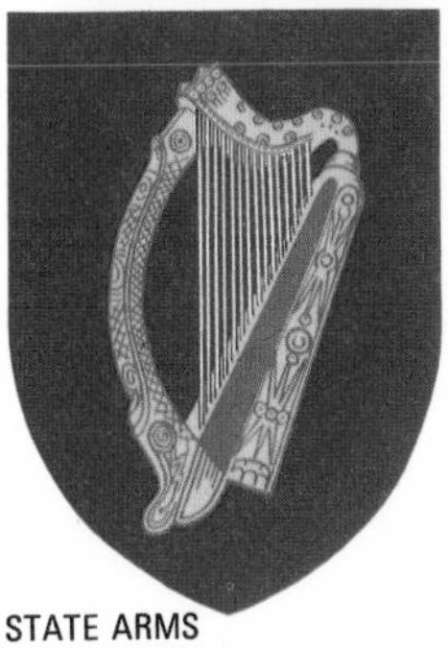

STATE ARMS

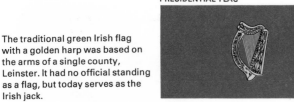

PRESIDENTIAL FLAG 1:2

The traditional green Irish flag with a golden harp was based on the arms of a single county, Leinster. It had no official standing as a flag, but today serves as the Irish jack.

1:2

CONNDAE CILL MANNTAIN WICKLOW COUNTY

41

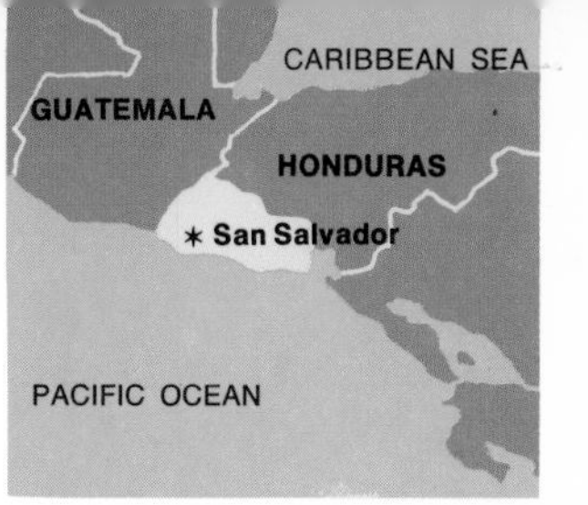

EL SALVADOR

EL SALVADOR

REPUBLICA DE EL SALVADOR

REPUBLIC OF EL SALVADOR

For further information see Guatemala, Honduras, Nicaragua, and Costa Rica.
Officially hoisted
ca. 27 September 1972.

For many years El Salvador flew a flag of stars and stripes based on that of the United States, but in 1912 the blue-white-blue flag of its early days of independence was reestablished. This flag is considered a symbol of solidarity with the other Central American nations.
The most recent flag law in El Salvador recognizes three official versions of the same basic design. One features the national motto – "God, Union, Liberty." Another includes this motto as part of the coat of arms.
The Masonic triangle of liberty and equality in the arms is framed by a wreath whose fourteen clusters of leaves correspond to the number of departments in El Salvador. The triangle contains a liberty cap, five volcanoes between two oceans, a rainbow, and the independence date "15 September 1821."

3:5

STATE ARMS

189:335

3:5

An ancient symbol of liberty, the Phrygian cap was revived during the French Revolution. Frequently represented in posters and printed media – as well as actually hoisted on poles – this cap spread from France to the New World. It may be seen in the arms of El Salvador, Argentina, Nicaragua, Cuba, Colombia, Bolivia, Honduras (1823–1866), Haiti (1803–1964), New York, and New Jersey; in the seals of Iowa and Paraguay (Treasury); and in the seal reverses of Pennsylvania and Virginia.

42

ESPAÑA

SPAIN

ESTADO ESPAÑOL

SPANISH STATE

More information on Spanish flags will be found on pages 124–129.

Since 1785 red and gold have been recognized as official Spanish colors, although their heraldic source is to be sought in the thirteenth century arms of Leon, Castile, Aragon, Navarre, and Granada.
The Spanish shield is accompanied by the arrows and yoke of the Catholic Monarchs, Ferdinand and Isabella. These symbols are also employed by the only legal party, the Spanish Phalanx.
The arms figure on the unofficial state flag: this has the proportions of the war flag, but the placement and size of the arms correspond to those found in the prime minister's flag.

Officially adopted 29 August 1936.

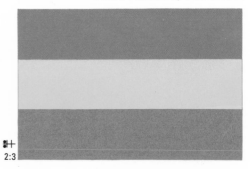

2:3

STATE ARMS

There are two versions of the personal standard of Generalissimo Francisco Franco, a square flag and one known as a *bandera cabdal* (see page 129). Officially purple, the background is in fact usually red.

2:3

HEAD OF STATE'S FLAG

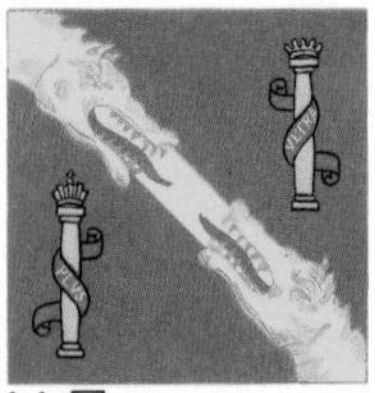

1:1

PRIME MINISTER'S FLAG

1:1

43

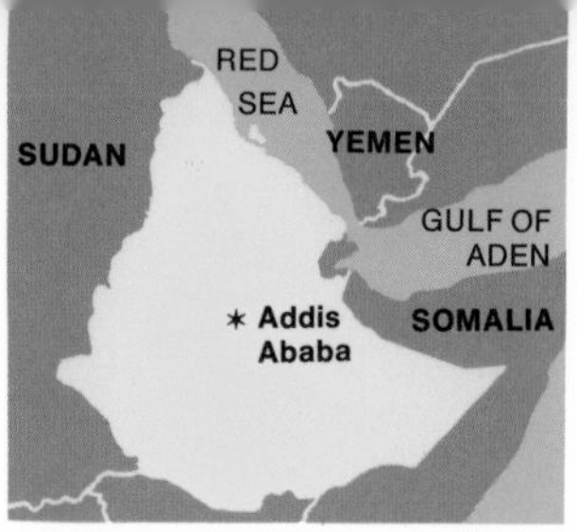

ETIOPIYA

ETHIOPIA

YE ETIOPIYA NIGUSA NEGAST MENGIST

EMPIRE OF ETHIOPIA

Contrary to Western heraldic rules, Ethiopia's lion faces the sinister.

Because of his supposed descent from Solomon, the Ethiopian emperor has been known as the Conquering Lion of Judah. The lion emblem of that ancient Jewish tribe figures as the Ethiopian state emblem, even though the emperor was deposed in 1974.
In the late nineteenth century three pennants were used together as a national flag. A rectangular flag (with the red stripe at the top) was established on 6 October 1897. The figure of St. George slaying the dragon is a symbol of the nation defeating its enemies.
Green, yellow, and red can be traced back many centuries in Ethiopian liturgical art. Various attributions are made of their symbolism: red is seen as the color of strength, the blood of patriots, or faith. Yellow is for the church, peace, natural wealth, or love. Green is seen as a symbol of the land or of hope. Others relate the colors to the Christian trinity or to three important Ethiopian provinces.

Usage reestablished ca. 5 May 1941.

2:3

STATE ARMS

2:3

STATE AND WAR FLAG (REVERSE)

2:3

2:3

44

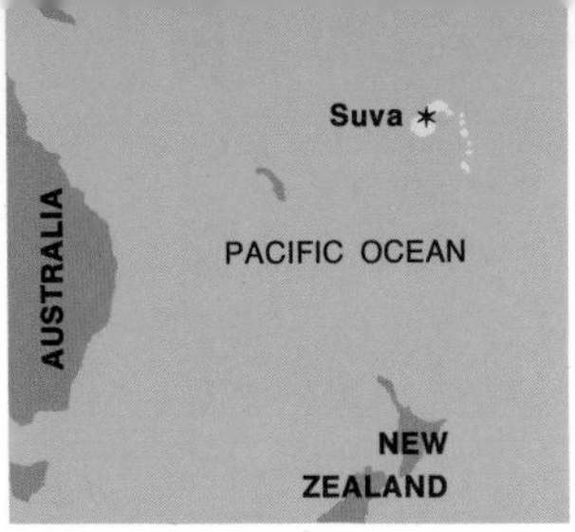

FIJI

FIJI

DOMINION OF FIJI

Officially hoisted 10 October 1970.

Links with Great Britain, which ruled Fiji between 1874 and 1970, are reflected in the Union Jack appearing in various Fiji flags. The shield of these flags, derived from the national coat of arms, dates from a royal warrant of 4 July 1908.

Two English symbols, the lion and cross of St. George, are combined in the arms with native agricultural produce – sugar cane, cocoanuts, and bananas. Both the dove with its olive branch and the motto (which translates "Fear God and Honor the King") date back to 1871 and the Kingdom of Fiji.

1:2

STATE ARMS

1:2

1:2

Alone among the flags of British Commonwealth governors-general, the Fiji flag includes a local symbol (a whale tooth).

1:2

GOVERNOR-GENERAL'S FLAG

11:15≈

45

FRANCE

FRANCE

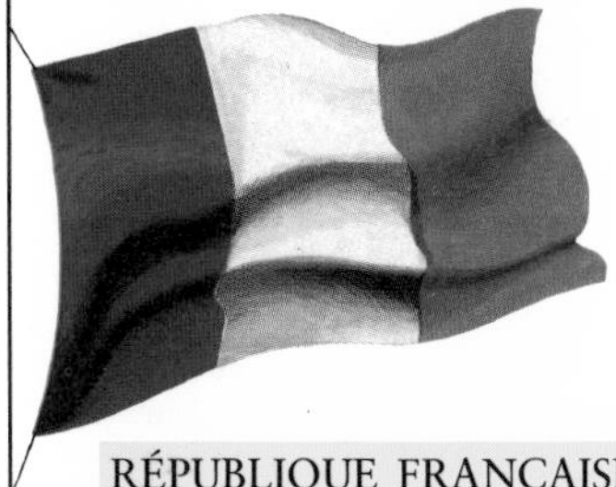

RÉPUBLIQUE FRANÇAISE

FRENCH REPUBLIC

There is no official coat of arms for the French Republic.

The Tricolor ranks as one of the most famous and most influential of national flags in history. It is a basic model for almost every official French government and military flag, and its three stripes have been copied by dozens of countries across the world. Further information on French flags will be found on pages 130–139.

A special version of the Tricolor, established on 17 May 1853 for use at sea, has stripes in relative proportions of 30:33:37. This is supposed to produce the visual impression of equality between the different colors when seen from a distance. On land the flag is frequently made square rather than oblong.

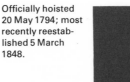

In 1974 the flag of President Giscard d'Estaing was given the traditional symbol of republicanism, a fasces, as its emblem.

Officially hoisted 20 May 1794; most recently reestablished 5 March 1848.

2:3

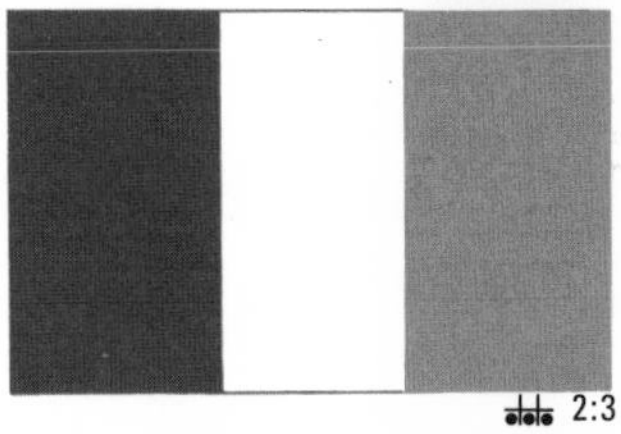

2:3

PRESIDENT'S FLAG

27:38/7:9≈

PRIME MINISTER'S FLAG

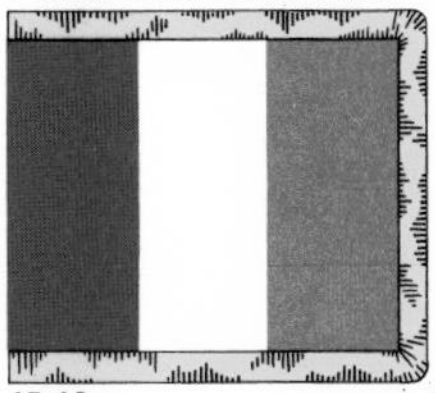

15:19≈

COMORES

5:7≈

The Muslim faith of the people and the four chief islands of the archipelago are symbolized in the Comoro flag. As of March 1975, independence has been scheduled for the Comoros, but no decision has been made on a possible change in its flag.

46

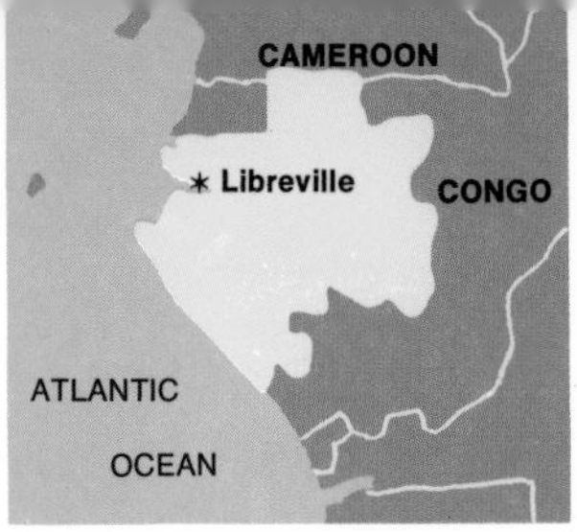

GABON

GABON

RÉPUBLIQUE GABONAISE

GABON REPUBLIC

Forests – whose lumber is a major contribution to the national economy – inspired the green stripe of the Gabon flag. An okumé tree displays and protects the shield of the national arms.
The blue and gold stripes emphasize that Gabon is a maritime nation through which the equator runs. Prior to independence the gold stripe was narrower than the other two, and the Tricolor of France, colonial master of Gabon, appeared as a canton.
The ship in the arms indicates an African nation traveling towards the brilliant future promised by its mineral wealth, as indicated by the gold discs at the top of the shield. In heraldry such discs are known as bezants, recalling the gold coins of the Byzantine Empire.
Two mottoes figure in the Gabon arms: the Latin translates as "United We Progress." The French slogan below proclaims "Union, Work, Justice."

Officially adopted
9 August 1960.

3:4

STATE ARMS

PRESIDENT'S FLAG

1:1

The armorial banner of the president of Gabon and the national arms were both designed by Louis Mühlemann, a Swiss heraldist and vexillologist. He chose panthers as supporters to symbolize the vigilance and courage of the president who protects the nation. Mühlemann, a founder of the International Federation of Vexillological Associations, also designed the coat of arms previously used by the Republic of the Congo.

47

THE GAMBIA

REPUBLIC OF THE GAMBIA

The blue stripe running through the center of the flag represents the Gambia River, which flows through the center of the country. The agricultural resources of The Gambia and the sun are symbolized by the green and red stripes; white stands for unity and peace.
In the coat of arms the blue, white, and green are given slightly different interpretations. The first is said to stand for love and loyalty; the white is for the law-abiding nature of the Gambian people and their friendliness. In addition to agricultural resources, green reflects hope and broadmindedness.

Officially hoisted
18 February 1965.

2:3

STATE ARMS

The agricultural implements – an ax and hoe – are seen as indications that the future prosperity of The Gambia depends upon the agricultural pursuits of its people. The lions are said to represent stateliness and dignity, but may also recall the British colonial regime that existed prior to independence.

It is a British Commonwealth tradition for the sovereign to grant a flag and coat of arms to a colony (such as The Gambia) upon its independence. An official painting of each is prepared by the College of Arms in London and signed by the British monarch.
The grant becomes effective on independence day; often no law is promulgated to which reference can be made for exact details of the flag design. In other countries the national flag is usually defined by a law or even by the constitution.

48

GHANA

REPUBLIC OF GHANA

Ghana's independence in 1957 began the decolonization of black Africa.

The green-white-red horizontal tricolor of the ruling Convention Peoples' Party and the green-yellow-red of Africa's oldest independent nation (Ethiopia) combined to inspire Ghana's flags. The black star is considered the lodestar of African freedom.
Symbols of local authority, the national economy, and Ghanaian history combine in a coat of arms of traditional Western pattern. In contrast, the emblem on the presidential flag is composed of authentic Ghanaian symbols meaning sovereignty, good luck, and sanctity.

Officially hoisted 6 March 1957; reestablished 28 February 1966.

2:3

STATE ARMS

2:3

2:3

In 1964, President Kwame Nkrumah, who had led the nation to independence, set up a one-party state in Ghana. The central stripe of the flag was changed to white until Nkrumah was overthrown two years later.

PRESIDENTIAL FLAG 7:12≈

49

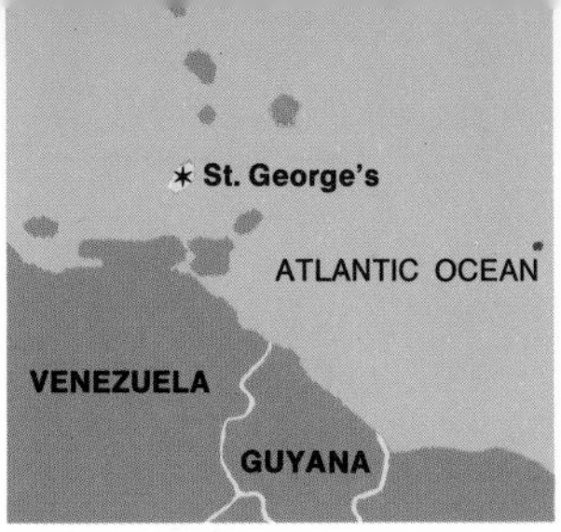

GRENADA

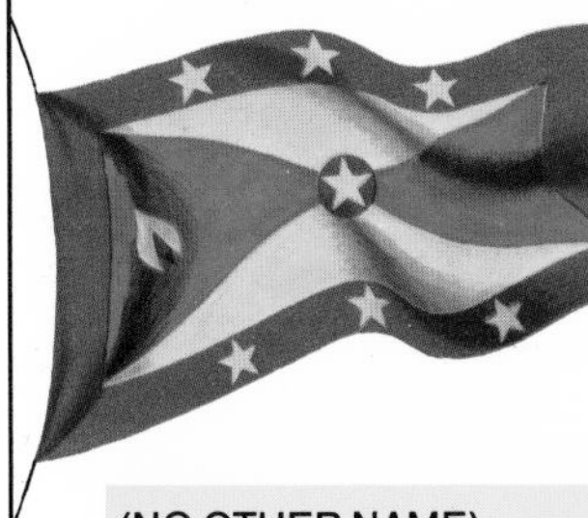

(NO OTHER NAME)

The Grenada flag design is unique in the world.

Only a island in the Caribbean, Grenada is the world's second largest producer of nutmeg – hence, the representation of a nutmeg in the hoist triangle of the flag. The country is divided into seven parishes, each represented by a star in the flag – St. George, St. John, St. Mark, St. Patrick, St. Andrew, St. David, and the Grenadines. These parishes are also represented by the seven roses in the crest of the coat of arms. The colors which figure in both the flags and coat of arms have the following symbolism. Yellow stands for the sun and the friendliness of the Grenadian people. Green represents the agricultural basis of Grenada's economy, while red is for harmony, unity, and courage. The ship and lilies in the coat of arms recall that Grenada was discovered by Columbus and has been Catholic for centuries.

Officially hoisted 7 February 1974.

3:5

STATE ARMS

1:2

In keeping with British Commonwealth practice, there are two versions of the same basic flag, differing in proportions when used at sea or on land.

50

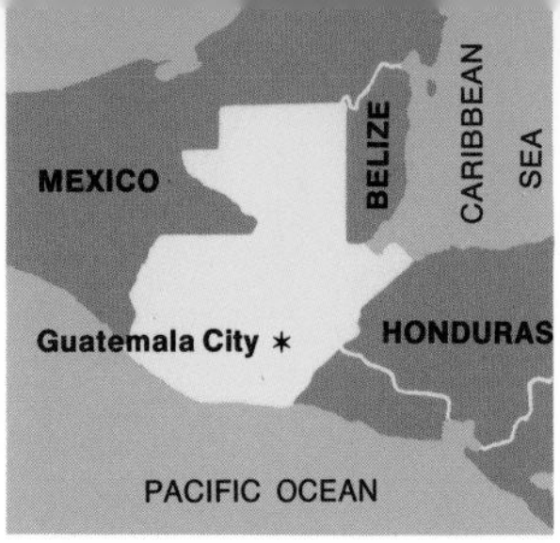

GUATEMALA

GUATEMALA

REPÚBLICA
DE GUATEMALA

REPUBLIC OF GUATEMALA

Officially adopted 15 September 1968.

Centuries ago the Aztec and the Maya-Quiche civilizations of Central America had gods in the form of feathered serpents (Quetzalcohuatl and Gugunatz). In artwork, the serpents' feathers would be represented by the brilliant green plumes of the quetzal. Today the national bird of Guatemala, the quetzal is considered a symbol of liberty because it supposedly cannot live in captivity. Gen. Justo Rufino Barrios introduced it as a national emblem in 1871, although the quetzal had been used decades earlier in the arms of the secessionist state of Los Altos.

5:8

STATE ARMS

Guatemala's arms bear a parchment scroll inscribed "Liberty 15 September 1821" in honor of the date when Central America broke with Spain. Like other former members of the United Provinces of the Center of America, Guatemala still uses a flag of blue, white, and blue.

5:8

Many attempts have been made to reunite Central America since its original confederation dissolved. Each such undertaking, whether by constitutional or other means, has had a symbol of unity associated with it. Not surprisingly, all have emphasized the traditional blue-white-blue stripes. When President Justo Rufino Barrios of Guatemala attempted to create such a union in 1885, the flag he designed was like the banner of Guatemala, except that the arms were "a quetzal on a column and on the latter the motto 'Liberty and Union, 15 September 1821, 28 February 1885.'"

51

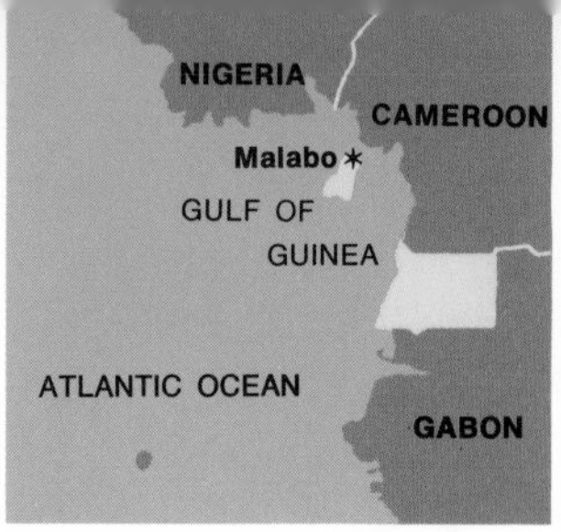

GUINEA ECUATORIAL

EQUATORIAL GUINEA

REPÚBLICA DE GUINEA ECUATORIAL

REPUBLIC OF EQUATORIAL GUINEA

The six stars in the arms of Equatorial Guinea represent the five islands (Fernando Po, Great Elobey, Little Elobey, Corisco, and Annobon) and the nation's mainland territory, Río Muni.

The country chose a significant date for its independence from Spain – Columbus Day or Hispanic Festival Day, as it is known locally. Recalling the discovery of the New World on 12 October 1492 and the subsequent spread of Spanish culture, this day is celebrated throughout Latin America and

Officially hoisted 12 October 1968.

2:3≈

STATE ARMS

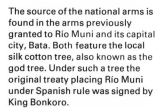

in the Philippines by the hoisting of the special Banner of the Race bearing on white three purple crosses and a golden rising sun.

The green stripe in the flag of Equatorial Guinea represents the natural resources of the land; blue is the water linking the mainland and islands.

2:3≈

The source of the national arms is found in the arms previously granted to Río Muni and its capital city, Bata. Both feature the local silk cotton tree, also known as the god tree. Under such a tree the original treaty placing Río Muni under Spanish rule was signed by King Bonkoro.

Equatorial Guinea follows the tradition of Spain and many Latin American countries in distinguishing its state flag from its civil flag by the addition of the state arms to the former.

White is for peace, and red for the independence struggle. The motto in the arms translates as "Unity, Peace, Justice."

52

GUINÉ-BISSAU

GUINEA-BISSAU

REPÚBLICA DA GUINÉ-BISSAU

REPUBLIC OF GUINEA-BISSAU

Officially hoisted
24 September 1973.

When the African Party for the Independence of Guinea-Bissau and the Cape Verde Islands (known as the PAIGC) began its liberation struggle against Portuguese colonial rule, other African countries were just becoming independent under flags of red, yellow, and green. These pan-African colors plus black were chosen in August 1961 by the PAIGC for its own flag.
The black star stands for the leadership of the party in this black African country. It may also correspond to the capital city (Bissau), which is located in the nation's coastal region, suggested by the red stripe.
The yellow and green may represent the savannahs of the north and the forests of the south, respectively. In other African countries they symbolize mineral wealth and agriculture.
Prior to the recognition by Portugal of the independence of this former colony, the PAIGC was in actual control of most of the territory of Guinea-Bissau. The party flag (which included the initials PAIGC in black below the star) was therefore the logical choice for a national flag when independence was unilaterally proclaimed in 1973.

1:2≈

STATE ARMS

There are several political and geographical names similar enough to be confused. These include Guinea-Bissau (formerly Portuguese Guinea), Equatorial Guinea (formerly a Spanish colony), and Guinea (formerly French) in Africa. In South America there are three Guianas – an overseas French department, a Dutch territory (properly known as Surinam), and a former British colony (now the independent nation of Guyana). The island of New Guinea, north of Australia, includes the nation Papua New Guinea.

53

GUINÉE

GUINEA

RÉPUBLIQUE DE GUINÉE

REPUBLIC OF GUINEA

The flag chosen following Guinea's proclamation of independence in 1958 reflected its years under French rule by the three vertical stripes. The flag colors are those of the organization that led the struggle for independence, the Democratic Party of Guinea. These also correspond to the pan-African colors previously adopted by Ethiopia, Ghana, and Cameroon.
Finally, the colors are seen as a reflection of the national motto "Work, Justice, Solidarity." Red is for the sweat running across the black bodies of the Guinean men and women who struggle to build their country and for the blood of patriotic martyrs. The golden sun which shines equally on all men suggests an identification of yellow with justice, although it is also an emblem of mineral wealth. The green of Guinea's vegetation evokes a spirit of solidarity among all citizens in the development of the national economy.
The commitment of Guinea's foreign policy to peace is symbolized by the dove and olive branch; the elephant is an emblem of strength used by the Democratic Party of Guinea.

Officially adopted
10 November
1958.

2:3≈

STATE ARMS

The flag of Guinea plays a role in the national campaign against illiteracy. When district headquarters of the Democratic Party achieve a 50 percent literacy rate, they are allowed to fly a red pennant. Additional yellow and green pennants are awarded for 75 and 100 percent literacy. This inspires competition for the honor of having the right to fly all three pennants whose colors form the national flag.

54

GUYANA

GUYANA

(NO OTHER NAME)

The author of this book designed Guyana's national flag.

"The Golden Arrowhead," as it is known to the Guyanese press, represents the golden future citizens hope will be built upon Guyana's mineral resources. The extensive water resources of the country are incorporated in the design through a white fimbriation that separates the arrowhead from the green field.

Green was chosen as an appropriate color for the flag background because green forests and fields cover more than 90 percent of Guyana.

Red is for zeal and sacrifice, elements of the dynamic nation-building process the Guyanese are engaged in. The black triangle border indicates the perseverance needed to achieve success in the undertaking.

Local attributes incorporated into the arms include a cacique's crown, diamonds, jaguars, agricultural products (sugar cane and rice), a pickaxe, and the national motto.

Officially hoisted 26 May 1966.

3:5

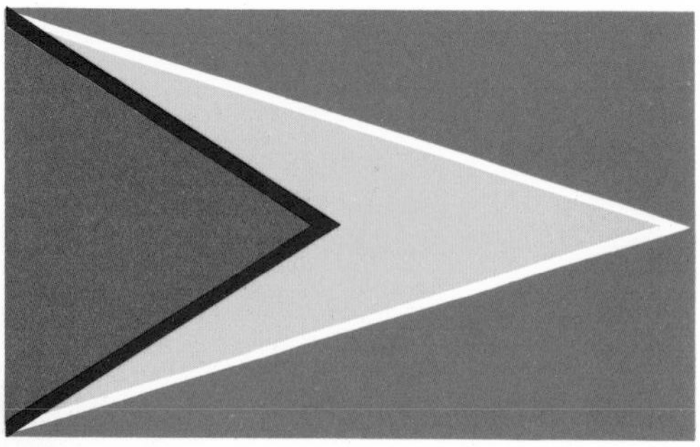

STATE ARMS

1:2

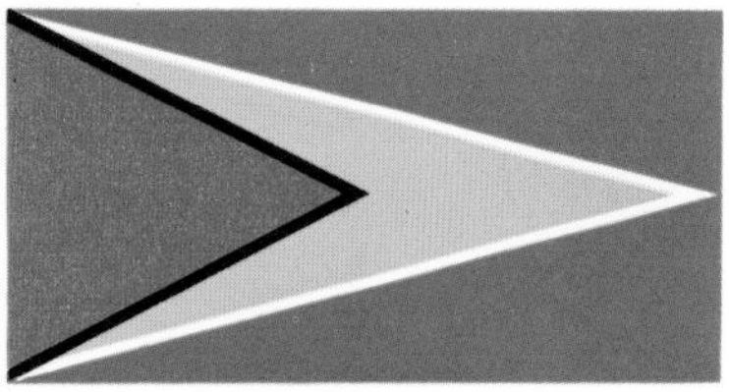

When Guyana became a republic in 1970, a presidential standard was developed from the national arms. To indicate leadership, the traditional Amerindian feathered crown was added to a banner of Guyana's arms; a canje pheasant and the national flower (the victoria regia lily) frame the shield on which this crown appears.

PRESIDENTIAL FLAG

1:1 ≈

55

HAÏTI

HAITI

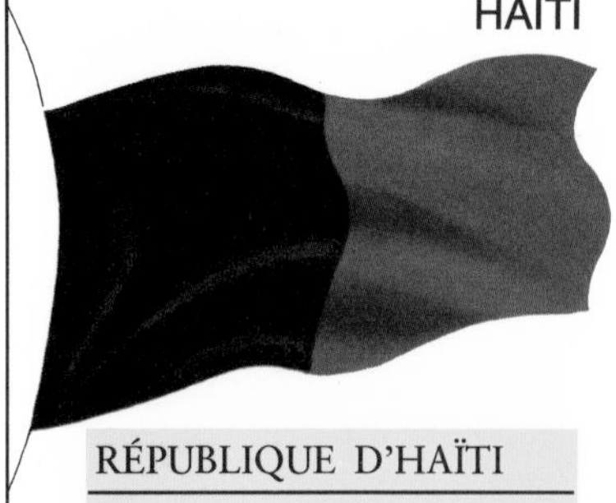

RÉPUBLIQUE D'HAÏTI

REPUBLIC OF HAITI

Officially hoisted 21 June 1964.

The concepts of liberty, democracy, and the natural rights of man preached by the French Revolution led the French colony of Saint Domingue to proclaim its independence on 1 January 1804 as the Republic of Haiti.

Its first flag consisted of blue and red stripes symbolizing blacks and mulattoes. The design omitted from the French Tricolor its central stripe, which Haitians saw as a symbol of the white slave holders.

Under Jean-Jacques Dessalines and Henri Christophe the blue was changed to black, but President Jean-Paul Boyer in 1822 established a horizontal blue-red flag which continued in use until 1964. At that time President François Duvalier brought back the early vertical black-red to stress links with Haiti's African heritage.

1:2 ≈

STATE ARMS

1:2 ≈

Haiti's motto is the same as the one in the arms of Belgium – "Union Makes Strength."

The emperor palm of the Haitian arms is considered a symbol of liberty. The patriot Toussaint L'Ouverture, on being deported to France in 1802, said, "In overthrowing me only the trunk of the tree of liberty of the blacks has been beaten in Saint Domingue; it will grow again from its roots because they are numerous and deep."

56

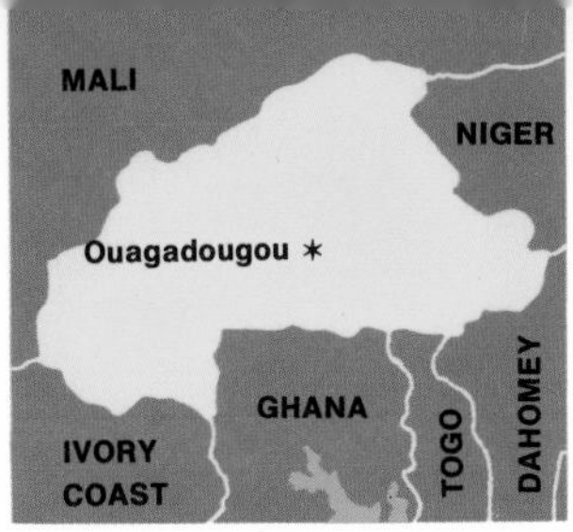

HAUTE-VOLTA

UPPER VOLTA

RÉPUBLIQUE DE HAUTE-VOLTA

REPUBLIC OF UPPER VOLTA

The upper reaches of the Red Volta, the White Volta, and the Black Volta flow through this land. They provided the country with its name and the inspiration for its national flag. Simple horizontal stripes corresponding to the names of the three rivers are repeated in the national flag, the national coat of arms, and the presidential standard.
The coat of arms, adopted in 1961, has two further charges indirectly related to the rivers. The water they provide is used to raise sorghum; consequently, this plant and the hoes used in its cultivation figure at the bottom of the arms. An appropriate symbol for an agricultural people, a hoe may also be found in the flag of the Congo and in the arms of Zambia, Tanzania, Rwanda, The Gambia, and Liberia.

Officially adopted 9 December 1959.

2:3

STATE ARMS

PRESIDENTIAL FLAG

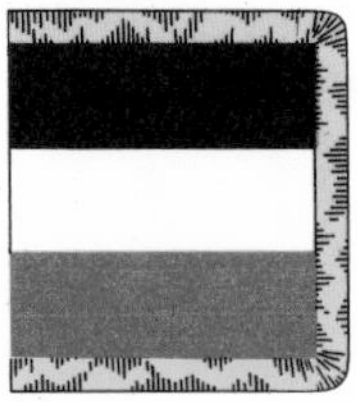

1:1

Except that its proportions are different (2:3 instead of 3:5), the national flag of Upper Volta is exactly like the civil ensign of the German Empire flown from 1867 until 1919. Other unintentional coincidences of design exist or have existed between the flags of Monaco and Indonesia; Italy and Mexico; and Chad, Romania, and Andorra.

In Central Europe there are numerous identical tricolors and bicolors, based on the heraldic colors, which have been adopted by districts, cities, and villages. Intentional coincidences of design in flags may be found in examples from Central America and the Arab world.

57

HELLAS

GREECE

HELLINIKI DIMOKRATIA

HELLENIC REPUBLIC

The first Greek republic existed between 1924 and 1935.

When in the early nineteenth century Christian Greeks rose in revolt against the Muslim Turks who controlled their land, the blue of their flag contrasted sharply with the red of Ottoman banners. Blue is said to stand for the sea and the sky, but it also has religious connotations dating back to the Byzantine Empire.
The basic form of the Greek flag was adopted in 1822 by its first government. The most recent form is slightly longer and has a darker shade of blue than the ones used previously. The latest flag law also eliminates different designs previously used for civil flag, civil ensign, and war ensign.

Officially hoisted 18 August 1970.

7:12

STATE ARMS

The cross in the canton is a reminder of the faith of the Greeks. It is said that the nine stripes of the flag correspond to the nine syllables in the war cry of independence, which translates as "Freedom or Death."

PRESIDENT'S FLAG

20:23

Although the establishment of a republic in Greece in 1973 did not alter the national flag, the royal arms were abandoned. Instead a traditional symbol was revived for use as the state emblem.
A phoenix being reborn from its ashes was previously used not only by the military junta that overthrew the monarchy in 1973, but the first Greek republic, Greek fraternal organizations, and many who struggled for independence in the nineteenth century. A new coat of arms based on the flag was created in 1975.

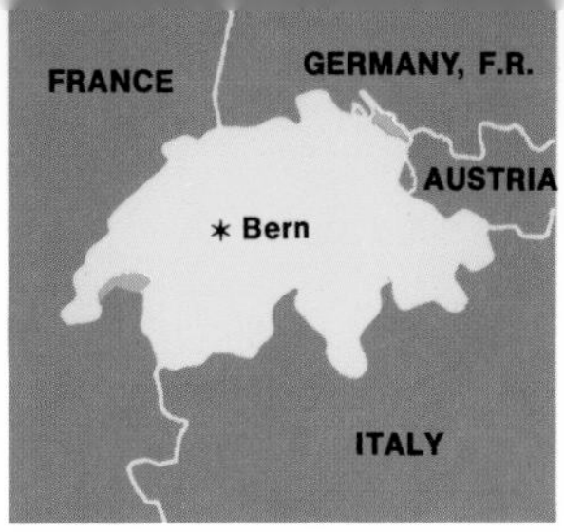

THE CANTONS OF SWITZERLAND

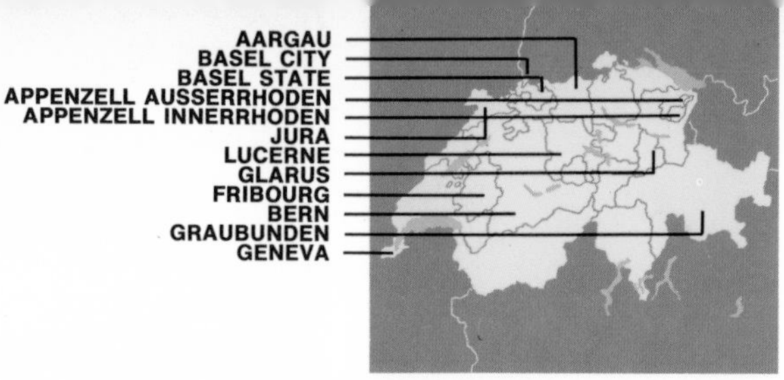

HELVETIA/SCHWEIZ/SUISSE/ SVIZZERA/SVIZZRA

SWITZERLAND

CONFOEDERATIO HELVETICA/ SCHWEIZERISCHE EIDGENOSSENSCHAFT/ CONFÉDÉRATION SUISSE/ CONFEDERAZIONE SVIZZERA/ CONFEDERAZIUN SVIZZRA

SWISS CONFEDERATION

On coins and stamps the Latin Helvetia joins the name of the country in its four official languages – German, French, Italian, and Romansch.

Through the ages Switzerland has provided thousands of the finest soldiers known to Europe, both in the service of other nations and in its own defense. Proud of the bold heraldic emblems of their own cantons (still used in the cantonal flags of today), these men also shared a common symbol – the Swiss cross. Emblazoned in white on the Blood Banner of the Holy Roman Empire, the Swiss cross appeared on those battlefields wherever the Swiss soldiers fought in the name of the confederation. While the similar emblem of the canton of Schwyz dates from 1240, for the confederation itself our first written record is more recent: troops leaving for the Battle of Laupen in 1339 "were marked with the sign of the Holy Cross, a white cross on a red shield. . . ."

The flag began to take on its present form during the nineteenth century. The Napoleonic wars caused great upheavals in Switzerland and led to a new political structure. When a new constitution was written for the confederation in 1848, the square red flag with a large white cross became standard for the army. The exact form of the present national flag dates from 12 December 1889.

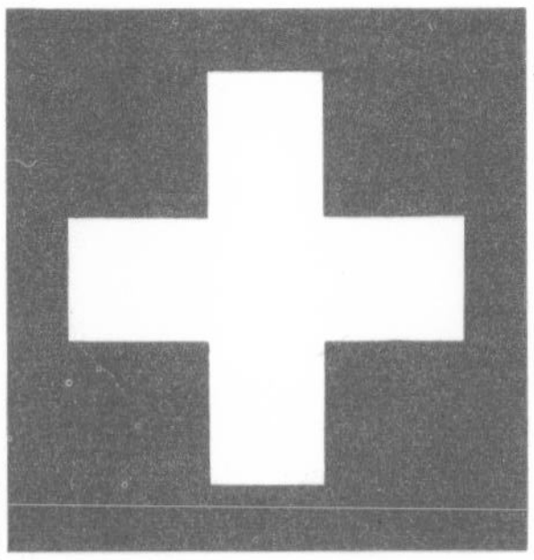

1:1

STATE ARMS

2:3

For many years "Admiral of the Swiss Navy" was considered a joke. Nevertheless during World War II an official version of the Swiss flag for use on water *(above)* was adopted, and today it is frequently seen, especially on the Rhine River and the lakes.

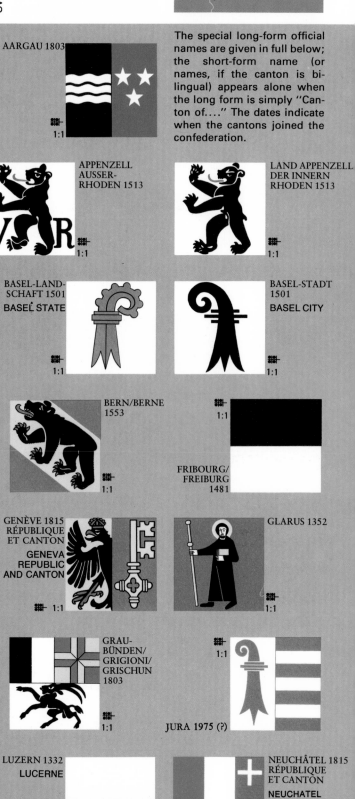

The special long-form official names are given in full below; the short-form name (or names, if the canton is bilingual) appears alone when the long form is simply "Canton of. . . ." The dates indicate when the cantons joined the confederation.

AARGAU 1803

1:1

APPENZELL AUSSER-RHODEN 1513

1:1

LAND APPENZELL DER INNERN RHODEN 1513

1:1

BASEL-LAND-SCHAFT 1501
BASEL STATE

1:1

BASEL-STADT 1501
BASEL CITY

1:1

BERN/BERNE 1553

1:1

FRIBOURG/ FREIBURG 1481

1:1

GENÈVE 1815 RÉPUBLIQUE ET CANTON
GENEVA REPUBLIC AND CANTON

1:1

GLARUS 1352

1:1

GRAU-BÜNDEN/ GRIGIONI/ GRISCHUN 1803

1:1

JURA 1975 (?)

1:1

LUZERN 1332
LUCERNE

1:1

NEUCHÂTEL 1815 RÉPUBLIQUE ET CANTON
NEUCHATEL REPUBLIC AND CANTON

1:1

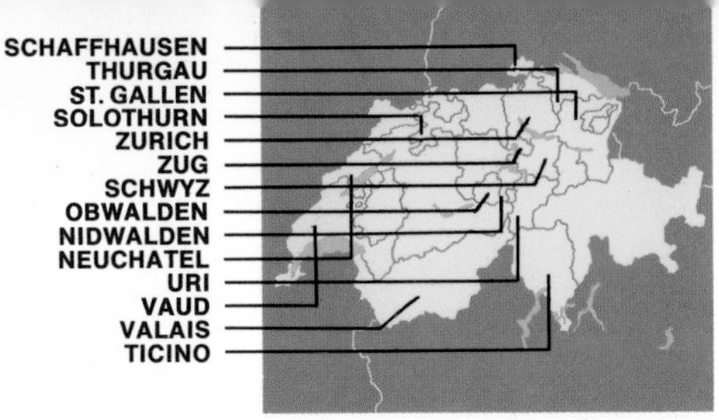

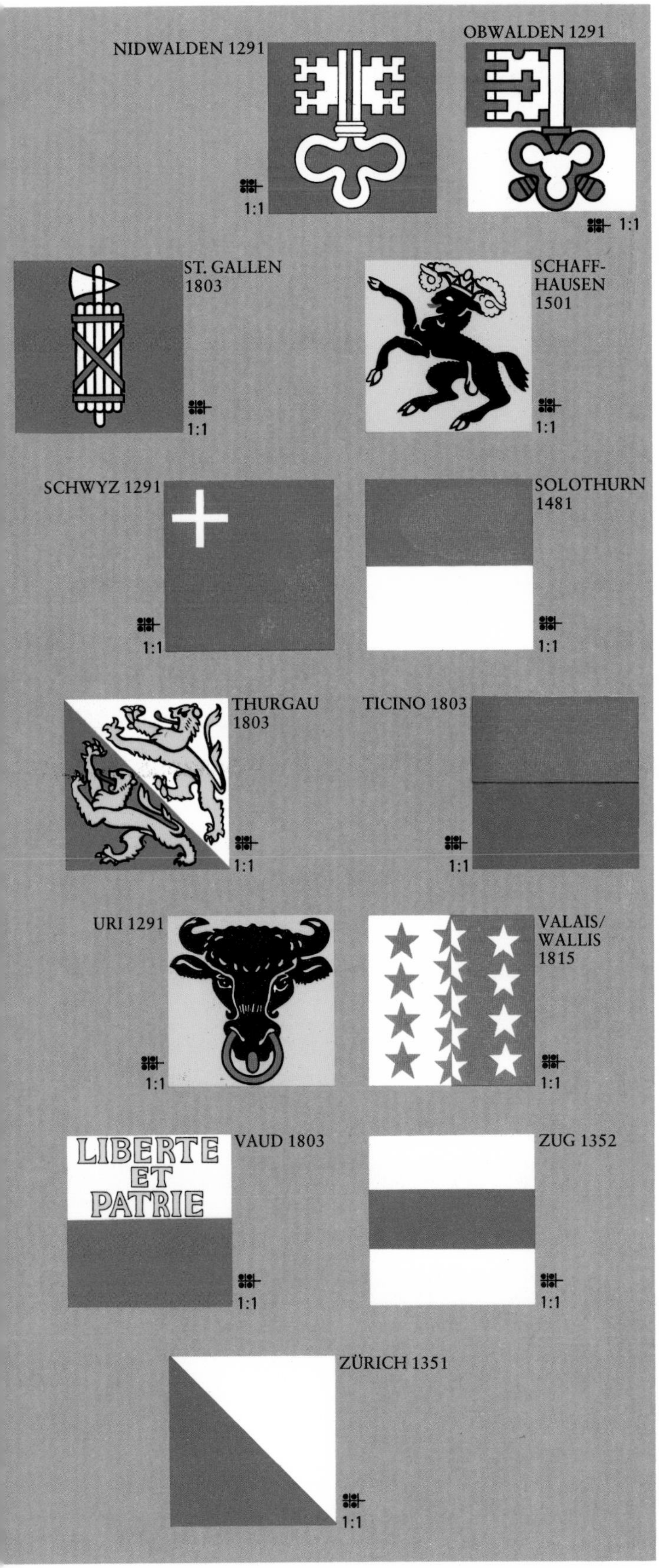

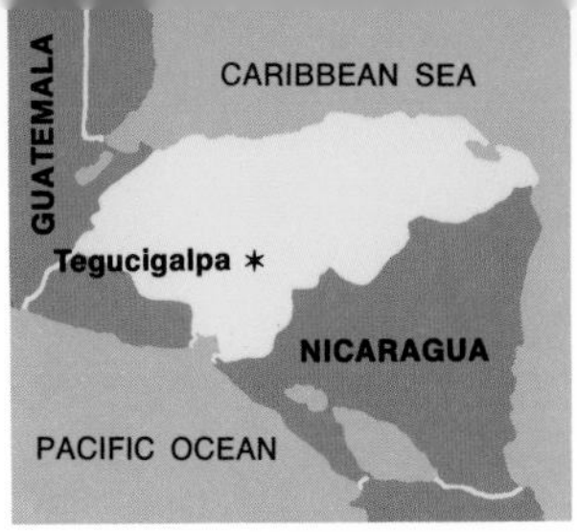

HONDURAS

HONDURAS

REPÚBLICA DE HONDURAS

REPUBLIC OF HONDURAS

Officially adopted 18 January 1949.

The flag of Honduras recalls its former union with Guatemala, Nicaragua, El Salvador, and Costa Rica by the five stars added to the central stripe in 1866; the tradition of the stripes goes back even further into the past.

The blue-white-blue horizontally striped flag of the United Provinces of the Center of America, based on the Argentine flag, was first hoisted in the independence struggle against Spain on 4 July 1818, when the commodore of an Argentine squadron, Louis Aury, proclaimed the first independent Central American state on islands off the eastern coast of Nicaragua.

STATE ARMS

Aury's government lasted until 1821, when Central America proclaimed its independence. Although it first became part ot the Mexican Empire in 1823, when complete independence was established the new national flag had stripes similar to, and apparently based on, those of the first free state on Santa Catalina.

In addition to the volcano, rainbow, triangle, and two oceans found in other Central American arms, the state arms of Honduras include several distinctive symbols.

A quiver for the original Indian population; cornucopias for agricultural wealth; mountains, mines, and mining tools for its mineral wealth; and trees for its sylvan resources all figure in the arms adopted in 1866 and modified in 1935.

60

INDONESIA

INDONESIA

REPUBLIK INDONESIA

REPUBLIC OF INDONESIA

Except for its proportions, the flag of Indonesia is the same as that of Monaco.

In 1293 when Prince Jayakatong led a revolt that ended the Kingdom of Singasari, a red and white flag was adopted by the new Majapahit Empire. Modern Indonesia looks back on that state as its predecessor and the source of its own *Merah-Putih* ("red-white") flag.

Its modern revival dates from 1922, for it was in that year the Indonesian Association formed by students in the Netherlands adopted the red-white flag. Taken up by the Indonesian Nationalist Party, it flew in Java for the first time in 1928. Indonesian independence, finally proclaimed at the end of World War II, required five more years of struggle before the new nation was recognized by the Dutch.

Indonesia's date of independence is reflected in the seventeen wing feathers and eight tail feathers of the Garuda in its coat of arms. The star, padi, and cotton of the arms are repeated as symbols in the presidential standard.

Officially hoisted 17 August 1945.

2:3≈

STATE ARMS

The motto "Unity in Diversity" refers to the many peoples and islands united in Indonesia. The shield of national defense bears symbols of the state philosophy, the Five Principles. The star refers to belief in god; the buffalo head, to popular sovereignty; the banyan tree, to national consciousness; and the padi and cotton (for food and clothing), to social justice. The chain, whose alternately square and round links represent women and men, is for equality.

PRESIDENTIAL FLAG

1:1/4:5

61

IRAN

IRAN

KESHVARE SHAHANSHAHIYE IRAN

EMPIRE OF IRAN

Iranian flags also appear on pages 34 and 100.

The lion and sun as a combined motif goes back to the thirteenth century A.D. and as a flag design is known from the mid-fifteenth century.

At first the lion and sun embodied astrological and religious symbolism, gradually acquiring royal and national meanings. The sword of Ali (see Morocco) is fairly recent, introduced by the Safadids in the sixteenth century.

In the nineteenth century Iran's flag was the lion and sun on white with borders of red and green. The basic tricolor dates from the constitution of 14 August 1905, with artistic alterations in 1912, 1933, and ca. 1964.

4:7

STATE ARMS

IMPERIAL ARMS

4:7

4:7

IMPERIAL FLAG

1:1≈

The imperial arms show emblems from the dynasties of the past. The inscription at the bottom reads "He Has Ordered Me to Be Just and He Himself Is the Highest Judge."

62

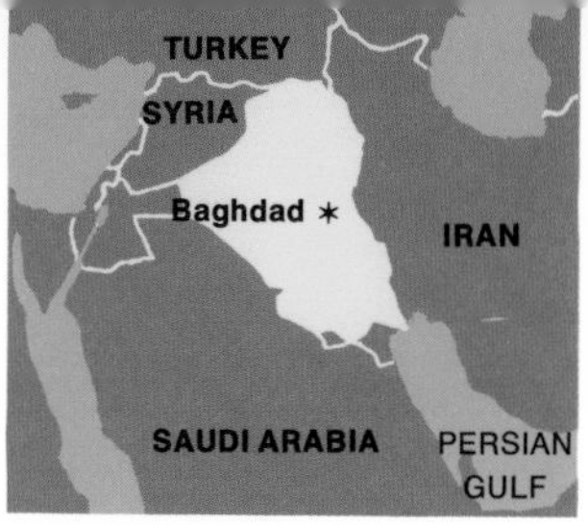

AL IRAQ

IRAQ

AL DJUMHURIYAH
AL IRAQIYAH
AL DIMUQRATIYAH
AL SHABIYAH

IRAQI DEMOCRATIC PEOPLE'S REPUBLIC

The development of Iraqi flags is shown on page 155.

The Arab Revolt of 1916 initiated by King Hussein of the Hijaz created a flag flown in Iraq until 1924; in 1958 it was briefly revived for the Arab Union which linked Iraq with Jordan. Hussein's son and great-grandson, Faisal I and Faisal II, were kings of Iraq under a flag based on the design created for the Arab Revolt. In 1959, after the overthrow of the monarchy, the new Republic of Iraq adopted a flag combining the four pan-Arab colors with a golden sun symbolic of the Kurds who inhabit northern Iraq.

In 1963 efforts were made by Iraq, Egypt, and Syria to reestablish the United Arab Republic. In anticipation of amalgamation, both Syria and Iraq altered their flags to the basic United Arab Republic design – red-white-black horizontal stripes with green stars in the center. The union failed to materialize, but the three stars of the Iraqi flag stand as a reminder of the aspiration to find common solutions to Arab problems.

The arms of Iraq, featuring the eagle of Saladin and the name of the state, were also adopted at this time.

Officially hoisted 31 July 1963.

2:3

STATE ARMS

The Confederation of Arab Republics introduced new flags in Syria, Egypt, and Libya in 1972, leaving the arms and flags of Iraq and the Yemens as the only current emblems based directly on the ones which characterized the move to Arab unity in the late 1950s and early 1960s.

63

ÍSLAND

ICELAND

LÝDHVELDIDH ÍSLAND

REPUBLIC OF ICELAND

For centuries blue and white were considered the national colors of Iceland, appearing in national costume and elsewhere. In the first flag designs proposed for Iceland, these colors predominated; they were also found in the arms used between 1903 and 1919 – a white falcon on a blue shield.

To indicate its links with other Scandinavian nations a Scandinavian cross flag was selected and the color red included when the definitive Icelandic flag design was established. At first the king of Denmark refused to approve the design; even when it became official, usage was restricted to land and to coastal waters. The appearance of the flag was unchanged when Iceland became independent in 1919 and when it became a republic in 1944. Iceland has also followed the custom common in Scandinavia and the Baltic of employing a swallow-tailed flagshape for official purposes.

Officially hoisted 19 June 1915; restrictions on use at sea lifted 1 December 1918.

18:25

STATE ARMS

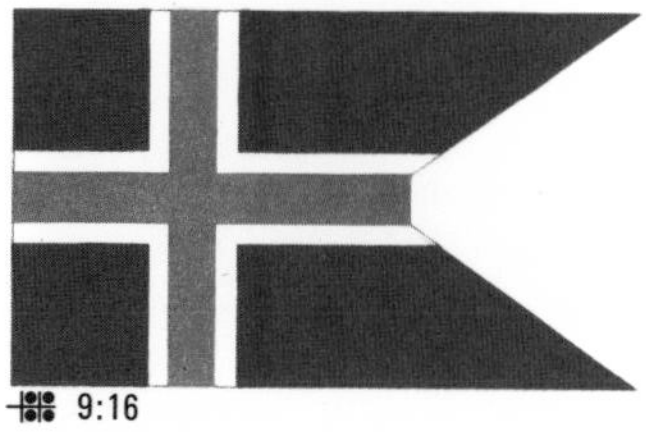

9:16

PRESIDENTIAL FLAG

9:16

The *Heimskringla* (the sagas of the Norwegian kings compiled by the Icelander Snorri Sturluson) relate a legend which is expressed graphically in the Icelandic arms: An evil spirit in the form of a whale sent to attack Iceland found the island protected on every side by fearsome monsters. Learning that a giant, a dragon, an eagle, and a bull guarded the land, the Danish king who had sent the whale decided not to execute his plans to invade the island.

64

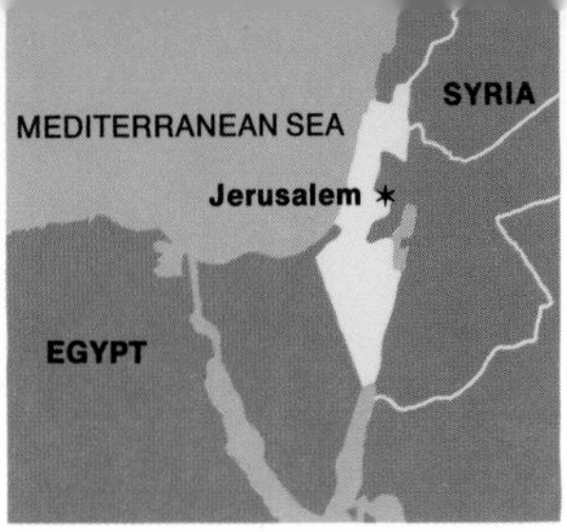

ISRAEL/ISRAIL

ISRAEL

MEDINAT ISRAEL/
DAULAT ISRAIL

STATE OF ISRAEL

Hebrew and Arabic are the official Israeli languages.

On 21 July 1891 at the dedication of Zion Hall in Boston, Massachusetts, the B'nai Zion Educational Society displayed a flag based on the *tallis* or Jewish prayer shawl. It was white with blue stripes; in the center was the ancient *Mogen David* (Star of David, often erroneously called Shield of David).

In 1897 this flag was submitted at the World Zionist Organization conference in Basel by the Boston delegate, Isaac Harris. Other Jews had conceived of similar designs; the flag quickly became accepted as the Zionist emblem, and in 1948 it was adopted by the State of Israel.

Officially confirmed 12 November 1948.

8:11

STATE ARMS

The State arms reflect other ancient Jewish symbols. The name of the state and the olive branches of prosperity frame a candelabra such as the Romans carried off in triumph after the destruction of Jerusalem in 70 A.D. The combination of the candelabra and branches is mentioned in Zechariah IV: 2–3 in the Bible.

2:3

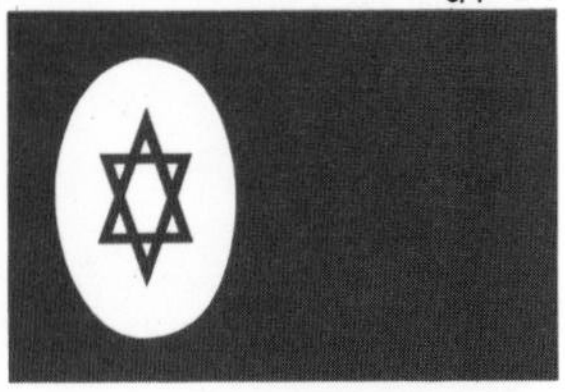

8:11

2:3

PRESIDENTIAL FLAG

1:1

65

ITALIA

ITALY

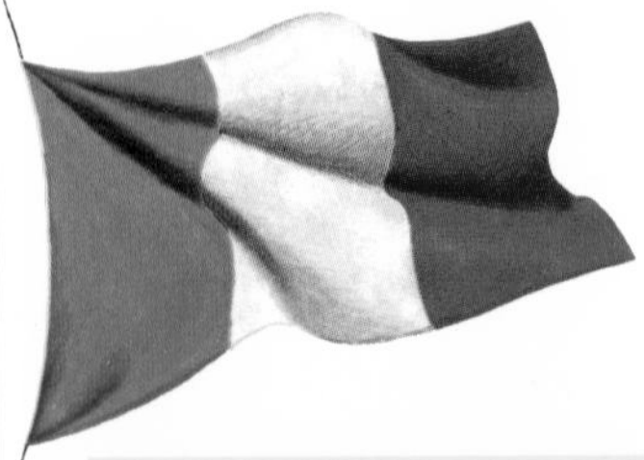

REPUBBLICA ITALIANA

ITALIAN REPUBLIC

Further information on Italian flags will be found on pages 140–147.

Since Italy was among the first nations to take up the revolutionary principles espoused by France in 1789, it is not surprising that the French Tricolor was chosen as the model for Italy's own national flag. The substitution of green for blue in the stripe at the hoist is said to have been a decision made by Napoleon himself.

Italy's Tricolor went through many political and military struggles before it achieved universal recognition by Italians as their national flag. The most recent form was established in 1946, when the monarchy was abolished and its coat of arms removed from the flag.

Officially adopted 19 June 1946.

2:3

STATE ARMS

The arms of the Italian Republic *(left)* feature a star, an emblem of the nation, set against a cog wheel standing for labor. It is framed by branches of oak and olive, representing strength and peace. The same arms figure in the presidential standard *(below).*

2:3

2:3

The crosses of Genoa, Amalfi, and Pisa and the winged lion of Venice recall Italy's glorious maritime heritage. In the war ensign *(top, right)* the lion holds a sword; in the civil ensign *(above)*, a book. The former also bears a "naval crown."

PRESIDENTIAL FLAG

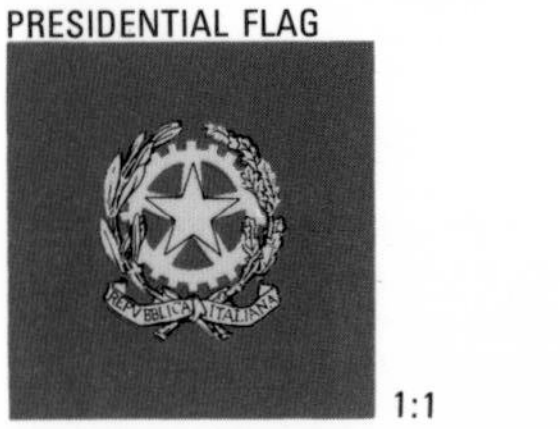

1:1

66

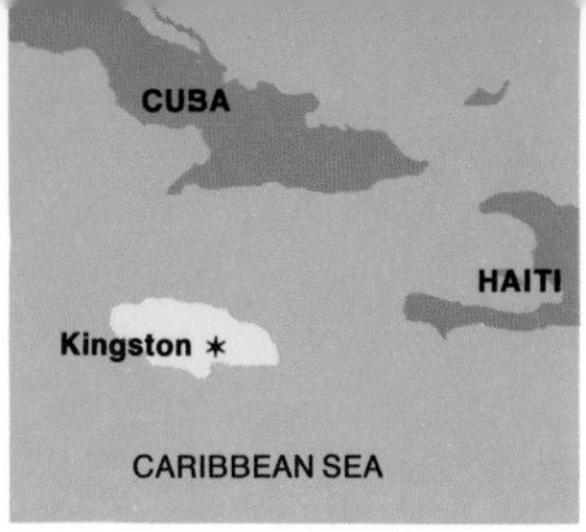

JAMAICA

JAMAICA

(NO OTHER NAME)

The original Jamaican flag proposal was discovered to resemble closely the flag of Tanganyika, although the design was approved by British authorities who should have been aware of the conflict. The current design was therefore substituted.

Green is a symbol of hope and of agriculture, gold of natural wealth and the beauty of sunlight. Black stands for the past and present hardships facing the country.

The arms are those originally granted in 1661; the pattern was modified in 1957 by having the motto and artistic rendition altered.

Officially hoisted 6 August 1962.

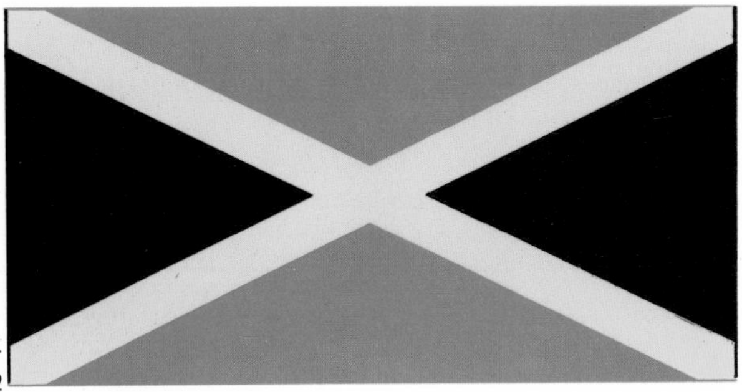

1:2

STATE ARMS

3:5

4:9

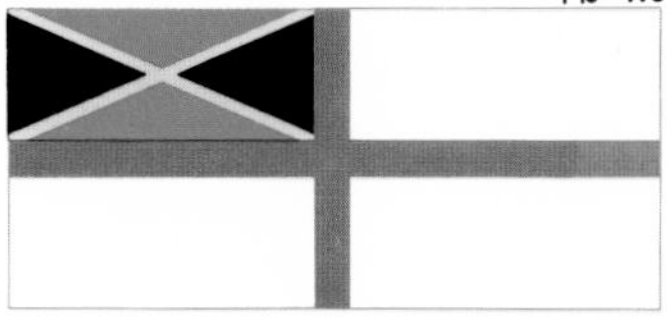

ROYAL FLAG

4:7≈

GOVERNOR-GENERAL'S FLAG

1:2≈

PRIME MINISTER'S FLAG

1:2≈

67

JUGOSLAVIJA

YUGOSLAVIA

SOCIJALISTIČKA FEDERATIVNA REPUBLIKA JUGOSLAVIJA

SOCIALIST FEDERATIVE REPUBLIC OF YUGOSLAVIA

The white, blue, and red have had two derivations: Imperial Russia, to which Slavs looked for support in seeking freedom from Austrian and Ottoman domination, flew a horizontal tricolor of white-blue-red. Also these same colors had appeared in the French republican banner familiar to Yugoslavs because its Illyrian area was annexed to France.

When the Kingdom of the Serbs, Croats, and Slovenes was proclaimed in 1917, the flag it adopted was blue-white-red with a coat of arms. Renamed Yugoslavia, the nation kept its flag unchanged. In September 1941, however, the Partisans led by Josip Broz (Tito) replaced the royal arms with their own red star. Having liberated their land from fascism, the victorious Partisans then officially confirmed the new flag on 31 January 1946. The Partisan star has also been introduced as a symbol into other Yugoslav flags.

1:2

STATE ARMS

2:3

2:3

Yugoslavia's arms, dating from 1944, salute national unity in the common flame which rises from six torches – one for each constituent republic. The date 29 November 1943 recalls the legislation beginning the country's new social and political system.

PRESIDENTIAL FLAG

1:1

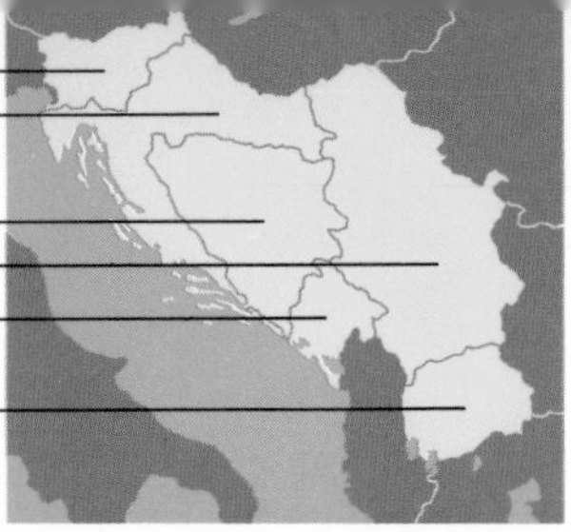

BOSNA I HERCEGOVINA

BOSNIA AND HERZEGOVINA

Officially adopted 31 December 1946. The red is for Communism.

1:2

CRNA GORA

MONTENEGRO

Officially adopted 31 December 1946. The Montenegrin tricolor dates from ca. 1880.

1:2

HRVATSKA

CROATIA

Officially adopted 18 January 1947. The Croat tricolor dates from 1848.

1:2

MAKEDONIJA

MACEDONIA

Officially adopted 31 December 1946. The historical arms were red with the gold lion.

1:2

SLOVENIJA

SLOVENIA

Officially adopted 16 January 1947. The Slovene tricolor dates from 1848.

1:2

Officially adopted 17 January 1947. The Serbian tricolor dates from 1835. The Autonomous Province of Vojvodina and the Autonomous District of Kosovo and Mitohija have no flags of their own but use the flag of Serbia, of which they are a part.

SRBIJA

SERBIA

1:2

Yugoslavia is one of many countries where the basic design of the national flag has been modified by governments of different ideologies through use of a special symbol.
In the past monarchist symbols appeared on the tricolors of Yugoslavia and its constituent parts in place of the red star of Communism. When Yugoslavia was dismembered in World War II, the fascist Ustashi inserted their party badge and the state arms in the flag of the Independent State of Croatia.

68

KAMPUCHEA

CAMBODIA

PREACH REACH ANAR CHAK KRUNG KAMPUCHEA

KINGDOM OF CAMBODIA

Both the traditional Cambodian flag (used until 1948) and the current design feature three elements – the national color (red as in neighboring Thailand and Laos), the royal color (blue), and the national symbol (Angkor Wat).
Angkor Wat is close to the Great City (Angkor Thom) which served from the twelfth through the fifteenth centuries as the capital of the Khmer Empire. The three towers are seen as manifestations of the sexual prowess of the king and his guarantee of the welfare and longevity of the land.

Officially adopted 29 October 1948.

2:3

ROYAL ARMS

At the center of the arms are ritual goblets and the divine sword presented to King Jayavarman VI in the late eleventh century. Above this is the royal crown spreading its light over the nation.
The parasols are royal symbols throughout Southeast Asia and appear in the flag of Laos and the former arms of Thailand. Here they are held by Kuchea Sey, the elephant-headed lion symbolizing authority, and Reachea Sey, the royal lion symbolizing strength.
The name of the state is inscribed below.

KAMPUCHEA
CAMBODIA

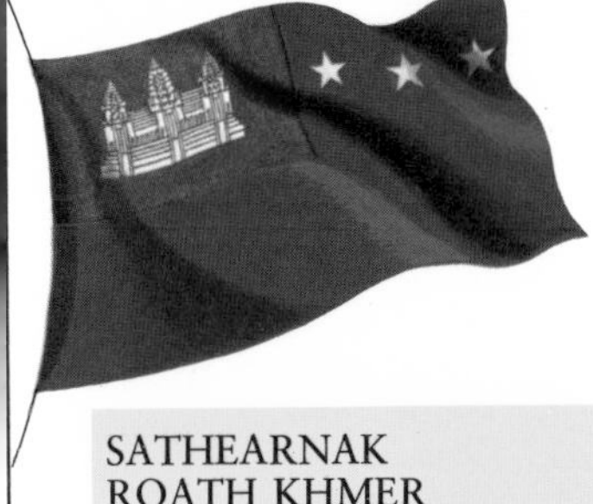

SATHEARNAK ROATH KHMER

KHMER REPUBLIC

The nation's name derives from the ancient Khmer Empire.

The three stars of the Khmer flag are said to be symbolic of the nation, its religion, and its republican government; upper, central, and lower Cambodia; the three parts of its government (legislative, executive, and judiciary); and the triple jewel of the Buddhist religious faith (Buddha, Dhamma, Sangha).
The representation of Angkor Wat, one of the mightiest architectural ruins of the world, symbolizes the golden age of the Khmer Empire. Blue is said to characterize the justice, happiness, and honesty of the Khmer people and red, their spirit of determination and courage. Buddhism is associated in the Khmer flag with white.
The stars and sunburst in the crest of the arms suggest that Khmers will rise to defend their land, religion, and republic. The ribbon at the bottom with the state name binds sheaves of rice which are represented in the shape of elephant tusks, to indicate the national solidarity that protects Angkor Wat. The flamelike dragons salute Khmer art; they flank two goblets which stand for the two chambers of the legislature and support the national constitution.

Officially hoisted 9 October 1970.

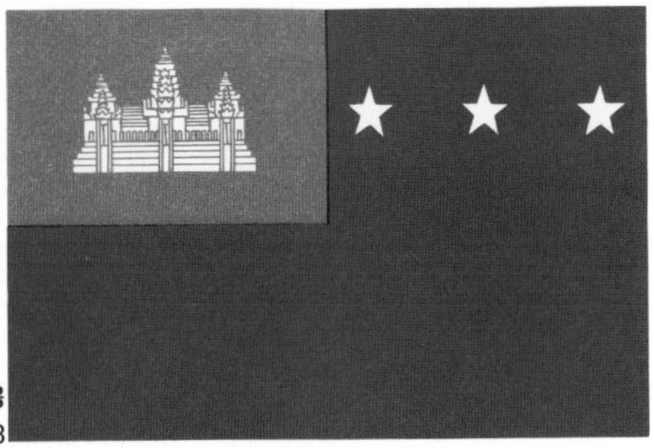

2:3

STATE ARMS

The Khmer Republic and the Kingdom of Cambodia both claimed sovereignty over the same territory and carried on a civil war from 1970 to 1975.

The Khmer Rouge forces of the royal government were victorious over the republicans in April 1975 and the flag and arms above are no longer in use.

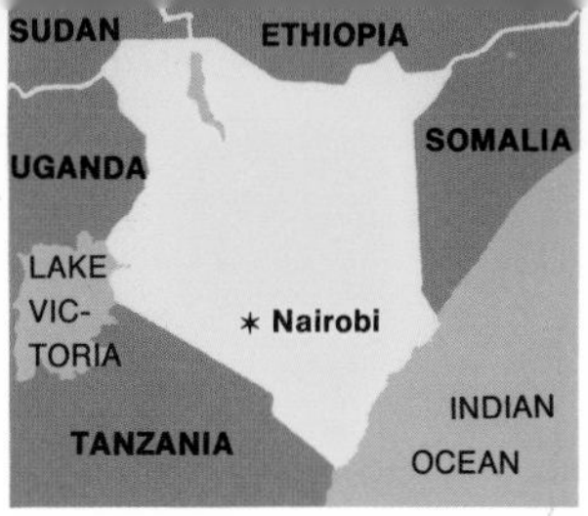

KENYA
KENYA

JAMHURI YA KENYA

REPUBLIC OF KENYA

A special shade known as "Kenya red" is used in the state and civil flag.

The long struggle for independence was led by the Kenya African National Union (KANU). In its flag horizontal stripes of black, red, and green symbolized the ethnic majority of Kenya, the blood they share in common with people everywhere, and the fertile fields and forests of the land.
In the national flag the same colors stand for the people of Kenya, their struggle for independence, and agriculture and natural resources. White fimbriations for peace and unity were added to separate the three stripes of the KANU flag. The traditional Masai tribal shield and the spears symbolize defense of freedom. They recall the somewhat similar design in the KANU flag.
The Swahili motto in the Kenyan coat of arms *(left)* means "Let's Pull Together." Mount Kenya serves as a compartment for the arms, while lions symbolic of protection constitute the supporters. Examples of local agricultural produce frame the shield at the bottom.

Officially hoisted 12 December 1963.

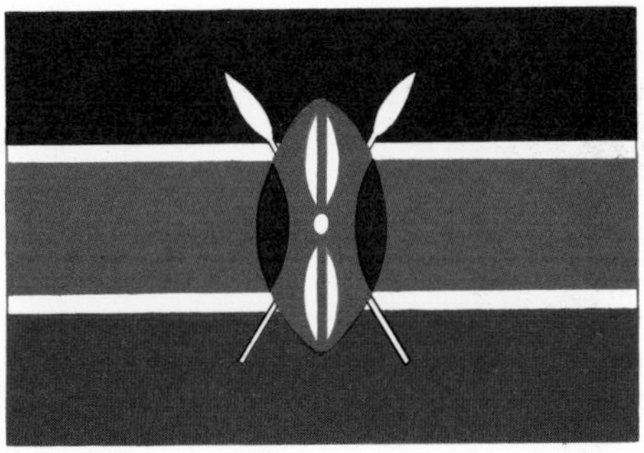

5:9≈

STATE ARMS

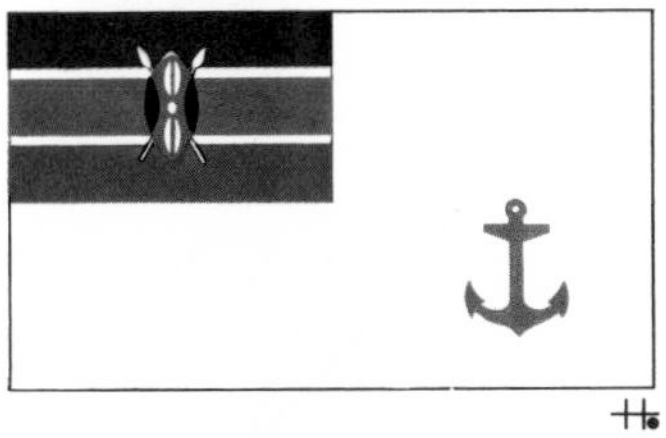

PRESIDENTIAL FLAG 2:3

While Kenya has followed a basically British pattern in its war ensign *(above, left)*, its presidential standard *(above, right)* is unique. Jomo Kenyatta, the man who led Kenya to independence, also served as its first president. His first name means "burning spear" – hence the spears on the presidential standard. Blue is for the skies over Kenya. The cockerel here and in the national arms is a traditional herald of a new and prosperous life, but it is also familiar to Kenyans as the emblem of the Kenya African National Union.

71

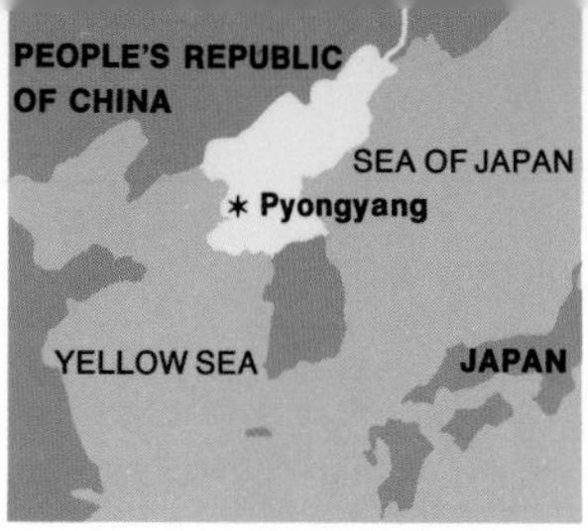

KORAI

KOREA

CHOSON MINCHU-CHUI IN-MIN GONG-HWA-GUK

KOREAN DEMOCRATIC PEOPLE'S REPUBLIC

Officially adopted 8 September 1948.

White has been the traditional color of the Korean nation and figures in the flag of the Korean Democratic People's Republic as a symbol of purity, strength, and dignity. The blue stripes represent a commitment to peace, while the red indicates that the nation is on the path to socialism.

The star is a symbol of the leading role played by the Korean Workers' Party in creating the new economic, social, and political structure of the country following World War II. The white disc on which the star appears may be reminiscent of the traditional Korean *T'aeguk,* symbol of the universe.

Because Korea is basically an agricultural nation, sheaves of rice surround the coat of arms adopted by the Korean Democratic People's Republic in 1948. The sheaves are bound by a red ribbon bearing the name of the state. At the center is a landscape reflecting the country's determination to industrialize. A hydroelectric station and dam, perhaps the ones built on the Amnokan River, figure prominently.

1:2

STATE ARMS

Vladimir Lenin – Communist theoretician and leader of the Russian Revolution, which led to the establishment of the first Communist state in the world – was well aware that the success of his undertaking would not be complete until it affected the everyday lives and beliefs of individual citizens. His statement that "Communism is Soviet power plus electrification of the whole country" has apparently been taken as the theme of the Korean Democratic People's Republic. Tractors and oil derricks are other symbols of industrialization that have been used as emblems of Communist states.

72

KORAI

KOREA

DAE-HAN MIN-GUK

REPUBLIC OF KOREA

When the Exclusion Doctrine, which closed the country to foreign intercourse, was ended in 1876, Korea recognized the necessity of a national flag. The flag hoisted in August 1882, when the first envoys were sent to Japan, became official on 27 January 1883. It differed from the present flag only in minor details. From 1910 to 1945 Korea was under Japanese occupation, followed by three years of American and Soviet administration. In 1948 the Republic of Korea reestablished the *t'aeguk* flag which was given its present form two years later.

Its white field stands for peace and the white clothing Koreans have traditionally worn. The *t'aeguk* in the center resembles the yin and yang of Chinese philosophy and expresses the diversity of forces in the universe and their interaction. The *kwae* on either side correspond to the four cardinal directions, the seasons, and the sun, moon, earth, and heaven.

Officially adopted 25 January 1950.

2:3

STATE ARMS

2:3≈

PRESIDENTIAL FLAG

2:3

In the state arms and presidential flag, the rose of Sharon takes a prominent place. It was chosen as a symbol because it is found in all parts of the Korean peninsula and is noted for its hardiness. The name of the state is written on a scroll beneath the blossom in the arms; in the presidential flag it is flanked by two phoenixes – symbols formerly used by the emperors of Korea.

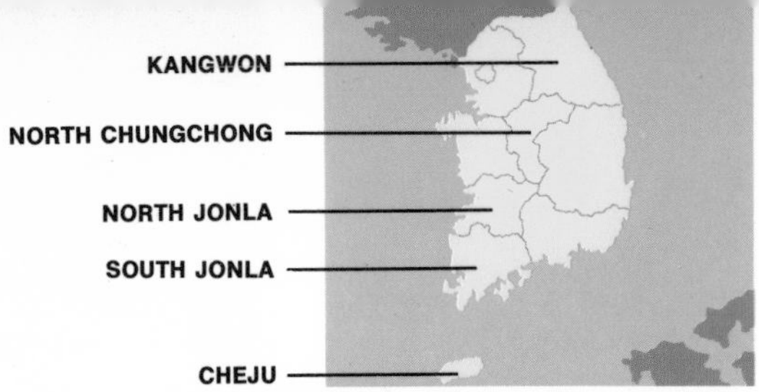

9:16≈

CHE-DJU
CHEJU
Officially hoisted 3 May 1966.

CHUNG-CHONG-PUK
NORTH CHUNGCHONG
Officially hoisted 1 February 1966.

2:3

3:4

DJON-LA-NAM
SOUTH JONLA
Officially hoisted 31 July 1969.

DJON-LA-PUK
NORTH JONLA
Officially hoisted 1 July 1964.

2:3

2:3≈

KANG-WON
Officially hoisted 20 October 1962.

The flags of the subdivisions of the Republic of Korea were all adopted within a few years of one another, as was the case in Japan, Canada, the Soviet Union, and a number of other countries around the world. There also tends to be a similarity of design among subdivision flags in a single country. The Korean flags *(above)* all have circular emblems, while the subdivisions of the Federal Republic of Germany favor striped flags with heraldic emblems and those of Colombia, simple flags of stripes.

In a number of ways the Korean provincial flags resemble the prefectural flags of Japan: both favor modern graphic design, the state name is used on the flag in many cases (as in the United States), and distinctive colors like brown and purple not often found in flags figure in these designs.

73

KYPROS/KIBRIS
CYPRUS

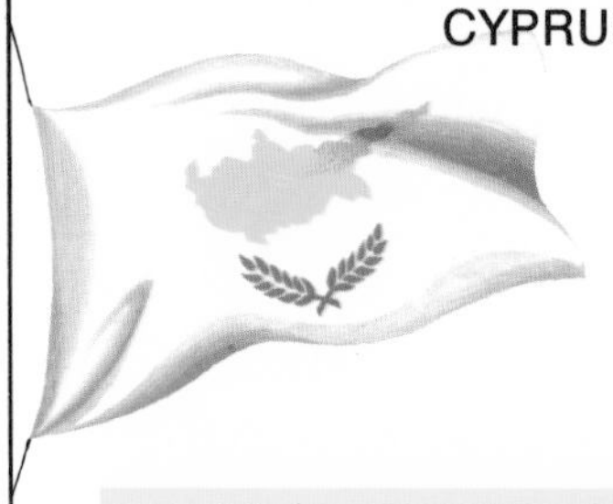

KYPRIAKI DIMOKRATIA/
KIBRIS CÜMHÜRİYETİ

REPUBLIC OF CYPRUS

Composed partially of Greek and partially of Turkish populations, Cyprus chose a flag of neutral design and colors when it became independent. The yellow color of the island is said to stand for the copper, mined since Roman days, which gave Cyprus its name. The olive branches below are for peace and prosperity; essentially the same symbolism is reflected in the coat of arms. The Greek and Turkish communities prefer, however, to fly only the flags of Greece and Turkey. Since 1974 the island has been physically divided between the two ethnic groups, and the Cypriote flag is rarely displayed.

Officially hoisted 16 August 1960.

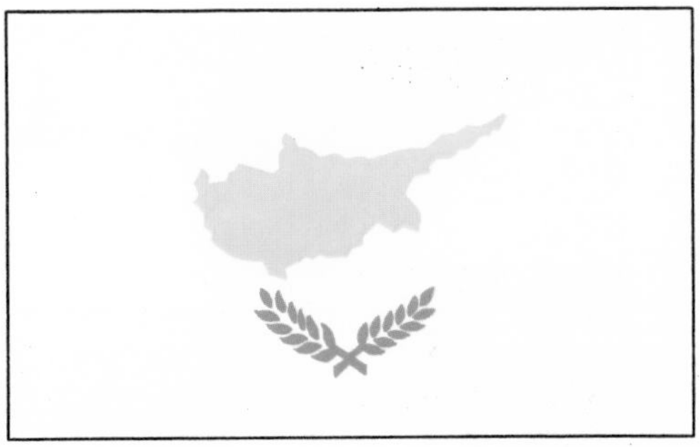

3:5

STATE ARMS

Certain parts of Cyprus known as the Sovereign Base Areas remain under the control of the former colonial power, Great Britain, and fly only the Union Jack. Neutral territory between the Greek and Turkish communities is manned by troops from the United Nations who display its blue and white flag.

The first proposal for a Cypriote flag had a white field with a large, rust-brown K (the first letter in the name "Cyprus" both in Turkish and Greek). Apparently considered too distinctive a design, this was rejected in favor of a flag similar to the present one. The first official version, in use for about a year, differed from the current one in having a white island with the yellow border instead of a solid yellow silhouette.

74

AL KUWAIT

KUWAIT

DAULAT AL KUWAIT

STATE OF KUWAIT

Officially hoisted
24 November 1961.

When Kuwaiti independence was achieved in 1961 at the termination of the British protectorate, the pan-Arab colors were chosen for the new flag. Black is interpreted to mean the defeat of enemies on the battlefield, their blood leaving the swords of the Arabs red. Arab deeds are seen as white or pure, their lands green and fertile.

The design of the new flag may have been influenced by those of Kuwait's neighbors, Iran and Iraq. The Iranian flag had horizontal stripes of green-white-red. The Iraqi flag, the only one in the world with a trapezium at the hoist, also had three horizontal stripes at that time.

A nation of seafarers and ship builders, Kuwait chose as the central emblem of its arms the traditional *dhow.* Falconry is the sport of kings in the Persian Gulf, and the falcon in the arms is seen as a symbol of Kuwaiti prowess. The full name of the state is written at the top of the emblem.

1:2

STATE ARMS

1:2

The Kuwaiti flag law specifies: "Anyone who is caught and convicted of flying the national flag on private buildings constantly... shall be subject to an imprisonment of not more than three months and/or a fine not exceeding twenty dinars."
Similar regulations exist in other countries, particularly in the British Commonwealth. While permitting use of the state flag on specified holidays, such countries make it clear that the national flag does not belong to the average citizen.

75

LAO

LAOS

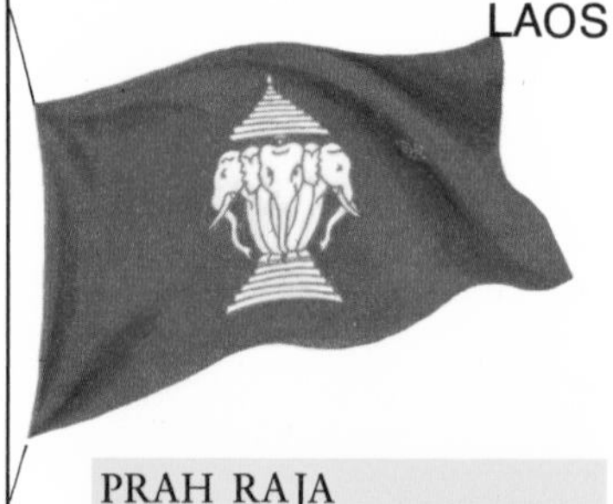

PRAH RAJA
ANACHAK LAO

KINGDOM OF LAOS

Laos has a seat of government (Vientiane) as well as a capital (Luang Prabang).

In the fourteenth century the Lao people were united in a powerful state known as Muong Lan Xang Hom Khao – Land of the Million Elephants and White Parasol. Khoun Borom, legendary founder of Lan Xang, is said to have arrived riding a white elephant and bearing the white parasol which has ever since been regarded as a symbol of royalty.

Red is recognized as the color of the sun and hence an appropriate color for a country in the Far East. The tricephalic elephant has been especially appropriate since 1947, when the three principalities into which Laos had been divided were reunited prior to the nation's release from French colonial rule.

The other symbols of the Lao national and royal flags stand for the five precepts of Buddhism (the stairs on which the elephant stands), the spiritual enlightenment of Buddhism (the urn and halo), prosperity (the golden cups), and the institution of monarchy (the parasols).

Officially adopted
11 May 1947.

2:3

ROYAL ARMS

An important flag in Laos, but one which has no international legal standing, is that of the Lao Patriotic Front. Commonly called the Pathet Lao, this Communist political organization and its People's Liberation Army are in actual administrative control of most of the territory and much of the population. Its flag consists of three unequal horizontal stripes (red, blue, red) with a white disc in the center.

ROYAL FLAG

2:3≈

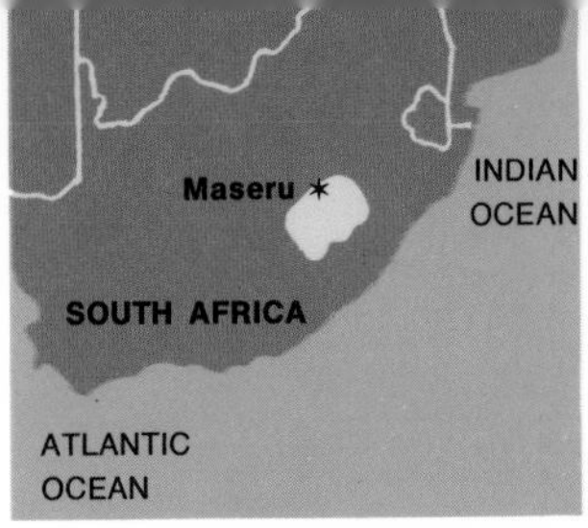

LESOTHO

LESOTHO

MUSO OA LESOTHO

KINGDOM OF LESOTHO

Lesotho was formerly known as Basutoland; its name is pronounced le *soo* too.

The national dress of Lesotho includes a conical hat woven of straw. There are many varieties, but the hat silhouetted on the national flag is typical. The blue field stands for the sky and rain and the white symbolizes peace. Green and red are, respectively, for the land and faith.

These themes are reflected in the motto of the national arms – "Peace, Rain, Plenty." Behind the traditional Sotho shield are nineteenth-century weapons, the assegai and kerrie.

When other black peoples of South Africa were being conquered by the British or Boers, King Moshoeshoe (pronounced moo *shway* shway) requested of Queen Victoria that he and his country "might rest under the great folds of her flag." Almost a century later Sotho independence was reestablished under King Moshoeshoe II.

Officially hoisted 4 October 1966.

2:3 ≈

STATE ARMS

ROYAL FLAG

2:3 ≈

The original coat of arms design drafted prior to independence bore a representation on its shield of Moshoeshoe I. Heraldic experts in South Africa advised that this was improper. Instead, the personal symbol of the king and his dynasty, a crocodile, was substituted. Immediately below the shield is a representation of Thaba Bosiu (Mountain of Night) where Moshoeshoe I first rallied his nation in their new homeland and where in 1870 he was buried.

LIBERIA

LIBERIA

REPUBLIC OF LIBERIA

Officially adopted 26 July 1847.

Until the twentieth century women were largely excluded from any association with national flags – except the sewing of them. The Liberian flag is exceptional in that it was designed and made by a committee consisting of seven women.

An American colony founded to provide a homeland for freed slaves returning to Africa from the United States, Liberia had had a flag since 1827. Understandably, the American flag constituted the basic design, except that a white cross substituted for the stars. In 1845 a Liberian ship flying that flag was seized by British authorities for lacking a recognized ensign; to give this flag international standing the decision was made to proclaim Liberian independence.

The basic form of the old flag was retained, but the number of stripes was reduced to eleven (the number of men signing the Liberian Declaration of Independence). A single white star on dark blue spoke of what was then the only independent nation in black Africa.

10:19

STATE ARMS

PRESIDENTIAL FLAG

1:1

The plow and spade in the coat of arms of Liberia represent the agricultural labor on which the national economy was founded. The palm tree is a reminder of the richness of the soil. The founding of the colony is reflected not only in the motto and the ship arriving on the coast, but also in the sun which heralds a new day. The dove with its scroll is symbolic of Liberia's message of goodwill and peace to the world.

LIBERIAN COUNTIES

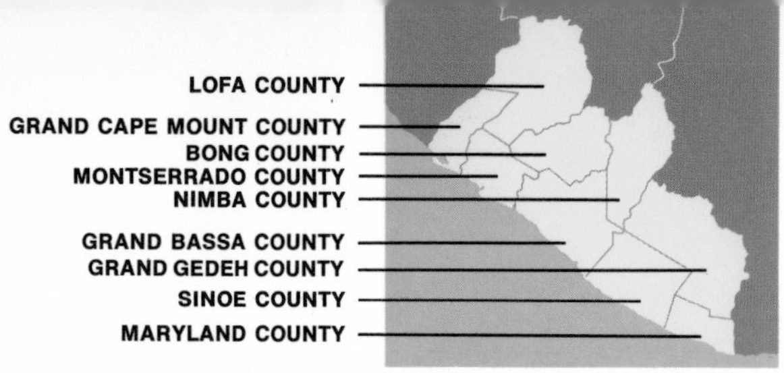

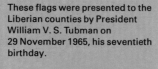

These flags were presented to the Liberian counties by President William V. S. Tubman on 29 November 1965, his seventieth birthday.

2:3≈

BONG COUNTY

The dawn of a new county (purple and orange), purity (white), and iron mining (tools) are symbolized.

2:3≈

GRAND BASSA COUNTY

Dark blue is for loyalty, the stripes for the four Grand Bassa men who signed Liberia's Declaration of Independence.

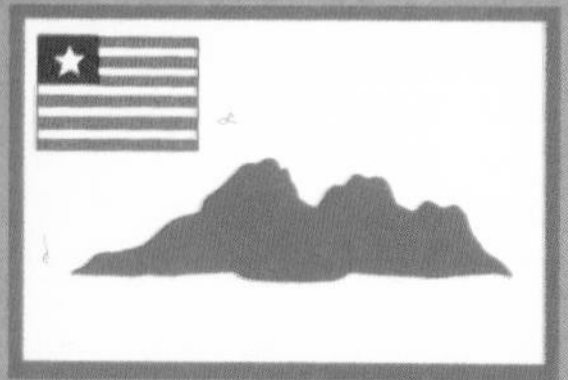

2:3≈

GRAND CAPE MOUNT COUNTY

Grand Cape Mount appears against a white field of peace and purity.

2:3≈

GRAND GEDEH COUNTY

The new county rises like its namesake mountain; white is for purity of heart, blue for peace and prosperity.

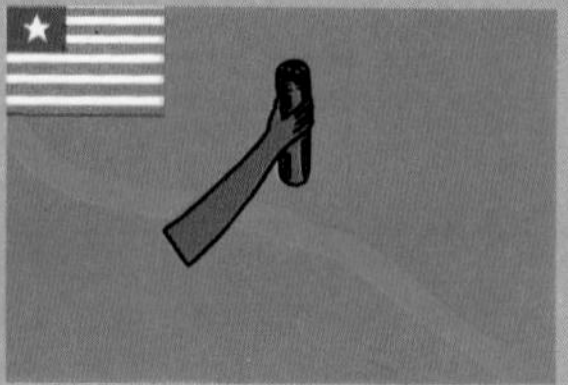

2:3≈

LOFA COUNTY

The arm and fagot symbolize unity across the forests and Lofa River.

2:3≈

MARYLAND COUNTY

Yellow stripes appeared in the flag of the Republic of Maryland before it joined Liberia in 1857.

2:3≈

MONTSERRADO COUNTY

Old and new cultures (blue and red) met on the county's Providence Island.

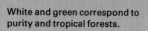

2:3≈

NIMBA COUNTY

Valor, purity, and fidelity are reflected in the flag's stripes.

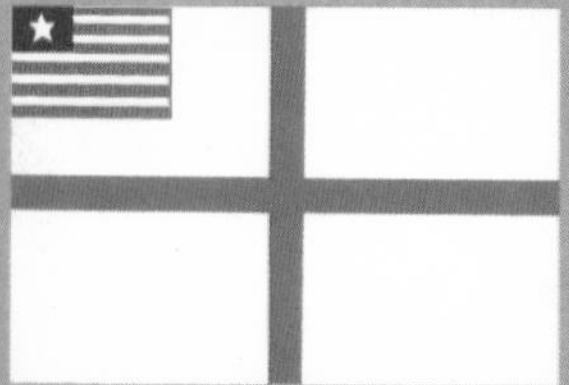

2:3≈

SINOE COUNTY

White and green correspond to purity and tropical forests.

78

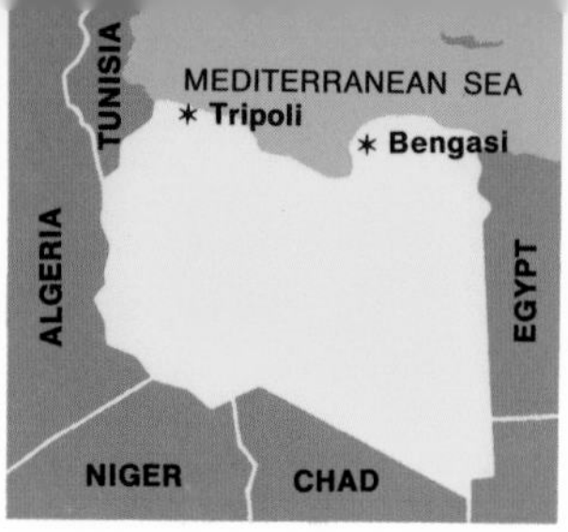

LIBIYA

LIBYA

AL DJUMHURIYAH
AL ARABIYAH
AL LIBIYAH

LIBYAN ARAB REPUBLIC

Further information on Libyan flags is on page 155.

During the early twentieth century Libya was under foreign occupation without a recognized flag of its own. Libya did have one flag tradition, however: the Senusi sect of Cyrenaica used flags of black, usually with inscriptions from the Koran.

In 1947 when the Senusi leader was recognized by the British as the amir of Cyrenaica, that region hoisted a black flag bearing a white star and crescent. In 1950 this was modified, red and green stripes being added at top and bottom to stand for the Fezzan and Tripolitania. Although it incorporated the four pan-Arab colors, the flag and the government it represented were conservative.

Following the revolution of 7 September 1969 a new national flag was adopted, based on the Arab Liberation Flag of neighboring Egypt. This red-white-black tricolor was modified two and a half years later to form the present Libyan flag. The arms are those of the Federation of Arab Republics with Libya's own name added.

Officially hoisted 1 January 1972.

2:3

STATE ARMS

On 17 April 1971 the presidents of Egypt, Libya, and Syria signed an agreement calling for confederation of their nations as a first step toward Arab unity. The Federation of Arab Republics came into existence on 2 September of that year, following referenda in the three lands.

The federation's constitution calls for a single flag for the federation and its three member states; this was hoisted on the first day of 1972. Nevertheless in actual practice some variations exist.

79

LIECHTENSTEIN

LIECHTENSTEIN

FÜRSTENTUM
LIECHTENSTEIN

PRINCIPALITY
OF LIECHTENSTEIN

The origin of the blue and red colors of the Liechtenstein flag is not known. However, in 1937 when the crown was first added to the flag, Head of Government Dr. Joseph Hoop stated: "We see in its blue the blue of the sky, in its red the glow of our evening fires, and in the gold of the crown we are made conscious of the fact that our people, our country, and our royalty are one heart and soul."

The royal flag is based on the inescutcheon of the arms which, crowned, serves as the lesser arms of the state.

Officially hoisted 25 July 1957.

2:3≈

STATE AND PRINCELY ARMS

The quarterings indicate the lineage of the ruling house by combining the arms of Silesia, the Kuenrings, Troppau, and East Frisia-Rietberg, with the horn of Jägerndorf at the bottom.

ROYAL FLAG

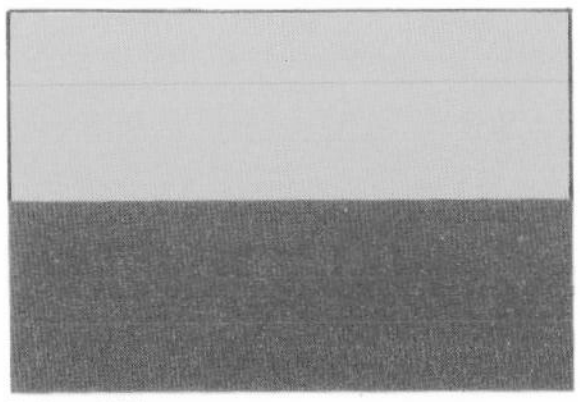

2:3≈

Blue and red were used as national colors in Liechtenstein during the nineteenth century and officially confirmed in the constitution of 1921. The Liechtenstein government learned during the 1936 Olympic Games, held in Berlin, that their flag was exactly the same as the civil flag and ensign of Haiti. To avoid potential international confusion, it was decided to modify the Liechtenstein flag by adding a princely crown.

80

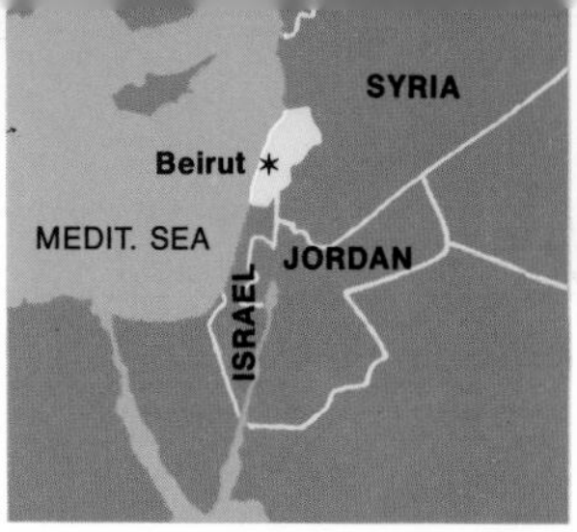

LUBNAN

LEBANON

AL DJUMHURIYAH
AL LUBNANIYAH

LEBANESE REPUBLIC

In the eighteenth and nineteenth centuries Maronite Christians in Lebanon used a white flag bearing a cedar. This tree – symbolizing holiness, eternity, and peace – is native to the area and is mentioned several times in the Bible. Psalms XCII:12 asserts that the "righteous shall grow... like a cedar in Lebanon." The red and white colors are those associated, respectively, with the Kayssites and Yemenites, opposing clans that divided Lebanese society between 634 and 1711. During the First World War the Lebanese Legion in French military service displayed a red saltire on a white flag, a cedar being represented in the center. Under the League of Nations mandate given to France, Lebanon displayed the French Tricolor with a cedar in the center; in 1943 when complete independence was gained the present flag was adopted.

No coat of arms has been created, although unofficially the cedar tree is frequently used as an emblem of state. It is sometimes represented in the center of a shield divided diagonally by red-white-red.

Officially adopted 7 December 1943.

2:3≈

Lebanon is one of a number of countries where official details of the flag are frequently ignored. The law provides that the cedar should touch the red stripes and be equal to one-third the length of the flag, but frequently it is shown considerably smaller. The traditional view has been that a flag is proper so long as it includes the essential design elements of colors and symbols, regardless of artistic rendition.

81

LUXEMBOURG/LUXEMBURG

LUXEMBOURG

GRAND-DUCHÉ
DE LUXEMBOURG/
GROSSHERZOGTUM
LUXEMBURG

GRAND DUCHY
OF LUXEMBOURG

The state flag differs from the Dutch flag in color shade and proportions.

The banner of Count Henry VI dating from 1288 is the earliest concrete reference we have to the flag today displayed as the civil ensign. Throughout the centuries references to a red lion on a white and blue striped field make clear the continuity of this tradition.

Under the influence of the French Revolution tricolors were created incorporating the red, white, and blue in different arrangements of horizontal stripes. On 12 June 1845 the government established the pattern now in use.

Officially adopted 16 August 1972.

1:2/3:5

GREATER STATE ARMS

LESSER STATE ARMS

5:7

GRAND DUCAL FLAG

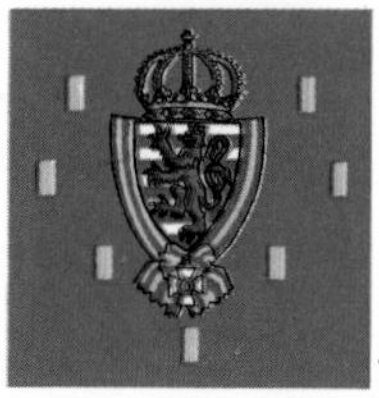

1:1

The personal standard of the grand duke bears the arms of Luxembourg surrounded by the collar of the Order of the Oaken Crown. The field of the flag is similar to the shield in the Netherlands. That both the grand duke of Luxembourg and the queen of the Netherlands are descendents of the House of Nassau is reflected in this shield. The duke also traces his ancestry to Hugues Capet, king of France in the tenth century.

82

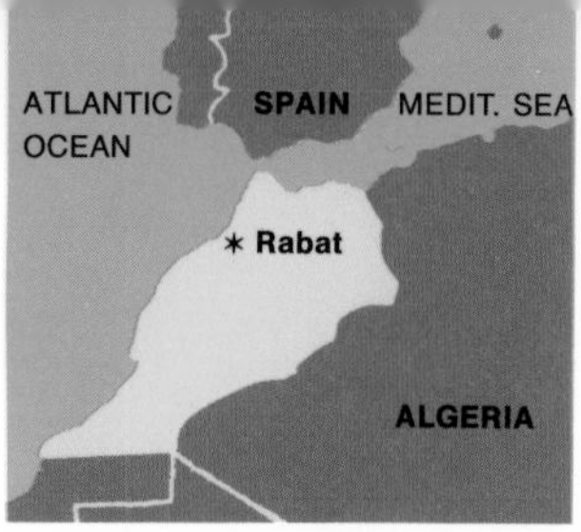

AL MAGRIB

MOROCCO

AL MAMLAKAH
AL MAGRIBIYAH

MOROCCAN KINGDOM

Al Magrib means "The West."

A number of Arab dynasties throughout Moroccan history were characterized by specific colors appearing as the fields of their military flags on which Koranic inscriptions were written. From the eleventh century until the beginning of the seventeenth, the principal color was white under the Almoravids, Marinids, and Saadians.

The red flags of the current dynasty have been used for the past three hundred years. Sometimes an emblem was added, but it was only in 1915 that the green Seal of Solomon was officially established. By then France and Spain had divided Morocco into five parts, and it was not until 1969 that the last of many colonial flags was lowered, leaving a single national flag in all parts of Morocco.

The Atlas Mountains of northern Morocco appear in the center of the royal arms. The inscription at the bottom reads "If You Assist God, He Will Also Assist You."

Officially adopted 17 November 1915.

2:3

ROYAL ARMS

2:3

Flag books have traditionally misrepresented a flag flown in the nineteenth century by the Sherifian Empire, as Morocco was then officially known. Across its red field and within its border of white triangles was the legendary sword known as *Thul Fuqar.* This had two blades because its owner, Ali (Muhammad's son-in-law) rived the sword when pulling it from the scabbard to which it had been nailed by his enemies. Ignorance of this tradition led European artists to represent the historic double-bladed saber as a pair of scissors.

83

MAGYARORSZÁG

HUNGARY

MAGYAR NÉPKÖZTÁRSASÁG

HUNGARIAN PEOPLE'S REPUBLIC

Five different official Hungarian flags existed between 1945 and 1957.

Tradition relates that Árpád, a ninth-century Hungarian ruler whose dynasty lasted 400 years, displayed a plain red flag. Hungarians also believe that a double-barred cross was given by the pope to St. Stephen, an early eleventh-century king, thus introducing the color white into the national coat of arms.

By the fifteenth century the Hungarian arms consisted of red and white horizontal stripes on the dexter half of a shield and the white cross, rising from green hills, on the red sinister. The green of the present national flag apparently derives from the color of the hills in the arms, as well as from military banners of the Hungarian army.

The influence of the French Revolution inspired use of the red, white, and green in three equal stripes. The Hungarian tricolor was in widespread use by the time of its first official adoption in 1848.

In the twentieth century the flag has undergone numerous changes in the coats of arms displayed on the white stripe. To eliminate their ideological associations, the present simple tricolor was legalized in 1957.

Officially hoisted 1 October 1957.

2:3≈

STATE ARMS

In March 1919 Hungary, following Russia and Bavaria, proclaimed itself the world's third Soviet republic. The red star used by this state as its emblem today serves as the crest in the arms of the People's Republic. Hungarian national traditions are reflected in the red-white-green ribbon and shield. Wheat, to symbolize the agricultural basis of the economy, was first introduced into the Hungarian arms following the establishment of the People's Republic in 1949.

84

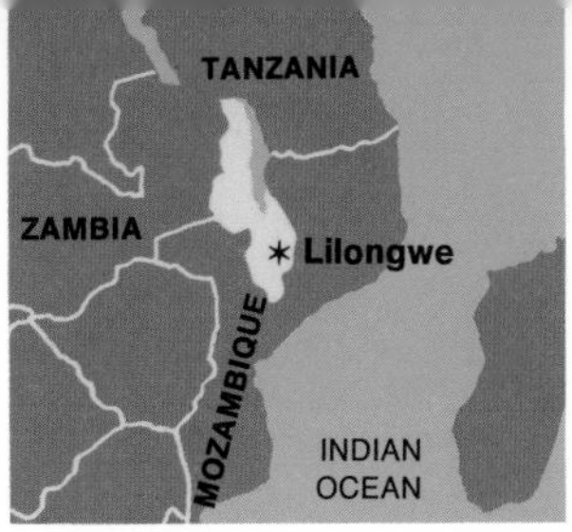

MALAWI

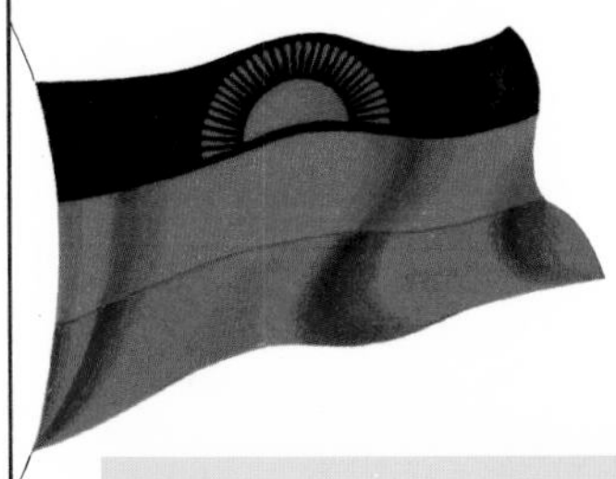

REPUBLIC OF MALAWI

As in many other African and Asian countries, the national flag in Malawi is based directly on the flag of the political movement which led the country to independence. The flag adopted by the Malawi Congress Party in 1953 differs from that used by Malawi itself only in the absence of the rising sun emblem.

In 1964, when its independence was obtained, Malawi added the sun to symbolize the dawning of a new day for Africa. The black stripe on which it rests stands for the people of the continent, and the red is for the blood of African martyrs in the cause of freedom. Green refers specifically to Malawi and the richness of its fields and forests.

The coat of arms of Malawi was granted by Queen Elizabeth II on 30 June 1964. Mount Mlanje, the tallest in the nation, appears as the compartment, while Lake Nyasa is symbolized by the wavy lines in the shield and crest. The fish eagle, leopard, and lions recall the abundant wildlife of Malawi.

Officially hoisted 6 July 1964.

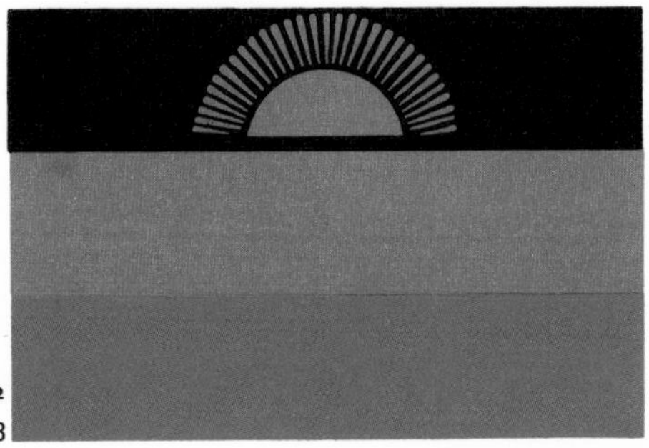

2:3

STATE ARMS

The sun has figured as an emblem in Malawi since 1914, when a coat of arms was granted by Royal Warrant to Nyasaland. (That name was replaced a half century later by Malawi – meaning "flaming waters," a reference to reflections of the sun in the surface of Lake Nyasa.) The theme of the sun was perhaps suggested by the Latin motto of Nyasaland, meaning "a light in the shadows." In any event it figured again in the arms granted to the short-lived Federation of Rhodesia and Nyasaland whose demise led to the independence of Malawi. In the current national arms the sun appears in both crest and shield.

STATES OF MALAYSIA

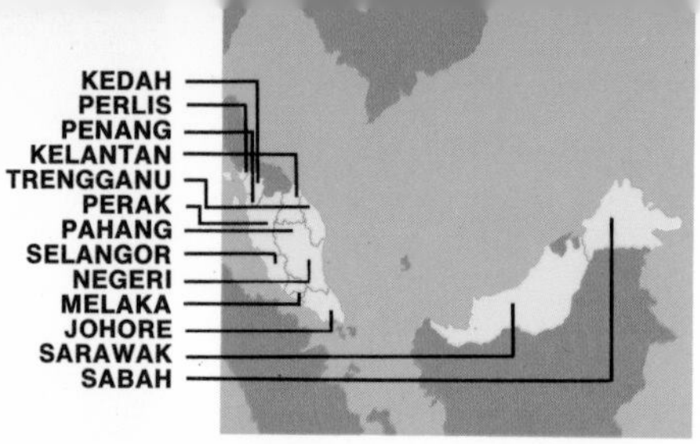

MALAYSIA

MALAYSIA

PERSEKUTUAN TANAH MALAYSIA

FEDERATION OF MALAYSIA

Officially hoisted
16 September 1963.

The Malaysian flag continued to bear fourteen stripes and a fourteen-pointed star even after 1965 when Singapore was excluded from the federation. Since the creation in 1974 of a federal capital territory (Kuala Lumpur), Malaysia again has fourteen constituent parts.
Many Malaysian states are kingdoms, so the royal color (yellow) was chosen for the crescent and star which symbolize Islam. Red and white are colors common to many flags in Southeast Asia (see Indonesia). Yellow also figures in the standard of Malaysia's elective Supreme Head of State *(below)*.

1:2

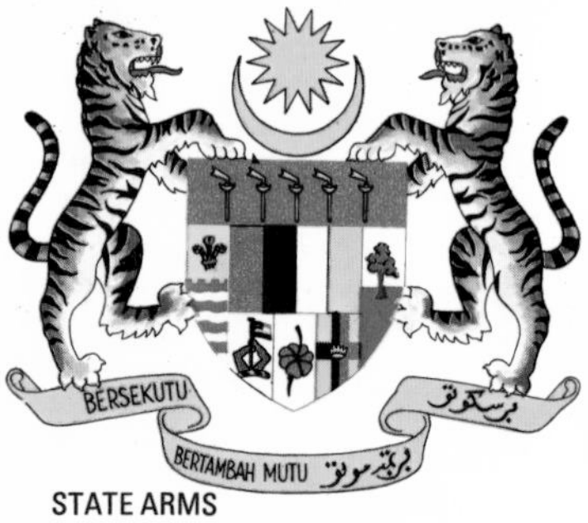

STATE ARMS

1:2

1:2

1:2

The designs of Malaysia's civil and war ensigns *(above)*, as well as their use of blue, recall the fact that Malaysia was long part of the British Empire. The traditional *kris* or dagger of the Malay warrior is featured twice in the war ensign. Five of them in the national coat of arms *(above)* stand for Johore, Kedah, Perlis, Kelantan, and Trengganu.
The royal tigers of these arms flank a shield also containing emblems for the other eight Malaysian states. The motto below, written in both Roman and Javi scripts, translates from the Malay as "Unity Is Strength."

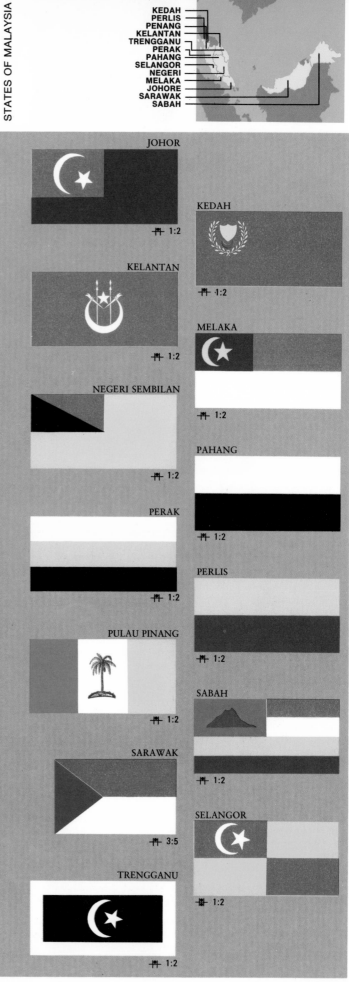

JOHOR

1:2

KELANTAN

1:2

NEGERI SEMBILAN

1:2

PERAK

1:2

PULAU PINANG

1:2

SARAWAK

3:5

TRENGGANU

1:2

KEDAH

1:2

MELAKA

1:2

PAHANG

1:2

PERLIS

1:2

SABAH

1:2

SELANGOR

1:2

86

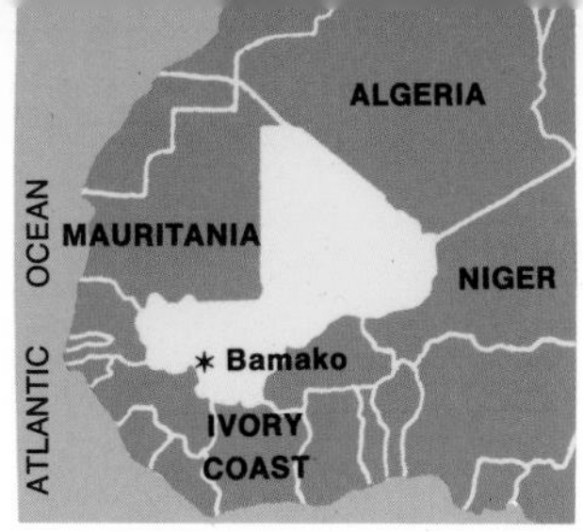

MALI

MALI

RÉPUBLIQUE DU MALI

REPUBLIC OF MALI

The inspiration for the design of the Mali national flag is clear. Being under French colonial rule, citizens of the future nation were familiar with the Tricolor of France and patterned their own national flag after it. It is quite similar to the flags of other French colonies which became independent at roughly the same time – Senegal, Guinea, Cameroon, Togo, and the Congo. The colors in the flags of all these African countries are the same – green, yellow, and red. The pan-African colors, as they are known, were probably influenced by the flags of two African countries which had previously gained independence,

Officially adopted 1 March 1961.

2:3

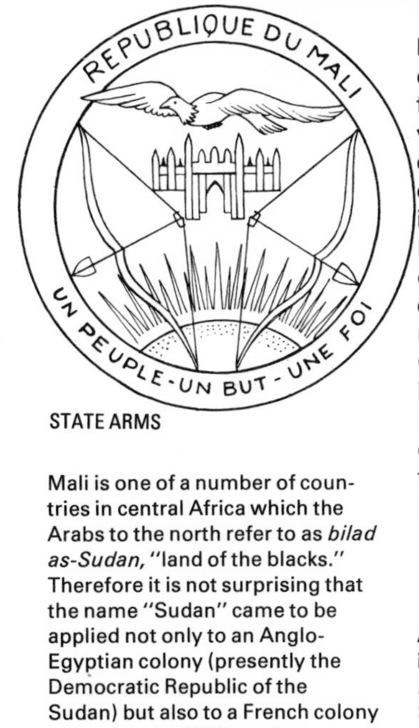

STATE ARMS

Ethiopia and Ghana. Probably even more important as an influence was the fact that green, yellow, and red were the party colors of the African Democratic Rally, which led Mali to independence.

Mali has never adopted a coat of arms. Its seal, used on official papers, bears the national motto – "One People, One Goal, One Faith." In the center is a walled city recalling Timbuktu and other important commercial and cultural centers of the medieval Mali Empire.

Mali is one of a number of countries in central Africa which the Arabs to the north refer to as *bilad as-Sudan*, "land of the blacks." Therefore it is not surprising that the name "Sudan" came to be applied not only to an Anglo-Egyptian colony (presently the Democratic Republic of the Sudan) but also to a French colony more than 2,400 kilometers (1,500 miles) to the west. Upon gaining independence in 1960, the French Sudan chose the name Mali, which had been used hundreds of years before by a powerful empire.

Another ancient symbol – a stylized figure of a man known as the *kanaga* – was also adopted. Shown in black in the center of the first Mali flag, it recalled the continuous use of that symbol in Mali for 2,000 years. Muslim purists, who objected to the representation of a human form, successfully campaigned for its omission from the flag.

87

MALTA

MALTA

(NO OTHER NAME)

The distinctive Maltese Cross employed by the Knights of St. John of Jerusalem figures in the arms and civil ensign of the country. Nevertheless, the knights ruled the island only from 1530 to 1798, and Malta legitimately lays claim to other historic symbols.

A simple vertical bicolor, its original flag, is reputed to date back to Count Roger the Norman, who took Malta from the Muslims in 1090. While undoubtedly very old, the flag has not been proved to date to the eleventh century. It was used under various foreign rulers, including the British who controlled the island between 1814 and 1964.

Officially hoisted 21 September 1964.

2:3

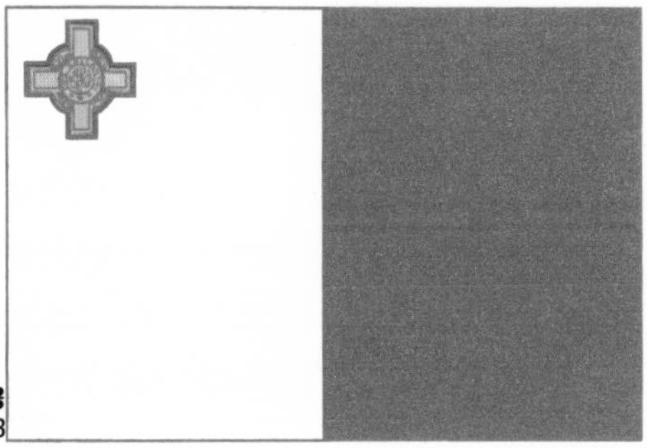

STATE ARMS

As an augmentation of honor for its valiant resistance to enemy attack in World War II, Malta on 28 December 1943 received royal permission to add the George Cross to its arms and flag and to bear the corresponding title (i.e., Malta, G.C.).

2:3

The maritime nature of the state is indicated in the arms by the stylized heraldic dolphins, as well as the waters from which they rise. The extensive fortifications of Malta – many built at the time it was ruled by the Knights of St. John – are represented by the crest emblem, technically known as a mural crown.

The motto translates as "By Virtue and Constancy."

88

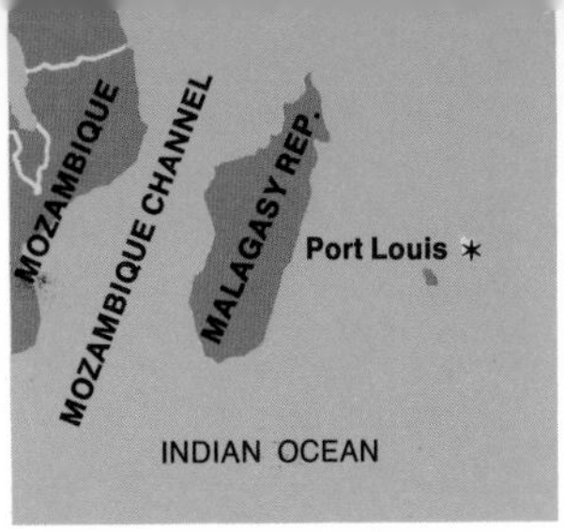

MAURITIUS

MAURITIUS

(NO OTHER NAME)

Like a number of new countries, Mauritius has no official long-form name.

The simple state flag of Mauritius contrasts with its complicated coat of arms – a contrast of vexillological simplicity and heraldic complexity that characterizes many other nations as well.

The flag speaks to the Mauritian people in direct terms about the things most important to them: the blue of the Indian Ocean surrounding them on all sides, the green of their land, the red of blood shed in the independence struggle, and the golden light of independence which now spreads over the island.

Granted in 1906, the arms refer to colonization from abroad (a ship), tropical vegetation (palm trees), and the strategic position of the island (the emblems referred to in the Latin motto, which translates as "The Star and Key of the Indian Ocean"). The supporters are the sambur deer, imported from Java in 1639, and the indigenous dodo bird which became extinct later in the sixteenth century.

Officially hoisted 12 March 1968.

2:3

STATE ARMS

1:2

1:2

1:2≈ GOVERNOR-GENERAL'S FLAG

89

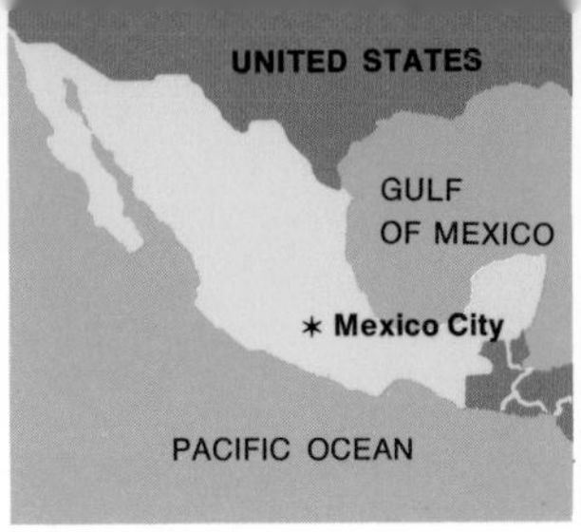

MÉXICO

MEXICO

ESTADOS UNIDOS MEXICANOS

UNITED MEXICAN STATES

More information on Mexican flags will be found on pages 74 and 148–151.

The Three Guarantees, which brought Mexicans together in the struggle to end the Spanish colonial regime, were independence, union, and religion. It was to symbolize these that a flag of three stripes – probably based on the French republican model – was adopted in 1821.

Many variations have occurred over the years in the coats of arms, but the green-white-red has remained constant. The central elements of the arms have always been the eagle and the cactus, recalling the legend of the founding of Tenochtitlan (now Mexico City). In the early fourteenth century Aztecs were promised their future home would be found where cactus grew from rocks. Thus the emblem manifests the Aztec origins of the state.

The latest versions of the arms and flag date from the time of the Olympic Games held in Mexico City. Alternate versions of the national arms in which the elements are represented in outline or in relief have been established for use in seals, official papers, coins, and medals. These also differ from the flag version of the arms in having the name of the state written at the top.

Officially hoisted 17 Sept. 1968.

4:7

STATE ARMS

Some nations issue no official specifications for the details of design, proportions, and color shades in their flags. Others publish these in an official law gazette or similar document.
Mexico is one of a small number of nations which has established models that are to be followed for representations of the flag and arms. These are preserved at the General Archives of the Nation, National Museum of History, and the Mint.

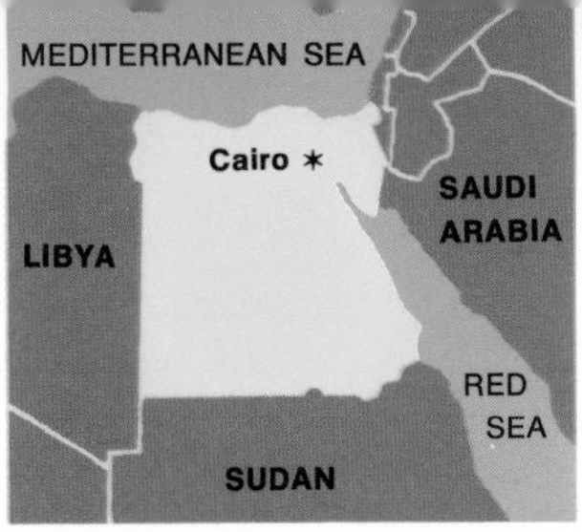

MISR

EGYPT

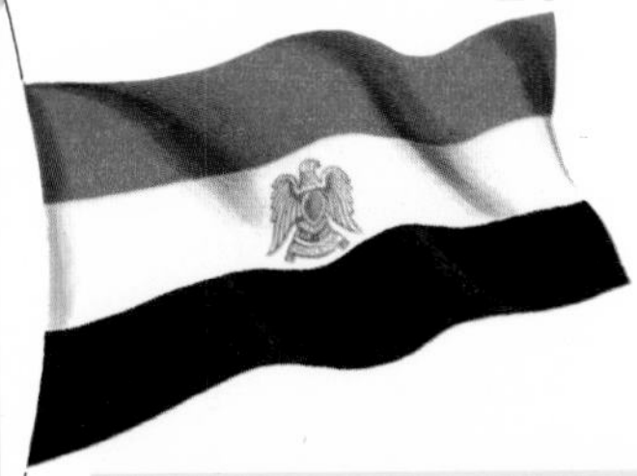

DJUMHURIYAH MISR AL ARABIYAH

ARAB REPUBLIC OF EGYPT

Further information on Egyptian flags will be found on pages 152–155.

The flag of the Federation of Arab Republics flown by Egypt (as well as by Libya and Syria, the other member states) is almost exactly like the Arab Liberation Flag first seen after the overthrow of the Egyptian monarchy in 1952. In that flag the coat of arms showed the eagle of Saladin – a symbol now replaced by the hawk of Quraish (see Syria) – later incorporated into the arms of the United Arab Republic.
The red, white, and black recall Egypt's revolution, its bright future, and the dark days of the past.

Officially hoisted 1 January 1972.

2:3

STATE ARMS

2:3

2:3

PRESIDENTIAL FLAG

2:3≈

Because of the intentional similarity between flags of many Arab countries, further information making clear the symbolism of the design and colors of Egyptian flags should be sought by the reader under Syria, Libya, Sudan, Jordan, Kuwait, both Yemens, and on page 155.

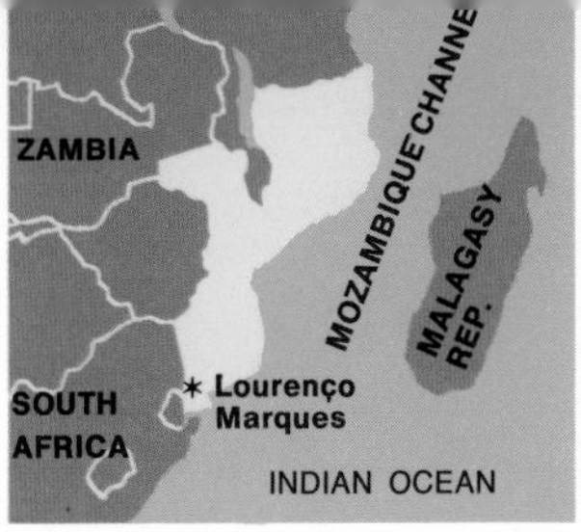

MOÇAMBIQUE

MOZAMBIQUE

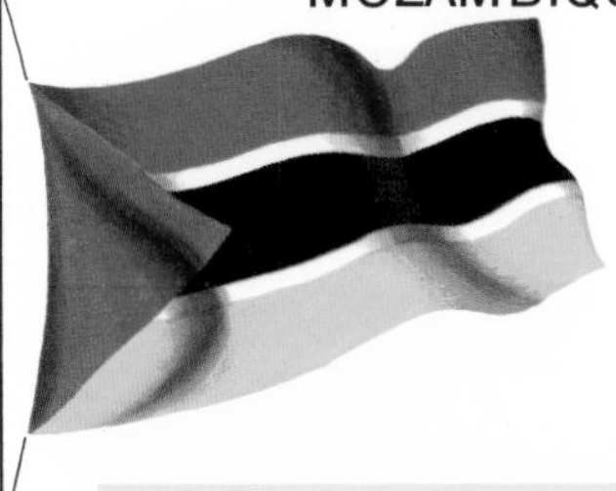

(NO OTHER NAME)

As an overseas province of Portugal, Mozambique had no flag of its own. Its coat of arms resembled those of the other colonies, incorporating an armillary sphere commemorating Portuguese exploration, the heraldic symbol for water, and the *quinas* – the historic Portuguese blue shields with white discs. On the sinister side appeared a local emblem, in the case of Mozambique arrows recalling the martyrdom of St. Sebastian – a reminder that the Portuguese colony had first been established on the small island of St. Sebastian of Mozambique.
In the 1960s a national liberation movement dedicated to establishing majority rule hoisted a flag of five colors. The success of FRELIMO (Front for the Liberation of Mozambique), speeded by a revolution in Portugal itself, led to the unofficial introduction of its banner as a national flag in 1974. It is expected that this will become official when Mozambique gains independence on 25 June 1975. The colors of this flag speak of the people, land, wealth, and freedom struggle.

Usage initiated 5 September 1974.

5:8≈

COLONIAL ARMS

Changes in political conditions around the world make it virtually impossible to produce a flag book which is absolutely up-to-date at the time of its publication. In the present book, for example, it is anticipated that official new flags will be needed for Angola, Mozambique, Cape Verde, and São Tomé and Príncipe (all former Portuguese colonies) between the time of writing and the book's publication, a period of less than six months.

92

MONACO

MONACO

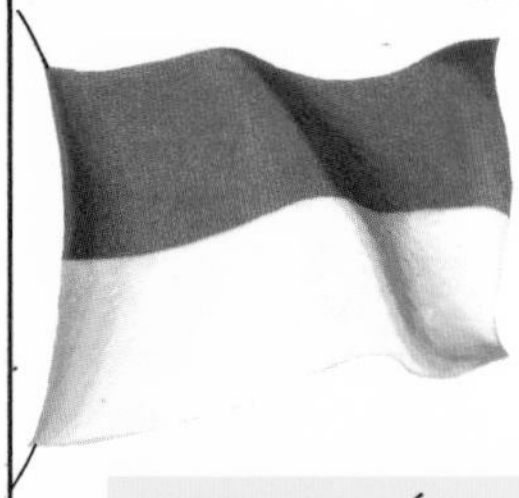

PRINCIPAUTÉ
DE MONACO

PRINCIPALITY OF MONACO

Except for its proportions, Monaco's flag is the same as Indonesia's.

Officially adopted
4 April 1881.

There is a tradition that the original Grimaldis, whose heirs rule Monaco to this day, were able to capture the fortress dressed as monks, their swords hidden under their cassocks. This explains the supporters in the arms and the motto "With God's Aid."
The flag colors of Monaco are attested as far back as 1339, although not in their present form. Banners of red and white lozenges – a design based on the arms – are found in the seventeenth century. On land it has been common since the last century to paint the pole from which the Monegasque flag is displayed with a red and white spiral.

4:5

PRINCELY ARMS

The arms of Monaco took their present form in the 1800s, although the basic form dates back hundreds of years. The shield is surrounded by a representation of the Order of St. Charles. The cipher of Prince Rainier figures on his personal flag.

4:5

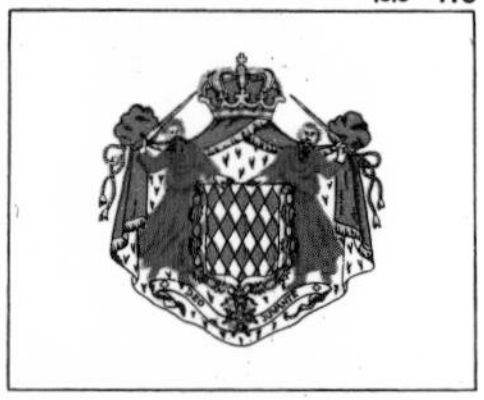

PRINCELY FLAG 5:6≈

Having created its flag in 1881, Monaco protested to Indonesia when the national flag of the latter (selected in 1945) became known. Relying on historical precedents at least as old as those on which the Monegasque flag is based, Indonesia refused to alter its design. There is little practical difficulty, however, in the similarity of the two flags since the two countries are on opposites sides of the earth and since Monaco is not a member of the United Nations. The red-over-white flag is also used by Vorarlberg and Salzburg in Austria.

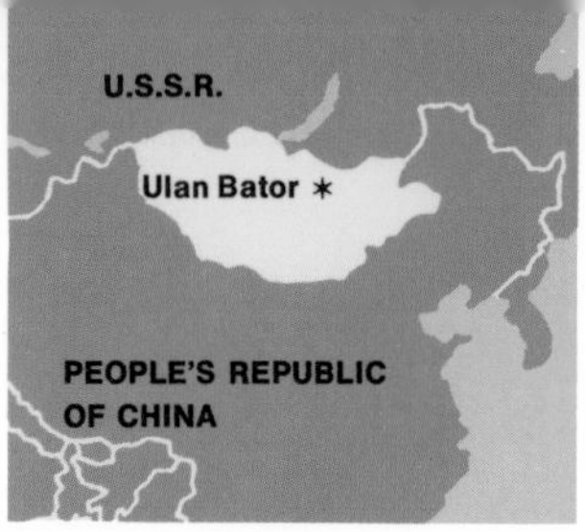

93

MONGGOL

MONGOLIA

BÜGÜD NAYRAMDAQ
MONGGOL ARAD ULUS

MONGOLIAN PEOPLE'S REPUBLIC

Officially confirmed
23 February 1949.

Even today largely a nomadic people, Mongolians have for centuries looked to the blue sky above them as a symbol. Light blue is considered the national color and as such figures in the center of the state flag.
The revolutionary path and socialist program of the Mongolian People's Republic, dating from 1924, is expressed graphically in the red stripes and gold star of the flag. Red banners had been carried by troops in 1921 under the leadership of Sukhe Bator and Choibalsan, the founders of modern Mongolia.
Along the hoist of the flag and at the top of the state arms appears the ancient symbol of Mongolia, called the *soyonbo.* Also in the arms are the wheat and cogwheel of agriculture and industry, linked by a ribbon bearing the initials of the state name. The landscape includes in stylized form the desert, steppe, and forest regions of Mongolia. The horseman racing into the sun – whose golden rays betoken prosperity – stands for the nation's advance toward Communism.

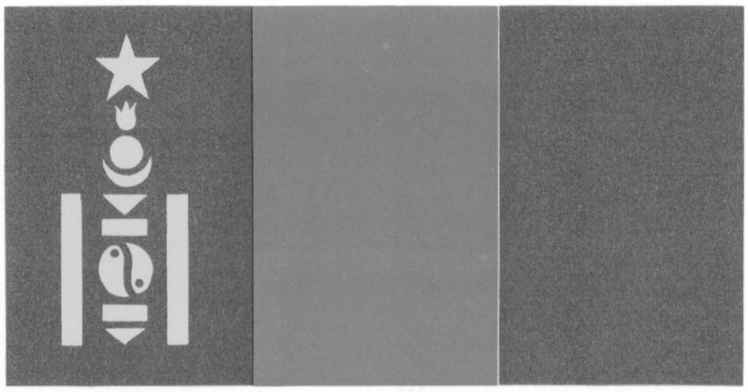

1:2

STATE ARMS

Mystical interpretations have been given to the *soyonbo* throughout Mongolian history. In 1686 a Buddhist monk created an entire alphabet for the Mongol language based on variations of the *soyonbo.* Today the flame at the top is seen as a promise of prosperity and progress. The sun and moon (as in the flag of Nepal) promise everlasting life for the nation. The triangles are arrowheads, threatening death to enemies of the people. The horizontal bars are for honesty and righteousness, the vertical ones for independence and strength. The ancient yin-yang symbol of the universe is here interpreted as two fish, an emblem of watchfulness on behalf of the state by men and women.

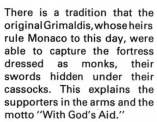

94

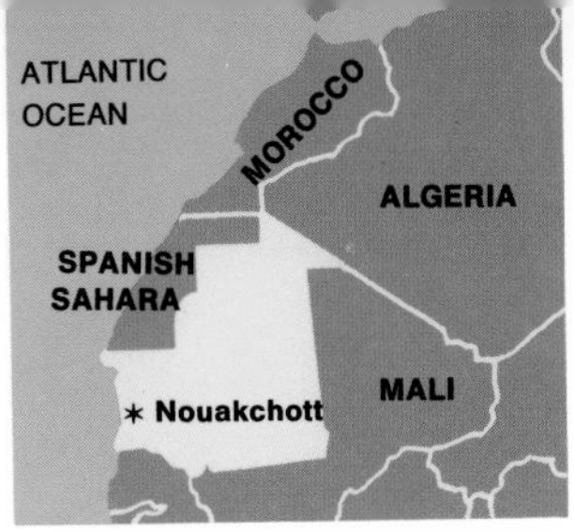

MURITANIYA/MAURITANIE

MAURITANIA

AL DJUMHURIYAH
AL ISLAMIYAH
AL MURITANIYAH/
RÉPUBLIQUE ISLAMIQUE
DE MAURITANIE

MAURITANIAN ISLAMIC REPUBLIC

The message of the flag and arms of Mauritania, emphasized by the official name of the state, is clear: both green and the star and crescent emblem symbolize Islam, the religion of the majority of the population. The green and gold colors of the flag also recall the pan-African red-yellow-green flags of nations to the south and the fact that Mauritania itself has a considerable black population, in addition to its Moorish majority. Although France had previously discouraged the creation of local symbols within its colonial empire, following the establishment in 1958 of the Fifth Republic that policy was reversed. Thus both the flag and arms of Mauritania were adopted in advance of its independence, achieved on 28 November 1960.

In addition to the name of the state in both official languages, the seal bears a palm tree and two slips of millet. The seal has a reverse bearing the inscriptions "In the Name of the Mauritanian People" and "Honor, Fraternity, Justice." These are framed by a wreath of palm and olive branches.

Officially adopted 1 April 1959.

2:3

STATE SEAL

Heraldry recognizes different kinds of crescents, depending upon the direction in which the horns face. The decrescent or moon on the wane has horns to the sinister; the increscent's waxing moon faces to the dexter. "Crescent" refers to one of the Mauritanian type with its horns upwards; the opposite position is called a crescent reversed.
These distinctions are never used in vexillology and even in heraldry are largely theoretical.

95

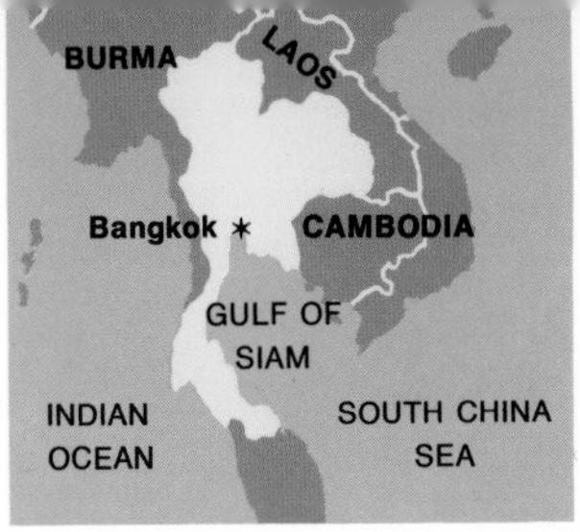

MUANG TAI

THAILAND

PRATET TAI

KINGDOM OF THAILAND

Tai means "free," and Thailand is one of the few Asian countries never under colonial domination.

In 1916 the king of Thailand was touring flood-stricken areas of his land when he spotted a national flag flying upside down: the four legs of the white elephant on the red flag were pointing skyward. The king resolved that the nation should have a new flag which could never be hoisted upside down.

A flag of red-white-red-white-red was first adopted, but the center stripe was changed to blue. This color, associated with the royal birthday, gave the new Thai flag the same three colors found in the flags of Thailand's World War I Allies – Britain, France, the United States, and Russia.

Officially adopted 28 September 1917.

2:3

ROYAL ARMS

The white of the *Trairong* ("Tricolor") symbolizes the purity of the people protected by their religion. The blood sacrificed by Thais for their nation is reflected in the red stripes.

2:3

2:3

The mythical Garuda serves in the royal arms and standard of Thailand. Bearer of the god of bravery, Phra Narai, Garuda is the enemy of all poisonous things. The golden yellow color of the Buddhist religion appears in the standard.

ROYAL STANDARD

1:1

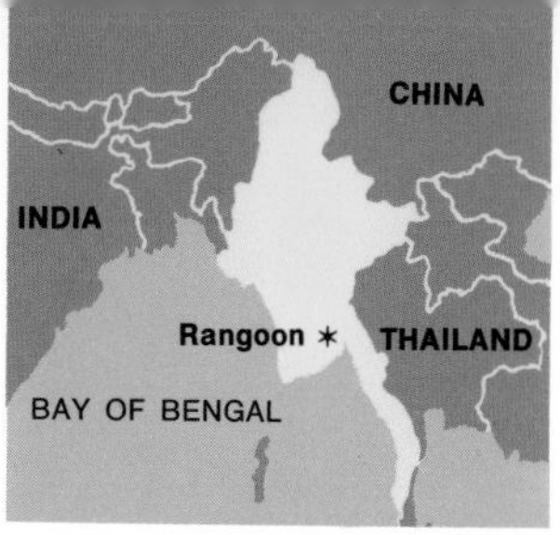

MYAN-MA

BURMA

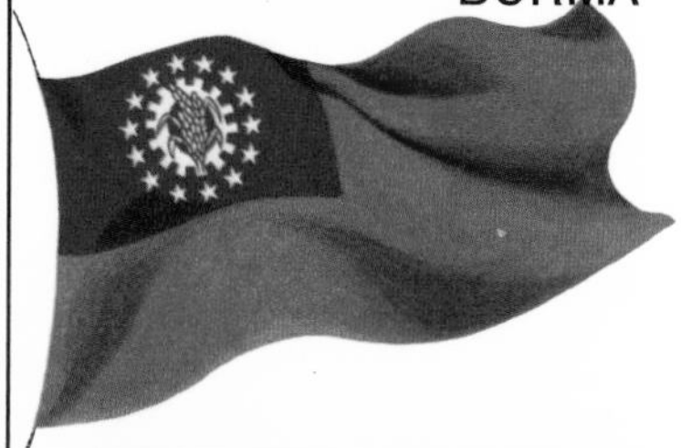

SOSIALIST PHAMADA PYI-DAUNG-SU MYAN-MA NAING-GAN DAW

SOCIALIST REPUBLIC OF THE UNION OF BURMA

Officially hoisted 3 January 1974.

Since the independence of Burma from Britain in 1948, its traditional color (orange) and peacock emblem have been little used. The star of independence originated during the struggle with the Japanese who occupied the country in World War II: the flag of the Anti-Fascist Resistance Movement was red with a white star in the upper hoist.
The first independent flag of Burma surrounded that white star with five smaller ones, all on a dark blue canton. This color symbolized peace and tranquility; the white purity, honesty, and truth. The red was seen as a symbol of courage, solidarity, and tenacity of purpose. The transformation of the country in 1974 into a socialist republic led to modifications of the flag. The gearwheel and rice are emblems of industry and agriculture. Instead of five stars for the principal ethnic groups, the flag now has fourteen stars, one for each state in the union. Similar changes were introduced into the arms.

5:9

STATE ARMS

Framing the central emblem of the arms and protecting it are two mythological lions known as *chinthe.* Familiar forms in ancient Burmese architecture, these lions incarnate ancient wisdom, bravery and strength, and purity and balance in the use of power.
The ribbon below the feet of the lions is inscribed with the official name of the state; a map of Burma appears in the center.

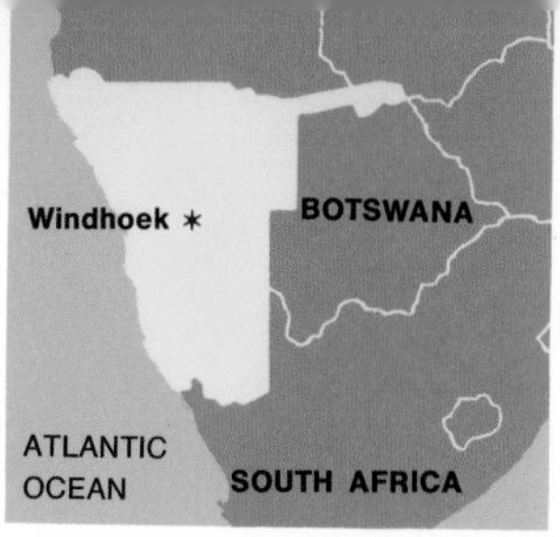

NAMIBIA

NAMIBIA

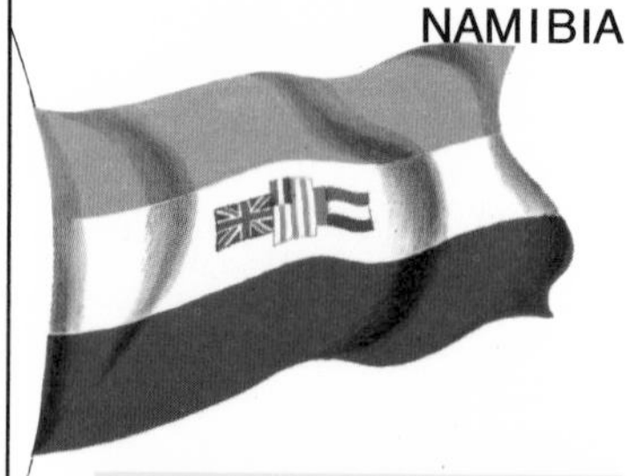

(NO OTHER NAME)

No official national flag exists for Namibia.

Following World War II South Africa refused to transfer its League of Nations mandate, which gave it legal authority over South West Africa, to the trusteeship system of the United Nations. Consequently that international organization has called for the independence of South West Africa, which it calls Namibia, although South Africa continues to administer it as a dependency under its own flag.
The South Africans have created two Bantustans with flags of their own and in 1961 a coat of arms was established for South West Africa by South African officials. The liberation movements of Namibia have distinctive flags of their own.

STATE ARMS

2:3≈ SWAPO

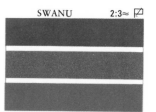

SWANU 2:3≈

KAVANGO 2:3

2:3 OVAMBO

NAOERO/NAURU

NAURU

REPUBLIC OF NAURU

Only 21 square kilometers (8 square miles), Nauru has no capital city.
Officially hoisted 31 January 1968.

The geographical position and people of Nauru find graphic expression in the symbolism of its flag, which has recently begun to appear on ships around the world.
The island is just one degree south of the equator in the Pacific Ocean to the east of the International Date Line, hence the yellow horizontal stripe on blue and the off-center star immediately below the stripe. The twelve points of the star are for the twelve tribes of Nauru – the Eamwit, Eamwidamit, Emea, Eano, Emangum, Eoaru, Eamwidara, Deiboe, Ranibok, Iruwa, Irutsi, and Iwi.
The economic base of the nation is the deposit of guano which is being mined for phosphates. The chemical symbol for phosphorus appropriately appears in the chief of the arms above a frigate bird and a spray of tomano flowers. Cocoa palm fronds frame the shield, while above is part of the ceremonial insignia of the Nauru chief, constructed of plaited fiber cords, local seeds, sharks' teeth, and frigate bird feathers.

1:2

STATE ARMS

Because the process of designing a national flag normally does not become public knowledge, vexillologists must in most cases rely on educated guesses about the intention of the designer(s). Official explanations of color and design symbolism do not always reveal or correspond to those intentions.

Among possible influences on the Nauru flag were a pattern submitted to the government by the author of this book and also the national flag of Australia, which flew over the island during several decades of trusteeship administration. Both these flags contained multipointed white stars on dark blue.

NEDERLAND

NETHERLANDS

KONINKRIJK DER NEDERLANDEN

KINGDOM OF THE NETHERLANDS

Dutch symbols are further discussed on pages 156–163.

Born during the Eighty Years' War for independence from Spain, the red-white-blue flag of the Netherlands gained further fame on the oceans of the world as the ensign of countless ships.
Over the years variations have arisen: six or nine stripes have been used instead of three, coats of arms have been added, and orange has been substituted for red. The plain tricolor of today was sanctioned by the Royal Decree of 21 September 1806. In addition to the eleven provinces constituting the Netherlands proper, the realm includes two self-governing territories with flags of their own–the Netherlands Antilles and Surinam.
The motto "I Will Maintain" in the royal arms *(left)* recalls the oath of Prince William. The lion holding a sword and bundle of arrows symbolizes protection of the rights of the Dutch provinces through their unity and constitutional government.

In use since the sixteenth century; confirmed by Royal Decree 19 February 1937.

2:3

STATE AND ROYAL ARMS

1:1 ROYAL STANDARD

On a field of the dynastic colors, orange (Orange) and blue (Nassau), the national shield and crown appear in the royal standard *(above, right)*. The collar of the Military Order of William frames the shield and the heraldic emblem of Orange (a horn) recalls the legendary William with the Horn who fought the Moors in Spain in the eighth century. The lion was the heraldic emblem of the Dutch provinces, as well as of the House of Nassau, long before the latter became the ruling dynasty.

PROVINCES OF NETHERLANDS

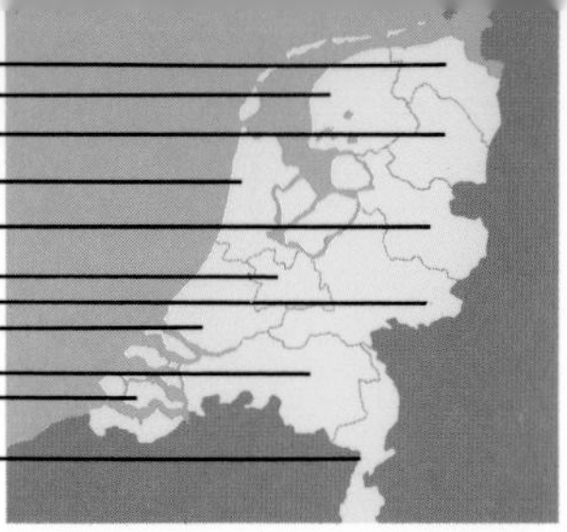

DRENTHE

9:13

FRIESLAND

9:13

GELDERLAND

9:13≈

GRONINGEN

2:3

LIMBURG

1:2≈

NOORD[NORTH]-BRABANT

2:3

NOORD[NORTH]-HOLLAND

2:3

OVERIJSSEL

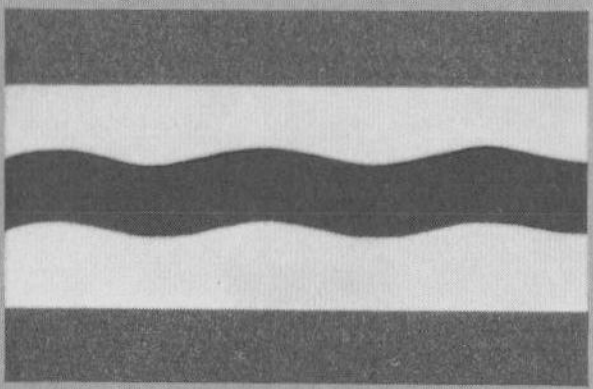

10:17

UTRECHT

9:13≈

ZEELAND/SEALAND

2:3

ZUID[SOUTH]-HOLLAND

2:3

NEDERLANDSE ANTILLEN
NETHERLANDS ANTILLES

2:3

SURINAME
SURINAM

2:3

100

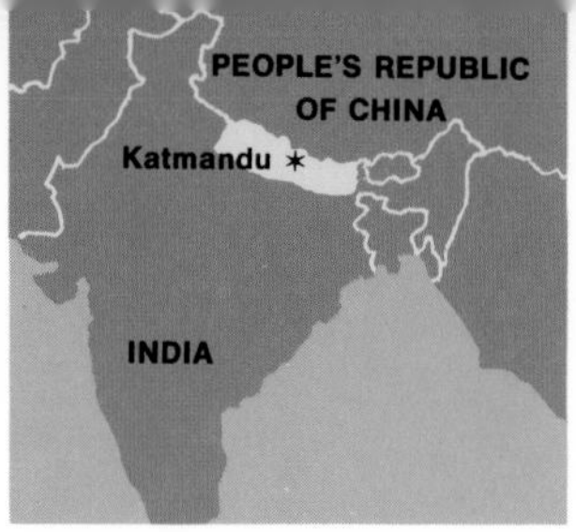

NEPAL

NEPAL

NEPAL ADIRAJA

KINGDOM OF NEPAL

Officially adopted
16 December 1962.

Official specifications issued in 1962 eliminated the facial features from the sun and moon and gave highly detailed measurements for all the dimensions of the flag, but it did not entirely "modernize" this banner. Nepal remains the only country in the world without a rectangular national flag. The two tails are said to represent the peaks of the Himalayas.

Crimson is the Nepali national color and dark blue and red frequently appear in religious and profane art in this country. The sun and moon express the hope that the nation may live as long as those celestial bodies.

4:3≈

STATE ARMS

ROYAL ARMS

Both the state and royal arms include diverse religious symbols – the footprints of the Buddha (born in what is now Nepal), the trident of Vishnu, the temple of Lord Pasupadineth, destroyer of evil. The crossed swords are the *khukari* used by the world famous Gurkha soldier in combat. Other charges are the sacred cow, pheasant, rhododendron, and motto "Mother and Motherland Are Dearer Than Heaven." The background landscape represents the country from the lowlands in the south to the Himalayas in the north.

ROYAL FLAG

2:3≈

101

NEW ZEALAND

DOMINION OF NEW ZEALAND

Officially adopted 12 June 1902.

Before the establishment of a British protectorate in 1840, among the flags flown by the Maori was the national flag of the United Tribes of New Zealand, adopted in 1834. It included stars and the colors red, white, and blue.

During the late nineteenth century British ensigns were flown by New Zealand with distinctive badges added in the fly. At the turn of the century the present flags were officially established: their designs and usage follow the British pattern of Red Ensign, Blue Ensign, and White Ensign.

1:2

STATE ARMS

1:2

1:2

17:19≈

ROYAL FLAG

1:2

GOVERNOR-GENERAL'S FLAG

COOK ISLANDS

1:2

102

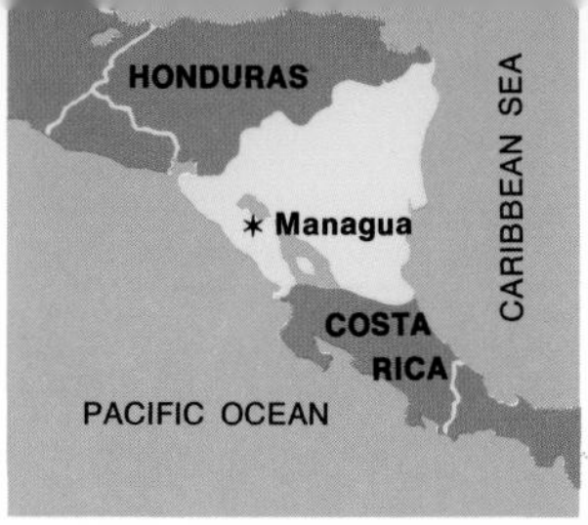

NICARAGUA

NICARAGUA

REPÚBLICA DE NICARAGUA

REPUBLIC OF NICARAGUA

The flag is related to those of El Salvador, Guatemala, Honduras, and Costa Rica.

The flag and arms of Nicaragua are almost exactly like those originally adopted in 1823 by the United Provinces of the Center of America. The independence of that state was proclaimed on 15 September 1821, but in January 1822 Emperor Iturbide of Mexico annexed the area, and freedom was not reestablished until June of 1823. Nicaragua reestablished the blue-white-blue after briefly substituting a flag of yellow, white, and mother of pearl.

The five volcanoes correspond to the five nations of the isthmus, washed by the waters of the Caribbean Sea and Pacific Ocean. Rays of liberty spreading throughout the land are shed by the liberty cap. The rainbow is for peace, and the triangle on which the entire design is represented symbolizes equality. Two related forces influenced the choice of these symbols – the French Revolution and masonry.

Officially hoisted 27 August 1971.

3:5

STATE ARMS

3:5

In South Africa and many Latin American countries it is the custom for the president to wear a sash as the symbol of his office on official occasions. In Nicaragua the presidential sash resembles the state flag: it is striped lengthwise in the national colors and bears in the center the official arms.

The official transmission of this sash corresponds roughly to the coronation ceremonies characteristic of monarchical countries.

103

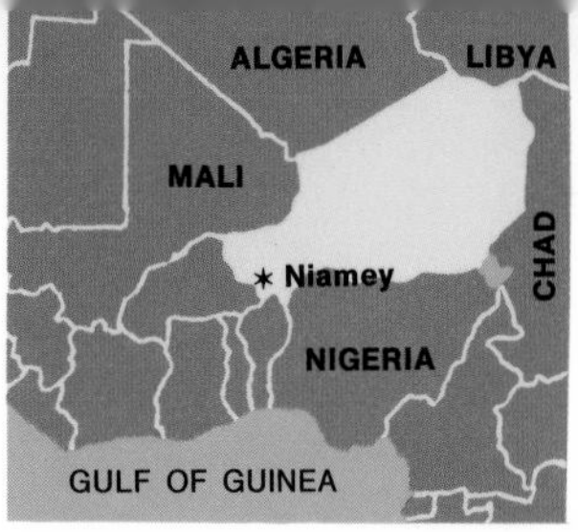

NIGER

NIGER

RÉPUBLIQUE DU NIGER

REPUBLIC OF NIGER

Vast portions of the east and north of Niger are part of the Sahara Desert, a region symbolized by the orange stripe of the flag. The grassy plains of the south and west – the latter nourished by the river from which the country takes its name – are the basis for the green stripe. Green also stands for fraternity and hope. The sun in the center is described as a symbol of the willingness of the Nigerois people to sacrifice themselves in defending their rights. White is both the good conscience of those who have done their duty and the mark of purity and innocence.
The sun is repeated in the coat of arms, where it is surrounded with emblems of animal husbandry and farming – a buffalo head and millet blades. The military valor of the people in the great empires of the past, ancestors of the modern Nigerois, is suggested by the crossed Touareg swords and spear.

Officially adopted
23 November 1959.

6:7≈

STATE ARMS

Orange being a very uncommon flag color, it is surprising that four of the flags incorporating orange should be quite similar in design. India displays a wheel instead of the sun, which appears in the flag of Niger, and the Ivory Coast and Ireland have vertical stripes with no emblem at all on the white. Yet all four flags are basically orange-white-green tricolors. The historical sources and symbolisms of these four flags are nevertheless quite distinct, and they were adopted quite independently of one another.

104

NIGERIA

NIGERIA

REPUBLIC OF NIGERIA

Officially hoisted 1 October 1960.

Flying over his native land on his way to London for university work, M. T. S. Akinkunmi was impressed by the virgin green land below him. He chose that color as the primary symbol for Nigeria in the flag he designed which was the winner in a contest that drew almost 3,000 entries.
The white stripe in the center signifies peace; the green stands for agriculture, which remains the backbone of the national economy. The red sun that Akinkunmi had included on the white stripe was omitted by the committee that approved the design for independence.

1:2

STATE ARMS

In the Nigerian arms black is said to refer to the rich soil of the land – irrigated by the Niger and Benue Rivers whose confluence is expressed heraldically by the Y-shaped "pall wavy argent." An eagle for strength and horses for dignity serve as the crest and supporters.

1:2

LAGOS STATE

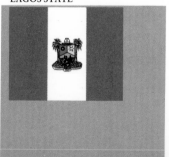

NIHON

JAPAN

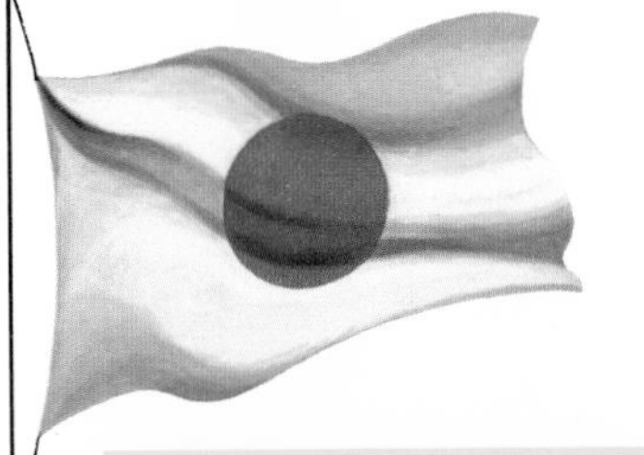

(NO OTHER NAME)

Although it has varied in shape and artistic rendition, the Japanese flag has been a red sun on white for many centuries. The design expresses the meaning of the country's name, Source of the Sun. The same motif has been interpreted differently for the military flags of Japan.
A chrysanthemum constitutes the *mon* or heraldic symbol of the emperor. This is a reminder of the hundreds of Japanese family banners regularly used in the past and still sometimes seen today.

More information on Japanese flags will be found on pages 164–173.

Officially adopted 5 August 1854.

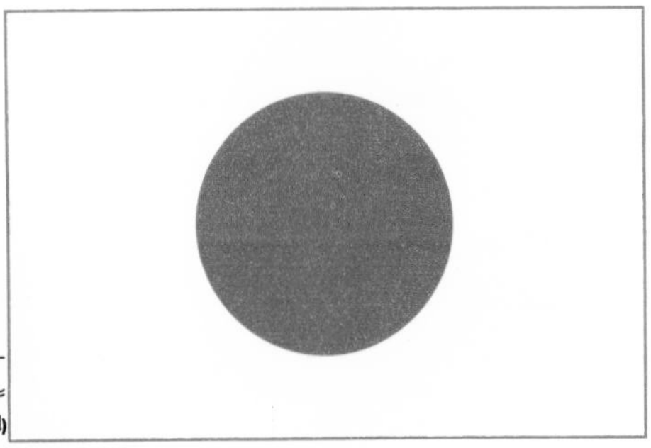

2:3≈

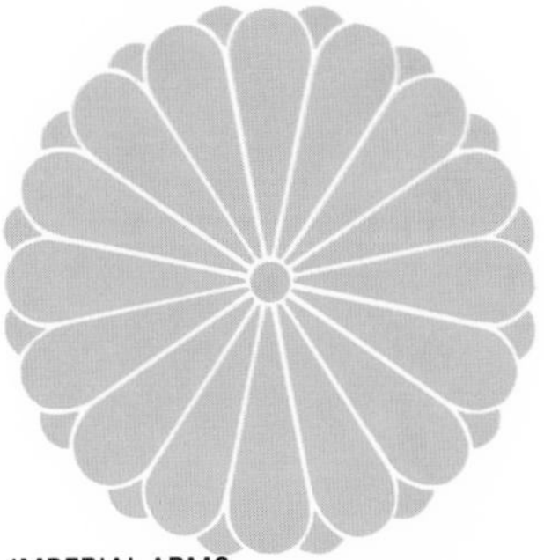

IMPERIAL ARMS

The concern of the Japanese for beauty and proportion in their flags is strikingly evident in those which have been adopted by the prefectures since 1945, when local autonomy began to increase. Many are based on the prefectural name or its first character; others incorporate a mountain, a flower, or other local symbol. Several feature colors (brown, lavender, crimson) rarely found in flags.

9:11≈

2:3

IMPERIAL FLAG

2:3

PRIME MINISTER'S FLAG

2:3≈

JAPANESE PREFECTURES

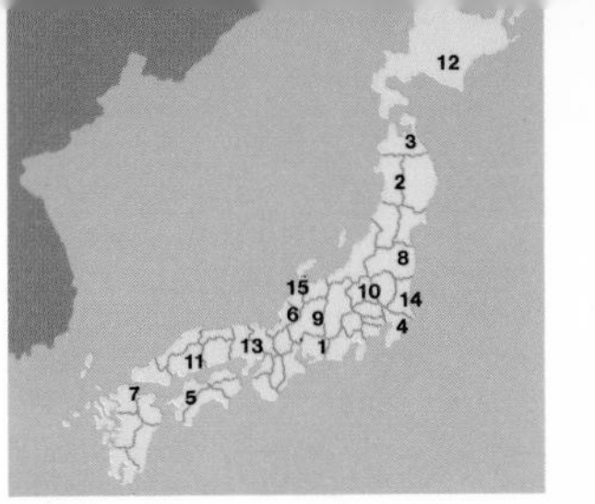

1 AICHI

2:3≈

2 AKITA

7:10

3 AOMORI

7:10

4 CHIBA

2:3

5 EHIME

2:3

6 FUKUI

2:3≈

7 FUKUOKA

2:3≈

8 FUKUSHIMA

2:3

9 GIFU

2:3≈

10 GUMMA

2:3

11 HIROSHIMA

7:10

12 HOKKAIDO

2:3

13 HYOGO

2:3≈

14 IBARAKI

2:3

15 ISHIKAWA

31:44

JAPANESE PREFECTURES

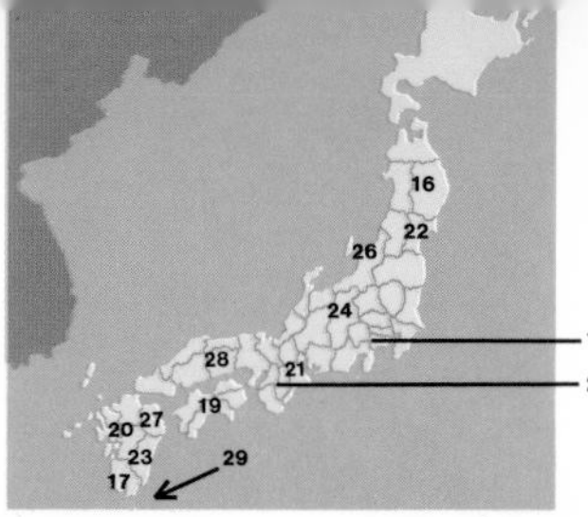

2:3 ≈

16 IWATE

2:3

17 KAGOSHIMA

7:10

18 KANAGAWA

2:3 ≈

19 KOCHI

2:3

20 KUMAMOTO

515:728

21 MIE

7:10

22 MIYAGI

5:7

23 MIYAZAKI

2:3

24 NAGANO

2:3

25 NARA

18:25

26 NIIGATA

7:10

27 OITA

2:3

28 OKAYAMA

7:10 ≈

29 OKINAWA

JAPANESE PREFECTURES

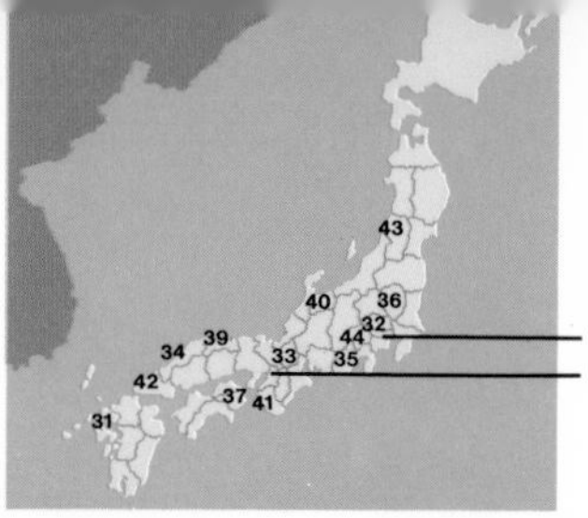

2:3

30 OSAKA

2:3

31 SAGA

2:3

32 SAITAMA

2:3

33 SHIGA

2:3 ≈

34 SHIMANE

2:3

35 SHIZUOKA

2:3 ≈

36 TOCHIGI

7:10

37 TOKUSHIMA

2:3

38 TOKYO

2:3

39 TOTTORI

2:3

40 TOYAMA

2:3

41 WAKAYAMA

2:3

42 YAMAGATA

2:3

43 YAMAGUCHI

7:10

44 YAMANASHI

NORWEGIAN COUNTIES

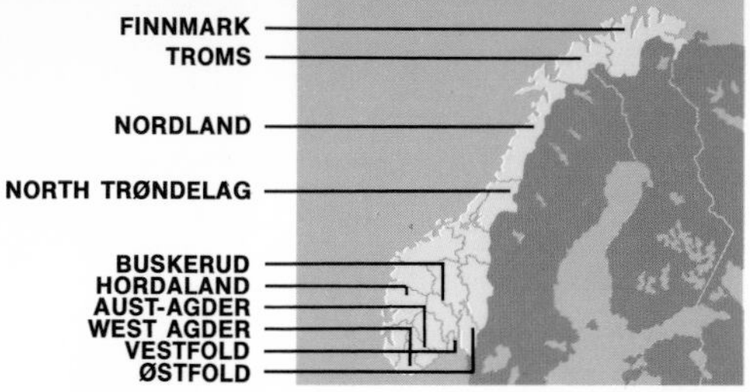

NORGE

NORWAY

KONGERIKET NORGE

KINGDOM OF NORWAY

Norway's flags are flown on several island territories belonging to that nation.

Officially approved 17 July 1821; restrictions on use at sea lifted 10 December 1898.

8:11

Centuries of rule by Denmark are reflected in Norway's flag – the Dannebrog with a blue cross added through the center. The choice of blue was probably influenced by the concept of red, white, and blue as colors of liberty.

Use of the Norwegian flag at sea was not achieved without a struggle. From 1814 until 1905 Norway was united with Sweden in a personal union under Swedish kings who wished ships of both countries to fly similar flags. The Norwegian struggle for a "clean flag," which achieved success in 1898, hastened the separation of Norway and Sweden six years later.

ROYAL ARMS

STATE ARMS

The royal arms *(above)* include a pavilion and a representation of the Order of St. Olav. The ax, personal symbol of this sainted king from the eleventh century, was introduced into the state arms

ROYAL FLAG 5:7

16:27

and royal standard about 1280. Various officers and branches of the government, such as the post office, have the right to add their own special emblems to the *splittflagg (left).*

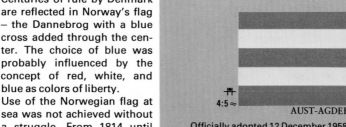

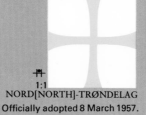

4:5≈

AUST-AGDER

Officially adopted 12 December 1958.

BUSKERUD

Officially adopted 1 April 1966.

1:1

1:1

FINNMARK

Officially adopted 6 January 1967.

HORDALAND

Officially adopted 1 December 1961.

7:9

1:1

NORD[NORTH]-TRØNDELAG

Officially adopted 8 March 1957.

NORDLAND

Officially adopted 15 January 1965.

1:1

1:1

ØSTFOLD

Officially adopted 26 September 1958.

TROMS

Officially adopted 15 January 1960.

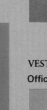

1:1≈

11:18≈

VEST[WEST]-AGDER

Officially adopted 12 December 1958.

VESTFOLD

Officially adopted 30 January 1970.

18:25≈

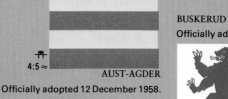

AUSTRIAN PROVINCES

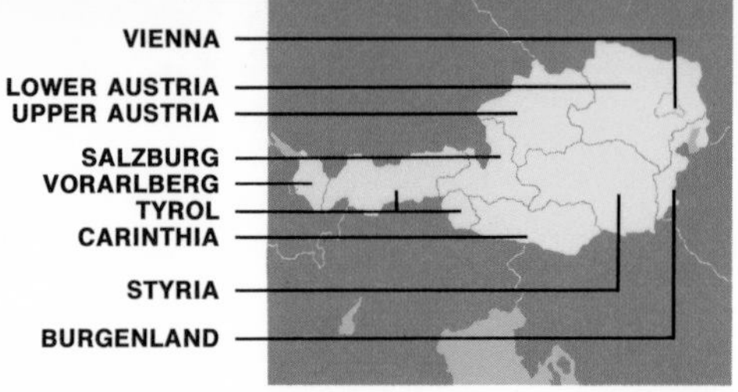

ÖSTERREICH
AUSTRIA

REPUBLIK ÖSTERREICH

REPUBLIC OF AUSTRIA

More information on the Austrian flag will be found on page 47.

The red-white-red shield of Austria goes back to the early thirteenth century, if not before. For centuries, however, it was eclipsed by other symbols when Austria formed part of the Hapsburg dominions in the Austro-Hungarian Empire. As a flag, the red-white-red stripes were first introduced in the war ensign of 1786. Different versions bearing royal ciphers or coats of arms were replaced in 1921 by the simple form reestablished after World War II.
Austrian symbols disappeared under Nazi rule from 1938 to 1945; following liberation in that year a broken chain symbolic of regained freedom was added to the eagle's legs.

Officially adopted 1 May 1945.

2:3

STATE ARMS

2:3

The historic Austrian eagle, often represented in the past with two heads, was originally an imperial rather than national symbol. Its lineage can be traced to the Roman Empire.
At the beginning of this century the wings of the eagle bore shields corresponding to the territories united under the emperor. Its two heads wore imperial crowns, and orders of knighthood hung around its necks.
The sickle, hammer, and civic crown of the eagle stand, respectively, for the peasants, workers, and middle class of modern republican Austria.

2:3 ≈

BURGENLAND

Officially adopted 25 June 1971.

NIEDERÖSTERREICH

LOWER AUSTRIA

Officially adopted 9 August 1954.

2:3 ≈

SALZBURG

Usage intiated 16 February 1921.

2:3 ≈

TIROL

TYROL

Usage initiated ca. 25 November 1945.

2:3 ≈

WIEN

VIENNA

Usage initiated ca. 1946.

2:3 ≈

KÄRNTEN

CARINTHIA

Officially adopted 18 June 1946.

2:3 ≈

OBERÖSTERREICH

UPPER AUSTRIA

Officially adopted 25 April 1949.

2:3 ≈

STEIERMARK

STYRIA

Officially adopted 1960.

2:3 ≈

VORARLBERG

Usage initiated ca. 1946.

2:3 ≈

108

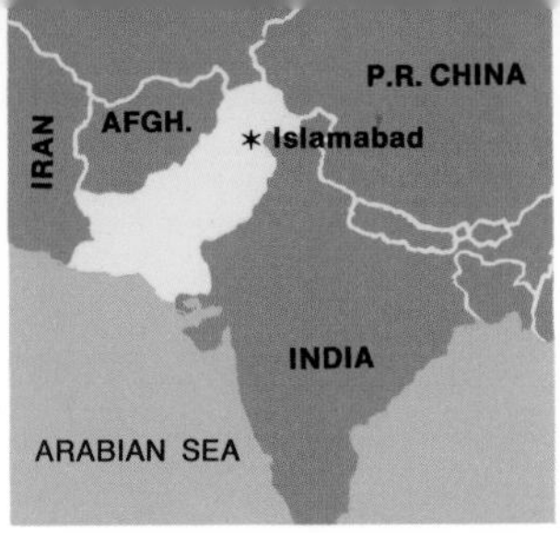

PAKISTAN

PAKISTAN

JAMHURIYAT
E PAKISTAN

REPUBLIC OF PAKISTAN

The Pakistani national color is known as tartan green.

On 30 December 1906 a flag was raised at Dacca (now in Bangladesh, formerly East Pakistan) when Muslims from all parts of British India gathered. The All-India Muslim League was formed as a result of that meeting, its aim being the achievement of an independent Muslim state. This was realized with the independence of Pakistan in 1947.

The flag of the Muslim League was green, long considered the chief religious color of Islam. The Muslim star and crescent were featured in the center of that flag.

But the party flag was not adopted directly by the nation; a white stripe was added at the hoist to represent minorities living in the state. Following British tradition, the presidential standard is dark blue: the name of the country is inscribed on it below the crescent.

Officially hoisted 14 August 1947.

2:3

STATE ARMS

2:3

1:2

PRESIDENTIAL FLAG

2:3≈

Above "Faith, Unity, Discipline" appear the products on which the national economy relies – cotton, tea, wheat, and jute. The flowers in the wreath are narcissi.

109

PANAMÁ

PANAMA

REPÚBLICA DE PANAMÁ

REPUBLIC OF PANAMA

In the Canal Zone, the Panamanian flag is flown together with that of the United States.

Throughout the nineteenth century Panamanian revolts sought to free the land from Colombia, of which it was then a part. The successful revolution which broke out on 3 November 1903 established the flag that has been flown by Panama ever since. It was baptized and officially saluted by civil and military authorities on 20 December of the same year.

The colors chosen corresponded to those used by the two traditional Panamanian political parties – the liberals (red) and conservatives (blue). White was to indicate peace between them, while the orderly division of the field suggested alternation of the parties at the helm of government. Blue and red also were associated with the Atlantic and Pacific Oceans, which flank Panama, and with the blood of patriots.

The blue star, according to the flag's designer, stands for the civic virtues of purity and honesty; the red star represents authority and law, which inculcate the former virtues. In the coat of arms there are nine stars corresponding to the provinces into which Panama is divided. Its green background (official, but rarely shown) is a reminder of the nation's tropical vegetation.

Officially confirmed 4 June 1904.

2:3≈

STATE ARMS

"For the Benefit of the World" proclaims the motto of Panama, referring to the canal which divides the country physically but provides it with a substantial portion of the national income. The arms incorporate other symbols as well. The civil wars of the past, represented by saber and rifle, have given way to the tools of peaceful labor, promising the prosperity and progress symbolized by the cornucopia and winged wheel. The sun and moon both appear in the central panel of the shield to indicate that independence was achieved at the hour of twilight.

PARAGUAY

PARAGUAY

REPÚBLICA DEL PARAGUAY

REPUBLIC OF PARAGUAY

Officially adopted 27 November 1842.

White, blue, and red flags were used by Paraguayan troops in 1806 when they went to the defense of Buenos Aires during the British invasion. The earliest mention of a red-white-blue tricolor in Paraguay seems to date from 15 August 1812. This bore on one side the arms of the capital city, Asunción, and on the other those of the king of Spain. The Star of May in the national arms recalls the date of independence, 14 May 1811. Defense of national liberty is symbolized by the lion guarding the liberty cap on the Treasury seal whose motto proclaims "Peace and Justice."

1:2≈ ≠

STATE ARMS

TREASURY SEAL

1:2≈

NATIONAL FLAG (REVERSE)

1:2≈

PRESIDENTIAL FLAG

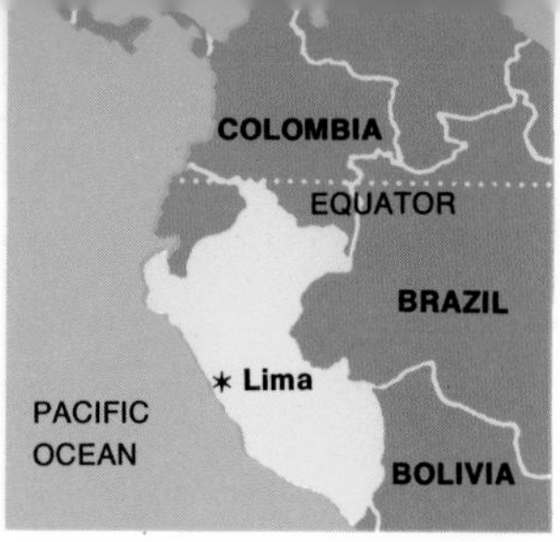

PERÚ

PERU

REPÚBLICA DEL PERÚ

REPUBLIC OF PERU

The flags of Peru have remained unchanged longer than most other national flags in the world. The choice of the colors red and white is said to date from an event in 1820 when the Argentine leader Captain General José de San Martín arrived to liberate Peru from Spanish domination. He is said to have taken as a good omen the flight of a number of flamingos at the time of his arrival; the colors of the birds thereupon became those of the flag of the Peruvian Legion which he founded. Several versions of the flag appeared in the period from 1820 to 1825 when the present form was established.

Officially adopted 25 February 1825.

2:3

STATE ARMS

The sun of the Incas, which San Martín had chosen as the heraldic emblem for the new republic, appears today in the presidential flag. Representations of the sun flank the national coat of arms, which is modified slightly for use in the state flag.

2:3

PRESIDENTIAL FLAG

2:3≈

The shield of the arms is divided into three parts, each representing one of the "kingdoms" over which the Inca Indians considered themselves master – the animal, vegetable, and mineral. These were symbolized by representative native forms – the vicuña, the cinchona tree, and coins of gold and silver spilling from a cornucopia. The shield in the flag is framed by palm and laurel, while the wreath which serves as a crest is holmoak.

112

PILIPINAS
PHILIPPINES

REPUBLIKA NG PILIPINAS

REPUBLIC OF THE PHILIPPINES

Officially hoisted 12 June 1898; most recently reestablished 14 October 1943.

The Katipunan, a revolutionary organization which initiated the liberation struggle against Spanish rule in the late nineteenth century, is symbolized by the white triangle of the flag. The three stars are for the main geographical areas of the Philippines – Luzon, the Visayas, and Mindanao. The eight provinces which first rose in revolt are honored by the eight rays of the sun.
Whenever the Philippines is at war the red stripe is flown at the top of the flag, the reverse of its normal position. This color stands for courage and bravery, while blue is for noble ideals, white for peace and purity.
The Americans and the Japanese, who occupied the islands at different times, officially outlawed the flag. Both were later forced to recognize as legal its use by Filipinos.

1:2

STATE ARMS

PRESIDENT'S FLAG

26:33

ANTIQUE

3:5≈

BENGUET

9:17

113

POLSKA
POLAND

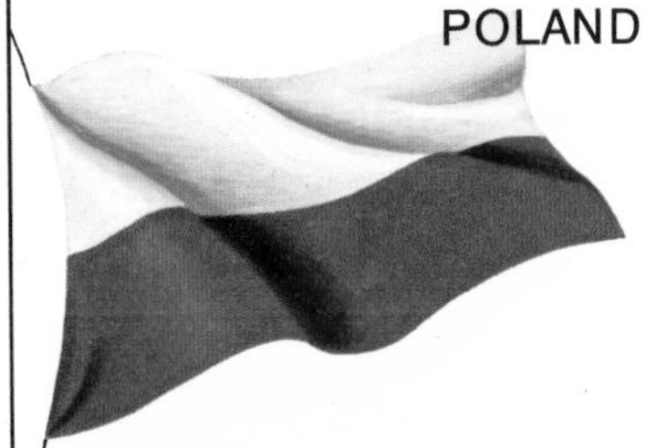

POLSKA RZECZPOSPOLITA LUDOWA

POLISH PEOPLE'S REPUBLIC

From the beginning of the thirteenth century the premier emblem associated with Poland has been theWhite Eagle. Its color and that of the red shield on which it appears have formed the basis for most Polish flags.
Over the centuries many variations of both arms and flags have been displayed by Polish ships, military forces, and rulers. In the nineteenth century, when Poland struggled to free itself from foreign domination and to unite the country, the White Eagle and variants of the bicolor based on it were rallying symbols for Polish patriots.
Although Poland has had a Communist government since the end of World War II, its symbols are little changed today from the forms established when the modern Polish nation was created following World War I. An exception is the omission of the crown from the head of the eagle.

Officially adopted 1 August 1919; reestablished 20 March 1956.

5:8

STATE ARMS

5:8

10:21

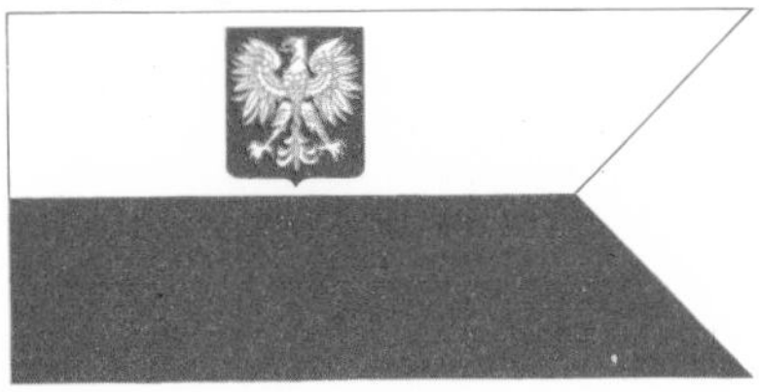

PRESIDENT'S FLAG

5:6≈

PORTUGAL

PORTUGAL

REPÚBLICA PORTUGUESA

PORTUGUESE REPUBLIC

See also Angola, Brazil, and Mozambique.

The armillary sphere – a navigational instrument symbolic of the Age of Discovery, when Portuguese sailors opened far parts of the world to European culture and commerce – was not officially added behind the shield in the state flag until the proclamation in 1815 of the United Kingdom of Portugal, Brazil, and the Algarves.

It had previously appeared on a number of other, earlier flags and was the personal symbol of King Manuel I (1495–1521) who had spurred Portuguese exploration.

The red and green of the flag, recalling the historic crosses of Avis and the Order of Christ, derive from a similar standard hoisted by the battleship *Adamastor* when it began the republican revolution. Below the laurel branches in the war flag is the motto "This Is My Good and Beloved Fatherland."

Approved 30 June 1911.

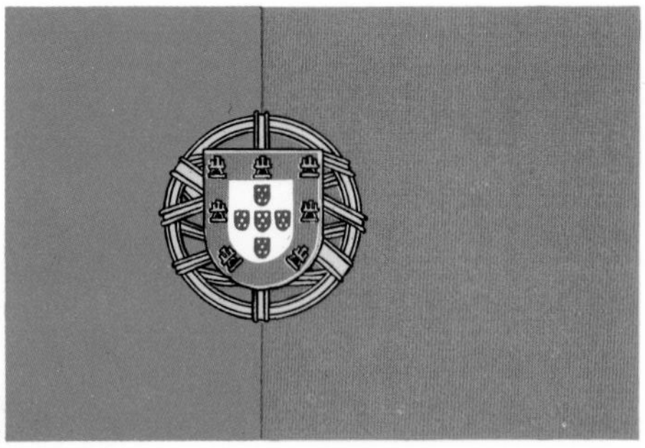

2:3

STATE ARMS

12:13

PRESIDENTIAL FLAG

2:3

Alphonso Henry (1112–1185) defeated the Castilians and established Portugal as an independent kingdom. According to the Portuguese national epic *Os Lusiades,* in 1139 Alphonso also defeated five Moorish kings after they had struck five shields from him in the battle of Ourique. The divine assistance which aided his victory is commemorated on each blue shield by five discs, representing the wounds of Christ. These continue to this day as the heart of the Portuguese arms.

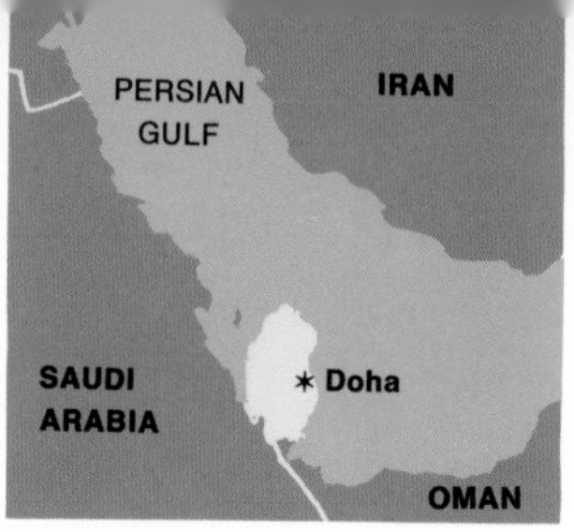

QATAR

QATAR

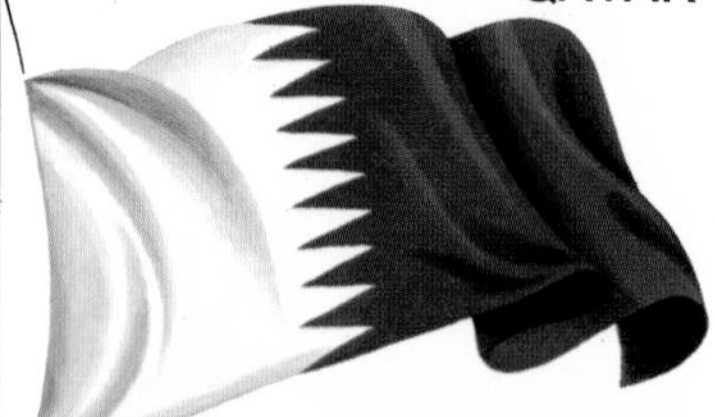

DAULAT QATAR

STATE OF QATAR

The pronunciation of Qatar is *Kah* tr.

Usage initiated ca. 1949.

The distinctive crimson or maroon characterizing the national symbols of Qatar apparently arose from the effect of the sun on the red natural dyes used in making flags. Because of the similarity of the Qatar flag to those of neighboring states (see Bahrain and the United Arab Emirates), the change was made official.

The flag was apparently first used under Shaikh Jasim bin Muhammad al-Thani about 1855. Variations existed over the years, including one in which the name of the country was inscribed in white on the crimson background. (In the coat of arms this name appears below a shell indicating the maritime pursuits of many Qatari citizens.)

Red is the traditional color of the Kharijite Muslims of eastern Arabia. In the early nineteenth century Great Britain was instrumental in having borders or stripes of white added to the previously all red flags. The serration between the two colors in the Qatari flag is purely a decorative motif.

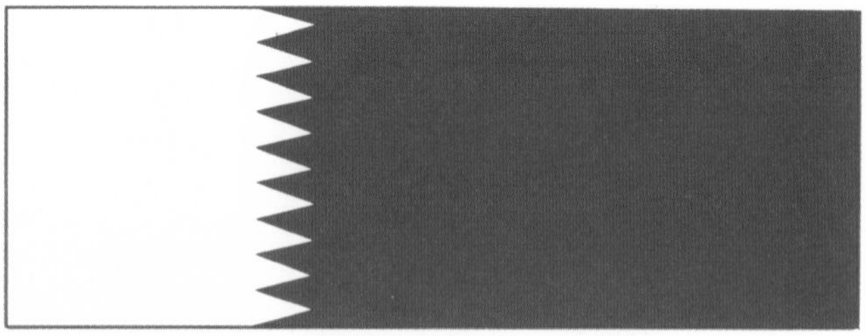

11:28

STATE ARMS

The overwhelming majority of flags are formed of six basic colors – red, yellow, green, blue, black, and white. However, for symbolic or historic reasons, orange, crimson, brown, and other special shades have been introduced into an increasing number of flags of nations and especially of national subdivisions (see, for example, the Japanese prefectures). Misrepresentation of such a color is in effect an error in the flag illustrated.

116

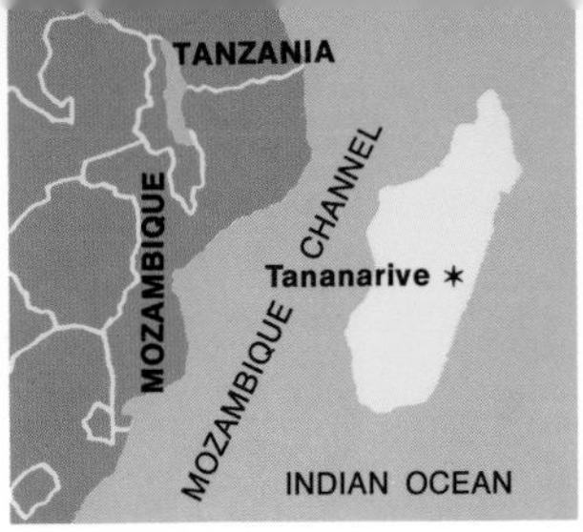

REPOBLIKA MALAGASY/ RÉPUBLIQUE MALGACHE

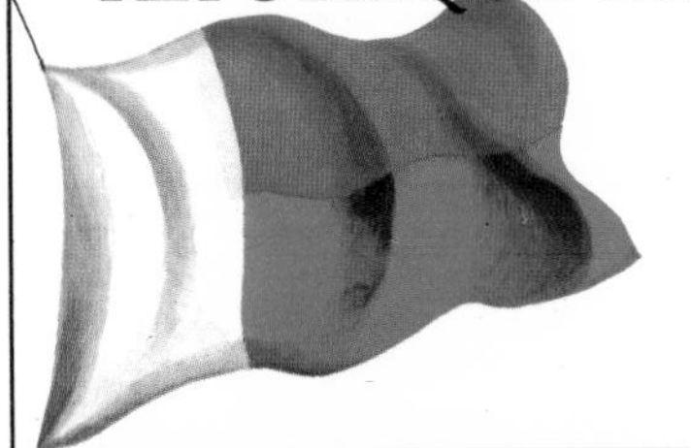

MALAGASY REPUBLIC

(NO OTHER NAME)

Many Malagasy are descended from settlers who originally came from Southeast Asia, suggesting that its red and white flags (see Indonesia) influenced similar red and white flags flown by the Hova empire in nineteenth-century Madagascar. Those Hova flags were the basis for the tricolor adopted shortly after Madagascar became the Malagasy Republic. Green was added for the coastal peoples.

Historically, red is associated with the Volamena and the white with the Volafotsi, princely families founded by King Andriandahifotsi (1610–1685). His personal emblem was a red bull, and the name of his kingdom was Menabe, "Great Red." Today the white is seen as a symbol of purity, the red of sovereignty, and the green of hope.

Officially hoisted 21 October 1958.

2:3≈

STATE ARMS

PRESIDENTIAL FLAG

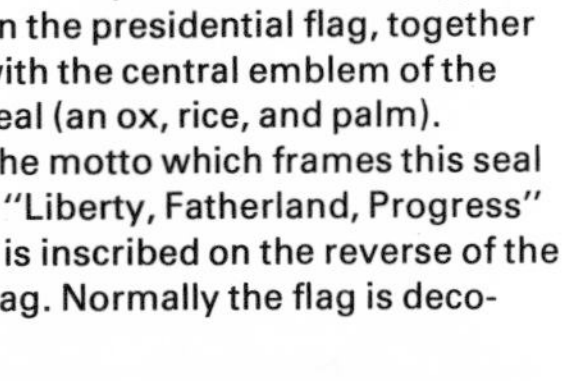

2:3 ≠

PRESIDENTIAL FLAG (REVERSE)

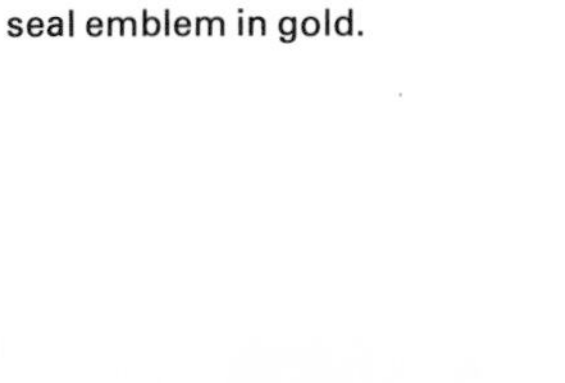

2:3

The initials of the country's name and the president's name appear on the presidential flag, together with the central emblem of the seal (an ox, rice, and palm).

The motto which frames this seal – "Liberty, Fatherland, Progress" – is inscribed on the reverse of the flag. Normally the flag is decorated with a cravat striped lengthwise white-red-green, bearing the seal emblem in gold.

117

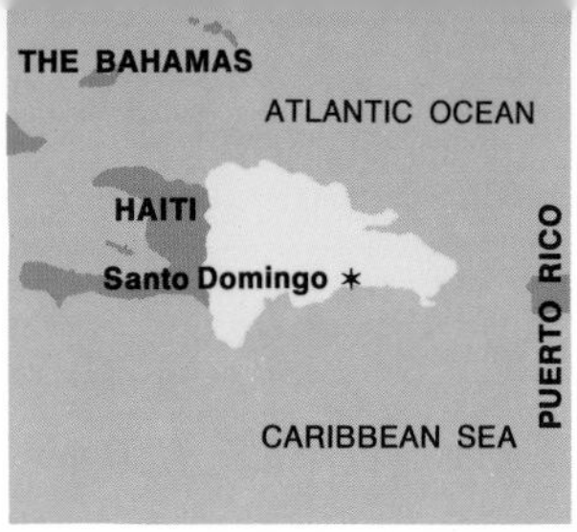

REPÚBLICA DOMINICANA

DOMINICAN REPUBLIC

(NO OTHER NAME)

Spain ruled this land 1494–1801, 1810–1821, and 1861–1863.

The early nineteenth century saw the Dominican people struggling for independence – against not only Spain and France, but also the Haitians with whom they share the island of Hispaniola. After several unsuccessful attempts, independence was finally achieved on 27 February 1844 under the banner still in use today.

The leader of the independence movement was Juan Pablo Duarte, who on 16 July 1838 had formed a secret revolutionary society, The Trinitarian. This name referred to the cells of three individuals who composed the group and also to their religious faith. The faith was asserted in the white cross the Dominicans added to the Haitian flag then flying over the island, which consisted of horizontal stripes of blue over red. Later the Dominican flag was modified to the extent of reversing the position of the blue and red quarters at the fly end of the flag.

Officially confirmed 6 November 1844; reestablished 14 September 1863.

2:3≈

STATE ARMS

2:3≈

The name of the country and "God, Fatherland, Liberty" appear on the national arms. Laurel and palm flank the shield which bears an open Bible, one of several symbols of Dominican religious faith incorporated in its national arms and flag.

The blue is said to stand for liberty, red for the fire and blood of the independence struggle. The white cross is a symbol of sacrifice.

118

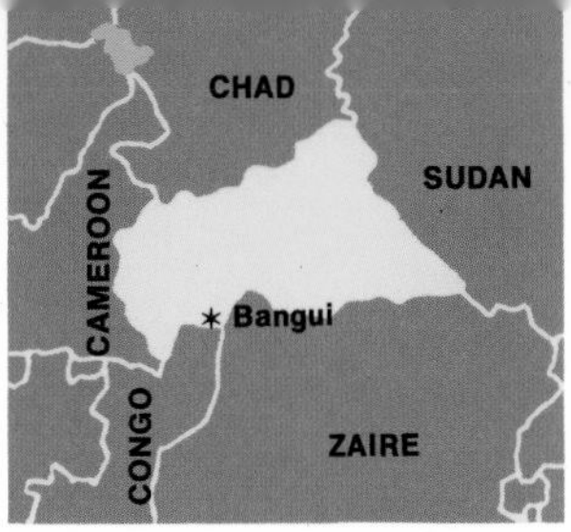

RÉPUBLIQUE CENTRAFRICAINE

CENTRAL AFRICAN REPUBLIC

(NO OTHER NAME)

"A Man Is a Man": the motto at the top of the state arms affirms a belief in the equality of all people, as graphically expressed in the national flag. The blue, white, and red of the French flag (which flew during the colonial regime) and the green, yellow, and red pan-African colors are united to show that Europeans and Africans must have respect and friendship for one another. Their common bond – the red blood of humanity – forms the vertical stripe in the Central African flag.

Officially hoisted 1 December 1958.

3:5 ≈

STATE ARMS

Green and yellow have been given specific meanings, the former representing the people of the forest region and the latter those of the savannah. The gold star of independence is a guide toward future progress.

PRESIDENTIAL FLAG

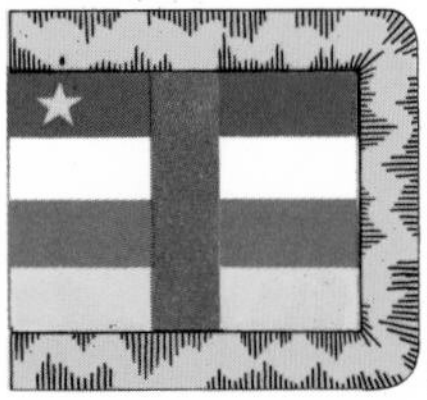

22:31 ≈

The black hand in the fourth quarter of the arms was the party emblem of the country's Movement for the Social Evolution of Black Africa prior to independence. The geographical position of the country is indicated by the star and map at the center of these arms. Below the shield is the Central African Order of Merit framed by the national motto ("Unity, Dignity, Work").

119

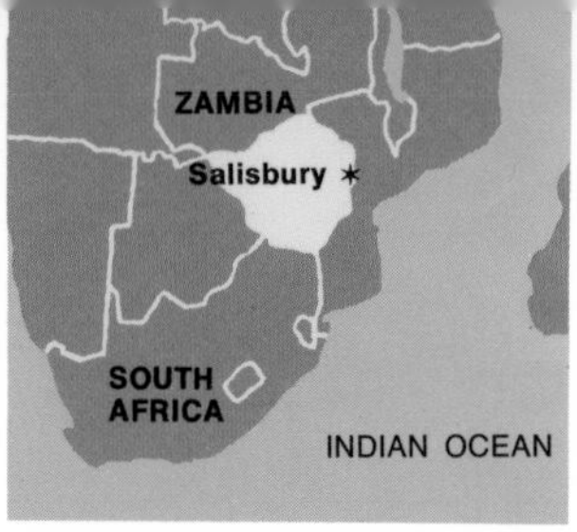

RHODESIA

(NO OTHER NAME)

Officially hoisted 11 November 1968.

Cecil Rhodes, the nineteenth-century British empire builder whose flag is described on page 77, left his mark in the symbols of central Africa. Southern Rhodesia (now Rhodesia) as well as Northern Rhodesia (now Zambia) were named for him; moreover, the lion and thistles of the Rhodes family arms now fill the chief in the Rhodesian state arms. The green portion of the shield and the green stripes in the flag allude to the agricultural basis of the Rhodesian economy. The gold pickax is a symbol of mining.

The armorial supporters, sable antelopes, recall the wildlife of Rhodesia while its ancient civilization is reflected in the representation of a bird. The original bird, carved in soapstone, was found in the Zimbabwe ruins. The Latin motto in the arms refers to the namesake of the country; it translates as "May [Rhodesia] Be Worthy of the Name."

1:2

STATE ARMS

1:1

PRESIDENTIAL FLAG

Rhodesia was a self-governing British colony until 11 November 1965 when it unilaterally proclaimed its independence – a status which has not been recognized by any other country. Although blacks constitute a majority of the population, they are restricted by the Rhodesian constitution to a minority position in the government. Leaders of the black community seek a majority-rule constitution for the country, which they call Zimbabwe. Such a change would undoubtedly alter the national symbols as well.

120

ROMÂNIA

ROMANIA

REPUBLICA SOCIALISTĂ ROMÂNIA

SOCIALIST REPUBLIC OF ROMANIA

The flag colors of Romania are heraldic; their origins may be found in ancient banners of Moldavia, Walachia, and Transylvania. One of the earliest combinations of the three colors was created in 1834 by permission of the Ottoman sultan at the request of the Prince of Walachia.
As a national symbol, a tricolor of blue-yellow-red became firmly established during the revolutionary events of 1848, although official recognition was not given until the union of Walachia and Moldavia in 1859. In subsequent years various governments altered the arms on its center stripe to reflect different ideologies.

Officially adopted 21 August 1965.

2:3

STATE ARMS

After the proclamation of a people's republic in 1947 a completely new coat of arms, bearing a tractor and three furnaces surrounded by a wreath of wheat, was decreed. A few months later the current basic design was substituted.

FLAG OF THE CHAIRMEN OF THE COUNCILS OF STATE AND OF MINISTERS

1:1

In addition to the name of the state (which received its present form in 1965) and the red star of Communism (added in 1952), the arms retain the essential form established in 1948.
The river, forests, oil derrick, wreath of wheat, and mountains all suggest important characteristics of the natural resources of Romania. The rising sun expresses the promise of a new day.

121

RWANDA

RWANDA

REPUBLIKA Y'U RWANDA
RÉPUBLIQUE RWANDAISE

REPUBLIC OF RWANDA

The R on the flag has not been given a precise official form.

The R of this banner obviously represents the name of the country over which the flag flies. Historically, it has further associations of equal importance – revolution, referendum, and republic.
Although nominally a Trust Territory of Belgium under United Nations supervision, Rwanda's internal power structure before independence was based on an ancient caste system and hereditary monarchy that maintained minority rule by the Tutsi clan. To free themselves of this feudal and authoritarian regime, the Hutu majority rose in revolt in November 1959. The Tutsi king fled and a republic was proclaimed in January 1961; the new, democratic political structure was confirmed in a referendum the following September. The flag hoisted in January had equal vertical stripes of red, yellow, and green, but since this was exactly the same as the flag of Guinea, an R was added after the September vote.
The red stripe represents blood shed in the revolution; yellow is for peace, tranquility, and liberation from the tyranny of the past; green is for hope in the future and the agricultural wealth of the land.

Officially hoisted ca. September 1961.

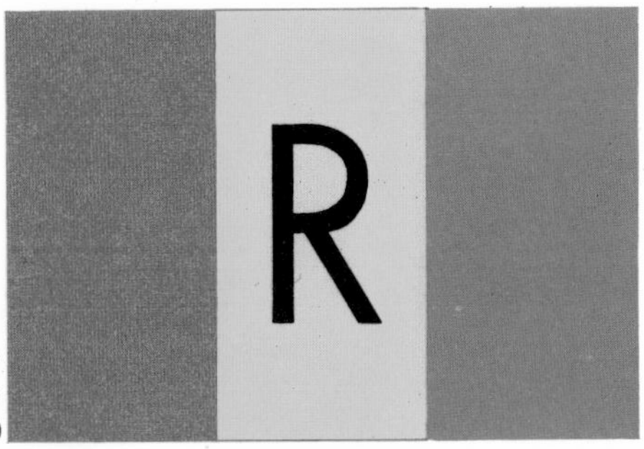

2:3≈

STATE ARMS

Under the Tutsi monarchy Rwanda's highest symbol of state was Kalinga, the royal drum from which the king himself supposedly derived authority. The coat of arms adopted by the republic displays the flag which replaced Kalinga as a symbol. It also includes the name of the state and its motto – "Liberty, Cooperation, Progress." A dove of peace surmounts a bow and arrow (for defense of democratic liberties) and the tools of an agricultural people, a hoe and pruning knife.

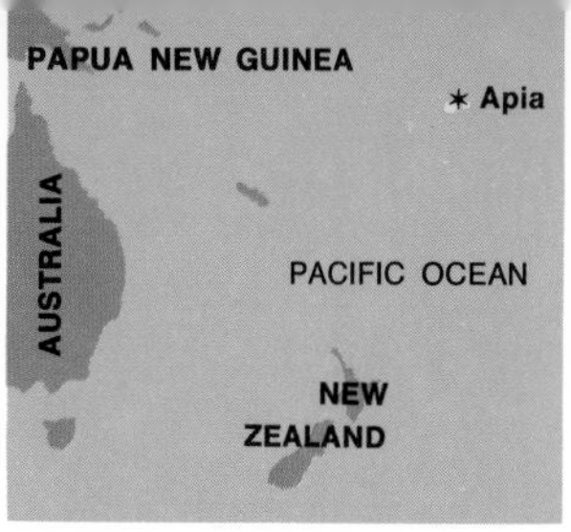

SAMOA I SISIFO
WESTERN SAMOA

MALOTUTO'ATASI
O SAMOA I SISIFO

INDEPENDENT STATE
OF WESTERN SAMOA

Officially adopted
24 February 1949.

The nineteenth-century independent kingdom of Samoa had several flags in which red and white were prominent. The colors were not used after 1900 when American and German colonial rule were established. They reappeared officially, however, in the Western Samoan flag hoisted in 1948. That design – to which a further star was added the next year – was created by Their Highnesses Tupua Tamasese Mea'ole and Malietoa Tanumafili II.
Until 1962 when independence was achieved under United Nations trusteeship, Western Samoa flew the flag of New Zealand at sea and, jointly with its own flag, on land. Today Western Samoa's sole official flag is honored in the national anthem, *Banner of Freedom.* Its colors are generally associated with courage (red), purity (white), and freedom (blue).
The constellation of the Southern Cross in the Western Samoan flag and arms links the nation with other flags from below the Equator – those of Brazil, Australia, New Zealand, the Falkland Islands, Papua New Guinea, and several Brazilian and Australian states. The motto in the coat of arms translates as "May God Be the Foundation of Samoa."

1:2

STATE ARMS

Traditionally white was the color of peace; since the formation of the United Nations (UN), light blue has begun to be a replacement – for example in the flags of the Republic of South Viet-Nam, certain counties of Liberia, and the former flag of Eritrea. Olive branches, originally an emblem of prosperity, have also come to symbolize peace (as in the Cypriote flag).
Western Samoa, a former UN Trust Territory, is the only country whose arms incorporate the seal of the United Nations in its own official arms.

SAN MARINO
SAN MARINO

REPUBBLICA DI
SAN MARINO

REPUBLIC OF SAN MARINO

Although San Marino has been a republic for centuries, it has a crown in its arms and flag.

This small republic, which according to tradition was founded in the third century by St. Marinus as a refuge, consists of a single mountain and some surrounding countryside. Both the flag and arms of the country express this topography very well. The sky is reflected in the blue of the flag and shield; white is for the clouds or for the snow that caps Mount Titano in the winter.
The emblem of the three towers surmounted by ostrich plumes goes back to at least the fourteenth century. They are not a heraldic fancy, but correspond to the three towers of the walled capital city that crowns the mountain. These towers – Guaita, Cesta, and Montale – have metal vanes at the top corresponding to the ostrich feathers in the national arms. It has been suggested that these plumes (*penne* in Italian) may be a reference to the Apennines of which Mount Titano is a part.

3:4 ≈

STATE ARMS

3:4 ≈

The traditional white and blue colors of the San Marinese arms were selected for the cockade adopted in 1797. The flag was probably created at about the same time, although there is no law regulating its design or usage even today. The current form of the arms dates from 6 April 1862.

The crown is a symbol of sovereignty, not of monarchy. The Latin motto ("Liberty") is the proud device of a country that has provided refuge for those fleeing from political or religious persecution.

124

SÉNÉGAL

SENEGAL

RÉPUBLIQUE DU SÉNÉGAL

REPUBLIC OF SENEGAL

Political principles developed in Senegal under years of French colonial rule – such as national unity, democracy, and equality – are symbolized by the equal vertical stripes of the Senegalese flag, which resembles the French Tricolor. Although the flag colors were found in Senegalese political party flags, they are considered pan-African colors as well, appearing in a dozen other national flags.

As France divested itself of its colonies in the late 1950s, new leaders – including Léopold Sédar Senghor of Senegal, whose initials appear today on the flag he displays as President of his nation – called for the unity of Africa. Senegal and the French Sudan established the Mali Federation in early 1959; it achieved independence on 20 June 1960. Its flag had vertical stripes of green-yellow-red, the center stripe bearing in black the figure of a man. Then two months later Senegal broke from the young federation and became independent. The symbol of the man was replaced with a green star, later incorporated into Senegal's coat of arms.

Officially adopted September 1960.

2:3≈

STATE ARMS

In addition to the three national colors, the arms of Senegal incorporate a representation of its national order and national motto ("One People, One Aim, One Faith"); the latter binds two palm branches. The shield bears symbols representing strength (a lion) and the Senegal River, which forms the nation's northern border. The tree in the sinister half of the shield is a baobab, found extensively throughout Senegal.

3:4≈ PRESIDENT'S FLAG

125

SHQIPËRIA

ALBANIA

REPUBLIKA POPULLORE E SHQIPËRISË

PEOPLE'S REPUBLIC OF ALBANIA

Albania means "White Land," Shqipëria "Land of the Eagle."

A century ago the black, double-headed eagle represented imperial Austria-Hungary, Russia, and the past glories of the Byzantine Empire. Its use by the Albanian national hero, George Castriota (known as Iskander Beg or Skanderbeg), was not entirely forgotten, however. When modern Albania became independent in 1912, the nation resurrected Skanderbeg's red flag with the double-headed eagle.

Since that time many symbols have accompanied the eagle on the flag – a star of independence, crown of royalty, fasces of Italian domination, and gold-bordered red star of Communism.

Officially confirmed 15 March 1946.

5:7

STATE ARMS

The Albanian war ensign is modeled on that of the Soviet Union – a stripe along the bottom edge of a white field bearing national symbols. The star and red ribbon of the arms proclaim the Communist philosophy of the state. The date heralds the National Anti-Fascist Congress of Liberation held in Permet.

2:3≈

2:3

Henry Longfellow wrote in his *Tales of a Wayside Inn:*
"The crescent banner falls /
And the crowd beholds instead /
Like a portent in the sky /
Iskander's banner fly /
The Black Eagle with double head. . . ."
Until his death in 1468, Skanderbeg was indeed able to keep the territory around his fortress of Kroia free from the Ottoman forces which had conquered Constantinople itself.

126

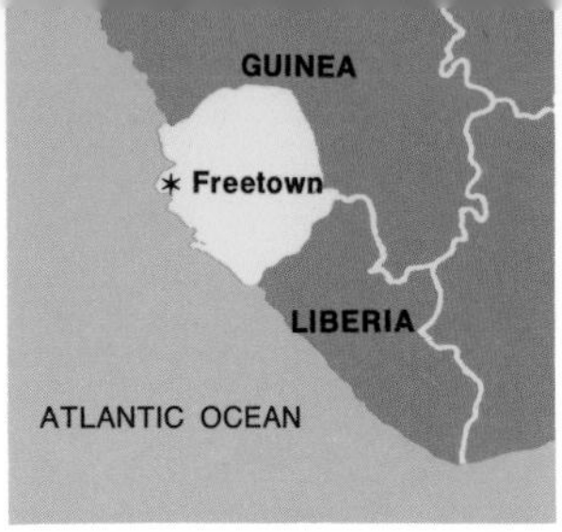

SIERRA LEONE

SIERRA LEONE

(NO OTHER NAME)

Because the terrain seemed wild and rough to them, Portuguese explorers named this country after the lion.

Sierra Leone has one of the few hilly areas on the West African coast; hence, green mountains were incorporated into its coat of arms. The green stripe in its flag symbolizes agriculture and natural resources as well as the mountains.
The blue in both the arms and the flag recall that the capital city, Freetown, has one of the best natural harbors on the African coast. The color stands for the hope that the nation may be able to make a contribution to world peace in the development of commerce through this harbor. The white stripe that separates the "cobalt blue" and "leaf green" in the state flag is an emblem of unity and justice. The lion of the arms refers to the national name and links Sierra Leone with its former colonial master, Great Britain.
Pride in the education its university colleges have provided to West Africa is evidenced in the flaming torches of enlightenment in the national arms.

Officially hoisted 27 April 1961.

2:3

STATE ARMS

The technical heraldic description of the Sierra Leone arms is as follows: "Vert [green] on a Base Barry wavy of four [stripes] Argent and Azure [white and blue] a Lion passant Or [gold] on a Chief dancetty of three points also Argent as many Torches Sable [black] enflamed proper [of natural color]. And for the Supporters: On either side a Lion Or supporting between the fore legs an Oil-palm proper: together with this Motto Unity Freedom Justice."

127

SINGAPURA/SINGAPORE/ HSIN-CHIA-P'O

SINGAPORE

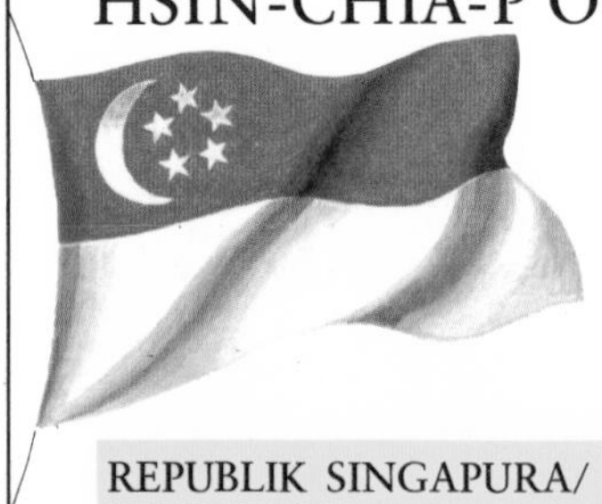

REPUBLIK SINGAPURA/
SINGAPORE
KUDIYARASU/
HSIN-CHIA-P'O
KUNG-HO-KUO

REPUBLIC OF SINGAPORE

The official interpretation is that the "crescent represents a young country on the ascent in its ideals of establishing democracy, peace, progress, justice, and equality as indicated by the five stars."
There are also official explanations for the symbolism of the red and white colors. The former stands for universal brotherhood and the latter for purity and virtue. Since the same colors are employed by many neighboring states, they may be considered as Southeast Asian regional colors.

Officially hoisted 3 December 1959.

2:3

STATE ARMS

The national motto – "Forward Singapore" – is also the title of the national anthem. The tiger in the arms recalls former associations with Malaysia, and the other supporter brings to mind the meaning of the name Singapore – "Lion City."

1:2

1:2

1:2

1:2 PRESIDENTIAL FLAG

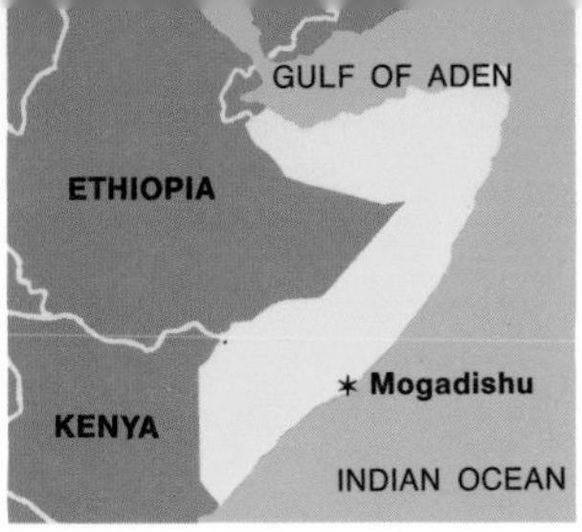

SOMALIA/SUMALIYA

SOMALIA

REPPUBLICA DEMOCRATICA DELLA SOMALIA/ AL DJUMHURIYAH AL SUMALIYAH AL DIMUQRATIYAH

SOMALI DEMOCRATIC REPUBLIC

Although bound by religion, ethnic ties, language, and history, the Somalis were divided in the nineteenth century by the British, French, and Italians. The modern Somali flag is a reminder of the nation's division.

Each of the points of the star stands for an area in which Somalis live – the Ogaden region of Ethiopia, the Northern Frontier District of Kenya, the French Territory of the Afars and Issas, former British Somaliland, and former (Italian) Somalia. The latter two, independent since 26 June and 30 June 1960, respectively, united to form the Somali Democratic Republic.

The field of blue recalls the blue flag of the United Nations under whose tutelage Somalia achieved its independence. This explains why Somalia is one of the two independent African nations to have a flag of light blue.

Officially hoisted 12 October 1954.

2:3≈

STATE ARMS

The coat of arms of Somalia obviously reflects the national flag, but its lineage also reaches back to the Italian colonial period. Following the conquest of Ethiopia in 1936, Somalia became one of five provinces constituting Italian East Africa. As such it had a coat of arms divided horizontally into three equal parts. The central band was blue, bearing a leopard with a white star over its head.

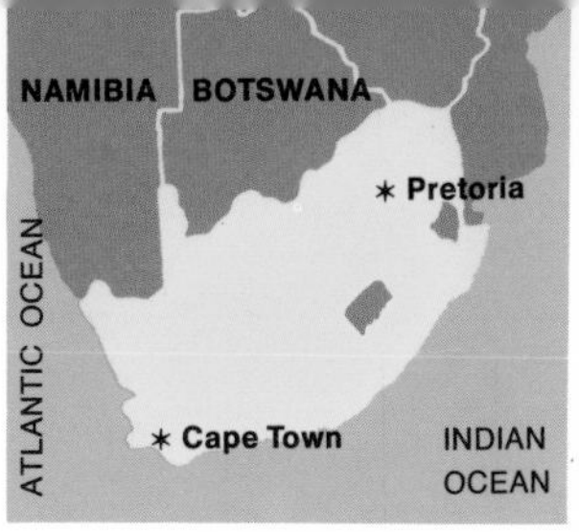

SOUTH AFRICA/SUID-AFRIKA

REPUBLIC OF SOUTH AFRICA/ REPUBLIEK VAN SUID-AFRIKA

The South African flag is composed of four flags.

Two British colonies (Natal and the Cape) and two formerly independent Boer states (the Orange Free State and the South African Republic) united to form South Africa. It was decided to combine the flags of the latter two with the Union Jack of the former as a special badge. This was added to the orange-white-blue flag originally brought to South Africa by Dutch settlers in the seventeenth century.

Until 1951 this flag was only flown on land and until 1957 it was always officially flown on public buildings jointly with the Union Jack. No change was made in the flag when South Africa became a republic in 1961.

The arms combine symbols of the provinces with the motto "Strength from Unity." The lion in the crest recalls both English and Dutch symbols.

Officially hoisted 31 May 1928.

2:3

STATE ARMS

2:3

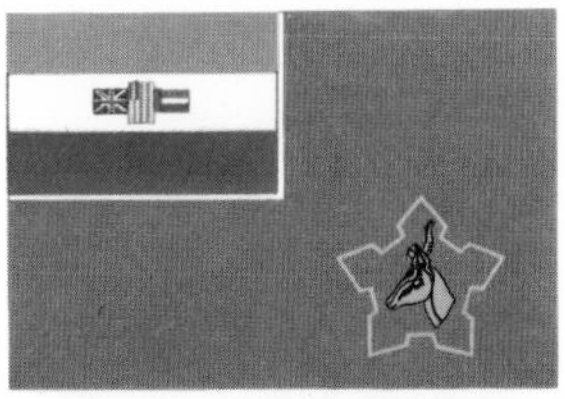

PRESIDENT'S FLAG

1:2

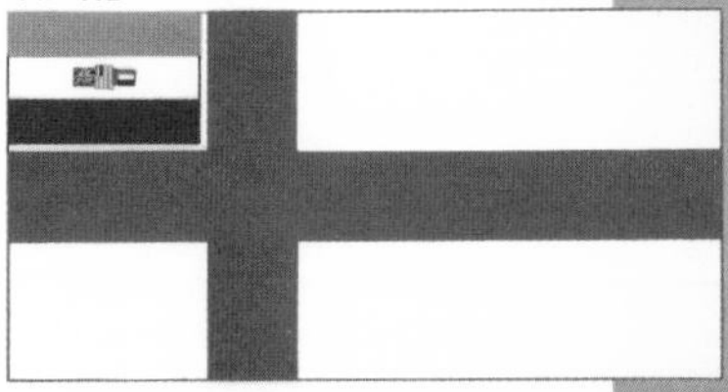

PRIME MINISTER'S FLAG

2:3

1:2

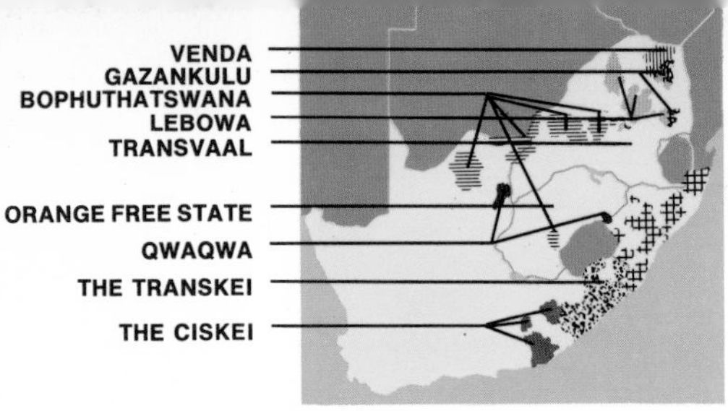

2:3≈

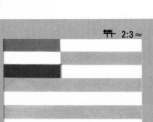

ORANJE-VRYSTAAT

ORANGE FREE STATE

Officially approved 28 February 1856; unofficial since 31 May 1902.

2:3≈

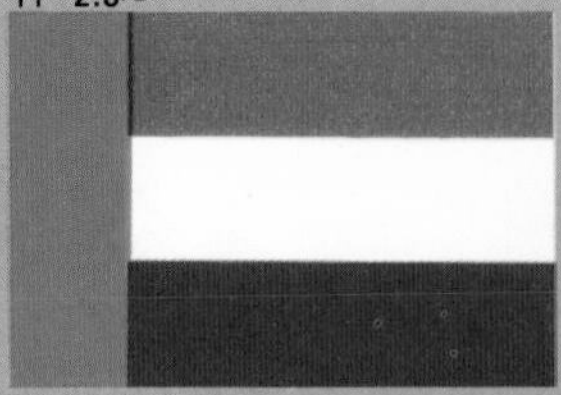

TRANSVAAL

Usage initiated 6 January 1857; unofficial since 31 May 1902.

2:3

BOPHUTHATSWANA

Officially approved 19 April 1973.

2:3

THE CISKEI

Officially approved 22 June 1973.

2:3

GAZANKULU

Officially approved 1973

2:3

LEBOWA

Officially approved 5 July 1974.

QWAQWA

Officially approved 1974.

2:3

THE TRANSKEI

Officially hoisted 20 May 1966.

2:3

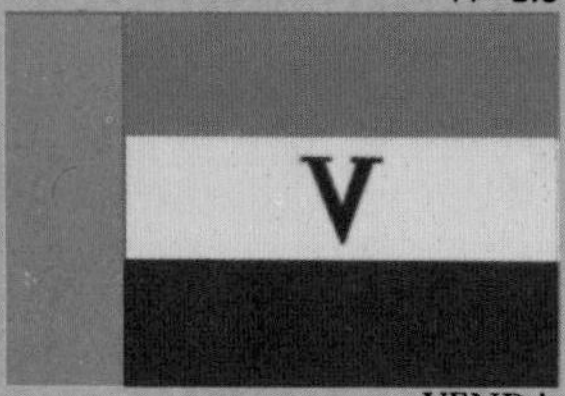

VENDA

Officially approved 1973.

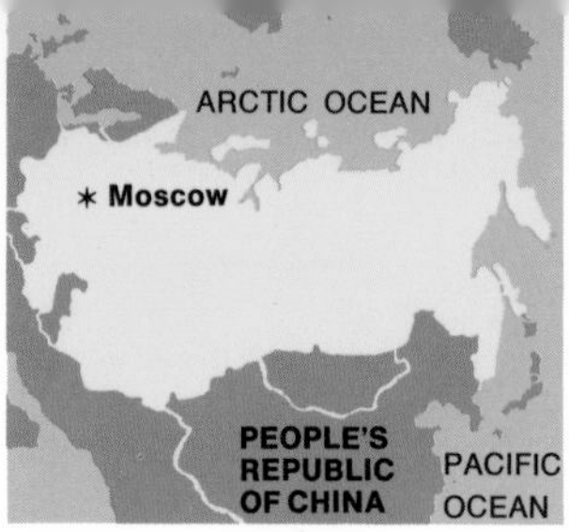

SOVYETSKII SOYUZ

SOVIET UNION

SOYUZ SOVYETSKIKH SOTSIALISTICHESKIKH RESPUBLIK

UNION OF SOVIET SOCIALIST REPUBLICS

Further data on Soviet symbols appear on pages 174–179.

Four symbols are common to most Soviet flags – the hammer, sickle, five-pointed star, and the color red. All reflect the Communist path which the country has followed since its 1917 October Revolution. The hammer and sickle stand for the proletariat and peasantry, who are guided by the Communist Party's red banner of revolution. The five star points suggest the unity of peoples in all five continents. The basic Soviet flag was added to the U.S.S.R. draft constitution on 12 November

1:2

1923; the present artistic rendition dates from 19 August 1955.

The Soviet coat of arms *(left)* graphically presents the dawn of a new day for the entire world. Its slogan, repeated in the fifteen national languages of the U.S.S.R., is "Workers of All Lands, Unite."

STATE ARMS

3:5

2:3

Soldiers of the Red Army, which did so much to ensure the stability and growth of the Soviet state during its early years, identified themselves by wearing large red stars on their headgear. Many soldiers also wore a red enamel star with a gold hammer and plow, a forerunner to the present hammer and sickle motif. Today's Soviet army flag *(above, left)* follows these traditions. The war ensign *(above, right)* recalls in its colors the "Andrew flag" of the Imperial Russian Navy – a blue saltire on a field of white.

UNION REPUBLICS OF THE U.S.S.R.

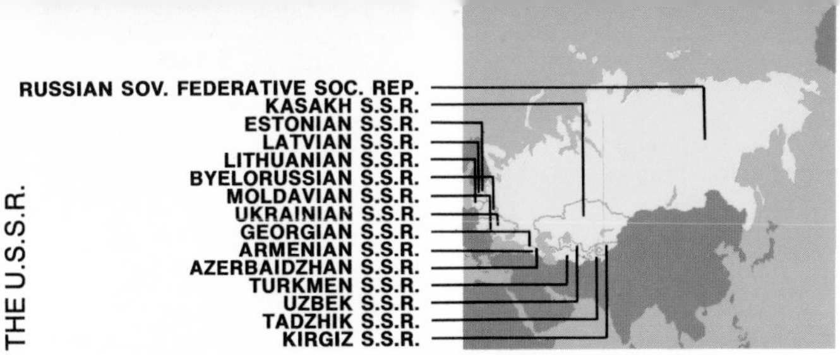

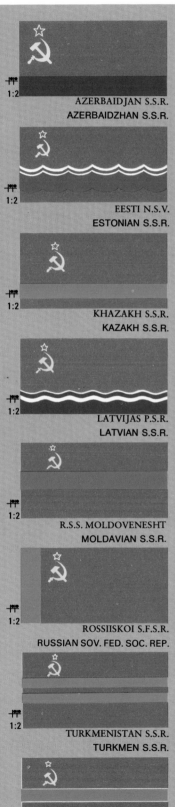

1:2
AZERBAIDJAN S.S.R.
AZERBAIDZHAN S.S.R.

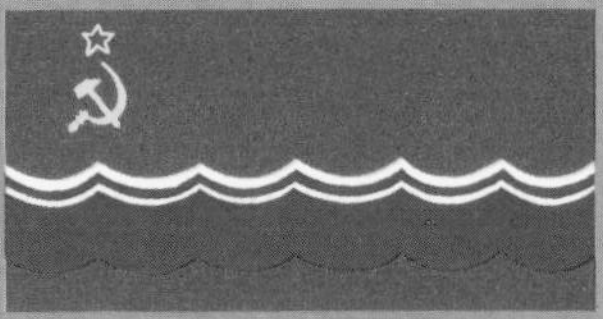
1:2
EESTI N.S.V.
ESTONIAN S.S.R.

1:2
KHAZAKH S.S.R.
KAZAKH S.S.R.

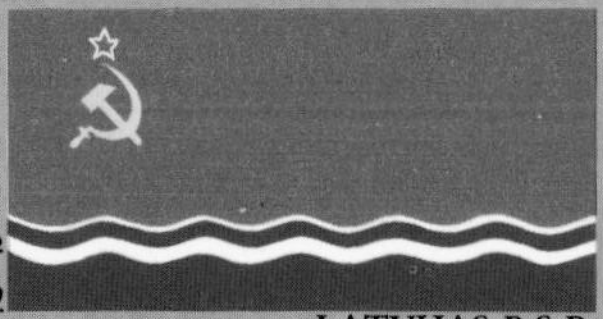
1:2
LATVIJAS P.S.R.
LATVIAN S.S.R.

1:2
R.S.S. MOLDOVENESHT
MOLDAVIAN S.S.R.

1:2
ROSSIISKOI S.F.S.R.
RUSSIAN SOV. FED. SOC. REP.

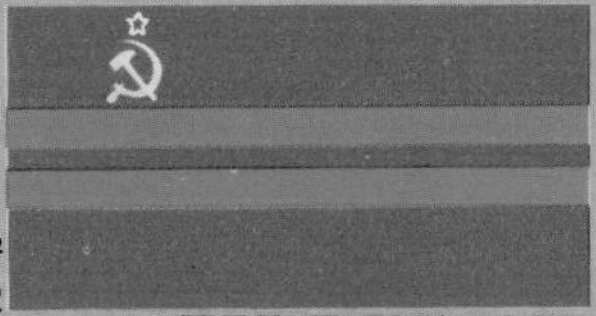
1:2
TURKMENISTAN S.S.R.
TURKMEN S.S.R.

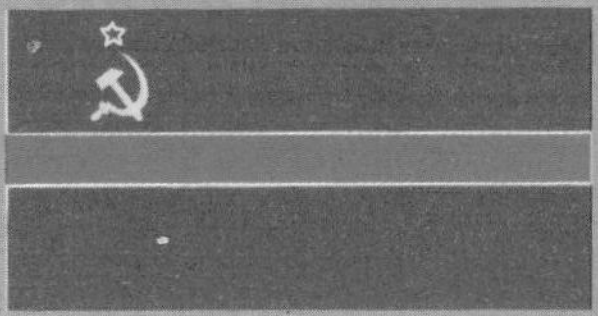
1:2
UZBEKISTAN S.S.R. **UZBEK S.S.R.**

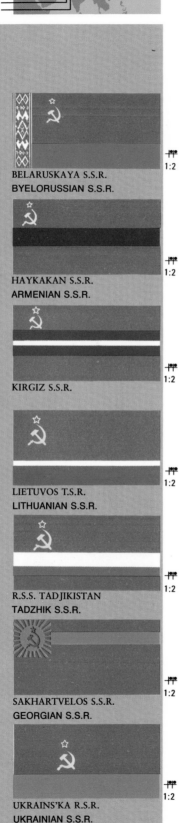

1:2
BELARUSKAYA S.S.R.
BYELORUSSIAN S.S.R.

1:2
HAYKAKAN S.S.R.
ARMENIAN S.S.R.

1:2
KIRGIZ S.S.R.

1:2
LIETUVOS T.S.R.
LITHUANIAN S.S.R.

1:2
R.S.S. TADJIKISTAN
TADZHIK S.S.R.

1:2
SAKHARTVELOS S.S.R.
GEORGIAN S.S.R.

1:2
UKRAINS'KA R.S.R.
UKRAINIAN S.S.R.

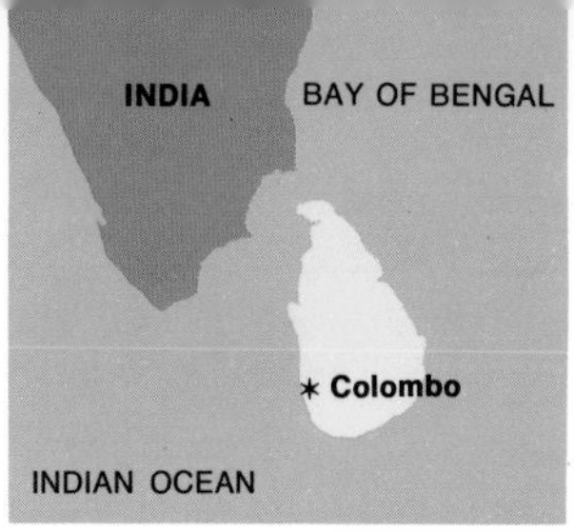

SRI LANKA
SRI LANKA

SRI LANKA JANARAJAYA

REPUBLIC OF SRI LANKA

Sri is Singhalese for "venerable" or "resplendent."
Officially hoisted 22 May 1972.

Legend credits Prince Vijaya, Aryan conquerer of Ceylon in the sixth century B.C., with descent from a lion. Ancient Singhalese royal palaces feature carved lions and a fifteenth century saga refers to a lion banner.
The flag of the last king of Kandy (later Ceylon and later still, Sri Lanka) was returned to Britain as war booty in 1815. Upon the restitution of Ceylonese independence in 1948, a replica of this banner was hoisted as the national flag, but three years later stripes of orange and green were added. These represented the Hindu and Muslim minorities, the Tamils and Moors.

5:9 ≈

STATE ARMS

The bo leaves of the sacred pipul tree in the corners are a symbol of the religion of the majority: Gautama is supposed to have received enlightenment, becoming the Buddha after meditation under a pipul tree.

3:5 ≈

PRESIDENTIAL FLAG
1:2

In the Sri Lanka arms the pot of rice is a symbol of prosperity; the sun and moon are for longevity as in the Nepal flag. At the top is a representation of the Buddhist Wheel of the Law, also found in the flag of India. Another Buddhist symbol, the lotus, surrounds the national lion and sword in the center. These arms appear on the presidential flag above the name of the country.

132

AL SUDAN

SUDAN

AL DJUMHURIYAH
AL SUDAN
AL DIMUQRATIYAH

DEMOCRATIC REPUBLIC OF THE SUDAN

Officially hoisted 20 May 1970.

Following the revolution of 1969 a competition was held to create a new flag which would better express the policies of the country, particularly its support for Arab unity. The pattern chosen to replace the old flag was designed by a Khartoum Art Institute graduate, Abdalrahman Ahmad Aljali.
A number of explanations were given to the colors incorporated in the flag, which was obviously patterned on the Arab Liberation Flag of Egypt. Red is seen as the color of revolution, progress, socialism, and national martyrs. White is for peace, optimism, and light; it also recalls the white flag flown in the 1924 revolution.
Sudan is an Arabic word meaning "black," and the country is partially in black Africa. Moreover, the flag of the Madhi was black (see p. 76). Green is hailed as a symbol of prosperity and Islam.

1:2

STATE ARMS

The native secretary bird is featured prominently in the coat of arms, together with the name of the state and the motto "Victory Is Ours."

PRESIDENTIAL FLAG 1:2≈

BAHR EL GHAZAL

2:3≈

NORTHERN KORDOFAN

2:3≈

133

SUOMI/FINLAND

FINLAND

SUOMEN TASAVALTA/
REPUBLIKEN FINLAND

REPUBLIC OF FINLAND

The Order of the Cross of Liberty appears in the canton of the presidential flag.

In the nineteenth century, Finland was part of Russia, although it had limited autonomy. Finns seeking to create a distinctive local flag looked to their national coat of arms for inspiration. Its red shield and gold lion, still the heraldic achievement used by Finland, inspired the basic colors.
Variations of the red and yellow were countered by proposals in which white and blue were prominently featured. Credit for suggesting the white of the snows and light blue of the lakes as appropriate Finnish colors is given to the poet Sakari Topelius. The struggle for Finnish independence and the civil war which followed it (in 1917–1918) produced new variations of both the red-yellow and white-blue flag designs. Today all four colors appear in the state flag.

Officially adopted 12 February 1920.

11:18

STATES ARMS

11:18

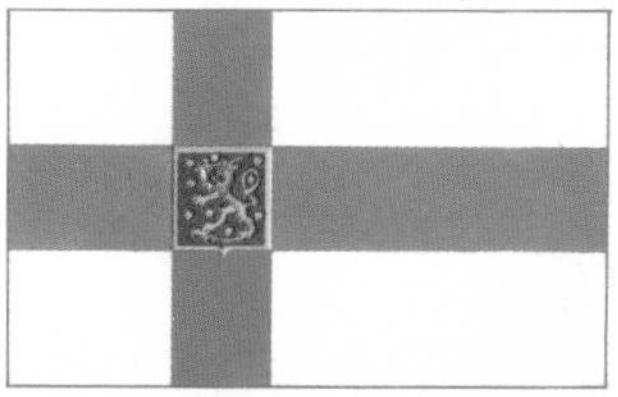

11:19

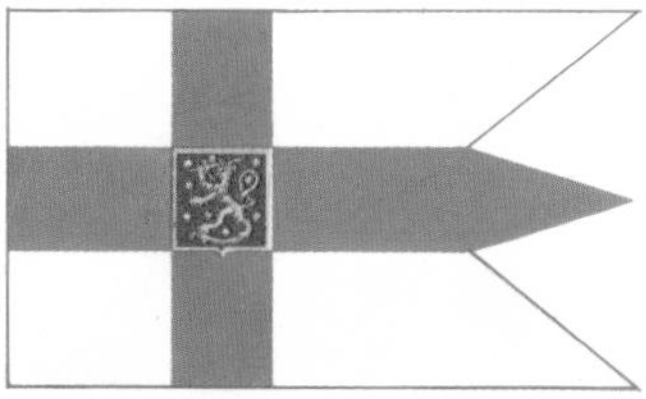

ÅLANDS

17:26

PRESIDENTIAL FLAG

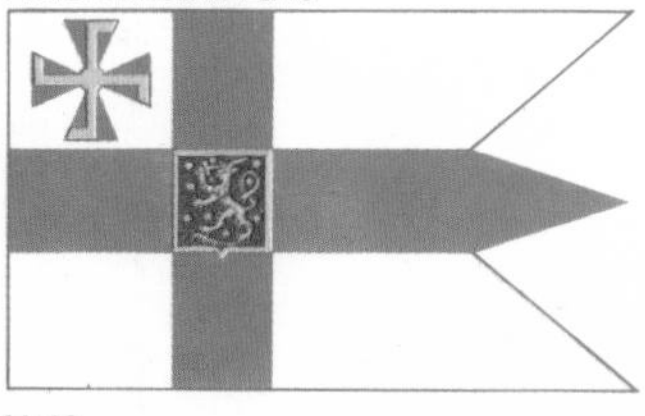

11:19

134

SURIYAH

SYRIA

AL DJUMHURIYAH
AL ARABIYAH
AL SURIYAH

SYRIAN ARAB REPUBLIC

The development of Syrian flags is shown on page 155.

Following the Second World War when most independent Arab states were monarchies, Syria had a republican form of government. The coat of arms Syria adopted at that time seems to have influenced the designing of later Arab republican coats of arms.
The central feature of the Syrian arms was the eagle emblem of General Khalid ibn al-Walid, Muslim conqueror of Damascus in the seventh century. The central shield bore the stars and colors of the Syrian flag; below were a wreath and ribbon with the name of the state.
The arms created in late 1971 for the Federation of Arab Republics shows a hawk, emblem of the Quraish tribe to which Muhammad belonged, but the artistic rendition is very similar to the original Syrian eagle. The shield is now plain and the ribbon bears the inscription "Federation of Arab Republics." (The Libyan and Egyptian versions add the names of those states at the bottom.)

Officially hoisted 1 January 1972.

2:3

STATE ARMS

In September 1971 Syria joined Libya and Egypt in the Federation of Arab Republics whose new flag and arms were established on the first day of the following year. From 1963 to 1972 Syria had used a flag of the same three colors, but with three green stars on the white stripe. A similar design constituted the Syrian flag from 1932 to 1958 and from 1961 to 1963. From 1958 to 1961 Syria joined Egypt in the United Arab Republic under a red-white-black tricolor bearing two green stars.

135

SVERIGE

SWEDEN

KONUNGARIKET
SVERIGE

KINGDOM OF SWEDEN

The blue and gold colors of the Swedish flag may be derived from the traditional arms of the nation – the gold crowns on blue were used as early as 1364.
The cross indicates the close ties between Sweden and other Scandinavian states. A gold cross on blue is found in a seal from 1449 employed by the Swedish king, but is today a national emblem.
In 1569 King John III ordered that the yellow cross be part of Swedish flags and in 1663 a special royal decree established the two basic forms of the flag still in use today. Swedes yearly celebrate 6 June as Flag Day.

Officially adopted 22 June 1906.

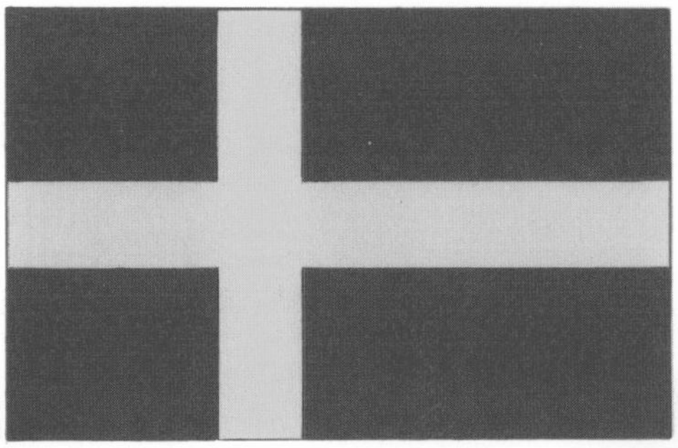

5:8

GREATER STATE ARMS

LESSER STATE ARMS

ROYAL FLAG

1:2

1:2

ROYAL COMMAND FLAG

1:1

136

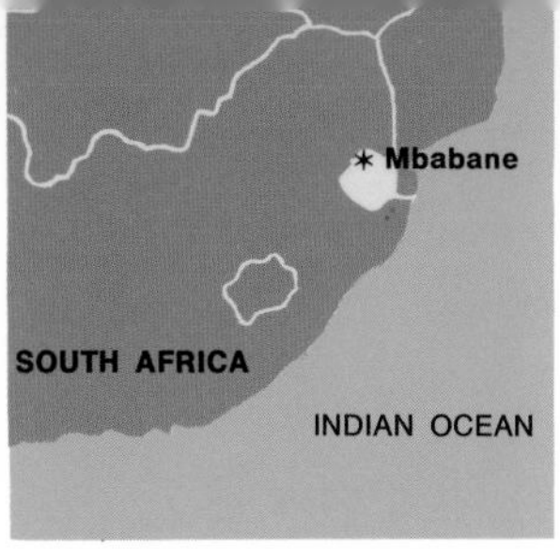

SWAZILAND

SWAZILAND

UMBUSO WE SWATINI

KINGDOM OF SWAZILAND

The Swazi Pioneer Corps which served with the British during World War II received their standard from King Sobhuza II in 1941 as a reminder of Swazi military traditions. More than a quarter century later, when Swaziland's independence from Britain was imminent, the corps color provided the basis for the design of the national flag. The new pattern, introduced on 25 April 1967, took its present form five months later.

Independence within the Commonwealth was achieved on 6 September 1967. The following year the king, then in the forty-seventh year of his reign, designed his own royal standard by adding his personal emblem (a lion) to the national flag.

The crimson in the flags is for the battles of the past, yellow for the wealth of mineral resources, and blue for peace. The shield reflects natural oxhide colors; the spears and staff bear feathers of the widow bird and lourie.

Officially hoisted 30 October 1967.

2:3

STATE ARMS

The supporters in the arms of Swaziland are not simply indigenous fauna: The lion stands for the king, the elephant for the queen mother. Jointly they proclaim "We Are the Fortress" – the motto appearing on the ribbon below. The royal headdress with its widow bird feathers rests on a shield bearing symbols similar to those found in the national flag. The weapons are those previously carried by the Emasotsha Regiment.

ROYAL FLAG

2:3

137

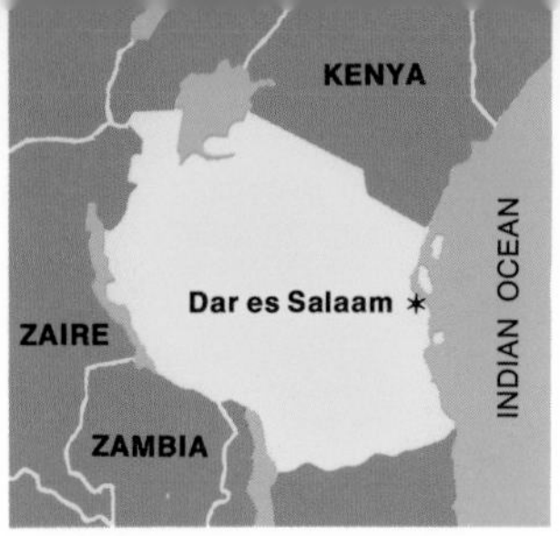

TANZANIA

TANZANIA

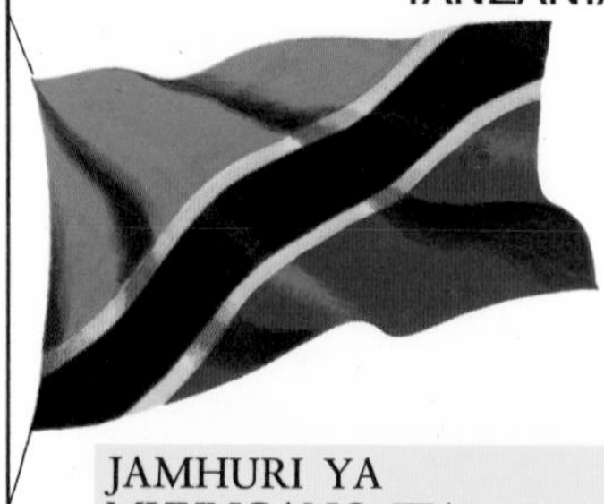

JAMHURI YA MUUNGANO WA TANZANIA

UNITED REPUBLIC OF TANZANIA

The flag of the Tanganyika African National Union (TANU) heralded the nation's fertile land by two horizontal stripes of green, separated by a black stripe to indicate the ethnic majority of the population. On 9 December 1961, when Tanganyika became independent, a national flag was hoisted: gold fimbriations were added to stand for Tanganyika's mineral resources.

After neighboring Zanzibar was amalgamated in 1964, the general form of the Tanganyikan flag was retained by Tanzania but in a diagonal rather than horizontal pattern. The introduction of blue reflected the flag of Zanzibar and the Indian Ocean.

The Swahili motto "Freedom and Unity" frames Mount Kilimanjaro in the Tanzanian arms. Among other symbols are found tools of development (an ax and hoe), a spear for defense, the flaming torch of freedom and knowledge, and leading agricultural resources (cotton and cloves).

Officially approved ca. 30 June 1964.

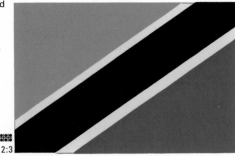

2:3

STATE ARMS

2:3≈

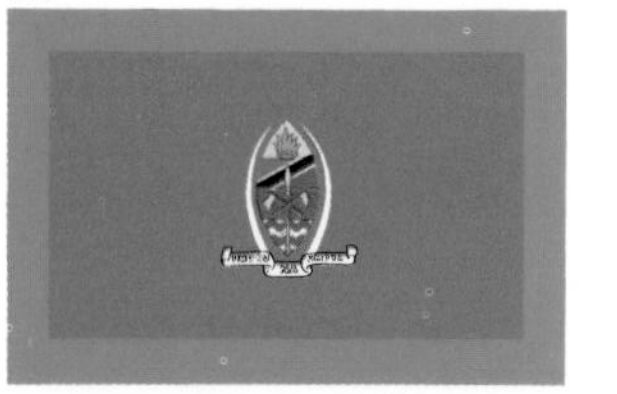

Between independence on 9 December 1963 and merger with neighboring Tanganyika on 25 April 1964, Zanzibar had four national flags. The fourth flag has continued to fly in Zanzibar since April of 1964 as a regional flag within Tanzania.

Derived from the flag of the ruling Afro-Shirazi Party, its stripes symbolize the sea, the people, and the land. A very narrow white strip at the hoist stands for peace. The green field and blue border of the presidential flag undoubtedly have the same color symbolism.

ZANZIBAR

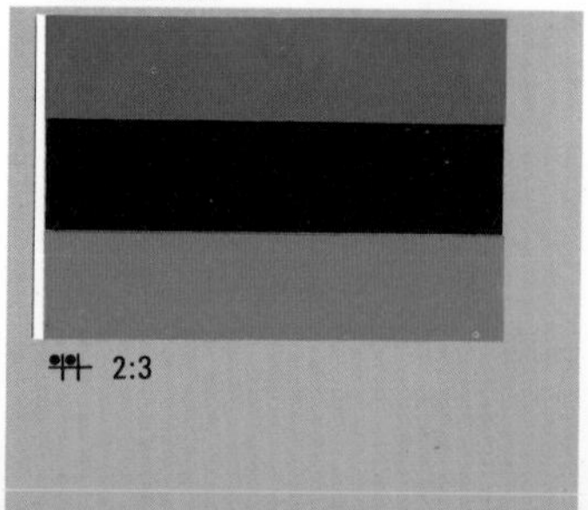

2:3

138

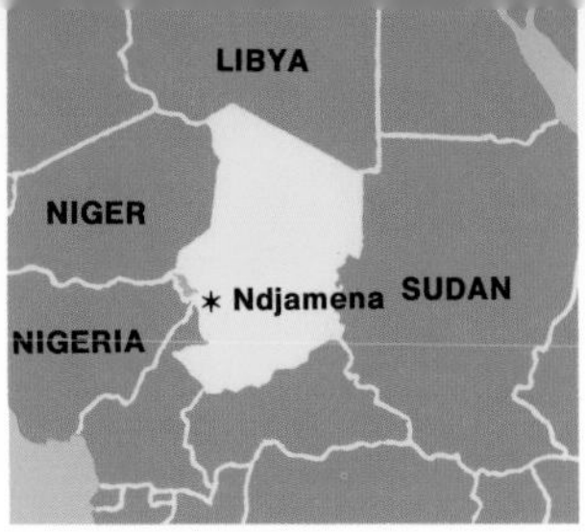

TCHAD

CHAD

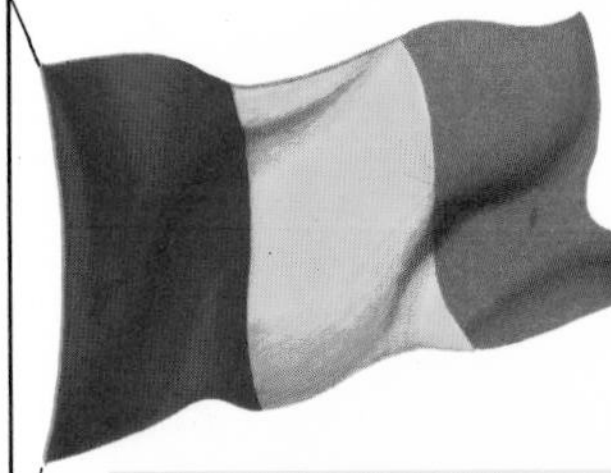

RÉPUBLIQUE DU TCHAD

REPUBLIC OF CHAD

Like some of the other former French colonies, Chad looked to the French Tricolor in creating its own national flag. Here the pan-African colors (green, yellow, and red) have been slightly altered in order that the flag not conflict with those of neighboring countries. The blue stripe has been officially described as a symbol of the sky, hope, agriculture, and the southern part of the country. Yellow is seen as a symbol of both the northern (desert) half of the country and the sun. Red stands for progress, unity, and the willingness of citizens to sacrifice themselves for the country.

The national coat of arms, designed by two Frenchmen in 1970, is in the European style. The national motto ("Unity, Work, Progress") appears on a ribbon at the bottom below a representation of the national order with its ribbon.

Officially adopted 6 November 1959.

2:3

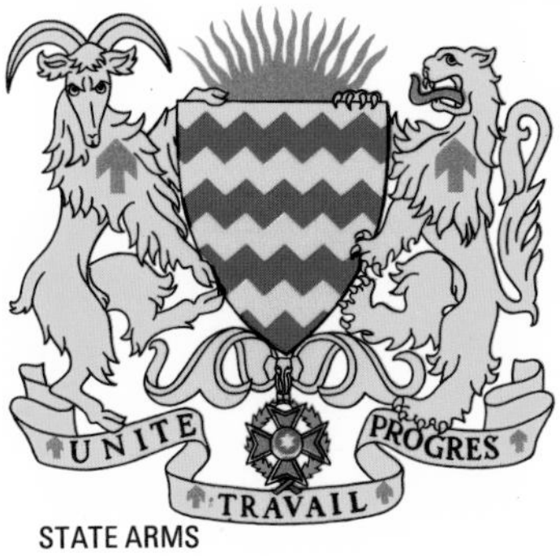

STATE ARMS

In the early days of heraldry, a coat of arms was one of the most personal possessions of an individual. Because a king and the area he ruled were intimately associated, his personal arms came to be considered as the state emblem – a situation that still exists in a few countries. In sharp contrast is the usage of coats of arms today, exemplified by the arms of Chad. Designed by foreigners and appearing largely on postage stamps and medals made expressly for sale to foreigners, the coat of arms is scarcely ever seen within Chad itself. The use of such an emblem is quite alien to the traditions of the country and it is ironic that it became official just at the time when a program of Africanization was introduced throughout the country. The importance of arms in former French colonies is weak, especially since France itself has long lacked an official coat of arms.

139

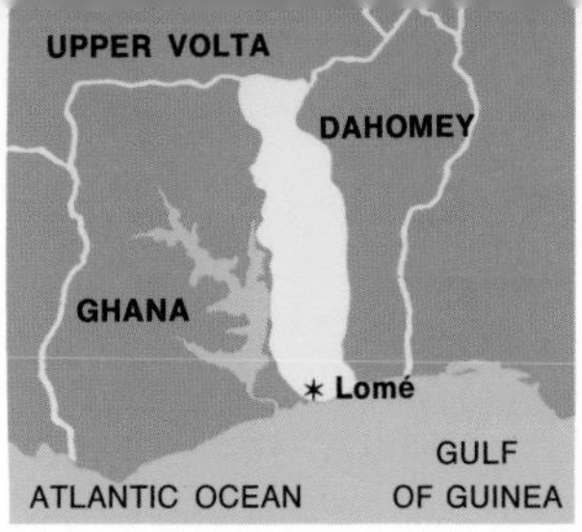

TOGO

TOGO

RÉPUBLIQUE TOGOLAISE

TOGO REPUBLIC

The green stripes in the Togo flag have a double symbolism – hope for the future and the agricultural work of the people on which that hope is founded. The yellow stripes indicate a faith in work as the basis of the moral and material well-being of the nation. The white star, an emblem of purity, is said to be a reminder to all citizens that they must show themselves worthy of their nation's independence. The red of the canton is officially described as "the color of charity, of fidelity, of love, of those cardinal virtues which inspire love of fellow humans and the sacrifice of one's life – if necessary – for the triumph of the principles of humanity and the pushing back of the frontiers of human misery."

Lions in the Togo arms reflect the courage of the people. The bows and arrows call on all citizens to be active in defense of the liberties of the country. The national motto inscribed at the top of the arms translates as "Work, Liberty, Fatherland."

Officially hoisted 27 April 1960.

3:5≈

STATE ARMS

Seeking to abolish the traditional privileges and prerogatives of feudal classes, French revolutionaries in the late eighteenth century introduced uniformity into all aspects of government. Although there have been many modifications of this policy over the years, it has produced a lasting effect in the flags used not only in France but equally in territories once under its control or influence. Thus in Togo, Dahomey, Mali, the Ivory Coast, and elsewhere there is a single flag employed for all purposes – private, public, and military display both on land and at sea. Visually, the usage of one flag instead of many reinforces the concepts of national unity and the responsibility of the central government for the ordering of the society.

140

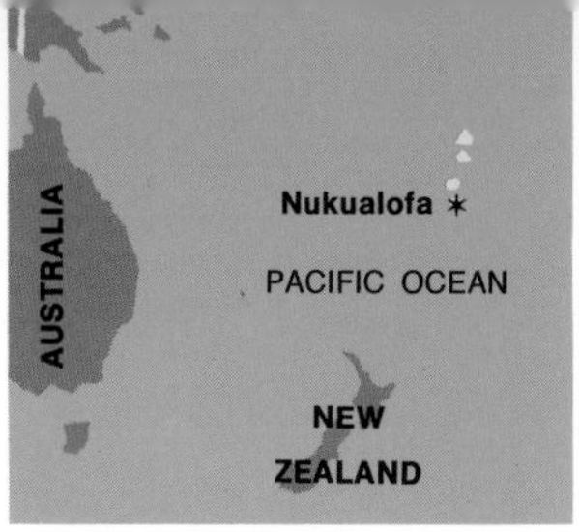

TONGA

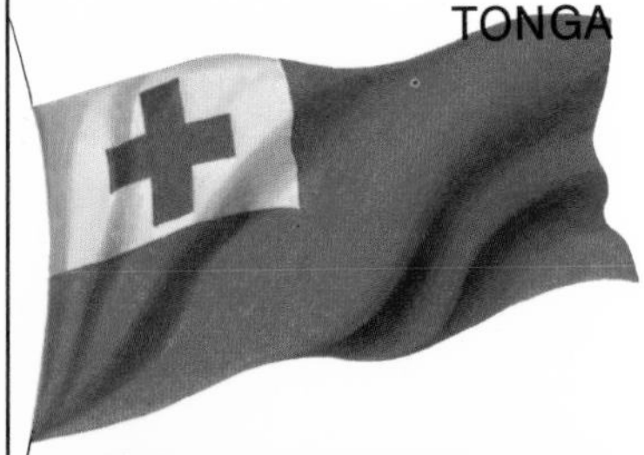

PULE'ANGA TONGA

KINGDOM OF TONGA

Officially confirmed
4 November 1875.

The importance of Christianity, introduced into Tonga in the early nineteenth century, is underscored by the national and royal flags and royal arms.

In the first parliament of the nation, held in 1862, King George Tupou I called for suggestions for a national flag. After much discussion he put forth his own concept in words tradition preserves thus: "It is my wish that our flag should have the cross of Jesus... and the flag should be red in colour to represent the blood shed on the Cross for our salvation." The actual forms of the flags and arms are credited both to Prince Uelingatoni Ngu Tupoumalohi and to Rev. Shirley Baker, a Wesleyan minister.

The 1875 constitution states that "the Flag of Tonga (the flag of King George) shall never be altered." Christianity's dove of peace in the royal banner holds a myrtle leaf, emblem of national unity.

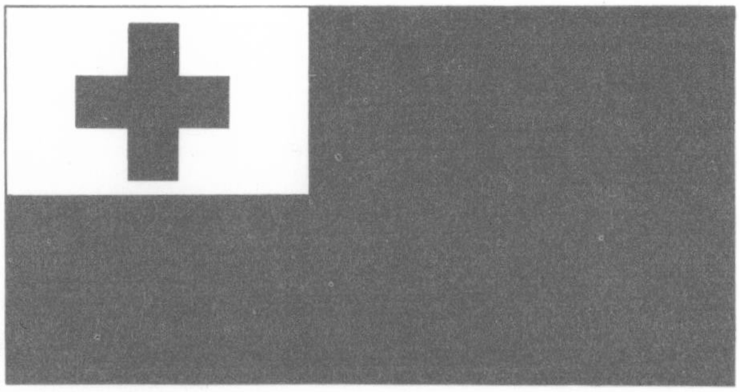

1:2

ROYAL ARMS

ROYAL FLAG

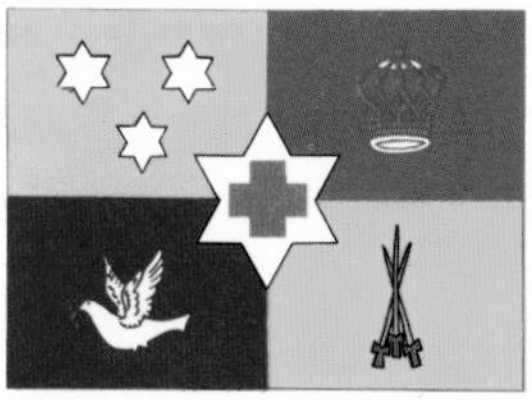

26:37

The stars in the royal flag stand for the main island groups united in Tonga – Tongatapu, Ha'apai, and Vava'u. The motto, chosen by King George Tupou I in 1862, reads "God and Tonga Are My Inheritance." The current royal family is successor to three lines of kings – hence the three swords.

Surrounding the crown are leaves of the chestnut tree, such as were worn by chiefs when they decided matters of life and death. Here they indicate that the sovereign's fate is in the hands of God.

141

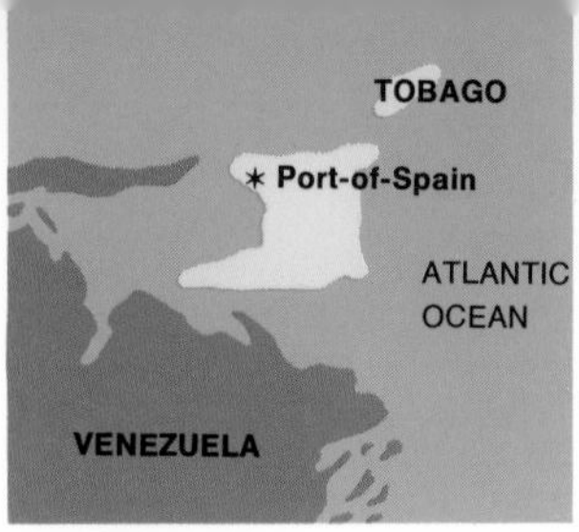

TRINIDAD AND TOBAGO

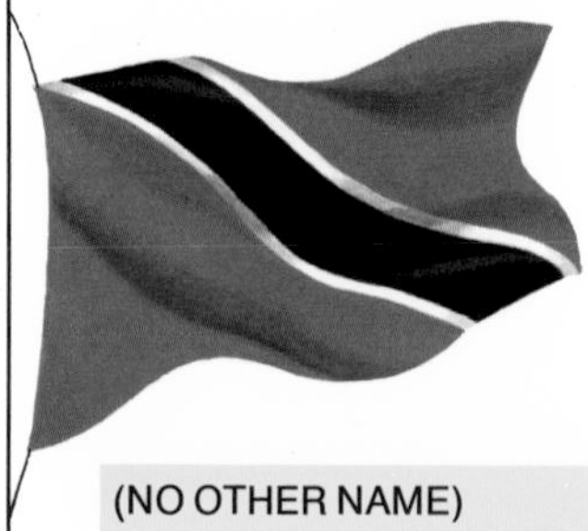

(NO OTHER NAME)

Several interpretations have been given to the colors combined in the arms and flag of this land. Red is said to express the vitality of the land and its peoples, the warmth and energy of the sun, and courage and friendliness.

White is a symbol of the sea, of the purity of national aspirations, and the equality of all men. Black is seen as an emblem of strength, unity, and purpose – as well as the wealth of the land.

Included in the arms are a scarlet ibis, a cocrico, and two hummingbirds – plus the three ships of Christopher Columbus.

Officially hoisted
31 August 1962.

3:5

STATE ARMS

1:2

1:2

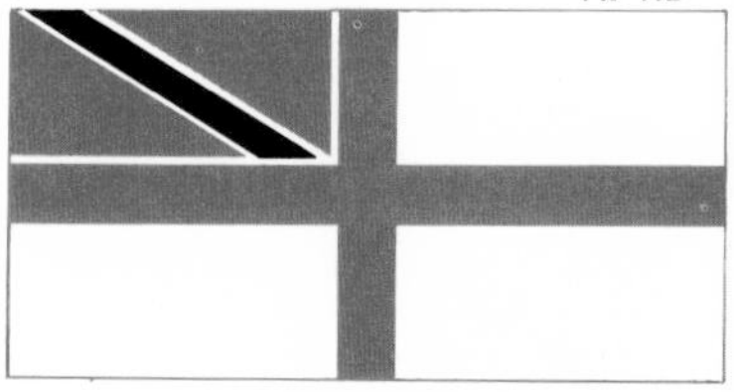

ROYAL FLAG

3:5 ≈

GOVERNOR-GENERAL'S FLAG

1:2 ≈

PRIME MINISTER'S FLAG

3:5 ≈

142

AL TUNISIYA

TUNISIA

AL DJUMHURIYAH
AL TUNISIYAH

TUNISIAN REPUBLIC

Although nominally under Turkish rule since the sixteenth century, Tunisia had considerable local autonomy in the early 1800s. This was expressed in the adoption by Hussain II, Bey of Tunis, of a flag slightly different from that of Turkey.

The new flag was distinctive enough to warrant official inquiries by the Sultan in Istanbul. These were never answered by the bey, and Tunisia's flag did not change. Even later, under French rule and following the abolition of the beylical dynasty, the flag stood unmodified.

Both the Tunisian national coat of arms and presidential standard incorporate the traditional Muslim star and crescent. The coat of arms also has the national motto ("Order, Freedom, Justice") and a ship, recalling that the earliest settlers arrived by boat from Phoenicia.

Usage initiated ca. 1835.

2:3

STATE ARMS

PRESIDENTIAL FLAG

1:1≈

Although the star and crescent had occasionally been employed by Islam in the past, the greatest impetus to that association came from usage by the Ottoman Empire from the fifteenth to the nineteenth centuries. Today the symbol is most common in countries (like Tunisia) that were once under Ottoman rule or in Muslim countries that are not part of the pan-Arab unity movement (which has adopted other symbols).

143

TÜRKİYE

TURKEY

TÜRKİYE CÜMHÜRİYETİ

REPUBLIC OF TURKEY

Red has been prominent in Turkish flags for seven hundred years. The star and crescent are Muslim symbols, but also have a long pre-Islamic past in Asia Minor.

The pagan city of antiquity known as Byzantium was under the protection of Diana, Goddess of the Hunt, whose symbol was a star. In 330 A.D. Constantine rededicated the city (which he called Constantinople) to the Virgin Mary, whose star symbol was added to the previous crescent. The fall of Constantinople in 1453 saw the end of the Byzantine Empire, but the old emblem continued in use. It eventually became the national badge of the new Ottoman rulers.

Although the design was standardized following the overthrow of the Ottoman sultanate and its religious counterpart, the caliphate, it has continued to be employed by the Republic of Turkey.

Officially confirmed 5 June 1936.

2:3

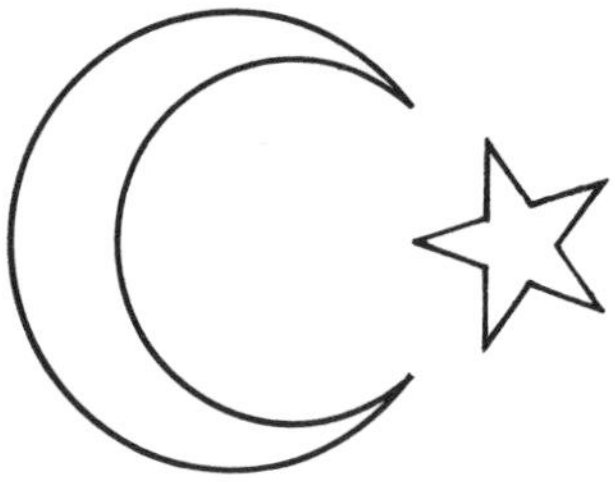

STATE ARMS

PRESIDENT'S FLAG

1:1

A reflection of the moon occulting a star, appearing in pools of blood after the Battle of Kossovo in 1448, led to the adoption of the Turkish flag by Sultan Murad II according to one legend. Others refer to a dream of the first Ottoman emperor in which a crescent and star appeared from his chest and expanded, presaging the dynasty's seizure of Constantinople. At least three other legends explain the flag.

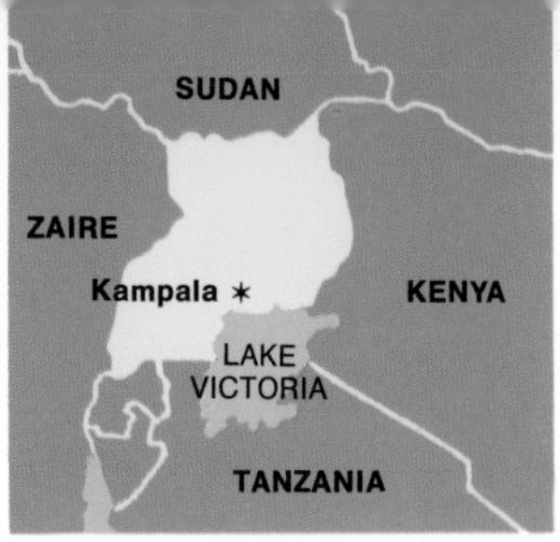

UGANDA

REPUBLIC OF UGANDA

Buganda was a kingdom formerly existing within Uganda.

The crested crane, not having been employed as the emblem of any kingdoms or tribes of Uganda, could therefore serve as a neutral national symbol. It first appeared in the colônial badge of Uganda under British rule.

The original proposal for the national flag was replaced in May of 1962 by a design based on the black-yellow-red flag of the Uganda People's Congress, the party which had just won a national election. The three colors were interpreted to symbolize the people of Africa, sunshine, and brotherhood. The design was suggested by the minister of justice, Mr. Grace Ibingira.

Officially hoisted 9 October 1962.

2:3≈

STATE ARMS

The drum, an important political symbol among traditional intralacustrine East African kingdoms, was incorporated in the flags of three Ugandan kingdoms before the abolition of flags and kingdoms in 1966.

PRESIDENT'S FLAG

1:2≈

Stylized heraldic waters at the top of the national shield are for the lakes and rivers of Uganda; those which flow beneath it indicate Lake Victoria, source of the White Nile. The equatorial position of the country is indicated by the sun, its agricultural economy by the cotton and coffee.

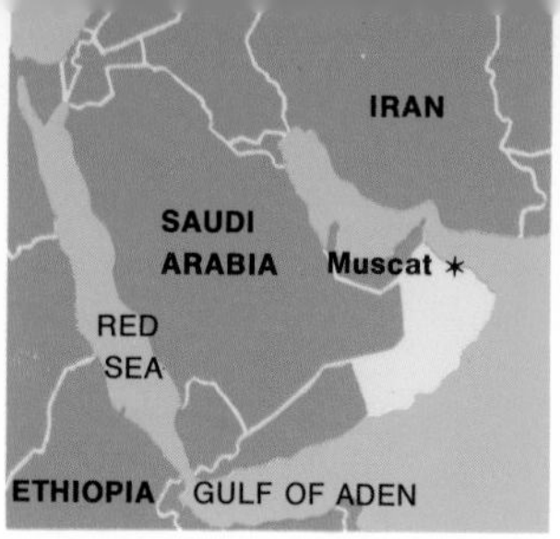

UMAN

OMAN

SULTANAT UMAN

SULTANATE OF OMAN

Until 1970 the official national name was the Sultanate of Muscat and Oman.

The Kharijite ("secessionist") Muslims of eastern Arabia adopted the color red centuries ago. Even in the twentieth century ships from Oman flew a plain red flag as they sailed throughout the Indian Ocean. To modernize this flag, the state arms – supposedly dating back to the middle of the eighteenth century – were added in the upper hoist. The crossed sword and dagger of the arms are traditional weapons among the Omani people.

The broad stripes of white and green were added to symbolize, respectively, peace and fertility. Historically, white had been associated with the imam, religious leader of Oman and at times a political rival to the ruling sultan. Green traditionally was associated with the Djebel al Akhdar (Green Mountains) and with the Hadji, those who had made the pilgrimage to Mecca.

Officially adopted 17 December 1970.

2:3

STATE ARMS

2:3≈

The modernization program of Oman has also resulted in the adoption of a war ensign.

In 1903 Omani vessels flying the French flag to cover their importation of slaves from Africa provoked an international incident. British and French warships were sent to the area, but eventually jurisdiction over the question was given to the International Court of Justice at the Hague. It rendered a decision severely restricting the right of Omani ships to use the French flag, a custom later completely abandoned.

UNITED KINGDOM
SUBDIVISIONS AND
DEPENDENCIES

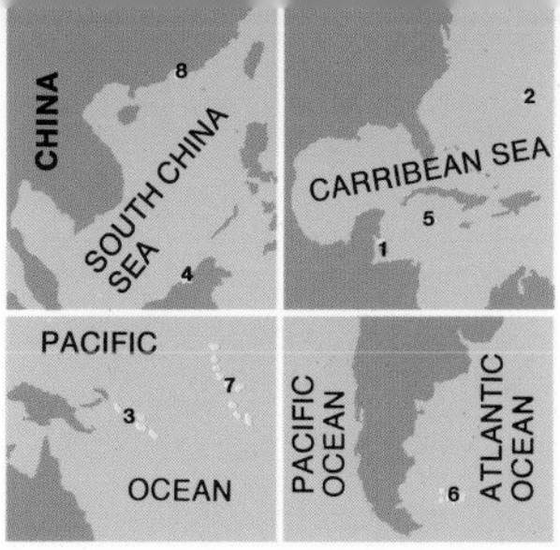

UNITED KINGDOM

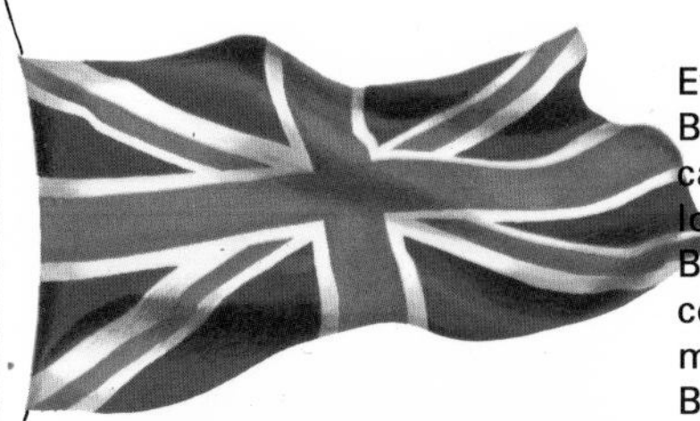

UNITED KINGDOM OF GREAT BRITAIN AND NORTHERN IRELAND

Officially hoisted 1 January 1801.

Even the special chapter on British flags (pages 180–189) can only hint at the rich vexillological history that Great Britain boasts of. The present columns illustrate a few of the many flags currently flown in Britain and the states associated with it in the Commonwealth of Nations.

Many British and Commonwealth flags incorporate the famous Union Jack with its combined crosses of SS. George (for England), Andrew (for Scotland), and Patrick (for Ireland). Others originated in one of the three historic naval flags of Britain – the Red Ensign, White Ensign, and Blue Ensign.

Finally, many such flags relate directly or indirectly to the royal arms of the United Kingdom. Used by elected government officials to show they are Ministers to the Crown, the arms may not without proper authorization be employed by private persons or commercial institutions under penalty of law.

1:2

ROYAL ARMS

The Queen of the United Kingdom is entitled to display a number of flags. In addition to the familiar "Royal Standard" *(above, right),* she is heralded on a ship by a flag with a gold anchor on red, symbolizing her position as Lord High Admiral. A new development since 1950 has been the use of a "personal" flag *(right)* to symbolize her position as Head of the Commonwealth, especially in member countries with republican forms of government. The Queen also has special royal standards for use in Canada, Jamaica, Trinidad and Tobago, Australia, and New Zealand which are illustrated under the sections on those lands.

1:2

1:2

1:2

2:3 ≈

1:2

ROYAL FLAG

1:1

2:3 ≈

1 BELIZE

1:2

2 BERMUDA

1:2

3 BRITISH SOLOMON ISLANDS

1:2

4 BRUNEI

1:2

5 CAYMAN ISLANDS

1:2

6 FALKLAND ISLANDS

1:2

7 GILBERT AND ELLICE ISLANDS

1:2

8 HONG KONG

UNITED KINGDOM SUBDIVISIONS AND DEPENDENCIES

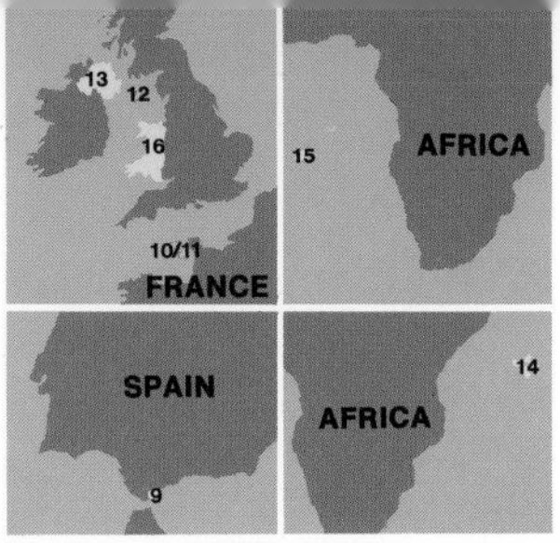

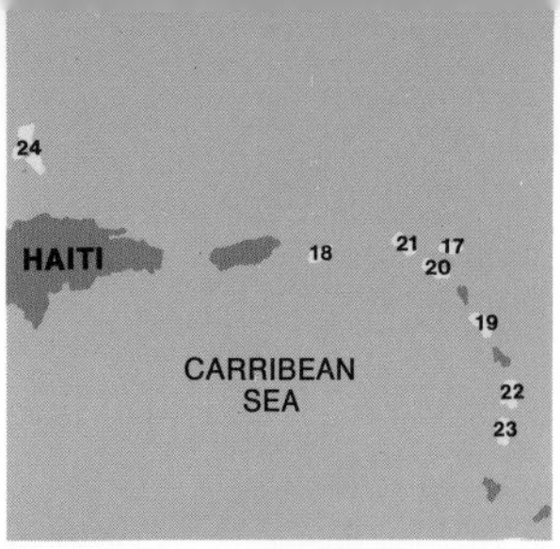

1:2
9 GIBRALTAR

2:3≈
17 ANTIGUA

1:2≈
10 GUERNSEY

1:2
18 BRITISH VIRGIN ISLANDS

1:2≈
11 JERSEY

1:2
19 DOMINICA

1:2
12 ISLE OF MAN

1:2
20 MONTSERRAT

1:2≈
13 NORTHERN IRELAND

1:2
21 ST. CHRISTOPHER NEVIS ANGUILLA

1:2
14 SEYCHELLES

5:8≈
22 ST. LUCIA

1:2
15 ST. HELENA

1:2
23 ST. VINCENT

2:3≈
16 WALES

1:2
24 TURKS AND CAICOS ISLANDS

147

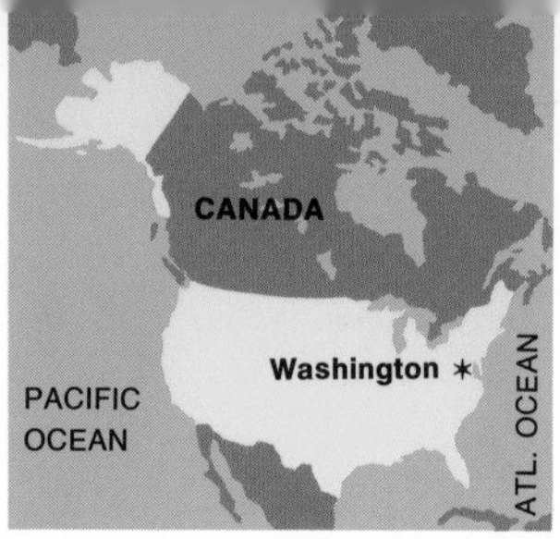

UNITED STATES

UNITED STATES OF AMERICA

Officially hoisted 4 July 1960.

Since its Declaration of Independence on 4 July 1776, the states have increased from thirteen to fifty and the "new constellation" of white stars referred to by the first flag law (14 June 1777) has grown correspondingly.

The original states are recalled in the flag stripes; in the arms they are symbolized by the stars, arrows, and bars on the shield. The motto in the arms, "One out of Many," suggests the federal system of government. More information on the development of the American flag will be found on pages 190–199.

The blue in the shield stands for Congress, the supreme governmental authority under the Articles of Confederation (replaced by the present constitution in 1787). The olive branch and arrows declare the power of Congress to decide matters of peace and war.

10:19

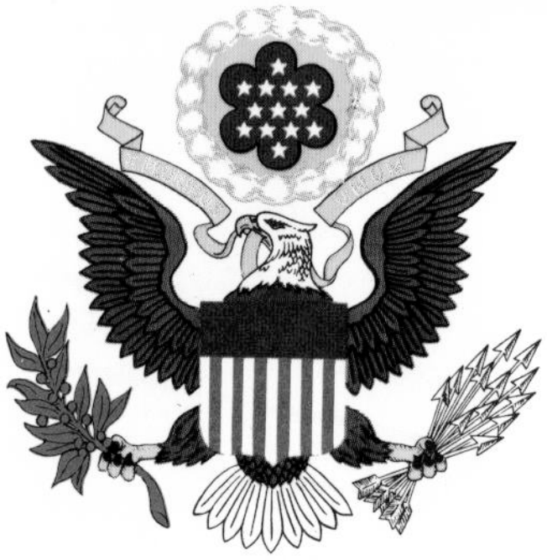
STATE ARMS

PRESIDENTIAL FLAG

26:33

Although many imperial eagles are found in flags and arms throughout history (in Rome, Byzantium, Austria, Germany, Russia, etc.), this is not the eagle's only symbolism.

The neoclassical spirit in America at the end of the eighteenth century looked to the ancient Roman Republic for many symbols, including the name of the upper chamber of its Congress (the Senate). In Rome the eagle began as a republican symbol; hence Americans chose their native bald eagle for the national arms in 1782.

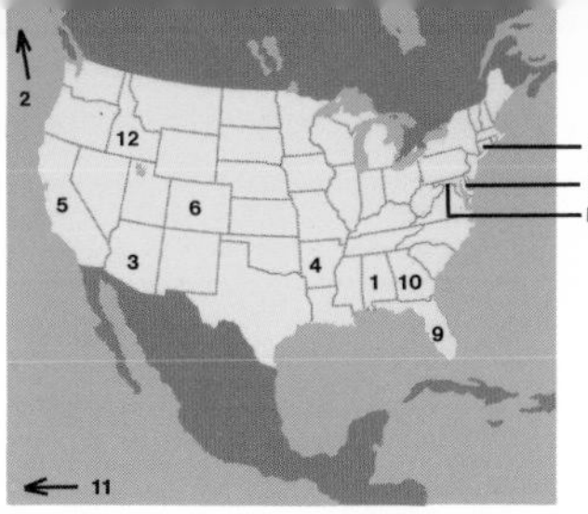

The information provided for each state is, sequentially:
1) the dates the states ratified the constitution (*) or joined the Union; 2) in what order; and
3) when their flags were adopted.

1 ALABAMA 1819 22 1895

1:1 ≈

2 ALASKA 1959 49 1927

125:177

3 ARIZONA 1912 48 1917

2:3

4 ARKANSAS 1836 25 1924

2:3 ≈

5 CALIFORNIA 1850 31 1911

2:3

6 COLORADO 1876 38 1964

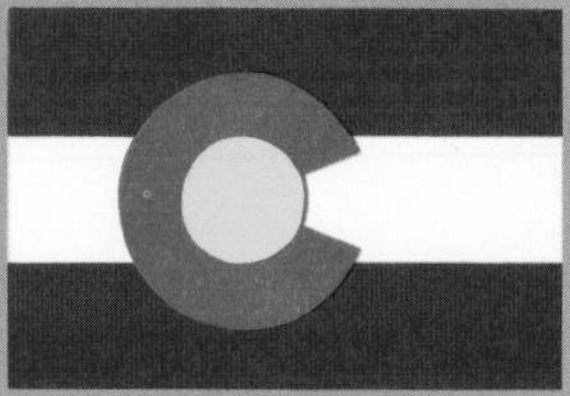

2:3

7 CONNECTICUT 1788* 5 1897

26:33

8 DELAWARE 1787* 1 1913

3:4 ≈

DISTRICT OF COLUMBIA

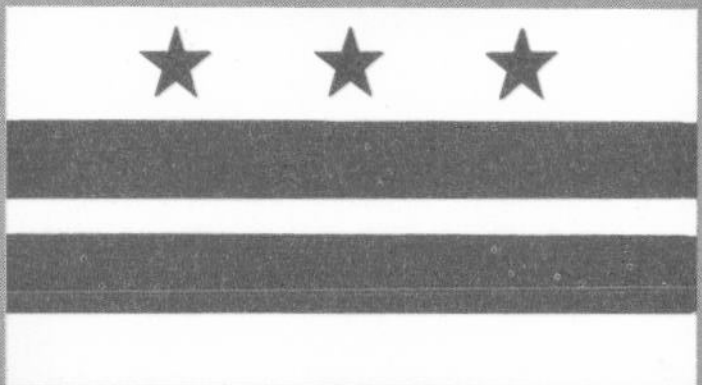

5:9

9 FLORIDA 1845 27 1900

2:3 ≈

10 GEORGIA 1788* 4 1956

2:3

11 HAWAII 1959 50 1845

1:2

12 IDAHO 1890 43 1927

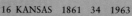

26:33

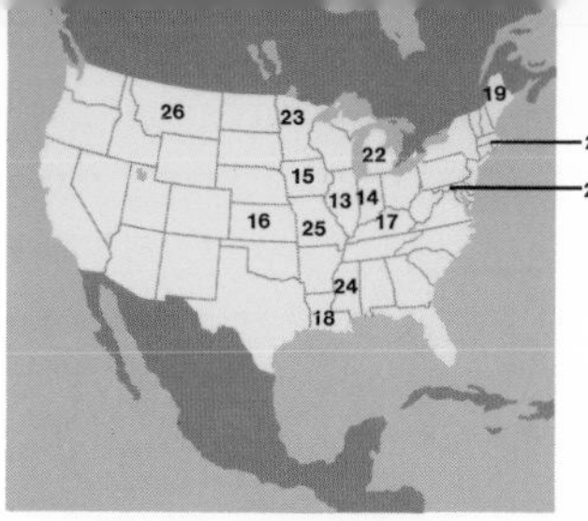

13 ILLINOIS 1818 21 1970

3:5 ≈

14 INDIANA 1816 19 1917

26:33

15 IOWA 1846 29 1921

3:4 ≈

16 KANSAS 1861 34 1963

3:5

17 KENTUCKY, COMMONWEALTH OF 1792 15 1963

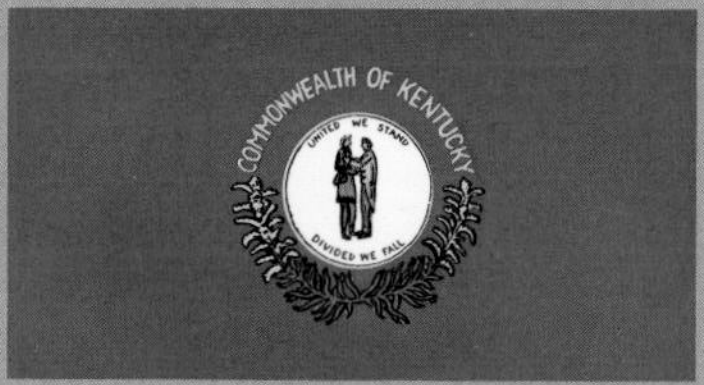

10:19

18 LOUISIANA 1812 18 1912

2:3 ≈

19 MAINE 1820 23 1909

26:33

20 MARYLAND 1788* 7 1904

2:3 ≈

21 MASSACHUSETTS, COMMONWEALTH OF 1788* 6 1971

3:5

22 MICHIGAN 1837 26 1911

2:3 ≈

23 MINNESOTA 1858 32 1957

3:5

24 MISSISSIPPI 1817 20 1894

2:3

25 MISSOURI 1821 24 1913

7:12

26 MONTANA 1889 41 1905

5:6 ≈

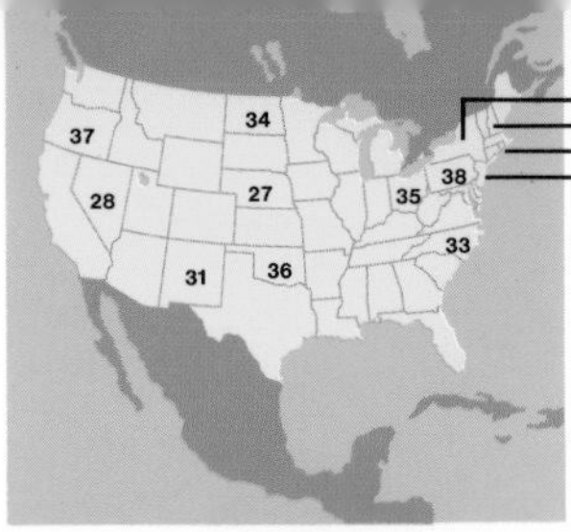

27 NEBRASKA 1867 37 1925

3:5≈

2:3≈

28 NEVADA 1864 36 1929

29 NEW HAMPSHIRE 1788* 9 1932

2:3≈

30 NEW JERSEY 1787* 3 1896

2:3≈

31 NEW MEXICO 1912 47 1925

2:3≈

32 NEW YORK 1788* 11 1901

10:19

33 NORTH CAROLINA 1789* 12 1885

3:4

34 NORTH DAKOTA 1889 39 1911

26:33

35 OHIO 1803 17 1902

8:13

36 OKLAHOMA 1907 46 1941

2:3≈

37 OREGON 1859 33 1925

500:833 ≠

37 OREGON (REVERSE)

500:833

38 PENNSYLVANIA, COMMONWEALTH OF 1787* 2 1907

27:37

39 RHODE ISLAND AND PROVIDENCE PLANTATIONS, STATE OF 1790* 13 1897

29:33

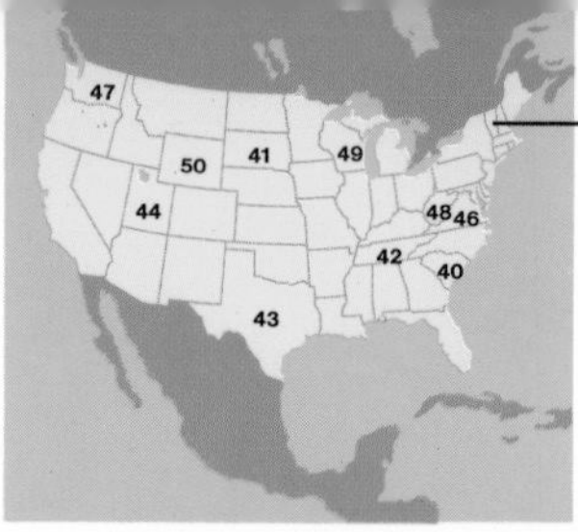

40 SOUTH CAROLINA 1788* 8 1861

2:3≈

3:5

41 SOUTH DAKOTA 1889 40 1963

42 TENNESSEE 1796 16 1905

3:5

43 TEXAS 1845 28 1839

2:3

44 UTAH 1896 45 1913

2:3≈

45 VERMONT 1791 14 1923

2:3≈

46 VIRGINIA, COMMONWEALTH OF 1788* 10 1861

2:3≈

47 WASHINGTON 1889 42 1923

2:3

48 WEST VIRGINIA 1863 35 1929

10:19

49 WISCONSIN 1848 30 1913

26:33

50 WYOMING 1890 44 1917

7:10

TERRITORIES
First row: American Samoa, flag adopted, 1960. Guam, 1917.
Second row: Puerto Rico, Commonwealth of, 1952. Trust Territory of the Pacific Islands, 1962. Virgin Islands of the United States 1921.

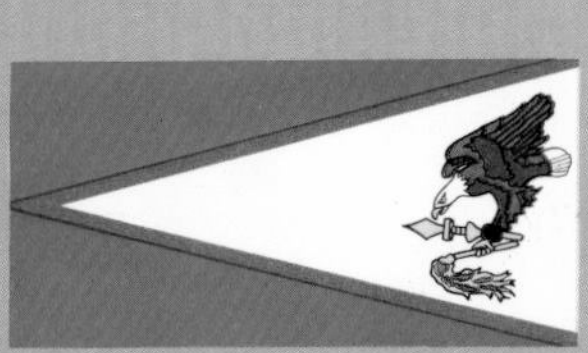

1:2≈

21:40

2:3≈

10:19

2:3≈

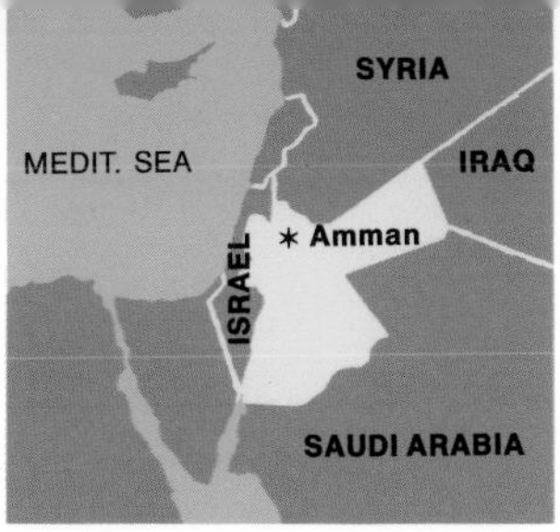

AL URDUN

JORDAN

AL MAMLAKAH
AL URDUNNIYAH
AL HASHIMIYAH

JORDANIAN HASHEMITE KINGDOM

King Hussein of the Hijaz (now part of Saudi Arabia) led the Arab Revolt against Turkey in World War I under the first flag to combine what came to be known as the pan-Arab colors (see also page 155).

In only slightly modified form this flag has continued to the present in Jordan, under the dynasty founded by Hussein; it also has influenced the design of many other Arab flags, including those currently displayed by the United Arab Emirates and Kuwait.

The seven points of the star refer to the seven verses basic to Islamic belief which open the Koran.

1:2

ROYAL ARMS

1:2 ≈

1:2 ≈

The Jordan state arms are similar to those formerly used by King Hussein of the Hijaz. The shield, helmet, and eagle emblem of Saladin figure prominently. The inscription reads: "The King of the Hashemite Kingdom of Jordan, al-Hussein bin-Talal bin-Abdulla, Beseeches the Almighty for Aid and Success."

ROYAL FLAG

1:2

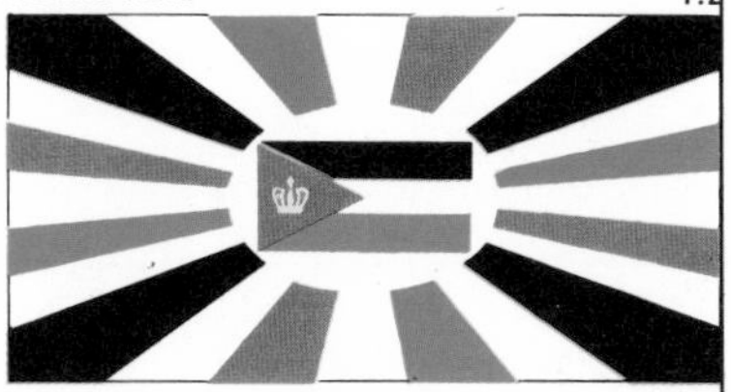

URUGUAY

URUGUAY

REPÚBLICA ORIENTAL DEL URUGUAY

REPUBLIC EAST OF THE URUGUAY

Prior to independence, Uruguay was known as the Eastern Strip.

As part of the United Provinces of the River Plate which rose against Spanish rule in 1812, Uruguay used the blue and white flag and gold sun, which to this day continue as national symbols of Argentina. Nevertheless, under the leadership of General José Artigas, Uruguay began very early to seek independence from Argentina as well. One version of Artigas's flag (blue-white-blue horizontal stripes crossed by a red diagonal) continues to be in use today as the Uruguayan jack.

Another banner associated with early Uruguayan patriot heroes is the flag of the Thirty and Three, a blue-white-red tricolor inscribed "Liberty or Death." This flag, raised in 1825 and still considered an official symbol, failed to become the national flag. Instead in 1828 when Uruguay achieved its definitive independence, a new banner was chosen. The nine blue stripes in that flag – and the nine blue and white stripes in the present flag – recall the nine departments into which Artigas had divided Uruguay.

Officially adopted 11 July 1830.

2:3

STATE ARMS

PRESIDENTIAL FLAG

3:5 ≈

The golden sun common to the Uruguayan flag and arms is a symbol of independence. The arms also include a balance (emblem of equality and justice) and the hill of Montevideo (symbol of strength). Liberty and plenty are seen in the horse and ox in the third and fourth quarters. Branches of olive and laurel bound with a ribbon of the national color complete the design.

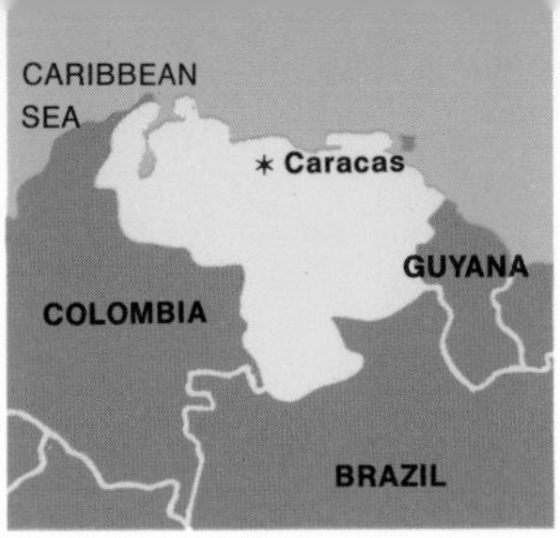

VENEZUELA
VENEZUELA

REPÚBLICA DE VENEZUELA

REPUBLIC OF VENEZUELA

The Venezuelan flag is related to those of Ecuador and Colombia.

The flag of Venezuela was first hoisted on the soil of America on 12 March 1806 by the leader in the independence movement, Francisco de Miranda. There is a tradition that the blue and red horizontal stripes were borrowed from the flag of Haiti, the place from which Miranda's invasion of Venezuela was launched. Nevertheless, a more likely source of the colors is the flag proposed by the leaders of the abortive Venezuelan revolution of 1797, Manuel Gual and José María España. Its stripes of white, blue, red, and yellow stood respectively for the whites, blacks, mulattoes, and Indians. The first use of the stars – one for each of the original provinces – dates from 1817; they became a permanent part of the flag in 1859. Since independence in 1830, Venezuela's flag has undergone only minor modifications – in its coat of arms and the arrangement of its stars.

Officially adopted 19 February 1954.

2:3

STATE ARMS

2:3

SUCRE

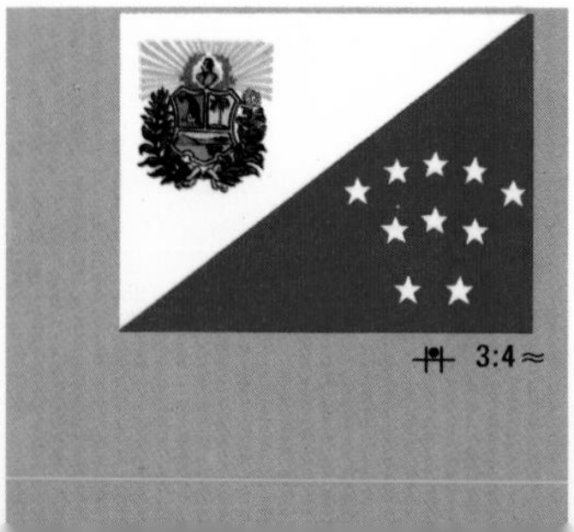

3:4≈

Since 1836 the Venezuelan arms have featured a running horse for liberty, cornucopias for plenty, a wheat sheaf for the unity of its provinces, and a display of weapons honoring independence.

VIỆT-NAM
VIET-NAM

CỘNG HÒA MIÊN NAM VIỆT NAM

REPUBLIC OF SOUTH VIET-NAM

In 1960 the South Viet-Nam National Liberation Front (NFL) was organized by Communists and their allies within the Republic of Viet-Nam. The flag chosen by the Front closely resembled that of the Democratic Republic of Viet-Nam in the north.

Gold is the traditional Viet-Namese color, and the star is a Communist symbol of long standing. The five points of the star in the NLF flag stand for the unity of intellectuals, peasants, workers, businessmen, and soldiers. Red is the traditional color of revolutionary struggle.

The sky blue is described as being emblematic of peace, although it may also have been adopted because that color has been used in the symbols of the Montagnards and other peoples of South Viet-Nam.

So far as is known, the Republic of South Viet-Nam has not adopted a coat of arms. Its flag continues to be used by the NLF, which dominates the country's Provisional Revolutionary Government.

Officially adopted 8 June 1969.

2:3

In January 1973, agreements were signed in Paris to end the direct involvement of the United States in the Viet-Namese civil war. Through its participation in the negotiation conference and signature of the agreements, the Republic of South Viet-Nam achieved international legal standing, as the Democratic Republic of Viet-Nam had nineteen years previously at another Paris conference concerning Viet-Nam. Cuba had been the first country to give diplomatic recognition to the Republic of South Viet-Nam, in March of 1969.

152

VIỆT-NAM

VIET-NAM

VIỆT-NAM CỘNG-HÒA

REPUBLIC OF VIET-NAM

Ceased to exist as an independent country on 30 April 1975.

Yellow was the traditional imperial color of Viet-Nam, even during the period when the country was under a French protectorate. Imperial flags showed a dragon, while national flags added one or more stripes of red (symbolic of success and good fortune) to the yellow background.
The earliest yellow and red striped flag appears to have been the one hoisted at the beginning of the nineteenth century when Emperor Gia Long sought to prevent his country from being conquered by the French. Under the Japanese puppet regime established in 1945, three red horizontal lines, the center

Officially adopted 14 June 1948.

2:3

one broken in the middle, were represented on a yellow flag. That symbol was the traditional hieroglyph for the "Land of the South."
In 1948 when negotiations for autonomy were being conducted with the French, the flag shown was established in which the three red stripes were introduced to represent the main regions of the country – Tonkin, Annam, and Cochin-China.

Different symbols were used, both officially and unofficially, by the Republic of Viet-Nam as state arms. These included a triangle bearing two pens, a scroll, and bamboo trees; a shield with the design of the national flag; and a disc of similar design flanked by dragons.

The best available information indicates that no coat of arms was officially recognized.

153

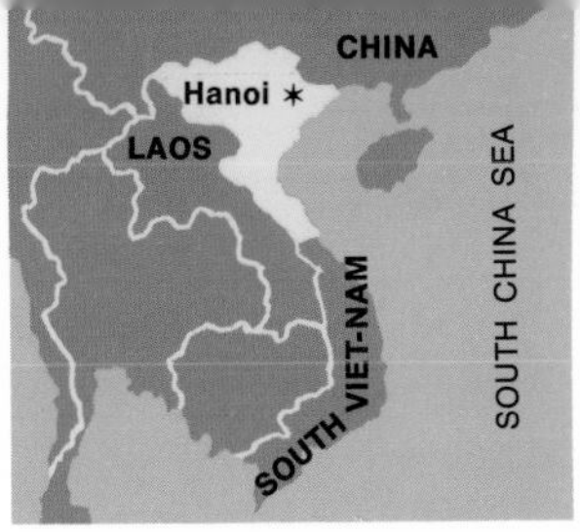

VIỆT-NAM

VIET-NAM

VIỆT-NAM DÂN CHỦ CỘNG HÒA

DEMOCRATIC REPUBLIC OF VIET-NAM

The independence of Viet-Nam seemed about to be realized in late August 1945. The Japanese, who had occupied all of Indochina in 1940, withdrew their troops and Emperor Bao Dai officially transferred his "mandate from heaven" to forces led by Ho Chi-minh. On 29 September 1945 a design dating from at least 1940 became the official flag of the Democratic Republic of Viet-Nam.
That flag differed only slightly from the one that replaced it in 1955 after ten years of struggle to preserve national independence and unity. Instead of the regular five-pointed star which is now official, the original flag had a wide-angle star, i.e., one in which the inner diameter equaled one-half the outer diameter. The wide-angle star is found in the symbols of certain other Communist countries; it is shown, for example, in the current arms of Romania and Lithuania. The national anthem of the Democratic Republic, *Marching to the Front,* states "...Our flag, red with the blood of victory, bears the spirit of our country.... Soldiers of Viet-Nam, we go forward, the gold star of our flag in the wind, leading our people, our native land, out of misery and suffering...."

Officially adopted 30 November 1955.

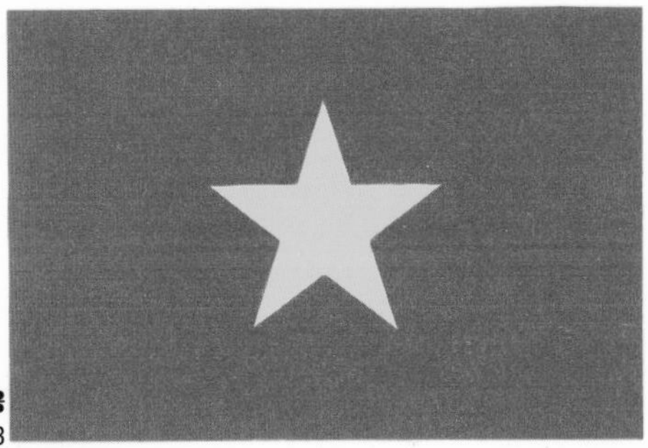

2:3

STATE ARMS

In the state arms of the Democratic Republic of Viet-Nam decreed in 1956, the central portion recalls the design of the state flag. Surrounding it is a wreath of rice, the chief crop of this largely agricultural land. The will to industrialize is reflected in the cogwheel at the bottom. Instead of a motto, the name of the state is written on the ribbon that binds the sheaves of rice.

154

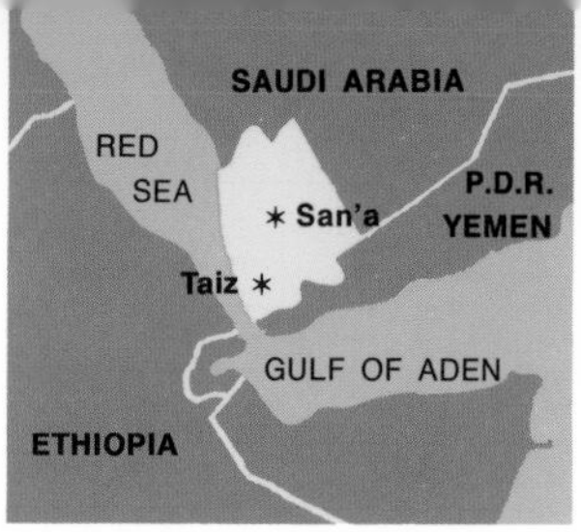

AL YAMAN

YEMEN

AL DJUMHURIYAH
AL ARABIYAH
AL YAMANIYAH

YEMEN ARAB REPUBLIC

Yemen experienced a revolution in 1962 which completely altered its national symbols. The red stripe in the new flag is the revolutionary spirit which motivated the Yemeni people in almost a decade of civil war that secured the establishment of the republic. Black is for the dark days of the past, and white expresses hope in a better future. The single star symbolizes unity and independence.
An eagle representing the strength of the Yemeni people overshadows a ribbon with the name of the state inscribed on it. The coffee plant on the shield is appropriate, mocha coffee being named for the Yemini city of Al-Mukha. Below the coffee is a representation of the Marib Dam, an important structure in the national irrigation system from the time of its building in the seventh century B.C. to the time of its collapse in the sixth century A.D.

Officially hoisted ca. 1 November 1962.

2:3

STATE ARMS

Further information on Yemeni flags will be found on page 155.
In 1958 Egypt and Syria created a unitary state, the United Arab Republic, and Iraq and Jordan formed a federation, the Arab Union. Both had distinctive flags. The same year Yemen and the United Arab Republic confederated under the name United Arab States. Because of the loose ties between the two member states, the United Arab States did not have a distinctive flag of its own.

155

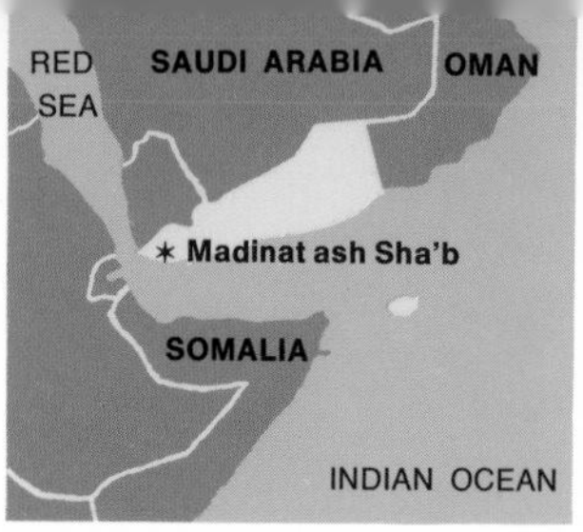

AL YAMAN

YEMEN

AL DJUMHURIYAH
AL YAMAN
AL DIMUQRATIYAH
AL SHABIYAH

DEMOCRATIC PEOPLE'S REPUBLIC OF YEMEN

The oppressive colonial and feudal regimes in Yemen's past are reflected in the flag's black stripe. White is for peace and red for revolution; the light blue triangle represents the people of the nation under the leadership of the National Liberation Front – symbolized by the red star.
The flag was based on the red-white-black banner of the National Liberation Front. That organization struggled for years to overthrow the almost two dozen local rulers who divided the land under British overlordship. The success of the front was such that, rather than granting independence as they had done in other colonies around the world, the British were forced to recognize a country which had already liberated itself. With the addition of the triangle and star, the flag of the front became that of the state.
The Yemeni coat of arms is based on the model in use by the United Arab Republic at the time Yemen achieved independence. The golden eagle of Saladin grasps a plaque with the name of the state.

Usage initiated ca. 30 November 1967.

2:3

STATE ARMS

Although it is officially the Democratic People's Republic of the Yemen, the nation is sometimes called Democratic Yemen or Yemen (Aden) to differentiate it from its western neighbor, the Yemen Arab Republic. The People's Democratic Republic of Yemen has had other names in the past – People's Republic of Southern Yemen, Federation of South Arabia, Federation of Arab Emirates of the South, and Aden Protectorate.

ZAÏRE

ZAIRE

RÉPUBLIQUE DU ZAÏRE

REPUBLIC OF ZAIRE

More information on Zaire flags appears on pages 200–203.

The original proposal for a new Zaire flag in 1971 displayed a narrow red horizontal stripe above the central yellow disc, recalling the blood of national martyrs. A corresponding stripe below the disc was blue, to symbolize the rivers and lakes of the country.
The stripes were omitted in the final design, which bears a modification of the emblem of the Popular Movement of the Revolution. The flag incorporates the pan-African colors of red, yellow, and green.
The presidential flag is displayed by the chief executive in his capacity as captain general of the Zaire Armed Forces. In addition to modern weapons, the flag shows the traditional lance and arrow framed by a palm branch and elephant tusk. The national motto ("Justice, Peace, Work") appears below the representation of a stone.

Officially hoisted ca. 20 November 1971.

2:3≈

STATE ARMS

PRESIDENT'S FLAG

3:4≈

Upon independence both the French territory known as Middle Congo and its neighbor to the south, the Belgian Congo, adopted the name Republic of the Congo. The names of their capital cities were often unofficially used to distinguish the two (Congo-Brazzaville and Congo-Leopoldville).
In part to avoid this confusion, the former Belgian colony changed its name first to the Democratic Republic of the Congo and later to the Republic of Zaire.

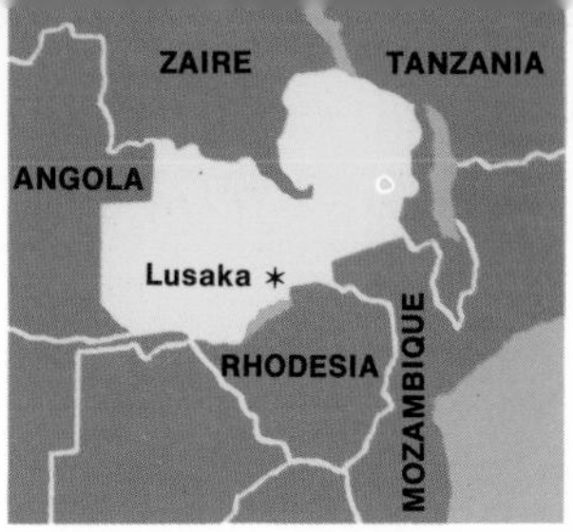

ZAMBIA

ZAMBIA

REPUBLIC OF ZAMBIA

The Zambian flag is exceptional in having its charges concentrated in its fly half.

Prior to the independence of Zambia, the United Nationalist Independence Party (UNIP), which spearheaded the struggle for freedom from Britain, employed a flag of four colors. The green field of the UNIP flag and its black and red colors survived in the state flag of Zambia; its yellow was changed to orange.
The symbolism of the colors has been altered slightly: green and orange are said to stand for natural resources and mineral wealth, black for the Zambian people, and red for the struggle for freedom. The eagle symbolizes the ability of the nation to rise above problems.

Officially hoisted 24 October 1964.

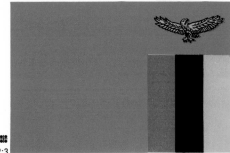

2:3

STATE ARMS

The arms of Zambia are closely related to its flag without repeating the design exactly. Here the eagle hovers over a heraldic representation of Victoria Falls, the white waters streaming over black rocks. This shield dates back to 1927 when, in a slightly different form, it was devised for use by the Colony of Northern Rhodesia.

PRESIDENTIAL FLAG

2:3

The men and women of Zambia (who figure as arms supporters) rely on the land whose mineral riches, wildlife, and agricultural produce figure in the mine shafthead, zebra, and ear of corn below the shield. The black shield (suggesting the black population) is a link to the Zambezi River from which the name of Zambia is derived. The motto at the bottom stresses the importance of national unity, while the eagle of liberty reflects a common aspiration to rise to greater things.

INTERNATIONAL FLAGS

In 1463 King George of Bohemia proposed a universal peace organization: Article 16 of the treaty upon which the organization would have been based provided for a distinctive international coat of arms and seal. No specific designs were mentioned nor was any flag anticipated, but these are nevertheless perhaps the oldest proposals for universal symbols.

Since that time, particularly in the twentieth century, there have been attempts to conceive of flags and other symbols that might encompass all humanity. White and blue are very popular colors in such flags; both stand for peace. Olive branches, also symbolic of peace, chains indicating the linking of peoples or nations, and stars of independence and unity are among the emblems popular with regional groupings whether they concern themselves with political unification, economic coordination, or military defence. The influence of the United Nations flag is evident in the designs of many other international flags.

The final six flags in the illustrations at right are only representative samples from among a great number of international flags used by nongovernmental organizations and movements. The Sovereign Military Order of Malta, founded in the Middle Ages, today runs hospitals and ambulance services. The Cooperative Movement, which seeks to reorganize the economic system, shows the colors of the rainbow for its flag. The Flag of the Race is flown throughout Spanish-speaking countries of the world to affirm their common cultural and linguistic ties.

Many religions and churches have adopted distinctive flags of their own, but few are so widely used as the Buddhist flag originally designed by an American convert living in Ceylon. While local organizations of each country in the Scout and Guide movement across the world have flags of their own, both the Boy Scouts and Girl Scouts have officially recognized international flags as well. Other organizations with social, fraternal, scholarly, technical, and other motivations have recognized the importance of a common symbol. The halyards on which actual flags are hoisted inspired the design of the flag adopted by the International Federation of Vexillological Associations. Finally, there are unofficial internationally recognized flags of plain color (page 15) whose usage is based on tradition rather than law or some other formal adoption procedure.

The flags opposite have been presented in a single shape and size. The correct proportions however are provided below each flag.

INTERNATIONAL INSTITUTIONS

UNITED NATIONS 2:3

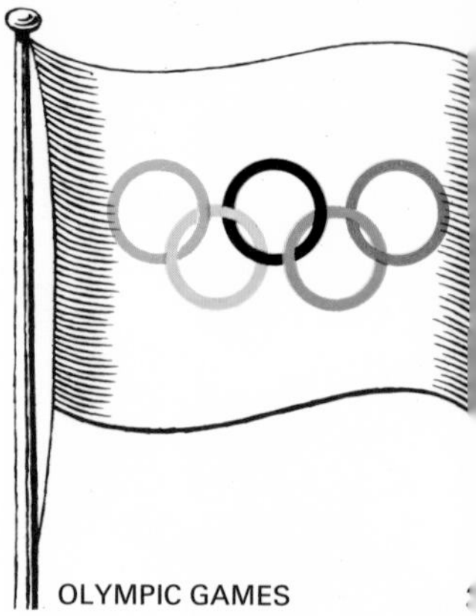
OLYMPIC GAMES

REGIONAL ORGANIZATIONS

COUNCIL OF EUROPE 2:3

LEAGUE OF ARAB STATES

ORGANIZATION OF AFRICAN UNITY 2:3

EAST AFRICAN COMMUNITY

OTHER INTERNATIONAL FLAGS

ORDER OF MALTA 2:3

COOPERATIVE MOVEMENT

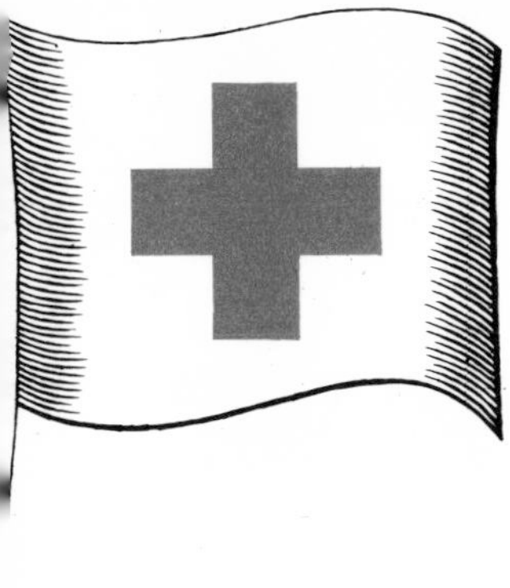

RED CROSS 1:1

RED CRESCENT 1:1

RED LION AND SUN 1:1

COMMONWEALTH OF NATIONS 1:2

ORGANIZATION OF AMERICAN STATES 2:3

SOUTH PACIFIC COMMISSION 2:3

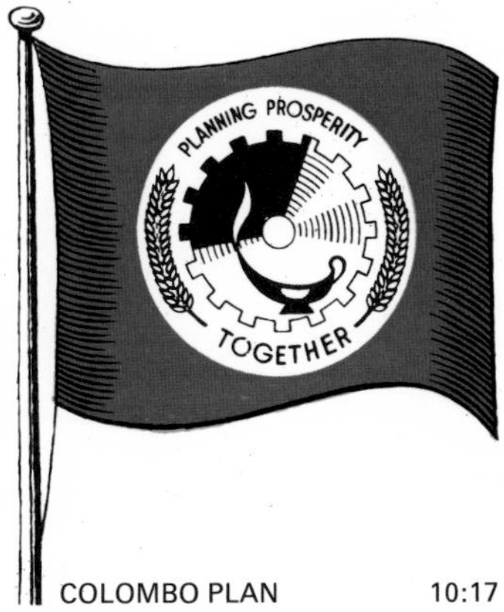

COLOMBO PLAN 10:17

ORGANIZATION OF CENTRAL AMERICAN STATES 2:3

SOUTH-EAST ASIA TREATY ORGANIZATION 2:3

NORTH ATLANTIC TREATY ORGANIZATION 2:3

CENTRAL COMMISSION FOR THE NAVIGATION OF THE RHINE 2:3

FOUR POWER JOINT MILITARY COMMISSION (VIET-NAM, 1973) 1:1

FLAG OF THE [HISPANIC] RACE 5:9

BUDDHIST FLAG 2:3

INTERNATIONAL FEDERATION OF VEXILLOLOGICAL ASSOCIATIONS 2:3

WORLD SCOUT FLAG 2:3

ETHNIC AND CULTURAL MINORITIES

The impulse to create and display a flag runs strong among the peoples of the world, even those who do not have nation-states of their own. Some of the flags illustrated here have official recognition, while others are illegal – their very appearance being considered an act of agression against an existing political system. Because of their unofficial nature, not all of these flags are accepted by those the flags purport to represent, nor are the designs as precise as most national flags. Among the major cultural and ethnic minorities of the world without flags of their own are the Eskimos, Maoris, the Cape Coloureds, American Indians and the Lapps.

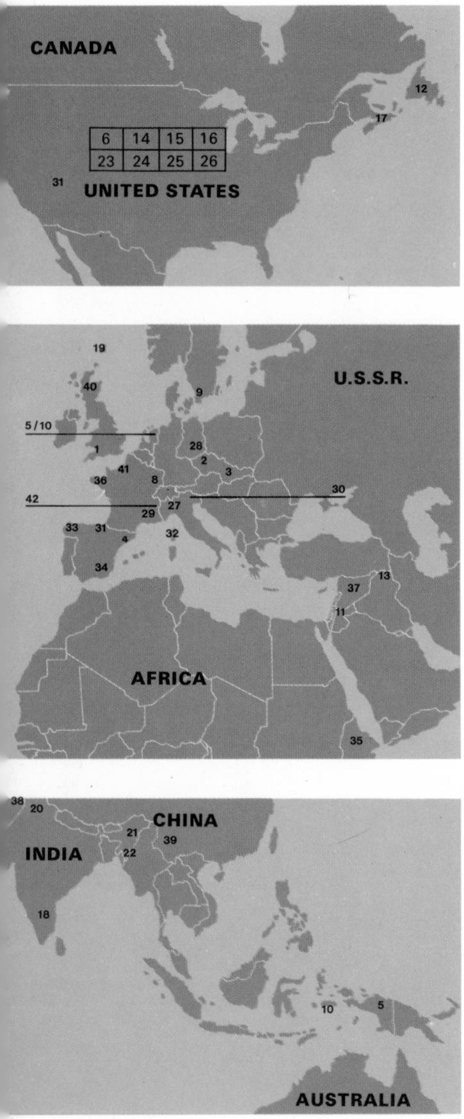

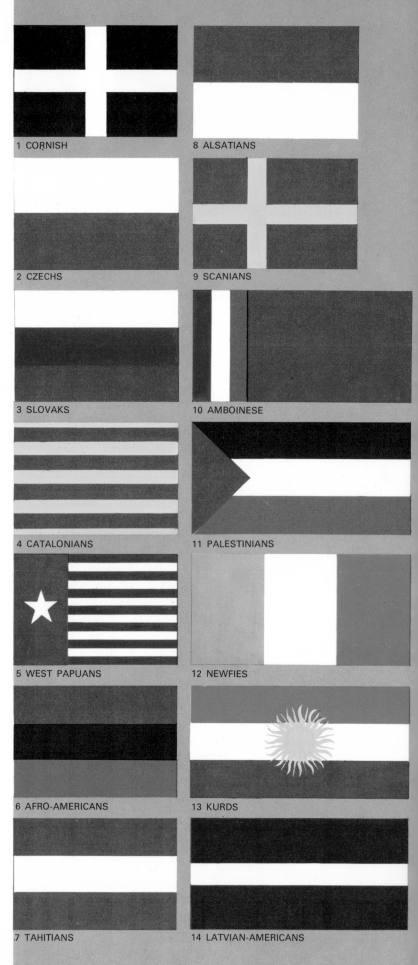

1 Cornish
2 Czechs
3 Slovaks
4 Catalonians
5 West Papuans
6 Afro-Americans
7 Tahitians
8 Alsatians
9 Scanians
10 Amboinese
11 Palestinians
12 Newfies
13 Kurds
14 Latvian-Americans
15 Larrakians
16 Armenian-Americans
17 Acadians
18 Tamils
19 Shetlanders
20 Sikhs
21 Nagas
22 Mizos
23 Irish-Americans
24 Ukrainian-Americans
25 Lithuanian-Americans
26 Estonian-Americans
27 Piedmontese
28 Sorbs
29 Provencals
30 Ladins
31 Basques
32 Corsicans
33 Galicians
34 Valencians
35 Eritreans
36 Bretons
37 Assyrians
38 Sindhis
39 Kachins
40 Scots
41 Normans
42 Occitanians

1 CORNISH

2 CZECHS

3 SLOVAKS

4 CATALONIANS

5 WEST PAPUANS

6 AFRO-AMERICANS

7 TAHITIANS

8 ALSATIANS

9 SCANIANS

10 AMBOINESE

11 PALESTINIANS

12 NEWFIES

13 KURDS

14 LATVIAN-AMERICANS

5 LARRAKIANS

6 ARMENIAN-AMERICANS

7 ACADIANS

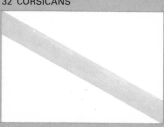

8 TAMILS

9 SHETLANDERS

0 SIKHS

1 NAGAS

22 MIZOS

23 IRISH-AMERICANS

24 UKRAINIAN-AMERICANS

25 LITHUANIAN-AMERICANS

26 ESTONIAN-AMERICANS

27 PIEDMONTESE

28 SORBS

29 PROVENCALS

30 LADINS

31 BASQUES

32 CORSICANS

33 GALICIANS

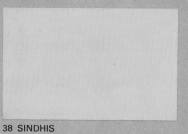

34 VALENCIANS

35 ERITREANS

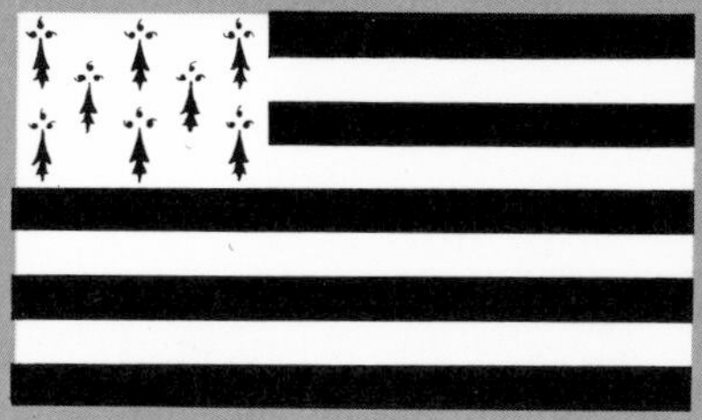

36 BRETONS

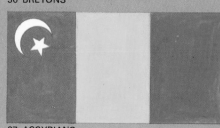

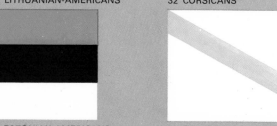

37 ASSYRIANS

38 SINDHIS

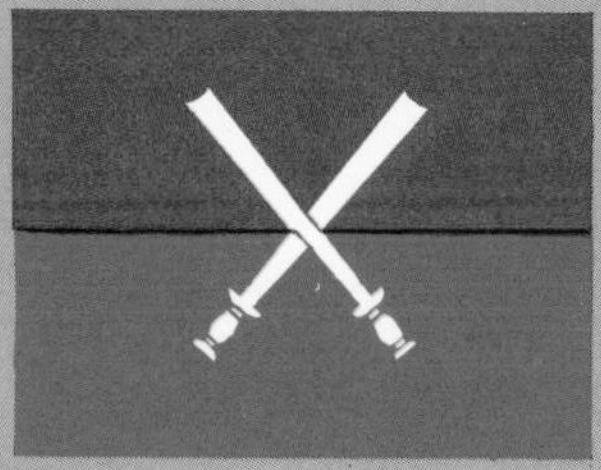

39 KACHINS

40 SCOTS

41 NORMANS

42 OCCITANIANS

"IT IS IN AND THROUGH *SYMBOLS* THAT MAN, CONSCIOUSLY OR UNCONSCIOUSLY, LIVES, WORKS, AND HAS HIS BEING."

Thomas Carlyle, *Sartor Resartus*.

SYMBOLS

The composition of the thousands of flags in existence around the world – such as those of Swiss towns *(right)* – depends on distinctive symbols. While each has a meaning and history behind it, these symbols, such as the daggers and sun in the flag of the queen of Nepal *(above)*, may simply be appreciated for their beauty.

What is the fundamental nature of humanity – Political Animal? Tool Maker? *Homo sapiens?* Each designation contains a good deal of truth, yet none would be possible if Man the Symbol-User did not exist. Symbols are perhaps the most important tool we have invented; they allow us to think by channeling the myriad sense impressions we constantly receive into manageable and orderly categories. Moreover, since these symbols are developed by groups rather than individuals, they provide us with a medium of communication fundamental to every social transaction – political, economic, artistic, religious, etc. Symbols are the link which humans forge between their internal selves and external conditions and events. If symbols do not always reflect reality accurately, at least they allow people to manipulate and reorder the world better to their liking.

Flags, of course, constitute only a small part of the great range of symbols invented. Aside from some overlapping influences, this book is not at all concerned with the symbols of art, religion, philosophy, mathematics, psychology, logic, linguistics, or literature. Even within political symbolism, of which flags are a major part, many areas cannot be dealt with in the scope of this book. Yet many of the same general principles of flag symbolism operate among other symbols as well. For example, in every area of life, sym-

R

The fourteenth century banner of Florence *(below)* bears a distinctive symbol – the fleur-de-lis – perhaps best known as the royal emblem of France. The same figure appears in the arms of North Dakota and Grenada and in the flag of

Quebec. It is a traditional symbol of the Virgin Mary. While we can catalog its modern uses, the origin of the fleur-de-lis is obscure. In the Middle Ages the French claimed that angels in the fifth century had crowned soldiers of King Clovis with fleurs-de-lis, yet we know the fleur-de-lis to have been used by ancient Egyptians and Persians. Among the possible sources suggested for the design have been the lily flower, the greek monogram of Christ, the head of a sceptre, a halberd or similar weapon, a bee, and even a frog. One plausible hypothesis posits that the fleur-de lis is modeled after the male genitalia in a form only thinly disguised by artistic and heraldic stylization.

A Spanish galleon, the *San Mateo,* wore this flag until it was captured in 1588 by a Dutch ship. Originally three meters (three yards nine inches) by twelve meters (thirteen yards), the flag has lost most of its length to souvenir hunters and decay since the sixteenth century. It retains however its principal motif – the Crucifixion. Made in an age when literacy was restricted to a small part of the population, this flag

served its function well. The holy nature of the enterprise for which the Spaniards went to battle was epitomized for them in this banner. It gave reassurance that any sacrifice which might be made would be rewarded.
While modern flags are rarely so explicit in their religious symbolism, soldiers and civilians alike are trained to believe that the colors and symbols of their national flag stand for all which is holy and just and that no sacrifice is too great when made in defense of such a flag.

bols are created and used *by humans:* their meanings, interpretations, and graphic and other expressions are not inherent in the objects and processes of nature. Symbols receive their emotional context from the meanings and usages people give them in actual situations. Over time a symbol may even "die," i.e., cease to be a medium of communication.

This is not to deny that there are both powerful forces in nature and continuities of usage which tend to encourage similarities in symbols, even between groups having little contact with one another. The association of the color green with agriculture is plausible because ultimately it rests on the fact that most plant life in human experience contains chlorophyll and is green. Other shapes and colors seem to be inevitable symbols, but logical associations and long usage are not the same as inherent meaning. Human society can change at will the emotional context of any symbol and frequently does so.

The question of meaning in a flag or some other symbol is difficult precisely because it involves neither a definable constant nor a legal norm. The state may legislate the correct artistic rendition of a flag, its proportions, the exact shades of color, when and where the flag may be used; but it can never enforce its own interpretation of meaning. The government in India has asserted that the saffron stripe of its flag stands for courage and sacrifice, its green stripe for faith and chivalry. Although it would take an extensive public opinion survey to prove the point, it seems clear that in fact these two colors represent to the majority of the population exactly what they did when the flag was first created – India's Hindu and Muslim communities. Likewise the flag of the Saar of 1948–1956 supposedly derived its blue, white, and red colors from the various districts composing the territory, yet those who wanted unity of the Saar with Germany could not help but see the flag as a symbol of French domination.

In analyzing symbols we must therefore keep in mind the historical sources of their designs and colors and current popular interpretations of them, as well as official statements – which are generally motivated by political considerations. It cannot be ruled out, of course, that certain elements in a flag or coat of arms may be arbitrary – added for artistic effect or at the whim of the designer and, consequently, bearing no ideological or historical connotation. To hold the whole of a design as a sacred inheritance from the past may lead to overemphasis on certain symbolic elements. For example, the date 1893 was retained in the revised version of the Minnesota state flag adopted in 1957, although in fact this date has no meaning except that it is the year in which the original flag was approved.

The very simplest function a given symbol may have is *referential:* such a symbol recalls a certain fact or helps us retain or order information with precision and speed. Signal flags, for example, fall into this category. Nevertheless the purely mnemonic function is rare in flags; they almost always evoke a certain mode, thought, or attitude or intensify an existing emotional condition. The referential symbol which has become familiar through constant use often acquires this evocative function. A striking example is the *tallis* or Jewish ritual prayer shawl which is bordered with blue stripes, as Numbers XV: 38 enjoins, "that ye may look upon it, and remember all the commandments of the Lord." When the Jewish nationalist movement began in the late nineteenth century, it was to this familiar

The eagle at left is from an eighteenth-century Austrian military color. With its halo it resembles the eagle of St. John, although in spirit and origin it is closer to that of the Caesars.

Most frequently a charge in heraldic design, the lion with wings and halo *(left)* is a special figure designating St. Mark, patron of Venice. This fourteenth century standard, captured by the Swiss in battle and recorded in a book of booty flags, shows the traditional book in the lion's paws and the inscription "St. Mark the Evangelist."

In ecclesiastic symbolism the bull represents St. Luke, as in this seventeenth century flag *(below)* from the Fribourg Abbey of St. Luke in Switzerland.

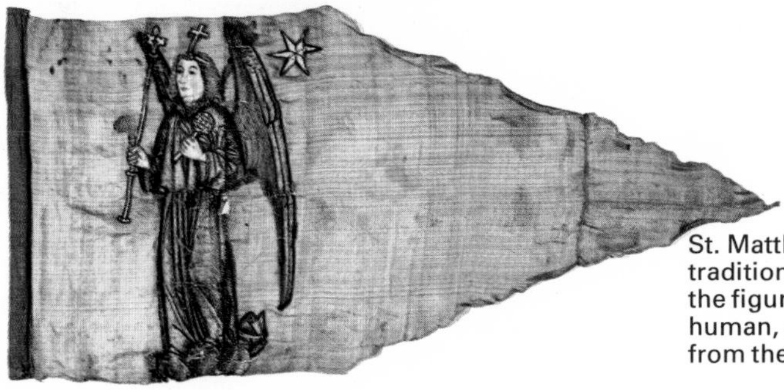

St. Matthew is represented in traditional inconography by the figure of a cherub or human, as in this flag *(left)* from the Engelberg Cloister.

pattern that Zionists turned as an inspiration for their national flag.

Beyond calling forth attitudes and emotions previously associated with it, such a symbol may incite or coerce an individual to act. Symbols whose functions are more than merely referential implicitly indicate rewards or threaten penalties. Courage, wisdom, justice, strength, sanctity, and similar virtues are latent in the seal that marks an official document, the coat of arms on a government building, the flag over a ship. It is difficult to be neutral toward such symbols because each constitutes the affirmation or rejection of some value.

Finally, there are interpretative symbols which do not simply recall a fact or happening known from the past with an incitement to act on that knowledge, but which broaden our understanding of that event or condition. The fragility of the Cypriot government and the possibility of

Despite Jewish and Muslim strictures against representational art, graphic symbolism has been strong in the Western religious tradition, easily surviving Puritan objections to its use. The close and long relationship between church and state inevitably left a strong influence of religious motifs on secular flags. Churches—such as the one in Sweden whose crucifixion is embellished with the attributes of four Evangelists *(left above)*—were a major source of art familiar to medieval society. It is little wonder that military flags reflect the themes developed in those churches.

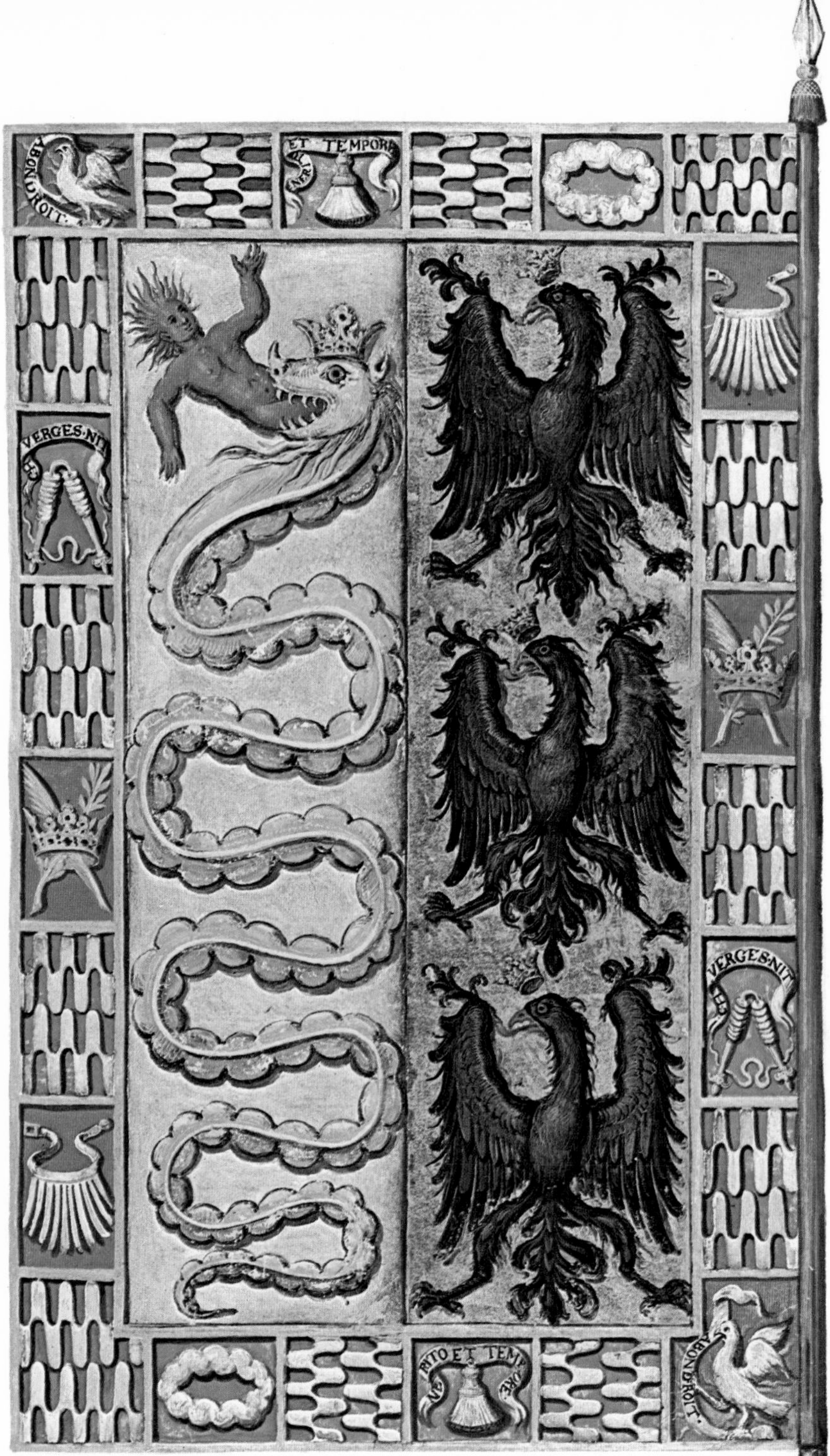

Massimiliano Sforza, Count of Pavia, displayed this handsome banner in the early years of the sixteenth century. It is replete with symbols, not simply for decorative purposes but to convey to the observer the impression of the majesty, power, and ancient heritage of the count and his family.
The central emblem is a combination of the arms of the Holy Roman Empire – a black eagle on gold (here repeated three times to fill the space better) and the arms of Milan. The latter shows a snake devouring a child.

the island's division (which actually occurred in 1974) might have been read clearly in the profound neutrality of the arms and flag adopted by Cyprus in 1960. Irredentism, clearly expressed in the flags of Hatay and the Ryukyus and their subsequent assimilation (to Turkey and Japan, respectively), was anticipated, even encouraged, in the very symbols which supposedly marked their existence as separate political entities. Particularly in newly independent countries where the nation-building process is a recent phenomenon, such interpretative symbols are a means of creating a new, higher consciousness and participation in wider groupings among populations previously characterized only by tribal or local loyalties.

The process is not actually limited to "new" countries: in Canada the pre-1965 flag expressed the national origins of many Canadian citizens by combining the arms of England, Scotland, Ireland, and France, but the mode of presentation was oriented to emphasizing the distinctions rather than the unity of such ethnic groups, their diverse past rather than their common future. The maple leaf flag on the other hand is an abstract, almost arbitrary symbol which effectively posits the necessity of all individuals – including the Ukrainians, Americans, Indians, Italians, Eskimos, and others omitted in the previous flag – working together to establish what the terms "Canada" and "Canadian" are to mean in the future.

Obviously, the manner in which symbols are generated and combined and displayed is a significant determinant of their social effectiveness. In an important sense to deny an institution or group of people a symbol of its own is to deny a distinctive personality. The flags of the Union Republics of the U.S.S.R. (page 283), by giving primacy to symbols of communism over those of nationalism, effectively negate the constitutional right of these states to secession and independence. In contrast the pluralism of the Brazilian and American societies is immediately evident in the flags chosen by the states into which they are divided.

In analyzing a flag then we must take many factors into consideration – historic sources, artistic composition, and symbolic meanings as seen by both the government and the people. It should be stressed that symbols are not pieces of furniture which can be rearranged at will, removed, added to, or dealt with individually if part of a composition. Traditional family heraldry has seen the shield as the essential core of a coat of arms with the crest, supporters, compartment, and other accessories having a secondary standing. There is some validity to this approach in personal arms, but state emblems (with specific exceptions) are indivisible units – in some cases the shield actually being one of the less important elements, as in the current arms of Egypt.

Nevertheless symbolic themes unbounded by time or political boundaries do exist and must be analyzed, even when this means dissection of an essentially indivisible achievement. In the following pages similarities and dissimilarities are examined in those motifs most commonly found in the arms and flags of the world's nations. From the apparent confusion of thousands of distinctive forms there arise a limited number of clearly defined categories and styles which are universal. The analysis presented here is not exhaustive, but is intended to create the framework which will allow the language of symbols – without losing any of the strength that has traditionally characterized it – to become less esoteric.

MOSAIC OF SYMBOLS

AFGHANISTAN	1	EGYPT	90	LIBERIA	77	SAN MARINO	123
ALBANIA	125	EL SALVADOR	41	LIBYA	78	SAUDI ARABIA	6
ALGERIA	37	EQUATORIAL GUINEA	51	LIECHTENSTEIN	79	SENEGAL	124
ANDORRA	3	ETHIOPIA	43	LUXEMBOURG	81	SIERRA LEONE	126
ANGOLA	4	FIJI	44	MALAGASY REPUBLIC	116	SINGAPORE	127
ANGUILLA	5	FINLAND	133	MALAWI	84	SOMALIA	128
ARGENTINA	7	FRANCE	45	MALAYSIA	85	SOUTH AFRICA	129
AUSTRALIA	8	GABON	46	MALDIVES	36	SOVIET UNION	130
AUSTRIA	107	THE GAMBIA	47	MALI	86	SPAIN	42
THE BAHAMAS	9	GERMANY	34,5	MALTA	87	SRI LANKA	131
BAHRAIN	10	GHANA	48	MAURITANIA	94	SUDAN	132
BANGLADESH	11	GREECE	57	MAURITIUS	88	SWAZILAND	136
BARBADOS	12	GRENADA	49	MEXICO	89	SWEDEN	135
BELGIUM	13	GUATEMALA	50	MONACO	92	SWITZERLAND	58
BHUTAN	38	GUINEA	53	MONGOLIA	93	SYRIA	134
BOLIVIA	15	GUINEA-BISSAU	52	MOROCCO	82	TANZANIA	137
BOTSWANA	16	GUYANA	54	MOZAMBIQUE	91	THAILAND	95
BRAZIL	17	HAITI	55	NAMIBIA	97	TOGO	139
BULGARIA	18	HONDURAS	59	NAURU	98	TONGA	140
BURMA	96	HUNGARY	83	NEPAL	100	TRINIDAD & TOBAGO	141
BURUNDI	19	ICELAND	63	NETHERLANDS	99	TUNISIA	142
CAMBODIA	68,9	INDIA	14	NEW ZEALAND	101	TURKEY	143
CAMEROON	20	INDONESIA	60	NICARAGUA	102	UGANDA	144
CANADA	21	IRAN	61	NIGER	103	UNITED ARAB EMIRATES	2
CENTRAL AFRICAN REPUBLIC	118	IRAQ	62	NIGERIA	104	UNITED KINGDOM	146
CHAD	138	IRELAND	40	NORWAY	106	UNITED STATES	147
CHILE	23	ISRAEL	64	OMAN	145	UPPER VOLTA	56
CHINA	24,5	ITALY	65	PAKISTAN	108	URUGUAY	149
COLOMBIA	27	IVORY COAST	30	PANAMA	109	VATICAN CITY	26
CONGO	28	JAMAICA	66	PARAGUAY	110	VENEZUELA	150
COSTA RICA	29	JAPAN	105	PERU	111	VIET-NAM	151-3
CUBA	31	JORDAN	148	PHILIPPINES	112	WESTERN SAMOA	122
CYPRUS	73	KENYA	70	POLAND	113	YEMEN	154,5
CZECHOSLOVAKIA	22	KOREA	71,2	PORTUGAL	114	YUGOSLAVIA	67
DAHOMEY	32	KUWAIT	74	QATAR	115	ZAIRE	156
DENMARK	33	LAOS	75	RHODESIA	119	ZAMBIA	157
DOMINICAN REPUBLIC	117	LEBANON	80	ROMANIA	120		
ECUADOR	39	LESOTHO	76	RWANDA	121		

The nations listed on the next four pages are numbered in alphabetical order based on the official name of each country in its own language. At left is the English-language name of each country and its corresponding number.

The following pages provide a synoptic view of the symbols used throughout the world in the national flags and coats of arms. These symbols have been grouped in eight categories which are then analyzed in detail in the remainder of this chapter or which may have already been discussed in the last chapter.

It is necessary to mention here the impossibility of depicting in all cases the complete symbol with all its details: certain signs were developed to represent entire categories, for example the tower for all buildings (i.e., Afghanistan, 1). Other signs were combined such as ship and helm (Bahamas, 9) or zebra and elephant (Angola, 4). Where a combination was not possible, due to lack of space, a general symbol ·:· has been inserted with a reference to that page on which the complete coat of arms and/or national flag are shown.

	AFGANISTAN 1	AMIRAT ARABIYAH MUTAHIDAH (Un. Arab Em.) 2	ANDORRA 3	ANGOLA 4	ANGUILLA 5	AL ARABIYA AL SAUDIYAH (Saudi Arabia) 6	ARGENTINA 7	AUSTRALIA 8	THE BAHAMAS 9	AL BAHRAIN 10	BANGLADESH 11	BARBADOS 12	BELGIQUE/BELGIË 13	BHARAT (India) 14	BOLIVIA 15	BOTSWANA 16	BRASIL 17	1
CELESTIAL OBJECTS	208				210		314	211	314						314		315	
TERRESTRIAL OBJECTS				336					212		336				336	336		
FLORA	208				332/334 335	332	335	320	212		213/334	332/334			216/336	216	217	2
FAUNA	318	208	325	209	325			211/320	320/325			320/325	214/322	215/323	320/336	324/325		3
HUMANS							211											
ARTIFACTS	318	208/336	209	209	330	330	211		212/337	328		214/331	328	331	216	331	217	2
ABSTRACT FORMS			338	209				211/316		338	338				317		217/316	3
INSCRIPTIONS	208	339	209	209	210	339		211	212			214	339	215	216	216	339	3

	EL SALVADOR 41	ESPAÑA (Spain) 42	ETIOPIYA 43	FIJI 44	FRANCE 45	GABON 46	THE GAMBIA 47	GHANA 48	GRENADA 49	GUATEMALA 50	GUINEA ECUATORIAL 51	GUINÉ-BISSAU 52	GUINÉE 53	GUYANA 54	HAÏTI 55	HAUTE-VOLTA (Upper Volta) 56	HELLAS (Greece) 57	HELVETIA 5
CELESTIAL OBJECTS	231																	
TERRESTRIAL OBJECTS	337													238				
FLORA	231	232		332/335 233		332	234	332	235	236	332		320	238/334	332	239		
FAUNA		318/323	322	320/322		325	323	235/318	235/320	236			324/320	320/324		324		
HUMANS				326														
ARTIFACTS	231	232/329	322	326/337		337	234/331	235/329	235	330				238/329	238/330	239		
ABSTRACT FORMS	337	232		233/316		234		235/316	235		236	237				239	317	3
INSCRIPTIONS	231	232		233		234	234	235	339	236	236	237	237	238	238	239		

	BURUNDI 19	CAMEROUN 20	CANADA 21	ČESKOSLOVENSKO 22	CHILE 23	CHUNG KUO (Peo. Rep. of China) 24	CHUNG KUO (Rep. of China) 25	CITTÀ VATICANO 26	COLOMBIA 27	CONGO 28	COSTA RICA 29	CÔTE D'IVOIRE (Ivory Coast) 30	CUBA 31	DAHOMEY 32	DANMARK 33	DEUTSCHLAND (Fed. Rep. of Germany) 34	DEUTSCHLAND (German Dem. Rep.) 35	DIVEHI (Maldives) 36	AL DJAZAIR (Algeria) 37	DRUK-YUL (Bhutan) 38	ECUADOR 39	ÉIRE/IRELAND 40
							314				337	314	314								336	
		331		322					336		337		336								336	
			334			222			223/335	224	224	332	225/336	332/335			228	332	229		230	
	323		322/323 321	322	221/320 324				320			324		324	226/322	318				229/321	320	
															326				229			
	330	219/331	220/331			222/329		328/331	223/336	224	337		225/336	226/329 337	328		331	228	229		230/336	331
	316	219	220	221	221/316	222/316			335	224	337		316/338	335	226/316			228/316	316	229		
	219	219	220		221				223		224	225		226				228		229	230	

	HONDURAS 59	INDONESIA 60	IRAN 61	AL IRAQ 62	ÍSLAND (Iceland) 63	ISRAEL/ISRAIL 64	ITALIA 65	JAMAICA 66	JUGOSLAVIJA 67	KAMPUCHEA (King. of Cambodia) 68	KAMPUCHEA (Khmer Rep.) 69	KENYA 70	KORAI (Dem. Peo. Rep.) 71	KORAI (Rep. of Korea) 72	KYPROS/KIBRIS (Cyprus) 73	AL KUWAIT 74	LAO 75	LESOTHO 76	LIBERIA 77	LIBIYA 78	LIECHTENSTEIN 79	LUBNAN (Lebanon) 80
	241		314																336			
	241												337		249	336		251	336			
	241	242/332				244	335	335	245		247	247	248	334	334				336	252		332
		318/325	322	318	243			245		246		320/323			320	250	324	251/324	336	252	318	
					326			326														
	41/329	318	322/328			331	331	245	245	246/329	329	247	337			336	250	251	336		328	
	241	317		243	316	317	317	317	317	246	247/316		248/317	328					317	252	253	
	241	242	242	243		339	244	245	245	246	247	247	248	248	249	250		251	251	252		

	81 LUXEMBURG	82 AL MAGRIB (Morocco)	83 MAGYARORSZÁG (Hungary)	84 MALAWI	85 MALAYSIA	86 MALI	87 MALTA	88 MAURITIUS	89 MÉXICO	90 MISR (Egypt)	91 MOÇAMBIQUE	92 MONACO	93 MONGGOL (Mongolia)	94 MURITANIYA	95 MUANG TAI (Thailand)	96 MYAN-MA (Burma)	97 NAMIBIA	98 NAOERO/NAURU
CELESTIAL OBJECTS		314		314		314							324					
TERRESTRIAL OBJECTS		254		255	336		257		258		336		324			330	331	26
FLORA			255		332/335		257	258/332	258	259			260	261/332		330	262	33
FAUNA	322	322		322/323 324	256/324	320	325	321/324	318	259			324		318	330	262/325	32
HUMANS					256							326	324					
ARTIFACTS	328	328		255	256/330	257/329	329/317	331/336			259	328/326	260			330	262/331	3
ABSTRACT FORMS	322	317	255		316			316		259	259	338	260/338	316		316/330		315/3
INSCRIPTIONS		339		255	339	257	257	258		259	259	260	260	261		339	339	33

	121 RWANDA	122 SAMOA I SISIFO (Western Samoa)	123 SAN MARINO	124 SÉNÉGAL	125 SHQIPËRIA (Albania)	126 SIERRA LEONE	127 SINGAPURA	128 SOMALIYA	129 SOUTH AFRIKA	130 SOVYETSKII SOYUZ (Soviet Union)	131 SRI LANKA	132 AL SUDAN	133 SUOMI/FINLAND	134 SURIYAH (Syria)	135 SVERIGE (Sweden)	136 SWAZILAND	137 TANZANIA	138 TCHAD
CELESTIAL OBJECTS		278								314	314/283							31
TERRESTRIAL OBJECTS		278/336	337	279		280				282							336/286	
FLORA	277	332/278		332/335	279	332		281	281/332	282	283/334			285			282	
FAUNA	277		377	323	318	322/323	323/324	325	322/325		322	320	322	285	285/322	322/324	286	323/
HUMANS									281				322				326	
ARTIFACTS	277/331		328/329			280		281	281	331	283		322		285/328	328/330	286/331	
ABSTRACT FORMS		298/317		316	316	322	280	316		317	283	284	316/322	285	285/317			287/
INSCRIPTIONS	339	278	278	279	279	280	280		281	282		284		285		286	286	28

No.	Country	1	2	3	4	5	6	7	8
9	NEDERLAND				22			22	63
100	NEPAL	337	337	264	264	326	264/328	264	264
101	NEW ZEALAND	315		265/335	325	326	331/336 328	315	265
102	NICARAGUA	315	315		325		315	315	265
103	NIGER	314		335			266		266
104	NIGERIA		336	266	318/324				266
105	NIHON (Japan)	314		334					
106	NORGE (Norway,				322		322/328	317	
107	ÖSTERREICH (Austria)				318		270/331		
108	PAKISTAN			334/335				316	339
109	PANAMÁ	314	314		271		271	271	271
110	PARAGUAY			272	272			316	272
111	PERÚ			272/332	325		331	272	
112	PILIPINAS (Philippines)	314		273	318/323		318	273/316	273
113	POLSKA (Poland)				318				
114	PORTUGAL			334			274	274	
115	QATAR			274	274		330	274	274
116	RÉPUBLIQUE MALGACHE (Malagasy)			275	325				275
117	REPÚBLICA DOMINICANA			275			275	316	275
118	RÉPUBLIQUE CENTRAFRICAINE	314	276	332	324	276	276	276/316	276
119	RHODESIA			276	276/325		276/331		276
120	ROMÂNIA	337	337	277			337	317	277

No.	Country	1	2	3	4	5	6	7	8
39	TOGO				322		7/322	316	287
140	TONGA			288	320		288/328 330	288/317	288
141	TRINIDAD/TOBAGO		288	288	320		288/331 337	337	288
142	AL TUNISIYA				323		331/337	316	289
143	TÜRKIYE							316	
144	UGANDA	314	290	290	320/325		290	290	290
145	UMAN						330		
146	UNITED KINGDOM			291	321/322 323		291/328	316	291
147	UNITED STATES	314		292	318		292	317	292
148	AL URDUN (Jordan)			295	328			292/317	339
149	URUGUAY	314	329	295	324/325		329	295	
150	VENEZUELA			296/335	324		296	316/335	296
151	VIÉT-NAM (Rep. of South V.-N.)							317	
152	VIÉT-NAM (Rep. of V.-N.)							297	
153	VIÉT-NAM (Dem. Rep. of V.-N.)			297			331	297	297
154	AL YAMAN (Yemen Arab Rep.)		298	298	298		298	298	298
155	AL YAMAN (Dem. Peo. Rep. of Yemen)				298			292/317	298
156	ZAÏRE			299	299/325	299	299/330	299	299
157	ZAMBIA		336	299	299/318	326	299		299

THE SUN

1 Iran (242)*
2 Malawi, flag (255)
3 Ivory Coast (225)
4 Central African Rep. (276)
5 Panama (271)
6 Morocco (254)
7 Malawi, Coat of arms (255)
8 The Bahamas (212)

1

2

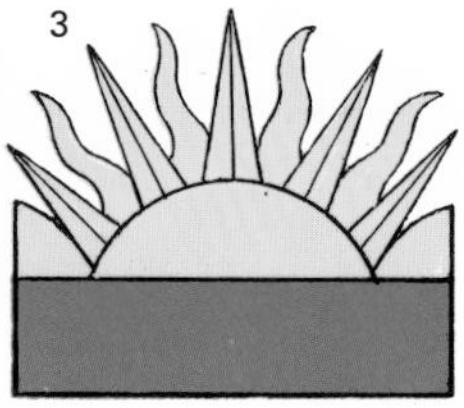
3

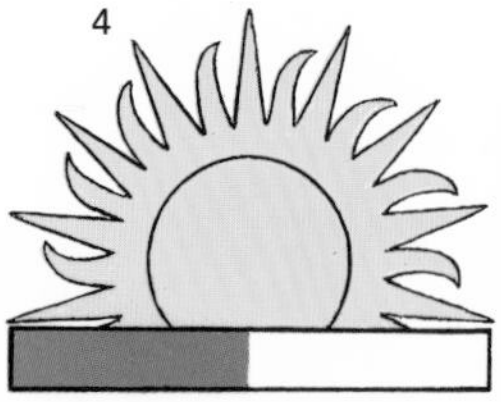
4

5

6

9 Cuba (225)
10 Soviet Union (282)
11 Mali (257)
12 Uruguay (295)
13 Sri Lanka (283)
14 Philippines (273)
15 China (Rep.) (222)
16 Malaysia (256)
17 Japan (267)
18 Uganda (290)
19 Argentina (211)
20 Niger (266)
21 United States (292)
22 Chad (287)
23 Bolivia (216)

Suns in landscapes are shown on pages 336/337:
Romania (277)
Mongolia (260)
Liberia (251)
Costa Rica (224)
Ecuador (230)

* The figures in parentheses indicate the pages on which the complete coat of arms or flag is reproduced.

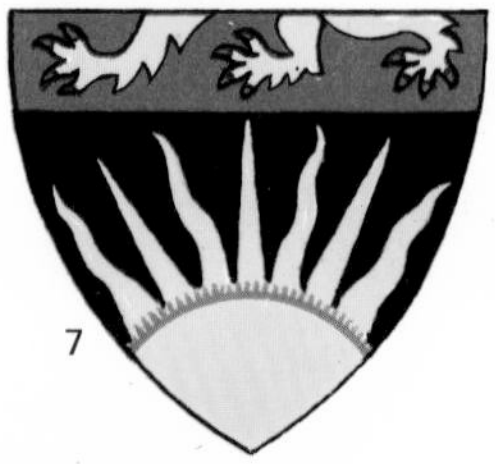
7

8

9

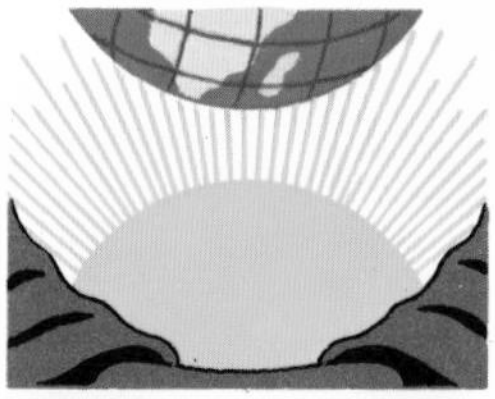
10

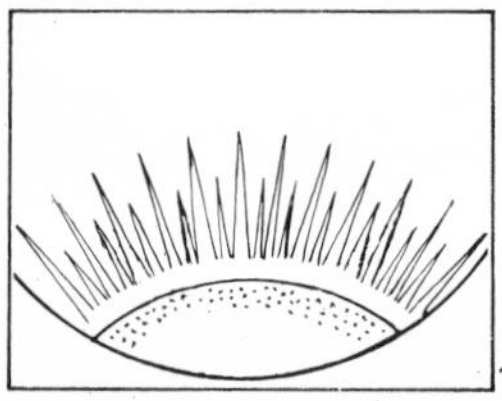
11

12

13

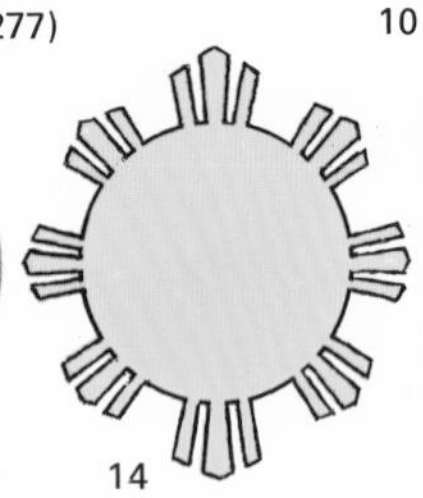
14

15

16

17

18

19

20

21

22

23

Perhaps because of the very universality of the sun in human experience, certain nations have given limited meanings to the sun symbol in their arms and flags.

A sun breaking through the clouds on independence day became an emblem associated with liberty in Argentina (19) and Uruguay (12). The Buddhists of Sri Lanka (13), the ancient Zoroastrinas of Iran (1), and the Incas in pre-colonial Peru recognized the sun as a religious symbol; later it was secularized into the forms now incorporated in the national arms. An entirely different meaning is found in the Philippine sun (14) whose eight rays correspond to the number of provinces originally leading the revolution for independence against Spain. The sun and the moon together in the arms of Panama (5) suggest the hour of twilight when the revolution for freedom in that country succeeded.

In a large number of other lands the sun is associated not so much with independence but with the promises it brings in the "dawn of a new day." Countries as diverse as Afghanistan (page 208), the Soviet Union (10), Mali (11), and the United States (21) have chosen this interpretation. Moreover, the sunbursts of Afghanistan

In the late fifteenth century Swiss soldiers captured as booty many flags carried by Burgundian troops, including the one shown below whose shape almost seems to have been designed especially for the sunburst design it displays.

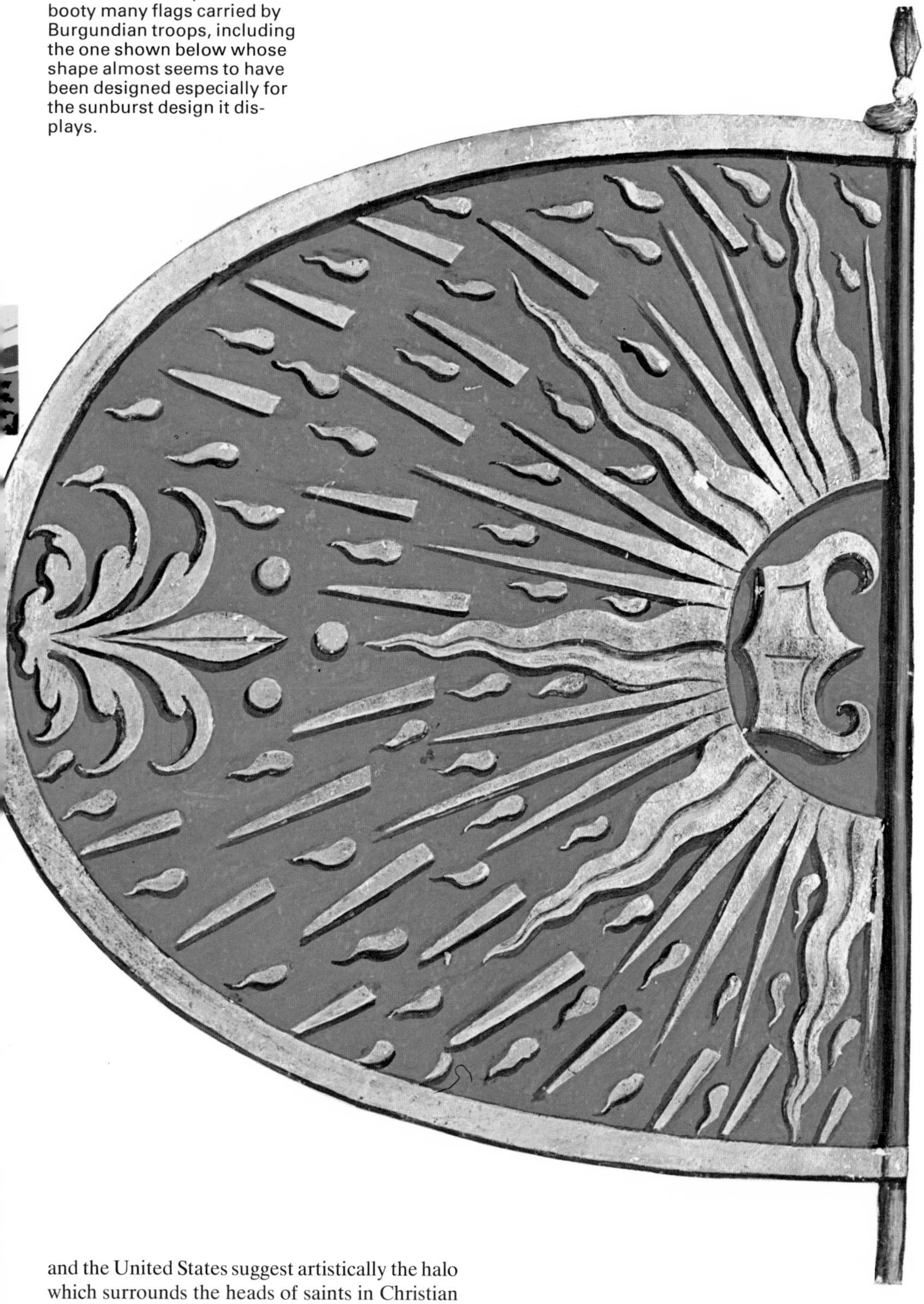

The sun and moon are not the only celestial objects featured in coats of arms. Constellations – as in the flags of Brazil *(above)* and New Zealand *(below, right)* – and even rainbows – as in the arms of Nicaragua *(below)* – are occasionally seen.

Nevertheless a high degree of stylization is often introduced in the artistic rendition of such objects. The "star" in the flag of Nauru *(below, left)* differs little from the Nepali sun (page 264), while the star in the flag of Mauritania *(below)* achieves the astronomically impossible by appearing in the center of a crescent moon.

and the United States suggest artistically the halo which surrounds the heads of saints in Christian iconography.

In other cases it is simply geographic location – near the equator, in the Far East, or the Far West – which has made the sun an appropriate symbol, as in Uganda (18), Japan (17), and Morocco (6).

The circular motion of the sun across the heavens readily suggests unceasing progress, as in the Republic of China sun (15). Finally, the sun and moon can express a prayer of longevity for the nation as in Nepal (page 264).

CRESCENTS, STARS, AND CROSSES

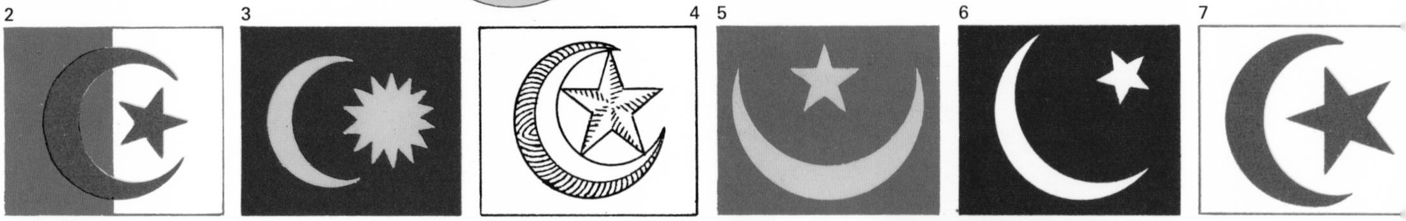

1 Malaysia, coat of arms (256)*
2 Algeria, flag (229)
3 Malaysia, flag (256)
4 Maldives, coat of arms (228)
5 Mauritania, flag (261)
6 Pakistan, flag (271)
7 Tunisia, flag (289)
8 Turkey, flag (289)
9 Soviet Union, arms (282)
10 Rep. of South Viet-Nam, flag (296)
11 Albania, coat of arms (279)
12 Bulgaria, coat of arms (218)
13 China, People's Rep., flag (222)
14 Ghana, flag (235)
15 Yugoslavia, coat of arms (245)
16 Korea, P.D.R., coat of arms (248)
17 Cuba, flag (225)
18 Liberia, flag (251)
19 Morocco, flag and coat of arms (254)
20 Romania, arms (277)
21 Paraguay, coat of arms (272)
22 Central African Republic, flag (276)
23 Somalia, flag and coat of arms (281)
24 Senegal, flag and coat of arms (279)
25 Togo, flag (287)
26 Yemen, P.D.R., flag (298)
27 Indonesia, coat of arms (242)
28 Israel, flag (244)
29 Jordan, flag (295)
30 Burma, flag (262)
31 Brazil, coat of arms (217)
32 Burundi, flag (219)
33 Chile, coat of arms (221)
34 Italy, coat of arms (244)
35 Bolivia, coat of arms (216)
36 Venezuela, flag (296)
37 United States, flag (292)
38 Philipines, coat of arms (273)
39 Surinam, flag (264)
40 Cambodia (Khmer Rep.), flag (247)

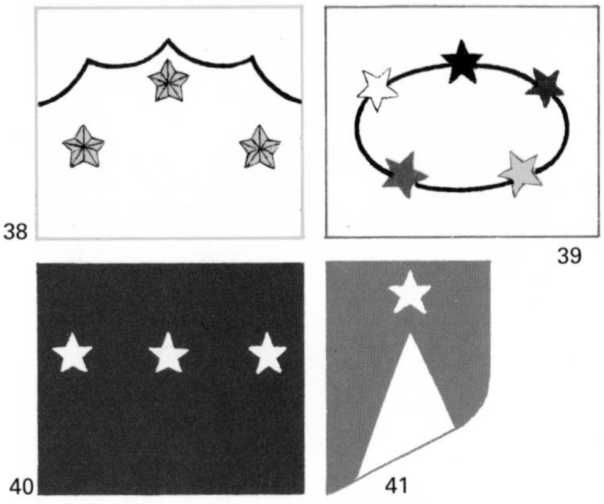

It is a general rule of symbolism that the larger and more diverse the entity, the simpler its chief symbols tend to be. Towns and cities almost always have more complex flags and coats of arms than nations; the emblems of obscure religious sects rarely achieve the concise graphic form of the Christian cross, the Buddhist lotus, or the Muslim star and crescent. The reason, perhaps, is that simple abstract geometric forms can be seen as symbolizing a great number of principles or qualities or events, whereas the more explicit emblems have a limited and obvious range of meaning.
Thus two of the simplest of symbols – the "star"

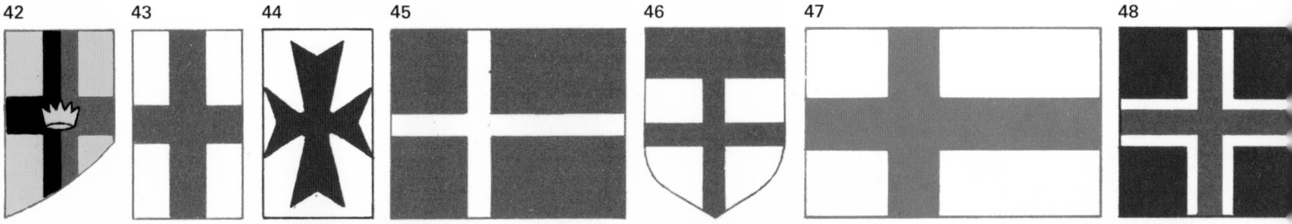

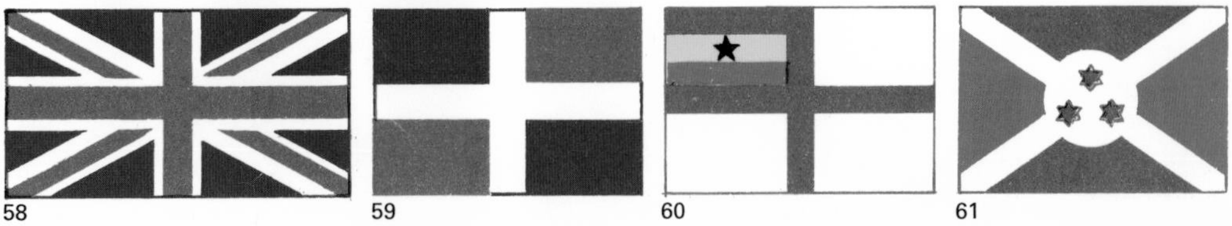

and the cross have found enormous popularity in the twentieth century. (The star is deservedly indicated in quotation marks because in fact it has little or nothing to do with the celestial objects also referred to by that name.) While it generally has meant independence or unity,

41 Mauritius, coat of arms (258)
42 Malaysia, coat of arms (256)
43 Australia, coat of arms (211)
44 Australia, coat of arms (211)
45 Denmark, flag (226)
46 Fiji, coat of arms (233)
47 Finland, flag (284)
48 Iceland, flag (243)
49 Greece, flag (239)

8

9

10

15

16

17

18

19

20

25
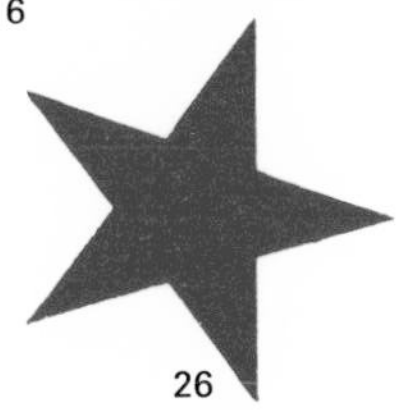
26

27
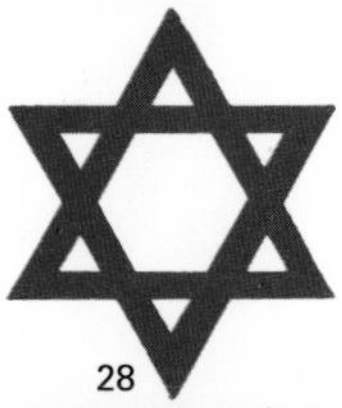
28

29

34

35

36

37

50 Jamaica, coat of arms (245)
51 Jamaica, flag (245)
52 Western Samoa, coat of arms (278)
53 Switzerland, flag and coat of arms (240)
54 Malta, flag and coat of arms (257)
55 Tonga, coat of arms and flag (288)
56 Norway, flag (269)
57 Sweden, flag (285)
58 United Kingdom, flag (291)
59 Dominican Rep., flag (275)
60 Ghana, flag (235)
61 Burundi, flag (219)

*The figures in parentheses indicate the pages on which the complete coat of arms or flag is reproduced.

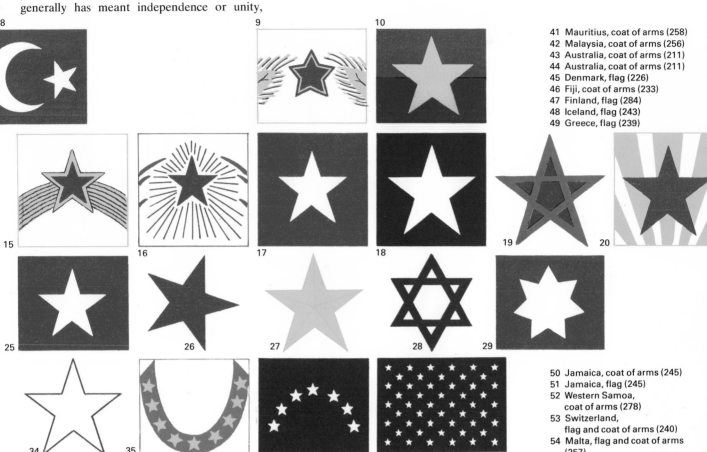

there is great flexibility both in the form and function of the star. In the Near East and Africa an outline star of five or six points is a good luck symbol; in the American tradition stars indicate the number of states or provinces constituting a country. In communist lands the five points of a star stand for the five continents of the world and thus the unity of humanity.

The cross is, of course, intimately associated with Christian concepts of salvation and sacrifice. Historically, flags with crosses in Europe were an affirmation of the sanctity of an undertaking, and in many cases flags and crosses were given by popes to monarchs as they went to war.

52

53

49

50
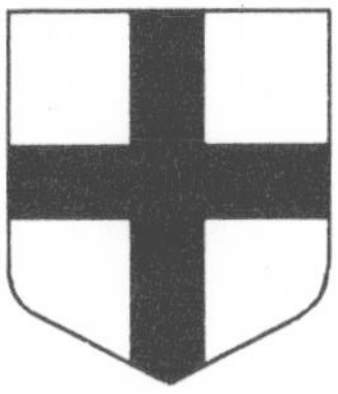
51
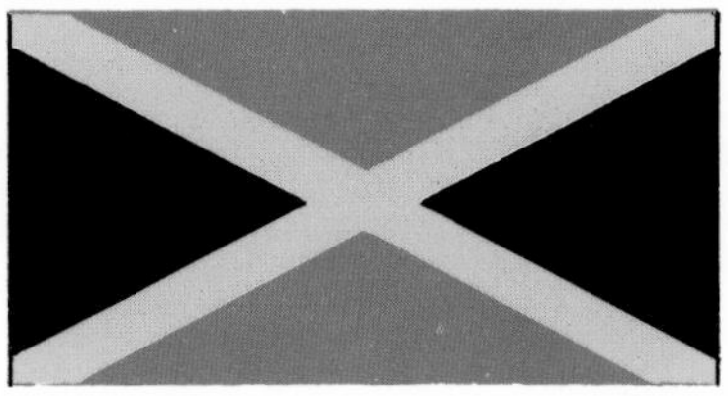

54
56

57

55

The cross has also been widely used in military decorations or simply as a pleasing geometric figure, providing an alternative to stripes as the basis for a simple flag design.

THE EAGLE

1

17

2

3

4

5

6

1 Afghanistan (208)*
2 Albania (279)
3 Poland (273)
4 Spain (232)
5 Philippines (273)
6 Federal Republic of Germany (227)

7

Few symbols have been so widely used and so variously interpreted as the eagle. Some are associated with the mystic origin of the country (1–3) or with a national hero or saint (14, 4). Indigenous kinds of eagles (13, 12, 17, 7) simultaneously express pride in the country represented as well as independence and strength, long recognized as the chief symbolic meanings of the eagle.

In the course of centuries Europe has produced some unusual interpretations of the eagle – with crowns, double heads, or even the bodies of human beings partially incorporated (2, 9, 10). Nevertheless, Europe is not alone in finding artistic value in anatomical impossibilities.

The *garuda* of Southeast Asia was, according to Hindu mythology, a man transformed into a bird in order to provide transportation for one of the gods. In the arms of Indonesia (15) the mythical bird's transformation is complete, but the royal arms of Thailand (16) portray both natures of the *garuda* simultaneously.

8

9

10

11

12

13

14

7 United States (292)
8 Nigeria (266)
9 Liechtenstein (253)
10 Liechtenstein (253)
11 Austria (270)
12 Mexico (258)
13 Zambia (299)
14 Iraq (243)
15 Indonesia (242)
16 Thailand (261)
17 Ghana (235)

*The figures in parentheses indicate the pages on which the complete coat of arms or flag is reproduced.

15

16

The banner of the Holy Roman Empire *(right)* shows the traditional eagle on a field of gold. This depiction is from *The Triumph of Maximilian I,* an early sixteenth century manuscript.

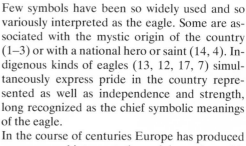

Schenckh

BIRDS AND FABULOUS BEASTS

1 Kenya, *Cockerel* (247)*
2 Cyprus, *Dove* (249)
3 Tonga, *Dove* (288)
4 Guinea, *Dove* (237)
5 Mali, *(Species not identified)* (257)
6 The Bahamas, *Flamingo* (212)
7 Uganda, *Crested crane* (290)
8 Trinidad and Tobago, *Scarlet Ibis* (288)
9 Trinidad and Tobago, *Cocrico* (288)
10 Barbados, *Pelican* (214)
11 Grenada, *Ramier* (235)
12 Chile, *Condor* (221)
13 Mauritius, *Dodo* (258)
14 Nauru, *Frigate* (263)
15 Guyana, *Canje pheasant* (238)

1

5

2

3

4

6

7

8

9

10

11

12

16 Australia, *Black swan* (211)
17 Australia, *Australian piping shrike* (211)
18 Fiji, *Dove* (233)
19 Trinidad and Tobago, *Humming birds* (288)
20 Bolivia, *Condor* (216)
21 Colombia, *Condor* (223)
22 Ecuador, *Condor* (230)
23 Sudan, *Secretary bird* (284)
24 Australia, *Emu* (211)

14

15

16

17

18

19

20

21

22

23

*The figures in parentheses indicate the pages on which the complete coat of arms or flag is reproduced.

24

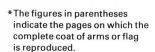

In addition to symbols such as flags or seals, many plants and animals are themselves honored as national emblems. For example, in the prefectures of Japan and the states of the United States, it is a common practice to recognize a distinctive bird, animal, flower, tree, and sometimes even insect as an official symbol – quite apart from any use it may have in the seal, coat of arms, and flag of the territory.
Distinctive birds have also been chosen, particularly among nations of the British Commonwealth, as charges or supporters of national arms. In a number of Latin American countries the crest is a condor, a huge bird which quite appropriately substitutes for the eagle characteristic of countries in other parts of the world.
In most cases there is no particular symbolism associated with a bird other than that it is a local species, familiar to the citizens. The crested crane of Uganda, for example, has been used in a number of versions not only since independence but during the era of colonialism; it appears today in the center of the national flag. A silhouette of a bird of paradise figures prom-

13

inently in the flag of Papua New Guinea, where a number of species of this brilliantly plumed bird live.

Other countries have not been content with what nature provides. Dragons, unicorns, griffins, and similar fabulous beasts are formed by joining parts of known animals in unlikely combinations – or by spurning biology altogether to create fantastic monsters (as in the arms of Iceland). These beasts have enriched heraldry since its earliest days.

The archiepiscopal crosier figures on Basel's shield in this eighteenth-century cavalry flag. Supporting it are cockatrices (or wyverns) – a cross between a cock and a lizard. Best known among imaginary symbolic animals in state symbolism are the

dragon of Bhutan *(above)* and the unicorn of Scotland in the arms of Britain *(right).*

THE LION

1

2

5

6

7

8

9

10

1 Ethiopia (232)*
2 Iran (242)
3 India (215)
4 Senegal (279)
5 Norway (269)
6 Netherlands (263)
7 Finland (284)
8 Luxembourg (254)
9 Belgium (214)
10 Czechoslovakia (221)

18

19

20

21

22

11 United Kongdom/Canada (291 and 220)
12 Philippines (273)
13 Spain (232)
14 Bulgaria (218)
15 Tunisia (289)
16 Togo (287)
17 Burundi (219)
18 United Kingdom/Canada (291 and 220)
19 Denmark (226)
20 Fiji (233)
21 Sierra Leone (280)
22 Denmark (226)
23 Malawi (255)
24 South Africa (281)
25 Canada (220)
26 Sri Lanka (283)

23
24

25

26

LIONS AS SUPPORTERS
27 Swaziland (286)
28 Sweden (285)
29 United Kingdom (291)
30 Netherlands (263)
31 Luxembourg (254)
32 Canada (220)
33 Morocco (254)
34 Morocco (254)
35 The Gambia (234)
36 Iran (242)
37 Sierra Leone (280)
38 Singapore (280)
39 Kenya (247)
40 Malawi (255)
41 Chad (287)

27

28

29

30

31

32

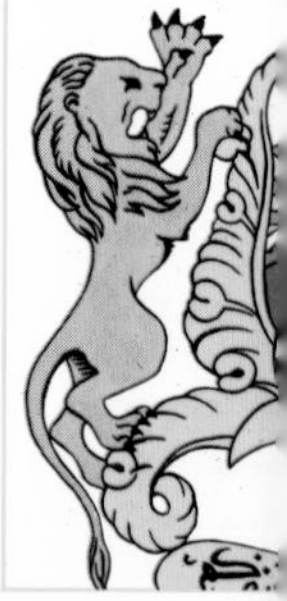

3

4

12

13

14

15

16

17

Belgium has lions as supporters in its arms (214)
Paraguay has a lion in the treasury seal appearing on the reverse of its flag (272)
Rhodesia has a lion in the chief of its arms (276)

*The figures in parentheses indicate the pages on which the complete coat of arms or flag is reproduced.

Strength, bravery, and the other real or imagined characteristics of the lion make it an ideal subject for an emblem of state. What is surprising, however, is the extent to which it has been so employed even in lands that have not known the lion in its natural state since prehistoric times. The prevalence of this beast in Scandinavia, Britain, and other countries of Europe may stem from one or two original sources from the time of the Crusades or earlier. This is borne out by the high degree of stylization seen in these lions, the frequent use in heraldry of the term "leopard" to refer to them, and the many symbols (especially crowns and swords) with which they are differentiated.
The lions of England (18) have had a direct impact on the symbols of a number of countries formerly part of the British Empire. "Cousins" include the lion of South Africa (24), the Canadian lions (18, 25), and the lions of several African countries (40, 35, 37, 39).

Elsewhere the lion has had an independent symbolic tradition of great antiquity. The *singha* or lion is the name source for the Singhalese people of Sri Lanka (26) and the island nation of Singapore (38). The Asiatic lion also figures in the arms of India (3) and in a modernized version of a very ancient Iranian emblem (2).
Although military leaders in Ethiopia (1) removed the cross from the staff and the crown from the head of the lion in 1975, its origins are still clear. The former imperial dynasty claimed direct descent from the Queen of Sheba and King Solomon; the latter's title, the Conquering Lion of Judah, was emloyed by his Ethiopian descendents. Long predating the stylization which has influenced modern heraldic lions, the Ethiopian beast faces to the sinister, which heraldry considers to be the less honorable direction.

34

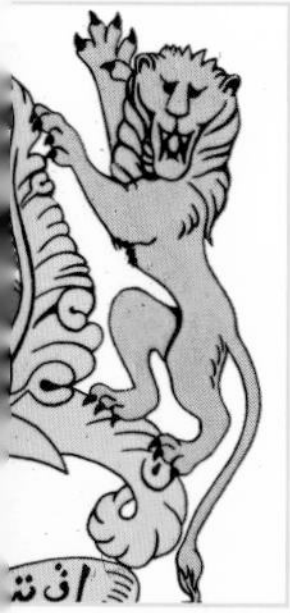

35

36

37

38

39

40

41

ARMORIAL ANIMALS

1

6

2

3

4

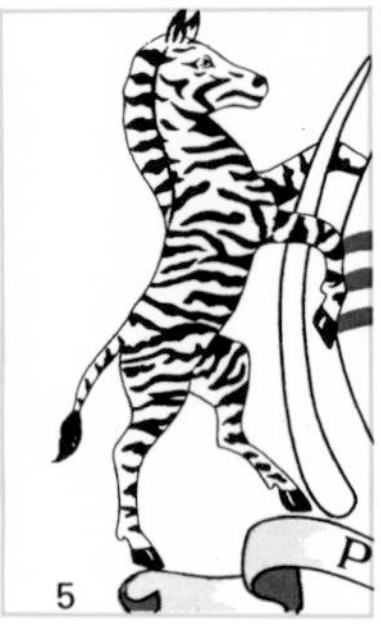
5

7

Horses and Zebras
1 Mongolia, *Rider and horse* (260)*
2 Nigeria, *Horse* (266)
3 Lesotho, *Horse* (251)
4 Upper Volta, *Horse* (239)
5 Botswana, *Zebra* (216)
6 Venezuela, *Horse* (296)
7 Uruguay, *Horse* (295)

Elephants
8 Ivory Coast, *Elephant head* (225)
9 Laos, *Three-headed elephant* (250)

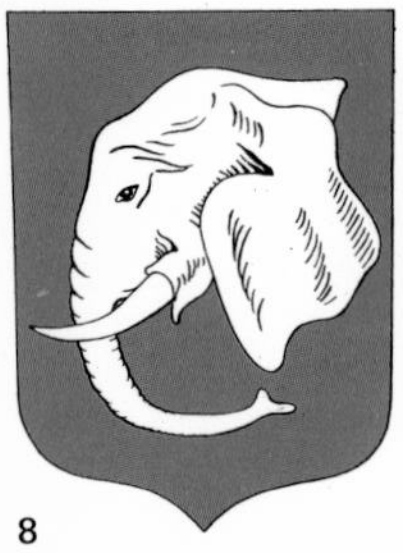
8

9

10

11

12

10 Central African Rep., *Elephant head* (276)
11 Guinea, *Elephant* (237)
12 Swaziland, *Elephant* (286)

Panthers, Tigers and Leopards
13 Malawi, *Leopard* (255)
14 Singapore, *Tiger* (280)
15 Malaysia, *Tiger* (256)
16 Guyana, *Jaguar* (238)
17 Dahomey, *Panther* (226)
18 Somalia, *Leopard* (281)
19 Gabon, *Black panther* (234)
20 Zaire, *Leopard head* (299)

Oxen, cows, llamas, and sheep
21 Niger, *Buffalo head* (266)
22 Andorra, *Cows* (209)
23 Malagasy Rep., *Ox head* (275)
24 Indonesia, *Ox head* (242)
25 Botswana, *Ox head* (216)
26 Peru, *Vicuña* (272)
27 South Africa, *Gnus* (281)
28 New Zealand, *Sheep* (265)
29 Uruguay, *Ox* (295)

Sealife
30 Anguilla, *Fish* (Species not indicated) (210)
31 Anguilla, *Dolphins* (210)
32 Barbados, *Dolphin* (214)
33 Malta, *Dolphin* (257)
34 The Bahamas, *Marlin* (212)

13

14

15

16

17

While the lion and eagle predominate as national emblems, certain other beasts are not to be forgotten in the catalog of armorial animals. The antelope, elephant, zebra, and panther are to be expected in African countries where such wildlife abounds; nevertheless, since the buffalo and horse have greater significance for national economies, they figure prominently in a number of African arms.

Other distinctive local animals such as the jaguar (Guyana), sheep (New Zealand), vicuña

35

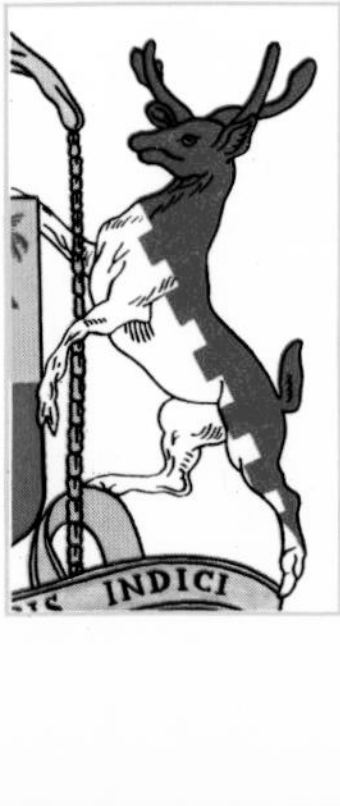

36

21

(Peru), and even the marlin (the Bahamas) and dolphin are to be found. The latter, frequently stylized in heraldry, stands as a general symbol for the sea in the traditions of Anguilla, Barbados, and Malta. In all cases we note a deep emotional attachment to historically significant forms of animal life, particularly as supporters to the national shield. Such symbols are rather rare in flags, at least those employed by modern nations. (They may, however, be found in flags of organizations and military units.) In part, the reason lies in the difficulty of achieving a satisfactory rendition of a living object with the piecing technique of manufacture which has largely replaced embroidery and painting.

22

23

24

25

26

27

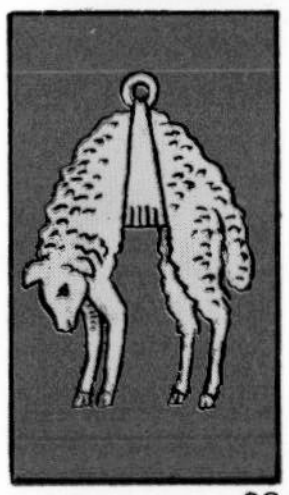

28

Deer and Antelopes
35 Mauritius, *Sambur deer* (258)
36 Chile, *Huemul* (221)
37 Namibia, *Springbok* (262)
38 Namibia, *Kudu* (262)
39 Chad, *Wild sheep* (287)
40 Uganda, *Uganda kob* (290)
41 South Africa, *Springbok* (281)
42 South Africa, *Oryx* (281)
43 Rhodesia, *Sable antelope* (276)

29

*The figures in parentheses indicate the pages on which the complete coat of arms or flag is reproduced.

20

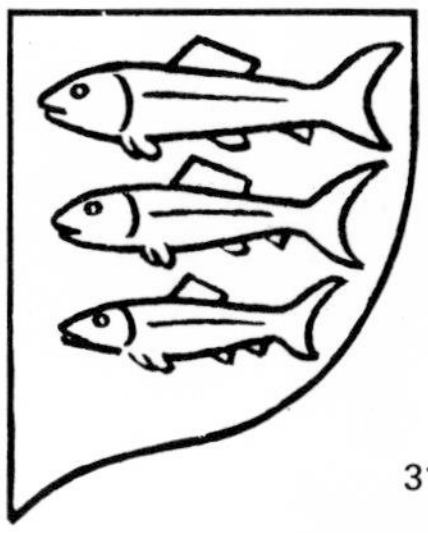

30

31

18

19

32

33

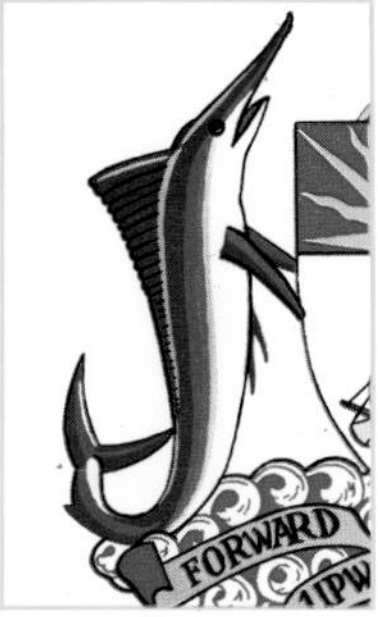

34

37

38

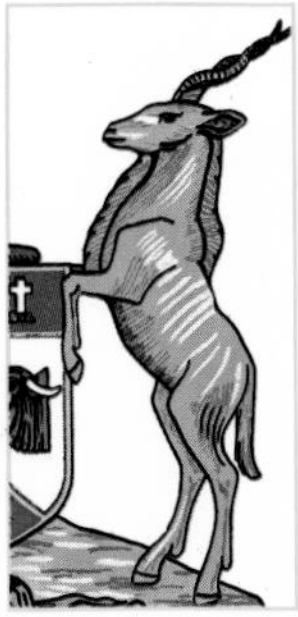

39

40

41

42

43

HUMAN BEINGS

1/2

1/2 Monaco, *monks* (260)*
3/4 Jamaica, *American Indians* (245)
5/6 Tanzania, *citizens* (286)
7/8 Denmark, *wild men* (226)
9/10 Zambia, *citizens* (299)
11/12 Nepal, *soldiers* (264)
13/14 Fiji, *citizens* (233)
15/16 New Zealand, *European and Maori* (265)
17 Iceland, *legendary hero* (243)

Human symbols also appear in the arms or flag of other countries:
Argentina, *two hands* (211)
Algeria, *hand* (229)
Central African Rep., *hand* (276)
Finland, *arm* (284)
Malaysia, *two arms holding flag* (256)
Mongolia, *man on horseback* (260)
South Africa, *female with anchor* (281)
Zaire, *arm with torch* (299)

Although humans rarely figure in flags today, they do appear in coats of arms – especially as supporters. These include the ones found in the arms of Monaco, Jamaica, Tanzania, Denmark, Zambia, Nepal, Fiji, New Zealand, and Iceland. A horseman appears in the arms of Mongolia (page 260). Human hands or arms are found in the coats of arms of Argentina (page 211), Algeria (page 229), the Central African Republic (page 276), and Finland (page 284). Humans were frequently represented on flags in the past, however. See, for example, pages 34, 54, 60, 65, 66, 67, and 70–75.

3/4

Among the Dogõ people of Mali there is a very ancient symbol, known as the *kanaga,* which resembles a man. When the Mali Federation was formed in 1960, a *kanaga* was placed on the center stripe of the green-yellow-red flag, sym-

5/6

7/8

9/10

11/12

bolizing the black men and women who, with feet firmly planted on the earth, raised their arms in supplication to the heavens for a new way of life. The following year when the federation was dissolved, Senegal replaced the *kanaga* with a star, and Mali omitted it entirely under the influence of Islam, which forbids the representation of living things.

With the end of the Mali Federation flag, humans have largely disappeared from the world's national flags. The exceptions are the monks on the state flag of Monaco, the human arms on the state flags of Zaire and Finland, and the human face on the sun of Uruguay's flag. Nevertheless men and women do appear on some British colonial and American state flags (see pages 291–294).
In coats of arms two kinds of humans predominate – figures symbolizing the original inhabitants of a land and those representing its typical modern citizens. The soldiers in the arms of Nepal, for example, are dressed in typical native and British fashion, indicating the respective armies in which they serve.

* The figures in parentheses indicate the pages on which the complete coat of arms or flag is reproduced.

13 14

15

16

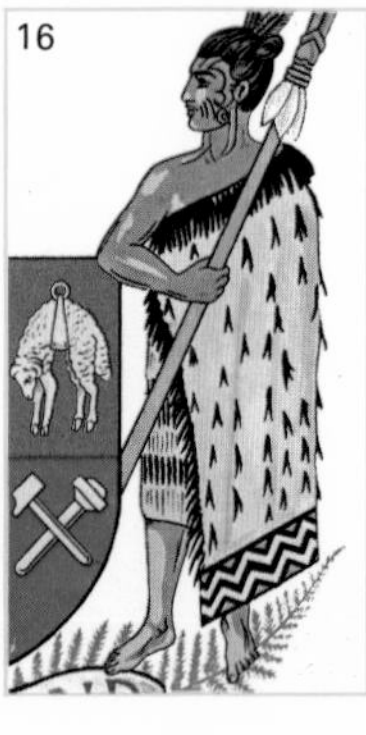

17

The standard on the opposite page represents the Holy Roman Emperor Charles V amid saltires and flames (his dynastic emblems). He is receiving divine approbation for his slaying of a Turk; the imperial arms and motto ("[There Is] More Beyond") and a representation of a saint complete the design.

CROWNS AND BUILDINGS

In British heraldic tradition, followed by Commonwealth nations, the helmet over a shield and below the torse and crown (or crest) indicates the rank of the bearer. Here the helmet in the arms of Malta reflects its status as a sovereign nation.

1

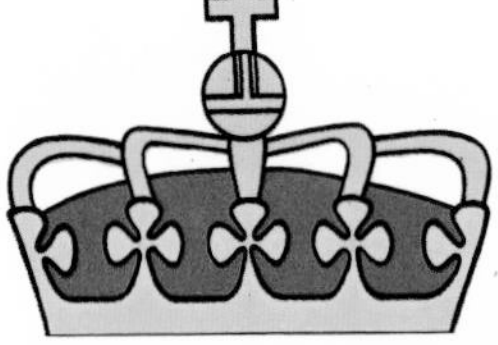
2

3

4

5

6

7

8

9

10

11

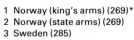

1 Norway (king's arms) (269)*
2 Norway (state arms) (269)
3 Sweden (285)
4 Belgium (214)
5 Denmark (state arms) (226)
6 Luxembourg (state arms) (254)
7 United Kingdom (291)
8 San Marino (278)
9 Canada (220)

12

13

14

15

16

10 New Zealand (265)
11 Tonga (288)
12 Liechtenstein (crown and pavilion) (253)
13 Netherlands (crown and pavilion) (253)
14 Belgium (crown and pavilion) (214)
15 Monaco (crown and pavilion) (260)
16 Jordan (crown and pavilion) (295)
17 Cambodia (crown and pavilion) (246)
18 Norway (crown and pavilion) (269)
19 Luxembourg (royal arms) (254)
20 Bahrain (213)
21 Guyana (238)
22 Vatican (223)
23 Morocco (254)
24 Nepal (264)
25 Denmark (crown and pavilion) (226)
26 Iran (242)
27 Swaziland (286)
28 Malta (257)

22

18

19

23

24

25

26

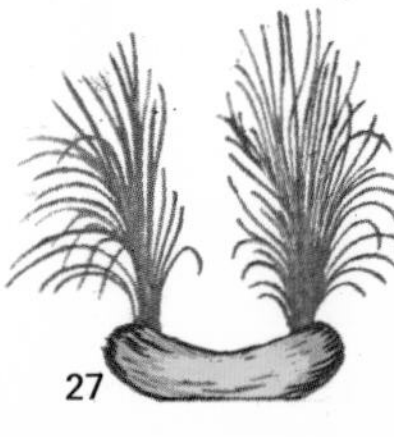
27

*The figures in parentheses indicate the pages on which the complete coat of arms or flag is reproduced.

28

CROWNS

The earliest crowns were generally very simple: a band of fur or a feather from a rare bird was enough to distinguish the chief from those under him. Today such crowns are used in only a few countries, chiefly in Africa and Asia. Ermine fur forms the base of many European crowns.

The gold bands, precious jewels, and velvet linings of the typical royal or imperial crown reflects the material wealth and ceremony which tended to characterize monarchies in the past. The heavenly origin of royal authority is suggested by the golden rays emanating from the Cambodian crown (17) and in the orb which surmounts almost all Western crowns. The ball of the orb is a symbol of the earth, its cross indicating the dominion of Christ over the world and its monarchs.

A recent innovation in state heraldry is the "mural crown" (28) which indicates nonmonarchical sovereignty.

17

The elegant tent or pavilion of medieval royalty was stylized into the decorative background found in many royal coats of arms. It is known as a mantle and appears to be different in origin from the mantling or lambrequin attached to the tops of helmets in certain personal coats of arms. Both have become extremely rare in flags since few monarchies have survived the political changes of the past century and a half.

20

21

BUILDINGS

Relatively few man-made endeavors have achieved status warranting stylization in flag design. Nevertheless, impressive structures of past civilizations do figure in the arms of certain countries (2, 4, 5, 9). The ancient temple at Angkor, for example, has been saluted by both royalists and republicans in Cambodia (1, 3).

The castle of Castile appearing in the arms of Spain (6) suggests the name of the territory; the capital of Uruguay is recalled in the arms of that country (8). The ostrich plumes at the tops of the three towers (7) actually exist in San Marino in the form of metal weathervanes.

1 Cambodia (Khmer Republic): Angkor Wat (247)*
2 China (P.R.): Tien An Men (Gate of Heavenly Peace), Peking (222)
3 Cambodia (Kingdom): Angkor Wat (246)

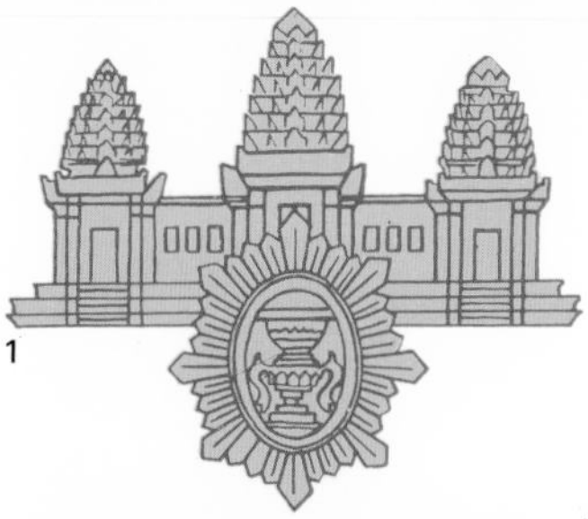
1

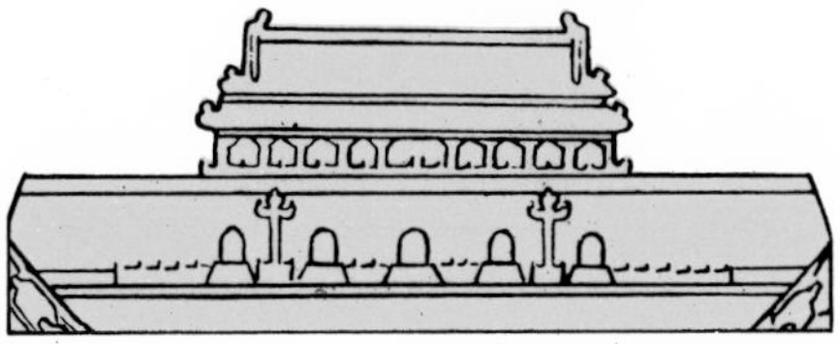
2

3

4 Mali: city walls of Timbuktu (257)
5 Ghana: unidentified fort (235)
6 Spain: unidentified (232)
7 San Marino: towers of Rocca, Cesta, and Montale (278)
8 Uruguay: city of Montevideo (295)
9 Dahomey: houses of the Somba people (226)
10 Honduras: unidentified castles (241)

4

5

6

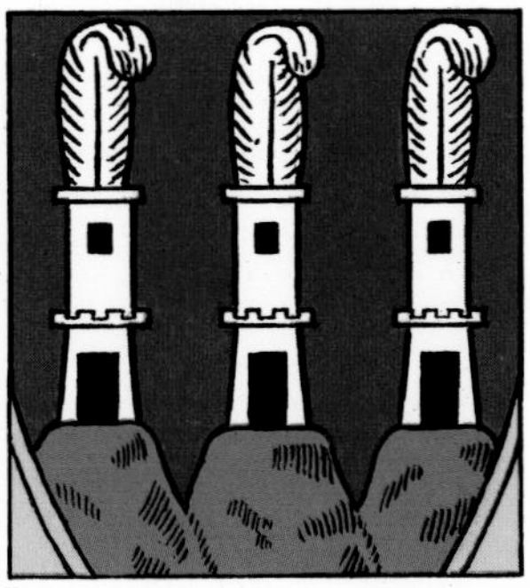
7

*The figures in parentheses indicate the pages on which the complete coat of arms or flag is reproduced.

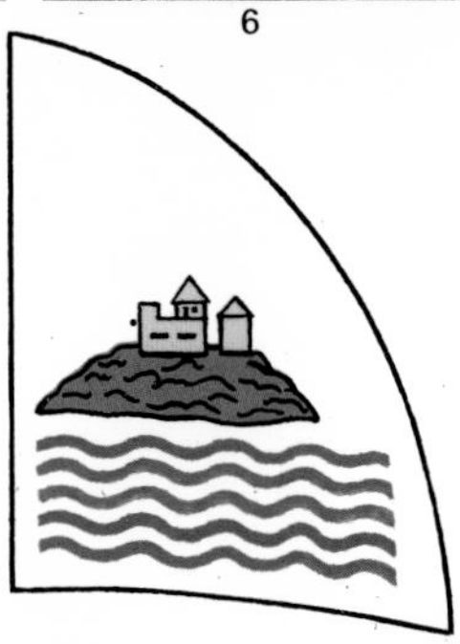
8

9

10

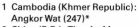

WEAPONS AND ARTIFACTS

1 Qatar, *Swords* (274)*
2 Anguilla, *Cannon* (210)
3 Saudi Arabia, *Swords* (210)
4 Burundi, *Spears* (219)
5 Zaire, *Arrow, spear* (299)
6 Swaziland, *Spears, staff* (286)
7 Haiti, *Cannon, cannonballs* (238)
8 Oman, *Swords, dagger* (290)
9 Malaysia, *Daggers* (256)
10 Tonga, *Swords* (288)
11 Guatemala, *Rifles, swords* (236)

1

2

3

4
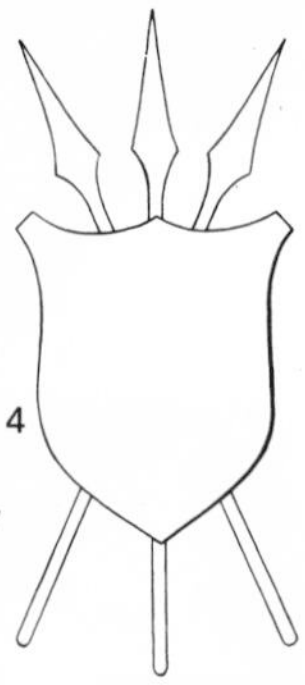

5
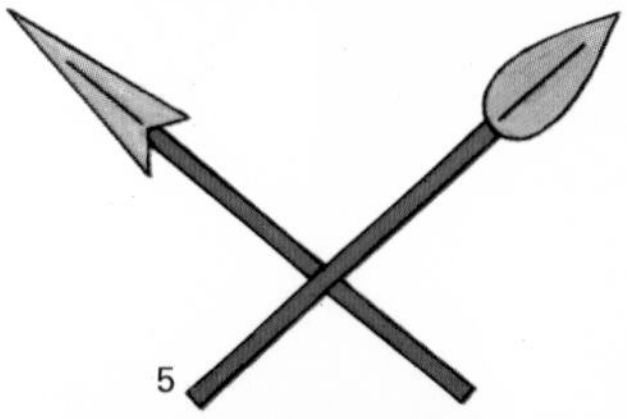

6
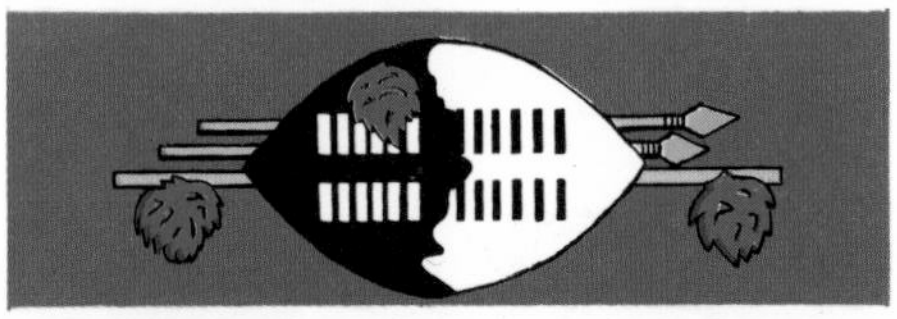

7

8
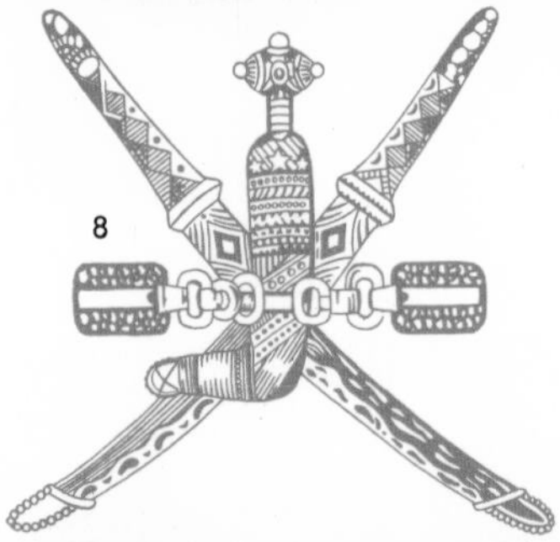

9
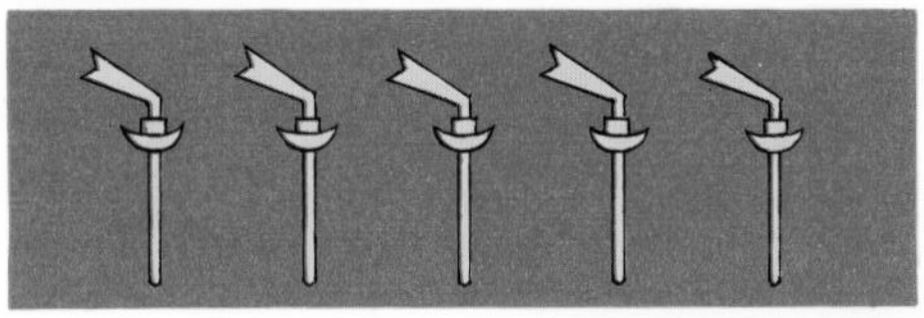

10
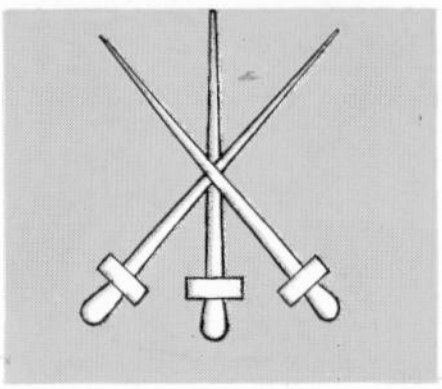

11

Other countries, not shown here, have weapons in their flag or coat of arms:
Bolivia, *Rifles, cannon, ax* (216)
Brazil, *Sword* (217)
Denmark, *Clubs* (226)
Spain, *Arrows* (232)
Ethiopia, *Spear* (232)
Fiji, *Spear, club* (233)
Ghana, *Swords* (235)
Upper Volta, *Spears* (239)
Honduras, *Arrows* (241)
Iran, *Sword* (242)
Kenya, *Spears* (247)
Lesotho, *Knobkerrie, assegai* (251)
Mali, *Bows and Arrow* (257)
Mozambique, *Arrows* (259)
Monaco, *Swords* (260)
Netherlands, *Sword, arrows* (263)
Nepal, *Rifle, bow and arrow* (264)
New Zealand, *Spear* (265)
Niger, *Swords, spear* (266)
Norway, *Ax* (269)
Panama, *Rifle, sword* (271)
Philippines, *Arrows* (273)
Rwanda, *Bow and arrow* (277)
Somalia, *Spears* (281)
Sri Lanka, *Sword* (283)
Finland, *Swords* (284)
Togo, *Bows and arrows* (287)
Tunisia, *Sword* (289)
Uganda, *Spears* (290)
United States, *Arrows* (292)
Jordan, *Swords, spears, bow and arrows* (295)
Venezuela, *Spear, swords* (296)

*The figures in parentheses indicate the pages on which the complete coat of arms or flag is reproduced.

In an important sense the coat of arms and flag of a nation are also arms (weapons) for its defense. To those who live in the country they make a succinct expression of past glories, future aspirations, and the principles upon which citizens are encouraged to act. For the outsider those symbols are a warning that the nation is willing to defend itself against those who would try to threaten its territory or rights.
Some countries are more overt than others in expressing symbolically their determination to defend themselves with force. More common in the past than now, rifles, swords, daggers, spears, and arrows are among the weapons to be found on shields or as accessories to them. The two hundred-year-old arms of the United States, for example, include a bundle of arrows and an olive branch to indicate the powers of the national Congress to decide questions of war and peace. The swords and daggers of Arab arms are associated with chivalric traditions in those countries, whereby adult males frequently wear such weapons as part of their normal attire and stand ready to use them if their honor is challenged.

16

A modern development of state heraldry is the substitution of tools of industry – hammers, hoes, gearwheels, and sickles, for example – indicating that true national strength is to be found as much in a strong economy as in armed forces. It is not generally known that the familiar hammer and sickle of communism has been replaced in certain communist states with local variants – e.g., a mattock and horsewhip (Eastern Mongolia), a sickle and rake (Tuva), and an anchor and pickaxe (Far Eastern Republic).
Other artifacts, such as keys and scales, are traditional heraldic emblems still found in a number of flags and arms. Scales are a symbol of justice revived by the neoclassical eighteenth century, when allegorical figures, such as Liberty, Agriculture, etc. were popular symbols.

TOOLS

1

2

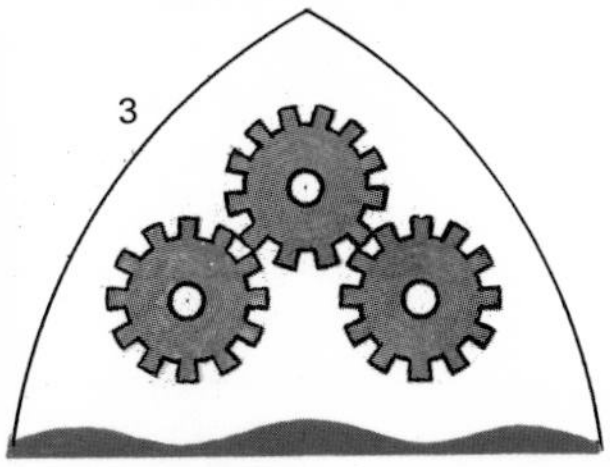
3

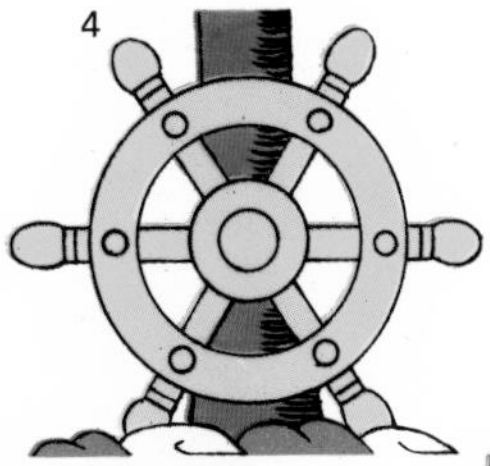
4

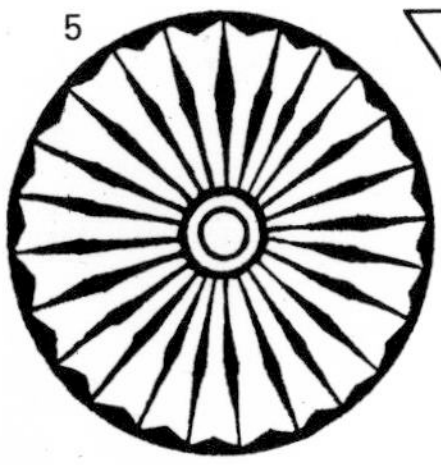
5

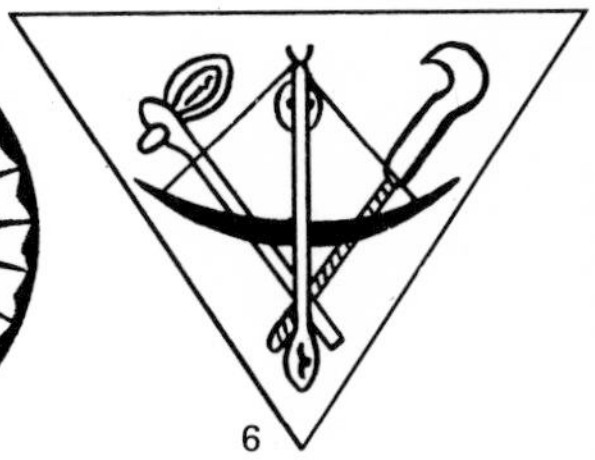
6

7

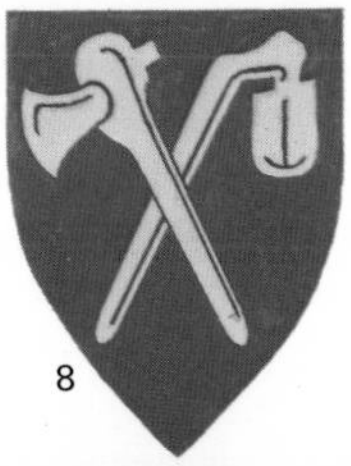
8

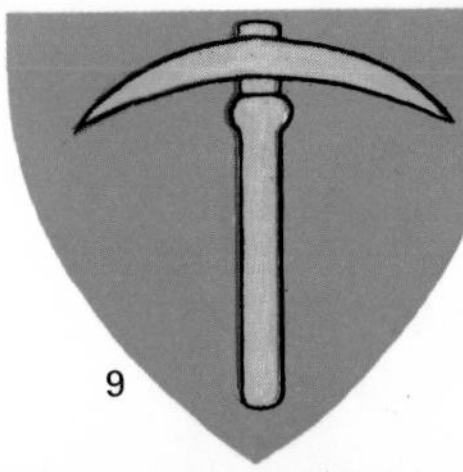
9

10

11

12

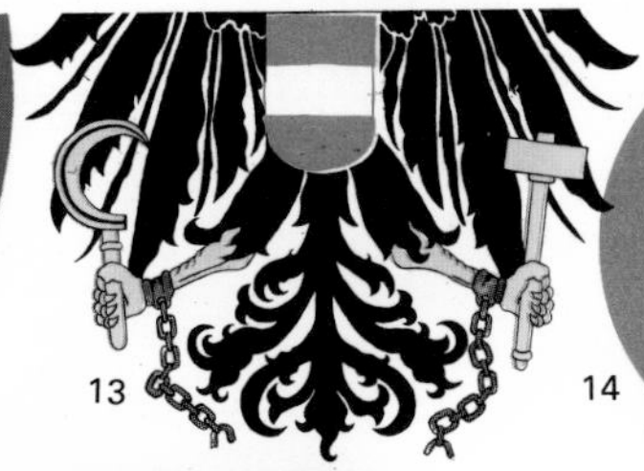
13

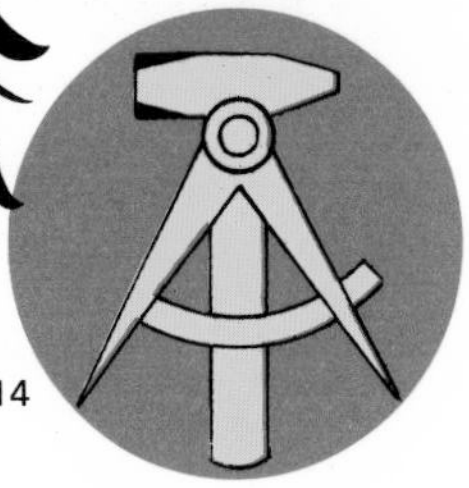
14

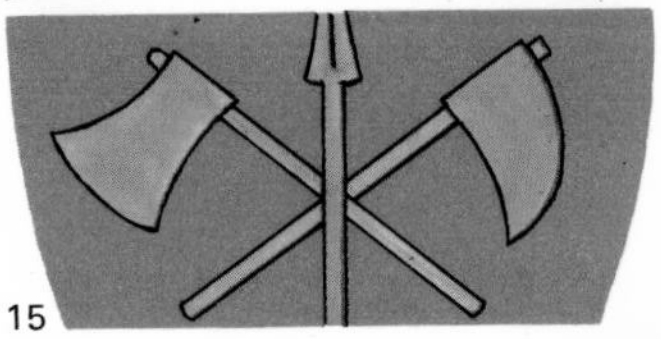
15

17

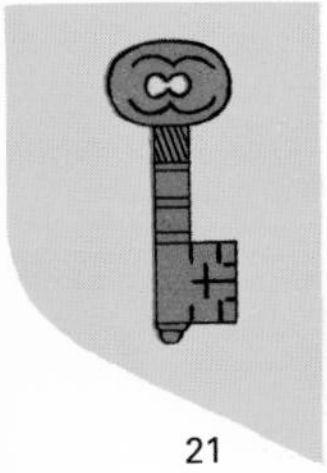
21

22

18

19

20

23

24

25

1 Italy, *Cogwheel* (244)*
2 Viet-Nam, *Cogwheel* (297)
3 Botswana, *Cogwheels* (216)
4 Trinidad and Tobago, *Ship's wheel* (288)
5 India, *Wheel* (215)
6 Rwanda, *Hoe, pruning knife* (277)
7 Soviet Union (arms), *Hammer and sickle* (282)
8 The Gambia, *Ax, hoe* (234)
9 Rhodesia, *Pick* (276)
10 Namibia, *Hammers* (262)
11 Soviet Union (flag), *Hammer and sickle* (282)
12 New Zealand, *Hammers* (265)
13 Austria, *Hammer, sickle, chains* (270)
14 German Dem. Rep., *Hammer, dividers* (228)
15 Tanzania, *Ax, hoe* (286)
16 Burma, *Cogwheel* (262)
17 Israel, *Menorah* (244)
18 Uruguay, *Scales* (295)
19 Cameroon, *Scales* (219)
20 Tunisia, *Scales* (289)
21 Mauritius, *Key* (258)
22 Vatican, *Keys* (223)
23 Ireland, *Harp* (231)
24 Peru, *Cornucopia* (272)
25 Barbados, *Trident* (214)

*The figures in parentheses indicate the pages on which the complete coat of arms or flag is reproduced.

THE TREE

1 Anguilla, *Mahogany* (210)*
2 Equatorial Guinea, *God-tree* (236)
3 Barbados, *Bearded fig* (214)
4 Mauritius, *Palm* (258)
5 Dahomey, *Oil palm* (226)
6 Mauritania, *Palm* (261)
7 Lebanon, *Cedar* (253)
8 Central African Republic, *(species not identified)* (276)
9 Sierra Leone, *Oil palm* (280)
10 Western Samoa, *Cocoanut palm* (278)
11 Haiti, *Emperor palm* (238)
12 Peru, *Cinchona* (272)
13 Fiji, *Cocoanut palm* (233)
14 Saudi Arabia, *Date palm* (210)
15 Malaysia, *Betel nut palm* (256)
16 Ivory Coast, *(species not identified)* (225)
17 Indonesia, *Banyan* (242)
18 Ghana, *Cocoa tree* (235)
19 South Africa, *Orange tree* (281)
20 Senegal, *Baobab* (279)
21 Gabon, *Okume* (234)
22 Maldives, *Palm* (228)

The "tree of life" motif was found extensively in the Near East as a religious symbol in antiquity. Today only a single national flag maintains that tradition – Lebanon prominently features the cedar as a symbol of immortality and holiness.
National coats of arms around the world include various types of trees, but the palm is most prominent. In those countries where it appears, it provides welcome shade, while its fruit gives both food and drink.
Trees are prominent in some of the past and present flags of American states (pages 293–294) – the palmetto of South Carolina, the magnolia of Mississippi, and the pine tree of Vermont, Maine, and Massachusetts. The latter emblem has been in use since 1628, and from 1686 until 1776 a pine tree emblem added in the upper hoist corner was the only distinction between the flags of New England and those of the mother country, Great Britain.
The district flag of Entlebuch, Switzerland *(right)* dates from 1394–1405. It epitomizes the tree in flags with its sturdy trunk for strength, roots for stability, and broad leaves promising the rejuvenation of human enterprise after the severest of winters.

1

2

3

4

5

6

7

8

9

10

11
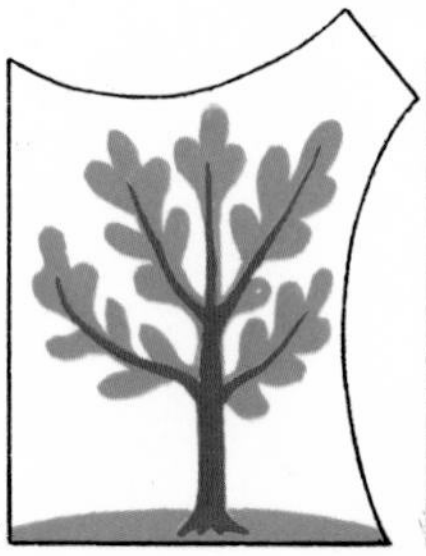
12

13

14
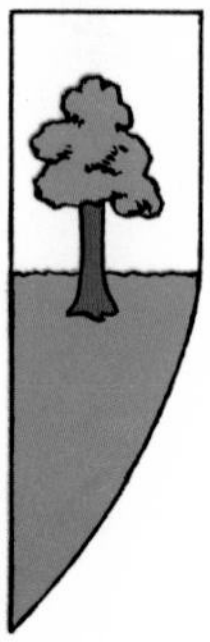
15

16

17

18

19

20
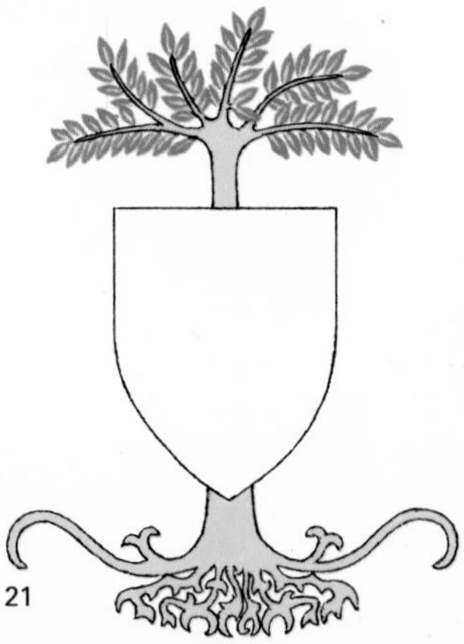
21

22

Other countries, not shown here, have tree symbols in their arms or flag:
Bolivia, *Breadfruit* (216)
Cuba, *Palm* (225)
Honduras, *Oak, pine* (241, 318)
Liberia, *Palm* (251, 320)
Nepal, *(species not identified)* (264, 330)
Malagasy Republic, *Ranivala* (275)
Romania, *(species not identified)* (277)

*The figures in parentheses indicate the pages on which the complete coat of arms or flag is reproduced.

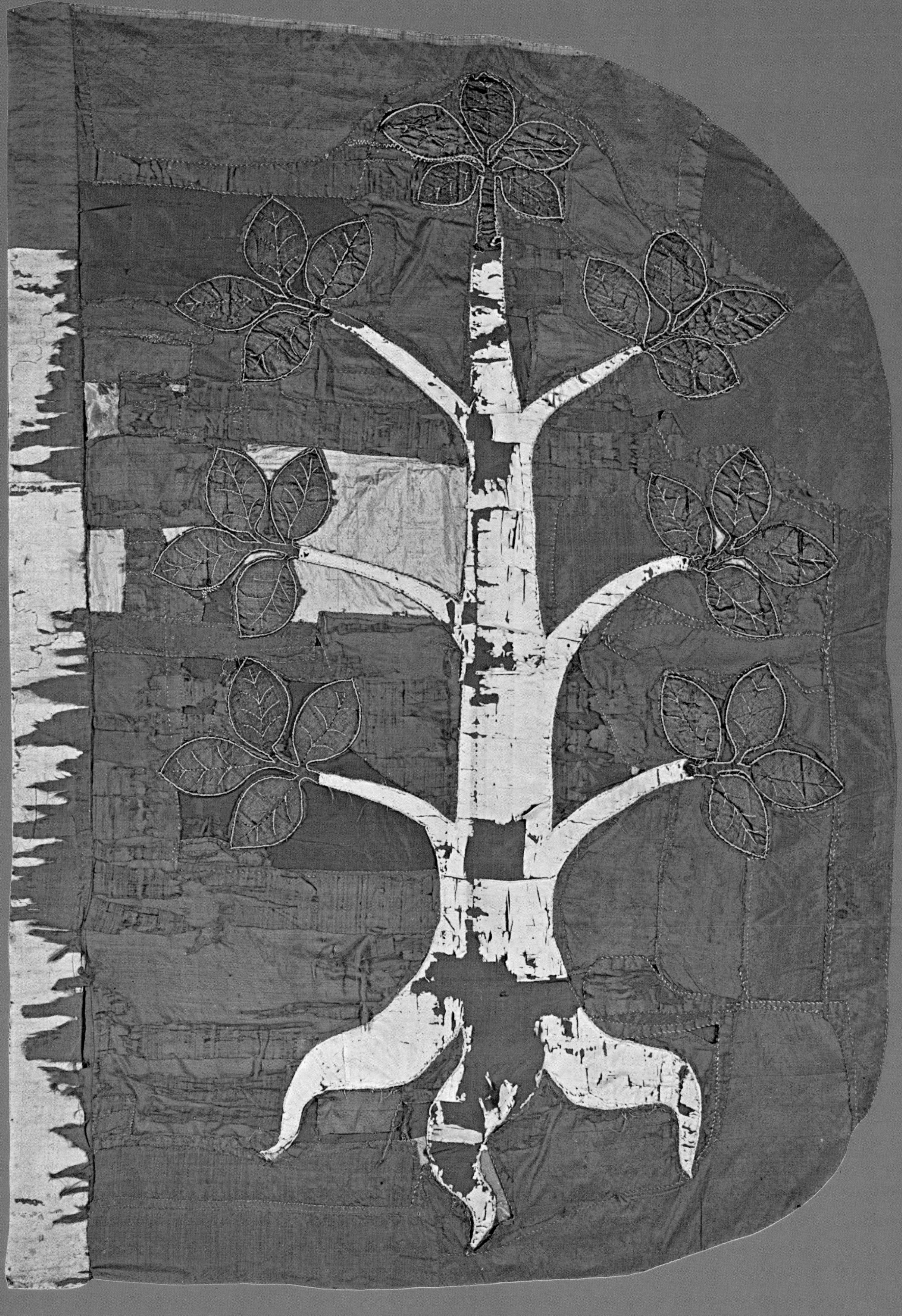

PLANTS AND FRUITS

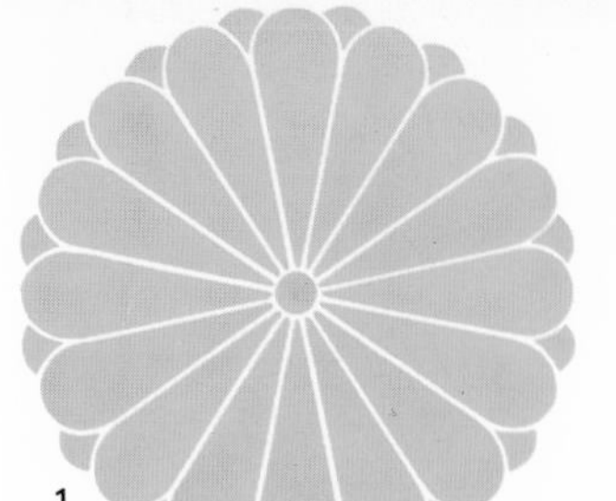
1

4

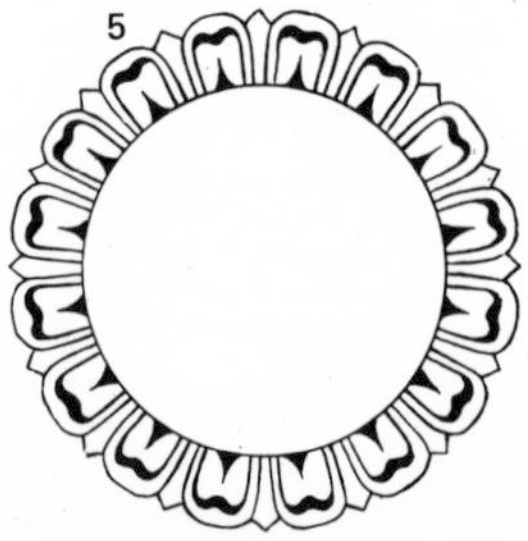
5

2

3

6

7

8

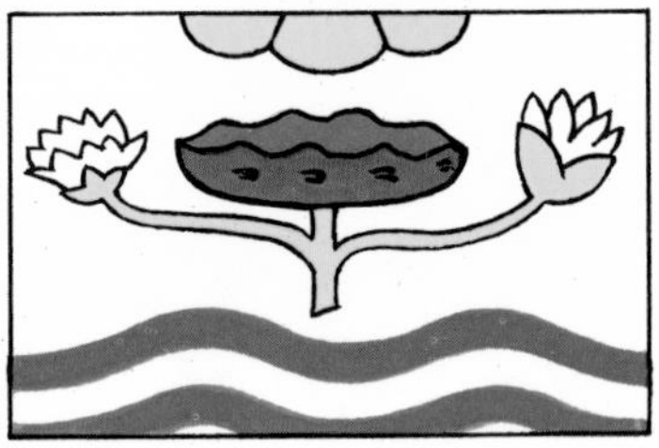
9

10

11

1 Japan, *Chrysanthemum* (267)*
2 Nauru, *Tomano* (263)
3 Barbados, *Pride of Barbados* (214)
4 Korea, Republic of, *Rose of Sharon* (248)
5 Sri Lanka, *Lotus* (283)
6 Anguilla *(unspecified)* (210)
7 Pakistan, *Tea* (271)
8 Bangladesh, *Water lily* (213)
9 Guyana, *Victoria regia lily* (238)
10 Canada, *Maple leaf* (220)
11 Canada, *Maple leaves* (220)
12 San Marino, *Laurel, oak* (278)
13 Pakistan, *Narcissus* (271)
14 Cyprus, *Olive branches* (249)
15 Portugal, *Laurel* (274)
16 Argentina, *Laurel* (211)
17 Democratic Republic of Viet-Nam, *Rice* (297)
18 Senegal, *Palm* (279)
19 Italy, *Olive, oak* (244)
20 Dahomey, *Corn (maize)* (226)
21 Colombia, *Pomegranate* (223)
22 Venezuela, *Fruits and flowers* (296)
23 Fiji, *Bananas* (233)
24 Niger, *Millet* (266)
25 Venezuela, *Wheat* (296)
26 Pakistan, *Wheat* (271)
27 Anguilla, *Fruit (species not specified)* (210)
28 Pakistan, *Jute* (271)
29 New Zealand, *Wheat* (265)
30 Malaysia, *Hibiscus* (256)
31 Pakistan, *Cotton* (271)
32 Jamaica, *Pineapple* (245)

*The figures in parentheses indicate the pages on which the complete coat of arms or flag is reproduced.

Ancient Greek tradition relates that the goddess Athena contended with the god Poseidon for the spiritual leadership of Athens. As represented in the west pediment of the Parthenon, the gifts they offered the people were an olive tree and a horse, symbolizing prosperity and strength, respectively. The Athenians chose the former, making the olive branch one of the earliest of men's floral symbols with political meaning.

Since olive trees flourished in times of peace, its branches – as in the modern arms of Cyprus and flag of the United Nations – have come to stand for peace. Other leaves and grains also have symbolic attributions, such as the oak for strength, laurel for victory, and wheat (or rice or maize) for prosperity.

12

13

14

15

Local agricultural products or distinctive flowers are featured in national coats of arms such as the bananas of Fiji, the tea leaves of Bangladesh, and the tomano flowers of Nauru. The pomegranate (*granada* in Spanish) was chosen for the emblem of Granada for obvious reasons; Colombia, once known as New Granada, continues the tradition. Agricultural produce spills from the cornucopia, a classical emblem of prosperity.

In some instances a floral emblem may have a deep religious and historical significance. This is the case with the chrysanthemum emblem of the Japanese emperors, the lotus in the arms of Sri Lanka and the former arms of Mongolia, and even the maple leaf of Canada. The crown of Tonga (page 288) is surrounded by chestnut tree

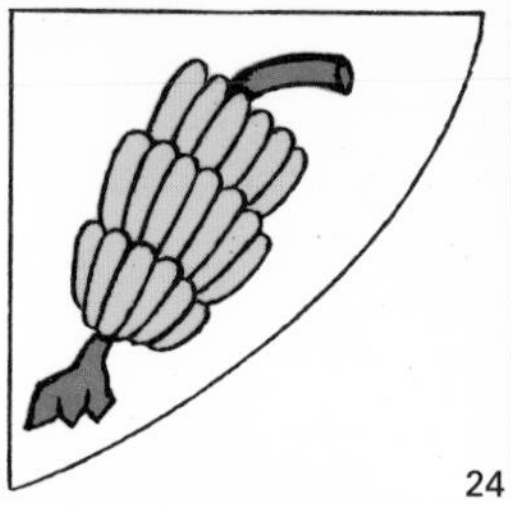

23

24

20

21

22

25

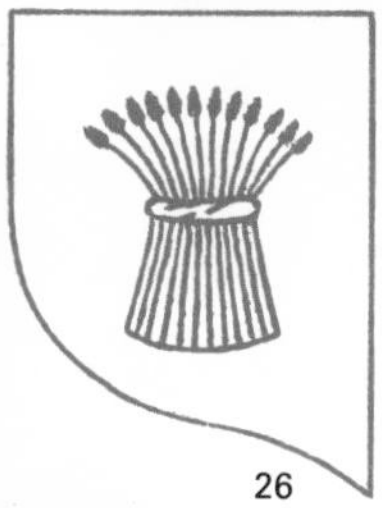

26

27

28

29

30

31

32

leaves because such leaves were worn by chiefs in the past when they made decisions of life and death. The leaf of the sacred bo tree under which the Buddha found enlightenment is represented in the flag of Sri Lanka.

Most coats of arms are symmetrical and present

16

17

18

19

in graphic form a "closed universe," suggesting that the nation encompasses everything needed by the citizen for a good and productive life. For that reason the arms may have typical plants, animals, or natural features; it may bristle with weapons; or it may have emblems that summarize the religious and political history of the land. Consistent with this interpretation the wreath around the outside of many arms may be looked at as a protective covering, a barrier to foreign intrusion. It corresponds to the human or animal supporters in other arms which fiercely guard the central shield. This reflects the modern realization that ultimately a strong agricultural base is at least as important as an army in defending national sovereignty.

WATER, LANDSCAPES, SHIPS

1
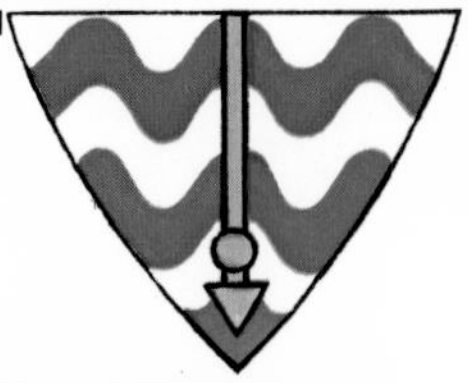
2
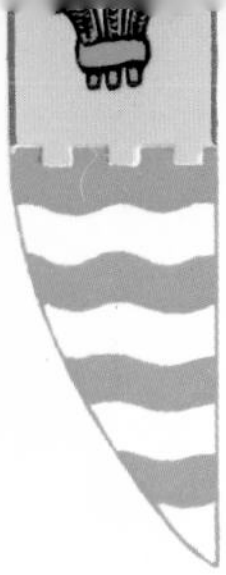
3

4

5
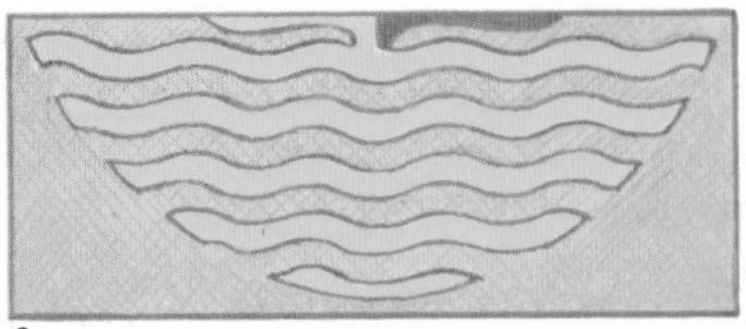
6

7

8

WATER
1 Tanzania (286)*
2 Malaysia (256)
3 Angola/Mozambique (209/259)
4 Nigeria: two rivers (266)
5 Botswana (216)

10

11

12

13

6 Bangladesh (213)
7 Western Samoa (278)
8 Zambia (299)

Other countries with this symbol in their flags or arms are:
Spain (232)
Ghana (235)
Honduras (241)
Korea, P.D.R. (248)
Kuwait (250)
Malta (257)
Mexico (258)
Trinidad and Tobago (288)
Yemen (298)
Guyana (238)

LANDSCAPES
9 El Salvador (231)
10 Bolivia (216)
11 Cuba (225)
12 Ecuador (230)
13 Liberia (251)
14 Costa Rica (224)
15 San Marino (278)
16 Romania (277)
17 Korea, P.D.R. (248)
18 Cuba (225)
19 Colombia (223)
30 Nepal (264)

Other countries with landscapes in their flags or arms are:
Honduras (241)
Lesotho (251)
Mongolia (260)
Nepal (264)

18

19
20

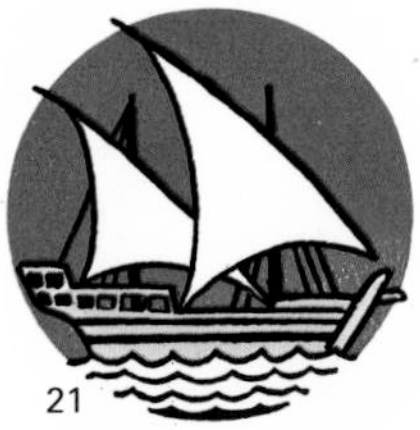
21
22

23

Any nation might choose distinctive native geographic features for representation in its coat of arms or its flag. Remarkably few countries have in fact done so, perhaps because traditional rules of heraldry in Western Europe forbade the presentation of topographical features; moreover, such features, when stylized, have a tendency to lose those distinctive aspects that make them acceptable as symbols.

Nevertheless modern state symbolism has developed a number of examples where a river or mountain or coastline serves to recall a specific country or a subdivision. The simplest mode of presentation is a stripe – perhaps green for forests or jungles, brown or orange for less fertile lands, and blue for water. These and similar stripes are found in a great number of flags, although their association with a certain aspect of nature is not always immediately apparent.

Quite close to the purity of this color symbolism

9

is the evocation of a lake or river or ocean by alternating wavy lines, usually of blue and white. Nigeria and Ecuador in their coats of arms have gone so far as to suggest artistically specific rivers, while the shield of Zambia is a heraldic presentation of Victoria Falls.
The flags of countries in the New World and of colonial territories would frequently have seascapes with ships because their original explorers and settlers arrived by ship from another country. Central American countries express with pride the fact that they are washed by both the

recognized a lymphad (as in the arms of New Brunswick and New Zealand) as the stylization of a ship, yet the ships of Columbus were specifically chosen for the arms of both the Bahamas and Trinidad and Tobago because of the discovery of those islands by those specific vessels.

Panama (271)
Zambia (299)
Nicaragua (265)

SHIPS
20 Kuwait (250)
21 United Arab Emirates (208)
22 New Zealand (265)
23 Mauritius (258)
24 Trinidad and Tobago (288)
25 Dahomey (226)
26 The Bahamas (212)
27 Gabon (234)
28 Fiji (233)
29 Tunisia (289)

14

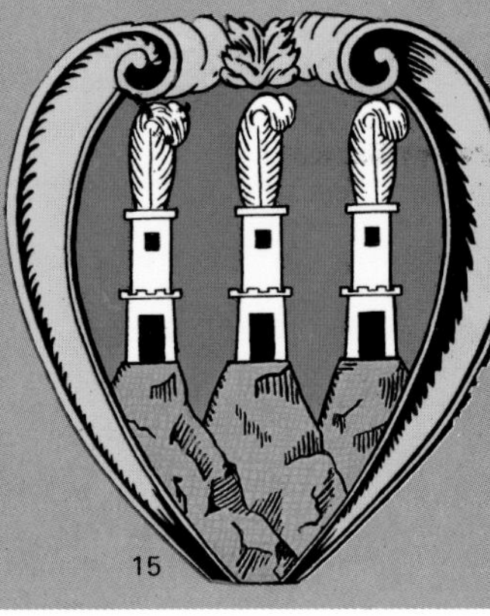

15

16

17

24

25

26

27

28

29

Atlantic and Pacific Oceans. Landscapes combining forests and mountains with such man-made features as railroads and dams are frequently in the arms of communist countries and in those of the states of the United States and Brazil.
Most of the ships represented in national arms are imprecise as to design or even era: the outrigger of Fiji and the *dhow* of several Arab states are exceptions. Heraldry has traditionally

30

SHIPS and LANDSCAPES
12 Ecuador (230)
13 Liberia (251)
14 Costa Rica (224)
19 Colombia (223)

*The figures in parentheses indicate the pages on which the complete coat of arms or flag is reproduced.

ABSTRACT FORMS AND INSCRIPTIONS

The *soyonbo* of Mongolia *(left)* has the stark simplicity of many modern commercial logos, yet its history dates back hundreds of years. Each element holds a specific symbolic meaning (see page 260).

The disc is frequently a symbol of the sun, but also sometimes of universality and harmony. It is particularly favored in the Far East, as in the flags *(right)* of the Republic of Korea, Bangladesh, and Japan.

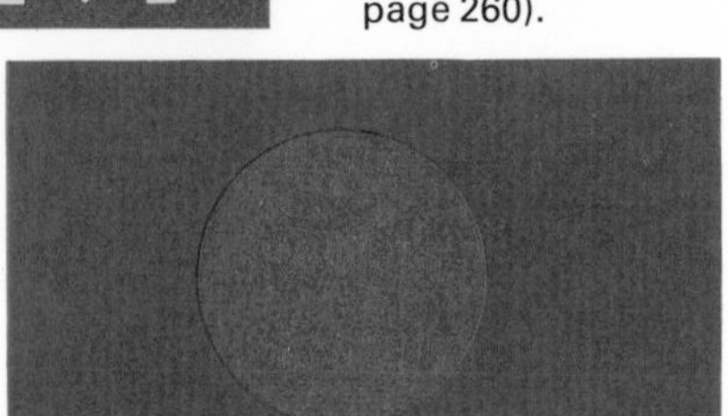

Bands of various colors are found in heraldry – here on the shields of Andorra and Cuba – and in numerous flags.

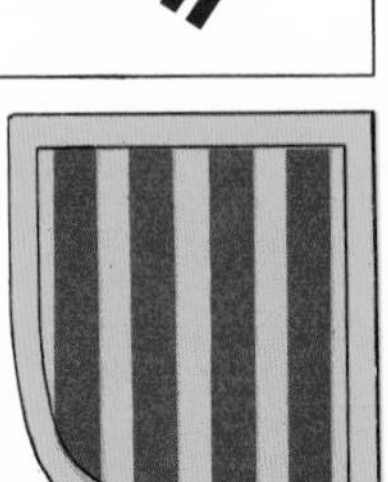

Heraldic forms, such as the lozenges of Monaco and zigzag stripes of Chad, are infrequently met with in national flags except when the arms on which they appear are reproduced on those flags.

A symbol is usually thought of as being a representation of a living thing or of an object, yet it may simply be a color or geometric shape. The latter type of symbol has come into special prominence in the past two hundred years, as complex nations have attempted to express in concise terms what they stand for. The ease and inexpensiveness of manufacturing geometric flags may also have had some effect upon their popularity.

Unlike more complicated symbols, stripes and bars and circles and similar designs have few stereotyped meanings. Limited only by imagination, men and women constantly develop new meanings and patterns for the symbols depicted on the arms and flags of nations, provinces, and cities.

Heraldry has traditionally argued against the use of words or even letters on coats of arms and flags. Words are verbal symbols, while flags are essentially visual symbols – the one presumably appropriate for use in certain circumstances, the other elsewhere.

Nevertheless from earliest times actual flags have borne inscriptions and words, and the increase in literacy among the peoples of the world is encouraging this trend. A single letter or character can be quite effective as a symbol, as several Japanese prefectural flags (pages 267–268) demonstrate. On flags of organiza-

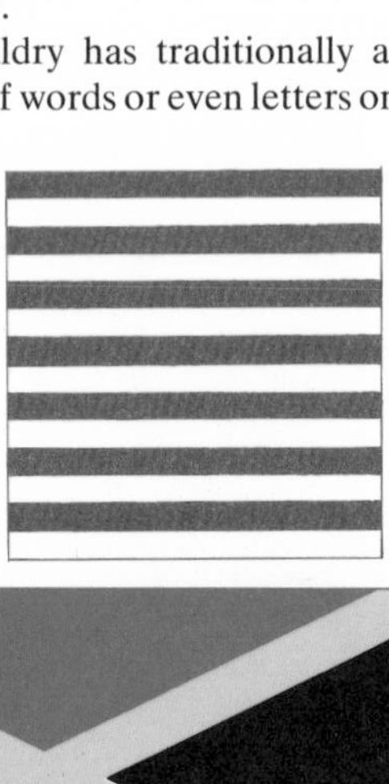

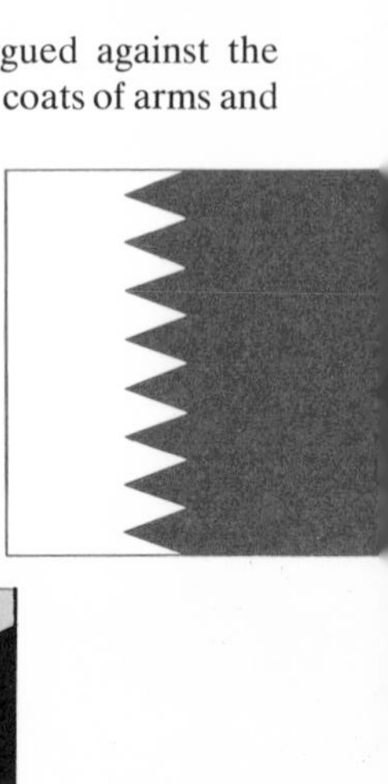

Particularly since the adoption of the United States flag in 1777, stripes have become one of the most widely used of all abstract designs in flags. The methods of rendering them are endless.

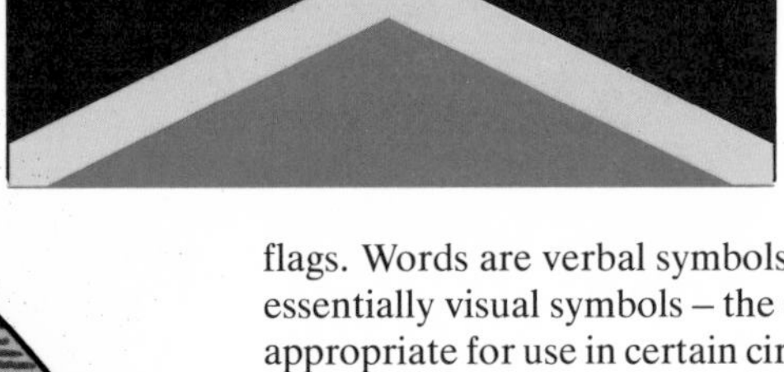

The stylized symbol and diapered background of medieval heraldry have found a modern application in the chief (upper part) of the Nauru arms *(right)*. Coconut fiber matting forms the background for the alchemical symbol for phosphorus, recalling the extensive deposits of guano on the island.

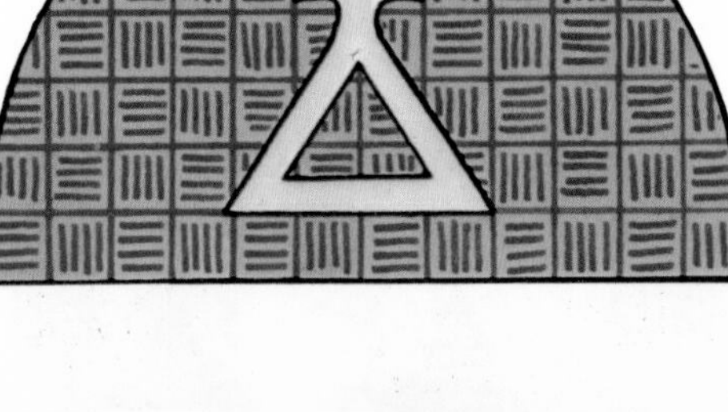

1

1 Saudi Arabia (210)*
2 Nauru (263)
3 Malaysia (256)
4 Belgium (214)
5 Jordan (295)
6 Pakistan (271)
7 Grenada (235)
8 Burma (262)
9 Bulgaria (218)
10 Morocco (254)
11 Israel (244)
12 Rwanda (277)
13 Brazil (217)
14 United Arab Emirates (208)
15 Namibia (262)
16 Romanian Regimental Flag

* The figures in parentheses indicate the page for complete coat of arms or flag.

tions or very small political entities, inscriptions are often necessary to identify one particular group or unit among the hundreds or even thousands of others with which it might otherwise be confused. Indeed it is a general rule that the most complex flags are of the smallest institutions and political entities.

In Muslim lands there is an added reason for the use of inscriptions. The Islamic injunction against the representation of living things has long encouraged the development of calligraphy, in flags as well as in architecture and art. Here the ability to decipher the written message is of secondary importance to its esthetic impression. The most striking modern examples include the personal standards of the sultan of Turkey and the king of Afghanistan, the national flag of Saudi Arabia, and military colors in a number of Muslim countries.

2

3

4

5

6

Although a great many of the inscriptions in national coats of arms are in the native language of the countries, such as Burmese (8) and Hebrew (11), a suprising number still rely on Latin; see, for example, the arms of South West Africa (15). The Arabic tradition of calligraphy has inspired a number of inscriptions, including Jordan's (5), the longest one of all. The only national flag composed chiefly of an inscription, that of Saudi Arabia (1), flies over the heartland of Islam. Inscriptions and letters appear infrequently on national flags, Rwanda (12) and Brazil (13) being exceptions, but are common on military colors where the name of the unit or its battle honors may be incorporated in the design. The 15th Regiment of Infantry of Romania (16) is a case in point.

7

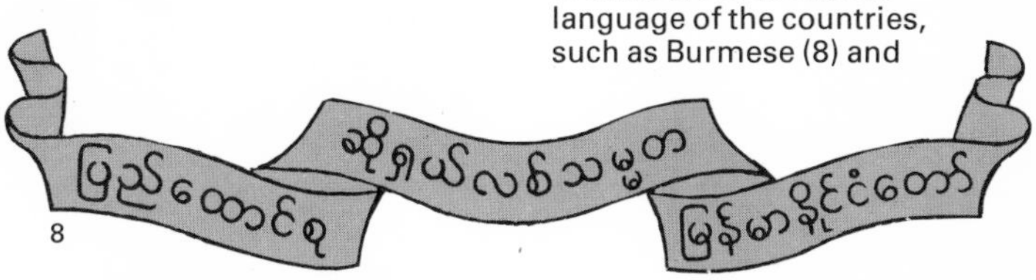

8

9

10

11

15

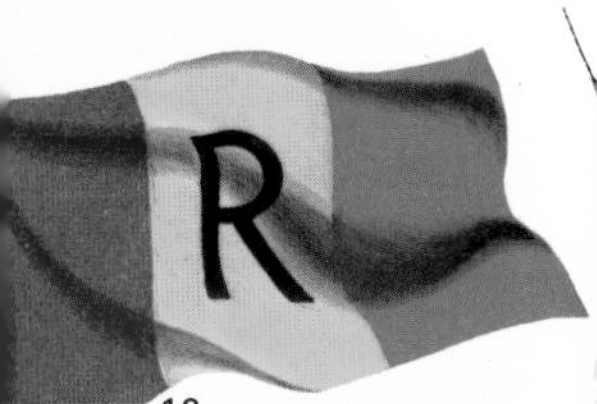

12

13

14

16

SYMBOLS IN POLITICS

Political parties and movements in all parts of the world express their policies and rally supporters with flags and symbols, of which a select number are shown on these pages. The choice here reflects the general characteristics of such flags – stripes, initials, and easily remembered symbols. While not all of those shown are still current, some may one day influence a change in a national flag – as political party emblems have in the past (see page 79).

1

4

5

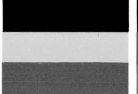
6

7

8

1 *National Party* (Turkey) Emblem centered on a red flag (2:3) above the words MİLLET PARTİSİ in white.
2 *Tupamaros* (Uruguay) 2:3.
3 *Progressive Nationalist Movement* (South Viet-Nam) 2:3.
4 *Convention People's Party* (Ghana) 2:3.
5 *Uganda People's Congress* (Uganda) 2:3.
6 *Sierra Leone Independence Party Youth Section* (Sierra Leone) 2:3.
7 *Swaziland Progressive Party* (Swaziland) 2:3.
8. *Popular National Alliance* (Colombia) 2:3.
9 *Bechuanaland People's Party* (Botswana) 2:3.
10 *Northern Elements Progressive Union* (Nigeria) 2:3.
11 *Movement for the Liberation of the Comoro Islands* (Comoro Islands) 2:3.
12 *Nepal Congress Party* (Nepal) 2:3.
13 *Kenya African National Union* (Kenya) 2:3.
14 *Democratic Republican Party* (Republic of Korea) Emblem in the middle of a flag (2:3) of white with a green triangle at each end.
15 *Korean Worker's Party* (P.D.R. Korea). Emblem in the upper hoist of a red flag (2:3).
16 *Italian Liberal Party* (Italy) 2:3.
17 *Nationalist Party* (Panama) 2:3.
18 *Bulgarian Communist Party* (Bulgaria) 2:3.
19 *Albanian Labor Party* (Albania) 2:3.
20 *New England State Movement* (Australia) Yellow emblem centered on a blue flag (2:3).
21 *Socialist Union of Youth* (Czechoslovakia).
22 *Nationalist Party* (Republic of China) Emblem in the middle of the flag (2:3).
23 *Free Social Union* (Federal Republic of Germany) Emblem in the middle of the flag (1:2).
24 *Country Party* (Finland) 1:1.
25 *Front for the Liberation of South Yemen* (P.D.R. Yemen) Emblem in the middle of a flag (2:3) of horizontal stripes of red-white-black.
26 *Norwegian Labor Party* (Norway) Emblem in upper hoist of the flag (2:3).
27 *Authentic Organization* (Cuba) Emblem in the middle of the flag (2:3).
28 *Independence Party* (Sudan) Emblem in the middle of the flag (2:3).

14

15

16

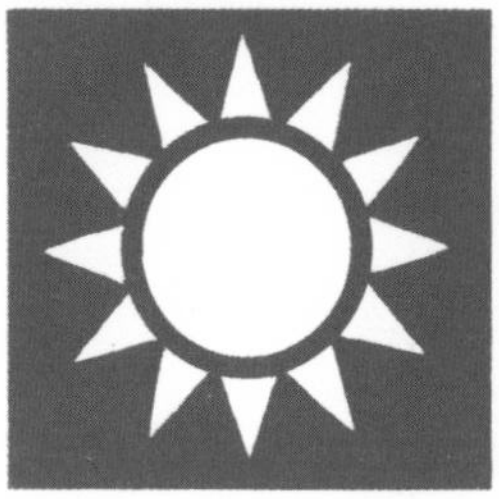
22

23

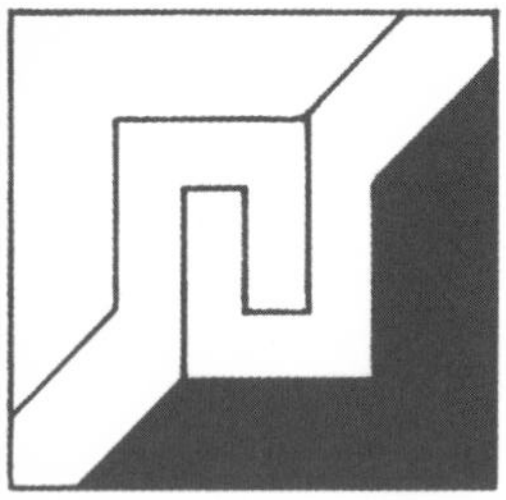
24

25

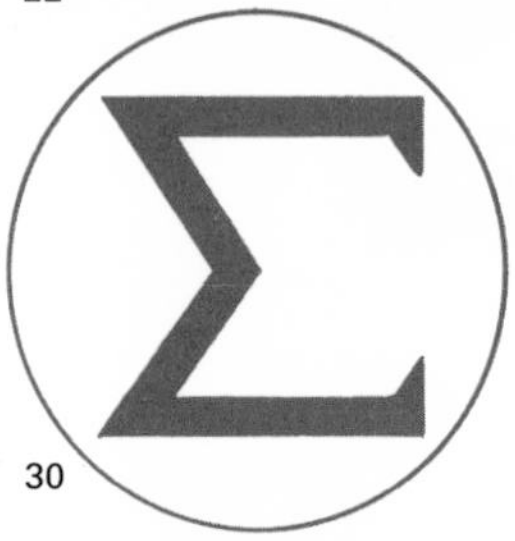
30

33

34

35

31

32

40

41

44

45

2

3

29 *Afro-Shirazi Party* (Tanzania) Emblem in the middle of the flag (2:3).
30 *Integralist Party* (Brazil) Emblem in the middle of a green flag (2:3).
31 *Vanguard Movement* (U.K.) Emblem in the fly of a white flag (2:3) with the Union Jack in the canton.

9

10

11

12

13

17

18

19

20

21

32 *United Force* (Guyana) Emblem in the middle of a blue flag (2:3).
33 *National Phalanx* (Spain) Emblem in the middle of a flag (2:3) vertically divided red-black-red in a ratio of 1:2:1.
34 *People's Action Party* (Singapore) Emblem in the middle of a white flag (2:3).
35 *Burmese Path of Socialism* (Burma) Emblem in the upper hoist (2:3).
36 *Party of the Radical Left* (Chile) Emblem in the middle of the flag (2:3).
37 *Swatantra Party* (India) Emblem in the middle of the flag (2:3).
38 *Lao Patriotic Front* (Pathet Lao) (Laos) Emblem in the middle of the flag (2:3).
39 *Nationalist Party* (South Africa) Emblem near the flagstaff of an orange triangular flag.
40 *14th of July Movement* (Dominican Republic) (2:3).
41 *People's Development Movement* (Belize).
42 *Khmer Rouge* (radical faction) (Cambodia) (2:3).
43 *United Malays National Organization* (Malaysia) (2:3).
44 *Lesotho National Party* (Lesotho) (2:3).
45 *Socialist Labor Action Party* (Costa Rica) (2:3).
46 *Independence Party* (Puerto Rico) (2:3).

26

27

28

29

36

37

38

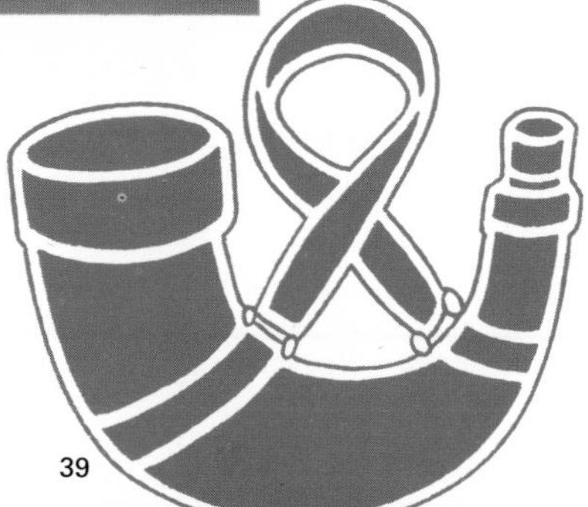
39

42

43

48
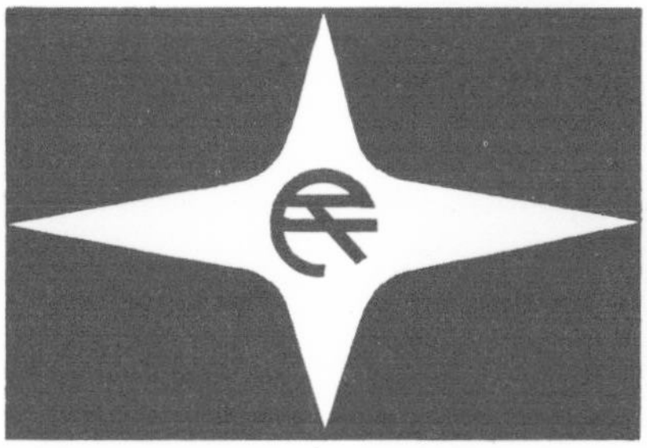

49

46

47

The symbols of some political parties are different in color when used on a flag from when they appear alone. On these pages only the flag version is shown, with an indication of the placement of the emblem and the color and proportions of the flag if it is not illustrated in full.

47 *Phalanx* (Lebanon) Emblem in the middle of a white flag (2:3).
48 *Democratic Socialist Party* (Japan) (2:3).
49 *National States Rights Party* (USA) (1:2).

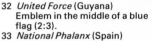

SYMBOLS IN THE SKY

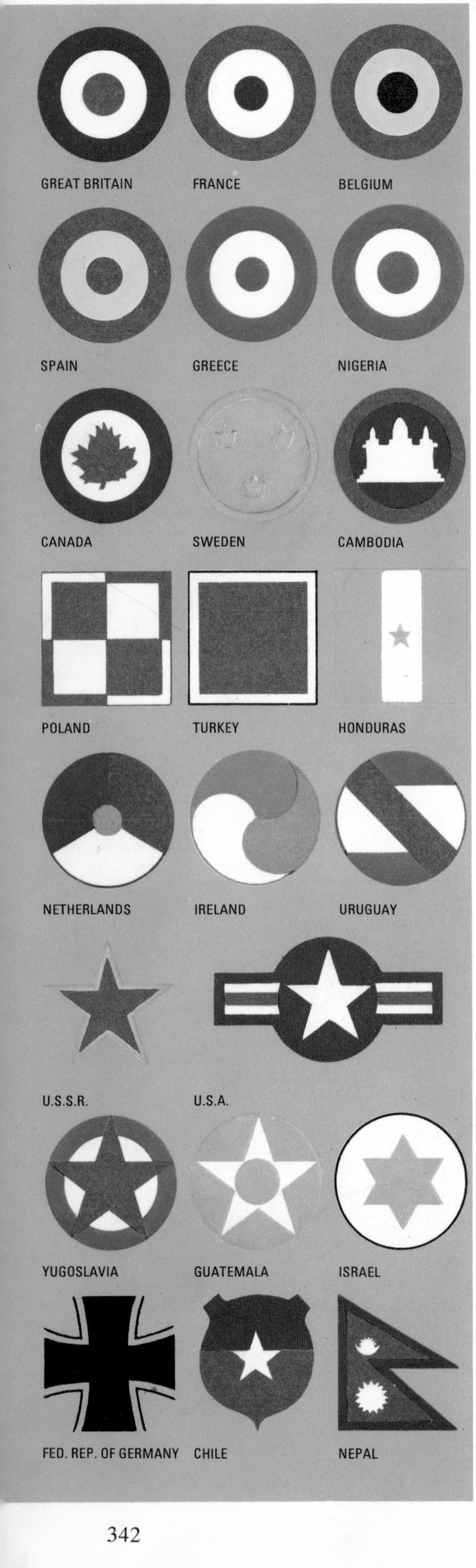

In the early days of ballooning – and even on the first heavier-than-air craft – actual flags were often hoisted to indicate nationality for the new vessels, just as ships at sea fly ensigns for identification. Very soon, however, the speed of the aircraft made it necessary to replace actual flags with painted ones or with flag-related emblems. Two main types developed, the roundels and fin flashes used by military aircraft *(left)* and the tail markings of civil aviation *(right)*. A number of these roundels and commercial symbols have found their way into flags flown on the ground at airports, but their most important function continues to be in their role as the "heraldry of the air."

Seven principal categories of design may be discerned in the seven rows of commercial tail markings at right. Many have simply taken the national flag or coat of arms or a principal element from these, translating it into the distinctive shape and surface of the new medium.

A second group has taken the theme of flight, generally expressed in the form of a bird or of stylized wings: national colors and graphics create the distinctions which are necessary for recognition purposes.

The name or abbreviation for the airline and/or its corporate logo is extensively used by a third group of airlines, while highly abstract lines and curves and color surfaces have been adopted by still others.

Traditional heraldry has relatively little impact in this modern field of symbolism, yet its basic rules – ease of interpretation, simplicity of rendition, and a sharp contrast of color – characterize the tail markings of a fifth grouping.

Finally, some airlines have chosen a picture of a flower, animal, or even a human face as the best means of maintaining public recognition.

Unfortunately space has not permitted the presentation of more than a fraction of the symbols in current use.

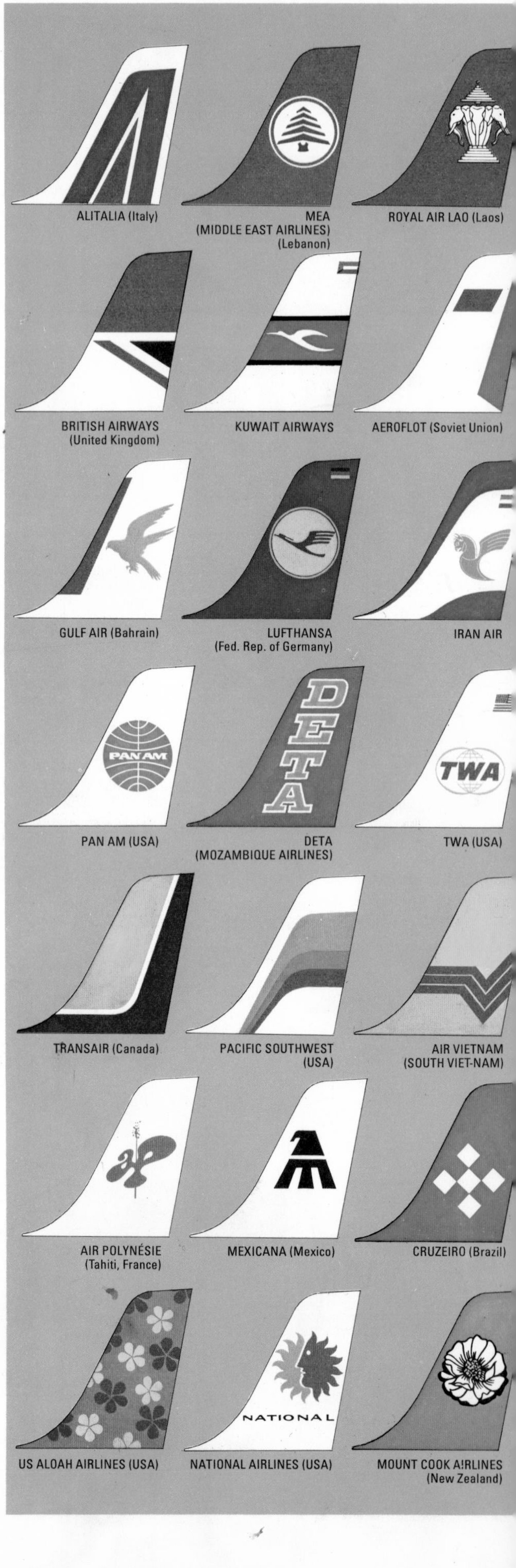

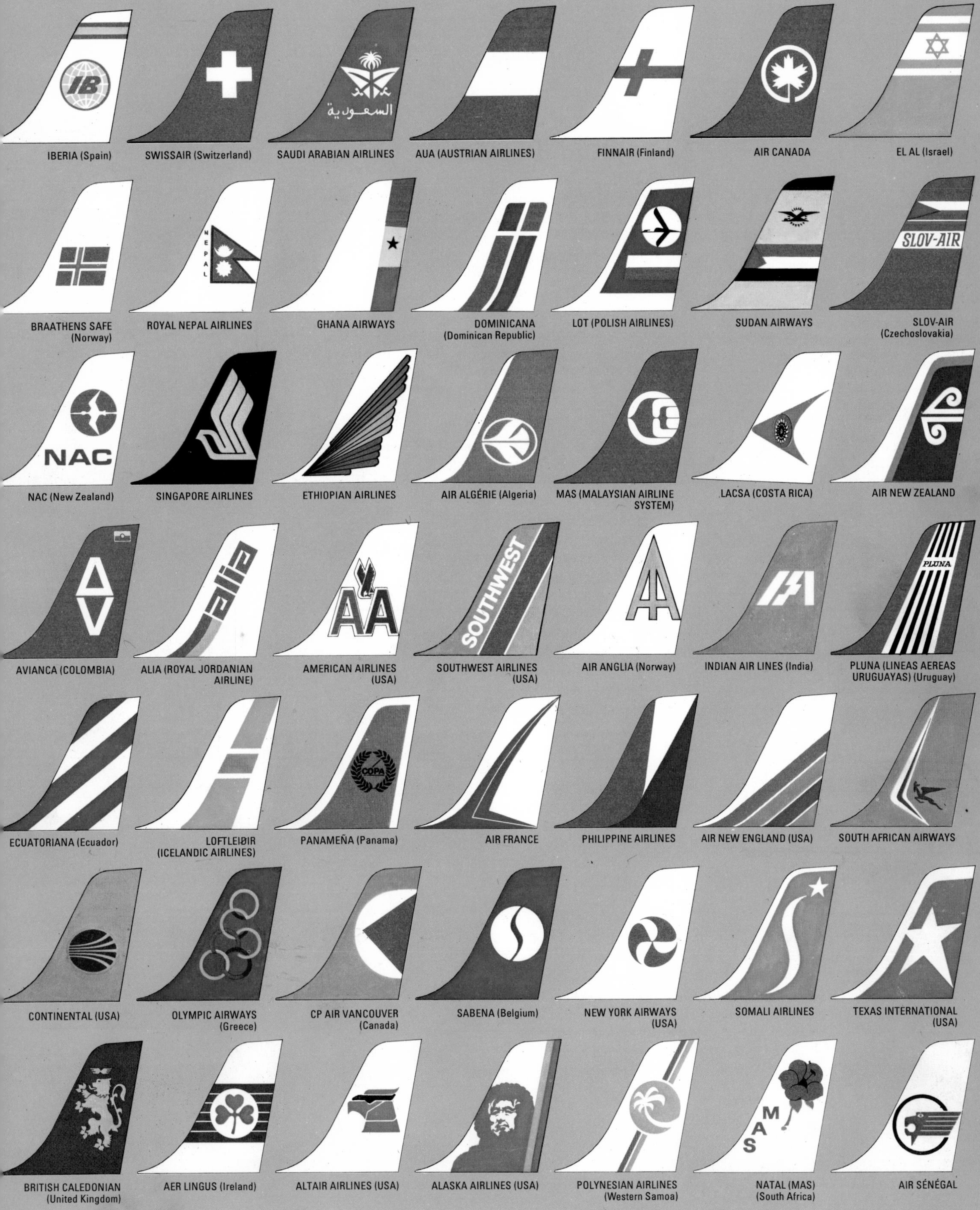

IBERIA (Spain) · SWISSAIR (Switzerland) · SAUDI ARABIAN AIRLINES · AUA (AUSTRIAN AIRLINES) · FINNAIR (Finland) · AIR CANADA · EL AL (Israel)

BRAATHENS SAFE (Norway) · ROYAL NEPAL AIRLINES · GHANA AIRWAYS · DOMINICANA (Dominican Republic) · LOT (POLISH AIRLINES) · SUDAN AIRWAYS · SLOV-AIR (Czechoslovakia)

NAC (New Zealand) · SINGAPORE AIRLINES · ETHIOPIAN AIRLINES · AIR ALGÉRIE (Algeria) · MAS (MALAYSIAN AIRLINE SYSTEM) · LACSA (COSTA RICA) · AIR NEW ZEALAND

AVIANCA (COLOMBIA) · ALIA (ROYAL JORDANIAN AIRLINE) · AMERICAN AIRLINES (USA) · SOUTHWEST AIRLINES (USA) · AIR ANGLIA (Norway) · INDIAN AIR LINES (India) · PLUNA (LINEAS AEREAS URUGUAYAS) (Uruguay)

ECUATORIANA (Ecuador) · LOFTLEIÐIR (ICELANDIC AIRLINES) · PANAMEÑA (Panama) · AIR FRANCE · PHILIPPINE AIRLINES · AIR NEW ENGLAND (USA) · SOUTH AFRICAN AIRWAYS

CONTINENTAL (USA) · OLYMPIC AIRWAYS (Greece) · CP AIR VANCOUVER (Canada) · SABENA (Belgium) · NEW YORK AIRWAYS (USA) · SOMALI AIRLINES · TEXAS INTERNATIONAL (USA)

BRITISH CALEDONIAN (United Kingdom) · AER LINGUS (Ireland) · ALTAIR AIRLINES (USA) · ALASKA AIRLINES (USA) · POLYNESIAN AIRLINES (Western Samoa) · NATAL (MAS) (South Africa) · AIR SÉNÉGAL

SYMBOLS AT SEA

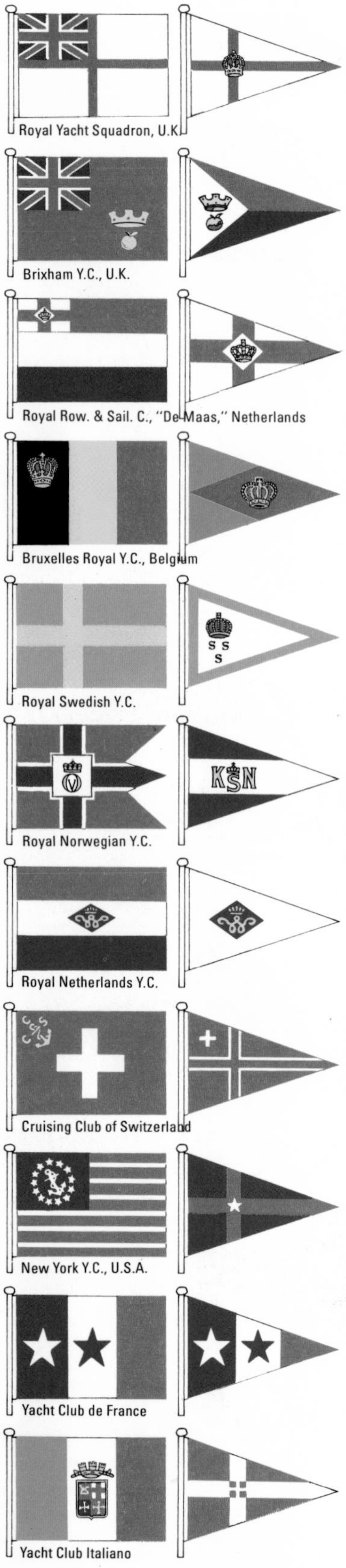

Although identifying names, number, and use of the civil ensign are required by law, the most distinctive naval symbols are those invented by the shipping lines, yacht clubs, and private boaters who display them. The use of such emblems began in the nineteenth century; today there are perhaps a thousand distinctive funnels and house flags for shipping lines (both cargo and tourist) and untold thousands of pennants, burgees, and flags representing clubs and individuals.

Because of the changing fortunes of commercial shipping in particular, these emblems are altered frequently, and it is almost impossible to maintain a current list. The flags and funnels shown here are compiled from the most up-to-date sources available. The great number of these "symbols at sea" has resulted in many design similarities. Specialized books listing this type of flag usually order them by the principal colors so that identification can be made readily.

There are other special flags and pennants to be seen on ships and boats, including those for racing and for official positions (e.g., treasurer) within a yacht club. Humorous flags – indicating, for example, that the owner of a vessel is on board, but asleep, are common in the United States. Sea rescue and lighthouse services, not to mention other non-military government organizations, have flags and pennants which they fly for identification in addition to the state ensign.

Many yacht clubs, particularly in Britain and the Commonwealth, have special permission to use a variation of the state ensign as a club flag *(left)*, although the burgee is still the principal means of identification for these clubs *(middle)*.

Private signals – the flags of individuals who own yachts or other vessels *(right)* – are properly displayed at the mainmast or main truck.

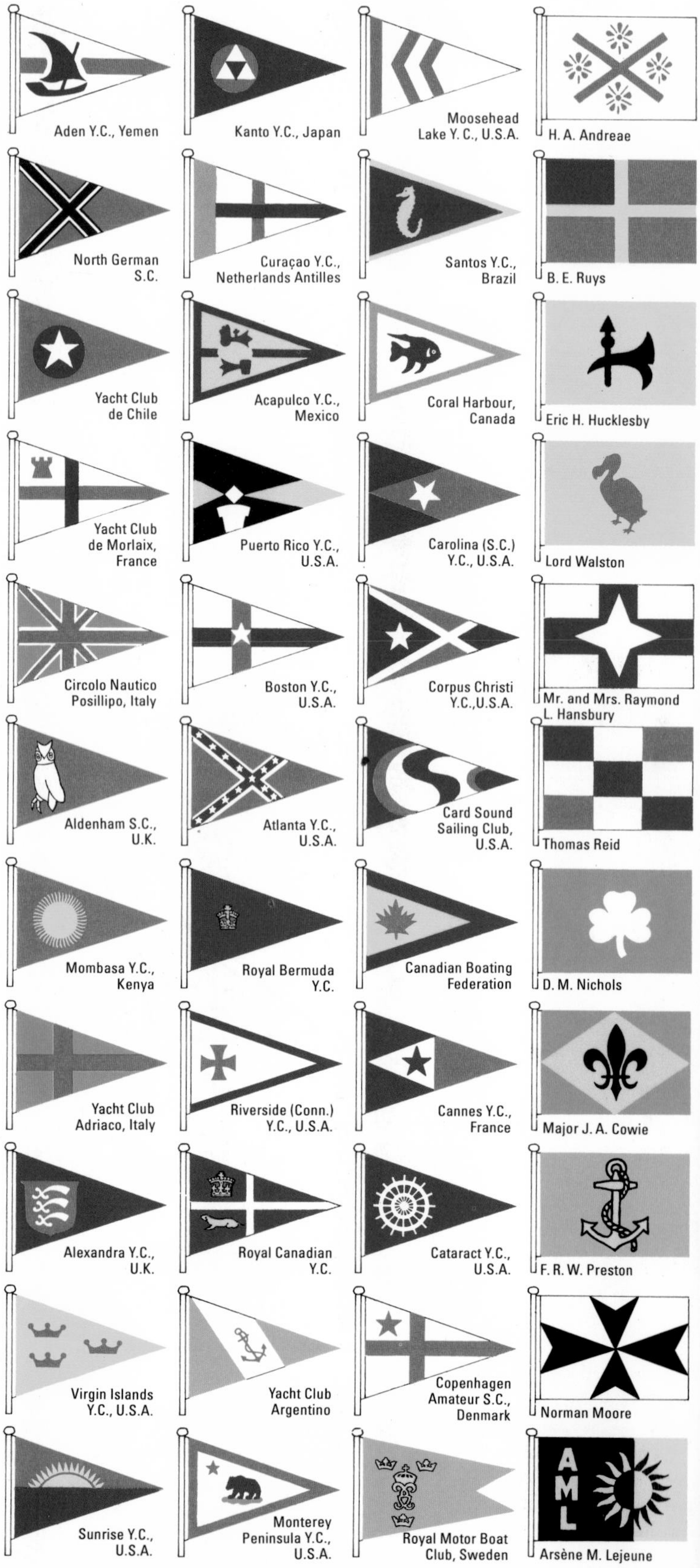

In the nineteenth century a large house flag flown at the mainmast identified a vessel at a distance. Today such flags are still used, but the funnel is a more important means of identification because it is larger, more prominent, and easier to see under differing weather conditions. Actually, the designs of the funnel and flag of a single company are frequently the same. The selection below indicates the propensity of the world's shipping lines to use stripes and letters, as well as a newer emphasis on commercially designed corporate logos.

Villain & Fassio, Genoa
Petterson, Soren, Gothenburg
British Rail, London
British & Irish Steam Packet Co. Ltd., Dublin
El Yam Bulk Carriers (1967) Ltd., Haifa
Henry Nielsen, A/B O/Y, Helsinki
South African Marine Corporation Ltd., Cape Town
Otto A. Müller, Hamburg
Lorentzens Rederi Co., Oslo
Union of Burma Five Star Line Corp., Rangoon
Tor Line Rederi A/B, Stockholm
Epitotiki Stship. Nav. Co., Piraeus
C.P. Ships-Canadian Pacific, Liverpool
Dahl, A/S Thor, Sandefjord
Nederlandse Erts-Tankers Maats N.V., Rotterdam
China, Government of the People's Republic, Peking
Cunard Line Ltd., Liverpool
Atid Cargo Lines Ltd., Haifa
Sealord Shipping Co. Ltd., London
Park Steamships Ltd., London
Fearnley & Eger, Oslo
Hunting & Son Ltd., Newcastle-upon-Tyne
Black Star Line Ltd., Accra
Shell Tankers (U.K.) Ltd., London
Cia. Nav. del Vapor Carmen, Madrid
Commodore Shipping Co., Ltd., Guernsey
Iraqi Maritime Transport Co. Ltd., Baghdad
de Vries – Tankreederei & Co., Hamburg
J.A. Zachariassen & Co., Usikaupunki
Soc. di Nav. Adriatica, Venice
Denholm Line Steamers Ltd., Glasgow
Arthur Hashagen, Rodenkirchen
Normandy Ferries, Southampton
Oregon Steamship Co. Ltd., London
Maranave S.A., Panama
United Carriers Ltd., Monrovia
Vergottis Ltd., London
Eastmount Shipping Corp., New York
Helmsing & Grimm, Bremen
Manila Interocean Lines Ltd., Manila
Albright & Wilson Ltd., Barrow-in-Furness
Kawasaki Kisen Kaisha, Kobe
Korean Shipping Corporation Ltd., Seoul
d'Amico Fratelli, Rome
New Zealand Shipping Co. Ltd., London
Efthymiadis Lines, Piraeus
American President Lines, San Francisco
Nigerian National Line Ltd., Lagos
Hansen-Tangen, H. E., Kristiansand

SYMBOLS IN SPORTS

At a tournament in medieval Europe *(right)*, both the judges and participants were characterized by coats of arms translated into the medium of a uniform. The former wore tabards – a coat whose front,

arms, and back bore the shield of the royal house which the herald served. His function was to be able to identify the similar arms belonging to individual knights who participated in the combat, such as the Lord of Gruthnyse shown *(right)* in this fifteenth-century illustration.
Across the center of the page is a modern adaptation of this ancient tradition – the stable colors of 190 racing stables from around the world. As the jockeys spur their mounts to win, it is often only the bright bits of color and their bold designs that allow the crowd to identify who is ahead and who is falling behind.
Thus, as in many other fields of symbolism, the practical function of identification remains the core in symbols of sport.

It is not simply a bull in the arena facing the red flag of the matador who finds stimulation in bright color and motion: the uniforms of modern sports teams convey

In the world of organized sports, flags are sometimes employed for the practical purpose of signaling and for identification, but the impulse to symbolism is not limited to these instances. Teams which originally chose distinctive colors or designs for their uniforms and helmets, so

Below and on page 348 are the persons or stables represented in the colors worn by the jockeys shown across these two pages.

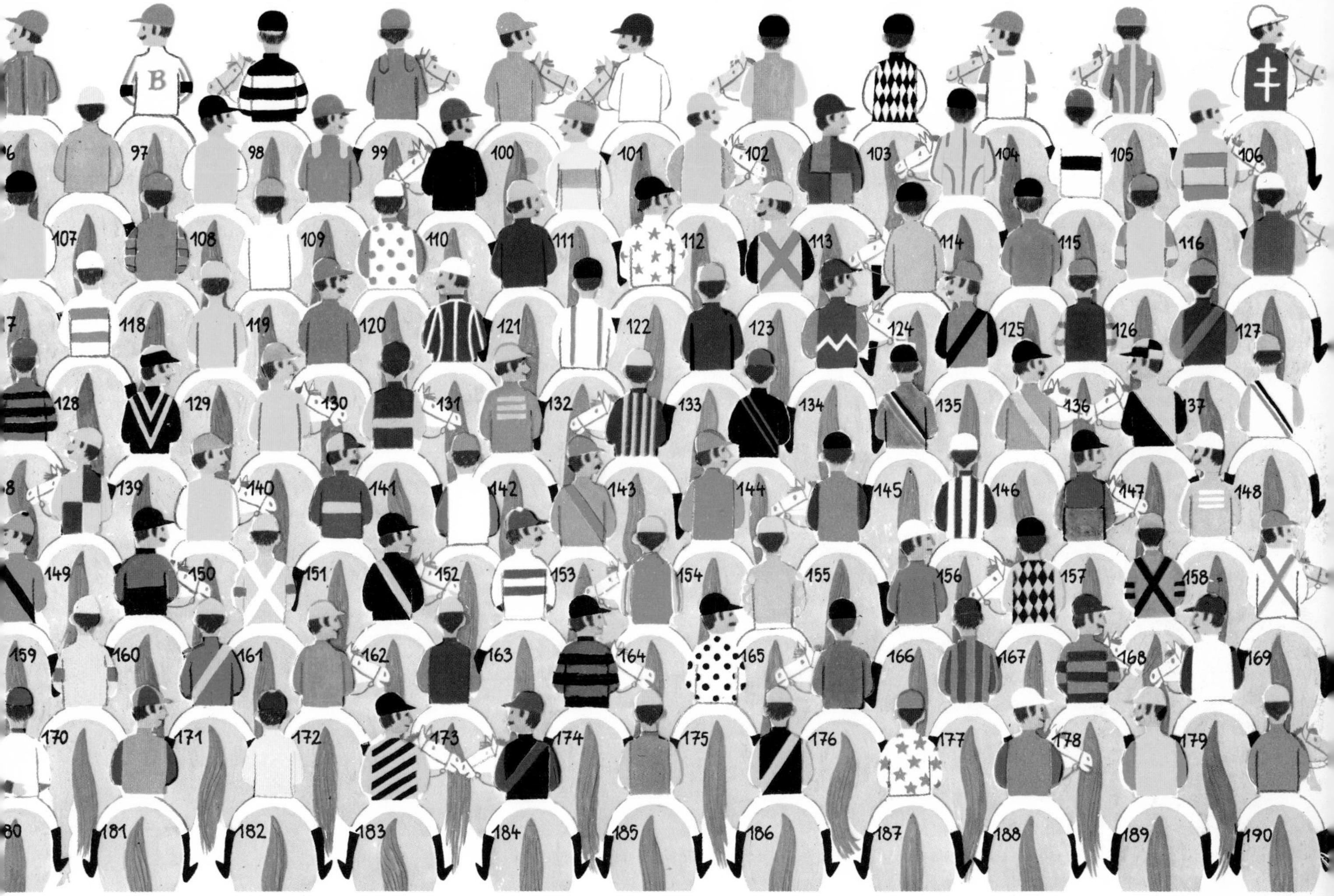

to spectators more than information about the course of the competition. They stir emotions to a high pitch and encourage the players themselves to do their best.

that they might be readily identified on the playing field, quickly discovered that those colors created a strong bond with supporters whose enthusiasm helped them to carry the day against opponents. Likewise the simple black and white checkered flag which originally indicated the end of the race quickly came to be considered a prize, triumphantly paraded by the victor.

Many of these symbols figure in flags furiously waved during competition by supporters of a particular team: obviously in such situations color and motion are primary, and design must be of the simplest possible form for easy recognition.

No catalog of all such symbols and flags has ever been compiled, although in certain sports (such as yachting) there are select lists giving a few hundred of the thousands in use. Both the vexillologist and collector of flags find in sports a realm of symbolism related to, but distinctly different from, those characterizing business, international politics, and other areas of life.

GREAT BRITAIN

1 H. M. Queen Elizabeth II of England
2 H. M. The Queen Mother
3 Anne, Duchess of Westminster
4 Lord Allendale
5 The Hon. J. J. Astor
6 Lord Carnarvon
7 Mrs. D. Thompson
8 Mr. E. R. Courage
9 Lord Derby
10 Mr. W. H. Gollings
11 Mrs. K. Hennessy
12 Mr. William Hill
13 Mr. L. B. Holliday
14 Mrs. V. Hue-Williams
15 Mr. H. J. Joel
16 Mr. Stanhope Joel
17 Lord Leverhulme
18 Mr. J. A. C. Lilley
19 Sir Reginald Macdonald-Buchanan
20 Lady Macdonald-Buchanan
21 The Duke of Norfolk
22 Mr. G. A. Oldham
23 The Hon. J. P. Philipps
24 Mr. F. W. Pontin

(Continued from previous page)

25 Mr. David Robinson
26 Mr. John Rogerson
27 Lord Rosebery
28 Lady Sassoon
29 Mr. Michael Sobell
30 Sir Humphrey de Trafford
31 Mrs. F. T. Walwyn
32 Lady Weir
33 Lady Zia Wernher
34 Mr. W. H. Whitbread
35 Mr. H. D. H. Wills

BELGIUM
36 Mme F. Beauduin
37 Le Baron de Crawhez
38 M. M. Janssens
39 Le Baron Lunden
40 Haras de la Rochette
41 M. Jacques du Roy de Blicquy

AUSTRALIA
42 Mr. T. L. Baillieu
43 Mr. Brian H. Crowley
44 Mrs. André Ozoux
45 Sir Frank Packer and Mr. L. K. Martin
46 Messrs. P. G., A. J. and K. Stiles
47 Messrs. D. G. and P. G. Tait

POLAND
48 Golejewko
49 Kozienice
50 Iwno
51 Janów Podlaski

UNITED STATES
52 Mrs. Edith W. Bancroft
53 Mr. James Cox Brady
54 Mr. C. T. Chenery (Meadow Stable)
55 Mr. Winifred S. Cheston (Brookmeade Stable)
56 Mr. Jack J. Dreyfus (Hobeau Farm)
57 Mr. John E. du Pont (Foxcatcher Farms)
58 Mrs. Richard C. du Pont (Bohemia Stable)
59 Mr. Rex C. Ellsworth
60 Mr. Michael Ford (Ford Stable)
61 Mr. John R. Gaines
62 Mr. John W. Galbreath (Darby Dan Farm)
63 Mrs. Frances A. Genter
64 Mr. Harry F. Guggenheim (Cain Hoy Stable)
65 Mr. Antony Imbesi
66 Mrs. Ethel D. Jacobs
67 Mrs. Ewart Johnston
68 Mr. Robert J. Kleberg, Jr. (King Ranch)
69 Mr. Lehmann
70 Mr. Charles E. Mather, II (Avonwood Stable)
71 Mrs. Lucille P. Markey (Calumet Farm)
72 Mr. Frank M. McMahon
73 Mr. Paul Mellon (Rokeby Stables)
74 Mr. John A. Morris
75 Mr. John M. Olin
76 Mr. William Haggin Perry
77 Mr. Ogden Phipps
78 Mrs. Gladys Phipps (Wheatley Stable)
79 Mr. John M. Schiff
80 Mrs. Gerard Smith
81 Mrs. Mary E. Tippett (Llangollen Farm)
82 Mr. Alfred G. Vanderbilt
83 Mr. R. N. Webster
84 Mr. Cortright Wetherill (Happy Hill Farm)
85 Mr. C. V. Whitney
86 Mr. John Hay Whitney (Greentree Stable)
87 Mr. George D. Widener
88 Mr. Louis E. Wolfson (Harbor View Farm)

IRELAND
89 The President of Ireland
90 Mrs. D. B. Brewster
91 Lord Donoughmore
92 Mr. C. W. Engelhard
93 Mr. Raymond Guest
94 Mr. B. Kerr
95 Major Dermot McCalmont
96 Mr. S. McGrath
97 Mr. John McShain
98 Mr. A. Willis

FRANCE
99 S. A. Aga Khan
100 M. Marcel Boussac
101 Comte de Chambure
102 M. Georges Courtois
103 M. Jean Couturié
104 M. Julien Decrion
105 M. Paul Duboscq
106 Mme Cino del Duca
107 M. François Dupré
108 Comte François de Ganay
109 M. M. Goudechaux
110 Lady Granard
111 M. Maurice Hennessy
112 Comte L. de Kérouara
113 Baron Louis de la Rochette
114 Baron S. de Lopez Tarragoya
115 Baron de Lustrac
116 Mme A. Mariotti
117 M. Martinez de Hoz
118 M. Ernest Masurel
119 M. Fabiani
120 Comte de Rivaud
121 Baron Guy de Rothschild
122 M. Jean Stern
123 Mme R. B. Strassburger
124 Comte de Talhouet-Roy
125 M. Jean Ternynck
126 Comtesse de la Valdène
127 Mme la Vicomtesse Vigier
128 Mme Léon Volterra
129 Baron G. de Waldner
130 M. A. Weisweiller
131 Mme P. Wertheimer
132 Mme P. A. B. Widener
133 M. G. Wildenstein

JAPAN
134 Mr. Kazuo Fujii
135 Mr. Kokichi Hashimoto
136 Mr. Yuzaku Kato
137 Mr. Yuji Kuribayashi
138 Mr. Mazaichi Nagata

GERMANY
139 Asta
140 Atlas
141 Gräfin Batthyany
142 Bona
143 Buschhof
144 Charlottenhof
145 Ebbesloh
146 W. Eichholz
147 Fährhof
148 Fohlenhof
149 Harzburg
150 Mydlinghoven
151 Niederrhein
152 H. Pferdmenges
153 Ravensberg
154 Röttgen
155 Schlenderhan
156 Waldfried
157 Werne
158 Zoppenbroich

CANADA
159 Mr. Bill Beasley
160 Max Bell of Calgary (Golden West Farm)
161 Mr. George Gardiner
162 Mr. Frowde Seagram
163 Mmes W. J. Seitz and V. P. Reid
164 Mr. John Smallman
165 Mr. E. P. Taylor (Windfields Farm)
166 Mr. Saul Wagman

ITALY
167 Allevamento Alpe Ravetta
168 Scuderia Castelverde
169 Razza Dormello-Olgiata
170 Scuderia Fert
171 Scuderia Mantova
172 Comm. Guido Ramazzotti
173 Razza di Rozzano
174 Razza del Soldo
175 Ettore Tagliabue
176 Razza Ticino

ARGENTINA
177 Félix de Alzaga Unzué
178 Fernando de Alzaga Unzué
179 Coronel Jorge Castro Madero
180 Ignacio Correas
181 Manuel José Gambin
182 C. y J. Monditegui

SOUTH AFRICA
183 Mr. P. Dolt
184 Messrs. A. R. and G. A. Ellis
185 Mr. S. C. Laird
186 Mr. and Mrs. H. F. Oppenheimer

SOVIET UNION
There are no stable colors in the Soviet Union. Every year the state which is the owner of the horses assigns racing colors to the jockeys. Consequently there are only riders' colors and they are changed from year to year.

LIST OF KEYS

An Index of the Reference Sections found throughout the Book

ACKNOWLEDGEMENTS

Agence Belga, Bruxelles: 202 (bottom); 203 (top);
Alabama Department of Archives and History: 195 (center, right);
Albany Institute of History and Art: 73 (bottom);
Altonaer Museum, Hamburg: 83;
American Heritage, New York: 148 (center);
Archiv C.J. Bucher, Lucerne: 58 (center, right); 106 (top, left); 104 (bottom); 346 -347 (center);
Archiv für Kunst und Geschichte, Berlin: 69 (top, right);
Archives Nationales, Paris: 66 (center, right);
Associated Press: 106 (top, second from left); 123; 199;
Atlas van Stolk, Rotterdam: 16 (bottom; Photo Hachette); 55; 159 (bottom);

Bayerische Staatsbibliothek, München: 116 (top, 3 pictures); 117 (left);
Bedford Public Library: 73 (top; photo William Ryerson); 191 (bottom; photo William Ryerson);
Benaki Museum, Athens: 87;
Bettman Archives, New York: 62 (top, left and right); 68 (top, right);
Biblioteca Apostolica Vaticana: 36 (top); 60 (Photo Scala);
Biblioteca Nacional, Madrid: 124 (bottom; Photo Oronoz);
Bibliothèque Nationale, Paris: 33; 40; 43 (top); 44 (bottom, left); 49 (left); 52; 53; 61 (top, left); 67 (top); 75 (top; Archives Estampes); 80 (left); 132 (left and right); 140 (center, right); 141 (top); 346 (top and bottom, left);
Bibliothèque Royale Albert Ier, Bruxelles: 26; 64 (center, left); 157 (top);
Nicolas Bouvier, Geneva: 50 (3 pictures); 170 (bottom);
The British Library Board: 44 (bottom); 99; 183;
British Museum: 46 (bottom, right); 83 (top, center); 156 (bottom);
The John Carter Brown Library, Brown University, Rhode Island: 28; 192 (center); 193 (center); 205;
Bunte Illustrierte: 96 (center, right); 98 (left); 100 (center, second from left);
Burgerbibliothek, Bern: 7; 21 (left); 181 (top, right);

Cairo Museum: 35 (Photo Rolf Ammon);
Calvin Bullock Collection: 135 (bottom, right);
Camera Press, London: 98 (top, right; Photo Tony Delano);
Century Photo Service, New York: 150 (top; Instituto National de Bellas Artes, Mexico City);
Chinese News Service: 112;
Collection Frank Cayley: 78 (top, left and center);
Collection Vezio Melegari: 96 (center, left); 144 (bottom);
Collection Neubecker: 114 (bottom); 118 (center, 3 pictures); 120 (center and bottom rows); 130 (bottom); 175 (bottom);
Collection Sturgis, New York 85;
Collection Sven TitoAchen: 64 (center, right);
Comet Photo, Zürich: 346 (bottom); 347 (bottom);

Companie Financière de Suez, Paris: 153 (top, left);
Cosmopress, Geneva: 31;
Culver Pictures, New York: 76 (top, left);

Danish Maritime Museum, Kronborg Castle: 64 (bottom);
Date Family: 165 (top and center, left); 172 (top, left);
De Lakenhal Museum, Leiden: 163 (top); 306 (right);
Dukas, Zürich: 105 (left and top, right); 188;

E. C. Armées, Fort d'Ivry: 138;
Editions Cercle d'Art, Paris: 72 (bottom); 174 (center);
Edito Service; Geneva: 16 (center); 18; 161 (top);
Escorial, Madrid: 41 (Photo Stierlin); 125 (top, right; Photo Stierlin);

Flag Research Center: 14; 15; 20 (bottom); 25; 27; 34 (top, right); 37 (top, left); 48; 55 (top and bottom, left); 58 (5 pictures); 61 (bottom, left); 63 (bottom, left); 74 (top and left); 75 (center and top, right); 76 (bottom, left); 79 (top and left); 109 (bottom, right); 110 (bottom, right); 111 (top, left and right); 117 (bottom, right); 119 (top, right and center, left); 121 (top); 128 (top); 129 (top); 134 (left); 136 (top); 137 (top); 143 (top, right and bottom row); 144 (top); 146 (top); 148 (bottom); 149 (top and center row); 152; 159 (top, right); 160; 161 (bottom); 162; 163 (bottom); 164 (bottom); 165 (bottom); 166; 167; 168 (bottom); 169 (bottom); 175 (top); 176 (top, left and bottom); 177 (bottom, left); 180 (top and bottom); 187 (center, right and bottom); 190 (top); 191 (top, right); 193; 197 (left); 198; 205; 304; 339 (bottom);

Giraudon, Paris: 46 (bottom, left; Condé, Chantilly); 66 (top, right); 68 (top, center); 75 (bottom; Louvre); 83 (bottom, second from left); 88 (Lauros); 125 (bottom, right; Condé, Chantilly); 131 (top, right);
Goso Family: 165 (right);

Hachette, Paris: 46 (center); 82 (center, right);
Hayashi Family: 164 (center, left);
Sven Erich Hedin: 107 (bottom, left);
Hispanic Society, New York: 125 (top, left);
Historia Photo: 44 (right, center);
Historiographical Institute of Tokyo University: 169 (top, left);
Historisches Museum, Basel: 49 (right); 70 (bottom);
Historisches Museum, Bern: 67 (bottom); 116 (bottom); 133 (top);
Historisches Museum, Frankfurt: 119 (top, left);
Historisches Museum, Schloss Heidegg: 333 (Photo Perret);
Historische Sammlung der Stadt Stein a. Rhein: 186 (left);
Hosokawa Family: 172 (top, center);

Ii Family: 164 (center, right);
Walter Imber, Laufen: 81; 106 (bottom, center);

Indiana Historical Society: 195 (top);

Japan Times: 106 (bottom, third from left); 173;
Japan Uni Literary: 172 (bottom);

Kantonsmuseum Baselland, Liestal: 321 (top);
Gottfried Keller Stiftung, Bern: 20 (top);
Kennedy Galleries, New York: 17 (center, right);
Keystone: 107 (top, left); 147; 110 (bottom, left);
Kloster Archiv, Engelberg: 307 (bottom; Photo Perret);
Kunsthistorisches Museum, Wien: 114 (top, right);

L. E. A., London: 102 (right);
Library of Congress: 177 (bottom, right);

Magnum: 58 (second row, left; Photo Eve Arnold); 102 (center, left; Photo Bruno Barbey); 104 (top; Photo René Burri); 105 (bottom, right; Photo Cornell Capa); 107 (top, right; Photo Burt Glinn); 106 (below, left; Photo René Burri); 107 (below, third from left; Photo Bruno Barbey); 111 (bottom; Photo Cartier-Bresson); 139 (Photo Bruno Barbey); 151 (Photo René Burri); 153 (bottom); 154 (top, right; Photo Azzi); 155 (Photo René Burri);
Mansell Collection, London: 42 (top); 68 (top, left); 72 (top); 79 (center, right);
Leonard von Matt, Buochs: 37 (top, right); 51; 70 (top); 96 (top); 142 (top);
Metropolitan Museum of Art, New York: 108 (center, left; Gift of the Dillon Fund); 180 (right; the Cloisters Collection, Munsey Fund, 1932);
Minneapolis Institute of Art: 109 (top, left);
Mondadori Press: 103 (bottom);
Monkmeyer Press Photo Service: 74 (bottom);
Bernhard Moosbrugger, Zürich: 100 (bottom, left);
Mount Vernon's Ladies Association: 192 (top);
Musée de l'Armée, Paris: 135 (top);
Musée des Monuments Français: 42 (left); 43;
Musées Nationaux, Paris: 134 (bottom, right; Musée de Versailles);
Museo Correr, Venezia: 141 (bottom);
Museo del Ejército, Madrid: 68 (bottom, right);
Museo Episcopal, Vich: 131 (top, left);
Museo Naval, Madrid: 84 (top);
Museo del Risorgimento, Milano: 56 (bottom; Photo Saporetti); 143 (top, left; Photo Saporetti);
Museo de Santa Cruz, Toledo: 126 (top; Property of Catedral Primada de Toledo);
Museum of Fine Arts, Boston: 38 (left and bottom); 39;
Museum für Kunst und Geschichte, Fribourg: 54 (bottom; Photo Rast); 306 (left; Photo Rast); 307 (top and bottom, right); 308; 315 (center);
Museum of National Antiquities, Stockholm: 100 (bottom, right);

NASA: 11;
Nationaal Scheepvaartmuseum, Antwerpen: 9;
National Archives Washington: 196 (left; Public Building Service);
National Army Museum, London: 76 (right);
National Geographic Society: 197 (top, right; Photo Dick Burbage);
National Maritime Museum, Greenwich: 17 (center, left); 86 (left); 127;
National Palace Museum, Taipei: 109 (bottom, left);
Navy Department, Washington: 84 (bottom);
Werner Neumeister, München: 305;
New York Historical Society: 93 (center, right); 191 (center); 194 (bottom, left); 195 (bottom, right);
New York Public Library, Slavonic Division: 177 (top);
New York Times: 203 (bottom);
Niedersächsische Hauptstaatsarchiv, Hannover: 117 (top, right);
Novosti: 97 (center, right); 179;

Old Print Shop, NYC, Courtesy Kenneth M. Newman: 90;
B. C. Olshak, Zürich: 101 (bottom, right; from "Mystic Art of Ancient Tibet", London and New York, 1973);

Paris Match: 30 (bottom); 59 (Photo Vital); 96 (center; Photo Habans); 97 (center, left); 101 (left); 103 (top, right) 107 (bottom, second from left); 136 (bottom, right); 137 (right); 188 (top); 189;
Photopress, Zürich; 93 (bottom); 97 (bottom); 98 (top); 122 (bottom, right);
Photothèque Laffont, Paris: 68 (left); 158 (Musée Royaux des Beaux-Arts, Bruxelles); 181 (top, left; Bibliothèque Nationale);
Presse Photo Baumann: 98 (bottom);
Publisher's Archives: 8; 16 (top); 17 (top); 34 (bottom); 45 (center, left); 54 (top); 63 (top); 64 (top); 65 (top); 70 (center, right); 71; 77; 82; 91; 92 (center, left); 93 (center, left); 96 (center, second from left); 97; 101 (center); 107 (bottom, right); 108 (top and bottom); 114 (top, left); 124 (top); 130 (top); 140 (top); 148 (top); 150 (center, right); 156 (top); 164 (top); 171; 174 (top); 190 (bottom); 193; 195 (left); 200; 201;

Rapho, Paris: 106 (top, right);
Rhodes House Library, Oxford: 77 (top);
Roger Viollet, Paris: 66 (top, left); 109 (top, right);
Royal Malta Library: 82 (center, left);
Ryksmuseum, Amsterdam: 159 (top, left);

Scala: 69 (top; Uffizi, Firenze); 100 (top; San Sepolcro, Museo); 142 (bottom; Museo di San Martino, Napoli); 145 (bottom); 146 bottom); 147 (Museo Correr); 186 (top);
Schweizerisches Landesmuseum, Zürich (Abteilung für Fahnen und Uniformen): 19 (center); 307 (top, left);
Bernard G. Silverstein: 130 (center);

ACKNOWLEDGEMENTS
(continued)

Sipa Press, Paris: 113;
Sirman Press, Geneva: 176 (top);
Skira, Geneva: 41 (top);
Smithsonian Institution, Freer Gallery of Art: 36 (left);
Southwest Museum, Los Angeles: 190 (center):
Sphere: 110 (top); 202 (center, left);
Staatsarchiv Koblenz: 114 (center);
Staatsbibliothek, Berlin: 69 (bottom); 118 (bottom, left); 120 (top, left);
Staatsbibliothek Preussischer Kulturbesitz, Berlin: 56 (top);
Stadtbibliothek Trier: 116 (top, right);
Stadtbibliothek (Vadiana), St. Gallen: 80 (right);
Stern, Hamburg: 122 (top);
Stiftsbibliothek, St. Gallen: 61 (right);
Swiss National Tourist Office: 101 (top);

Tass Agency: 178 (top);
Teikoku Kanko Treasury: 169 (top, right);
Television Rencontre, Lausanne: 92 (center, right); 319;
Three Lions: 96 (bottom);
T'ien-kung K'ai Wu: 38;
Time: 154 (left; Photo Eddie Adams);
Top Capi Library, Istanbul: 92 (center, third from left; Photo Henri Stierlin);

Uesugy Family: 168 (left);
Ullstein: 115 (top, row); 119 (top, right and bottom); 120 (top);
Unpoji Temple: 168 (center);
UPI: 106 (top, third from left); 121 (center); 129 (bottom; Photo S.O.F.); 154 (top, left);
USIS: 93 (left); 103 (top, left);

Victoria and Albert Museum, London: 83 (bottom, left);
Ville de Bayeux: 181 (bottom, left);

Wehrgeschichtliches Museum, Rastatt: 19 (top); 21 (right);

Yale University Art Gallery: 192 (bottom);

Zenpukuji Temple: 168 (center, right);
Zentralbibliothek, Zürich: 92 (center, second from left);
Zodiaque: 307 (center, left);

BIBLIOGRAPHY

The following entries have been selected from the thousands of books and articles relating to vexillology as being the most valuable and most readily available. *The Flag Bulletin* publishes articles of all kinds relating to flags; it is issued by the Flag Research Center, Winchester, Massachusetts, 01890, U.S.A. This journal, a quarterly from 1961 to 1973 and a bimonthly since then, is referred to for the sake of brevity as *FB* in the listing that follows, with an indication of volume and issue number (e.g., XIII:2).

National newsletters devoted exclusively to material on flags are published in a number of countries:

Flagmaster (Chester, England)
Liehuvat Värit (Korso, Finland)
Nava News (Oaks, Pennsylvania, U.S.A.)
Vexilla Helvetica (Zollikon, Switzerland)
Vexilla Italica (Via Vallarsa 22, 10135 Turin, Italy)
Vexilla Nostra (Muiderberg, Netherlands)
Vexillologia (28 rue de la Sablière, Paris 14, France)
Vexilologie (Kalininova č.20, Prague, Czechoslovakia)

Further excellent material is found in the biennial *Reports* of the International Congresses of Vexillology and in heraldic journals published in Switzerland, Great Britain, Germany, South Africa, Canada, Denmark, and Belgium.

GENERAL SOURCES

Barraclough, E. M. C., *Flags of the World* (New York and London: Warne, 1971).
Ivanov, K. A., *Flagi gosudarstv mira* (Moscow: Transport, 1971).
Pedersen, Christian F., *The International Flag Book in Color* (New York: Morrow, 1970).
Rabbow, Arnold, *dtv-Lexikon politischer Symbole* (Munich, 1970).
Smith, Whitney, *The Bibliography of Flags of Foreign Nations* (Boston: Hall, 1965).
Smith, Whitney, *Flags of All Nations*, a wallchart (Glasgow: Brown, Son & Ferguson, 1975).
Tanino, Atsuo, *Sekai no kokki* (Osaka: Nunoi-shobo, 1964).

TERMS DEFINED

Heraldry Society Flag Section, *Dictionary of Flag Terminology* (London: Heraldry Society, 1969).
Sierksma, Klaes, *Vlaggekundig Woordenboekje* (Muiderberg: Stichting voor Banistiek en Heraldiek, 1971).

THE HISTORY OF FLAGS

Adam, Paul, "Les enseignes militaires du Moyen Age et leur influence sur l'héraldique," *Receuil du Ve Congrès International des Sciences Généalogique et Héraldique* (Stockholm: Almquist & Wiksell, 1961).
Artin, Yacoub, *Contribution à l'étude du blason en Orient* (London: Quaritch, 1902).
Gayre, Robert, *Heraldic standards and other ensigns* (Edinburgh: Olivèr & Boyd, 1959).
Horstmann, Hans, *Vor- und Frühgeschichte des europäischen Flaggenwesens* (Bremen: Schünemann, 1971).
Neubecker, Ottfried, "Fahne," *Reallexikon für deutsche Kunstgeschichte* (Munich: Druckenmüller, 1972).
Neubecker, Ottfried, *Fahnen und Flaggen* (Leipzig: Stackmann, 1939).
Neubecker, Ottfried, *Historische Fahnen* (Hamburg: Altona Zigarettenbilderdienst, 1932).
Rabbow, Arnold, *Visuelle Symbole als Erscheinung der nicht-verbalen Publizistik* (Münster: Universität Münster, 1968).
Renel, Charles, *Cultes militaires de Rome: les enseignes* (Paris: Foutemoing, 1903).
Siegel, Rudolf, *Die Flagge* (Berlin: Reimer, 1912).
Smith, Whitney, *Prolegomena to the Study of Political Symbolism* (Boston, 1968).
Wescher, H., "Flags," *Ciba Review*, December 1949.
Walker, Rodney C., "The Earliest Flags," *FB*, IV:2.

FLAGS THAT MADE HISTORY

Achen, Sven Tito, "Dannebrog," *FB*, VIII:4.
Agrawala, Vasudeva, *The Wheel Flag of India* (Benares: Prithivi Prakashan, 1964).
Beguin, Antoine, "Le Comte de Chambord et le drapeau blanc," *Miroir de l'histoire*, September 1962.
Carr, H. G., "Y ddraig goch," (in English), *FB* XII:2.
Desjardins, Gustave, "Oriflamme de Charlemagne," *Recherches sur les drapeaux français* (Paris: Morel, 1874).
Desroches, M. J. P., *Le labarum* (Paris, 1894).
Egger, Rudolf, *Das Labarum, die Kaiserstandarte der Spätantike* (Vienna: Rohrer, 1960).
Fox, Len, *The Strange Story of the Eureka Flag* (Darlinghurst, New South Wales, 1963).
Holt, P. M., "Correspondence [on the flag of the Mahdi]," *Sudan Notes and Records* (1955).
Lux-Wurm, Pierre C., "Columbus: What Was His Flag?" *FB*, VIII:2.
Mäder, Peter, "The Julius Banners," *FB*, X:2–3.
Smith, Whitney, "The Bedford Flag," *FB*, X:2–3.
Smith, Whitney, "Činggis Qan's Flags," *FB*, III:1.
Smith, Whitney, "La Virgen de Guadelupe," *FB*, IX:4.
Steinmann, Ulrich, "Die Bundeschuh-Fahnen des Joss Fritz," *Deutsches Jahrbuch für Volkskunde*, 1960.
Szala, John R. B., "Joan of Arc's Standard," *FB*, XI:4.
Zvegintsov, V. V., *Znamena i shtandarty russkoi armii* (Paris, 1964).

CUSTOMS AND ETIQUETTE

Barraclough, E. M. C., *Yacht Flags and Ensigns* (London: Yachting World, 1951).
Chapman, Charles F., "Flag Etiquette," *Piloting, Seamanship, and Small Boat Handling* (New York: Motor Boating, 1970).
Edwards, D. J., *Standards, Guidons, and Colours of the Commonwealth Forces* (Aldershot, England: Gale & Polden, 1953).
Irving, John, *The Manual of Flag Etiquette* (London: Seeley, Service, 1938).
Lovette, Leland P., *Naval Customs, Traditions and Usage* (Annapolis: United States Naval Institute, 1939).
Mittlebeeler, Emmet, "Flag Profanation and the Law," *Kentucky Law Journal*, 1972.
Sierksma, Klaes, "Bannistique et esthétique," *Recueil du IIe Congrès International de Vexillologie* (Zurich: Société Suisse de Vexillologie, 1968).
Stenzel, Al, *Your Flag* (North Brunswick, N.J.: Boy Scouts of America, 1973).

FLAGS ACROSS THE WORLD

The items in this section have numbers corresponding to those given to the countries in the above chapter (pages 208–299); this part of the bibliography also serves for the countries in the national flag histories section. For the coats of arms of these countries, insofar as they are not covered by the following entries, refer to the series by Ottfried Neubecker in *Heraldische Mitteilungen des Heraldischen Vereins "Zum Kleeblatt,"* 1965ff.

1. "Republic of Afghanistan," *FB*, XIII:2.
2. "The United Arab Emirates," *FB*, XI:2.
5. "Anguilla," *FB*, VIII:1.
7. Cánepa, Luis, *Historia de los símbolos nacionales argentinos* (Buenos Aires: Albatros, 1953).
8. Cayley, Frank, *Flag of Stars* (Adelaide: Rigby, 1966).
9. "Commonwealth of the Bahamas," *FB*, XIII:4.
11. "Bangladesh," *FB*, X:4.
12. "Barbados," *FB*, VI:1–2.
13. Harmignies, Roger, "Les emblèmes nationaux de la Belgique," *Receuil du Ve Congrès International des Sciences Généalogique et Héraldique* (Stockholm: Almquist & Wiksell, 1961).
14. Ministry of Information and Broadcasting, Publications Division, *Our Flag: Origin, Adoption, Description, Use* (Delhi: Government of India, 1952).
15. Ocampo Moscoso, Eduardo, *Historia de la bandera nacional* (Cochabamba: Amigos del Libro, 1954).
16. "Botswana," *FB*, V:4.
17. Coimbra, Raimundo Olavo, *A bandeira do Brasil* (Rio de Janeiro: Fundação Instituto Brasileiro do Geografia e Estatística, 1972).
18. Stamatov, C., *Bulgarskite durzhavni simvoli i rituali* (Sofia: Tsentralna Komsomolska Shkola "G. Dimitrov" pri Tsk na DKMS, 1970).
19. "Burundi" *FB*, V:4.
20. "Federal Republic of Cameroun," *FB*, I:2.
21. Stanley, George F. G., *The Story of Canada's Flag* (Toronto: McGraw-Hill Ryerson, 1972).
22. Česak, Josef, "The 50th Anniversary of the Flag of Czechoslovakia," *FB*, IX:2.
23. Valencia Avaria, Luis, "Las banderas de Chile," *Memorial del ejército de Chile, March–June* 1963.
25. *Wo mên ti tang ch'i ho kuo ch'i* (Taipei, Chung-kuo kuo min tang chung yang wei yüan hui ti ssu tsu, 1955).
26. Galbreath, Donald Lindsay, *Papal heraldry* (London: Heraldry Today, 1972).
27. Ortega Ricaurte, Enrique, *He-*

ráldica nacional (Bogotá: Banco de la República, 1954).
28. "The Congo," *FB*, IX:2.
29. Solera Rodríguez, Guillermo, *Símbolos nacionales: el himno, la bandera, el escudo* (San José: Lehmann, 1955).
31. Gay-Calbó, Enrique, *Los símbolos de la nación cubana* (Havana: Sociedad Colombista Panamericana, 1958).
33. Henningsen, Henning, *Dannebrog og Flagføring til søs* (Copenhagen: Handels og Søfartsmuseet, 1969).
34. Davis, Brian L., *Flags and Standards of the Third Reich* (London: Macdonald Jane's, 1975).
34. Friedel, Alois, *Deutsche Staatssymbole* (Frankfurt: Athenäum, 1968).
34. Valentin, Veit and Ottfried Neubecker, *Die deutschen Farben* (Leipzig: Quelle & Meyer, 1928).
34. Wentzche, Paul, *Die deutschen Farben* (Heidelberg: Winter, 1955).
35. "German Democratic Republic," *FB*, XIII:1.
36. Didi, Hassan Ali, "The Flag [of the Maldives]," *The Maldives Islands Today* (Colombo: Office of the Maldivian Government Representative, ca. 1960).
37. Barbour, Neill, "The Flags of Algeria, Past and Present," *FB*, I:1.
38. "The Symbolism of the National Flag of the Kingdom of Bhutan," *The Kingdom of Bhutan* (Calcutta, ca. 1972).
39. Dirección de Estudios (Guayas), *La bandera, el escudo, el himno patrios* (Guayaquil: Jouvin, 1917).
40. "Flags of Ireland," *Heraldry Society Flag Section Newsletter*, Winter 1970.
41. *Historia y símbolos patrios* (San Salvador: Casa Presidential, ca. 1970).
42. Puelles y Puelles, Antonio, *Símbolos nacionales de España* (Cadiz: Cerón, 1941).
43. Chojnacki, S., "Some notes on the history of the Ethiopian national flag," *Journal of Ethiopian studies*, 1963.
44. "Fiji," *FB*, IX:3.
45. Bouillé du Chariol, Louis A.M.L. de, *Les drapeaux français de 507 à 1872* (Paris: Dumaine, 1872).
45. Rey, Jean, *Histoire du drapeau* Paris: Techener, 1837).
45. Sepet, Marius, *Le drapeau de la France* (Paris: Palmé, 1873).
47. "The Gambia," *FB*, IV:3.
48. "Ghana," *FB*, V:3.
49. "Grenada," *FB*, XIII:1.
50. Gálvez, G., María Albertina, *Emblemas nacionales* (Guatemala: Ministerio de Educación Pública, 1958).
51. "Equatorial Guinea," *FB*, VII:4.
52. "Guinea-Bissau," *FB*, XII:4.
53. Touré, Sékou, "L'emblème," *Expérience guinéenne et l'unité africaine* (Paris: Présence Africaine, 1961).
54. "Guyana," *FB*, V:3.
55. Aubourg, Michel, *Le drapeau dessalinien* (Port-au-Prince: Théodore, 1964).
57. "Hellenic Republic," *FB*, XII:4.
58. Bruckner, Albert Theophil and Berty Bruckner, *Schweizer Fahnenbuch* (St. Gallen: Zollikofer, 1942).
58. Mader, Robert, *Die Fahnen und Farben der Schweizerischen Eidgenossenschaft und der Kantone* (St. Gallen: Zollikofer, 1942).
59. Fonseca Flores, Abel, *Folleto Cívico* (Tegucigalpa, 1965).
60. Yamin, Muhammad, *6000 tahun sang mérah-putih* (Jakarta: Siguntang, 1954).
61. Ackerman, Phyllis, "Standards, banners, and badges," *A Survey of Persian Art* (London: Oxford University, 1939).
61. Kasravi Tabrizi, Ahmad, *Tarikhče šir va khoršid* (Teheran: Shargh, 1958).
62. "Iraq," *FB*, VI:3.
63. Thorlacius Birgir, *Fáni Íslands og Skjaldarmerki* (Reykjavik, 1964).
64. Hom, Ze'ev, *Ha-degelim* (Haifa: Israeli Seamanship Association 1953).
65. Gerbaix di Sonnaz, Albert, *Bandiere, stendardi e vessili* (Turin: Frassati, 1896).
65. Ghisi, Enrico, *Il tricolore italiano (1796–1870)* (Milan: Societá nazionale per la storia del risorgimento italiano, 1931).
65. Ziggioto, Aldo, "Le bandiere degli stati italiani," *Armi Antiche*, 1967 *et seq.*; reprinted as "Flags of Italy," *FB*, VI:4 *et seq.*
66. Bustamante, Alexander, *Jamaican National Flag* (Kingston: Jamaican Parliament, 1962).
67. *Flags and State Emblems of the Federal People's Republic of Yugoslavia and Its Component People's Republics* (Belgrade: Information Service, 1960).
68, 69. "Cambodia," *FB*, IX:1.
70. "Kenya," *FB*, III:2.
71. Smith, Whitney, "Symbols of the KDPR," *FB*, XIII:5.
72. Kim, Il-su, "T'aeguk: The History of the Korean National Flag," *FB*, XII:3.
72. Sin, Ui-sop, *Uri Kukki* (Seoul: Hanmi mun hwa sa, 1954).
74. "Kuwait," *FB*, I:2.
74. Smith, Whitney, "The Flag of Laos," Nava News, June 1974.
76. "Lesotho," *FB*, VI: 1–2.
77. de Graaf, G., "Flags over Liberia," *FB*, XII:1.
78. "Libya," *FB*, IX:1.
79. Neubecker, Ottfried, "Die Flagge von Liechtenstein," *Archivum Heraldicum*, 1960.
80. Philippe, Lucien, "Vlaggen in Libanon," *Vexilla Nostra*, 1969.
81. Wirion, Louis, *Origine et historique du drapeau luxembourgeois* (Luxemburg: Bourg-Bourger, 1955).
82. Dubreuil, B., *Les pavillons des états musulmans* (Rabat: Université Mohammed V, 1962).
83. Varkonyi, Endre, *A magyar cimer utja* (Budapest: Kossuth, 1957).
84. "Malawi," *FB*, III:4.
85. *Bendera dan lambang negara dan negeri² Malaysia / National and state flags and crests of Malaysia* (Kuala Lumpur: Department of Information, 1963).
86. Smith, Whitney, "The Political Milieu," *Prolegomena to the Study of Political Symbolism* (Boston: Boston University, 1968).
87. "Malta," *FB*, IV:2.
88. "Mauritius," *FB*, XI:4.
89. Carrera Stampa, Manuel, *El escudo nacional* (Mexico, 1960).
89. Romero Flores, Jesus, *Banderas históricas mexicanas* (Mexico: Costa-Amic, 1973).
90. Zaki, 'Abd-al Rahman, *Al-a'lam wa sharat al-mulk fi wadi al-nil* (Cairo: Dar al-ma'arif, 1948).
91. "Mozambique," *FB*, XIII:5.
92. Pasch, G., "Symbols of Monaco," *FB*, V:4.
93. "Mongolia," *Liehuvat Värit*, September–October 1972.
95. Suradej Sri-ithayakorn, "...the National Flag," *Bangkok World*, 15 March 1964.
96. "Socialist Republic of the Union of Burma," *FB*, XIII:3.
97. "Namibia," *FB*, XIII:5.
98. "Nauru," *FB*, VII:2.
99. Sierksma, Klaes, *Nederlands vlaggenboek* (Utrecht: Prisma, 1962).
99. Sierksma, Klaes, *Vlaggen: symbool, traditie, protocol* (Bussum: Dishoek, 1963).
100. Landon, Perceval, "Armorial Bearings and Flags," *Nepal* (London: Constable, 1928).
101. Glue, W.A., *The New Zealand Ensign* (Wellington: Government Printer, 1965).
102. *Escudos de armas coloniales de Nicaragua* (Managua: Oficina de control de especies postales y filatelia, 1961).
104. Smith, Whitney, "A Tribute to Nigeria," *The Coat of Arms*, October 1960.
105. Takahashi, Kenichi, *Buke no Kamon to Hatajirushi* (Tokyo, 1973).
105. Wedemeyer, A., "Über die Sonnenflagge Japans," *Asia major*, 1932.
106. Grahl-Madsen, Atle, *Forslag til Lov om Flagg og Flaggbruk* (Bergen: Norges Handelshøyskole, 1972).
107. Mell, Alfred, *Die Fahnen des österreichischen Soldaten im Wandel der Zeiten* (Vienna: Bergland, 1962).
108. Department of Films and Publications, *The Pakistan Flag* (Karachi: Government of Pakistan, 1964).
109. Castillero Reyes, Ernesto, *Historia de los símbolos de la patria panameña* (Panama: Librería Selecta, 1959).
110. Vargas Peña, Benjamín, *La bandera del Paraguay* (Buenos Aires: Argentina, 1946).
111. Fernandez Stoll, Jorge, *La bandera* (Lima: Sociedad Bolivariana de Lima, 1957).
112. Gagelonia, Pedro A., *The Philippine National Flag* (Manila: Department of Education, 1963).
113. Russocki, Stanislaw, Stefan K. Kuczyński, and Juliusz Willaume, *Godlo, barwy i hymn Rzeczypospolitej* (Warsaw: Wiedza Powszechna, 1970).
114. Mattos, José, *As gloriosas bandeiras de Portugal* (Porto: Mattos, 1961).
117. Fuentes, G.J., "República Dominicana," *Billiken*, 4 August 1947.
118. Épron, J.G.M., *Drapeau et devise de la République Centrafricaine* (Bangui: Présidence de la République, 1963).
119. "Rhodesia," *FB*, VII:4.
120. Benson, Gary S., "Two Early National Flags of Walachia & Moldavia," *FB*, IX:2.
121. Smith, Whitney, *Political Symbolism in Rwanda* (New York, Flag Research Center, 1963).
123. Morganti, Luigi, "La bandeira," in Giuseppi Rossi (ed.), *La Serenissima Repubblica di San Marino, guida ufficiale* (San Marino: Vogarte, 1963).
127. "Singapore," *FB*, VI:1–2.
128. Mancini, Marcello, "Una bandiera azzurra," *Corriere della Somalia*, 12 October 1954.
129. Pama, Cornelius, *Lions and Virgins* (Cape Town: Human & Rousseau, 1965).
130. Ivanov, K.A., *Flagi gosudarstu mira* (Moscow: Transport, 1971).
130. Semyonovich, N.N., *Istoriya russkogo voenno-morskogo flaga* (Leningrad: Gosudarstvennyi Ermitazh, 1946).
130. "Soviet State Symbolism," *FB*, XI:1.
131. House of Representatives, *Report of the National Flag Committee* (Colombo: Ceylon Government Press, 1951).
132. Brožek, A., "Vlajky Sudanu," *Vexilologie*, 1974.
133. Hulkko, Jouko, *Siniristilippumme* (Helsinki: Otava, 1963).
134. "Syria," *FB*, III:3.
135. Åberg, Alf, "The National Flags of Sweden," *The American Scandinavian Review*, March 1974.
135. Justice Department, *Rikets Vapen och Flagga* (Stockholm: Norstedt & Söner, 1966).
136. "Swaziland," *FB*, VII:2.
137. "Tanganyika and Zanzibar," *FB*, IV:1.
141. *Our Flag and Other National Emblems* (Port-of-Spain: Government of Trinidad and Tobago, 1962).
142. Hugon, Henri, *Les emblèmes des Beys de Tunis* (Paris, 1913).
143. Kurtoglu, Fevzi, *Türk bayraği ve ay yildız* (Ankara: Türk Tarih Kurumu, 1938).
144. "Uganda," *FB*, II:1.
145. "Oman," *FB*, X:4.
146. Cumberland, Barlow, *History of the Union Jack* (Toronto: Briggs, 1900).
146. Milne, Samuel M., *The Standards and Colours of the Army* (Leeds, Goodall & Suddick, 1893).
146. Perrin, W.G., *British Flags* (Cambridge, 1922).
147. Mastai, Boleslaw and Marie-Louise d'Otrange Mastai, *The Stars and the Stripes* (New York: Knopf, 1973).
147. Smith, Whitney, *The Flag Book of the United States* (New York: Morrow, 1975).
149. Aparicio, Juan F., "Uruguay: The History of Its Flags," *FB*, VI:1–2.
150. Vargas, Francisco A., *Estudio histórico sobre la bandera* (Caracas: Instituto de Estudios Históricos Mirandino, 1973).
151. "Notes from the News," *FB*, V:2.
152. *Quôc-ky Viêt-Nam / The National Flag of Viet-Nam* (Saigon: Viên Dinh Chu'ân, 1969).
153. Dumoutier, G., *Les symboles* (Paris: Leroux, 1891).
154. Avendaño, José L. de, "The New Republic of Yemen," *FB*, II:3.
155. "South Yemen," *FB*, VII:1.
156. Harmignies, Roger, "Histoire du drapeau du Congo," *Recueil du IIe Congrès International de Vexillologie* (Zurich: Société Suisse de Vexillologie, 1968).
157. "Zambia," *FB*, IV:1.

SPECIAL FLAGS

"Europese Volksgroepen en hun Vlaggen," *Vexilla Nostra*, 1973.

Flags, Club Burgees, and Private Signals (New York: Lloyd's Register, 1973).

Harding, Brooks, *World Flag Encyclopedia* (Washington: U.N. Honor Flag Committee, 1948).

Pereira, Harold B., *Aircraft Badges & Markings* (London: Adlard Coles, 1955).

Stewart, John, *Yacht Club Burgees* (Southampton: Adlard Coles, 1957).

Styring, John S., *Brown's Flags and Funnels* (Glasgow: Brown, Son & Ferguson, 1971).

INDEX

NOTE: Illustrations are indicated by the page number appearing in italics.

AFTERWORD

Historically, there has been only one important way for a person to become involved with flags. Aside from the very few who create the designs that inspire millions and those who execute these designs in cloth, there have been only the followers of flags – those patriots who supported causes great and small and the soldiers who stood ready to shed their own blood and that of enemies in contending for the supremacy of one flag over another.

Today any person can become directly involved in the world of flags in an entirely different manner – through the study of their forms and symbolisms and usages. The number of such persons is not large, yet in some way each is coming to understand the nature of human society better as vexillology offers insights into the hopes, the achievements, and the fond beliefs embraced in the folds of every flag.

It is particularly appropriate in this book to mention the associations of vexillologists which have been formed around the world. Such groups bring individuals together and focus attention on national problems of flag research and development, often publishing their results in a newsletter or in monographs. These societies are linked by the International Federation of Vexillological Associations, founded in 1967 at the Second International Congress of Vexillology in Zurich. The federation sponsors such congresses biennially and recognizes the bimonthly *Flag Bulletin* as its official journal for the publication of articles on all aspects of flags.

Participation in flag-related activities can mean considerably more than joining a vexillological association and subscribing to a journal, however. It may involve collecting actual flags, displaying and/or lecturing about flags, designing and making flags, collecting items such as postage stamps or coins on which flags figure, promoting educational projects among young people on the subject of flags, or simply taking notes and making illustrations of flags for one's personal pleasure. Many have found enjoyable a topic of specialization within vexillology – such as flags of businesses or cities in a certain area, military flags of a particular war, the development of a special kind of flag, or flag references in historical literature.

Those who become intrigued by any aspect of flags may make contact with other vexillologists, as well as activities and publications relating to flags, by writing to the Flag Research Center. As director of the center since 1962, it has been my mission to make the world of flags more widely and more deeply known through books and articles, conferences and exhibits, and especially *The Flag Bulletin* which the center publishes. The present book indeed is part of an ongoing process; its pages rely on hundreds of colleagues, government officials, librarians, academicians, and countless others who over the years have assisted me. The lack of space to list their names in no way diminishes my gratitude to them.

Whether or not the reader finds sufficient inspiration from this book to join the growing activities of vexillologists in all parts of the globe, may he or she at least finish by concurring with the comment made by Henri Châtelaine in 1720 when he described vexillology as "an intriguing and fascinating study not only for those who sail or live in maritime cities, but as well for all who are inquisitive."

Dr. Whitney Smith
Flag Research Center
Winchester, Massachusetts
U.S.A.

POLAND
PORTUGAL
QATAR
ROMANIA
RWANDA
SAUDI ARABIA
SENEGAL

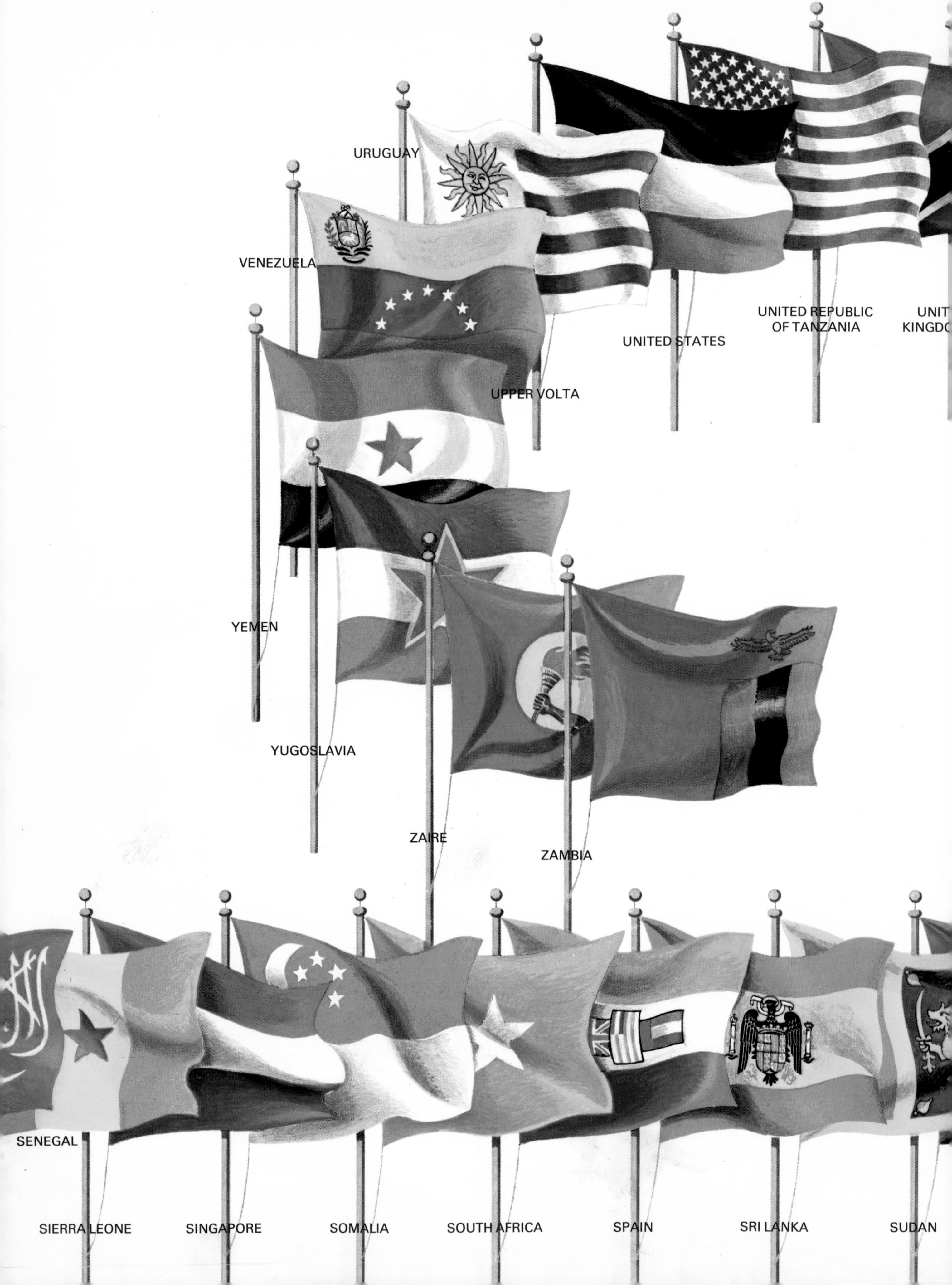
URUGUAY
VENEZUELA
UNITED STATES
UNITED REPUBLIC OF TANZANIA
UPPER VOLTA
YEMEN
YUGOSLAVIA
ZAIRE
ZAMBIA
SENEGAL
SIERRA LEONE
SINGAPORE
SOMALIA
SOUTH AFRICA
SPAIN
SRI LANKA
SUDAN

UNITED ARAB EMIRATES
U.S.S.R.
UKRAINIAN S.S.R.
UGANDA
TURKEY
TUNISIA
TRINIDAD
&
TOBAGO
TOGO
THAILAND
SYRIA
SWEDEN
SWAZILAND

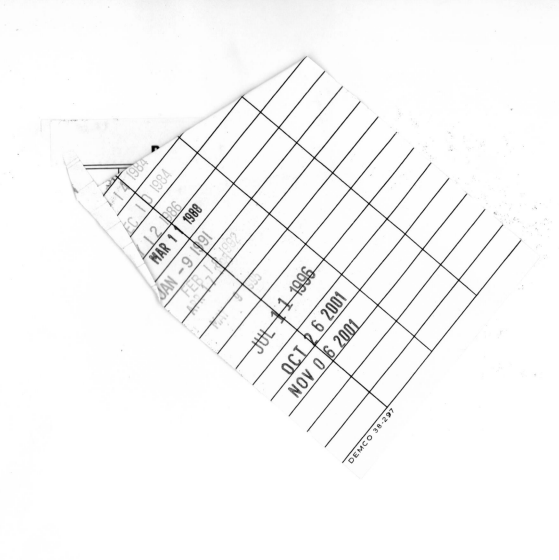